PORTUGAL

CARRIE-MARIE BRATLEY

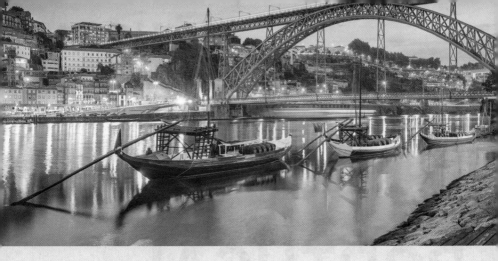

Contents

Although every effort was made to make sure the information in this book was accurate when going to press, research was impacted by the COVID-19 pandemic and things may have changed since the time of writing. Be sure to confirm specific details, like opening hours, closures, and travel guidelines and restrictions, when making your travel plans. For more detailed information, see page 444.

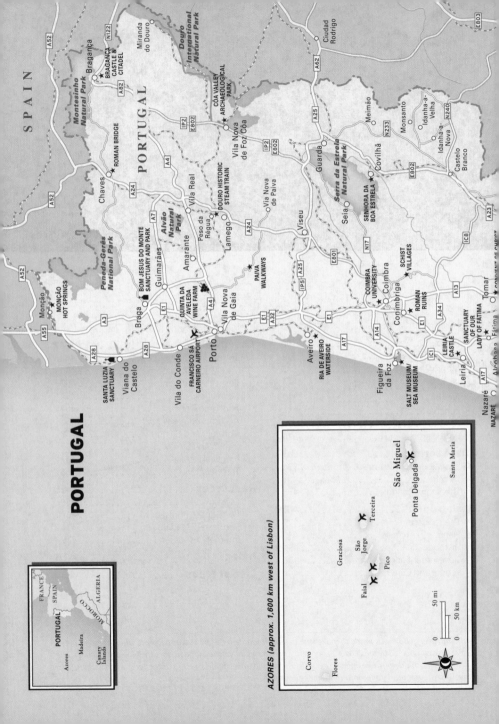

DISCOVER
Portugal

Like the sardine that has become symbolic of Portuguese gastronomy and its formidable seafaring heritage, Portugal is small but packs a mighty flavorful punch. Hemmed by the seemingly infinite Atlantic to the west and south, its northern and eastern borders fused with Spain, Portugal forms the most southwesterly corner of Europe, occupying about a fifth of the Iberian Peninsula.

Small, bright, and breezy, steeped in staunch tradition and culture, Portugal has tons to offer beyond the beaches and golf courses for which it gained a reputation in the '80s. Languid rivers flanked by lacy vineyards that produce the country's acclaimed wines characterize the mountainous north; capital city Lisbon is an exciting and fast-paced modern metropolis; rolling golden wheat-covered plains carpet the Alentejo region; snow-capped ski resorts are an unexpected surprise in a country famed for its Mediterranean climate; and medieval castles, historic palaces, Roman ruins, and ancient slate villages pepper the mystical Centro.

As birthplace of the Age of Discoveries and center of the first global empire, Portugal has always been a country of intrepid adventurers and pioneering explorers. Remnants left by ancient peoples including the Celts, Romans, Visigoths,

Clockwise from top left: surfing in the Algarve; the Alcobaça Monastery; Miradouro Santa Luzia in Lisbon; Benagil sea cave; *piripiri* chicken; boats in Carvoeiro.

and Moors who once occupied Portugal pay testament to its historic desirability, while the growing numbers of tourists who visit annually are proof that the country today still has major appeal. Despite once being one of Europe's poorest countries, Portugal's resilient people, in addition to being proud of their rich heritage, are experts at reinventing the wheel. They also have an innate love of a good *festa;* making time for coffee and a cake is a key part of the daily ritual, and family and football are sacred.

Portugal caters for all tastes in travel: glamorous modern metropolises, rural hideaways, barefoot surfy towns, and paradisiacal beach resorts are just some of its compelling features. Add into the mix two fascinating archipelagos—Madeira and the Azores—a gastronomy that is second to none, people who are genuinely warm and welcoming, and year-round fine weather, and it's easy to see why Portugal is consistently among Europe's top destinations.

Clockwise from top left: *levada* trail on Madeira; the Glória Funicular in Lisbon; the eggy custard tart *pastel de nata;* Livraria Lello, the famous bookshop in Porto.

10 TOP
EXPERIENCES

1 Kayaking on the Azores' emerald green **Sete Cidades** crater lakes, or gazing down at them from above (page 396).

2 Wandering through layers of history in **Évora,** from its chilling 16th-century Chapel of Bones, to its medieval cathedral, to a well-preserved Roman Temple (page 137).

3 Tasting Portugal's **authentic cuisine,** from grilled sardines and chicken *piripiri* to the famous *pastel de nata* (page 28).

4 Sipping **wine in the Douro Valley,** whose breathtaking vineyards can be explored by river cruise, car, or train (page 330).

5 Soaking in a performance of Portugal's mournful folk music in the **fado houses of Lisbon** (page 78).

6 Strolling into the past in the **lost-in-time villages** of rural Portugal (page 30).

7 Dolphin-watching and eating seafood in authentic villages on the windswept **Setúbal Peninsula** (page 115).

8 Whizzing down vertiginous streets in one of **Funchal's wicker toboggan sleds,** used for transportation on the island of Madeira since the 1850s (page 361).

9 Climbing the walls of the glorious **castles of the Alentejo** to learn about Portuguese history and for incredible views of rolling plains (page 166).

>>>

10 Finding the Algarve's less crowded side in the dazzling salt pans and bird-dotted sand barriers of **Ria Formosa Natural Park** (page 203).

>>>

Planning Your Trip

Where to Go

Lisbon

Located at the mouth of the Tagus River, Portugal's buzzing, cosmopolitan capital is a show-stopping gateway to southern Europe. Home to **fado** music and a vivid **nightlife** scene, the "City of Seven Hills" oozes charm and cool in equal measures. With tile-clad facades and red-brick roofs that tumble toward the Tagus, its **historic, maze-like neighborhoods** beckon to be explored. By day you can wander along Lisbon's scenic **riverfront,** amble beautiful **boutique-lined boulevards,** visit one of many grandiose **museums,** enjoy a *pastel de Belém* custard tart, or trundle around the narrow, cobbled backstreets on a rickety old **tram.** Jam-packed with tantalizing activities that stimulate all the senses, Lisbon is a city not just for sightseeing, but for living and experiencing.

Around Lisbon

With Lisbon as a base, visitors are perfectly positioned to enjoy a smorgasbord of exciting day trips, all within an hour's drive of the capital. Among the most popular day trips from Lisbon are chic **Estoril** and **Cascais**, on an up-market stretch of coastline with great **beaches** also known as the **Portuguese Riviera.** A little farther inland is **Sintra,** filled with fairy-tale **castles.** The stunning **Setúbal Peninsula,** where the iconic statue of *Christ the King* stands with arms outstretched, is a short hop south from Lisbon across the **Tagus River.** Visit the

view from the Miradouro da Graça in Lisbon

Lisbon's MAAT—Museum of Art, Architecture and Technology and 25 de Abril Bridge

If You Have...

A LONG WEEKEND

Head to lovely **Lisbon** or charismatic **Porto** to squeeze as much Portuguese culture as you can out of your quick trip to Portugal.

ONE WEEK

Dedicate a few days to really unearthing the charms of **Lisbon** before tacking on a day trip or two to **Estoril, Cascais,** and **Sintra,** or **Óbidos** and **Nazaré.** Then, head south to the **Setúbal Peninsula** and inland to explore rural, untouched **Alentejo**—don't miss one of its finest towns, **Évora,** and an obligatory stop at **a winery.** Or, from **Porto,** you can treat yourself to a trip up the **Douro Valley,** indulging in some of its fabulous wine farms and pretty riverside towns. But if R&R

is what you want from your holiday, head straight south to the **Algarve** and spend the week sunning yourself while indulging in the delights of Portugal's premier holiday region.

TWO WEEKS

Two weeks is plenty of time to see the best of Portugal. Short, cheap **flights** between **Lisbon, Porto,** and the **Algarve** mean you can hop from one region to the next in under an hour. Then, hop over to one of the archipelagos, **Madeira** or the **Azores,** for a long weekend. Another option is to see real Portugal by **car.** Ideally, start at one end and work your way toward the other, through Portugal's lesser-seen landscapes, like the **Alentejo** and the **Centro.**

seafood-rich village of **Sesimbra** and the popular summer resort **Costa da Caparica,** with infinite beaches and authentic fisherman culture.

Évora and the Alentejo

All of Portugal is laid-back, but nowhere more so than the rolling plains of the Alentejo, where the rhythm is dictated by the crops and the seasons. Famous for its **wine** as well as its **marble,** this underrated area offers **rural escapes,** charming **hamlets,** and some of the **warmest weather** in the country, all under one big, blue sky. Its largest city, **Évora,** is home to distinctive monuments, like a Gothic cathedral, the skeleton-packed Chapel of Bones, and a Roman temple.

The Algarve and the Southern Beaches

The Algarve is Portugal's number one spot for sun-drenched holidays. Buzzing in summer and beautiful in winter, this year-round destination has stunning stretches of **golden sand, crystalline coves,** and heady **nightlife. Golfers** and road-trippers flock to the Algarve

in winter and spring, when almond trees flourish with snowy white petals.

Coimbra and the Centro

A visit to Central Portugal can feel like a journey into the past. The region captivates with its ethereal **schist villages, medieval monuments,** and the Catholic pilgrimage site at **Fátima.** Yet Central Portugal is also about the future, boasting the largest university city in the country, **Coimbra. Serra da Estrela Natural Park** is Portugal's only **skiing** destination. This is also where you'll find the town of **Nazaré,** one of the world's top spots for big-wave **surfing,** not far from the atmospheric medieval walled town of **Óbidos,** whose ginger liqueur in chocolate cups attracts the crowds.

Porto and the Norte

With a cooler, grayer climate, Northern Portugal also has a lusher landscape. It's famous for producing Portugal's most celebrated tipple: **port.** Cruises along the **Douro River** and through the **winemaking Douro Valley** are the number one pull, while cultural attractions, particularly in the up-and-coming city of **Porto,** are also popular. Farther north are **Guimarães,** the "cradle of the nation"; medieval **Bragança;** and lively fishing port **Viana do Castelo.**

Madeira

The Madeira archipelago has long been a favorite among Europeans seeking an **offbeat nature destination.** The main and biggest eponymous island and Funchal, its capital, are famous for tropical vegetation, **wicker toboggans** that slide down lush hills, **New Year's fireworks,** and sweet and sticky **Madeira wine.**

The Azores

The volcanic Azores are one of Europe's last, best-kept secrets. These nine unspoiled islands, each distinct and characterful, can be reached in two hours by plane from the mainland. The main island, **São Miguel,** home to the archipelago's capital, **Ponta Delgada,** is famed for its rusty-red **hot springs,** jungle-like scenery, and tasty **local cuisine.** The three islands of the **Azores**

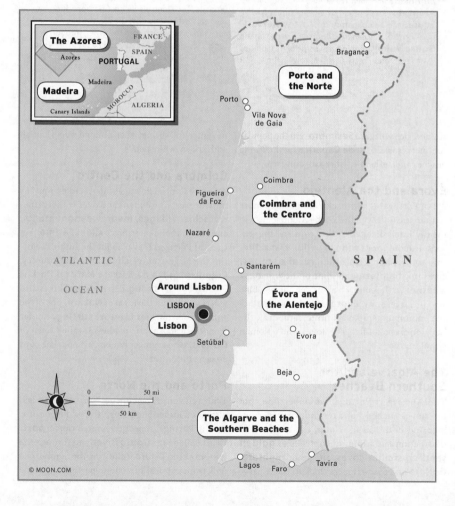

© MOON.COM

Triangle (São Jorge, Pico, and Faial) are legendary **trans-Atlantic sailors' haunts.** One thing all the islands have in common is the herds of **cows** that roam lush pastures and provide the delicious **cheeses and meats** for which the Azores are also renowned.

When to Go

Portugal is a year-round destination. That said, hotel prices in **Lisbon** peak in **summer** and during major events, like the hugely popular **Santo António festivities** in June.

The **Algarve,** though beautiful all year, is best visited when the weather is hot to take full advantage of the **beaches;** it's busiest and hottest in **July and August/early September,** when temperatures can hit the high 30s C (86°F and up). **Spring** and **autumn** are cheaper, milder, and less crowded. Hotel prices are at a premium in high season and over New Year's.

Northern Portugal is generally **cooler and grayer** than the rest of Portugal, while the **Centro** and **Alentejo** experience **weather extremes,** very hot in summer and very cold in winter, and always **less crowded** than the rest of the country.

Portugal does have rainy months, **December** being the wettest. Portugal's only ski resort, in the **Serra da Estrela mountain range,** is one of very few places in Portugal where it snows and has its high season in winter.

The **Azores** are fantastic to visit in any season, though they can experience "four seasons in one day" any time of year. **Madeira** is also **mild year-round,** and particularly spectacular on **New Year's** or during its famous **Flower Festival,** staged yearly in April or May.

traditional tiled facade in Porto

Madeira Botanical Garden in Funchal

Know Before You Go

Getting There

The three main **airports** on mainland Portugal are **Lisbon, Porto** in the north, and **Faro** in the south. Most flights from outside the European Union are to Lisbon. Porto also has regular direct flights from outside the EU, although far fewer than Lisbon. Faro has almost exclusively European flights.

FROM NORTH AMERICA

Portugal is served by regular **direct flights** from North America. Airlines such as **TAP, United** (www.united.com), **SATA,** and **Air Canada** (www.aircanada.com) have regular flights, which run 7-9 hours and start around €600 round-trip.

FROM NEW ZEALAND, AUSTRALIA, AND SOUTH AFRICA

There are no direct flights to Portugal from Australasia. Getting here will usually require a **layover** in the Middle East or elsewhere in Europe. A number of major international carriers code-share flights with European partners. Flying in from Australasia will usually take more than 24 hours. The average one-way fare will be around €1,800-3,000. At the time of writing, there were also no direct flights to Portugal from South Africa; trips from South Africa usually require a stop in Luanda or a major European destination such as Paris, London, Munich, Amsterdam, or Madrid. However, Portugal's national flag-carrier TAP (www.flytap.com) recently announced a direct flight from Lisbon to Cape Town for 2021.

FROM ELSEWHERE IN EUROPE

Traveling to Portugal from anywhere within Europe is quick and easy—and even better, cheap, thanks to the growing number of **low-cost airlines.** There are numerous flights from myriad cities in Europe to **Lisbon** and **Porto;** flights to Portugal within Europe can be found for less than €100 round-trip.

Bus and **train** services connect Portugal with Spain, France, Belgium, the Netherlands, and the United Kingdom. **Driving** to Portugal is also possible thanks to a good international road network and the EU open-borders policy.

Getting Around Portugal

Thanks to its compact size and a good road network, Portugal is easily traveled by **car.** Renting a car also provides greater flexibility for exploring off the beaten track. But an efficient bus and train network also connects most major towns and cities. **Train travel** can often be more **scenic** and **cheaper** than bus, but train stations can sometimes be located far outside town centers. **Bus travel** is almost always **quicker** than train.

Portugal's archipelagoes, **Madeira** and the **Azores,** are within a two-hour flight from the mainland, with direct flights from Lisbon and Porto.

Passports and Visas

All travelers entering Portugal are required to have a **valid ID.**

European Union nationals traveling within EU or Schengen states do not require a visa for entering Portugal for any length of stay. They do require a valid passport or official ID card. European citizens traveling between **Schengen** countries are not required to present an identity document or passport at border crossings, as an open-borders policy is in effect. However, it is recommended that travelers have ID documents with them.

Citizens of the **United Kingdom** and **Ireland** must produce a passport to enter Portugal, valid for the duration of the proposed stay, and can stay for up to three months.

People from **non-EU countries** always require a passport, valid for at least six months; some may require a visa. **Australian, Canadian,** and **US** travelers require a valid passport but do not need a visa for stays of up to 90 days in any six-month period. While it is not obligatory to have an onward or return ticket, it is advisable.

South African nationals need to apply for a Portugal-Schengen visa. This should be done three months before travel. Applicants must have a South African passport valid for six months beyond date of return with at least three blank pages.

What to Pack

What to pack depends on when you are due to visit. Summer requires **beach wear,** loose-fitting light clothing like shorts and T-shirts, sunscreen, and a cap. Shoulder seasons are all about **layers:** You'll need lighter clothing for daytime and warmer clothing for the evenings.

A light windbreaker, long-sleeved shirt, a shawl for around the shoulders, or roll-up rain jacket are all useful. In winter you'll need **good footwear** and **warm clothing,** including a coat, hat, scarf, and gloves, especially for January. If heading to Madeira or the Azores, don't forget a good pair of **hiking boots.** The dress code in Portugal is mostly relaxed, except in higher-end eateries where smart dress is expected.

You'll also need an **adapter** (Portugal uses standard European round two-pin plugs; electrical items are 220-240V). **Sunglasses** are handy most of the year, and a small fold-up **umbrella** is useful, particularly if visiting the wetter northern region or islands. A discreet **travel pouch** for carrying money and ID cards is always a good idea. And don't forget a **camera!**

Praia do Camilo, Lagos

Explore Portugal

The Best of Portugal

Not so long ago, Portugal was seen predominantly as a beach and golf destination, with the Algarve taking center stage for tourists. But tourists have gradually discovered the rest of the country's appeal as a holiday destination, boasting wine, nature, and adventure tourism. Both Lisbon and Porto have also achieved an enviable status as two of Europe's most up-and-coming getaway destinations, and are well-connected to flights throughout Europe, so you could start your trip in either city. Here are some ideas for building your itinerary, dividing your time into the north and south of the country as well as Lisbon in the center. The itinerary can be done in reverse or broken into smaller pieces, depending on how much time you have.

North
DAY 1: PORTO

The *azulejo* tile-clad **São Bento Railway Station,** the spindly **Clérigos Tower,** the amazing **Livraria Lello** bookshop, and the opulent **Stock Exchange Palace** are must-sees in Portugal's second city, all within walking distance of one another, as is the glorious **riverfront,** lined with rainbow-colored buildings. Stop at a riverside restaurant for lunch.

After lunch, stroll across the **Dom Luís I bridge** to **Vila Nova de Gaia** and visit one of the famous **port wine cellars** for a tour and a tasting. Round the day off with a **cable car** ride up the hill.

the riverfront promenade in Porto

terraced hills covered in grapevines in the Douro Valley

DAY 2: DOURO VALLEY

Take a daylong **river cruise** to see the enchanting **Douro Valley.** (One leg of the trip, either upriver or downriver, is often by train.) Choose a trip that incorporates a visit to a wine farm or at least allows time to explore one of the riverside towns, such as lovely **Peso da Régua,** where the **Douro Museum** offers an introduction to the valley's history and traditions. Back in Porto, have dinner and stop for a drink at one of the local nightspots.

DAY 3: COIMBRA AND TOMAR

Begin heading south to Coimbra (just over an hour south of Porto). Tour the famed university campus, including the opulent 18th-century **Joanina Library.** Then, make your way through the cobbled streets down to the riverside, stopping at the striking **Old Cathedral.** Walk across the bridge over the Mondego River and visit one of the city's quirkiest attractions, the miniature village of **Little Portugal.**

Continue just under an hour south to the Templar city of **Tomar,** where you'll have a few hours to explore the magnificent **Convent** **of Christ** complex as well as visit the **Tomar Synagogue** and wander the tree-lined riverside before heading to your hotel for the night.

DAYS 4-5: ÓBIDOS AND NAZARÉ

Move west toward the coast, stopping en route in **Alcobaça,** a traditional river-valley town famous for its huge **monastery** and local sweet **confectionary.** Spend a night in surfy **Nazaré,** and the next day, get up early and head to enchanting **Óbidos.** Allow a couple of hours to stroll the **castle walls** and soak up the medieval feel, before heading back to your hotel in Nazaré.

Lisbon and Around

DAY 6: LISBON'S HISTORIC CENTER

Start your exploration of Portugal's capital at the bustling riverfront **Comércio Square.** From here, you can catch the famed yellow **tram 28,** which trundles through Lisbon's most historic neighborhoods, and take trips on the **Santa Justa Elevator** and **Glória Funicular.** Worthwhile stops along the way include the **Lisbon Cathedral** and the **Portas** do Sol Viewpoint, which has a café where you can enjoy lunch with a panoramic view. In the afternoon, choose between a climb to the São Jorge Castle, for still more amazing views, or head to the elegant Estrela Basílica and gardens. Then, spend the evening in the atmospheric Alfama neighborhood for dinner and a fado show (make your reservation well in advance).

DAY 7: BELÉM

The next day, get an early start for sightseeing in Belém, a short trip west of the city center. Admire the city's most iconic monuments—the sprawling Jerónimos Monastery and riverside Belém Tower. Stop for lunch and indulge in a *pastel de Belém* custard tart at the famous Pastéis de Belém bakery for dessert. Return to Lisbon for a little rest at your accommodation before heading out again for a sunset cocktail at a rooftop bar, such as the one at Hotel Mundial. Then, make your way to the bohemian Bairro Alto to enjoy dinner and hit some nightspots.

DAY 8: THE PORTUGUESE RIVIERA

Leave metropolitan Lisbon and head west to the affluent stretch of coast known as the Portuguese Riviera. Stop first in Estoril. Park up near the glitzy casino and its manicured lawns and have a stroll, stopping for a pastry at the famed Pastelaria Garrett. Weather allowing, bask on one of Estoril's golden beaches, then head to neighboring Cascais, where you can have lunch and rent a bike to cycle to windswept Guincho Beach. Make sure to stop at the dramatic Boca do Inferno rock formation en route. Head back to Cascais to indulge in its colorful culinary and nightlife scene before returning to Lisbon.

DAY 9: SINTRA

Today, make your way to Sintra. En route, stop at Cabo da Roca, Europe's most westerly point, for a photo. Allocate a full day for Sintra's iconic attractions, like the whimsical Pena Palace and Regaleira Estate. Head back to Lisbon for your final night in the capital city.

Sintra's Moorish Castle wall, with Pena Palace in the distance

Top Beaches

Portugal is renowned for its dramatic sea cliffs, snug coves, and, of course, sweeping stretches of golden sand.

- **Guincho Beach** (Cascais, near Lisbon): Head to this windswept beach, popular among surfers and windsurfers, to enjoy sweeping views of the ocean and plains (page 109).

- **Marinha Beach** (Carvoeiro, Algarve): Encased by sheer ocher cliffs, this beach has craggy rock formations that stretch out over the soft, golden sand to a calm, translucent sea. It's one of the most beautiful beaches in the country (page 228).

- **Dona Ana Beach** (Lagos, Algarve): Surrounded by golden cliffs and fronting cool crystalline water, this romantic beach is postcard-perfect (page 237).

- **Franquia Beach** (Vila Nova de Milfontes, Alentejo): With shallow waters that are warmer than others along the coast, this crescent-shaped swath of sand is a magnet for families (page 176).

- **Nazaré Beach** (Nazaré, Central Portugal): Fringed by a long seafront avenue, this huge

Marinha Beach near Carvoeiro

half-moon of glimmering sand is one of the most famous places in the world for big-wave surfing (page 262).

South

DAY 10: SETÚBAL PENINSULA

Start your exploration of the Setúbal Peninsula south of Lisbon with **Cabo Espichel**, an eerie headland occupied by a ghostly abandoned hermitage. From here, make the short drive to the charming fishing village of **Sesimbra** and enjoy a grilled fish lunch at one of the down-to-earth dockside restaurants. Drive on to Setúbal city, passing through the amazing natural scenery of the **Arrábida Natural Park.** In Setúbal city, join a **dolphin-watching** boat tour on the **Sado Estuary.**

DAYS 11-12: THE ALGARVE

Settle in at the charming fishing village of **Carvoeiro** for two nights. Take a grotto trip from **Carvoeiro Beach** to see the amazing **sea caves** along the coast. After lunch, hit the sand at **Marinha Beach,** one of the most famous and beautiful in the country. Choose from Carvoeiro's colorful selection of bars and restaurants for dinner and a cocktail (or two) before turning in.

Make a side trip to the fortified city of **Silves** to admire its wonderful **hilltop castle** before heading back up north to the heart and "capital" of the Alentejo region, Évora.

DAYS 13-14: ÉVORA

Historic Évora lies in the heart of the rustic Alentejo. Évora's charming walled city center is best enjoyed at a leisurely pace. Take in the grand **Évora Cathedral** with its splendid rooftop views, the regal columns of the well-preserved **Roman Temple of Évora,** and the morbidly fascinating **Chapel of Bones.**

Explore Portuguese Cuisine

Portugal is known for fine wines and liqueurs, the freshest seafood, and a gastronomy that comes from the heart and the land. Here are some of the country's iconic dishes and where to try them.

LISBON

- *Pastel de nata:* This eggy custard tart is ubiquitous in Portugal, found in every café and cake shop. Lisbon's Belém neighborhood has its own version of the *pastel de Nata,* known as *pastel de Belém,* which still follows the original local recipe. It's Portugal's most famous sweet.

- *Bacalhau:* Cod is Portugal's go-to fish, and the country is said to have as many recipes for cod dishes as there are days of the year. Lisbon has several restaurants dedicated solely to cod.

ÉVORA AND THE ALENTEJO

- *Porco preto:* A delicacy found widely throughout the Alentejo region, black pig pork meat is moister and more succulent than regular pork, and derives from acorn-fed pigs.

ginja de Óbidos

THE ALGARVE

- Chicken *piripiri:* The Algarve town of Guia is the capital of this spicy, charcoal-grilled chicken dish, made with *piripiri* hot sauce.

- Grilled sardines: Any waterfront restaurant serves grilled sardines. They're simple finger food, served with a slice of rustic bread. Portimão has a trademark row of riverside sardine restaurants and hosts a festival in August dedicated to the fish.

- *Cataplana:* Found widely in restaurants along the coast, the *cataplana's* birthplace is believed to be the Algarve. It takes its name from the shell-shaped copper dish in which the original seafood and meat stew is cooked.

COIMBRA AND THE CENTRO

- *Ginja de Óbidos:* This strong cherry liqueur (known as *ginjinha* in the rest of the country) is served in

---

After lunching on local delicacies like cured meats and regional cheeses, explore one of the upper Alentejo's wine farms. Located a 30-minute walk (5-minute drive) north of Évora's city center, the **Cartuxa Estate** is one of the most revered names among Alentejo wines. The century-old organic vineyard offers guided tours and tastings. For an unforgettable overview of the vast rolling plains of the vine-meshed Alentejo, book a sunset **hot-air balloon ride.**

shops in the medieval village of Óbidos, usually in a chocolate cup.

- *Sopa da pedra:* Stone soup is a fabled meat-and-bean soup born from a local legend originating in the small village of Almeirim, in the Santarém region.

- *Polvo á lagareiro:* Soft, pressure-cooked octopus covered in lashings of olive oil, typically served in Nazaré.

PORTO AND THE NORTE

- **Port wine:** This traditional fortified wine is produced solely in the Douro Valley. Traditionally sweet and red in color, it's generally served as a dessert wine. Across the Douro River from Porto, Vila Nova de Gaia's legendary port wine cellars date back centuries.

- *Francesinha:* Northern Portugal's most iconic dish, the *francesinha* is a monster of a sandwich, made up of layers of various types of cured and cooked meats, covered in melted cheese and a hot, spicy tomato and beer sauce.

port wine tasting

MADEIRA

- **Madeira wine:** This robust fortified wine is produced exclusively on the Madeira Islands, with a history dating back to the Age of Discoveries at the end of the 15th century. Ranging from dry to sweet, Madeira wine is consumed as an aperitif or dessert accompaniment.

- **Nikita:** A divisive drink found exclusively in Câmara de Lobos on Madeira Island, it is an intriguing mix of wine, beer, and homemade pineapple ice cream.

- *Espetadas da Madeira:* An icon of Madeira cuisine, these are hanging kebabs, traditionally laurel sticks, skewered with chunks of juicy beef, native to the Câmara de Lobos region of Madeira Island.

THE AZORES

- *Cozido das Furnas:* Every region has its own interpretation of this meat-and-vegetable stew. The Azores' version is slow-cooked underground in the natural volcanic heat of São Miguel Island.

- *Alcatra:* A melt-in-the-mouth beef rump and red wine stew typical of the Azores' Terceira Island.

Despite its sleepy feel, Évora has a youthful buzz, thanks to the local university population, which means there are a good selection of **hip eateries** and **cool bars** to try out before you turn in for the night.

The next day, explore the **Almendres Cromlech** on your way back to Lisbon for your return flight.

Lost-in-Time Villages

If it's a lesser-seen side of Portugal that you want, take a trip back in time with a tour of central Portugal's characterful rural villages. **Rent a car** and start in the university town of **Coimbra,** easily accessible from Porto, and close to the hub of ancient schist, or slate-built, villages, known as the *aldeias do xisto.* Then, head farther south to the dramatic castles protecting the historic towns that dot the **Alentejo.**

Day 1

Start in **Coimbra,** Portugal's atmospheric university city, often overlooked and underexplored by visitors. Visiting the amazing, historic **Coimbra University** campus in the older part of town, perched on top of a hill, should be at the top of your list. Drive or take public transport up, and then meander your way back down; the **São Miguel Chapel, University Tower,** and the **Joanina Library** are must-sees. On your way back down to Coimbra's bustling Baixa downtown, stop at the **Old Cathedral.** Choose a nice café for a light lunch, and spend the afternoon exploring the other side of the Mondego River, visiting the **Santa Clara-a-Velha Monastery** and **Little Portugal,** fun for kids of all ages. Follow dinner with some Coimbra-style **fado.**

Day 2

From Coimbra, head south to **Conímbriga,** the site of an ancient Roman settlement. Spend a few hours exploring this unique archeological treasure before heading south on a driving tour of the area's famed schist villages, **Casal de São Simão, Cerdeira,** and **Talasnal,** which still appear much as they have for centuries. Return back to your hotel in Coimbra after a day of exploring.

Day 3

Head two hours southeast through picturesque countryside to **Marvão,** up against the Spanish border, in the heart of the **São Mamede Mountain Range Natural Park.** This is authentic Portugal: Visit Marvão's famous **castle** with its sweeping views over Spain, and enjoy a **hike** in the park. Pack a lunch or buy supplies at a supermarket or café to enjoy a picnic en route. When your legs start to get tired, start making your way toward **Portalegre,** a stone's throw from Marvão, at the foot of the mountains. Spend the afternoon taking in sights such as the **cathedral, Tapestry Museum,** and **Santa Clara Convent.** For dinner, head to one of Portalegre's cozy little eateries that serve classic Alentejo fare.

Day 4

From Portalegre, venture deeper into the Alentejo via the N246 to the fascinating walled town of **Elvas,** an hour's drive south. Take a walk along its incredible star-shaped **bulwarks,** built to defend the country from invasion from Spain. From Elvas, head west to **Estremoz.** Stop off to see the bustling market town's **castle;** its tower is regarded as one of the most impressive in Portugal. Next, make the short drive south toward the whitewashed town of **Borba,** one of the main towns on the **Marble Route,** a trail of towns that demonstrate the prominence of the marble industry that once operated in this region. See Borba's marble **Fonte das Bicas** fountain, and then keep driving south to **Vila Viçosa,** known as the "Princess of the Alentejo." Here, visit the **marble museum,** the **Ducal Palace,** and pop into the exuberant **Marmoris Hotel,** a shrine to all things marble, and then set off for whimsical and charming old-world **Monsaraz,** a 45-minute drive south. Explore for an hour or so before heading west to larger **Reguengos de**

Getting Outside

With over a dozen natural parks and reserves and one huge, stunning national park, in Portugal there's no shortage of terrain for hiking, biking, canyoning, and kayaking. Dotted throughout the country, the parks are managed by the Institute for Nature and Forest Preservation (ICNF; www.icnf.pt).

FOR HIKERS AND CLIMBERS

The country's only classified national park, **Peneda-Gerês National Park** in northeastern Portugal is home to stunning mountains, magical woodland, cascading waterfalls, indigenous flora and fauna, traditional mountain communities, and nooks and crannies that beg to be climbed and trekked (page 338).

FOR PADDLERS

In southern Portugal, stretching over 60 kilometers (37 mi) along the Algarve coastline, **Ria Formosa Natural Park** is a labyrinth of translucent lagoons, golden sand barriers, and dazzling salt pans, inviting for leisurely boat trips and water sports like stand-up paddling and canoeing (page 203).

surf in Nazaré

FOR SURFERS

There's also no shortage of water-based fun in Portugal; the country's ultimate surf spot is **Nazaré,** home of one of the most famous big-wave surf spots on the planet, where the surf is epic (page 260).

FOR DIVERS

Head to the mid-Atlantic **Azores archipelago** for some of the best dive spots in the hemisphere (pages 393 and 408).

FOR SNOW BUNNIES

Serra da Estrela Natural Park comprises rolling mountains and lakes and the highest point on mainland Portugal, as well as the country's only winter sports resort (page 291).

Monsaraz, which has a larger selection of accommodations and restaurants.

Day 5

Enjoy a leisurely breakfast before making the 40-minute drive west to **Évora,** an easy drive along the IP2 motorway. Spend the day here; don't miss the eerie **Chapel of Bones,** the amazing **cathedral,** and theatrical **Roman Temple.** Enjoy a light lunch in one of Évora's busy cafés that flank the main **Giraldo Square.** In the afternoon, pay a visit to the **Cartuxa Estate** on the outskirts of town for a tour and wine-tasting.

Lisbon

Portugal's magnificent capital is one of Europe's best—vibrant and culturally rich, where the historic blends seamlessly with the cool and contemporary. At the mouth of the Tagus River (Rio Tejo), the "City of Seven Hills" is buzzing and cosmopolitan, home to melodic fado music and a vivid nightlife scene. Traditional tile-clad facades and redbrick roofs conceal a tangle of charming cobbled streets and elegant avenues that beckon to be explored.

Lisbon's notable history is shaped by its strategic position at the mouth of the Tagus River, evolving from an important seafaring port to one of the main gateways to Europe for Africa and South America. From the Neolithic period through Christian reconquest in the 12th and 13th centuries, Lisbon was inhabited by a succession of

Highlights

Look for ★ to find recommended sights, activities, dining, and lodging.

★ **São Jorge Castle:** On a hilltop in the heart of Lisbon, this imposing Moorish monument commands spectacular views of the historic city center and the Tagus River (page 45).

★ **Avenida da Liberdade:** An appealing mix of historic and contemporary buildings, high-end boutiques, and tree-shaded cafés lines the country's most famous avenue (page 49).

★ **Carmo Convent:** Once the largest church in Lisbon, these ruins starkly show the devastation of the 1755 earthquake (page 50).

★ **Belém Tower:** At the mouth of the Tagus River, this fortified tower was the last and first sight the country's intrepid sailors had of their homeland when setting off and returning from their voyages (page 55).

★ **Jerónimos Monastery:** Home to the national archaeological and naval museums, Belém's stunning centerpiece is a marvel of ornate Manueline architecture and took the entire 16th century to construct (page 57).

★ **Fado:** A night of soulful fado in its reputed birthplace is a can't-miss, unforgettable experience (page 78).

Iberians, Celts, Phoenicians, Greeks, Romans, Visigoths, and Moors. All left their marks on the city, adding layer upon layer to Lisbon's cityscape and heritage, from fascinating underground Roman galleries to ancient fortifications like the stunning São Jorge Castle and Moorish medieval walls still standing in parts of the city. It was during the 15th and 16th centuries that Lisbon really flourished, establishing itself as Portugal's colonial base, the beating heart of a rapidly expanding and ambitious empire.

The city, along with vast swaths of Portugal, was practically razed in the 18th century following the 1755 Lisbon earthquake and tsunami. Being rebuilt in a mishmash of contemporary national and international architectural trends gave Lisbon its unique and distinctive look, most noticeable in its elegant downtown Baixa area.

Today Lisbon is a cosmopolitan, fast-paced city, and its rush hour is a frenzied crescendo of beeping horns and packed subway stations, subsiding to a gentler flow at lunch and dinnertime. Locals good-naturedly jostle with throngs of tourists for barstools at trendy hangouts after hours.

Lisbon's impressive monuments, historic neighborhoods, and edgy vibe welcome visitors to drink in stunning bird's-eye views from many panoramic *miradouro* viewpoints or hip hotel rooftop bars. Stroll chic boulevards lined with boutiques, admire striking riverfront monuments, learn from world-class museums, or take the famous tram 28 around the city's historic nooks and crannies before enjoying mesmerizing fado music in one of the many authentic haunts in Alfama or Bairro Alto.

ORIENTATION

Hilly Lisbon is divided into many neighborhoods and parishes, or *bairros*. The heart of Lisbon's historic area is the **Baixa**

Pombalina, often simply referred to as the Baixa; it's the main downtown commercial and banking area along the river. Baixa is immediately fringed by several of the city's other most famous neighborhoods: labyrinth-like **Alfama** and hilltop **São Vicente,** cultural and hip nighttime hangout **Chiado** and **Bairro Alto,** cool and arty **Cais do Sodré,** and chic **Estrela** and **Lapa. Alcântara,** a former docks area currently enjoying a hipster revival, is west of the downtown area.

Heading north from downtown is the **Avenida da Liberdade,** one of the city's most famous avenues, surrounded by some excellent museums and historic monuments. On the western extremity of the heart of Lisbon is the culturally rich area of **Belém,** while at the opposite side, on the northeast, is the modern area of **Park of Nations (Parque das Nações),** dramatically developed for the 1998 World Exposition.

Baixa

Fronted by the Tagus River, the Baixa Pombalina (BYE-shah pom-bah-LEE-nah), or just Baixa, or "downtown Lisbon," is the city's central shopping and banking district—and its tourist hub. The name derives from the distinctive Portuguese Pombaline architectural style employed to rebuild the city after the 1755 earthquake, under the guidance of Sebastião José de Carvalho e Melo, the 1st Marquis of Pombal, characterized by uniform, elegant neoclassical facades and patterned cobbled streets.

Lisbon's main squares, **Rossio Square** and **Comércio Square,** with their monuments and museums, are here, and its two main streets, **Rua Augusta** and **Rua da Prata,** are laden with buzzing shops and restaurants. The main Metro stops in the Baixa area are Avenida, Restauradores, Rossio, Baixa-Chiado, and Terreiro do Paço, on the Green and Blue Lines.

Previous: Lisbon; Belém Tower; Jerónimos Monastery.

Alfama

Alfama (al-FAH-mah), just east of Baixa, is Lisbon's oldest and most soulful neighborhood and claims to be the birthplace of fado (although Bairro Alto to the west also makes this claim). Inhabited from the 5th century by the Visigoths, the narrow cobbled streets of this unpolished neighborhood create a stepped labyrinth of historic houses and quirky shops. It was once rough, home to dockworkers and seafarers, but as the city's port prospered, so did Alfama—although its rugged charisma remains. Alfama is home to the main **Lisbon Cathedral**, traditional **fado houses**, and many fabulous **viewpoints** along its slopes.

In the northern part of Alfama, the stately and traditional area around **São Jorge Castle** is known as Lisbon's birthplace and often called **Castelo.** It's one of the city's finest neighborhoods, with beautiful views from almost every street corner.

São Vicente

Two major monuments, the **National Pantheon** and the **São Vicente de Fora Church,** are in São Vicente (sown vee-SENT), among a cascade of historic homes on the hillside toward the east of Alfama. Peaceful and poised most of the week, São Vicente comes alive every Saturday morning for the famous **Feira da Ladra Flea Market,** next to the National Pantheon.

Avenida da Liberdade

This broad, leafy avenue running north from Baixa is home to some of Lisbon's most upscale **shops** and priciest real estate. The Avenida terminates in **Marquês de Pombal Square,** with the towering statue of the marquis guarding the entrance to **Eduardo VII Park,** and is surrounded by some of the city's best museums, such as the **Calouste Gulbenkian Museum.**

Chiado and Bairro Alto

Just northwest of Baixa, centered on **Chiado Square,** the Chiado (SHEE-aah-doo) neighborhood is the core of Lisbon's cultural scene—a district packed with **theaters, museums,** and **galleries.** The emblematic square is lined with traditional commerce and fashionable boutiques galore. Named after acclaimed Portuguese poet Almeida Garrett, **Rua Garrett** is flanked by handsome cultural venues, such as the **São Carlos National Theater, Livraria Bertrand,** believed to be one of the oldest bookstores in the world, and

Comércio Square

Lisbon

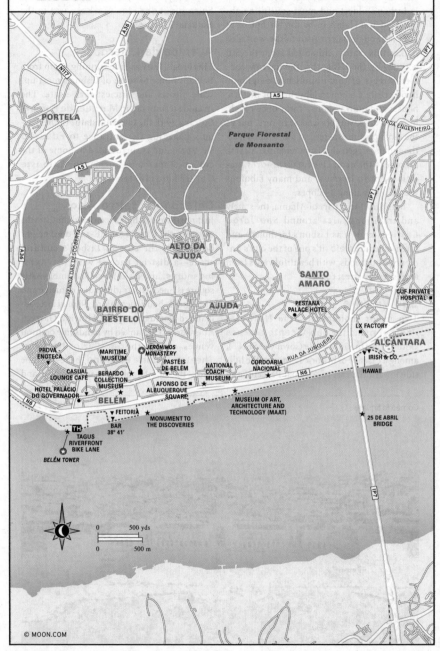

PORTELA

Parque Florestal
de Monsanto

AVENIDA ENGENHEIRO

ALTO DA
AJUDA

SANTO
AMARO

CUF PRIVATE
HOSPITAL

BAIRRO DO
RESTELO

AJUDA

PESTANA
PALACE HOTEL

LX FACTORY

ALCÂNTARA

PROVA
ENOTECA

MARITIME
MUSEUM

JERÓNIMOS
MONASTERY

PASTÉIS
DE BELÉM

NATIONAL
COACH
MUSEUM

CORDOARIA
NACIONAL

RUA DA JUNQUEIRA

IRISH & CO.

HAWAII

CASUAL
LOUNGE CAFÉ

BERARDO
COLLECTION
MUSEUM

AFONSO DE
ALBUQUERQUE
SQUARE

N6

HOTEL PALÁCIO
DO GOVERNADOR

BELÉM

MUSEUM OF ART,
ARCHITECTURE AND
TECHNOLOGY (MAAT)

N6

FEITORIA

BAR
38° 41'

MONUMENT TO
THE DISCOVERIES

25 DE ABRIL
BRIDGE

TH
TAGUS
RIVERFRONT
BIKE LANE

BELÉM TOWER

0   500 yds

0   500 m

© MOON.COM

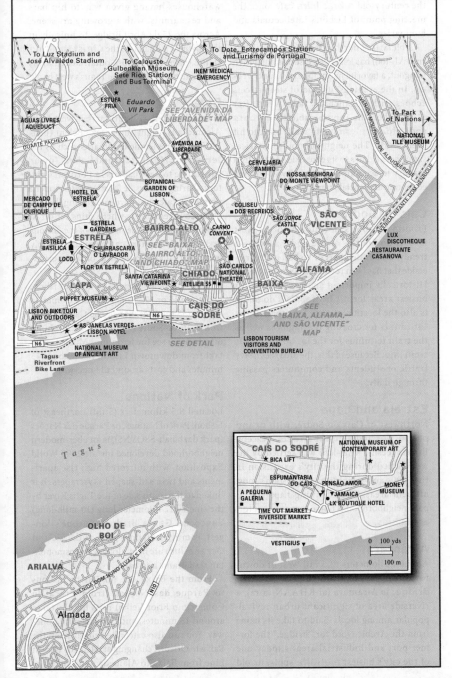

To Luz Stadium and José Alvalade Stadium

To Calouste Gulbenkian Museum, Sete Rios Station and Bus Terminal

To Dote, Entrecampos Station, and Turismo de Portugal

INEM MEDICAL EMERGENCY

To Park of Nations

ESTUFA FRIA

Eduardo VII Park

SEE "AVENIDA DA LIBERDADE" MAP

NATIONAL TILE MUSEUM

ÁGUAS LIVRES AQUEDUCT

DUARTE PACHECO

AVENIDA DA LIBERDADE

AVENIDA MOUZINHO DE ALBUQUERQUE

AVENIDA INFANTE DOM HENRIQUE

CERVEJARIA RAMIRO

NOSSA SENHORA DO MONTE VIEWPOINT

MERCADO DE CAMPO DE OURIQUE

HOTEL DA ESTRELA

BOTANICAL GARDEN OF LISBON

COLISEU DOS RECREIOS

SÃO JORGE CASTLE

SÃO VICENTE

LUX DISCOTHEQUE

ESTRELA GARDENS

BAIRRO ALTO

CARMO CONVENT

RESTAURANTE CASANOVA

ESTRELA

ESTRELA BASÍLICA

CHURRASCARIA O LAVRADOR

SEE "BAIXA, BAIRRO ALTO AND CHIADO" MAP

LOCO

FLOR DA ESTRELA

SÃO CARLOS NATIONAL THEATER

ALFAMA

LAPA

SANTA CATARINA VIEWPOINT

CHIADO

BAIXA

PUPPET MUSEUM

ATÉLIER 55

LISBON BIKE TOUR AND OUTDOORS

CAIS DO SODRÉ

SEE "BAIXA, ALFAMA, AND SÃO VICENTE" MAP

N6

AS JANELAS VERDES LISBON HOTEL

N6

NATIONAL MUSEUM OF ANCIENT ART

LISBON TOURISM VISITORS AND CONVENTION BUREAU

Tagus Riverfront Bike Lane

SEE DETAIL

Tagus

OLHO DE BOI

ARIALVA

AVENIDA DOM NUNO ÁLVARES PEREIRA

N10

Almada

CAIS DO SODRÉ

BICA LIFT

NATIONAL MUSEUM OF CONTEMPORARY ART

ESPUMANTARIA DO CAIS

PENSÃO AMOR

MONEY MUSEUM

A PEQUENA GALERIA

JAMAICA

LX BOUTIQUE HOTEL

TIME OUT MARKET / RIVERSIDE MARKET

VESTIGIUS

0   100 yds
0   100 m

the century-old **A Brasileira** café, once the meeting point of Lisbon's intellectuals and luminaries.

A bit farther northwest, Bairro Alto (BYE-rroo AL-too) has long been Lisbon's bohemian hangout, a favorite haunt for artists and writers. In the evenings, its grid of steep streets echoes with melancholic fado. Visit after 11pm, when the innumerable **small bars** and **colorful nightspots** really start to hit their stride. The neighborhood's historical significance dates to its expansion in the 16th century to accommodate the city's booming economic and social transformation.

Cais do Sodré

Fronting Lisbon's downtown to the west is Cais do Sodré—or the Sodré Docks—a trendy, underrated part of Lisbon on the riverside that has been revitalized in recent years. Historically important and one of the city's busiest areas for **nightlife,** Cais do Sodré is also the location of one of the main **ferry terminals** for crossing the Tagus as well as the train terminus for the **Lisbon-Cascais train line.** Because of this, the area sees heavy traffic of students and commuters passing through daily.

Estrela and Lapa

Northwest of Cais do Sodré, with **grand properties** and **elegant streets,** peaceful Estrela (eesh-TREH-lah) was settled by the well-heeled during the city's expansion in the 1700s and remains one of Lisbon's most affluent areas. The adjoining Lapa (LAH-pah) neighborhood is home to many **foreign embassies.**

Alcântara

About 4 kilometers (2.5 mi) west of downtown, directly beneath the **25 de Abril Bridge,** is Alcântara (al-KHAAN-ta-ra), a riverside area of significant urban revival, popular among locals. Said to take its name from the Arabic word for "bridge," the former port and industrial area is today one of the city's busiest **nightlife** spots, its old warehouses having given way to hip bars and restaurants, with a growing art scene. Across the 25 de Abril Bridge, technically in the town of Almada, is the **Christ the King** statue (page 119), whose outstretched arms dominate the skyline of the Tagus's west bank.

Belém

Four kilometers (2.5 mi) farther west from Alcântara is bright and breezy Belém (beh-LAYN), where iconic landmarks such as the **Jerónimos Monastery** and **Belém Tower** pay tribute to key chapters in Portugal's history, sharing a riverside location with modern museums, cafés, and gardens. During the Age of Discoveries, this is where ships set off to explore the globe. Belém, home of the famous *pastel de Belém* tart, can be uncomfortably busy, particularly in the heat of summer; expect long queues.

To get to Belém from downtown Lisbon, take tram 15 or 127 from the main Comércio Square (35 minutes; €4), or the Cascais train from Cais do Sodré (7 minutes; €1.35). Jump off when you see the Jerónimos Monastery. A taxi from downtown Lisbon takes about 15 minutes and costs around €14 one-way.

Park of Nations

Located 8.5 kilometers (5 mi) northeast of Lisbon, Park of Nations, or Parque das Nações (park dazh nah-SSOYNS), is an über-modern neighborhood developed for the 1998 World Exposition, with mirrored high-rise apartments and twin sail-shaped skyscrapers. It is linked to the south side of the Tagus River by the sinewy 17-kilometer-long (10-mile-long) **Vasco da Gama Bridge,** Europe's longest. Family attractions such as the **Lisbon Oceanarium** are here, along with cosmopolitan restaurants and bars.

From the Baixa, the no. 781 or 210 bus to Parque das Nações (from Praça do Comércioto Prior Velho) runs hourly, takes around 15 minutes, and costs about €2 one-way. You can also catch the subway from the Baixa to Oriente, changing at Alameda (Green Line from Baixa to Alameda and Pink Line from Alameda to Oriente), which will take around 20 minutes and cost €1.50 for a single fare. A taxi takes under 10 minutes and will cost around €11.

SAFETY

As with many tourist destinations, Lisbon is afflicted by petty and opportunistic crime. Take basic precautions such as not walking along dark streets alone at night, not leaving valuables in rental vehicles, and not carrying large amounts of cash. Pickpockets are an issue, so wear backpacks in front in crowded areas and on public transport, or better still, use separate concealed pouches for your cash and documents. If you have an issue, call **PSP tourist police** (tel. 213 421 623) or visit the nearest police station. In an emergency, call **112.**

PLANNING YOUR TIME

Much of Lisbon's city center can be covered in a day, but it's worth spending at least 2-3 days here. Set aside more days if you want to explore the many **day trips** within a few hours' drive of the city (page 91).

While in Lisbon, don't miss the landmark São Jorge Castle, eating a *pastel de Belém*, drinking a rooftop cocktail, and trundling around the city on the iconic tram 28. An absolute must is dinner at a **fado restaurant** in Bairro Alto. If you've had enough of the

monuments and hustle and bustle, head out of the capital to any of the day trip destinations within an hour away. But to really soak up Lisbon's atmosphere and charisma, you should slow down, find a nice café somewhere along the riverside, and simply people-watch. Wander the cobbled maze-like streets of historic quarters like Alfama, or take a moment to sit and admire the views from one of the city's fabulous viewpoints.

A great way to cover the must-sees is either a **hop-on hop-off bus** that stops at all main attractions and landmarks, or **tram 28,** which circumnavigates Lisbon's main neighborhoods. Other good options to explore include the neatly organized **subway,** nifty *tuk-tuk* carts, and a **hop-on hop-off ferryboat.**

In mid-June, the traditional **Santo António festivities,** dedicated to the city's patron saint, explode into party mode. In December, **Christmas** trimmings and roasted chestnuts bring warmth to the city. July and August can get very hot, and even though many of the city's residents head south for summer vacation, it is still packed with tourists. **Summer** and **New Year** are tourism high seasons, when hotel prices soar and the city is full of visitors. Good times to visit are **March-May** and **September-October,** when the weather is pleasant and the hotels less expensive.

Itinerary Ideas

DAY 1: BAIXA AND BAIRRO ALTO

1 Spend the morning discovering downtown Lisbon. Explore famous **Comércio Square** and its museums and landmarks—they're all within walking distance. Make sure you climb to the top of the Triumphal Arch on Rua Augusta.

2 A few streets back from the main square is the **Santa Justa Elevator,** also called the Carmo Lift. This historical contraption transports passengers from downtown up to the famous Bairro Alto neighborhood. Hop onto the elevator and admire how the old-fashioned machinery comes to life, taking you to the viewing platform at the top.

3 Once up in Bairro Alto, visit the **Carmo Convent,** a once-magnificent building

Itinerary Ideas

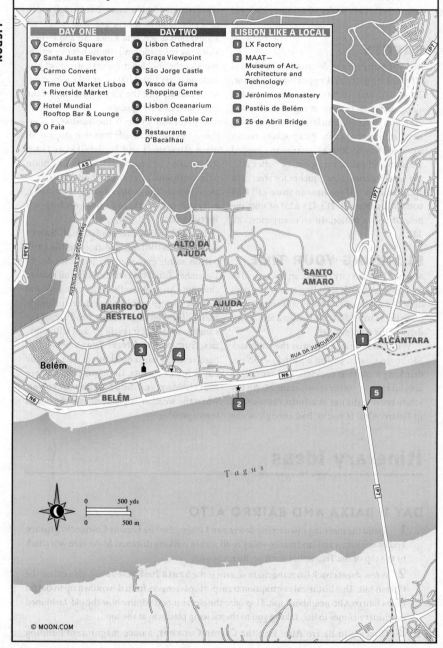

DAY ONE	DAY TWO	LISBON LIKE A LOCAL
1 Comércio Square	1 Lisbon Cathedral	1 LX Factory
2 Santa Justa Elevator	2 Graça Viewpoint	2 MAAT— Museum of Art, Architecture and Technology
3 Carmo Convent	3 São Jorge Castle	
4 Time Out Market Lisboa + Riverside Market	4 Vasco da Gama Shopping Center	3 Jerónimos Monastery
5 Hotel Mundial Rooftop Bar & Lounge	5 Lisbon Oceanarium	4 Pastéis de Belém
6 O Faia	6 Riverside Cable Car	5 25 de Abril Bridge
	7 Restaurante D'Bacalhau	

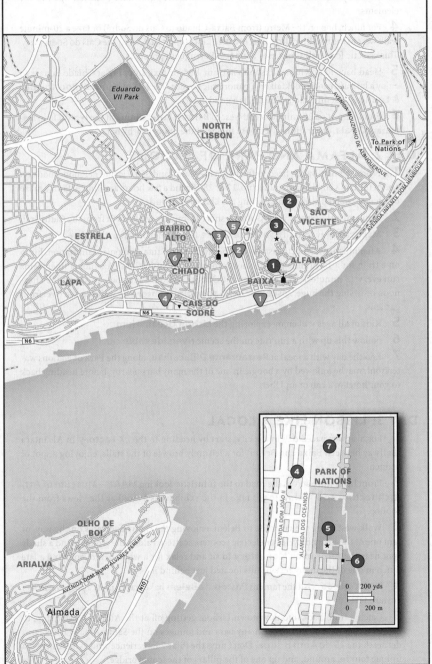

destroyed by a dramatic earthquake whose dramatic ruins have been left open to the elements.

4 For lunch, hop on the Metro (from Baixa-Chiado to Cais do Sodré) or take a 20-minute walk west to the bustling **Time Out Market Lisboa,** set back from the Cais do Sodré quay. This eclectic food hall showcases the finest Portuguese products.

5 Head back to downtown Lisbon via tram, bus, or taxi, stopping at Chiado Square to enjoy a late-afternoon cocktail on a panoramic terrace. The **Hotel Mundial Rooftop Bar & Lounge,** just off Chiado Square, is a good choice.

6 From here, it's a 20-minute stroll west to Bairro Alto for dinner at the typical fado restaurant **O Faia.** After dinner, let loose in one of the many nearby bars.

DAY 2: ALFAMA AND PARK OF NATIONS

1 From Lisbon's Baixa, head to the historic Alfama and São Vicente neighborhoods on one of the city's emblematic trams (no. 12 or 28). Spend a few hours ambling Alfama's maze of ancient cobbled streets and visiting the **Lisbon Cathedral.**

2 Don't miss the **Graça Viewpoint,** a short 15-minute walk north from the Cathedral.

3 Make your way toward **São Jorge Castle** for a spot of lunch with a view.

4 After lunch, walk northeast toward the river to the Santa Apolónia train station. Jump on a train for a 10-minute journey north toward Park of Nations (Azambuja line; trains run every 15 minutes). Exit at modernist Oriente station. Here you can spend the afternoon browsing the huge **Vasco da Gama shopping center** and walking the riverfront gardens.

5 Kids of all ages will enjoy exploring the **Lisbon Oceanarium.**

6 Follow this up with a fun ride on the scenic **riverside cable car.**

7 End the day with a meal at **Restaurante D'Bacalhau,** along the Park of Nations waterfront, maybe followed by a boogie in one of the many bars nearby, before heading back to your hotel in a cab or an Uber.

DAY 3: LISBON LIKE A LOCAL

1 For a slower-paced day in the city, start by heading to the **LX Factory** in Alcântara (halfway between Baixa and Belém) for a leisurely browse of the stalls, enjoying a spot of brunch.

2 From here, walk across the road to the futuristic-looking **MAAT—Museum of Art, Architecture and Technology;** take in the exhibitions as well as the views from the rooftop.

3 Walk west along the riverside to Belém, enjoying the sights and cafés on the way, or rent one of the many bicycles or electric scooters scattered along the stretch. Find a shady spot near the **Jerónimos Monastery** to sit and relax for a while before enjoying a late lunch in one of the many restaurants located just behind it.

4 Now it's time to visit the famous **Pastéis de Belém** bakery to sample a *pastel de Belém* custard tart.

5 Catch a train back into downtown Lisbon, getting off at the Alcântara-Mar stop, to enjoy a sundowner at one of the many bars and lounges on the Santo Amaro Docks underneath the **25 de Abril Bridge.** Don't miss the Pilar 7 Experience while you're here—a unique tour in, around, and up one of the pillars of the iconic bridge.

Sights

BAIXA
Comércio Square
(Praça do Comércio)

This vast square, with views of the Tagus River, bustles with visitors and features a statue of King José I on his horse. The impressive colonnades that frame it on three sides house several ministries, museums, shops, and restaurants. It's one of the city's main transport hubs, with many trams and buses running from here; it's also directly across from the Cais do Sodré ferry terminal.

THE LISBON STORY CENTRE

Praça do Comércio 78; tel. 211 941 099; www. lisboastorycentre.pt; daily 10am-8pm; €7; Metro Terreiro do Paço, Blue Line

The Lisbon Story Centre recounts the key chapters of Lisbon's history through state-of-the-art interactive multimedia.

AUGUSTA TRIUMPHAL ARCH
(Arco da Rua Augusta)

Praça do Comércio; tel. 210 999 599; www.visitlisboa. com; daily 9am-8pm; viewing terrace €2.50; Metro Terreiro do Paço, Blue Line

The formal entrance to the Baixa neighborhood, the decorative Augusta Triumphal Arch was built to mark the city's resilience and glorious rebirth following the 1755 earthquake. Historical Portuguese figures such as explorer Vasco da Gama and the Marquis of Pombal adorn the gateway's six columns, gazing over Comércio Square and out to the river. Inside the arch, a narrow spiral staircase made from solid stone climbs to a viewing terrace that offers sweeping views of the plaza.

Archaeological Center of Rua Correeiros
(Núcleo Arqueológico da Rua Correeiros)

Rua dos Correeiros 15-23; tel. 211 131 004; Mon.-Sat. 10am-6pm; free; Metro Baixa-Chiado, Green/Blue Lines

Overlooked by many tourists, the Archaeological Center of Rua Correeiros showcases a wealth of Roman artifacts uncovered during the construction of the bank next door. Free guided tours of Roman ruins beneath the streets of Lisbon must be booked in advance and are available in English.

Santa Justa Elevator
(Elevador de Santa Justa)

www.carris.pt; daily 7:30am-11pm May-Oct., daily 7:30am-9pm Nov.-Apr.; round-trip €5.15; Metro Baixa-Chiado, Green/Blue Lines

Also called the **Carmo Lift,** the 19th-century neo-Gothic, wrought-iron Santa Justa Elevator is the only vertical lift in Lisbon, connecting the Baixa area to the Bairro Alto neighborhood, saving a steep climb. Inaugurated in 1902, it is classified as a national monument. Standing at 45 meters (148 ft) tall, it was designed by engineer Raoul Mesnier du Ponsard in a style similar to that of the Eiffel Tower. The lift is stunning at night when lit up and has a fabulous viewing platform at the top. Intriguingly, it can transport more people going up than coming down. It is accessed via Rua do Ouro at the bottom, or Carmo Square at the top. The viewing platform (€1.50) is also accessible directly from Carmo Square, up the hill behind the lift.

Rossio Square
(Praça Dom Pedro IV)

Metro Rossio, Green Line

The beating heart of Lisbon, located downtown, Rossio Square has long been one of the city's main meeting places, a lively, genteel square of Pombaline architecture lined with cafés, trees, and two grand Baroque fountains at either end. Housed in the impressive buildings framing the square are the stately **Dona Maria II National Theater** and the historic

Café Nicola, which dates to the 18th century and was one of the first cafés to emerge in Lisbon. Also nearby is the ornate Rossio train station, which is typically Manueline in its architecture. One of the square's distinguishing features is the wavy black-and-white cobblestone paving.

Glória Funicular
(Elevador da Glória)

www.carris.pt; Mon.-Thurs. 7:15am-11:55pm, Fri. 7:15am-12:25am, Sat. 8:45am-12:25pm, Sun. and holidays 9:15am-11:55pm; round-trip €3.60; Metro: Restauradores, Blue Line

The quirky Glória Funicular puts the "fun" in funicular. It has become an emblem of Lisbon, its graffiti scrawl only adding to its charm, mirroring its urban surroundings. Inaugurated in 1885, it connects the Restauradores Square in the Baixa to the São Pedro de Alcântara Viewpoint in Bairro Alto via a steep track that cuts straight through a dense residential area packed with 19th-century buildings. Practical for locals, it's a treat for visitors.

ALFAMA
★ São Jorge Castle
(Castelo de São Jorge)

Rua de Santa Cruz do Castelo; tel. 218 800 620; www.castelodesaojorge.pt; daily 9am-9pm Mar.-Oct., daily 9am-6pm Nov.-Feb.; €8.50; tram 28 or Castelo Bus, line 737

The São Jorge Castle sits on a summit high above historic Baixa. One of Lisbon's most recognizable landmarks and historically important monuments, the original fortress was built by the Visigoths in the 5th century and expanded by the Moors in the mid-11th century because of its prime defensive location. It was expanded again during Christian rule and today contains the medieval castle, ruins of the former royal palace, stunning gardens, and part of an 11th-century citadel that housed the city's elite.

1: Glória Funicular 2: Rossio Square 3: Augusta Triumphal Arch

The site itself is vast and impressive, hemmed in by towering ancient walls. It boasts amazing panoramic views of Lisbon, especially if at sunset. The well-kept castle grounds teeming with regal peacocks are beautiful to wander; visitors can soak up the enchanting atmosphere of the garden, search for the surviving traces of Moorish influence in the design and décor, climb towers where watchmen once kept their protective sights on Lisbon, roam the ruins of the citadel's former Royal Palace, and discover the castle's many secrets, like the Door of Treason, through which elusive messengers snuck in and out.

A permanent exhibition of relics uncovered here includes objects from the 7th century BC to the 18th century. The Black Chamber, a camera obscura, provides 360-degree views of the city through an optical system of mirrors and lenses, while an open-air viewpoint looks over the city center and the Tagus River. Renowned restaurant Casa do Leão (www.pousadas.pt) and a casual café are also within the castle walls.

Lisbon Cathedral
(Sé de Lisboa)

Largo da Sé; tel. 218 866 752; www.patriarcado-lisboa.pt; daily 9am-7pm; main cathedral free; tram 28 or 12

Between the Alfama neighborhood and Castelo, Lisbon Cathedral is the oldest and most famous church in the city. Its official name is the Church of Santa Maria Maior, but it is often simply called the Sé. Construction began in 1147, and successive modifications and renovations span the centuries. Its exterior is austere, with two robust towers. Inside, a wealth of decorative features reflects different eras. The neoclassical and rococo main chapel contains the tombs of King Afonso IV and his family. You'll also see lofty Gothic vaults, sculptured Romanesque motifs, stained-glass rose windows, and a Baroque sacristy. The Cloister (Mon.-Sat. 10am-5pm, Sun. 2pm-5pm, extended hours until 7pm May-Sept.; €2.50) houses Roman, Arab, and medieval relics excavated during

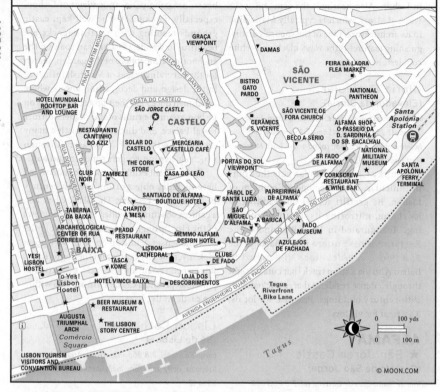

Baixa, Alfama, and São Vicente

(map showing locations including:) GRAÇA VIEWPOINT, DAMAS, FEIRA DA LADRA FLEA MARKET, SÃO VICENTE, NATIONAL PANTHEON, Santa Apolónia Station, HOTEL MUNDIAL / ROOFTOP BAR AND LOUNGE, BISTRO GATO PARDO, SÃO JORGE CASTLE, CASTELO, SÃO VICENTE DE FORA CHURCH, CERÂMICS S. VICENTE, ALFAMA SHOP Ó PASSEIO DA D. SARDINHA E DO SR. BACALHAU, RESTAURANTE CANTINHO DO AZIZ, SOLAR DO CASTELO, MERCEARIA CASTELLO CAFÉ, BECO A SÉRIO, SR FADO DE ALFAMA, NATIONAL MILITARY MUSEUM, SANTA APOLÓNIA FERRY TERMINAL, THE CORK STORE, CLUB NOIR, ZAMBEZE, CASA DO LEÃO, PORTAS DO SOL VIEWPOINT, CORKSCREW RESTAURANT & WINE BAR, SANTIAGO DE ALFAMA BOUTIQUE HOTEL, FAROL DE SANTA LUZIA, PARREIRINHA DE ALFAMA, TABERNA DA BAIXA, CHAPITÔ À MESA, SÃO MIGUEL D'ALFAMA, A BAIUCA, FADO MUSEUM, ARCHAEOLOGICAL CENTER OF RUA CORREEIROS, PRADO RESTAURANT, MEMMO ALFAMA DESIGN HOTEL, ALFAMA, AZULEJOS DE FACHADA, YES! LISBON HOSTEL, BAIXA, LISBON CATHEDRAL, TASCA KOME, CLUBE DE FADO, To Yes! Lisbon Hostel, HOTEL VINCCI BAIXA, LOJA DOS DESCOBRIMENTOS, Tagus Riverfront Bike Lane, BEER MUSEUM & RESTAURANT, AUGUSTA TRIUMPHAL ARCH, THE LISBON STORY CENTRE, Comércio Square, LISBON TOURISM VISITORS AND CONVENTION BUREAU, Tagus

0 100 yds
0 100 m

© MOON.COM

archaeological digs. The **Treasury** (Mon.-Sat. 10am-5pm; €2.50) on the second floor contains jewels from various periods. Tram 28 stops right outside the cathedral's door.

Fado Museum
(Museu do Fado)

Largo Chafariz de Dentro 1; tel. 218 823 470; www. museudofado.pt; Tues.-Sun. 10am-6pm; €5; Metro Santa Apolónia, Blue Line

The Fado Museum showcases traditional fado, a soulful and often mournful musical genre that is to Portugal what the blues are to Memphis. Fado's origins are debated, but the consensus is that it was born in Alfama in the 1820s. This interactive museum hosts a permanent exhibition with photographs, records, and instruments. There are also sometimes live performances.

National Military Museum
(Museu Militar)

Largo Museu da Artilharia; tel. 218 842 300; www. exercito.pt; Tues.-Fri. 10am-5pm, Sat.-Sun. and holidays 10am-12:30pm and 1:30pm-5pm; €3; Metro Santa Apolónia, Blue Line

Across the square from the Santa Apolónia train station, the National Military Museum is Portugal's largest and oldest military museum. Beautiful, lofty, tile-clad rooms contain 26,000 pieces of military paraphernalia spanning centuries, including the former Royal Arsenal. The building is a striking monument, built on the site of a 16th-century foundry.

Lisbon's Best Views

Because Lisbon is laid out over seven hills, gorgeous views can be found throughout the city. Public viewing points (*miradouros*) offer views of the cityscape. Some are enhanced with cafés and restaurants, landscaped gardens, and even chic lounges. Best of all, they're free. Visit at sunset for a truly special experience.

- The **Portas do Sol Viewpoint** (Miradouro Portas do Sol; Largo Portas do Sol) overlooks the charismatic Alfama neighborhood.

- The **Graça Viewpoint** (Miradouro da Graça; Calçada da Graça) peers over São Jorge Castle.

- The famous **São Pedro de Alcântara Viewpoint** (Miradouro São Pedro de Alcântara; Rua São Pedro de Alcântara) provides panoramic views over São Jorge Castle and Alfama, as well as Lisbon Cathedral and the Tagus.

- The **Santa Catarina Viewpoint** (Miradouro Santa Catarina; Rua de Santa Catarina) offers the best views over the 25 de Abril Bridge and Lisbon's ship-lined docks, as well as amazing sunset vistas.

- The romantic **Nossa Senhora do Monte Viewpoint** (Miradouro da Nossa Senhora do Monte; Largo Monte) is the highest viewpoint, offering bird's-eye views over the old quarters and castle all the way to the Tagus River.

Along with the *miradouros*, the **São Jorge Castle** has possibly the best views in the city. Panoramas can also be enjoyed from hotel rooftop bars, such as the **Hotel Mundial** (Praça Martim Moniz 2), where the Sunset Parties have a cult following.

SÃO VICENTE
National Pantheon
(Panteão Nacional)

Campo de Santa Clara; tel. 218 854 820; Tues.-Sat. 10am-6pm Apr.-Sept., Tues.-Sat. 10am-5pm Oct.-Mar.; €4; Metro Santa Apolónia, Blue Line

The National Pantheon—otherwise known as the Church of Santa Engrácia—has Baroque architecture and a distinctive domed roof that can be seen from most of central Lisbon. It is on the site of the original Santa Engrácia church, which began renovations in 1681 and took more than 300 years to complete. Construction dragged on for so long that the Portuguese call any lengthy project "work of Santa Engrácia." In 1916, the church was converted into a pantheon, a process that took another 50 years. Today, the building boasts a majestic nave with a polychrome marble decoration typical of Portuguese Baroque architecture. It is home to tombs of historic personalities such as writer Almeida Garrett, fado singer Amália Rodrigues, legendary soccer star Eusébio, and Portuguese presidents.

The views from the front steps and the terrace around the dome are breathtaking.

São Vicente de Fora Church
(Igreja de São Vicente de Fora)

Largo de São Vicente; tel. 218 824 400; www. patriarcado-lisboa.pt; Tues.-Sun. 10am-6pm; €5; Metro Santa Apolónia, Blue Line

In its present guise, the São Vicente de Fora Church, or Monastery of São Vicente de Fora, is considered one of the finest examples of mannerist architecture in the country. Rebuilt from a 12th-century church, it dates to the 16th century and houses one of the biggest collections of Baroque glazed tiles in the world, used to clad the cloisters, stairways, and aisles. There are also two mausoleums, one belonging to the Royal House of Braganza and the other to the city's archbishops, known as the Patriarchs of Lisbon. The must-see Patriarchate's Museum showcases beautiful historic works of religious art. Enjoy fabulous views from the roof terrace.

National Tile Museum
(Museu Nacional do Azulejo)

Rua da Madre de Deus 4; tel. 218 100 340; www.
museudoazulejo.gov.pt; Tues.-Sun. 10am-6pm; €5;
Metro Santa Apolónia, Blue Line

Located in a 16th-century convent, the National Tile Museum contains a collection of traditional hand-painted *azulejo* ceramic tile plaques, some dating from the 15th century. It explores the history and tradition behind the art and craft of tilework, and the building is a splendid example of the magnificence of Portuguese Baroque, with carved and gilded wood features, old paintings, and historical *azulejo* panels.

★ AVENIDA DA LIBERDADE

Stretching 1.5 kilometers (0.9 mi) between the Baixa downtown area and the Eduardo VII Park, the Avenida da Liberdade is Lisbon's main boulevard, an elegant, regal main avenue running through the heart of the city. Lined with leafy trees, it's dotted with distinguished statues and monuments, high-end designer boutiques, lovely little coffee kiosks, arts and crafts stalls, chic hotels, and trendy bars and restaurants. With exquisitely patterned cobblestone walkways and magnificent period architecture lining the stately boulevard, enhanced by cool, leafy gardens, it's often compared to Paris's Champs-Élysées, and it was originally intended for Lisbon's wealthy. Most buildings along the avenue date from the 19th century, built after the devastating 1755 earthquake that razed most of Lisbon. Its main terminuses are **Restauradores Square** in the Baixa and the noble **Marquês de Pombal Square** in front of the **Eduardo VII Park.**

This bustling artery adopts the spirit of each season, with cute Christmas markets in winter, spring sales for shoppers, an alfresco atmosphere in summer when it plays host to the popular saints festivities, and falling golden brown leaves in autumn. Along this lavish avenue there are lovely water features, and it boasts the typical grandiose classical architecture of 19th-century Portugal. A fantastic place for window-shopping and people-watching, everything about the Avenida da Liberdade is distinguished and grand. A walk downhill down this street is a great introduction to Lisbon.

Marquês de Pombal Square
(Praça Marquês de Pombal)

Metro Marquês de Pombal, Blue/Yellow Lines

The massive statue of the Marquis of Pombal towering in the middle of this busy roundabout is one of Lisbon's most recognizable landmarks. Sebastião José de Carvalho e

Avenida da Liberdade

To Estufa Fria
RUA JOAQUIM ANTÓNIO DE AGUIAR
Eduardo VII Park
RUA CASTILHO
AV FONTES PEREIRA DE MELO
MARQUÊS DE POMBAL SQUARE
FOOD MARKET
O CACHO DOURADO
THE GREAT AMERICAN DISASTER ▼
LUIS ONOFRE
AVENIDA DA LIBERDADE
RUA ALEXANDRE HERCULANO
DELIDELUX
RUA ROSA ARAÚJO
RUA RODRIGUES SAMPAIO
RUA DE SANTA MARTA
★ MEDEIROS E ALMEIDA HOUSE-MUSEUM
RUA CASTILHO
RUA BARATA SALGUEIRO
PRADA
AVENIDA DA LIBERDADE
RUA DO PASSADIÇO
RUA DO SALITRE
LOUIS VUITTON LISBONNE
TIVOLI FORUM
GUCCI
OTRO PERFUME CONCEPT
BABY LIBERDADE
BOUTIQUE DOS RELÓGIOS PLUS
RUA DA ALEGRIA
▼CHAFARIZ DO VINHO
RUA DA CONCEIÇÃO DA GLÓRIA
RUA DO TELHAL
BOUTIQUE HOTEL HERITAGE AVENIDA DA LIBERDADE

0   200 yds
0   200 m

© MOON.COM

1: São Jorge Castle **2:** tile from the National Tile Museum **3:** Fado Museum **4:** Eduardo VII Park

Melo, the 1st Marquis of Pombal, was prime minister in the 18th century. His soaring statue faces the Tagus River, strategically between **Eduardo VII Park** and the cosmopolitan Avenida da Liberdade, the start of several main thoroughfares.

Medeiros e Almeida House-Museum
(Casa Museu Medeiros e Almeida)
Rua Rosa Araújo 41; tel. 213 547 892; www.casa-museumedeirosealmeida.pt; Mon.-Sat. 10am-5pm; €5; Metro Marquês de Pombal, Blue/Yellow Lines

Once a private residence, this museum is another of Lisbon's lesser-known attractions and is definitely worth a visit. Its more than two dozen rooms house a massive collection of 17th- to 20th-century artifacts, including furniture, clocks, Chinese porcelain, European paintings, silverware, and, word has it, Napoleon Bonaparte's tea service. Set aside 1-2 hours to take in the priceless private collection, amassed by the house's former owner, businessman Antonio Medeiros e Almeida, who had an eye for fine arts and rare pieces. The grandiose manor home is replete with extraordinary artifacts that reflect a lifetime of travels and deals. The house itself is a handsome, stately mansion fit for one of the most successful Portuguese businessmen of the 20th century. Visitors will also see how upper-class homes were designed, styled, and furnished in 20th-century Lisbon.

Calouste Gulbenkian Museum
(Museu Calouste Gulbenkian)
Av. de Berna 45A; tel. 217 823 461; www.gulbenkian. pt/museu; Wed.-Mon. 10am-6pm; €14; Metro São Sebastião, Blue/Red Lines

A major hub of the arts, the Calouste Gulbenkian Museum is one of Lisbon's less-celebrated treasures despite being considered by many as one of the great museums of the world. Ranging from Greco-Roman antiquity to contemporary pieces, with 18th-century French art well represented, this is the personal collection of wealthy Armenian entrepreneur and philanthropist Calouste Sarkis Gulbenkian, who spent his final years in Lisbon. Following his death in 1955, his will established his desire to create an eponymous foundation to the benefit of the community.

The museum is housed in two separate buildings—the Founder's Collection and the Modern Collection—connected by a lovely garden, and both with cafeterias. A full morning or afternoon should be set aside to see the entire collection and enjoy the grounds. The Founder's Collection showcases over 6,000 excellently presented and well-curated exotic and ancient artifacts from all over the world, while the Modern Collection celebrates works of art from the 20th century onward and is considered to be the most complete collection of modern Portuguese art in the world. The stunning works of French glass and jewelry designer René Lalique (1860-1945) are a highlight. Visiting exhibitions regularly feature works by acclaimed and emerging national and international artists and artisans, such as experimental projects by Dutch video artist Manon de Boer and renowned Portuguese artist Sarah Affonso. Art lovers could probably spend the whole day wandering this fascinating and underrated museum.

At the time of writing, the Modern Collection building was closed for renovation with reopening scheduled for 2022.

CHIADO AND BAIRRO ALTO
★ Carmo Convent
(Convento do Carmo)
Largo do Carmo; tel. 213 478 629; www. museuarqueologicodocarmo.pt, Mon.-Sat. 10am-6pm May-Sept., Mon.-Sat. 10am-5pm Oct.-Apr.; €4; Metro Baixa-Chiado or Rossio, Green/Blue Lines

Once Lisbon's largest church, the Carmo Convent is a stark reminder of the vast devastation caused by the 1755 earthquake that razed the city and large swaths of Portugal. Originally built in 1389 by order of Nuno Álvares Pereira, an influential knight who led the Portuguese army, the church and convent sit on a hill directly opposite the São Jorge Castle. Today only its naked Gothic ruins still stand.

The convent's walls are solid, but the roof of the main nave is just a web of bare vaulted Gothic arches against the sky, a melancholy and dramatic sight. The roof is said to have crumbled onto the congregation during mass when the 1755 earthquake struck. The convent was in the process of being rebuilt when religious orders were abolished in Portugal in the 1830s, leaving it half-finished. There's an eerie magic about wandering the spindly remains of the roofless site. Its former grandeur is apparent, and the many artifacts inside, such as ancient stone tools and a Peruvian mummy, are unique, but most of all, its skeletal state is a thought-provoking reminder of the twists and turns of history.

The site is also home to the **Museu Arqueológico do Carmo,** a museum with a collection of relics from dissolved monasteries, including sarcophagi and the grisly but well-preserved Peruvian sacrificial mummies. There are also various tombs in the archeological museum, including that of King Ferdinand I.

National Museum of Contemporary Art
(Museu Nacional de Arte Contemporânea do Chiado; MNAC)

Rua Serpa Pinto 4; tel. 213 432 148; www. museuartecontemporanea.gov.pt; Tues.-Sun. 10am-6pm; €4.50; Metro Baixa-Chiado, Green/Blue Lines

Established by government decree in 1911, the National Museum of Contemporary Art—Museu do Chiado is housed in what was the old convent of São Francisco da Cidade. The convent was severely damaged by the 1755 Lisbon earthquake, and later by a huge fire in 1988; it was redesigned by French architect Jean-Michel Wilmotte and re-inaugurated in 1994. It specializes in 19th- and 20th-century Portuguese contemporary art, divided into temporary exhibitions and a permanent collection displaying thematic exhibitions that span Portuguese Romantic, naturalist, modern, and contemporary art.

São Roque Church and Museum
(Igreja e Museu de São Roque)

Largo Trindade Coelho; tel. 213 235 065 or tel. 213 235 449; http://mais.scml.pt/museu-saoroque; Mon. 2pm-7pm, Tues., Wed., Fri.-Sun. 10am-7pm, Thurs.

Carmo Convent

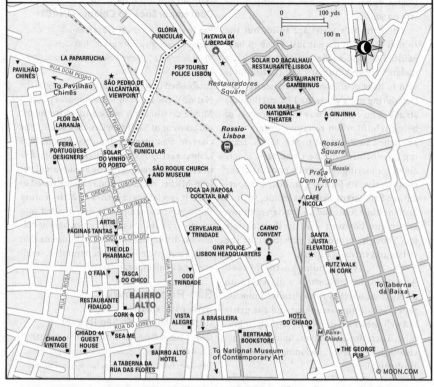

Baixa, Bairro Alto, and Chiado

10am-8pm; church free, museum €2.50 (children free), Sun. 10am-2pm free; Metro: Baixa-Chiado, Green/Blue Lines

One of the first art museums to open in Portugal, the São Roque Museum was originally created to house an important collection of Italian art. Since its founding it has occupied a 17th-century cloister adjacent to the Church of São Roque, which had been donated to the Holy House of Mercy of Lisbon in 1768, after the expulsion of the Jesuits. Throughout the 20th century it was subject to a series of extensive refurbishments, allowing the museum to greatly expand its permanent exhibition area. Today comprising over 100 years of history, the São Roque Museum is said to be one of the most beautiful and complete museums of Portuguese religious artifacts and paintings.

The building itself is also a treat to visit. Its plain exterior belies the exquisiteness of its lavish gold-leaf interior and ornate embellishments. From the outside it may well be one of the city's least remarkable churches, but on the inside, it is one of the most opulent—and said to be home to one of Europe's most expensive chapels (the fourth on the left). This church was also one of only a handful of buildings in Lisbon's westerly quarters to withstand the 1755 earthquake without major damage.

Botanical Garden of Lisbon (Jardim Botânico da Universidade de Lisboa)

Rua da Escola Politécnica 56/58; tel. 213 921 800;

The 1755 Earthquake

On the morning of Saturday, November 1, 1755, the ground shook violently in Portugal. What followed was one of the most devastating and deadliest earthquakes Europe had seen. The 1755 earthquake—also referred to as the Great Lisbon Earthquake—destroyed not only vast swaths of Lisbon but also much of Portugal, and it triggered a tsunami that tore up the Tagus River, washing out most of Lisbon's downtown area. Portugal happened to be celebrating All Saints Day on the day of the quake; widespread fires were caused by lit candles toppling in homes and churches.

With most of its buildings destroyed or greatly damaged, the decision was made to raze what was left of Lisbon's entire downtown quarter and rebuild with an orderly, spacious, grid-like layout. This massive undertaking was spearheaded by Sebastião José de Carvalho e Melo, the 1st Marquis of Pombal and then a Minister of the Kingdom of Portugal. As a tribute, his name was lent to the architecture that today characterizes downtown Lisbon—the Pombaline style, hence, the *Baixa Pombalina*. This thorough renovation saw a revolutionary anti-seismic building method, centered on the *gaiola Pombalina* (Pombaline cage), a masonry building reinforced with an internal wood-lattice cage that was both sturdy and earthquake-resistant. The innovative technique was among the earliest quake-proof constructions in Europe, making Lisbon one of the first truly modern cities in the world.

While the handsome Pombaline buildings continue to stand firm and proud, other landmarks still bear the scars of one of Portugal's darkest days:

- **Augusta Triumphal Arch:** This majestic archway was built purposely after the 1755 earthquake to signal the rebirth of Lisbon (page 43).

- **Carmo Convent:** The naked bones of the roofless Carmo Convent are a stark reminder of the extent of the devastation caused by the 1755 earthquake. Built in 1389, the once magnificent Gothic building was left ruined beyond repair (page 50).

- **National Museum of Contemporary Art:** This museum is housed in the former São Francisco da Cidade convent, a complex of monastic buildings severely damaged by the earthquake. In 1988, the area was again devastated by a raging fire; the museum was completely overhauled and re-inaugurated in 1994 (page 51).

- **São Roque Church:** Home to "the world's most expensive chapel," São Roque Church was one of few buildings in the westerly quarters to survive the Great Lisbon Earthquake with only minor damage (page 51).

www.museus.ulisboa.pt/pt-pt/jardim-botanico-lisboa; daily 9am-7:30pm Oct.-Mar., daily 9am-8pm Apr.-Sept.; €3; Metro Rato, Yellow Line

Once declared the finest botanical garden in southern Europe, the Lisbon Botanical Garden is an enchanting oasis of cool and calm. Covering 10 acres on the Olivete Hill, on the northern fringe of Bairro Alto, it is resplendent with rare and exotic tree and plant species, comprising flora from all over the world. Created between 1858 and 1873, it is still home to one of the largest collections of subtropical vegetation in Europe. The garden is particularly rich in tropical species from New Zealand, Australia, China, Japan, and South America, and it creates its own microclimate.

CAIS DO SODRÉ

Cais do Sodré has recently undergone a much-needed facelift that elevated the neighborhood from seedy to swanky. Gone are the days when swashbuckling sailors sought their thrills during layovers in Lisbon and fishermen told their colorful tales in the many tackle shops that dotted the area; nowadays the tackle shops have been converted into cool hangouts, brothels into trendy bars, and the hip Time Out Market Lisboa is where new gastro trends are set.

Bica Lift
(Ascensor da Bica)

*Calçada da Bica Pequena 1; tel. 213 613 000;
Mon.-Sat. 7am-9pm, Sun. and public holidays
9am-9pm; €3.80 round-trip, purchased on-board*

Inaugurated in 1892, this funicular connects Lisbon's downtown to the Bica and Bairro Alto neighborhoods, running every 15 minutes between Rua de São Paulo, near Cais do Sodré's Time Out Market Lisboa, and Largo do Calhariz (Calhariz Square). Its route takes passengers up one of Lisbon's steepest hills, Rua da Bica de Duarte Belo, on what is arguably one of the city's most picturesque funicular routes, passing quaint houses and traditional commerce. The funicular's traction system was originally powered by steam engines before being electrified in 1914. It was declared a National Monument in 2002 and is one of the city's most popular tourist activities. Once up at the top, make sure to visit the **Santa Catarina Viewpoint,** which offers stunning bird's-eye views of the city.

Money Museum
(Museu do Dinheiro)

*Largo de São Julião; tel. 213 213 240; www.
museudodinheiro.pt; Wed.-Sun. 10am-6pm; free;
Metro Baixa-Chiado or Terreiro do Paço, Blue Line*

Part of the Bank of Portugal's premises, this fascinating, interactive multimedia museum is probably one of Lisbon's more underrated sights. It takes visitors on a trip covering the entire history of global currency, from pre-currency civilization to payments in the modern world. In a lofty converted 17th-century church, you can handle a real bar of gold, visit old Roman ruins in the basement, see currency from all over the world, and learn about how money is made, before popping into the on-site café.

ESTRELA AND LAPA
Estrela Basílica
(Basílica da Estrela)

*Praça da Estrela; tel. 213 960 915; www.
patrimoniocultural.gov.pt; daily 7:30am-8pm; free;
tram 25 or 28*

The neoclassical Estrela Basílica was built in the 18th century by order of Queen Maria I, whose tomb it houses. The interior walls and flooring are clad in swaths of yellow, pink, and gray marble in stunning geometric patterns. Twin bell towers stand atop the striking facade, while the dome provides views over the city. The Estrela Basílica was the first church in the world dedicated to the Sacred Heart of Jesus.

National Museum of Ancient Art
(Museu Nacional de Arte Antiga)

*Rua das Janelas Verdes; tel. 213 912 800; www.
museudearteantiga.pt; Tues.-Sun. 10am-6pm; €6*

Housed in a former 17th-century palace on one of the city's toniest streets, this opulent museum is laden with artifacts that span the 12th-19th centuries. The collection includes paintings, sculptures, textiles, and furniture. Among the most celebrated pieces are the *Panels of St. Vincent,* which depict a cross-section of 15th-century Portuguese society gathered to venerate a saint. To get here, take the Cascais-bound train or the Santos-o-Velho bus from Cais do Sodré to Santos.

Puppet Museum
(Museu da Marioneta)

*Rua da Esperança 146; tel. 213 942 810; www.
museudamarioneta.pt; Tues.-Fri. 11am-5pm, Sat.-Sun.
10am-6pm; €5; tram 25 or 28*

One of Lisbon's more unusual collections, the puppet museum is small but entertaining. It houses a colorful collection of marionettes from all over the world, which are odd and amusing in equal proportions. Check it out online in advance to see when live shows are on, and don't forget the obligatory puppet selfie on your way out. Audio tour included in entry price, on request.

Águas Livres Aqueduct
(Aqueduto das Águas Livres)

*main entrance at the EPAL Municipal Water Museum
ticket office, Calçada da Quintinha 6, Campolide*

neighborhood; tel. 218 100 215; www.epal.pt;
Tues.-Sun. 10am-5:30pm; €3

Climb above the city to explore the formidable Águas Livres Aqueduct, whose name translates as "Aqueduct of the Free Waters." Built between 1731 and 1799 to supply the city with water from Sintra, it's a remarkable example of 18th-century engineering, snaking over 58 kilometers (36 mi) along the trajectory of an old Roman aqueduct. Despite its size, it blends into its surroundings. Visitors can walk the main portion of the platform, crossing the 1-kilometer (0.6-mi) stretch over the Alcântara Valley, the aqueduct's highest point at 68 meters (223 ft), with views of Lisbon. Guided **tours** (first Sat. every month, 11am) require advance booking.

Take the Portas da Benfica bus 758 (every 15 minutes; €2) from the Glória Funicular to Campolide, then walk west for 5 minutes to the aqueduct. A taxi from central Lisbon to the aqueduct costs around €8.

ALCÂNTARA
25 de Abril Bridge
(Ponte 25 de Abril)

tel. 212 947 920; www.lusoponte.pt; tolls €1.85-7.20
(northbound only)

Lisbon's iconic 25 de Abril Bridge dominates the skyline from most directions. Stand underneath it and the buzz of the vehicles whooshing above is hypnotic. It was inaugurated in 1966, and prior to the Carnation Revolution it was named the Salazar Bridge, after statesman António de Oliveira Salazar. Post-independence it was renamed the 25 de Abril Bridge, in tribute to the bloodless uprising that overthrew Salazar's dictatorial regime and gave Portugal independence and democracy, on April 25, 1974. Spanning 2,277 meters (1.4 mi), the bright red suspension bridge connects Lisbon to Almada, on the south bank of the Tagus River. The upper deck carries six vehicle lanes, and the bottom deck is a double electrified rail track, added in 1999. Crossed by some 150,000 cars every day, it offers the most incredible views of Lisbon for those who come into the city over the bridge.

The bridge is also home to one of Lisbon's newest tourist attractions, the **Pilar 7 Experience** (Avenida da Índia N6 34; tel. 211 117 880; www.visitlisboa.com/en/places/pilar-7-bridge-experience; daily 10am-8pm; €6), an interactive museum that allows visitors to explore inside one of the famous bridge's pillars. Those with a head for heights can take an elevator to a 72-meter-high (236-ft-high) panoramic glass viewing platform adjacent to the pillar. Vertigo-sufferers be warned—the floor is glass, too (but the views are worth the shaky legs)!

BELÉM
★ Belém Tower
(Torre de Belém)

Av. Brasília; tel. 213 620 034; www.torrebelem.gov.
pt; Tues.-Sun. 10am-5:30pm Oct.-Apr., Tues.-Sun.
10am-6:30pm May-Sept.; €6; train: Belém Station,
bus 714, 727, 728, 729, 751, 113, 144, 149, tram 15, 18

Jutting into the Tagus River, magnificent Belém Tower is one of Portugal's most recognizable monuments and a UNESCO World Heritage Site, acknowledging Belém's significance as a launchpad during the Age of Discoveries. The decorative Manueline tower was originally built in the 16th century, part of a coastal defense system to guard the Tagus River mouth and the entrance to Lisbon. Today it is symbolic of one of the most significant chapters in Portugal's history. As well as protecting Lisbon, the tower also marks the spot where Portuguese explorers started and ended their journeys to the "New World."

The frilly Manueline tower became a ceremonial landmark, often the last and first sight sailors had of their homeland. The sturdy little tower's ornate stonework incorporates figures related to the Age of Exploration, such as exotic animals, ropes and knots, and a statue of Our Lady of Safe Homecoming, a symbol of protection for sailors on their voyages. The navigators who set sail from Belém, in study wooden caravels and *nau* ships built in shipyards in Lisbon and the Algarve, laid the blueprints for Portugal's colonial empire. Setting up Atlantic trade routes brought Portugal

considerable wealth and established Lisbon as Europe's main trading center for spices, silk, and precious gems like pearls and diamonds. It also brought historic tragedies, namely the damage inflicted to Indigenous peoples by colonialism, and the country's role in the Atlantic slave trade.

Having also been used as a lighthouse, a customs house, and a prison, the fortification is today one of Portugal's most visited tourist sites. Its elaborate exterior belies the starkness inside: Entering the tower over an ancient drawbridge, visitors access a bulwark housing artillery, in the middle of which is a small courtyard flanked by Gothic arches. Inside the tower are the Governor's Room on the first floor, the opulent King's Hall on the second floor, the Audience Room on the third floor, and a chapel on the fourth floor. All rooms are devoid of furnishings, showcasing only the bare stonework. The floors all boast lovely balconies, connected by a narrow spiral staircase topped by a viewing terrace. It's worth the climb for views over the Tagus estuary and Belém's monuments.

National Coach Museum
(Museu Nacional dos Coches)

Av. da Índia 136; tel. 210 732 319; www. museudoscoches.pt; Tues.-Sun. 10am-6pm; €6; bus 28, 714, 727, 729, 751, tram 15

Before cars, there were horses and carriages, and Portugal has some fine examples of horse-drawn vehicles on permanent display at the National Coach Museum. From elaborately decorated Berlins that transported royalty to children's carriages and mail buses, the various collections of 16th- to 19th-century coaches are fascinating. Located on the fringe of the **Afonso de Albuquerque Square** (Praça Afonso de Albuquerque), the museum also hosts a number of collections of other stately items, such as ceremonial clothing, instruments, tapestries, and horse tack.

1: Jerónimos Monastery 2: Belém Tower
3: Monument to the Discoveries 4: MAAT Museum

★ Jerónimos Monastery
(Mosteiro dos Jerónimos)

Praça do Império; tel. 213 620 034; www. mosteirojeronimos.gov.pt; Tues.-Sun. 10am-5pm Oct.-Apr., Tues.-Sun. 10am-6pm May-Sept.; €10, ticket including the Maritime Museum and the Archaeology Museum €12; bus 727, 728, 729, 714, 751, tram 15

Parallel to the Tagus River, with the stately Imperial Square Gardens sprawling in front of it, the exuberant Jerónimos Monastery is Belém's breathtaking centerpiece. A prime example of ornate Manueline architecture, it is also a UNESCO World Heritage Site. Construction on the impressive landmark began in 1501 on the order of King Manuel I, who wanted to honor the memory of explorer Henry the Navigator, as well as to demonstrate his own devotion to Saint Jerome. The vast building took 100 years to complete. Its several architectural styles include Renaissance and the lavishly ornate Spanish plateresque style. The magnificent riverside facade has a figure of Our Lady of Belém, while inside is the Latin-cross-shaped Church of Santa Maria, the final resting place of explorer Vasco da Gama and one of Portugal's greatest poets, Luís Vaz de Camões.

Also located in the expansive wings of the Jerónimos Monastery is the **National Archaeology Museum** (Museu Nacional de Arqueologia; €4, ticket including Jerónimos Monastery and the Maritime Museum €12), devoted to ancient Iberian art. Among its collections are ancient jewelry, busts, mosaics, and epigraphs, as well as metal artifacts, medals, and coins. The **Maritime Museum** (Museu de Marinha; €6.50, ticket including the Jerónimos Monastery and the Archaeology Museum €12), also often referred to as the Navy or Naval Museum, occupies the western wing of the Jerónimos Monastery as well as a modern annex to the north. It grew from a collection started by King Luís I (1838-1889), an accomplished navigator who had a keen interest in oceanographic studies. It currently comprises more than 17,000 pieces and is widely regarded as one of the most important maritime museums in Europe.

Monument to the Discoveries
(Padrão dos Descobrimentos)

Av. Brasília; tel. 213 031 950; www.
padraodosdescobrimentos.pt; daily 10am-7pm
Mar.-Sept., Tues.-Sun. 10am-6pm Oct.-Feb.; €3;
Train: Belém Station, bus 714, 727, 728, 729, 751,
tram 15

A short stroll from Belém Tower along the Tagus riverside is the Monument to the Discoveries. First erected in 1940 and made permanent in 1960 to mark 500 years since Henry the Navigator's death, the monument celebrates the Age of Discoveries in the 15th and 16th centuries with statues of Henry the Navigator, Pedro Álvares Cabral, and Vasco da Gama, leaders of Portugal's maritime voyages. The Discoveries cemented Portugal's reputation as a maritime powerhouse, a complicated legacy given subsequent exploitation, violence, and slave trade. Shaped like the bow of a caravel—a small Portuguese sailing ship—it also houses an auditorium and a museum with changing exhibitions and has a viewing platform on top. In the square out front is the stunning **Compass Rose,** an elaborate decorative work of paving art shaped like a compass, 50 meters (164 ft) across, in black and red *lioz* limestone, in the center of which is a map of the world during the Age of Discoveries surrounded by decorative figures like mermaids, stars, and leaves.

MAAT–Museum of Art, Architecture and Technology
(Museu de Arte, Arquitetura e Tecnologia)

Av. Brasília; tel. 210 028 130; www.maat.pt;
Wed.-Mon. noon-8pm; €5; Train: Belém Station, bus
201, 714, 727, 751, tram 15E, 18E

Inaugurated in 2016 in a contemporary building in stark contrast with its classical peers, MAAT is one of Lisbon's newest cultural additions. The new building, by British architect Amanda Levete, has a curved design and white-tiled facade that juts out over the river like a low, gleaming spaceship. It sits next to a striking old industrial power plant and hosts national and international exhibitions and collections of contemporary art, architecture, and technology, showcasing the likes of experimental installations, abstract paintings, and cutting-edge sculptures, and is connected to the city by a footbridge. It is free to climb to the roof from outside for views over the Tagus at what has become an iconic location.

Berardo Collection Museum
(Museu Colecção Berardo)

Praça do Império; tel. 213 612 878; www.
museuberardo.pt; daily 10am-7pm; €5 (free entry on
Sat.); tram 15, bus 714, 728

Lisbon's most-visited museum is indeed a must-see for modern art lovers. Comprising a vast selection of carefully curated modern and contemporary art, spanning all genres from Cubism to Pop Art, the outstanding Berardo Collection Museum is a private collection that features iconic pieces by the greats—works by Mondrian, Picasso, Duchamp, Andy Warhol, Jackson Pollock, Salvador Dalí, and Francis Bacon can all be found here—as well as emerging artists. The permanent collection occupies the entire second floor, with rotating exhibitions on the lower floor.

Cordoaria Nacional

Av. da Índia; tel. 213 637 635; www.
patrimoniocultural.gov.pt; Mon.-Fri. 10am-7pm,
Sat.-Sun. 10am-8pm; bus 727, 728, 751, 756

The Cordoaria Nacional is a former naval rope-making factory in Belém that now functions as an exhibition center. The original factory is believed to have been built on the order of the Marquis of Pombal circa 1771, and was completed in 1779. Located on the main road running alongside the Tagus River, it produced sisal ropes, cables, sails, and other equipment for the Portuguese Navy and other ships. Widely revered as an outstanding example of 18th-century industrial architecture, it is now used as a space for rotating exhibitions, which have featured internationally acclaimed artists such as Banksy.

Park of Nations

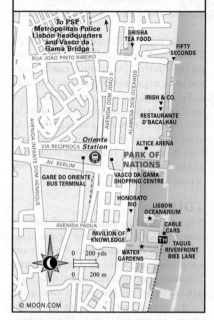

© MOON.COM

PARK OF NATIONS

In the modern Park of Nations (Parque das Nações) neighborhood, **cable cars** (daily 11am-6pm, until 8pm in summer, closed in bad weather; €3.95 one-way, €5.90 round-trip) run between the Oceanarium and the modern 145-meter (476-ft) Vasco da Gama tower, gliding over the waterfront.

Lisbon Oceanarium
(Oceanário de Lisboa)

Esplanada Dom Carlos I s/n; tel. 218 917 002; www. oceanario.pt; daily 10am-8pm late Mar.-Oct., daily 10am-7pm Nov.-mid-Mar.; adults €16.20, children 4-12 €10.80; Metro: Oriente Station, Red Line

Inaugurated in 1998 for the World Exposition, the Lisbon Oceanarium, Europe's largest indoor aquarium, is home to a huge assortment of marine species, from seagulls to sea lions, sea dragons, and surgeonfish. The star attraction is a huge tank that houses exotic sea life, including rays, sharks, moray eels, barracudas, and sunfish.

Vasco da Gama Bridge
(Ponte Vasco da Gama)

tel. 212 328 200 (Mon.-Fri. 8:30am-6pm); www. lusoponte.pt; tolls €2.70–€11.70 (northbound only)

Snaking across the Tagus River to link eastern Lisbon to the South Bank, the Vasco da Gama Bridge is Europe's longest bridge. Measuring 17.2 kilometers (10.7 mi), it was purpose-built for the 1998 Lisbon World Fair Exposition, in the Park of Nations area east of Lisbon's city center. Flanked by viaducts, the elegant and sturdy cable-stayed bridge is a feat of engineering and design. The six-lane structure sees more than 62,000 vehicles cross it daily.

Pavilion of Knowledge– Living Science Center
(Pavilhão do Conhecimento, Centro Ciência Viva)

Largo José Mariano Gago; tel. 218 917 100; www. pavconhecimento.pt; Mon.-Fri. 10am-6pm, weekends and holidays 11am-7pm (closed Mon. Sept.-May);adults €9, children €6-7; Metro Gare do Oriente, Red Line

Children of all ages will enjoy spending a couple of hours at this highly interactive technological center dedicated to science. It comprises a vast number of exhibitions and activities, covering wide-ranging themes that aim to be fun, stimulating, and educational at the same time. Located next to the Oceanarium, it offers a superb option for a rainy or really hot day. Main attractions include a suspended Skyline Bike Ride and robotics games.

Sports and Recreation

PARKS

EDUARDO VII PARK
(Parque Eduardo VII)

Just behind the Marquês de Pombal Square is a sprawling, manicured garden of lush lawns and box hedges that give it a regal feel, consistent with the historic buildings surrounding it. Stand at the top of the park and enjoy magnificent views down to the Baixa and the Tagus River. Covering 26 hectares (64 acres), the park was renamed in 1902 for Britain's Edward VII, who visited Portugal that year. It is also home to the **Estufa Fria** (Cold Greenhouse; www.estufafria.cm-lisboa.pt; €3.10), one of the most important gardens in the city center, comprising lakes, waterfalls, brooks, statues, and hundreds of different plant specimens from all over the world. It's a great place to take refuge on a hot day.

ESTRELA GARDENS
(Jardim da Estrela)

The exquisitely landscaped Estrela Gardens are colloquially referred to as the Central Park of Lisbon, a tranquil, lush oasis in the heart of this affluent neighborhood, bordered by the main Rua da Estrela and Avenida Ávares Cabral, with the Estrela Basílica at the bottom and a statue of explorer Pedro Álvares Cabral at the top. Stroll past duck ponds, browse the library, and enjoy open-air concerts hosted in the wrought-iron bandstand on summer evenings.

WATER GARDENS
(Jardins d'Água)

Ulisses boardwalk; open 24/7

Fronting the Park of Nations area are the attractive Water Gardens, which provide leafy, cool refuge on a warm day. This peaceful oasis is a perfect complement to the neighborhood's contemporary feel and lends the built-up area some much-needed greenery. A number of pretty water features offer splendid views over the Tagus and Vasco da Gama Bridge. The sculpted gardens hide several intriguing points of interest, such as the exotic plants and trees, large wind chimes, water volcano, and sculptures, and have plenty of seating. It's the ideal spot to sit and enjoy a book with the calming sound of running water in the background. Just behind the gardens, set back from the riverfront, is a string of restaurants and bars that form the backbone of the Park of Nations's nightlife.

TOURS

Personalized walking tours by locals have become popular in Lisbon, allowing you to explore the city at a leisurely pace. Guided tours are available in English, and many are free. Tours take place rain or shine, and their duration can range from just over 1.5 hours to the full day. On free tours, payment is in the form of tips—a suggested tip is €5-12 per person. Specialist walking-tour companies include **Discover Walks Lisbon** (www.discoverwalks.com) and **Discover Lisbon** (tel. 932 060 800; www.discoverlisbon.org).

LISBON SEGWAY TOURS

www.lisbonsegwaytours.pt; from €35

Lisbon Segway Tours are a fun way to zip around the city and really get into its nooks and crannies. Tours visit different areas, including a riverside tour, a tour of Alfama, a city center tour, and a Belém tour. More unusual itineraries are a Lisbon by Night tour, a gastronomic tour to discover the city's foodie delights, and a three-hour super tour that covers most of the city's main spots.

CYCLING AND CYCLING TOURS

Lisbon City Hall has created an extensive shared-bicycle network called Gira and around 90 kilometers (55 mi) of cyclable paths to explore. There's also a "green corridor" from Lisbon center to the verdant Monsanto Forest Park, a protected forest city-park approximately 8 kilometers (5 mi) northwest of the Baixa.

TAGUS RIVERFRONT BIKE LANE

Cycling Distance: *16.5 kilometers (10.2 mi) one-way*

Cycling Time: *1.5 hours one-way*

Trailhead: *Lisbon Oceanarium in Park of Nations or Belém Tower*

Information and Maps: *www.cm-vfxira.pt/pages/2519?poi_id=309*

Among the most popular routes enjoyed on two wheels is the Tagus Riverfront ride, a shared pedestrian-bike path stretching all the way from Park of Nations to Belém, passing dozens of Lisbon's riverfront attractions on the way, including Comércio Square, Cais do Sodré, and the Monument to the Discoveries. A wonderful way to spend an afternoon touring Lisbon.

GIRA

tel. 211 163 060; www.gira-bicicletasdelisboa.pt

The shared-bicycle scheme Gira comprises about 50 stations around the city, with 500 electric and standard bicycles. Download the app, buy a day pass for €2, and pedal away.

LISBON BIKE TOUR AND OUTDOORS

Rua Presidente Arriaga 112; tel. 912 272 300; www.lisbonbiketour.com

Lisbon Bike Tour and Outdoors have designed exciting tours—all downhill—that cover key historic areas.

RENT-A-FUN

www.rent-a-fun.com

Rent-a-Fun includes some uphill climbs on its tours, but its bicycles are electric. Standard bike tours take 3 hours and cost €32 adults, €15 children. Rent-a-Fun also rents out electric, regular, and folding bicycles (daily 9am-9pm; €25), including delivery, a helmet, and a lock.

BOAT TOURS

A nice view of Lisbon is on approach from the opposite side of the Tagus River, and, given the nation's seafaring history, a boat trip offers a uniquely appropriate vantage point to see the city.

LISBON BY BOAT

tel. 933 914 740; www.lisbonbyboat.com

Lisbon by Boat offers a variety of tours, from guided sightseeing trips to romantic sunset cruises, but all promise unforgettable views of the Portuguese capital. By motorboat or by yacht, trips range 1-6 hours, starting from around €35 pp for an hour-long historic Lisbon sightseeing cruise.

YELLOW BOAT TOUR

www.yellowbustours.com; from €18

An alternative way to explore Lisbon is on the hop-on hop-off Yellow Boat Tour. Purchase a 24-hour ticket that gives you access at points of interest on both sides of the Tagus. A nonstop circuit takes 1.5 hours, with a running commentary on sights in a number of languages, including English.

SOCCER (FOOTBALL)

LUZ STADIUM
(Estádio da Luz)

Av. Eusébio da Silva Ferreira; tel. 217 219 500; www.slbenfica.pt; Metro Colégio-Militar/Luz or Alto-dos-Moinhos, Blue Line

The 64,642-seat Luz Stadium (Estádio da Luz), the Stadium of Light, is the home of soccer team **Benfica,** one of the country's Big Three (along with cross-city rivals Sporting and northern team Porto). Architecturally impressive, its wavy roof of steel arches is designed to feel light and transparent. At the stadium there is a store, a museum, and 20-minute guided tours (daily 10am-6pm; €12.50, with museum €17.50). Game tickets start around €30.

JOSÉ ALVALADE STADIUM
(Estádio José Alvalade)

Rua Professor Fernando da Fonseca; tel. 217 516 164; www.sporting.pt; Metro Campo Grande, Green Line
A short distance from Luz Stadium is José Alvalade Stadium (Estádio José Alvalade), or Lions' Stadium, home to the soccer team **Sporting**, "the lions." Predominantly green to echo its home team's colors, the stadium was designed by architect Tomás Taveira in a mall complex with a 12-screen movie theater, a health club, and a soccer museum. There are four daily guided tours of the stadium and museum (from €14). Game tickets start at €30.

Arts and Entertainment

PERFORMING ARTS

DONA MARIA II NATIONAL THEATER
(Teatro Nacional Dona Maria II)
Praça Dom Pedro IV; tel. 213 250 800; www.tndm.pt
Prestigious Dona Maria II National Theater is a national jewel and cultural heavyweight on noble Rossio Square. Built between 1842 and 1846 in neoclassical style, it celebrates the performing arts with a full agenda of plays, shows, and concerts.

SÃO CARLOS NATIONAL THEATER
(Teatro Nacional de São Carlos)
Rua Serpa Pinto, 9; tel. 213 253 000; see https:// tnsc.bol.pt for program; Metro Baixa-Chiado, Green/ Blue Lines
Portugal's national opera house, the São Carlos National Theater, was inaugurated on June 30, 1793, built by order of Queen Maria I to replace the Tejo Opera House in Comércio Square, which was destroyed by the 1755 earthquake. Inspired by Italy's grandiose La Scala theater in Milan and the San Carlo Theater in Naples, it is the only Portuguese theater that produces and showcases opera and choral and symphonic music still today. Classified a National Monument, the beautiful neoclassical building with ornate rococo touches has long been a centerpiece of the country's cultural scene.

COLISEU DOS RECREIOS
Rua Portas de Santo Antão 96; tel. 213 240 580; www.coliseulisboa.com
Inaugurated in 1890, the famed Coliseu dos Recreios regularly welcomes international productions, traditionally from the realm of ballet, theater, and opera, as well as pop stars, circus troupes, and comedians. Architecturally, the Coliseu was ahead of its time with cutting-edge ironwork, seen in its spectacular German-made iron dome and iron roof.

CALOUSTE GULBENKIAN FOUNDATION
(Fundação Calouste Gulbenkian)
Av. de Berna 45A; tel. 217 823 461; www.gulbenkian.pt
One of Lisbon's newer cultural venues, the Calouste Gulbenkian Foundation has offerings beyond the world of art and exhibitions, with jazz, choral, and orchestral concerts, sometimes held in the lovely gardens.

FESTIVALS AND EVENTS
Lisbon loves to party, and these annual events draw crowds. The Santo António festival is without a doubt Lisbon's main event, the biggest traditional religious celebration in the country. Lisbon hosts an array of music festivals and fairs and concerts throughout the year, mostly at **Altice Arena** (Rossio dos Olivais; tel. 218 918 409; http://arena.altice. pt) in the Park of Nations.

Spring
CARNIVAL
(Carnaval)
throughout Lisbon; mid-Feb.-early Mar.
Portugal goes into party mode for Carnival, and Lisbon has a succession of colorful floats and costumed dancers shimmying through

the city's main avenues in a cloud of colorful confetti and streamers to the energetic rhythms of hot South American and popular Portuguese folk music, regardless of the weather. Carnival typically falls around mid-February or early March and lasts a number of days, during which concerts, masquerade balls, and street events are also held.

LISBON FISH AND FLAVORS (Peixe em Lisboa)

Carlos Lopes Pavilion, Av. Sidónio Pais 16; tel. 916 442 541; www.peixemlisboa.com; early Apr.; €6-15

Discover the amazing flavors of the sea with gastronomic Lisbon Fish and Flavors, showcasing the best fish and seafood by innovative and well-known chefs and restaurants. The event takes place over 10 days and involves food and market stalls, cooking demonstrations, and discussions.

Summer
SANTO ANTÓNIO AND JUNE FESTIVITIES

throughout Lisbon; June

Dedicated to Saint Anthony, the city's patron, Santo António is Portugal's biggest traditional religious festival. Celebrations are staged throughout the capital for the whole month of June, reaching their peak on June 12, with jubilant parades and processions into the night. On June 13, the time-honored **Casamentos de Santo António** (Santo António weddings) are held. Established in 1958, these are a mass wedding of a dozen of the city's most impoverished couples, selected from hundreds of applicants. The entire ceremony, from the bridal outfits to the honeymoon, is funded by city hall and other sponsors. Over these two days, the city parties to pay homage to "matchmaker" Saint Anthony, from the afternoon through the early morning.

During Santo António, Lisbon is at its prettiest. Every garden and square is decked out with colorful trimmings and lights. Food and drink stalls, tables, and chairs are set up with small stages for local artists to perform traditional folk songs. Grilled sardines, sangria, and traditional *caldo verde* (potato and kale) soup are served from stalls to fuel the merriment. The neighborhoods of **Alfama** and Bica are the most popular for Santo António. Each neighborhood also designs a float and takes part in a grand procession along the city's main avenues in the pinnacle of the celebrations to decide which neighborhood wins. Santo António shouldn't be missed if you're in Portugal in June, but be sure to book accommodations far in advance if you decide to visit during this time.

Shopping

Lisbon has a sophisticated shopping scene, from upscale stores along stylish **Avenida da Liberdade** to smaller boutiques and craft shops in the neighborhoods surrounding **Baixa**. It also has shopping centers galore and plenty of open-air markets.

Baixa itself, between **Rossio Square** and the riverside plazas and smaller boulevards, is the heart of commerce in Lisbon, where mainstream chain stores adjoin traditional grocery stores, boutiques, and souvenir shops. The two main shopping streets in the Baixa are **Rua da Prata** and **Rua Augusta,** parallel to each other from the main Comércio Square up to Rossio. However, for more unique souvenirs, you may want to venture farther afield to neighborhoods like Alfama, Chiado, and Bairro Alto.

ALFAMA
Tiles and Ceramics
LOJA DOS DESCOBRIMENTOS

Rua dos Bacalhoeiros 14B; tel. 218 865 563; www. loja-descobrimentos.com; daily 9am-7pm

Loja dos Descobrimentos is a shop and workshop selling brightly colored hand-painted tiles and ceramics in styles from all over Portugal. Meet the artisans in the atelier and watch as they work on tiles, or paint your own.

AZULEJOS DE FACHADA

Beco do Mexias 1; tel. 966 176 953; www.azulejosdefachada.com; Mon.-Fri. 10:30am-12:30pm and 2pm-5:30pm

Another top place for authentic hand-painted tiles and ceramics with a bright modern twist, Azulejos de Fachada will also take custom orders and ship overseas.

ALFAMA SHOP - O PASSEIO DA D. SARDINHA E DO SR. BACALHAU

Rua dos Remédios 169; tel. 917 393 675; http://alfamashop.blogspot.com; Mon.-Sat. 9am-3pm

This lovely little family-run souvenir shop on a bustling Alfama street sells everything from traditional handicrafts made by local artisans to Portugal's best-loved drinks and foods. All the top souvenirs—handmade soaps, embroidery, canned sardines, mini bottles of port, and cork products—can be found here.

THE CORK STORE

Rua do Espírito Santo 5; tel. 218 861 620; daily 10:30am-7pm

This interesting specialty store carries a trove of all things cork, fashioned into a whole manner of items, from caps to wallets and purses and bracelets.

SÃO VICENTE

Ceramics
CERÂMICA S. VICENTE

Rua de São Vicente 31; tel. 917 743 529; https://ceramica-svicentelisboa.com; Tues 10am-5:30pm, Wed.-Fri. 10am-2:30pm, Sat. 10am-1pm

This stunning little family-run shop and workshop atelier sells realistic reproductions of traditional pieces, such as patterned plates and tiles, all handmade to traditional craft processes. Watch the ceramics being made as you browse. Original and customized pieces also available.

Market
FEIRA DA LADRA FLEA MARKET

Tues. and Sat. 9am-6pm

Dating to the 12th century, the São Vicente Feira da Ladra Flea Market, which literally translates as "Thieves' Fair," is a chance to experience the sights and sounds of old-time Lisbon. With an eclectic mix of antiques and secondhand family heirlooms, vendors tout everything from jewels to junk. The vast market starts by the São Vicente Archway, near a stop for tram 28, and fills the streets around the Campo de Santa Clara square. While some of the traders have properly laid-out stalls, others simply pile their wares onto blankets on the ground.

AVENIDA DA LIBERDADE

Lisbon's most famous avenue, and priciest real estate, Avenida da Liberdade has serious shopping. At 90 meters (295 ft) wide and more than 1 kilometer (0.6 mi) long, this fancy street—the busiest in Portugal—has fashion's biggest players, including **Louis Vuitton Lisbonne** (Av. da Liberdade 190; tel. 213 584 320; www.eu.louisvuitton.com; Mon.-Thurs. 10am-7:30pm, Fri.-Sat. 10am-8pm), **Prada** (Av. da Liberdade 206; tel. 213 199 490; Mon.-Sat. 10am-7:30pm), and **Gucci** (Av. da Liberdade 180; tel. 213 528 401; www.gucci.com; Mon.-Sat. 10am-7:30pm).

Food and Wine
DELIDELUX

Rua Alexandre Herculano 15A; tel. 213 141 474; www.delidelux.pt; Mon.-Fri. 8am-11pm, Sat.-Sun. 9am-11pm

Just off the Avenida da Liberdade at Rua Alexandre Herculano is the stylish DeliDelux, stocked with beautifully packaged gourmet products like wine, olive oil, and canned fish, which make great gifts.

Clothing and Accessories
LUÍS ONOFRE

Av. da Liberdade 247; tel. 211 313 629; www.luisonofre.com; Mon.-Sat. 10am-7:30pm

Women's shoe designer Luís Onofre built his brand on generations of family shoemaking history; the shoes are manufactured at a state-of-the art workshop in northern Portugal.

BABY LIBERDADE

Av. da Liberdade 144G; tel. 213 432 142; www.babyliberdade.com; Mon.-Sat. 10am-7:30pm

You'll find high-end childrenswear from leading international brands for the coolest kids in town at this shop.

BOUTIQUE DOS RELÓGIOS PLUS

Av. da Liberdade 129; tel. 213 430 076; https://boutiquedosrelogios.pt; Mon.-Sat. 11am-7pm

Home to some of Lisbon's most expensive luxury wrist-pieces (the guards at the door might give it away), Boutique dos Relógios Plus sells high-end, handmade timepieces by renowned international names such as Breitling, Bvlgari, Cartier, Montblanc, and Rolex, as well as from brands such as Balmain, Calvin Klein, Omega, Seiko, Swatch, and Tissot.

Shopping Malls
TIVOLI FORUM

Av. da Liberdade 180; tel. 213 530 208; www.facebook.com/TivoliForum; daily 10am-8pm

This modern and elegant mini-mall contains a selection of high-end, luxury boutiques, perfume shops, and jewelers, such as Gucci, Fashion Clinic, and Be Code. The mall also has a food court and is located right in the heart of Avenida da Liberdade.

Perfumes
OTRO PERFUME CONCEPT

Galerias Tivoli Forum, D, Loja 6, Av. da Liberdade 180; tel. 216 062 636; www.otroperfume.com; Mon.-Sat. 10am-7pm

This high-end luxury boutique sells exclusive and unique perfumes handpicked from around the globe for the national market.

CHIADO AND BAIRRO ALTO
Arts and Crafts
ATELIER 55

Rua António Maria Cardoso, 70-74; tel. 213 474 192; www.atelier55.blogspot.com; Mon.-Sat. 11am-7pm

A trove of authentic Portuguese arts and crafts, Atelier 55 brims with handmade ceramics, embroidery, and paintings from local artists.

VISTA ALEGRE

Largo do Chiado 20-23; tel. 213 461 401; https://vistaalegre.com/pt; daily 10am-7pm

A short walk from the Carmo Convent, Vista Alegre is one of the highest-held names in Portuguese porcelain and crystal-ware, established in 1824. The pieces aren't cheap, but they are heirlooms.

CHIADO VINTAGE

Rua Chagas 17; tel. 926 257 740; https://m.facebook.com/pages/category/Vintage-Store/Chiado-Vintage-452788734825761; Mon.-Sat. noon-7pm

Snap up vintage treasures at Chiado Vintage, a trove of unique furniture, decorative items, and art from bygone eras.

Books
BERTRAND BOOKSTORE (Livraria Bertrand)

Rua Garrett 73-75; tel. 213 476 122; www.bertrand.pt; daily 9am-10pm; Metro Baixa-Chiado, Green/Blue Lines

Distinguished by Guinness World Records as the oldest working bookshop in the world, the Bertrand Bookstore in Chiado is housed in a beautiful old building clad in traditional blue and white Portuguese *azulejo* tiles. Open since the mid-1730s, this wonderful bookshop has several rooms packed with literature from some of Portugal's greatest authors—including José Saramago, Eça de Queiroz, Almada Negreiros, Alexandre Herculano, and Sophia de Mello Breyner—as well as a cozy café where visitors are encouraged to "try before you buy" (the books, not the cakes or coffee!).

Cork
CORK & CO

Rua das Salgadeiras 10; tel. 216 090 231; www.corkandcompany.pt; Mon.-Sat. 11am-8pm, Sun. 5pm-8pm

Best Souvenirs

Two of Portugal's most distinctive products are cork goods and beautiful *azulejo* tiles and ceramics.

CORK

Once used to create only bottle stoppers for prestigious champagnes, today Portuguese cork has become fashionable for shoes, handbags, jewelry, and even clothing. **Bairro Alto** is a good place to go cork-hunting, especially **Cork & Co** (page 65) and **Rutz Walk in Cork** (page 66).

AZULEJOS

Azulejo hand-painted tile plaques adorn walls throughout the city. Many smaller-size replicas of plaques and tiles are now produced as souvenirs. **Alfama** is the place to head for *azulejos,* with shops offering miniature versions of these ceramic squares; try **Loja dos Descobrimentos** (page 63) or **Azulejos de Fachada** (page 64).

Everything at Cork & Co, from hats to shoes and all accessories, is made from natural cork.

RUTZ WALK IN CORK

Rua dos Sapateiros 181; tel. 212 477 039; www.rutz.pt; daily noon-8pm

Rutz Walk in Cork is a Portuguese brand specializing in shoes, bags, accessories, and gifts made from cork.

Clothing
FERN - PORTUGUESE DESIGNERS

Rua da Rosa 197; tel. 213 470 208; www. fernandapereira.net; daily 10am-9pm

FERN carries unique and individual items of clothing by arty Portuguese fashion designer Fernanda Pereira.

CAIS DO SODRÉ
Arts and Crafts
A PEQUENA GALERIA
(The Little Art Gallery)

Avenida 24 de Julho, 4C; tel. 213 950 356; www. apequenagaleria.com; Wed.-Sat. 5pm-7:30pm; free; Metro Cais do Sodré, Blue Line

The Little Art Gallery is a collective project that occupies a snug space right on the riverside, aimed at exhibiting, informing about, and selling art. In the same vein as The Little Galleries of the Photo-Secession—later known as the 291 Art Gallery—in New York, this funky gathering place mainly focuses on photography.

ALCÂNTARA
Arts and Crafts
LX FACTORY

Rua Rodrigues de Faria 103; tel. 213 143 399; www. lxfactory.com; daily 6am-4am; free; tram 15

Less factory, more arty-hive, this historical industrial complex comprises more than 200 restaurants, shops, businesses, and offices under one roof. Converted from an old fabric-production plant spanning 23,000 square meters (248,000 sq ft), today LX Factory is a hive of cool creativity and a rising tourist attraction. The LX Factory's first floor is entirely dedicated to an ethical market. There is also a food court, and open-plan workspaces allow visitors to see artisans in action. Enjoy the laid-back hipster vibe and grab a drink on one of the terraces overlooking the iconic 25 de Abril Bridge. Live music performances and other events are also staged on occasion; check the website.

PARK OF NATIONS
Malls
VASCO DA GAMA SHOPPING CENTER

Av. Dom João II 40; tel. 218 930 601; www. centrovascodagama.pt; daily 9am-midnight; Metro Oriente, Red Line

Directly opposite the Oriente main transport hub in Park of Nations is the huge Vasco da Gama shopping center—one of the largest shopping malls in Portugal. The modern multilevel mall comprises more than 160 stores under its glass roof, housing all European high-street favorites plus a range of national specialty boutiques, movie theaters, and a vast food court. From here it is a short walk to all of Park of Nations's other main attractions, including the concert arena, riverfront gardens and bars, cable cars, Oceanarium, and Pavilion of Knowledge—Living Science Center. The Oriente Metro is also directly connected to Lisbon airport.

Food

Lisbon's food scene is a crossroads of traditional and contemporary, offering everything from street food and vegan restaurants to gourmet market stalls. One thing that sets Lisbon apart from other European capitals is value for money.

BAIXA
Bustling Baixa is a hub of restaurants, cafés, and bars, plenty of them arranged around the main Comércio Square, promising people-watching and alfresco dining.

Portuguese
TABERNA DA BAIXA

Rua dos Fanqueiros, 161-163; tel. 218 870 290 or 919 847 419; www.tabernadabaixa.pt; daily noon-3pm and 7pm-10:30pm; €15

This little gem is the perfect place to sample Lisbon's flavors. With a cozy, rustic-chic feel, the small restaurant showcases regional produce in the likes of shared cold platters paired with handpicked wines, and its signature dish, slow-cooked black pig cheeks in red wine. Live shows can also be enjoyed at the venue (check the website for dates).

BEER MUSEUM & RESTAURANT (Museu da Cerveja)

Terreiro do Paço, East Wing 62-65; tel. 210 987 656; www.museudacerveja.pt; daily noon-midnight; €20

Located in the Praça do Comércio, fashionable Museu da Cerveja showcases the finest beers produced in Portugal and Portuguese-speaking countries—a great place to both learn about beer and try it! A range of snacks and meals includes famous codfish cakes that complement the brews.

RESTAURANTE GAMBRINUS

Rua das Portas de Santo Antão 23; tel. 213 421 466; www.restaurante-gambrinus.business.site; daily noon-12:30am; €20-40

Established in 1936, acclaimed Restaurante Gambrinus has a dedicated following for its tapas and seafood, served in a classic setting with polished dark wood and crisp white tablecloths.

PRADO RESTAURANT

Travessa das Pedras Negras 2; tel. 210 534 649; www. pradorestaurante.com; Wed.-Sat. noon-3:30pm and 7pm-11pm, Sun. noon-5pm; €30

Spearheaded by rising young chef António Galapito, Prado takes clean, fresh flavors of the farm and the sea and magics them into contemporary dishes for the table. The restaurant is housed in a lofty, bright former factory, and the menu is a celebration of seasonal Portuguese produce, concocted into dishes such as black pork tenderloin with quinces and chocolate peppers and Barrosã beef sirloin steak and lettuce salad. Reservations are compulsory for groups of more than six.

Appetizers Aren't Free

As soon as you sit down at any table in Lisbon, waiters will almost immediately bring you an array of mouthwatering appetizers, such as a fresh bread basket, butter and pâtés, fritters, and olives and cheeses. Beware—these are not a complimentary welcome gift; the tab is totting up from the moment you butter that bread. Anything you don't want, don't be afraid to politely decline or send back. Always be clear on prices beforehand, as some cheeses and sausages can be pricy, and make sure you pay only for what you eat.

Café
★ CAFÉ NICOLA

Praça Dom Pedro IV 24-25; tel. 213 460 579; daily 8am-midnight; €8

With a prime position on posh Rossio Square, the landmark Café Nicola epitomizes European coffee culture with its art deco interior, excellent coffees, and top-notch breakfasts. It was a favorite of poet Manuel du Bocage, who is memorialized in a statue out front. The celebrated café is excellent for people-watching, but prices are high.

International
RESTAURANTE CANTINHO DO AZIZ

Rua de São Lourenço 5; tel. 218 876 472; www.cantinhodoaziz.com; daily 11am-11pm; €15

At popular family-run Restaurante Cantinho do Aziz, savor exotic flavors from Mozambique in fare such as samosas, crab curry, and traditional Yuca Malaku and Yuca Miamba curries. The atmosphere is relaxed. Sit inside or on the long outdoor street terrace.

TASCA KOME

Rua da Madalena 57; tel. 211 340 117; www.kome-lisboa.com; Tues.-Thurs. noon-2:30pm and 7pm-10pm, Fri. noon-3pm and 7pm-10pm, Sat. 12:30pm-3pm and 7pm-10pm; €15

Established by powerhouse Japanese chef Yuko Yamamoto, whose Lisbon supper clubs were sell-out events, Tasca Kome is a Japanese tavern in the heart of the Baixa. Serving authentic Japanese fare, staples on the menu include miso soup, sushi and sashimi, plus house specials such as fried octopus balls, salmon zuke-don, and parmesan cheesecake.

Seafood
★ SOLAR DO BACALHAU

Rua do Jardim do Regedor 30; tel. 213 460 069; www.solardobacalhau.com; daily noon-3pm and 7pm-midnight; €20

Cod is king at charming Solar do Bacalhau, one of the best spots to enjoy the Portuguese specialty *bacalhau*. It also serves other meat and fish dishes in a setting with natural stone walls and elegantly laid tables.

ALFAMA
Portuguese
CORKSCREW RESTAURANT & WINE BAR

Rua dos Remédios 95; tel. 215 951 774; www.thecorkscrew.pt; Thurs.-Sat. noon-2am, Sun.-Wed. 1pm-midnight; €10

CorkScrew Restaurant & Wine Bar serves great Portuguese tapas of cheeses, cured meats, and fish preserves, accompanied by fantastic Portuguese wines.

★ CHAPITÔ À MESA

Costa do Castelo 7; tel. 218 875 077; www.chapito.org; Mon.-Sat. noon-6pm and 7pm-1:30am, Sun. 7pm-1:30am; €25

Part of a famous circus arts school, Chapitô à Mesa offers fun, flamboyant cuisine alongside gorgeous views of Lisbon. Choose the snack bar, an alfresco grill terrace, or the elegant restaurant. Menu favorites include grilled shrimp with tropical fruit and pork cheeks with clams and sautéed potatoes.

★ CASA DO LEÃO

Castelo de São Jorge; tel. 218 880 154; www.pousadas.pt; daily 12:30pm-9pm; €28

Located inside the São Jorge Castle, Casa do Leão takes advantage of its architectural features, including a vaulted brick ceiling, to create an elegant atmosphere. Its culinary masterpieces are concocted from fresh seasonal ingredients. Seafood *cataplana* and Portuguese-style steak are highlights. Even more remarkable are the views from the terrace outside, overlooking the city.

Café
MERCEARIA CASTELLO CAFÉ

Rua das Flores de Santa Cruz 2; tel. 218 876 111; daily 10am-8pm; €8

Tradition meets cool at Mercearia Castello Café, a funky little eatery and grocery store. Its wood-clad interior harks back to the old days, and its location at the top of the hill near the castle is second to none. The fresh homemade fare includes quiches, crêpes, and sandwiches made from quality regional products—it hits the spot after climbing to the castle.

International
RESTAURANTE CASANOVA

Av. Infante Dom Henrique Loja 7; tel. 218 877 532; www.pizzeriacasanova.pt; daily 12:30pm-11pm; €10

Canteen-style Restaurante Casanova has a privileged riverside location with long tables conducive to sharing authentic Italian food. Try the wood-oven-baked pizza.

ZAMBEZE

Calçada Marquês de Tancos, Edifício EMEL, Mercado Chão do Loureiro; tel. 218 877 056 or 925 200 631; www.zambezerestaurante.pt; daily 10am-11pm; €30

Situated in the historic heart of Alfama, Zambeze is housed in a restored historic marketplace. The clean and minimalistic interior accentuates the intriguing fusion of Euro-African flavors. An alfresco terrace boasts fantastic views over downtown Lisbon and the Tagus River. Set menu of chef's suggestions available for €19.50.

Seafood
FAROL DE SANTA LUZIA

Largo de Santa Luzia 5; tel. 218 863 884; Mon.-Sat. 12:30pm-10pm; €18

Rustic Farol de Santa Luzia is set in an 18th-century building directly opposite the Santa Luzia Viewpoint, near São Jorge Castle. Menu favorites include octopus salad, shellfish *açorda* (a soupy bread dish), and pork *cataplana* with shrimp, clams, and *chouriça* sausage.

outdoor café in Alfama

SÃO VICENTE

One of the city's oldest and more traditional areas, São Vicente has a more grown-up attitude that is reflected in its restaurants, which offer classic Portuguese and Mediterranean fare and cozy bistro-type eateries.

Café
BISTRO GATO PARDO

Rua de São Vicente 10; tel. 934 696 871; Fri.-Tues. noon-10pm; €15

With its exposed stone wall and brick floor, hidden hole-in-the-wall Bistro Gato Pardo is inviting for a snack, coffee, or a cozy meal. Tasty lamb, risotto with fish, and shrimp dishes are favorites.

International
DAMAS

Rua da Voz do Operário 60; tel. 964 964 416; daily 9:30am-10:30pm; €10

At no-frills hipster hangout Damas, craft beers and excellent food accompany live music. The menu is scribbled on the tile-clad wall and changes daily. Dishes from across the Mediterranean include smoked lamb, almond tagine with falafel, and seitan meatballs. On weekends, DJ sets and live concerts are held in a small back room.

BECO A SÉRIO

Calçada de São Vicente 42; tel. 218 872 805; www. facebook.com/becoaserio; daily 12:30pm-10:30pm; €20

A selective menu packed with simple, clean flavors is what Beco a Sério is all about. Choices are limited, but the menu includes tapas, vegetarian, salads, children's menu, vegan, gluten-free, and fish and meat entrées, with homemade starters and desserts. Quality Portuguese dining in a small, family-friendly restaurant located up a quaint alley.

Seafood
★ CERVEJARIA RAMIRO

Av. Almirante Reis 1-H; tel. 218 851 024; www. cervejariaramiro.pt; Wed.-Mon. noon-12:30am; €20

Established in 1956, authentic beer house Cervejaria Ramiro is a famed institution featured on many travel programs. Expect long queues outside the restaurant. The rainbow of seafood includes prawns *al guilho*. The *prego no pão* is a steak sandwich with a cult following, which many eat at the end of meals in lieu of dessert. Wash it down with a chilled beer.

AVENIDA DA LIBERDADE
Portuguese
CHAFARIZ DO VINHO

Rua da Mãe d'Água; tel. 213 422 079; www. chafarizdovinho.com; Tues.-Sat. 3pm-11pm; €25

Located in the Príncipe Real neighborhood just north of Baixa, between Rossio and Marquês de Pombal (near the Lisbon University Botanical Gardens), Chafariz do Vinho is a unique gem of a find. It is a fascinating wine and tapas bar housed in an ancient aqueduct with a vast wine cellar and tasty nibbles to accompany the drink.

DOTE

Avenida da República 51C; tel. 217 961 104; www.dote. pt; daily noon-1am; €12

Boasting a stylish modern brewery concept, popular Dote oozes designer cool. Its menu bridges signature dishes of Lisbon and Porto as well as international favorites. This is where you can enjoy sticky ribs with slaw, a typical Porto *francesinha,* or traditional Portuguese cod fish and steak dishes, washed down with a selection of great Portuguese beers, in the heart of the capital.

Market
FOOD MARKET

Av. Fontes Pereira de Melo 6; tel. 210 199 258; daily 8am-10pm; from €5

Just off the Marquês do Pombal roundabout (northeast), Food Market covers breakfast, brunch, lunch, and dinner. The eclectic food hall's stalls tout everything from oysters to éclairs, grilled chicken to smoked fish, to eat in or take out.

Local Specialties

Ask anyone what Lisbon's most typical dishes are, and here's some of what you will hear:

- **Salted codfish (*bacalhau*),** for which the Portuguese claim to have a different recipe for each day of the year. Head to **Solar do Bacalhau** in Lisbon's Baixa, a shrine to codfish with around a dozen different codfish dishes on the menu (page 68).

- **Seafood** features heavily on menus throughout the city, with other popular dishes including *caldeirada* (fish stew), shellfish, and octopus creations. **Cervejaria Ramiro** is famed for its rainbow of fresh seafood dishes washed down with a chilled beer (page 70).

- **Bite-size snacks** like codfish pasty (*pastéis de bacalhau*), green bean fritters (*peixinhos da horta*), and codfish fritters (*pataniscas de bacalhau*) are also popular, available at most restaurants and snack bars, to be washed down with a cold beer. Lisbon's **Beer Museum & Restaurant** on the Praça do Comércio square is a great place to enjoy some savory snacks with one of Portugal's renowned beers (page 67).

ginjinha cherry liqueur

- Try a *ginjinha* cherry liqueur at its home, the historic **A Ginjinha** bar in the Baixa's São Domingos Square (page 76).

International
THE GREAT AMERICAN DISASTER

Praça Marquês de Pombal 1; tel. 213 161 266; daily noon-midnight; €12

Take a step back in time in this theatrical 1950s-America burger and fries joint—a slice of fun if you fancy a break from the local fare. The obligatory pink and black décor, red booths, and milkshakes are all here.

Seafood
O CACHO DOURADO

Rua Eça de Queiroz 5; tel. 213 543 671; www. ocachodourado.com; Sun.-Fri. 7:30am-11:30pm; €15

Specializing in authentic Portuguese fish and seafood dishes, O Cacho Dourado is off the tourist track but always busy with regulars. If you visit on a Friday, try the famous codfish dish that has been served on Fridays only for nearly half a century.

CHIADO AND BAIRRO ALTO

Bohemian Bairro Alto might be better known for its nightlife, but it doesn't disappoint when it comes to restaurants, with a rainbow of international flavors.

Portuguese
A TABERNA DA RUA DAS FLORES

Rua das Flores 103; tel. 213 479 418; Mon.-Sat. noon-11:30pm; €15

This long, narrow, typically Portuguese eatery, located in an old greengrocer's store, retains original vintage features such as its door and floor tiles. The cozy tavern is popular among locals and tourists alike, serving traditional tapas of yesteryear with a contemporary twist.

RESTAURANTE FIDALGO

Rua da Barroca 27; tel. 213 422 900; www.
restaurantefidalgo.com; Mon.-Sat. noon-3pm and
7pm-11pm; €20

A traditional, family-run Portuguese restaurant founded in 1972, Fidalgo serves good old-fashioned Portuguese food at reasonable prices. All the classics—rabbit stew, fresh fish, octopus, and codfish dishes—are on the menu, along with homemade desserts and an excellent selection of national wines that line the walls of the cozy eatery.

★ CERVEJARIA TRINDADE

Rua Nova da Trindade 20C; tel. 213 423 506; www.
cervejariatrindade.pt; Mon.-Fri. noon-10:30pm; €30

One of Portugal's oldest and most beautiful breweries, bright and bold Cervejaria Trindade dates from the mid-1800s, when it was the choice for writers, poets, and politicians. Its huge medieval banquet rooms can accommodate groups of up to 200. National and international beers are accompanied by a different dish of the day, as well as typical Portuguese fish and meat dishes like steak in beer sauce.

Café

A BRASILEIRA

Rua Garrett 122; tel. 213 469 541; www.abrasileira.pt;
daily 10am-8pm; €5

The century-old A Brasileira café is one of the oldest and most famous cafés in Lisbon. The emblematic venue has an air of antique grandeur, with its art deco chandeliers, wooden booths, mirrored walls, and checkerboard floors. It is a time-honored meeting place for Lisbon's coffee-lovers and has a fascinating history, having once been frequented by the city's intellectuals, artists, writers, and free thinkers. A regular, allegedly, was famous Portuguese poet Fernando Pessoa, and a bronze statue of him sits permanently outside the busy café in tribute. Today it is a mustsee tourist attraction, but the coffee is still as popular as it was when A Brasileira opened in the 19th century.

International

FLOR DA LARANJA

Rua da Rosa 206; tel. 213 422 996; daily 7pm-11pm;
€14

At welcoming and intimate Flor da Laranja, authentic Moroccan food is handmade by the Morocco-born chef, who is also the owner and the waiter. Reservations are required.

LA PAPARRUCHA

Rua Dom Pedro V 18-20; tel. 213 425 333; www.
lapaparrucha.com; daily 1pm-11pm; €25

Modern meets rustic and meat rules at La Paparrucha, a firm favorite among locals. Almost everything is cooked on an authentic Argentinean grill.

Seafood

SEA ME

Rua do Loreto 21; tel. 213 461 564; www.
peixariamoderna.com; Mon.-Thurs. 12:30pm-3:30pm
and 7:30pm-midnight, Fri. 12:30pm-3pm
and 7:30pm-1am, Sat. 12:30pm-1am, Sun.
12:30pm-midnight; €28

Modern, informal Sea Me pays homage to Lisbon's fishmongers with seafood purchased from the counter to be cooked in the kitchen, in a fusion of Japanese and Portuguese cuisines.

CAIS DO SODRÉ

This waterfront wharf has shed its former seedy image and is now a cool place to eat, drink, and be merry. It's also the location of hip **Pink Street,** which makes it a convenient spot to spend an evening.

Portuguese

ESPUMANTARIA DO CAIS

Rua Nova do Carvalho 39; tel. 213 470 466; daily
7pm-4am; €15

Located on Cais do Sodré's famous Pink Street, swanky and minimalistic Espumantaria do Cais is a marble-clad quayside tapas and Champagne bar. Pop open a

---

1: Time Out Market Lisboa **2:** A Ginjinha **3:** Pastéis de Belém

bottle of bubbly, order a sharing platter like the popular cheeseboard or salmon tacos, and have a wonderful evening with some fizz.

Market
★ TIME OUT MARKET LISBOA + RIVERSIDE MARKET
(Mercado TimeOut + Mercado da Ribeira)

Avenida 24 de Julho 49; tel. 213 951 274; Sun.-Wed. 10am-midnight, Thurs.-Sat. 10am-2am; free; Metro Cais do Sodré, Blue Line

After its concession was taken over by the team behind the Lisbon edition of *Time Out* magazine, this landmark market hall—the historic Mercado da Ribeira, or Riverside Market, formerly one of Europe's most renowned markets—is today among the city's coolest hangouts. Despite being more than 100 years old (it first opened in the 1890s) this market is livelier than ever, with a huge, often chaotic food court that boasts a vast variety of gourmet stalls showcasing innovative and traditional Portuguese fare. The two-dozen-plus stands are allocated to chefs and restaurants handpicked by *Time Out*'s food writers. The eastern portion of the building still houses the traditional fruit and veg market, which also sells fresh fish, flowers, bread, and souvenirs. It operates 6am-2pm and offers early risers a glimpse of genuine Lisbon market trading. Live music adds to the ambience.

ESTRELA AND LAPA

Estrela's culinary scene follows the same feel as the neighborhood: refined and upscale with a pinch of cool.

Portuguese
FLOR DA ESTRELA

Rua João de Deus 11; tel. 213 967 278; Mon.-Thurs. noon-10pm, Fri. noon-10:30pm, Sun. noon-3pm; €12

Behind the traditional tile-clad exterior with its decorative cobblestone paving, Flor da Estrela is another unassuming little eatery that serves honest home-cooked Portuguese fare.

CHURRASCARIA O LAVRADOR

Calçada da Estrela 193; tel. 213 961 807; Tues.-Sun. 11:30am-3:30pm and 6:30pm-10pm; €15

A proper local's favorite and aptly called "Farmer's Grill," this modest restaurant serves fresh meat and fish straight off the grill with hearty helpings of potatoes and salad.

Market
MERCADO DE CAMPO DE OURIQUE

Rua Coelho da Rocha 104; tel. 211 323 701; Sun.-Thurs. 10am-11pm, Fri.-Sat. 10am-1am; €10-20

Lisboetas love to meet at trendy Mercado de Campo de Ourique, a neighborhood gastro market with a buzzing food court that feels both traditional and contemporary. Explore the many different stalls and choose what takes your fancy.

Fine Dining
LOCO

Rua Navegantes 53; tel. 213 951 861; www.loco.pt; Tues.-Sat. 7pm-10:30pm; €85

Each meal at ultra-swanky Loco is a masterpiece. With two different tasting menus, this culinary experience is twice as nice.

BELÉM
Portuguese
PROVA - ENOTECA

Rua Duarte Pacheco Pereira 9E; tel. 215 819 080; www.facebook.com/ProvaEnoteca; Tues.-Sat. 11:30am-2pm and 7pm-10pm; €10

As the name of this trendy deli and wine bar indicates (it loosely translates as "try"), the aim here is to sample excellent local produce with a good wine. Plates of cured cold meats and cheeses, salads, veg platters, and fish tapas are all there for the taking, to be paired with a careful selection of great Portuguese wines.

FEITORIA

Altis Belém Hotel & Spa, Doca do Bom Sucesso; tel. 210 400 208; www.restaurantefeitoria.com; Tues.-Sat. 7pm-11pm; €100

Enjoying on a prime position overlooking the Tagus River, Feitoria is a swish, cool,

Pastel de Belém vs. Pastel de Nata

It might look like Portugal's omnipresent *pastel de nata* (custard tart), it might even taste like the ubiquitous *pastel de nata*, but the *pastel de Belém* is a tart in its own right.

HISTORY

While the *pastel de nata* is found throughout Portugal, the *pastel de Belém* is found only in Belém. History has it that the *pastel de Belém's* secret recipe emerged in the 19th century from the Jerónimos Monastery.

In 1834, when all the monasteries and convents of Portugal were forced to close, the workers decided to start selling the sweet treats to make a living, in the same spot where the **Pastéis de Belém** bakery is today. The bakery was officially inaugurated in 1837.

WHERE TO TASTE

To this day the tarts are handmade following the same ancient original recipe that came from the Jerónimos Monastery. This recipe is a closely guarded secret, known only by a handful of master bakers at the Belém bakery, which has become one of the area's top tourist attractions.

pastel de Belém

There's an old saying that states going to Belém without trying a *pastel de Belém* is like going to Rome without seeing the Pope, and judging by the queues that form outside the bakery every day, there might be some truth in it.

Michelin-star-awarded eatery renowned for its contemporary take on Portuguese classics. Located in the Altis Belém Hotel & Spa, it is an exciting choice for a special occasion.

Bakery
★ PASTÉIS DE BELÉM

Rua Belém 84-92; tel. 213 637 423; www. pasteisdebelem.pt; daily 8am-8pm; €5

No visit to Lisbon is complete without a taste of the humble, iconic *pastel de nata* custard tart. It can be found throughout Portugal, but Belém is its birthplace. Pastéis de Belém started making the delectable tarts in 1837, following a secret recipe from the Jerónimos Monastery. The buttery pastry contains a creamy, eggy filling, slightly caramelized top, and a sprinkling of cinnamon. Other fresh-baked sweet and savory treats can be enjoyed in the large seating area, which is always packed full.

PARK OF NATIONS

The modern Park of Nations is home to eateries offering a kaleidoscope of cuisines, most located along the riverfront.

Fine Dining
FIFTY SECONDS

Cais das Naus, Torre Vasco da Gama; tel. 211 525 380; www.fiftysecondsexperience.com; Tues.-Sat. 12:30pm-3pm and 7:30pm-11pm; €150

Located on the top floor of the Vasco da Gama Tower, Fifty Seconds is spearheaded by Spaniard Martín Berasategui, a multi-Michelin-star-awarded chef. An extraordinary culinary experience with mind-blowing 360-degree views over the Tagus, Fifty Seconds takes its name from the time it takes to climb the 120 meters (393 feet) to the restaurant in the elevator. Pricy, but an absolutely unique experience. Taster menus start from around €120.

International
HONORATO RIO

Alameda dos Oceanos, Lote 2, Unit F/G; tel. 932 561 524 or 218 967 207; www.honorato.pt; daily 12:30pm-10pm; €10

Chic fast-food joint Honorato Rio boasts the best handmade gourmet burgers in Lisbon.

Seafood
RESTAURANTE D'BACALHAU

Rua da Pimenta 45; tel. 218 941 296 or 967 353 663; www.restaurantebacalhau.com; daily noon-5pm and 7pm-11pm; €20

As its name indicates, bright Restaurante D'Bacalhau specializes in codfish dishes from across the country, including a platter of four of the most traditional *bacalhau* concoctions; you can also enjoy a classic fish pasty.

Bars and Nightlife

Bohemian and cosmopolitan in equal measures, Lisbon's nightlife has a different vibe in each part of the city, from giddy Bairro Alto and atmospheric Alfama to the funky Pink Street in Cais do Sodré and the trendy Park of Nations.

BAIXA

In comparison to other parts of Lisbon, and with the exception of peak seasons like summer and Christmas, nightlife in the Baixa is rather tame. It's more about having a quiet drink at the end of the day than a big night out.

Bars and Pubs
A GINJINHA

Largo São Domingos 8; tel. 218 145 374; daily 9am-10pm

Home to Portugal's award-winning *ginjinha* cherry liqueur, A Ginjinha is a historic hole-in-the-wall serving tiny glasses of the sweet drink over its sticky slab of marble bar top. *Ginjinha* is served as a shot, with a cherry in the glass if you ask. Soft drinks and beer are also available. This place is standing room only and crowded.

HOTEL MUNDIAL ROOFTOP BAR & LOUNGE

Praça Martim Moniz 2; tel. 218 842 000; www.hotel-mundial.pt; daily 10:30am-10pm

The swanky terrace of Hotel Mundial Rooftop Bar & Lounge has stunning views. During the warmer months, it is a fashionable in-crowd hangout, popular for sunset parties. The views over Lisbon's downtown are worth a visit, but drinks are pricy, and the terrace can get crowded.

THE GEORGE PUB

Rua do Crucifixo 58-66; tel. 213 460 596; www.facebook.com/thegeorgelisbon; daily noon-2am

A good old-fashioned British pub in the heart of downtown Lisbon, the George is the kind of place where everyone knows your name (especially if you're an expat regular) and also has a following for its famous eggs Benedict. Comfy couches and gleaming wooden surfaces lend original pub charm to this top spot for a refreshing pint and live sports.

CLUB NOIR

Rua da Madalena 201; tel. 919 191 919; www.club-noir.wixsite.com/home; Sat. 6pm-10pm

Rock out at colorful Club Noir, an underground hangout that is a must for lovers of all genres of rock music—from post-punk, hard rock, and glam rock to heavy metal and indie rock. This trendy alternative venue is popular among Goths; don't miss the gorgeous brick-rimmed vaulted roof.

ALFAMA
Clubs
LUX DISCOTHEQUE
Av. Infante Don Henrique, Warehouse A; tel. 218 820 890; www.luxfragil.com; Thurs.-Sat. 11pm-6am; cover €10-20

Co-owned by actor John Malkovich, Lux Discotheque is one of Lisbon's most exuberant nightspots, renowned throughout Europe as the place to go to see and be seen. On two different levels, it regularly puts on live acts and DJs. Upstairs the music is mainstream, while the groove on the bottom floor is left to the resident or guest DJ. Outside is a huge terrace where you can watch the sun come up over the Tagus River.

CHIADO AND BAIRRO ALTO

A quaint and traditional part of Lisbon that is sleepy during the day, bohemian Bairro Alto comes to life at night. The cobbled streets are packed with people and cool nightspots ranging from chic wine bars to historic fado houses and renowned jazz clubs.

Bars and Pubs
ODD TRINDADE
Rua Nova da Trindade 9D; tel. 933 687 974; Mon.-Sat. 10pm-2am

Hidden away in the basement beneath the Trindade Theatre, groovy ODD Trindade is a must for beer lovers, home to more than 170 brands of craft beer. It also has a vast selection of quality liquors, regular live music, and is the café-bar that serves the theater.

TOCA DA RAPOSA COCKTAIL BAR
Rua da Condessa 45; tel. 965 463 262; www.facebook.com/Tocadaraposabar; Tues.-Sun. 6pm-midnight

An ode to the art of mixology, stylish Toca da Raposa (the fox den) is a cocktail-lovers' paradise. Only fresh Portuguese ingredients are used to make the drinks, served on the solid marble bar.

PAVILHÃO CHINÊS
Rua Dom Pedro V 89; tel. 213 424 729; Mon.-Sat. 5pm-midnight, Sun. 5pm-2am

Take a trip back in time at Pavilhão Chinês, a sumptuously upholstered tearoom with a web of nooks and crannies spread over five rooms. The walls and cabinets of this popular hangout, converted from a grocery store, are filled with a vast private collection of shiny treasures and relics: mugs, plates, books, and ancient maps. Besides more than 40 different types of tea, the Pavilhão Chinês (which translates as "Chinese Pavilion") also serves wine, beers, cocktails, and liquors.

Live Music
PÁGINAS TANTAS
Rua do Diário de Notícias 85; tel. 966 249 005; Tues.-Sun. 6pm-midnight

Partake in some foot-tapping at Páginas Tantas, a popular jazz bar with live music. The instrument-themed décor and portraits of jazz greats give the club a colorful, contemporary vibe. Rising and established musicians jam live nightly on a little stage in the corner.

Wine Bars
THE OLD PHARMACY
Rua do Diário de Notícias 73; tel. 920 230 989; daily 5:30pm-midnight

The Old Pharmacy is a quirky bar that offers a wide selection of wines by the glass or bottle. Wine bottles now fill the cabinets that were once stocked with medicines. Dim lighting and wine-barrel tables add to the allure.

ARTIS
Rua do Diário de Notícias 95; tel. 213 424 795; Tues.-Sun. 5:30pm-2am

Iberian-rustic Artis is the ideal place for long conversations over wine, cheese, and tapas.

SOLAR DO VINHO DO PORTO
Rua São Pedro de Alcântara 45; tel. 213 475 707; Mon.-Fri. 11am-midnight, Sat. 3pm-midnight; glasses from €2

Directly opposite the romantic São Pedro de Alcântara Viewpoint and housed in an

☆ A Night of Fado

Enjoy dinner and a show with spellbinding fado. This moving, soulful genre of music can be traced back to Lisbon in the early 19th century, often associated with darkened backstreet taverns where singers, the *fadistas*, accompanied by musicians of traditional Portuguese instruments like guitars and violas, would entertain crowds with melodic tales of longing and daily hardships of the era, with songs ranging from mournful and melancholic to upbeat and jovial. Some of Portugal's biggest musical stars were fado singers, who, like the great Amália Rodrigues, the Queen of Fado, became revered personalities.

As fado gained popularity as a tourist attraction, it became mainstream for shows to be preceded by a set-priced dinner. Most fado restaurants are cozy and offer traditional Portuguese dining; many fado houses have a minimum fee that covers dinner and the show. It is customary for spectators to be silent while melodic fado is being sung, out of respect for the *fadista* and the accompanying musicians. With livelier songs, however, guests and even the staff join in. Reservations are strongly recommended.

In Lisbon, the best neighborhoods to see fado are Alfama and Bairro Alto; Alfama is widely believed to be the birthplace of fado, but Bairro Alto is popular for its maze of streets with intimate little fado restaurants and characterful bars.

ALFAMA

Sr. Fado de Alfama

Rua dos Remédios 176; tel. 218 874 298; www.sr-fado.com; Wed.-Thurs. and Sat.-Sun. 7:30pm-11pm; €35
Family-run Sr. Fado de Alfama belongs to *fadista* Ana Marina and is a cultural mainstay, with good traditional Portuguese food and a healthy dose of fado.

São Miguel d'Alfama

Largo de São Miguel; tel. 968 554 422; www.saomigueldalfama.com; daily 7pm-midnight; €25
Intimate, arabesque-styled São Miguel d'Alfama is famous for its fado and traditional Portuguese food.

Clube de Fado

Rua de São João Praça 86-94; tel. 218 852 704; www.clube-de-fado.com; daily 8pm-10:30pm; €40
In the heart of Alfama, behind an unremarkable exterior, famous Clube de Fado serves excellent

18th-century palace, Solar do Vinho do Porto is run by the Port Wine Institute. It showcases more than 300 different types of port, many of which can be sampled by the glass, including rarer vintages that date as far back as 1937.

CAIS DO SODRÉ

Created through a clever urban renewal program, the Pink Street project has taken a part of town that once was a red-light district and turned it into one of the hippest hangouts in Lisbon, with varying ambience along a short, colorful stretch.

Bars and Pubs

PENSÃO AMOR

Rua do Alecrim 19; tel. 213 143 399; www. pensaoamor.pt; Sun.-Wed. 2pm-3am, Thurs.-Sat. 2pm-4am
A former inn that once rented rooms to sailors and ladies of the night, Pensão Amor is now a lively and bohemian hangout.

JAMAICA

Rua Nova do Carvalho 6; tel. 213 421 859; www. jamaica.com.pt; Tues.-Sat. midnight-6am; women free, men minimum about €8
Jamaica, one of Lisbon's best-known bars, is

Portuguese cuisine to the sound of the Portuguese guitar accompanying the *fadista*. It has a warm, romantic, and almost mystic atmosphere.

A Baiuca
Rua São Miguel 20; tel. 218 867 284; Thurs.-Mon. 4pm-midnight; €25 minimum pp includes dinner, drinks, and dessert
An authentic, classic fado dinner haunt, tiny tavern A Baiuca serves tasty home-cooked Portuguese fare on long tables where patrons sit snugly together. The convivial atmosphere is conducive to a great evening enjoying the magic of fado and new friends.

Parreirinha de Alfama
Beco do Espírito Santo 1; tel. 218 868 209; www.parreirinhadealfama. com; Tues.-Sun. 8pm-1am; minimum consumption per person €40
Small and atmospheric, Parreirinha is one of Lisbon's oldest and most popular fado haunts. A legendary restaurant inextricably intertwined with fado, it was established in 1939 and is owned by acclaimed fado singer Argentina Santos. Some of Portugal's most famous fado singers have graced the stage of Parreirinha over the years, including the great Amália Rodrigues. Its food is equally renowned, based on typical Portuguese flavors. Mains include monkfish rice and roast kid. Fado is sung nightly. Cash payments only.

BAIRRO ALTO

O Faia
Rua da Barroca 54-56; tel. 213 426 742; www.ofaia.com; Mon.-Sat. 8pm-1:30am; minimum €50
Founded in 1947, O Faia is a famed fado house with a cult following; it hosts nightly shows and has a restaurant that serves traditional Portuguese cuisine with a contemporary twist.

Tasca do Chico
Rua do Diario de Noticias 39; tel. 961 339 696; daily 7pm-2am; €15
Unlike other fado venues, Tasca do Chico is more of a fado bar than a restaurant. Dim lighting in this tiny tavern enhances the atmospheric experience. Drinks and typical Portuguese tapas, such as plates of cured meats, are served. There is no minimum consumption fee, but it's cash only.

the place to go to drink and dance. It's not huge, so the dance floor can get crowded, but the DJs play a mix of '70s, '80s, rock, and current hits.

VESTIGIUS
Cais do Sodré 8, tel. 218 203 320, www.vestigius.pt, daily 11am-7pm
A popular wine and gin bar (more than 100 gins on the menu!) with vintage retro décor and two outdoor waterfront esplanades.

ALCÂNTARA
Situated directly beneath the 25 de Abril Bridge, the **Santo Amaro Docks,** or Docas, have long been one of Lisbon's most popular nightlife spots. A long row of old port warehouses belonging to Lisbon Docks were renovated in 1995 and are enjoying a second lease on life as cool bars, restaurants, and clubs catering to a multitude of tastes, flanked by sports courts and street food to enjoy at sunrise. It overlooks a smart recreational marina, and the constant hum of traffic crossing the bridge overhead adds to the atmosphere. Take tram 15 or a train from Cais do Sodré to get there, getting off at Alcântara-Mar. Trains run every 20 minutes.

Bars and Pubs
IRISH & CO.
Edifício Topo Nascente, Doca de Santo Amaro; tel. 213 959 885; www.irishco.pt; Mon.-Fri. noon-10:30pm, Sat.-Sun. 9am-1pm

Popular among the expat community, Irish & Co. is a welcoming Irish bar with a relaxed feel and great *craic*. Reputedly the oldest Irish pub in Lisbon.

HAWAII
Warehouse 1, Doca Alcântara; tel. 213 900 010; daily 7pm-6am

A longstanding favorite on the Docas, especially among the younger crowds, Hawaii is the place to dance the night away. Good cocktails and open until dawn.

BELÉM
Bars and Pubs
BAR 38° 41'
Avenida Brasília BP; tel. 210 400 210; www.altishotels.com; daily 11am-1am

Sit and watch the world sail by at this trendy dockside lounge-bar with guest DJs Thursday through Sunday in summer.

CASUAL LOUNGE CAFÉ
Rua Bartolomeu Dias 148b; tel. 213 019 024; www.facebook.com/casuallounge; Mon.-Fri. 1pm-10pm

A laid-back, arty lounge in which to chill out with a cocktail, coffee, or a glass of wine.

PARK OF NATIONS
Enjoy dinner and a drink in style in this funky new part of town.

Bars and Pubs
IRISH & CO.
Rua Pimenta 57; tel. 218 940 558; www.grupodocadesanto.com.pt; Mon.-Fri. noon-10:30pm, Sat.-Sun. 9am-1pm

For authentic Irish warmth and good *craic*, head to the traditional pub Irish & Co., where you'll find a friendly ambience with live music. With its vast open front on the riverside and a pub menu, it's a great place to spend a convivial few hours.

SHISHA TEA FOOD
Alameda dos Oceanos 44301M; tel. 215 940 508; www.shishateafood.pt; daily noon-2am

Shisha Tea Food is a funky Middle Eastern-inspired hookah bar and lounge with a warm Moroccan vibe and exotic *shisha* (water pipes) and great drinks, including teas and cocktails, and an alfresco esplanade.

Accommodations

Lisbon is awash with cool and interesting places to stay, from historic townhouses to converted palaces. The Baixa area is central and convenient. Lodging is generally pricy, but there are quality budget hostels and guesthouses.

BAIXA
Under €100
★ YES! LISBON HOSTEL
Rua de São Julião 148; tel. 213 427 171; www.yeshostels.com; €32 dorm, €140 d with shared bath

Yes! Lisbon Hostel has it all: an excellent location, good service, and budget-friendly prices. Custom-made bunks ensure a good night's sleep, and reception is happy to provide tips on how to get the most out of your stay.

€100-200
★ HOTEL MUNDIAL
Praça Martim Moniz 2; tel. 218 842 000; www.hotel-mundial.pt; €130-200 d

Despite its plain exterior, four-star Hotel Mundial is an institution because its rooftop has a great view. Décor is tasteful, beds are comfortable, and the location is second to none. A short walk from Rua do Comércio.

HOTEL VINCCI BAIXA

Rua do Comércio 32-38; tel. 218 803 190; www. vinccibaixa.com; €180-250 d

Square, elegant four-star Hotel Vincci Baixa embodies class and comfort in a prime location.

ALFAMA
€100-200
★ SOLAR DO CASTELO

Rua das Cozinhas 2; tel. 218 806 050; www. solardocastelo.com; €160-200 d

Small, romantic Solar do Castelo is the only hotel within the walls of the São Jorge Castle. Converted from an 18th-century mansion, this eco-retreat with medieval and contemporary style even has specially commissioned furniture to enhance its uniqueness.

★ MEMMO ALFAMA DESIGN HOTEL

Travessa Merceeiras 27; tel. 210 495 660; www. memmoalfama.com; €150-250 d

Cool and contemporary Memmo Alfama Design Hotel is a 44-room urban retreat fast earning a reputation for its chic, clean design, which blends well with the historic Alfama neighborhood.

€200-300
SANTIAGO DE ALFAMA BOUTIQUE HOTEL

Rua de Santiago 10 a 14; tel. 213 941 616; www. santiagodealfama.com; €200-300 d

A former 15th-century palace has been reborn as cosmopolitan Santiago de Alfama Boutique Hotel, which oozes authenticity from its tiled floors to its prime location in Alfama. It's one of Europe's most outstanding urban hotels.

AVENIDA DA LIBERDADE
€200-300
BOUTIQUE HOTEL HERITAGE AVENIDA DA LIBERDADE

Av. da Liberdade 28; tel. 213 404 040; www. heritageavliberdade.com; €200-300 d

Set back from leafy Avenida da Liberdade, the stately Boutique Hotel Heritage Avenida da Liberdade is in an elegant 18th-century townhouse, a pleasant stroll from the Baixa area.

CHIADO AND BAIRRO ALTO
€100-200
CHIADO 44 GUEST HOUSE

Rua Horta Seca 44; tel. 930 544 457; www. chiado44.pt; €120-200 d

Set in the heart of Chiado in a typical 19th-century building, Chiado 44 is a simple and relaxed three-star hotel with cool, clean décor and river views.

HOTEL DO CHIADO

Rua Nova do Almada, 114; tel. 213 256 100; www. hoteldochiado.pt; €170-250 d

The charming Hotel do Chiado is housed in historic former warehouses that were renovated by leading Portuguese architect Siza Vieira following the catastrophic 1988 neighborhood fire. It's famed for stunning city views from its seventh-floor rooftop terrace and its afternoon tea.

Over €300
★ BAIRRO ALTO HOTEL

Praça Luis de Camões 2; tel. 213 408 288; www. bairroaltohotel.com; €350-400 d

Wedged between bohemian Bairro Alto and trendy Chiado, the five-star Bairro Alto Hotel enjoys a dominant position on the main square and has handsome 18th-century architecture. Within walking distance of shops, restaurants, and bars, the 55 rooms are twins, doubles, and suites.

CAIS DO SODRÉ
€100-200
LX BOUTIQUE HOTEL

Rua do Alecrim 12; tel. 213 474 394; www. lxboutiquehotel.com; €100-200 d

Overlooking the Tagus River, the decadently decorated LX Boutique Hotel is an atmospheric 19th-century hotel conveniently at the nexus of Chiado, Baixa, and Cais do Sodré.

ESTRELA AND LAPA
€100-200
AS JANELAS VERDES LISBON HOTEL

Rua das Janelas Verdes 47; tel. 213 968 143; www. asjanelasverdes.com; €120-200 d

A night at the plush 18th-century As Janelas Verdes Lisbon Hotel feels like staying in someone's very grand home, with stunning views from the rooftop terrace.

HOTEL DA ESTRELA

Rua Saraiva de Carvalho 35; tel. 211 900 100; www. hoteldaestrela.com; €150-200 d

Occupying an old-school building, the 19th-century Paraty Palace, the small Hotel da Estrela blends contemporary with quirky.

ALCÂNTARA
€100-200
★ HOTEL PALÁCIO DO GOVERNADOR

Rua Bartolomeu Dias 117; tel. 212 467 800; www. palaciogovernador.com; €150-250 d

Poised and polished five-star Hotel Palácio do Governador occupies the 16th-century Governor's Palace, carefully conserving its original features. With 60 rooms and two pools, it is a whitewashed and manicured oasis of tranquility in one of Lisbon's prettiest neighborhoods.

BELÉM
€200-300
PESTANA PALACE HOTEL

Rua Jau 54; tel. 213 615 600; www.pestana.com; €200-300 d

Feel like royalty with a stay at five-star Pestana Palace Hotel, in an exquisite 19th-century palace with gorgeous gardens.

Information and Services

VISITOR INFORMATION

"Ask Me" tourist information desks can be found throughout Lisbon, at the airport, major bus and train stations, and monuments. Most are open daily about 9am-6pm. Also available are the main **Lisbon Tourism Visitors and Convention Bureau** (Rua do Arsenal 21; tel. 210 312 700; www.visitlisboa.com; Mon.-Fri. 9:30am-7pm) and the national tourist board, **Turismo de Portugal** (Rua Ivone Silva, Lote 6; tel. 211 140 200; www.visitportugal.com, www.turismodeportugal.pt; Mon.-Fri. 9am-1pm and 2:30pm-5:30pm).

EMBASSIES

- **United States:** Av. das Forças Armadas 133C; tel. 217 273 300; https://pt.usembassy. gov; Mon.-Fri. 8am-5pm
- **Canada:** Av. da Liberdade 196; tel. 213 164 600; www.canadainternational.gc.ca; Mon.-Fri. 9am-noon
- **United Kingdom:** Rua de São Bernardo 33; tel. 213 924 000; www.gov.uk; Mon., Wed., and Fri. 9:30am-2pm
- **Australia:** Av. da Liberdade 200; tel. 213 101 500; www.portugal.embassy.gov.au; Mon.-Fri. 10am-4pm

MONEY

In Lisbon, most hotels, currency exchanges, travel agencies, some banks, and even some shops have currency exchange facilities. Or you can use your debit card to make a withdrawal from an ATM *(multibanco)*, which can be found throughout the city. The currency exchange company **Unicâmbio** (www.unicambio.pt) has more than 80 offices around the country, including the airports at Lisbon, Faro, and Madeira, the Rossio train station in central Lisbon, the Cais do Sodré station in

Baixa, and El Corte Inglês shopping mall (Av. António Augusto de Aguiar 31).

HEALTH AND EMERGENCIES

- **GNR Police Lisbon headquarters:** Largo do Carmo 27; tel. 213 217 000; www.gnr.pt

- **PSP Metropolitan Police Lisbon headquarters:** Av. Moscavide 88; tel. 217 654 242; www.psp.pt

- **PSP Tourist Police Lisbon:** Praça dos Restauradores, Palácio Foz; tel. 213 421 623

- **INEM medical emergency:** Rua Almirante Barroso 36; tel. 213 508 100; www.inem.pt

- **Lisbon Fire Brigade:** Av. Dom Carlos I; tel. 218 171 470; www.cm-lisboa.pt

- **CUF Private Hospital:** Travessa do Castro 3; tel. 213 926 100; www.saudecuf.pt

- **24-Hour pharmacy:** Farmácia Largo do Rato, Av. Alvares Cabral 1; tel. 213 863 044; www.farmaciasdeservico.net

Getting There and Around

GETTING THERE
Air
LISBON PORTELA AIRPORT
(Aeroporto de Lisboa)

LIS; Alameda das Comunidades Portuguesas; tel. 218 413 500; www.ana.pt

Lisbon's airport, also known as Humberto Delgado Airport, is Portugal's biggest and busiest international airport. European flights tend to be shorter than 4 hours and inexpensive. Portugal's national airline, **TAP-Air Portugal** (www.flytap.com), has expanded its operations to the United States and operates several direct daily flights between Portugal and US cities. A number of US airlines also fly to Lisbon.

GETTING TO AND FROM THE AIRPORT

Lisbon's airport is 7 kilometers (4.3 mi) north of the city center. The **Metro** runs direct from the airport to Lisbon; the Red Line runs from just outside the airport's main entrance and connects with the Green Line at Alameda station, which runs to the Baixa and Cais do Sodré riverfront, and ends on the Blue Line, at the São Sebastião station. A journey to downtown Lisbon (€1.25) requires one transfer and takes 20 minutes. The **Aerobus** (www.aerobus.pt) shuttle bus runs regularly to the city center and to the financial district from outside the arrivals terminal (daily 7:30am-11pm; €3.15 one-way). Municipal bus company **Carris** (www.carris.pt; €1.85 one-way) runs five bus routes between Lisbon Airport and the city center. **Taxis** can be found outside the arrivals terminal; a trip to Lisbon city center should cost up to €15. Alternately, call an **Uber** (www.uber.com).

The cheapest and easiest way to get around Lisbon is to buy a **7 Colinas/Viva Viagem card,** available at the airport from the newsagent on the second floor, or from main bus or Metro stations. The cards are prepaid and can be recharged. The card itself costs €0.50, and they are accepted on all local buses and Metro subways, trams, funiculars, and ferryboats. Most single trips on any mode cost €2-3. A one-day travel option has a flat rate of €6.

Bus
SETE RIOS BUS TERMINAL

Rua Professor Lima Basto 133, opposite Lisbon Zoo; tel. 707 223 344; ticket office 7am-11:30pm daily; Metro Jardim Zoológico, Blue Line

GARE DO ORIENTE BUS TERMINAL

Av. Dom João II, Park of Nations; tel. 218 956 972; Metro Oriente, Red Line

The two main bus terminals in Lisbon are

Sete Rios, a Rede Expressos' hub, and the modern Gare do Oriente, closest to the airport. **Eurolines** (www.eurolines.com) operates regular international bus service between Lisbon and cities such as London, Madrid, and Paris. National intercity bus company **Rede Expressos** (tel. 707 223 344; www.rede-expressos.pt) operates express bus trips to Lisbon from most of the country's regions, including the Algarve and Porto, each around 3 hours' journey. Algarve bus company **Eva** (tel. 289 899 760; www.eva-bus.com) also runs daily routes between main bus stations in the Algarve and Lisbon.

Train

Getting to Portugal from other European countries by train isn't as straightforward as by air, and can sometimes be more expensive, usually involving passing through a hub such as Paris or Madrid, and a few transfers. There are two overnight sleeper trains from Spain: the **Lusitania Hotel Train** (www.cp.pt) from Madrid and the **Sud Expresso** (www.cp.pt) from San Sebastian. Traveling from Europe by train can make sense if you're using a rail pass such as the **Eurail** pass.

Trains run to Lisbon from most major towns across the country, and train travel can be a cheap and scenic option. The two types of trains for long-distance travel are the slower Intercidades (intercity) and the Alfa-Pendular (high-speed) train. All trains in Portugal have a first-class option and are operated by **Comboios de Portugal** (CP; tel. 707 210 220; www.cp.pt).

The four main railway stations in Lisbon are **Entrecampos** (Rua Dr. Eduardo Neves), **Oriente** (Av. Dom João II), **Sete Rios** (Rua Professor Lima Bastos), and **Santa Apolónia** (Av. Infante Dom Henrique). The Alfa-Pendular runs from Oriente, Santa Apolónia, and Entrecampos.

Car

Two main motorways connect Lisbon to the country's extremities: the **A1** to the north (Porto) and the **A2** to the south (Algarve). The **A6** is the main motorway from the east. From outside Portugal, you'll cross the entire country from any border point to get to Lisbon. The scenery makes up for any potholes or wrong turns you might endure.

There are two crossings to Lisbon from the south over the Tagus River: the **25 de Abril Bridge,** to the western end of the city, or the newer **Vasco da Gama Bridge**—the longest in Europe—to the Park of Nations area. Both provide stunning views of the city on approach.

Cruise Ship

Lisbon has become a popular port-of-call for many transatlantic and European cruise itineraries and has a busy year-round docking schedule. There are two main cruise hubs; **Alcântara** (Alcântara Docks, Port of Lisbon; tel. 213 611 000; www.portodelisboa.pt), west of the main downtown area (Baixa) or **Santa Apolónia** (Avenida Infante Dom Henrique Warehouse B, Shop 8; tel. 213 611 000 (Port of Lisbon); www.portodelisboa.pt), east of the Baixa. Santa Apolónia, a brand-new, state-of-the-art-terminal, is slightly closer to the downtown (1.5 km/1 mi) and more convenient to explore on foot. If you only have a few hours, head straight to the Baixa (downtown) and medieval Alfama districts to see the sights there. Taxis will be readily available from both hubs. Day trips organized by the cruise company are good options to fit in as much as possible, but often expensive. A **hop-on hop-off bus** is always a good option to see the essential sights in a short time.

GETTING AROUND

Getting around Lisbon can be cheap and easy on public transport, or expensive if you opt for novelty transport like the city's mushrooming *tuk-tuks.*

Lisboa Card

The Lisboa Card (www.lisboacard.org), Lisbon's official tourist pass, includes unlimited travel on public buses, trams, the Metro, elevators, and funiculars as well as travel on CP train lines to Sintra and Cascais; free access to 26 museums, monuments, and UNESCO World Heritage Sites; and deals and discounts on tours, shopping, and nightlife. The cost is €20 for a 24-hour card, €34 for a 48-hour card, and €42 for a 72-hour card. Children's cards are half price. These cards can be purchased online, for which a voucher is given that can be exchanged at main tourist points such as the Lisboa Welcome Center, Foz Palace, and Lisbon Airport.

Public Transit

Single trips on buses, trams, ferryboats, and the Metro generally cost under €1.50, and the rechargeable **7 Colinas/Viva Viagem card** can be bought at most newsagents and kiosks, stations, and terminals for €0.50. A **24-hour public transport pass** can be loaded onto the card; it costs €6 and covers all forms of local public transport (buses, trams, and Metro). Add ferryboat trips to the 24-hour pass and it costs €9, or €10 to also include trains to nearby Sintra and Cascais. Some public transport timetables can vary depending on the season, with hours extended later in summer.

Lisbon's main transit hubs are the **Sete Rios bus station** (Rua Prof. Lima Basto 133), a major station for Rede Expressos intercity coaches, which links with the train and subway, approximately 4 kilometers (2.5 mi) north of the Baixa district and 4.2 kilometers (2.6 mi) from the airport. Another major transport hub is the **Oriente Station** (Edifício Gare do Oriente, Av. Dom João II) in the Park of Nations neighborhood, which also brings together major intercity bus and train transport with local networks and the Metro subway. Lisbon's main train station is **Rossio Station** (Rua 1º de Dezembro 125), the main station for the local and the Lisbon-Sintra network

BUS

The capital has an efficient bus service, **Carris** (www.carris.pt), which also manages the city's tram system. It provides good coverage of the city, as well as service to neighboring towns and suburbs, and is inexpensive, with most trips under €2. Most buses run 6am-9pm daily, with the busiest lines running until midnight. Tickets can be purchased from the driver (cash only) or at main transport hubs. Buying tickets from the driver is more expensive than using the 7 Colinas/Viva Viagem card.

TRAM

Carris (www.carris.pt) operates a network of historic trams and funiculars, a unique way to get into the city's backstreets. Five tram routes carry 60 trams, most of which are vintage vehicles. The star of the show is the famous **tram 28,** which circumnavigates Lisbon's historic neighborhoods Bairro Alto, Alfama, Baixa, and Chiado. A downside is that it is plagued by petty thieves, so stay alert. Trams and funiculars generally operate 6am-11pm daily. Tickets can be purchased onboard from the driver, although this is more expensive than using the 7 Colinas/Viva Viagem card.

METRO

Inaugurated in 1959, Lisbon's **Metro** (www.metrolisboa.pt) has consistently grown, including a stop beneath the airport, making travel fast and easy. The Metro has four main lines—Green, Yellow, Red, and Blue—and is simple to navigate. Trains run regularly and reliably. It is divided into two zones: central Lisbon and the outskirts. All main tourist attractions are within zone 1, the wider city center. A 24-hour pass that also covers funiculars, trams, and buses costs €6. The Metro runs 6:30am-1am daily. All metro stations have ticket vending machines and manned stations. The most useful lines for tourists are the **Blue** and **Green** Lines, which run through the main downtown area, and the **Red** Line, which connects to Park of Nations and the airport.

FERRY

Commuter ferries chug continuously across the Tagus River between Lisbon and Setúbal, operated by **Transtejo & Soflusa** (tel. 808 203 050; www.transtejo.pt) generally 5am or 6am to 1am daily, although crossings are more frequent on weekdays. Boats get busy during rush hours (before 9am and after 4:30pm weekdays) and depart from three terminals along Lisbon's riverside: Terreiro do Paço, Cais do Sodré, and Belém. The five stops on the Setúbal side are Montijo, Barreiro, Seixal, Cacilhas, and Porto Brandão-Trafaria. The Cais do Sodré-Cacilhas crossing is the busiest.

Commuter ferries are much cheaper than tourist boats, with single trips under €3. A charged 7 Colinas/Viva Viagem public transport card can be used to pay for tickets. Crossings provide awesome views of Lisbon's iconic 25 de Abril Bridge and of the city.

Taxi and Ride-Share

Taxis in Portugal are plentiful and easy to spot: beige or black with a minty green roof. Each is identified with a number, usually under the driver's side mirror. There are lots of taxi stands throughout the city at train and bus stations, central plazas, and near shopping malls. Hotel reception desks will call a taxi for you, or simply hail one on the street. The main taxi firms in Lisbon are **Taxis Lisboa** (tel. 218 119 000; www.taxislisboa.com), **Cooptaxis** (tel. 217 932 756; www.cooptaxis.pt), and **Teletaxis** (tel. 218 111 100; www.teletaxis.pt).

Uber cars are also now popular and widely available in Lisbon, giving taxi drivers a run for their money.

Tuk-Tuk

A novel way of exploring Lisbon is to jump on a *tuk-tuk*. These nifty little vehicles have taken the city by storm in recent years; it's rare to turn a street corner without hearing or seeing one of the colorful three-wheelers buzzing along. They have the advantage of fitting on streets and lanes where cars can't go, and they're cute and comfortable—but they are more expensive than public transport or taxis. *Tuk-tuk* operators include **Tuk Tuk Lisboa** (www.tuk-tuk-lisboa.pt), **City Tuk** (www.citytuk.pt), **Eco Tuk Tours** (www.ecotuk-tours.com), and **Tuga Tours Tuk Tuk** (www.tugatours.pt). Expect to pay €55-70 pp for an hour's tour of the sights.

Car

Getting around Lisbon without a car is easy and convenient thanks to the comprehensive public transport network. A car is only necessary to visit outlying areas. Book one online and pick it up at the airport, or ask your

the famous tram 28

hotel to help. In and around Lisbon Airport, the many vendors include **Europcar** (tel. 218 401 176; www.europcar.com), **Hertz** (tel. 219 426 300; www.hertz.com), and **Budget** (tel. 808 252 627; www.budget.com.pt).

Driving in Lisbon can be fast, furious, and overwhelming. Main arteries such as the Segunda Circular ring road, which bypasses the airport, can become gridlocked during rush hour; signage is hit-or-miss (although it's slowly improving), and there are one-way roads to contend with. Lisbon's historic areas are a web of narrow, steep streets that can be daunting to drive, and finding parking, particularly in the busy city center, can be challenging. Most public parking spaces, including car parks, entail a hefty fee.

If you do rent a car to drive in Lisbon, check whether your hotel has private **parking** (which will entail additional cost), or find an underground car park that offers lower-cost "holiday fees," such as the one in Marquês de Pombal Square.

Hop-On Hop-Off Bus

Lisbon has various companies operating modern hop-on hop-off buses, which are an excellent way to see everything the city has to offer in a relatively short amount of time. An audio guide is available onboard in various languages to provide an explanation of the city's history and main monuments—although the quality and sound of the narrative can be poor. Due to their—and Lisbon's—popularity, there can be long queues for the buses. A good tip is to first stay onboard for the entire circuit, and then get off at what interests you the second time around. There are three main companies operating hop-on hop-off tours; tickets start from around €20 for 24-hour tickets on basic routes:

- **Yellow Bus – Carristur:** www.yellowbus-tours.com
- **Cityrama Gray Line:** www.cityrama.pt
- **City Sightseeing:** www.city-sightseeing.com

Around Lisbon

A rich tapestry of towns and villages blankets the outskirts of Lisbon. Just a short drive from the city, the hamlets of Estoril, Cascais, Sintra, and Mafra are worlds away from the bustle of the capital. The stunning coastline linking Estoril, Cascais, and Sintra is called the Portuguese Riviera and the Coast of Kings. During World War II, Portugal's neutral status made it a safe haven for European monarchs, aristocrats, and spies. Today it's still a playground for the rich and famous. Nestled on the coast between Cascais and Sintra is raw and rugged Guincho, a spot of untamed beauty that forms a transition between the up-market elegance of Cascais and the verdant charm of the Sintra mountain range.

Packed with elaborate mansions, grand monuments, and quirky

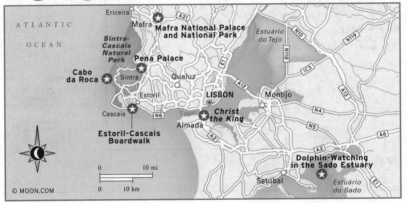

Highlights

Look for ★ to find recommended sights, activities, dining, and lodging.

ATLANTIC OCEAN

Ericeira
Mafra
Mafra National Palace and National Park
Estuário do Tejo
A21
N10
N119
N118
IC3
Sintra-Cascais Natural Park
Pena Palace
E1
A12
A13
Cabo da Roca
Sintra
Queluz
LISBON
Montijo
N4
Estoril
N6
Tagus
Christ the King
Almada
N5
A6
Cascais
Estoril-Cascais Boardwalk
A2
A2
E1
Dolphin-Watching in the Sado Estuary
Setúbal
Estuário do Sado

0   10 mi
0   10 km

© MOON.COM

★ **Pena Palace:** Magnificent Pena Palace is a bold and beautiful hilltop castle surrounded by dense green forest, straight out of a fairy tale (page 93).

★ **Estoril-Cascais Boardwalk:** Join locals getting their steps in with stunning views of the coastline just west of Lisbon along this romantic boardwalk, lined with bars and restaurants on one side and lovely beaches on the other (page 99).

★ **Cabo da Roca:** Feel the power of the Atlantic's tides and winds from mainland Europe's most westerly point (page 110).

★ **Mafra National Palace and National Park:** Explore this rich tapestry of flora and fauna with an outstanding 18th-century Baroque palace at its heart, a former royal game reserve (page 113).

★ *Christ the King:* Take in panoramic views of Lisbon from across the Tagus River as you climb Christ the Redeemer, protective arms outstretched over Portugal's capital city (page 119).

★ **Dolphin-Watching in the Sado Estuary:** Few memories are as magical as seeing playful and inquisitive dolphins in their natural habitat; in this case, it's one of Europe's few pods that resides in an estuary (page 122).

Around Lisbon

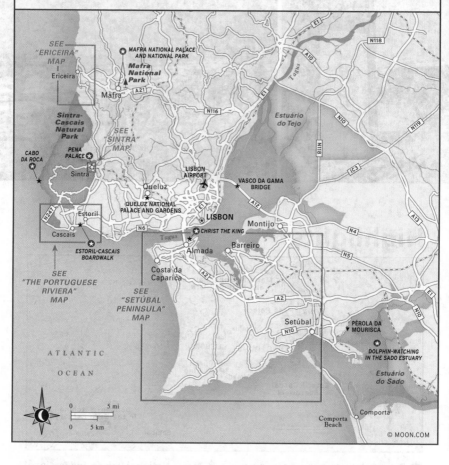

SEE "ERICEIRA" MAP

MAFRA NATIONAL PALACE AND NATIONAL PARK

Ericeira

Mafra National Park

Mafra

N116

Estuário do Tejo

Sintra-Cascais Natural Park

SEE "SINTRA" MAP

CABO DA ROCA

PENA PALACE

Sintra

LISBON AIRPORT

Queluz

QUELUZ NATIONAL PALACE AND GARDENS

VASCO DA GAMA BRIDGE

LISBON

Estoril

Cascais

Tagus

CHRIST THE KING

Montijo

Barreiro

ESTORIL-CASCAIS BOARDWALK

Almada

SEE "THE PORTUGUESE RIVIERA" MAP

Costa da Caparica

SEE "SETÚBAL PENINSULA" MAP

Setúbal

PÉROLA DA MOURISCA

DOLPHIN-WATCHING IN THE SADO ESTUARY

ATLANTIC OCEAN

Estuário do Sado

0   5 mi
0   5 km

Comporta Beach

Comporta

© MOON.COM

attractions—and often much cooler than the rest of Lisbon—Sintra is a wonderful place with its own microclimate that offers so many amazing vistas and experiences that it should definitely be top of the agenda when visiting Lisbon.

The coastline south of Lisbon, across the Tagus, is replete with popular seaside resorts. Costa da Caparica and the Setúbal Peninsula are go-to places among Lisbon locals wanting to beat the frenzy of the city and wind down on the beach or savor a slow seafood lunch.

PLANNING YOUR TIME

Most of the destinations in this chapter can be done as a **day trip,** but some warrant an **overnight** stay, or could even be grouped together. For example, the beachy seaside resort of **Costa da Caparica** can easily be done as a day trip, but fishing

Previous: Pena Palace; the lighthouse at Cabo da Roca; Estoril-Cascais Boardwalk.

Day Trips from Lisbon

Driving even less than an hour from Lisbon's city center in any direction reveals a different side of Portugal, and an extraordinary variety within a relatively small area. That said, many of these destinations, especially Sintra and the beaches in summer, can become very crowded. An **overnight stay** will allow you to visit the most popular spots outside the usual day-tripper hours, when it might be quieter and queues shorter.

SINTRA

An extravaganza of historic mansions, fairy-tale palaces, striking castles, and magical forests: You can easily spend a full day taking in Sintra's top sights, among which are some of Portugal's most recognizable and popular monuments. Be warned—Sintra, a short 30-minute drive northwest of Lisbon, is a very popular tourist hotspot; the tour buses roll in from early morning and the main attractions can become crowded (page 92).

THE PORTUGUESE RIVIERA

Enjoy a splash of glitz and glamour and indulge your inner people-watcher and window-shopper as you take in elegant beach resort Estoril and affluent Cascais. Drive 25 minutes west of the capital and stay overnight in either town to really enjoy the best of both. Relax on the beach by day, and enjoy cosmopolitan bars and restaurants by night (page 98).

MAFRA AND ERICEIRA

Veer a little off the beaten track in less-touristy Mafra and Ericeira; the former is home to one of Portugal's most extravagant royal palaces and game reserves, and the latter is a laid-back, barefoot surf town. Mafra is a 45-minute drive northwest of Lisbon, and then it's another 10 minutes west to Ericeira, on the coast (page 113 and 110).

COSTA DA CAPARICA

This is a go-to spot in summer for Lisbon locals, who make the short 22-minute drive south over the Tagus to enjoy the spacious golden sands of Caparica's endless beaches. Traffic over the river can jam on weekends when the weather is good (page 116).

SETÚBAL PENINSULA

If excellent seafood and getting out on the water are your thing, then the Setúbal Peninsula has you covered. Under 45 minutes south from Lisbon, a plethora of waterside seafood eateries, boat and dolphin-watching trips, and down-to-earth local communities await (page 115).

village **Sesimbra** and industrious port town **Setúbal** coupled justify an overnight stay. The same can be said of **Estoril, Cascais,** and **Sintra,** all north of Lisbon. Each can be visited individually from Lisbon as an excursion, but it's lovely to spend a day on the beach in Estoril and a fun night in glamorous Cascais before heading up to Sintra early the next day, passing the wild and windy **Guincho Beach** and **Cabo da Roca** viewpoint en route.

If heading to beaches near Lisbon in **summer,** remember that while the city itself might be quieter as the locals head off on their holidays, the main roads will be busy, especially on weekends. In Sintra, expect **crowds** most of the year; it pays to get there as early as possible.

Sintra

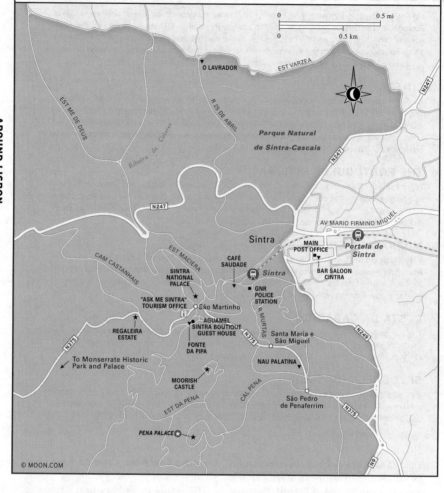

Sintra

If Sintra had to be summed up in just one word, it would be "magical"—a whimsical resort set into the picturesque green foothills of the Sintra Mountains. Inland from the windy Atlantic coast, this fairy-tale forest town has a misty microclimate all its own, cooled by the Atlantic breeze that comes whooshing up the plains from the coast, made fragrant by the pine trees that cover the hills (pack a windbreaker, just in case!). This cooler climate made Sintra a popular spot for summer residences for Europe's aristocrats and wealthy artists, whose flamboyant mansions were inspired by the Romanticism of the era. The hilltop Pena Palace is straight out of a Disney movie, the gothic Sintra National Palace impresses, while the town center's multihued historic mansions are swaddled by lush greenery. It's a little hub of theatrical extravagance.

Most sights in the historic town center are within walking distance; **Sintra National Palace,** often referred to as the "Town Palace," is in the heart of the city. **Pena Palace,** the **Regaleira Estate,** and the **Moorish Castle** are all located in the hills west of the town center; walking here from the center is recommended only for avid hikers.

SIGHTS
Sintra National Palace
(Palácio Nacional de Sintra)

Largo Rainha Dona Amélia; tel. 219 237 300; www. parquesdesintra.pt; daily 9:30am-7pm late Mar.-late Oct., daily 9:30am-6pm late Oct.-late Mar.; €10; take train from Lisbon's Rossio station to Sintra (roughly every 30 minutes, journey takes 40 minutes; approx. €5 round-trip) or a taxi from Lisbon (about 30 minutes, €35 one-way)

Sintra National Palace was the residence of Portugal's royal families from the 15th to 19th centuries and today is the first stop for many visitors to Sintra. Its white Gothic exterior, with some Manueline features, is minimalist, a counterpoint to the extravagance of the fanciful Pena Palace on the hilltop. The wow factor of the detailed interior makes up for the exterior. A bird motif is evident in the Magpie Room and the Swan Room, with its octagonal paneled ceiling. The rudimentary Moorish kitchen is topped with huge conical chimneys. Most splendid is the 16th-century Coats of Arms room, where the paneled ceiling contains the coats of arms of 72 aristocratic families. **Guided tours** (daily 2:30pm, 90 minutes; €5) are available in Portuguese, English, and Spanish. Reservations and online discounts are available via the website.

Regaleira Estate
(Quinta da Regaleira)

Rua Barbosa do Bocage 5; tel. 219 106 650; www. regaleira.pt; daily 9:30am-5pm; €6; bus 435

If the Pena Palace is a fairy tale, the sprawling Regaleira Estate, near the town center, is out of a scary movie. It's a spooky Gothic palace awash with gargoyles and spiky pinnacles and topped with a striking octagonal tower. Inside, a warren of hallways and stairways lead to rooms spread over five floors. The lush surroundings have hidden passages and secret spots with lakes, grottoes, wells, and fountains. The estate once belonged to the Viscountess of Regaleira, who was from a wealthy merchant family in Porto. The current building was completed in 1910.

A tourist bus—the **435**—connects Sintra train station to the Regaleira Estate (a short walk from Sintra center), and Monserrate Palace, among others.

★ Pena Palace
(Palácio Nacional da Pena)

Estrada da Pena; tel. 219 237 300; www. parquesdesintra.pt; daily 9:30am-8pm; €14; bus 434

Portugal's finest example of 19th-century Romantic architecture, perched on a rocky peak often shrouded in clouds, the colorful, whimsical Pena Palace wouldn't look out of place in a Disney movie. Commissioned in 1838 by the young German-born King Ferdinand II for his wife, Portuguese Maria II, and built on the site of an abandoned 16th-century monastery, the project was entrusted to amateur architect Wilhelm Ludwig von Eschwege. The imitation medieval fortress that resulted includes a jumble of watchtowers, turrets, terraces, a tunnel, and even a drawbridge.

The bold pink, gray, and ocher can be seen for miles. The interior is just as eccentric, with stuccos, trompe-l'oeil murals, and *azulejo* plaques. Note the exquisite carved chairs and vaulted ceiling in the Royal Dining Room, the rich upholstery in the Noble Room, and the orchestra of brass pots and pans in the kitchen. The Queen's Terrace and a clock tower offer the best views. **Guided tours** (daily 2:30pm, 90 minutes; €5) are available in Portuguese, English, and Spanish, and require prior

booking. Reservations and online discounts are available via the website.

Pena Palace is on top of a particularly steep hill; taking the **434 tourist bus** from the train station is recommended.

Moorish Castle
(Castelo de Mouros)

Estrada da Pena, Parque de Monserrate; tel. 219 237 300; www.parquesdesintra.pt; daily 9:30am-8pm late Mar.-late Oct., daily 9:30am-7pm late Oct.-late Mar.; €8; bus 434

Surrounded by lush forest, the crumbling old Moorish Castle provides excellent views from its towering stone walls and extensive ramparts. Built in the 9th century during Moorish occupation, the castle fell into disrepair after the Christian reconquests but was later restored in the 19th century by Ferdinand II, who incorporated it into the vast gardens surrounding the Pena Palace. As one of Portugal's most recognizable landmarks, the hilltop Pena Palace is a feast of architectural geniality, one of the most remarkable examples of 19th century Romanticist castles in the country as well as one of its most unique and theatrical tourist attractions. A series of ornately decorated rooms, fanciful details, and stunning views await those who make their way to this fairy-tale palace.

Monserrate Historic Park and Palace
(Parque e Palácio de Monserrate)

Rua Visconde de Monserrate; tel. 219 237 300; www.parquesdesintra.pt; park daily 9:30am-8pm late Mar.-late Oct., daily 9:30am-7pm late Oct.-late Mar., palace daily 9:30am-7pm late Mar.-late Oct., daily 9:30am-6pm late Oct.-late Mar.; €8; bus 435

The award-winning gardens are the main attraction at the 19th-century Monserrate Historic Park and Palace, 4 kilometers (2.5 miles) west of Sintra town. The flora ranges from romantic to wild to exotic, with species from around the world. The estate was bought

in 1856 by wealthy English textile magnate Francis Cook, who commissioned architect James Knowles to design the small palace with Gothic, Indian, and Moorish influences.

FOOD

Strong meaty flavors and delicious sweets are staples in this part of Portugal. *Vitela à Sintrense* is a slow-roasted veal dish served with roast potatoes. The traditional *queijadas de Sintra* are a decadent sweet treat, with a creamy filling of fresh cheese and cinnamon wrapped in delicate, crisp pastry.

CAFÉ SAUDADE

Av. Doutor Miguel Bombarda 6; tel. 212 428 804; Wed.-Mon. 9am-6pm; €10

The Portuguese word *saudade* roughly means "longing." This pretty eatery across from the train station fulfills longings for tasty meals and treats with an extensive menu that includes sandwiches, fresh soups and salads, coffee, and freshly baked pastries and snacks.

NAU PALATINA

Calçada de S. Pedro 18; tel. 219 240 962; Tues.-Sat. 7pm-midnight; €10

Nau Palatina is a cute little place with scrumptious Mediterranean and Portuguese haute-rustic tapas, including regional specialties like pork cheeks, traditional Alentejo delicacies, and many vegetarian-friendly options.

O LAVRADOR

Rua 25 de Abril 36; tel. 219 241 488; http:// restaurantelavrador.business.site; Tues.-Sat. noon-3pm and 7:30pm-10pm, Sun. noon-3pm; €20

Small, traditional Portuguese restaurant O Lavrador, on the main 25 de Abril road out of Sintra, has specialties that include *naco de carne na pedra* (chunks of beef on hot stone) and prawn and bacon skewers. Don't miss the Portuguese pottery hanging overhead.

BARS AND NIGHTLIFE
FONTE DA PIPA

Rua Fonte da Pipa, 11-13; tel. 219 234 437; daily 12:30pm-2am

1: Pena Palace 2: Sintra National Palace 3: Monserrate Historic Palace 4: Moorish Castle

Queluz National Palace and Gardens

Queluz National Palace

If you want a taste of fantasy even closer to Lisbon than Sintra, commuter suburb Queluz (keh-LOOZH) is home to the Palácio Nacional de Queluz e Jardins (Largo Palácio de Queluz; tel. 219 237 300; www.parquesdesintra.pt; daily 9am-6pm late Oct.-late Mar., daily 9am-7pm late Mar.-late Oct., last entry 1 hour before closing time; €10, audio guide €3), about 20 minutes northwest of Lisbon. The fanciful royal palace and splendid gardens make this a historic hot spot. This is a great place to visit if you'd like to see a spectacular palace but aren't quite ready to journey as far as Sintra yet.

THE HISTORY

Built in the 18th century as a summer residence, Queluz National Palace soon became a royal favorite for leisure and entertaining. Portugal's royal family lived here permanently before fleeing to Brazil in 1807 to escape French invasions. The palace's extravagance is a heady blend of **Baroque, neoclassical,** and **rococo styles,** and its French-inspired gardens draw comparisons with the Palace of Versailles.

INSIDE THE PALACE

Inside are the **Corridor of Azulejos;** the **Throne Hall,** dripping with shimmery mirrors and chandeliers; the **Lantern Room,** which houses the palace's biggest portrait; and the opulent **Ambassadors' Hall,** in which every square centimeter is gilded. Outside, visitors can wander gardens decorated with fountains and statues. **Corte em Queluz,** a 2-hour reenactment of 18th-century life inside the palace, is staged once a month (check dates beforehand; reservations required). The €10 fee includes entrance to the palace.

GETTING THERE

Queluz is a 20-minute drive, 14 kilometers (8.7 miles) north of Lisbon. Take the **N117** or the **A37** roads. A taxi will cost around €15 one-way. From Lisbon's **Oriente** and **Rossio** stations, **CP trains** (tel. 707 210 220; www.cp.pt; €1.60) run on the Sintra Line every 10 minutes during the week and every half hour on the weekend. The journey to the **Queluz-Belas** or **Monte Abraão** station takes 20-25 minutes; both are about a 1-kilometer (0.6-mi) walk to the palace.

A popular meeting place for young people and locals, Fonte da Pipa, in Sintra's town center, is a lively, down-to-earth drinking hole with a selection of Portuguese beer and wines.

BAR SALOON CINTRA

Avenida do Movimento das Forcas Armadas N 5; tel. 914 462 761; daily 8pm-2am

Boasting a huge range of spirits, crafts beers, and cocktails, Bar Saloon Cintra, on the southern outskirts of town, is a quirky little bar with something for everyone, good music, and nibbles.

ACCOMMODATIONS

★ AGUAMEL SINTRA BOUTIQUE GUEST HOUSE

Escadinhas da Fonte da Pipa 3; tel. 219 243 628; www.aguamelsintra.com; €120 d

In the heart of the historic center, family-run Aguamel Sintra Boutique Guest House offers a deluxe home-away-from-home experience. Contemporary on the inside, this cozy 19th-century property is a slice of history with a superb location in the town center.

INFORMATION AND SERVICES

- **GNR police station:** Rua João de Deus 6; tel. 213 252 620; www.gnr.pt
- **"Ask Me Sintra" tourism office:** Praça República 23; tel. 219 231 157; daily 9:30am-6pm
- **Main post office:** Praça Dom Afonso Henriques 7; tel. 219 241 623

GETTING THERE
Car

Sintra is 25 kilometers (15.5 miles) west of **Lisbon** on the main **A16** motorway, a 30-minute drive. Taking the train is strongly recommended over driving to Sintra—the train is frequent, cost-efficient, and convenient. Parking is limited in the town center, restricted to residents, city buses, emergency services, commercial vehicles, and taxis. There are a few **parking lots** on the outskirts,

a couple of which offer free parking, within walking distance of the historic center (www.cm-sintra.pt/car-parking-in-sintra). The roads to and in Sintra are rather narrow, and the center can become heavily congested, particularly in summer when the flux of traffic and tourist buses is at its peak.

Train
SINTRA TRAIN STATION

Avenida Dr. Miguel Bombarda; tel. 707 210 220; ticket office Mon.-Fri. 6:45am-8:30pm, Sat., Sun., and public holidays 7am-8:30pm

CP trains (tel. 707 210 220; www.cp.pt) to Sintra run from Lisbon's Rossio station many times daily, roughly every half hour. A one-way ticket costs €2.25 and takes about 40 minutes. Sintra train station is approximately 1.5 kilometers (1 mi) from town (about a 20-minute walk), but the **434 and 435 Sintra tourist buses** connect the station, the town center, and the main attractions such as Pena Palace.

GETTING AROUND

Sintra's compact town center can be covered **on foot,** but most sights are farther afield. A number of private companies, such as **Turislua Tourist Entertainment** (tel. 219 243 881), operate *tuk-tuks* near the train station and in the town center, which you can rent for a single trip or for a full day's sightseeing. This is a costly alternative to the bus, at around €30/hour.

Tourist Bus

The hop-on hop-off **Scotturb tourist buses** (tel. 214 699 125; www.scotturb.com) connect all the main sights. The **434 route** (€6.90 hop-on hop-off, €3.90 one-way) includes stops at Sintra train station, the historic town center, Pena Palace, and Moorish Castle. The **435 route** (€5 hop-on hop-off) goes to the Regaleira and Monserrate palaces. A full-day pass for all lines costs €15.

Tourist Train

The **Sintra tourist train** (tel. 918 258 001;

www.comboiodesintra.pt) takes visitors on a leisurely (and at times bumpy, thanks to the cobblestone roads) trip around the town and its attractions. It does a tour of the most emblematic locales in Sintra, including the National Palace, Regaleira Estate, Moorish Castle, and Pena Palace. The starting point is in the **old town center** (a 2-minute walk south from the National Palace), and there's a stop on Estrada da Pena for Pena Palace visitors. The complete tour lasts 45 minutes and costs €8 (children age 6-12 €5).

The Portuguese Riviera

The coastal area to the west of Lisbon is often referred to as the Portuguese Riviera, encompassing the popular coastal towns of Estoril and Cascais, as well as Boca do Inferno, a rocky coastal formation dramatically named "The Mouth of Hell." The **Marginal Road,** also known as the N6, is a popular Sunday drive from Lisbon along the Portuguese Riviera, and one of Portugal's most iconic routes. A very scenic drive, the N6 passes countless interesting sights en route, including museums and forts, gorgeous beaches, and parks.

The Marginal starts at Lisbon's Cais do Sodré docks and ends in Cascais, which at a leisurely drive takes between 45 minutes and 1 hour, depending on traffic. However, the road is generally busy; it is widely used by commuters and tourists, even more so on weekends when the locals head out of the city for a change of pace. An early morning drive or late-night cruise of the Marginal offers a certain romantic quality and should be less congested. It's also very easy to take the train to most of the Portuguese Riviera's prettiest spots and avoid the traffic if needed.

Estoril is approximately 25 kilometers (16 mi) west of Lisbon, and Cascais a little farther along, about 30 kilometers (19 mi). A popular **seafront promenade** runs between the two towns. These beautiful coastal retreats are popular among Lisbon locals and holidaymakers looking for an antithesis to the hustle and bustle of the capital. Many Lisboetas drive to Cascais and Estoril for a coffee and a stroll on a Sunday, and they flock to their beaches in summer.

ESTORIL

Glitzy São João do Estoril, better known as just Estoril (EEZH-too-reel), is a stylish seaside resort home to the largest casino in Europe. Beaches are long and spacious, with a series of rocky outcrops and piers; calm, clean water; and a laid-back, romantic ambience. It is a popular escape for families and couples on weekends. Estoril is spread over a lengthy stretch of coastline fronted by a glorious promenade and a string of cosmopolitan restaurants and bars and dotted with intriguing historic properties and lush green spaces.

Estoril's heyday was in the mid-1900s, when it was a playground for the Portuguese aristocracy and European high society. During World War II, the resort's reputation as a hangout for spies gave it a sense of intrigue. This is where Ian Fleming wrote the first part of *Casino Royale,* which launched the James Bond series. Mainstream tourism has stripped Estoril of a little of its elitism, but it is still one of the most glamorous beach destinations in Portugal.

Sights

Watch out for the quizzical clifftop **Castelinho São João do Estoril** (EN6, São João do Estoril seafront), also known as the Little Castle, located along the main Marginal Road just before Estoril. Though not open to visitors, it's reputedly one of the most haunted places in Portugal, and it has an austere, Gothic-like exterior that plays up its spooky reputation.

ESTORIL CASINO

Av. Dr. Stanley Ho; tel. 214 667 700; www.
casino-estoril.pt; daily 3pm-3am

The largest casino in Europe, Estoril Casino is in the heart of Estoril, separated from the coast by sprawling, manicured gardens that slope gently upward toward the glitzy casino building. During World War II, the casino was a convergence point for spies and dispossessed royals. Its colorful history also provided inspiration for Ian Fleming's James Bond 007 novel *Casino Royale*. With nightly entertainment and myriad slot machines, Estoril Casino is the ultimate place for dinner and a show. As well as the main games area, it has restaurants, bars, nightclubs, and a theater.

Walks

★ ESTORIL-CASCAIS BOARDWALK

Walking Distance: *3 kilometers (2 mi) one-way*
Walking Time: *30 minutes one-way*
Trailhead: *São João do Estoril Station (or Cascais Station)*
Information and Maps: *www.cascais.pt/galeria-de-imagens/paredao*

The Estoril-Cascais boardwalk, locally known as the **Paredão,** is an enjoyable promenade that hems the beachfront between the two towns. Trimmed by bars and restaurants on one side and stunning beach views on the other, it is popular among exercise-loving locals who take advantage of its smooth, flat surface to jog and power-walk. The promenade is bookended by two train stations: the São João do Estoril Station at the eastern end and the Cascais terminus at the western end. Along the route are interesting historical buildings and some of the finest beaches in the region, particularly wonderful on a balmy summer's evening.

Beaches

Lining the Estoril-Cascais coastline is a string of lovely bay-like beaches, ranging from the busier and bigger **Tamariz** Beach to the small and rocky **Poça** Beach. **Carcavelos** Beach is the biggest on the stretch of coast between

Lisbon and Cascais and closest to Lisbon. It's popular among locals and **surfers,** with plenty of parking, space, and recreational facilities. Most of the main beaches, including all of those listed below, are served by the **Lisbon-Cascais urban train line,** with stations a short walk to the beach.

CARCAVELOS BEACH
(Praia de Carcavelos)

Avenida Marginal, 15-minute drive from Lisbon along Marginal Road; good parking; open 24/7; lifeguards on duty during beach season, roughly May-Oct.

A quick 20-minute train ride from Lisbon's Cais do Sodré station, exiting in Carcavelos, it is one of the largest beaches in the Lisbon region, with 1.5 kilometers (0.9 mi) of soft, golden sands. Carcavelos Beach has excellent facilities, including plenty of sun beds and parasols, surf and sports equipment rentals, and restaurants. An array of sport and surf facilities and clean, safe water attract a young, active crowd, as well as families. The waves are usually moderately sized, except late autumn and winter, when swells grow and the surf is rougher, enjoyed by more experienced surfers. At the eastern end of the beach is the imposing **São Julião da Barra fort** (Forte de São Julião da Barra; Av. Marginal 10), one of the largest and most impressive military defense complexes remaining in Portugal. This sprawling, popular beach has plenty of parking, though it does fill up fast in the warmer months.

TAMARIZ BEACH
(Praia do Tamariz)

Avenida Marginal, directly in front of Estoril train station; no parking; open 24/7; lifeguards on duty during beach season, roughly May-Oct.

A medieval castle overlooks family-friendly Tamariz Beach, long, wide, calm, and clean but crowded in summer. Facilities include sun beds and umbrellas, lifeguards, public restrooms, and reasonably priced restaurants and bars. Adjacent to the beach is a saltwater pool, great for swimming when the waves get rough.

The Portuguese Riviera

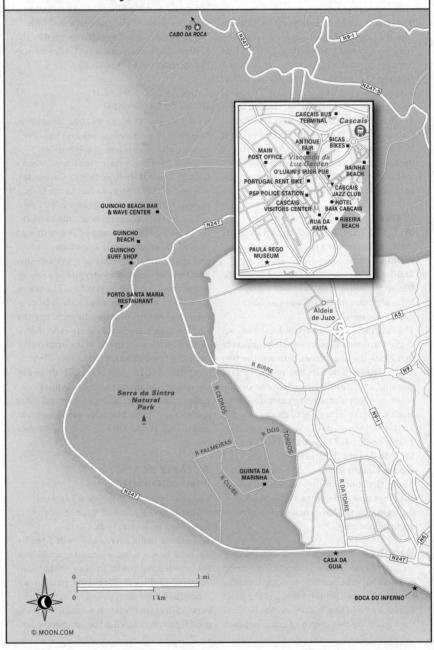

TO
CABO DA ROCA

N247

N9-1

N247-5

CASCAIS BUS
TERMINAL

Cascais

ANTIQUE
FAIR

BICAS
BIKES

MAIN
POST OFFICE

*Visconde da
Luz Garden*

O'LUAIN'S IRISH PUB

RAINHA
BEACH

PORTUGAL RENT BIKE

CASCAIS
JAZZ CLUB

PSP POLICE STATION

CASCAIS
VISITORS CENTER

HOTEL
BAÍA CASCAIS

RUA DA
RAITA

RIBEIRA
BEACH

PAULA REGO
MUSEUM

GUINCHO BEACH BAR
& WAVE CENTER

N247

GUINCHO
BEACH

GUINCHO
SURF SHOP

PORTO SANTA MARIA
RESTAURANT

Aldeia
de Juzo

A5

R BIRRE

N9

Serra da Sintra
Natural
Park

R CEDROS

R PALMEIRAS

R DOS
TORDOS

R CLUBE

QUINTA DA
MARINHA

R DA TORRE

N9-1

N247

N9

CASA DA
GUIA

BOCA DO INFERNO

0   1 mi
0   1 km

© MOON.COM

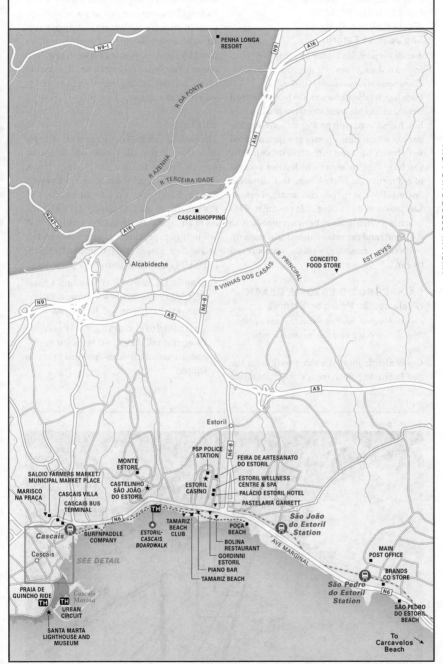

PENHA LONGA RESORT

N9-1

N9

A16

R DA PONTE

R AZENHA

R TERCEIRA IDADE

A16

CASCAISHOPPING

N247-5

N9

Alcabideche

A16

R VINHAS DOS CASAIS

R PRINCIPAL

CONCEITO FOOD STORE

EST NEVES

A5

N6-8

A5

Estoril

PSP POLICE STATION

N6-8

FEIRA DE ARTESANATO DO ESTORIL

MONTE ESTORIL

SALOIO FARMERS MARKET/ MUNICIPAL MARKET PLACE

CASTELINHO SÃO JOÃO DO ESTORIL

ESTORIL CASINO

ESTORIL WELLNESS CENTRE & SPA

PALÁCIO ESTORIL HOTEL

PASTELARIA GARRETT

MARISCO NA PRAÇA

CASCAIS VILLA

CASCAIS BUS TERMINAL

N6

TH

SÃO JOÃO do Estoril Station

Cascais

SURFNPADDLE COMPANY

ESTORIL-CASCAIS BOARDWALK

TAMARIZ BEACH CLUB

POÇA BEACH

AVE MARGINAL

Cascais

SEE DETAIL

BOLINA RESTAURANT

GORDINNI ESTORIL

PIANO BAR

TAMARIZ BEACH

MAIN POST OFFICE

BRANDS CO STORE

Cascais Marina

SÃO PEDRO do Estoril Station

N6

PRAIA DE GUINCHO RIDE

TH

URBAN CIRCUIT

SÃO PEDRO DO ESTORIL BEACH

SANTA MARTA LIGHTHOUSE AND MUSEUM

To Carcavelos Beach

POÇA BEACH (SÃO JOÃO DO ESTORIL BEACH)
(Praia da Poça/Praia de São João de Estoril)

Avenida Marginal, São João do Estoril; limited parking in vicinity; open 24/7; lifeguards on duty during beach season, roughly May-Oct.

Poça Beach (also known as São João do Estoril Beach) in São João do Estoril is a small, sandy beach smattered with rocky patches, along the back of which runs a pretty promenade lined with beach bars and cafés. It is delimited by two large cliffs on top of which stand a couple of old fortresses: Forte Velho, also known as Forte da Poça, at the one end, and the Forte de São Teodósio da Cadaveira at the other. This beach is located halfway between the São João do Estoril and the main Estoril train stations, so it's easily accessible by public transport and by car.

SÃO PEDRO DO ESTORIL BEACH
(Praia de São Pedro do Estoril)

Avenida Marginal, São Pedro do Estoril; open 24/7; lifeguards on duty during beach season, roughly May-Oct.

Conveniently located a short walk from the São Pedro do Estoril train station, this wide wedge of golden sand is not as big as some of its neighbors, but it is just as popular. It appeals to an array of visitors: The choppy surf attracts surfers, while the low tidepools are loved by families. Nestled between beautiful ravines, São Pedro do Estoril Beach is particularly popular among body-boarders and is very busy in summer.

Surfing

The number one spot in this area for all types of surfing is rugged, windswept **Guincho Beach** (page 109), a short drive from Cascais on Portugal's west coast. **Carcavelos Beach, São Pedro do Estoril Beach,** and **Bolina Beach** are also all popular with surfers of all capabilities, from learners to pros. A few outfitters provide surf equipment rentals and lessons, as well as stand-up paddleboarding (SUP) classes and board repair.

- **Brands Co Store:** Rua Sacadura Cabral 40; tel. 215 879 869; www.brandsco.store; Mon.-Fri. 9am-7pm, Sat. 10am-7pm
- **SurfnPaddle Company:** Praia da Duquesa; tel. 933 258 114; www.surfn-paddle.com; daily 9am-7pm (may vary in winter)

Tamariz Beach

Spas
ESTORIL WELLNESS CENTER & SPA

Termas do Estoril, Rua Particular Hotel Palácio; tel. 214 658 600; www.estorilwellnesscenter.pt; daily 8am-9:30pm

The Estoril Wellness Center & Spa harnesses the natural properties of the local springs for soothing treatments, including whirlpools and massages.

Shopping
FEIRA DE ARTESANATO DO ESTORIL

FIARTIL, Av. Amaral; tel. 214 677 019 or 912 590 249; Mon.-Fri. 6pm-midnight, Sat.-Sun. 5pm-midnight June-early Sept.

A nightly summer handicraft fair called Feira de Artesanato do Estoril is held behind the Estoril Casino, featuring about 300 artisans working on their wares, as well as food stands. The traditional Portuguese entertainment starts at around 9pm nightly.

Food and Bars
★ PASTELARIA GARRETT

Av. Nice 54; tel. 214 680 365; Wed.-Mon. 8am-6pm; €5

Open since 1934, celebrated bakery and cake shop Pastelaria Garrett was once frequented by royalty and remains a popular haunt for Portuguese celebrities. Its displays are crammed with colorful sweet treats. It's busiest at lunchtime, and in December queues for traditional Christmas cakes spill into the street.

GORDINNI ESTORIL

Av. Marginal 7191; tel. 214 672 205; www.gordinniestoril.com; Thurs.-Tues. noon-3:30pm and 7pm-11pm; €15

In the heart of Estoril with views over the bay, cozy Gordinni Estoril has a huge menu of freshly baked pizzas and pastas and is famous for its sangria and *caipirinha* cocktails.

BOLINA RESTAURANT

Rua Olivença 151; tel. 214 687 821; www.bolina.fish; Mon.-Fri. 10am-6pm, Sat.-Sun. 9am-1pm; €20

With a prime position on the boardwalk, long-established Bolina Restaurant specializes in simple grilled fish, seafood, and meats—and sunset views.

TAMARIZ BEACH CLUB

Av. Marginal 7669; tel. 919 573 899; Wed.-Sun. 11:30pm-4:30am

Fashionable Tamariz Beach Club is a popular place to be seen with a cocktail in hand. It has great views over the coast and gets lively after the sun goes down.

Accommodations
★ PALÁCIO ESTORIL HOTEL

Rua Particular and Av. Biarritz; tel. 214 648 000; www.palacioestorilhotel.com; €270 d

Built in 1930, the storied Palácio Estoril Hotel was the refuge of choice for royalty fleeing World War II. Frequented by artists, writers, and spies, it later served as a set for the James Bond movie *On Her Majesty's Secret Service*. The hotel still retains many of its original features, décor, and beautiful gardens.

Information and Services

- **PSP police station:** just behind Estoril Casino; tel. 214 646 700; www.psp.pt
- **Main post office:** Rua 9 de Abril 371; tel. 214 649 977

Getting There

Estoril is a 25-kilometer (16-mi) drive west of **Lisbon.** The easiest and fastest route (20 minutes) is the **A5** motorway, which has tolls. The scenic **Marginal coastal road (N6)** is toll-free but takes a little longer (about 45 minutes) and gets busy at commuter rush hours and on weekends. Once in Cascais, **parking** (particularly free parking) can be hard to find, especially on weekends and during summer. But there are plenty of paid car parks; there's an underground car park right next to the beachfront, metered parking along the marina and main streets and by the train station, and covered parking in the **Cascais Villa** shopping center. Hourly rates vary according to time and season.

Local urban **Scotturb bus** (tel. 214 699 100; www.scotturb.com; €3.35) Lines 406, 407, 411, 412, and 416 run between Estoril, Cascais, and Sintra, departing from outside Estoril train station.

SÃO JOÃO DO ESTORIL STATION

Quinta da Carreira, 2765-472; ticket office Mon.-Fri. 6:45am-8:30pm, Sat.-Sun. 7am-8:30pm

CP trains (tel. 707 210 220; www.cp.pt) run about every half hour from Lisbon's Cais do Sodré train station 36 minutes along the coast to the São João do Estoril Station (€2.25 one-way) and continue to Cascais. Trains are less frequent after dark. There are four stations in Estoril: **São Pedro do Estoril, São João do Estoril, Estoril** (for the town, the casino, and Tamariz Beach), and **Monte Estoril** (halfway between Estoril and Cascais).

Getting Around

The town of Estoril is easily covered **on foot.** A lovely and safe 3-kilometer (2-mi) **seafront promenade** connects Estoril to Cascais, providing an enjoyable walk between the two.

CASCAIS

Perched on the western tip of the coastline, cosmopolitan little Cascais (kash-KAIZH), with its picturesque bay and elegant marina, is one of Lisbon's wealthiest suburbs. King Luís I of Portugal made the seaside hamlet his summer home in the 1870s, and it has been a magnet for the rich and famous ever since. Despite hosting some of the most exclusive resorts in the country, Cascais retains the charm of a fishing village. On weekends, city dwellers drive the scenic Marginal coast road from Lisbon to Cascais to enjoy people-watching in its cafés and bars.

Sights
CASCAIS MARINA

Casa de São Bernardo; tel. 214 824 857; www. mymarinacascais.com

With a capacity for several hundred vessels, Cascais Marina regularly hosts sailing competitions and international events. It's also home to elegant restaurants and boutiques.

SANTA MARTA LIGHTHOUSE AND MUSEUM
(Farol Museu de Santa Marta)

Praceta Farol; tel. 214 815 328; www.cascais. pt; Tues.-Fri. 10am-5pm, Sat.-Sun. 10am-1pm and 2pm-5pm; €5

Built in 1868, the distinctive blue-and-white-striped Santa Marta lighthouse peers over Cascais Marina. Located to the south of Cascais center, it is a beacon for sailors around the bay. The quadrangular tower stands 8 meters (26 ft) tall and houses an interesting little museum in a neighboring building dedicated to lighthouse history. The views over Cascais from the top of the tower are fantastic, but it can be climbed only on Wednesdays.

PAULA REGO MUSEUM
(Casa das Histórias Paula Rego)

Avenida da República, 300; tel. 214 826 970; www.casadashistoriaspaularego.com; Tues.-Sun. 10am-6pm; €5

An intriguing building dedicated to one of Portugal's most famous and divisive current artists, the Paula Rego Museum was designed by acclaimed Portuguese architect Eduardo Souto de Moura at the artist's personal request. Paula Rego is a Portuguese-born visual artist best known for her thought-provoking storybook-based paintings and prints, whose descriptions range from disturbing to brilliant. Inaugurated in 2009, the ochre-red pyramidlike building sits in stark contrast with its azure, palm-tree-lined, Riviera-like surroundings. Consisting of four wings, comprising permanent collections and temporary

1: main square in Cascais **2:** Santa Marta Lighthouse **3:** Paula Rego Museum **4:** Boca do Inferno

exhibitions, it also has an auditorium, a café, and a gift shop; the collection includes 15 paintings by Rego's late husband, Victor Willing.

BOCA DO INFERNO

1.5 kilometers (1 mi) west of Cascais town

The dramatically named Boca do Inferno (Hell's Mouth) is a striking rock formation carved by relentless tides. After the ceaseless pounding caused the original cave to give way, it left behind an intriguing rock formation in the shape of a grotto and a large archway. Stunning coastal views can be enjoyed from the paths up and down the cliff. In summer, when the seas are calmer, the translucent turquoise water laps gently around the formation's base. In winter, huge waves lash the rock and cliffs—at times the spray from the crashing waves can dwarf the cliffs themselves. It's about 1.5 kilometers (1 mi) west of Cascais town, roughly a half-hour stroll along the coast. A scattering of cafés and market stalls selling souvenirs and gifts can be found here. You'll probably need around an hour to walk around the site, admire the views and the waves crashing against the cliffs, take a few photos, and enjoy a coffee or an ice cream from one of the nearby cafés.

There are a number of routes to **walk** from Cascais town center to Boca do Inferno, which all generally take 20-40 minutes (depending on the pace). The most enjoyable is perhaps along the mostly flat **Avenida Rei Humberto II de Itália,** a seaside route that offers delightful ocean views as you walk past Cascais marina and lighthouse. You can also **bike** along the cycle path, or take a **cab.**

CASA DA GUIA
(Guia House)

Avenida Nossa Senhora do Cabo 101; tel. 214 843 215; http://casadaguiacascais.com; daily 9am-2am; free

A 40-minute (2-km/1.2-mi) walk from Cascais town center, this 19th-century manor house is surrounded by 2 hectares (5 acres) of lovely gardens. Within the walls of the historic mansion are arts and crafts stalls, novelty shops,

cafés and restaurants, and glorious ocean views, which altogether makes it worth spending an hour or two here. There is limited parking on the road outside the mansion, which runs between Cascais and Guincho Beach.

Beaches
RIBEIRA BEACH
(Praia da Ribeira)

Main town front; underground car park within walking distance; open 24/7; lifeguards on duty in summer

Cascais's main beach, Praia da Ribeira, also often referred to as Praia dos Pescadores, or Fishermen's Beach, is a charming little chunk of sand directly in front of the main town center. Overlooking Cascais's marina and docks, the beach can get pretty crowded in summer and on weekends, but there are plenty of parking lots in the vicinity. The water is very calm and cool, and the beach is just a short walk from Cascais Train Station.

RAINHA BEACH
(Praia da Rainha)

200 meters (650 ft) walk west of Cascais town; no dedicated parking, limited metered street parking in vicinity or use Largo da Estação car park and walk; open 24/7; lifeguards on duty during summer

Just before Cascais's main Ribeira Beach, heading west from Estoril to Cascais, is Rainha Beach, a small, clean, bay-like beach with crystalline waters and soft sands studded with rock formations. Compact and picturesque, it has sun beds and umbrellas available to the public to rent for around €20 per day in summer. The beach is a 50-meter (150-ft) walk from Cascais high street and a 200-meter (650-ft) walk to Cascais Train Station.

Cycling

In addition to **Portugal Rent Bike** (Rua da Palmeira 39A; tel. 934 432 304; www.portugalrentbike.com; daily 9am-9pm) in the heart of Cascais, **Bicas Bikes** (Rua Dra. Iracy Doyle 5; https://mobi.cascais.pt; daily 9am-7pm) has three stations in Cascais: one by the train station, one at the tourist bureau near the Paulo Rego Museum, and one at Casa da Guia. Each station has some 20 basic bikes, which can be picked up from and returned to different stations. Rentals start from a couple of euros for an hour and go up to about €6 per day.

URBAN CIRCUIT

Cycling Distance: 3.8 kilometers (2.4 mi) round-trip
Cycling Time: 15 minutes round-trip
Trailhead: Cascais Marina
Information and Maps: www.ciclovia.pt/ ciclovias/3lisboa/1lisboa/cascais/ccircuito.html

This designated cycle path is a sort of figure-eight shape and takes cyclists along a scenic route through Cascais's urban center and main attractions. Sights along the way include the Boca do Inferno rock formation, Paula Rego Museum, up to the roundabout before Casa da Guia, and through the heart of the town back down to the town center, seafront, and marina.

PRAIA DE GUINCHO RIDE

Cycling Distance: 10 kilometers (6 mi) round-trip
Cycling Time: 35 minutes round trip
Trailhead: Castro Guimarães Museum, west of the marina
Information and Maps: www.ciclovia.pt/ ciclovias/3lisboa/1lisboa/cascais/cguincho.html

Enjoy one of Cascais's most popular bike rides along a flat and smooth purpose-made cycle path between Cascais and the stunning surfing beach of Guincho Beach. It's an enjoyable half-day activity, taking in dramatic coastline, cliffs, beautiful beaches, and numerous interesting sights such as the Boca do Inferno and Casa da Guia. Stop at Guincho Beach for a fresh seafood lunch at the swanky beach-shack-chic Porto Santa Maria Restaurant (www.portosantamaria.com).

Golf

PENHA LONGA RESORT

Estrada da Lagoa Azul Sintra Linhó; tel. 219 249 031; www.penhalonga.com

The Penha Longa resort is home to one of Europe's top-30 golf courses, the 18-hole Atlantic Championship course (€74 per round) with rolling greens, world-class facilities, and the Sintra Mountains as a backdrop.

Shopping

The lovely pedestrian street **Rua da Raita** is Cascais's main shopping street. It's a pleasant, pedestrianized, cobbled street with a distinctive black and white wavy pattern, lined with European fashion boutiques and the obligatory tourist souvenir shops.

Every Saturday and Sunday, **antiques and handicrafts fairs** are held in the Visconde da Luz garden in the heart of the town center and at nearby **Casa da Guia.**

VISCONDE DA LUZ GARDEN ANTIQUE FAIR

Visconde da Luz Garden, Av. dos Combatentes da Grande Guerra; Wed. only 9am-8pm

Soak up the sights, sounds, and smells of yesteryear at this bustling antique market brimming with interesting paraphernalia and collectors' items, from silverware to books and vinyl records.

SALOIO FARMERS MARKET/ MUNICIPAL MARKET PLACE

Rua Padre Moisés da Silva 29, Municipal Market Place; tel. 214 825 000; Wed. and Sat. 7am-1pm

Get your fill of tasty fresh produce or pack for a picnic at the Saloio Famers Market, which showcases the best regional delicacies like cured meats and cheeses.

CASCAIS VILLA

Avenida Dom Pedro; tel. 214 828 250; www. cascaisvilla.pt; daily 10am-10pm

Located on the road heading out of town toward Estoril, the Cascais Villa shopping center is small but perfectly formed, with its interesting blue glass feature front, a decent selection of shops and restaurants in the food court, and a supermarket.

CASCAISHOPPING

Estrada Nacional 9; tel. 210 121 628; www. cascaishopping.pt; daily 10am-11pm

The larger of Cascais's shopping malls, CascaiShopping is a good place to bear in mind if the weather turns cool or rainy. Packed with trendy shops, from high street names to designer brands, and fun eateries, the mall also has wheelchairs and baby strollers available on request, a medical center, and a movie theater.

Food and Bars
★ MARISCO NA PRAÇA

Rua Padre Moisés da Silva 34; tel. 214 822 130; daily noon-midnight; €20

Don't miss the Marisco na Praça for old-fashioned seafood. In the town center, this no-frills *marisqueira* is both market stall and eatery, offering fresh catch. Have the seafood cooked here and served at the table.

CONCEITO FOOD STORE

Rua Pequena; tel. 218 085 281; www. conceitofoodstore.pt; Tues.-Sat. 7:30pm-11pm; €30

Traditional Portuguese cuisine is given a modern overhaul at Conceito Food Store, an in-demand restaurant with minimalist décor. Products from local suppliers are transformed into contemporary masterpieces.

CASCAIS JAZZ CLUB

Largo Cidade da Vitória 36; tel. 962 773 470; www.facebook.com/cascaisjazzclub; Wed.-Sat. 8pm-12:30am, Sun. 11am-2pm and 8pm-12:30am

This surprisingly agreeable little jazz house has live jazz sessions every Thursday, Friday, and Saturday night and Sunday afternoon.

O'LUAIN'S IRISH PUB

Rua da Palmeira 4; tel. 214 861 627; daily noon-2am

There's always good *craic* at this typical Irish pub in the heart of old town Cascais, just back from the main beach. With live music on Fridays, Saturdays, and Sundays, it's a popular hangout among expats and holidaymakers.

Accommodations
★ HOTEL BAÍA CASCAIS

Av. Marginal; tel. 214 831 033; www.hotelbaia.com; €130 d

In the heart of Cascais, on the beachfront, the large three-star Hotel Baía Cascais offers a first-rate location at accessible prices. Ideal for families or groups, it has 113 rooms, 66 of which have sea-view verandas.

Information and Services

- **PSP police station:** Rua Afonso Sanches 26; tel. 214 814 060; www.psp.pt
- **Cascais Visitors Center:** Praça 5 de Outubro; tel. 912 034 214; daily 9am-8pm
- **Main post office:** Av. Ultramar 2; tel. 214 827 281

Getting There and Around

Cascais is 35 kilometers (22 mi) west of Lisbon's city center. The two main routes are the **A5** motorway, which has tolls, or the more scenic but often much busier **Marginal coastal road (N6),** which runs parallel to the A5, passing pine-tree countryside, luxury villas, and old forts. On a good day, both routes take 30 minutes. With traffic, the Marginal can crawl, but the scenery is lovely. It's busiest at rush hour on weekdays and on weekends in good weather.

Once you arrive, compact Cascais itself is easily covered **on foot.** Cascais is also a pleasant 3-kilometer (2-mi) walk west from Estoril along a lovely flat seafront promenade with lots to see—tide pools, cafés and bars, and quirky old houses.

CASCAIS TRAIN STATION

Largo da Estação, 2750-340; Mon.-Fri. 7am-9:30pm

During the day, **CP trains** (tel. 707 210 220; www.cp.pt) run approximately every 30 minutes from **Cais do Sodré** station in Lisbon along the coast to Cascais (€2.25 one-way). The journey takes approximately 40 minutes. Trains are less frequent after dark but still run until around 1:30am. The train station is a 10-minute stroll east of the town center.

The CP train on the Lisbon-Cascais line runs frequently and is the quickest way to travel between Cascais and **Estoril's** seafront station. The journey takes just 3 minutes, and a one-way ticket (€1.30) can be bought at the station from machines or the ticket office.

CASCAIS BUS TERMINAL

Av. Costa Pinto 74, 2750-642

The local urban **Scotturb bus** (tel. 214 699 100; www.scotturb.com) runs between Estoril, Cascais, and Sintra. The main **bus terminal** in Cascais is beneath the Cascais Villa shopping mall (level 0), just north of the Cascais railway station and town center. From here, buses depart at least once an hour for the main destinations of Guincho Beach, Cabo da Roca, and Sintra. Lines 406, 407, 411, 412, and 416 run frequently between Cascais and Estoril, while Line 418 runs between Cascais and Sintra. Line 403 passes Cabo da Roca, and Lines 405 and 415 run to Guincho Beach.

The West Coast

North of Cascais is a stretch of coast that remains unspoiled and untamed. Buffeted by the winds that roll in from the Atlantic Ocean, rugged and raw, the west coast comprises the famously wild Guincho Beach, with its sandy dunes, Cabo da Roca, mainland Europe's most westerly point, and top surf spot Ericeira.

GUINCHO BEACH
(Praia do Guincho)

Northwest of Cascais on the windswept Atlantic Coast, Guincho Beach is rugged and unbridled, with vast coastal dunes that make the landscape almost desolate. The waves that roll in from the Atlantic make it popular for surfing, windsurfing, and kitesurfing, rather than for relaxation. The beach has good facilities, including public showers and toilets, beach bars, restaurants, and surf shops.

Surfing

- **Guincho Surf Shop:** Praia do Guincho Estalagem Muchaxo; tel. 214 850 286; www. guinchosurfshop.com; daily 9am-6pm

- **Guincho Beach Bar & Wave Center:** tel. 214 647 013 or 918 500 041; www.bardogu-incho.pt/en/wave-center; daily 9am-late

Food
PORTO SANTA MARIA RESTAURANT

Estrada do Guincho; tel. 214 879 450; www. portosantamaria.com; daily noon-11pm; €60

Having undergone a lavish refurbishment in late 2019, Porto Santa Maria has been elevated from time-honored favorite beachside seafood shack to an über-swanky place to see and be seen. Stylish and glamorous, the restaurant serves exceptional and fresh food from the docks or the in-house tanks. It even has its own wine cellar boasting rare wines. On the menu are seafood classics like lobster, crab and oysters, sea-salt baked fish, and seafood pastas, complemented by a range of succulent meat dishes and locally grown sides.

Getting There

Guincho is a 15-minute drive (7 km/4.3 mi) northwest from **Cascais,** following the **Rua Joaquim Ereira** road or the **N247** coastal road. The local urban **Scotturb bus** (tel. 214 699 125; www.scotturb.com) Lines 405 and 415 run between Cascais (from the main terminal beneath the Cascais Villa shopping center) and Guincho at least once an hour. Tickets cost about €2. Alternately, rent a **bicycle** in Cascais from **Portugal Rent Bike** (www. portugalrentbike.com) to ride the scenic 5-kilometer (3-mi) cycle path from Cascais to Guincho.

★ CABO DA ROCA

www.cm-sintra.pt

For invigorating sea air, stand on mainland Europe's most westerly point at Cabo da Roca, flanked by gigantic granite boulders and dramatic vertical cliffs that drop 100 meters (328 ft) to the Atlantic. A solitary rock monument marks the spot with a crucifix and an engraved quote from Portugal's greatest poet, Luís de Camões, who declared in his epic *Os Lusíadas* that this is where "land ends and sea begins." A short walk away, Portugal's first purpose-built **lighthouse** has a **gift shop** that offers certificates confirming that visitors set foot on the western edge of Europe. Pack a jacket; this promontory is blustery and cold.

Getting There

Cabo da Roca is 40 kilometers (25 mi) west of **Lisbon,** a 40-minute drive on the **A5,** and 15 kilometers (9.3 mi) north of **Cascais,** a 25-minute drive following the **N247** road. **Scotturb bus** (tel. 214 699 125; www.scotturb.com; €4) Line 403, which runs from Cascais to Sintra, also stops here once an hour during the day, but services are irregular; check the schedule in advance.

ERICEIRA

On the coast north of Lisbon, laid-back Ericeira is a little gem, not especially picturesque but with stunning ocean vistas and beautiful beaches. A jumble of whitewashed fishermen's cottages are piled atop high-backed cliffs that encircle the cove-like main beach and harbor, and it is a place where you can walk around barefoot and carefree. The village attracts surfers and big-name surfing competitions. The Save the Waves Coalition has even declared it a World Surfing Reserve, the second in the world and the only one in Europe.

What Ericeira lacks in picturesqueness it makes up for with vibrant nightlife and excellent seafood. Still not quite on the mass tourism radar, Ericeira has managed to strike the perfect balance between traditional and cool, which makes for a fun and heady combination that keeps visitors coming back.

Sights

Life in Ericeira centers on the **Praça da República** square, a cobbled hub fringed with lovely cafés and cake shops, set back off the main **Praia dos Pescadores (Fishermen's Beach)**. **Rua Dr. Eduardo Burnay** is the buzzing main street that runs south from the square

Cabo da Roca

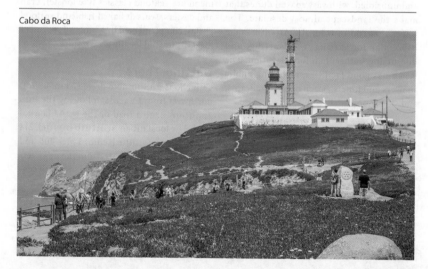

Ericeira

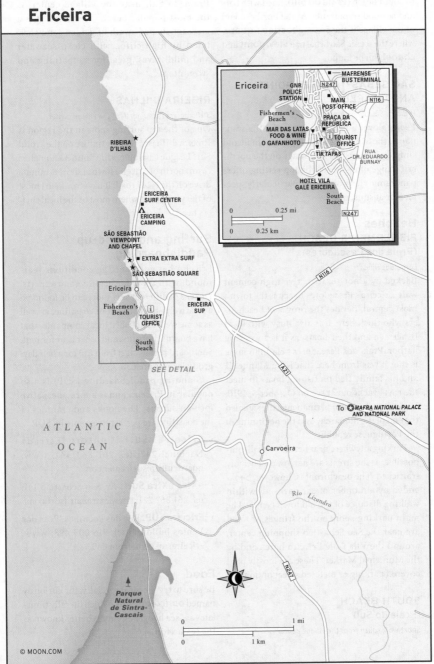

Ericeira

- MAFRENSE BUS TERMINAL
- GNR POLICE STATION
- MAIN POST OFFICE
- N247
- N116
- Fishermen's Beach
- PRAÇA DA REPÚBLICA
- MAR DAS LATAS FOOD & WINE
- O GAFANHOTO
- TOURIST OFFICE
- RUA DR. EDUARDO BURNAY
- TIK TAPAS
- HOTEL VILA GALÉ ERICEIRA
- South Beach
- N247

0   0.25 mi
0   0.25 km

RIBEIRA D'ILHAS

ERICEIRA SURF CENTER

ERICEIRA CAMPING

SÃO SEBASTIÃO VIEWPOINT AND CHAPEL

EXTRA EXTRA SURF

SÃO SEBASTIÃO SQUARE

Ericeira

Fishermen's Beach

TOURIST OFFICE

ERICEIRA SUP

South Beach

SEE DETAIL

N116

N247

A21

To ⚫ MAFRA NATIONAL PALACE AND NATIONAL PARK

ATLANTIC OCEAN

Carvoeira

Rio Lizandro

N247

Parque Natural de Sintra-Cascais

0   1 mi
0   1 km

© MOON.COM

to South Beach (**Praia do Sul**), lined with bars and seafood restaurants. At the northern end of the village is the **São Sebastião Square,** where the scenic São Sebastião **viewpoint** and **chapel** can be found.

SÃO SEBASTIÃO VIEWPOINT AND CHAPEL

Praia de São Sebastião

Peering over a beach that goes by the same name, the São Sebastião chapel is a small and simple whitewashed hermitage on the northern fringe of town. Its clifftop setting offers panoramic views out to sea, particularly spectacular at sunset.

Beaches

FISHERMEN'S BEACH (Praia dos Pescadores)

Largo das Ribas

Backed by a not-so-attractive high cement wall, Ericeira's Pescadores Beach is the town's most central. Besides the droves of beachgoers who flock here, it is also busy with local fishermen and their boats, as it is a working harbor. Praia dos Pescadores's claim to fame is that it was from here that King Manuel II and his family fled on fishing boats to meet the royal yacht out at sea on October 5, 1910. Their departure into permanent exile signaled the end of the monarchy and the beginning of the Portuguese republic.

Parking anywhere near here is virtually impossible, as the streets are narrow and heavily trafficked. The beachfront is, however, bookended by a number of car parks all within walking distance of the old town center. The main parking spots on the fringes of town are near the São Sebastião shopping center, around the Vila Galé Ericeira hotel, and by the Municipal Market. These are mostly paid covered parking or metered street options.

SOUTH BEACH (Praia do Sul)

Short walk south from the village center

Praia do Sul, near the village center, is the most popular beach in Ericeira. It is a crescent-shaped swath of golden sand sheltered by high cliffs, with clean seawater and mild waves, great for sunbathing and swimming.

RIBEIRA D'ILHAS

3 kilometers (2 mi) north of the village center

One of the top surfing spots in the region is Ribeira d'Ilhas, a regular fixture on the World Surf League Championship Tour, 3 kilometers (2 mi) north of Ericeira town, a short 8-minute drive on the N247 road. It has strong surf most of the year and is where most of the local surfers head.

Surfing and Stand-up Paddleboarding

Ericeira has good surfing conditions year-round, with spots for beginners to experts. Dozens of different surf spots can be found on a relatively short stretch of coastline, as well as some well-established local companies that have boards, wetsuits, and other gear for rent. Surfboard rentals start from €15 for a half day; group lessons are €30-35 pp.

Stand-up paddleboarding (SUP) is also popular in Ericeira and is a nice alternative for non-surfers. The nooks and crannies of the coastline are perfect to explore by SUP.

- **Ericeira Surf Center:** Estrada Nacional 247; tel. 261 864 547; www. boardculturesurfcenter.com
- **eXtra eXtra Surf:** Av. São Sebastião 14I; tel. 261 867 771; www.extraextrasurf.com
- **Ericeira SUP:** Rua dos Pocinhos, Rosa dos Ventos building; tel. 916 009 498; www. ericeirasup.com, from €40

Food

Be sure to try the local specialty, the curiously named *ouriço-do-mar* (which literally translates as "sea hedgehog" but is better known as the sea urchin).

☆ Mafra National Palace and National Park

A 10-minute drive southeast of Ericeira, Mafra is famed for its extravagant palace and Mafra National Park, a former royal game reserve.

MAFRA NATIONAL PALACE
(Palácio Nacional de Mafra)
Terreiro Dom João V; tel. 261 817 550; www. palaciomafra.gov.pt; Wed.-Mon. 9am-6pm; €6

On a hilltop above the town center, this monumental palace is the finest example of 18th-century Baroque architecture in Portugal, built during the reign of John V (Dom João V) to fulfill a promise he made that if his wife bore him children, he would build a convent. The first stone was laid in 1717, and it took 13 years and 52,000 workers to complete it.

The original plan was a monastery for 13 monks, but the project grew to immense proportions, eventually housing 300 monks and including a basilica and a royal palace. The sprawling monument's limestone facade measures 220 meters (722 ft). The beautiful exterior, painted in sunny yellow, features twin bell towers that frame the central basilica.

Mafra National Palace

The lavish interior comprises 1,200 rooms and 5,000 windows and doors. The Old Library is a trove of 36,000 ancient books, and the basilica has no fewer than six organs. Outside are a lovely, bird-filled courtyard and vast decorative patio. Guided tours of the palace are available with prior booking.

MAFRA NATIONAL PARK
(Tapada Nacional de Mafra)
Portão do Codeçal; tel. 261 817 050; www.tapadademafra.pt; daily 9:30am-6pm

A 10-minute drive northeast of Mafra town on the N9-2 road, the 8-square-kilometer (3-sq-mi) Mafra National Park is a sprawling royal game reserve created for the Mafra National Palace. Today it is still verdant and varied habitat for free-roaming deer, wild boars, wolves, foxes, badgers, and birds of prey. Activities include hiking, mountain biking, horseback riding, archery, and falconry, staged mostly on weekends. For more information on these activities, inquire at the main ticket office at the entrance (tel. 261 814 240; daily 9:30am-6pm) or the park website.

There are four different hiking routes, ranging from 4.5 km (2 mi) to 8.2 km (5 mi). Guided footpath tours are also available. BTT (all-terrain mountain bike) routes (8 km/5 mi-24 km/15.5 mi) are open 9am-4pm. Rental bikes are available at the trailhead of the white route (adults €10, children). The price to enter the park varies by activity; hikes are €4 on weekdays, €6.50 on weekends.

GETTING THERE

Mafra is 40 kilometers (25 mi) northwest of Lisbon, about a 40-minute drive. Follow the A8 motorway from Lisbon, taking junction 5 and then heading west on the A21. There is a spacious paid parking lot just next to the Mafra Palace (parking costs a couple of euros for a few hours) and also a large parking lot just outside the Tapada that is free for paying visitors.

Mafrense buses (tel. 707 201 371; www.mafrense.pt) run hourly from Lisbon's Campo Grande main bus station, stopping in front of Mafra National Palace. The trip takes 1 hour each way and costs €4.30. Buses are less frequent on weekends.

AROUND LISBON
THE WEST COAST

O GAFANHOTO

*Rua da Conceição 8; tel. 261 864 514; https://
brunomata17.wixsite.com/gafanhoto; Wed.-Mon.
noon-4pm and 7pm-10:30pm; €10*

In the town center, O Gafanhoto (The Grasshopper) is typically Portuguese on the outside, with its *azulejo* tiles and sky-blue trim, and typically Portuguese on the inside, with a menu that features good old-fashioned favorites like *cozido à Portuguesa* (Portuguese stew), Portuguese-style liver, and the Transmontana bean stew. Daily special menus are available in full or half portions.

TIK TAPAS

*Rua do Ericeira 15; tel. 261 869 235; Tues.-Thurs.
7pm-midnight, Sat.-Sun. 12:30pm-3pm and
7pm-midnight; €10*

A rainbow of tasty meat, fish, and vegetarian tapas is served in this vibrant little eatery, with its bright-blue bar and tables and burnt-orange walls.

MAR DAS LATAS FOOD & WINE

*Rua Capitão João Lopes 24A; tel. 912 218 423; www.
facebook.com/mar.das.latas; Thurs.-Tues. 6pm-11pm;
€30*

This classy, modern-traditional eatery serves fine wine, accomplished cuisine based on fresh local ingredients, and sunset drinks with a view. From the kitchen of a talented young chef come tasty starters such as ceviche, fried squid, and tuna tartar, while entrées range from delectable leg of lamb to cod curry, beetroot risotto, and Wagyu beef.

Accommodations

HOTEL VILA GALÉ ERICEIRA

*Largo dos Navegantes 1; tel. 261 869 900; www.
vilagale.com; €100-200 d*

This large, grand dame-style hotel is located on the Ericeira cliffs, facing South Beach on the southern edge of town. Vila Galé Ericeira has comfortable rooms and two pools, one of which is saltwater, both overlooking the ocean.

ERICEIRA CAMPING

*Estrada Nacional 247; tel. 261 862 706; www.
ericeiracamping.com; 2 people + 1 tent approx. €20
pp/night high season (July-Aug.), classic 4-person
bungalow €110 pp/night (July-Aug.)*

Free your inner adventurer and stay at the modern and well-equipped Ericeira Camping park. It offers traditional camping among shady trees as well as bungalows and mobile homes for accommodation, catering, and a surf school right next door.

Information and Services

- **GNR police station:** Largo Domingos Fernandes 7; tel. 261 860 710; www.gnr.pt
- **Tourist office:** Rua Dr. Eduardo Burnay 46; tel. 261 863 122; daily 10am-6pm
- **Main post office:** Rua do Paço 2; tel. 261 860 501

Getting There

Ericeira is 50 kilometers (31 mi) northwest of **Lisbon,** 46 kilometers (28.5 mi) north of **Cascais,** and 9.5 kilometers (5.9 mi) west of **Mafra.** The quickest and easiest way to get to Ericeira from Lisbon is by car along the **A8** motorway, then the **A21** road west to the coast. It's about a 45-minute drive.

MAFRENSE BUS TERMINAL

R. dos Bombeiros Voluntários 3

Regular bus services operated by **Mafrense** (tel. 707 201 371; www.mafrense.com) run throughout the day between Lisbon's **Campo Grande terminal** and Ericeira (€6.25 one-way). Buses leave Campo Grande hourly, and the journey takes 1 hour; the bus drops off at the **Mafrense terminal,** 250 meters (275 yards) north of Ericeira town center. Buses are less frequent on weekends.

Getting Around

Most sights in Ericeira are within **walking** distance—covering the entire length of the village, from São Sebastião viewpoint to South Beach, takes around 20 minutes (1.5 km/1 mi). **Parking,** however, is limited. Ericeira's streets

Setúbal Peninsula

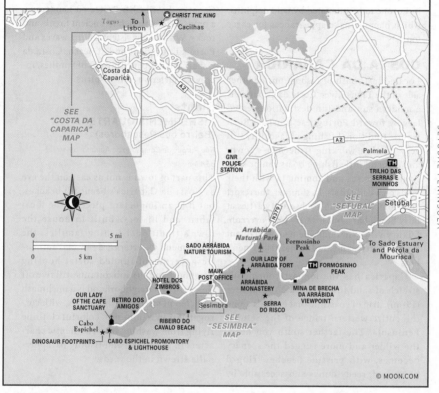

are narrow and can get very crowded, especially during summer. There is plenty of parking in free parking lots set back from the main beachfront, or limited paid parking within the village.

Setúbal Peninsula

Across the Tagus River, the Setúbal Peninsula is connected to Lisbon by the historic 25 de Abril Bridge and the Vasco da Gama Bridge, Europe's longest. It's an enthralling, underexplored region, with great beaches, wines, and seafood.

On the fringes of the Sado Estuary Natural Reserve, the main city, Setúbal, a 50-minute drive south of Lisbon, is an industrialized working port, home to the country's largest fish market. Setúbal makes no apologies for its unrefined, unpolished character, but the unbridled natural beauty surrounding it makes up for what it lacks in airs and graces. A few kilometers west in sprawling Arrábida Natural Park, wild birds of prey soar over dramatic coastal scenery. Farther on are charming fishing town Sesimbra and the vertiginous

Cabo Espichel. But one of the major draws to Setúbal is its estuary, one of few water inlets in Europe to be inhabited by wild dolphins, which happily make appearances for eager tourists.

COSTA DA CAPARICA

Located just south of Lisbon, on the other side of the Tagus River, Costa da Caparica is a modern sun-and-fun destination geared largely toward Portuguese tourists. Born from a traditional fishing village, it is still very much a working fishermen's town, and colorful little fishing boats can be seen going out to sea and coming in with their loads on a daily basis. In summer, the resort area comes alive with cool sunset parties at busy beach bars, but it rarely feels overrun. Luxury villas sit alongside neat apartment blocks, hotels, and traditional fishermen's huts.

Caparica has the longest continuous stretch of sand in Europe, a 30-kilometer (19-mi) strip of coastline that extends along the entire western fringe of the Setúbal Peninsula. The farther south you head, the wilder and more rugged the scenery becomes, with pristine beaches fringed by rugged, reedy dunes and accessible by car or by an adorable tourist train. Also along this stretch of coast is the Costa da Caparica Fossil Cliff Protected Landscape, a nature preserve rich in ancient fossils and rocks. With its consistent rolling waves and Portugal's original nudist beach, Costa da Caparica is a hip melting pot of families, in-crowds, surfers, and free spirits.

Sights
FISHERMEN'S QUARTERS (Bairro dos Pescadores)

Rua Parque de Campsimo de Almada; on-street parking

This part of town is not as easy on the eye as Costa da Caparica's beautiful beaches, but it is an important piece of the local fabric and history. Built to house the town's traditional fishing families, the Fishermen's Quarters is a raw and authentic government-funded social housing neighborhood. Its inhabitants still live off the sea. Their neighborhood is a mishmash of different sized boxy buildings, with corrugated iron trimmings, colorful clothing flying from washing lines, authentic characters in the street, and fishing paraphernalia strewn in the yards.

Costa da Caparica Fossil Cliff Protected Landscape

Costa da Caparica

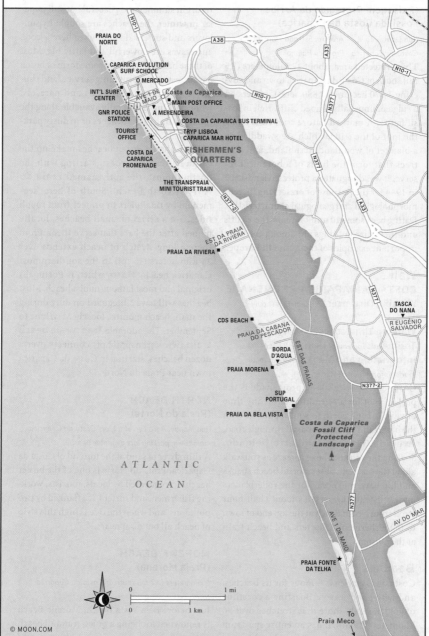

PRAIA DO NORTE

CAPARICA EVOLUTION SURF SCHOOL

O MERCADO

INT'L SURF CENTER

AVE 1 DE MAIO

Costa da Caparica

MAIN POST OFFICE

GNR POLICE STATION

A MERENDEIRA

COSTA DA CAPARICA BUS TERMINAL

TOURIST OFFICE

TRYP LISBOA CAPARICA MAR HOTEL

COSTA DA CAPARICA PROMENADE

FISHERMEN'S QUARTERS

THE TRANSPRAIA MINI TOURIST TRAIN

N377-2

EST DA PRAIA DA RIVIERA

PRAIA DA RIVIERA

TASCA DO NANA

R EUGÉNIO SALVADOR

CDS BEACH

PRAIA DA CABANA DO PESCADOR

EST DAS PRAIAS

BORDA D'AGUA

PRAIA MORENA

N377-2

SUP PORTUGAL

PRAIA DA BELA VISTA

Costa da Caparica Fossil Cliff Protected Landscape

ATLANTIC

OCEAN

AVE 1 DE MAIO

N377

AV DO MAR

PRAIA FONTE DA TELHA

0   1 mi

0   1 km

To Praia Meco

© MOON.COM

COSTA DA CAPARICA FOSSIL CLIFF PROTECTED LANDSCAPE (Paisagem Protegida da Arriba Fossil da Costa da Caparica)

Rua Dom João V, 17, Aroeira, Estrada Florestal da Costa de Caparica - Praia da Rainha

This protected area, about 12 kilometers (7.5 mi) south of Costa da Caparica town and covering 1,570 hectares (3,880 acres), centers on a ridge of unusually shaped cliffs, rich in fossil fauna. A marked nature trail runs along the foot of the cliffs, which are swaddled by a blanket of woodland, scrubland, and pine trees that form the basis of a botanical reserve. It was designated a protected landscape in 1984 for the purpose of preserving its geomorphological and geological characteristics. Dating back some 10 million years, these cliffs and their surroundings are among the most important examples of their kind in Europe.

Walks

COSTA DA CAPARICA PROMENADE

Walking Distance: *2.6 kilometers (1.6 mi) one-way*

Walking Time: *30 minutes one-way*

Trailhead: *Top end of town near P2 car park*

Information and Maps: *Inquire at local tourist information center*

Costa da Caparica's long promenade is the perfect spot for a refreshing stroll any time of year. It runs north to south, parallel with the beach and the main coastal through-road, **Avenida General Humberto Delgado.** Soak up the sun and the sea breeze as you walk along the seafront, past colorful beach shacks and hip bars; make way for the rollerbladers and cyclists and joggers. It's about a half-hour stroll from North Beach at the top end of town to the Fishermen's Quarters and beach train at the bottom.

Beaches

Costa da Caparica is famous for its beaches, and with good reason. Boasting a coastline of golden sandy shore that stretches over 30 kilometers (19 mi), it has an entire spectrum of beaches for all purposes and ambiences:

Surfing, naturist, families, gay, you name it, Costa da Caparica has a beach for it. A lively resort in summer and peaceful but still popular in winter, the beaches are sought by sunlovers and surfers alike. The sea here is cool, and waves are powerful and fairly big. Most of these beaches will have some form of beach bar or restaurant providing service, and usually a concession with beds and parasols, while parking is generally available along the roads leading to the beaches or in dusty parking lots.

More than a dozen beaches make up the Costa da Caparica coast, starting with the northernmost, the aptly named **Praia do Norte** (North Beach). South of here, segmented by tidal piers to protect from rough tides, are a series of small beaches, locally named after the bars that serve them. From there a long stretch of beach extends over 24 kilometers (15 mi) to the southernmost Caparica beach, **Meco,** which is Portugal's original and most famous nudist beach. Most beaches will have a lifeguard on duty during the main beach months, loosely May/June to September. The adorable **Transpraia beach train** (www.transpraia.pt) connects over a dozen beaches, starting in Costa da Caparica town near Praia do Norte.

NORTH BEACH (Praia do Norte)

Rua Manuel Agro Ferreira 1, off Costa da Caparica main town; parking lots available nearby

A thin sliver of sand at the top end of Costa da Caparica, Praia do Norte is one of the busier beaches, frequented by locals, tourists, working fishermen, and surfers. It's flanked by two pontoons, and when the tide is high this strip of beach all but disappears.

MORENA BEACH (Praia Morena)

6 kilometers (3.7 mi) south of Costa da Caparica town

Just before Bela Vista Beach, Morena Beach is renowned for being a quiet, tranquil beach with plenty of space, easy parking, and

☆ Christ the King

Dominating the skyline of the Tagus's south bank is the *Christ the King* **statue** (Cristo Rei; Alto do Pragal, Av. Cristo Rei; tel. 212 751 000 or 212 721 270; www.cristorei.pt; daily 9:30am-6:30pm; €4), standing with arms outstretched and epitomizing Portugal's Catholic faith. The idea to build the monument came after the Cardinal Patriarch of Lisbon visited Rio de Janeiro in 1934 and was impressed by its imposing Christ the Redeemer statue. Built on an isolated clifftop, the statue stands 192 meters (630 ft) above the Tagus River. An express lift whizzes visitors to a viewing platform at 82 meters (269 ft), which affords dazzling views over the city. At the statue's base is a chapel. The statue's interior contains a library, a large café, two halls, and another chapel.

translucent, calm waters that make it ideal for stand-up paddleboarding.

BELA VISTA BEACH
(Praia da Bela Vista)
7 kilometers (4.3 mi) south of Costa da Caparica town
An official nudist beach, Praia da Bela Vista is a wide, peaceful beach of fine white sand, flanked by cliffs and dunes. It is accessed by a dirt road and has its own parking lot.

FONTE DA TELHA BEACH
(Praia da Fonte da Telha)
10 kilometers (6 mi) south of Costa da Caparica town
Fonte da Telha Beach is famous for its mud; it's not uncommon to see people caked head to toe in the restorative sludge.

MECO BEACH
(Praia do Meco)
30 kilometers (18.6 mi) south of Costa da Caparica town
Wide and rugged, Meco, the Costa's original and most famous nudist beach, is at the southernmost extremity.

Surfing and Stand-up Paddleboarding
Waves along this stretch are consistent but not in the same category as Guincho or Ericeira, which makes Costa da Caparica perfect for less-experienced surfers. Top spots for surfing are **CDS Beach** (Costa da Caparica town, off the main avenue) and **Praia da Riviera** (2 km/1.2 mi south of CDS Beach). Local

surf schools, shops, and guesthouses have flourished in the vicinity. Board plus wetsuit rental is around €15 for a half day; lessons are around €15.

- **Caparica Evolution Surf School:** Estrada da Muralha, Marcelino Beach-K bar; tel. 939 124 758; www.kevolutionsurf.com; daily 9am-8pm May-Oct., daily 10am-6pm Nov.-Apr.

- **International Surf Center:** Rua Praia do CDS, Apoio Praia 11; tel. 912 530 689; www.caparicasurf.com; daily 9am-8pm

- **SUP Portugal:** Praia da Bela Vista; tel. 967 697 039; www.sup-portugal.com; daily 10am-7pm

Food
Costa da Caparica excels in seafood. *Canja de carapau* (mackerel soup) is a local specialty.

A MERENDEIRA
Rua dos Pescadores 20; tel. 212 904 527; www.amerendeira.com; Sun.-Thurs. 10am-1am, Fri.-Sat. 10am-2am; €6
A Merendeira's wholesome soups, freshly baked *chouriço* rolls, and traditional puddings make it the perfect pit stop for a quick lunch.

TASCA DO NANA
Rua Eugénio Salvador 23; tel. 933 240 178; www.nanapetiscos.pt; Tues.-Sun. noon-10:30pm; €8
Typical *tasca* (simple, small Portuguese eatery) Tasca do Nana serves a rainbow of *petiscos*, which are fish and meat snacks perfect for sharing.

BORDA D'AGUA

Praia da Morena s/n; tel. 212 975 213; www.
bordadagua.com.pt; daily 10am-midnight; €15

The name of Borda d'Agua translates as "waterside," and it makes the most of its beachside location, with a large deck for alfresco dining as well as enclosed indoor seating for breezier days. It's a must-visit for delicious fresh fish with a sea breeze.

O MERCADO

Avenida 1° de Maio 36D; tel. 218 235 099; www.
facebook.com/pg/omercadocc; Tues.-Sat.
12:30pm-3pm and 7:30pm-10pm; €15

A rustic-chic gastropub in the center of Costa da Caparica that serves typical Portuguese fare made from the freshest market produce, with a contemporary international flourish; don't miss the octopus tempura.

Accommodations

Hotels in Costa da Caparica are varied and cheaper than most in central Lisbon.

★ TRYP LISBOA CAPARICA
MAR HOTEL

Av. Gen. Humberto Delgado 47; tel. 212 918 900;
www.tryplisboacaparica.com; from €138 d

The ultimate beachfront hotel, four-star Hotel Costa da Caparica is family-friendly, with a nice swimming pool. Some of the 354 rooms over seven floors have views over the Atlantic.

Information and Services

- **GNR police station:** Rua Pedro Álvares Cabral 29; tel. 265 242 590; www.gnr.pt
- **Tourist office:** Av. da República 18; tel. 212 900 071; Mon.-Sat. 9:30am-1pm and 2pm-5:30pm
- **Main post office:** Praça de 9 de Julho

Getting There

Costa da Caparica is roughly 16 kilometers (10 mi) from downtown **Lisbon.** From Lisbon, take the **A8** motorway over the 25 de Abril Bridge southbound, before heading west on the **A38** to Costa da Caparica. This is the fastest road route between Lisbon and Costa da Caparica and takes around 20 minutes if traffic is flowing normally.

There are two ways of getting from Lisbon to Costa da Caparica by public transport. For a more roundabout, but possibly more fun journey, take the **ferry** from Cais do Sodré (Metro Green Line) to Cacilhas (€1.25 one-way), before catching the **Transportes Sul do Tejo** (TST; www.tsuldotejo.pt) express bus from Cacilhas to Costa da Caparica. From there take the express bus (TST 135 or 124) to Costa da Caparica. The TST 135 bus runs once or twice per hour and is the faster, more direct service at 20 minutes. The 124 runs 3-4 times per hour and takes around 40 minutes. Both cost €2.40 and can be purchased straight from the driver.

COSTA DA CAPARICA
BUS TERMINAL

Praça Padre Manuel Bernardes

The most direct route to Costa Caparica by public transit is taking the 161 bus operated by **Transportes Sul do Tejo** (TST; www.tsuldotejo.pt) from Praca do Areeiro (Metro Green Line) in Lisbon. There two departures every hour 8am-7pm, and at 15 and 45 minutes past the hour on weekends. Monday to Friday, departures are on the hour and 30 minutes past the hour. A one-way ticket costs €3.20 (buy from the driver) and the journey takes 40-60 minutes, depending on traffic. The 161 bus goes straight to the Costa da Caparica terminal, around 500 meters (550 yards) from the beach and 1 kilometer (0.6 mi) south of the town center.

Getting Around

Costa da Caparica's main sights—the main beach and town center, **Fishermen's Quarter,** and **tourist train**—are all within walking distance.

TRANSPRAIA MINI TOURIST TRAIN

Rua Parque Infantil; tel. 212 900 706; www.
transpraia.pt; daily 9am-8pm June-Sept.

The Transpraia mini tourist train carries

Setúbal

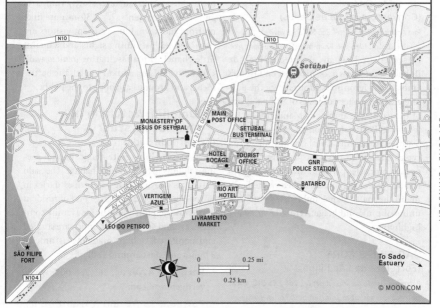

beachgoers from one end of Costa da Caparica to the other. It's a bumpy but scenic way to discover Costa's best beach spots. It runs 9 kilometers (5.6 mi) from Caparica town to Fonte da Telha, which takes around 25 minutes, with four little stations and 15 stops en route. The track is divided into **zone 1** (€5 round-trip) and **zone 2** (€8 round-trip). The train operates only in high season (June-Sept.). There are two departures per hour from each end, one on the hour and the other at half past. In Caparica, the Transpraia train leaves from in front of the children's beachside play park in the main town center.

SETÚBAL AND THE SADO ESTUARY

The unpolished port town of Setúbal is divisive. Many are charmed by its lovely old town square, busy waterfront, and unrepentant lack of pretension; others are unable to see past its gritty industrial facade. Colorful fishing boats and commuter ferries run beside leisure vessels, a sure sign that tourism is buoying the city. With good hotels and restaurants, Setúbal is well placed as a base for exploring the wildlife-heavy Sado Estuary.

Originating in the deep Alentejo in the Vigia mountain range, the Sado River flows into the sea south of Setúbal. The humid and fertile Sado Estuary Natural Reserve covers 23,000 hectares (89 sq mi) of rich wetlands. It is a protected nature reserve, one of 30 officially protected areas in the country, where mirrorlike wetlands and surrounding banks and thickets host more than 200 bird species, including white storks and pink flamingos. Once one of the most important salt-producing areas in the country, it is now a hot spot for bird- and dolphin-watching. A pod of bottlenose dolphins has long resided in the estuary's calm waters, a phenomenon unique in Portugal and rare in the world.

Sights

MONASTERY OF JESUS OF SETÚBAL

(Convento e Igreja de Jesus)

Rua Acácio Barradas 2; tel. 265 537 890; www. mun-setubal.pt; Tues.-Sat. 10am-6pm, Sun. 2pm-6pm; free

Designed in 1494 by architect Diogo de Boitaca (best known for his work on Lisbon's emblematic Jerónimos Monastery), the austere gray Monastery of Jesus of Setúbal is one of the earliest examples of Manueline architecture in Portugal. Among its distinguishing features are soaring spiral granite pillars and typical *azulejo* murals. Outside, gargoyles and twisted pinnacles perforate an otherwise plain facade. Inside, an intricate ribbed vaulted ceiling in the main chapel and twisted-rope columns of pink and beige Arrábida stone are highlights.

SÃO FILIPE FORT

(Forteleza de São Filipe)

Estrada Castelo de São Filipe; tel. 265 545 010; www. sintracascaissesimbra.com/setubal/Setubal-castle-Forte-Sao-Filipe.html; open 24/7

Sitting atop a swollen mound on the western skirts of the city center, the 16th-century São Filipe (Saint Phillip) Fort (also referred to as Setúbal Castle) is one of Setúbal's top attractions. Peering over the city, its fishing port, and the Sado beyond, it is an imposing sight, with its austere, sturdy ramparts and solid battlements. It's a 30-minute hike up from the town, but persistent visitors are rewarded with stunning sights and a quaint little chapel with a fascinating *azulejo* wall. Currently housing a luxury hotel, the battlements and grounds are open to the public.

★ Dolphin-Watching in the Sado Estuary

(Estuário do Sado)

There's something quite magical about seeing dolphins in their natural habitat. The Sado Estuary is one of very few known estuaries in Europe to be home to a large pod of resident bottlenose dolphins. This unique family comprises around 40 mammals, which are studied and monitored. Dolphin-watching last around 3 hours and start around €30.

- **Vertigem Azul:** tel. 265 238 000; www. vertigemazul.com
- **Portugal Sport and Adventure:** tel. 910 668 600; www.portugal-sport-and-adventure.com
- **Sado Arrábida Nature Tourism:** tel. 265 490 406 or 915 560 342; www.sadoarrabida.pt

dolphin tour in the Sado Estuary

GALLEON SAL SADO TRIPS

tel. 265 227 685; www.sal.pt; 3 hours; €25

A different way to explore the Sado is aboard a historic *sal* (salt) galleon. These wooden ships were converted from small fishing vessels, first used to transport salt and later used for fishing and cargo. The restored boats are now used for coastal and estuary cruises. **Sal Cruises** runs cruises on the Sado, Tagus, and Zêzere rivers.

Food

You'll often see locals sitting alfresco, sharing a plate of local specialty *choco frito* (fried squid) with a cold beer.

LIVRAMENTO MARKET (Mercado do Livramento)

Avenida Luísa Todi 163; tel. 265 545 392; Tues.-Sun. 7am-2pm

One of the most famous markets in Portugal, lively Mercado do Livramento bursts with fantastic fresh produce and buzzes with activity. Regional cheeses, the freshest fish and seafood, and fruit and vegetables galore are all in their finest glory to be seen and sampled. Originally inaugurated in 1876, it houses a diversity and character that visitors would be hard-pressed to find elsewhere in Portugal. Widely considered one of Portugal's best markets, it is also one of the country's biggest.

★ LEO DO PETISCO

Rua da Cordoaria 33; tel. 265 228 340; Mon.-Sat. noon-3pm and 7pm-10pm; €8

Head for the simple café-snack bar Leo do Petisco in Setúbal's town center to try local delicacy *choco frito* served on a plate or—interestingly—in a sandwich.

PÉROLA DA MOURISCA

Rua da Baía do Sado 9; tel. 265 793 689; Wed.-Sun. 12:30pm-3:30pm and 7pm-10:30pm, Mon. 12:30pm-3:30pm; €10

With the best sea and river produce, down-to-earth Pérola da Mourisca is best known for its shellfish tapas but also cooks seafood-based rice and pasta dishes.

BATAREO

Rua das Fontainhas 64; tel. 265 234 548; Tues.-Sun. noon-3:30pm; €15

Small, simple dockside Batareo does only fish and shellfish. Fish move straight off the boat and into the glass display case.

Accommodations

Hotels in Setúbal are located in and around the town center and the port.

HOTEL BOCAGE

Rua de São Cristóvão 14; tel. 265 543 080; www.hoteisbocage.com; €80-100 d

Just off Setúbal's main drag, Avenida Luísa Todi, in the heart of the historic part of town, two-star Hotel Bocage provides an unfussy, comfortable stay. Its sister, Bocage Guest House, is on a side street just around the corner.

RIO ART HOTEL

Av. Luísa Todi 117; tel. 965 801 988; www.rioarthotel.pt; €100-150 d

In the heart of Setúbal, the Rio Art Hotel retains some original features of its historic exterior. The renovated interior is gleaming and contemporary, with 23 colorful, spacious rooms and vintage-chic touches.

Information and Services

- **GNR police station:** Av. Jaime Cortesão; tel. 265 242 500; www.gnr.pt
- **Tourist office:** Travessa Frei Gaspar 10; tel. 265 539 120; daily 10am-7pm
- **Main post office:** Av. Mariano Carvalho s/n; tel. 265 528 621

Getting There

Located 50 kilometers (31 mi) southeast of Lisbon Airport, Setúbal is a 45-minute drive from **Lisbon.** By car the main route is over the 25 de Abril Bridge, following the **A2** motorway. The Sado Natural Reserve is located approximately 90 kilometers (56 mi) south of Lisbon; it envelops the immediate fringes of Setúbal and is about 38 kilometers (24 mi) east from Sesimbra. The best way to explore the protected wetlands is with an **excursion** from Setúbal or Sesimbra.

SETÚBAL TRAIN STATION

Praça do Brasil; tel. 707 210 220; www.cp.pt; daily 6:45am-11am and 11:30am-2:15pm

CP trains (tel. 707 210 220; www.cp.pt) run every hour from Lisbon's Santa Apolónia and Cais do Sodré stations and take around 2 hours. Single-trip tickets cost €11.20. The train station is about 1 kilometer (0.6 mi) east of the main town center in Praça do Quebrado (Quebrado Square), near the main bus stops on **Avenida 5 de Outubro.**

SETÚBAL BUS TERMINAL

Av. 5 Outubro/Av. Dr. Manuel de Arriaga 2; tel. 265 525 051; www.tsuldotejo.pt

Setúbal's main **bus terminal** is set a few streets back from the waterfront, about 150 meters (500 ft) from the city center. **Transportes Sul do Tejo express buses** (tel. 707 508 509; www.tsuldotejo.pt) run directly from Lisbon's **Praça da Espanha** (Lines 561 and 563) and **Gare do Oriente** (Lines 562 and 563) stations, departing once an hour; the trip takes 50 minutes and costs €4.45 one-way. National express-bus company **Rede Expressos** (tel. 707 223 344; www. rede-expressos.pt) operates a dozen buses per day between Lisbon's **Sete Rios terminal** and Setúbal (45 minutes; €6).

Getting Around

Setúbal's downtown area, with the main sights, attractions, and restaurants, can easily be explored **on foot.** Set back from the ferry terminal and the waterfront is the historic old town and its maze of quaint cobbled streets dotted with hip boutiques and eateries.

ARRÁBIDA NATURAL PARK
(Parque Natural da Arrábida)

www.natural.pt

Blanketing a chunk of coastline between the city of Setúbal and the village of Sesimbra, the Arrábida Natural Park covers 16,500 hectares (64 sq mi). A rugged belt of deep green, the Serra da Arrábida mountain range is separated from the Atlantic by thin white-gold beaches. Its tallest peak stands 499 meters (1,637 ft), and the chalky Arrábida massif is covered by a thick rug of plant life, including rare species like rockroses and purple star thistle as well as typical Mediterranean *maquis* and *garigue* scrubland. To protect the vegetation, some areas can only be accessed with an authorized guide.

Opt for a leisurely activity such as biking or hiking, or join certified guides who lead mountain climbing, caving, and diving excursions. The translucent turquoise waters along the jagged coast are also perfect for SUP, kayaking, and canoeing. For information, contact the **park office** (Praça da República, Setúbal; tel. 265 541 140).

Sights
OUR LADY OF ARRÁBIDA FORT
(Forte de Santa Maria da Arrábida)

Portinho da Arrábida; tel. 212 189 791; Tues.-Fri. 10am-4pm, Sat. 3pm-6pm; €3.50; access to the fort is via the park's narrow, winding roads, roadside parking available in the vicinity of the fort

Perched above translucent seawater and overlooking one of the prettiest beaches in the region, Portinho da Arrábida, the Arrábida Fort was built in 1676 as part of a strategic coastal defense line. An **oceanographic museum** now occupies the historic cliff-foot fort. Inside, make sure to visit the chapel and its stone image of Our Lady.

ARRÁBIDA MONASTERY
(Convento da Arrábida)

tel. 212 180 520; www.foriente.pt; on-site parking

The park is also home to the enigmatic Arrábida Monastery. This 16th-century complex is situated higher in the hills above the fort, amid 25 hectares (62 acres) of dense shrubbery. The cluster of religious buildings includes two former convents, chapels, a garden, and a sanctuary. It can be **toured** (Wed. and Sat.-Sun.; €5) if you reserve in advance.

Hiking

The park itself is crossed by signposted footpaths, tailored to varying degrees of physical aptitude. There are three main hikes.

FORMOSINHO PEAK

Hiking Distance: *6.6-kilometer (4-mi) loop*
Hiking Time: *3 hours round-trip*
Trailhead: *Convento da Arrábida*
Information and Maps: *www.wikiloc.com/hiking-trails/beyond-lisbon-hiking-guide-percurso-walk-17-pico-do-formosinho-16323090*

This is a demanding trail to the highest point of the Arrábida Mountain Range, **Formosinho Peak** (500 m/1,640 ft).

SERRA DO RISCO

Hiking Distance: *8-kilometer (5-mi) loop*
Hiking Time: *2.5 hours round-trip*
Trailhead: *Mina de Brecha da Arrábida viewpoint (above Jaspe quarry), just west of the Portinho da Arrábida*
Information and Maps: *www.wikiloc.com/hiking-trails/serra-do-risco-arrabida-setubal-6680279*

Another scenic route also popular with mountain bikers is the trail from the Mina de Brecha da Arrábida viewpoint to Serra do Risco (Risk Point).

TRILHO DAS SERRAS E MOINHOS (Mountain Ranges and Windmills Trail)

Hiking Distance: *21.4-kilometer (13-mi) loop*
Hiking Time: *5-6 hours round-trip*
Trailhead: *Palmela parish*
Information and Maps: *www.alltrails.com/es/trail/portugal/alentejo/trilho-das-serras-e-moinhos-via-serra-do-louro-e-vale-dos-barris*

A longer, well-signed route, the Trilho das Serras e Moinhos takes hikers through dramatic valleys, from the village of Palmela along a path dotted with traditional windmills and local flowers.

Information and Services
ARRÁBIDA PARK OFFICE

Praça da República, Setúbal; tel. 265 541 140; Mon.-Fri. 9am-12:30pm and 2pm-5:30pm

Contact the park office for more information on opening times, hiking and cycling routes, and other park activities.

Getting There and Around

Arrábida Natural Park is 2.5 kilometers (1.6 mi) west of **Setúbal,** a 5-minute drive along the **Avenida General Daniel de Sousa** and the **N10** road. Public transport is infrequent; the best way to reach the Arrábida Natural Park is by car, or by asking about excursions at your hotel or the local tourist office. A taxi from Setúbal should cost around €13. From **Sesimbra,** the 10-kilometer (6.2-mi) drive east takes about 20 minutes on the **N378** road and **Avenida 25 de Abril.** A taxi should cost €18. The Arrábida Natural Park is located approximately 40 kilometers (25 mi) south of **Lisbon;** the fastest route is following the **A2** motorway over the 25 de Abril Bridge (50 minutes).

SESIMBRA

At the foot of the Arrábida Mountain Range (Serra da Arrábida) in a protected bay, the authentic fishing town of Sesimbra (seh-ZEEM-brah) has marvelous beaches but remains largely undiscovered, allowing its genuine seaside charm to shine. It's also located at the western edge of the **Arrábida Natural Park,** making it a gateway to unspoiled natural beauty.

Nestled at the foothills of the Arrábida Mountain Range, the town centers on the beach, with a small fishing port and its authentic fresh fish restaurants at the western end, while at the opposite end are a couple of swanky modern hotels. The two ends are bound by a sweep of golden sand and a pretty seafront road and promenade, **Avenida dos Naufrágios,** with all the other main hotels, bars, and restaurants found in between.

Beaches
OURO BEACH
(Praia do Ouro)

Avenida dos Náufragos

Praia do Ouro (just west of the town center) is

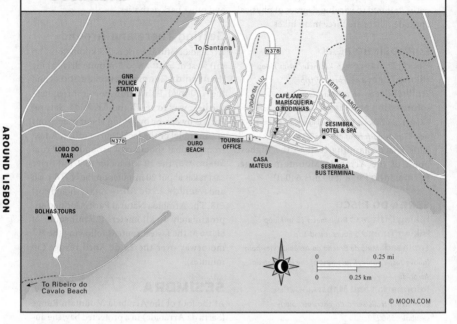

Sesimbra

To Santana

N378

GNR
POLICE
STATION

R. JOÃO DIA LUZ

CAFÉ AND
MARISQUEIRA
O RODINHAS

ESTR. DE ARGEIS

SESIMBRA
HOTEL & SPA

N378

LOBO DO
MAR

OURO
BEACH

TOURIST
OFFICE

CASA
MATEUS

SESIMBRA
BUS TERMINAL

BOLHAS TOURS

0   0.25 mi
0   0.25 km

To Ribeiro do
Cavalo Beach

© MOON.COM

a generous strand of golden sand sloping gently toward calm, clear water, along Sesimbra's main seaside avenue. Find comforts like sun beds, beach bars, and a children's play area.

RIBEIRO DO CAVALO BEACH
(Praia do Ribeiro do Cavalo)

Rua Baía de Sesimbra

Smaller Praia do Ribeiro do Cavalo is on a cove with rocky beds teeming with sea life, making it perfect for diving or snorkeling. There are no diving outfitters on the beach, so bring your own gear. It's a 3-kilometer (2-mi) drive west of town, but you can reach it by **boat** from Sesimbra's port for €10 round-trip.

Fishing

Fishing trips are the main excursions in Sesimbra, and deep-sea fishing is the most popular. Tours vary but generally last around 5 hours and are suitable for the whole family.

- **Bolhas Tours—Follow Sensations:** tel. 910 658 555 or 916 205 429; www.bolhastours.com, from €35

Food

Sesimbra's gastronomy is all about the sea. Local specialties include *arroz de marisco* (a rich, well-sauced rice stew packed with gently boiled seafood and spices) and *peixe-espada preto* (black scabbard fish).

★ CAFÉ AND MARISQUEIRA
O RODINHAS

Rua Marques de Pombal 25; tel. 212 231 557; www.marisqueiraorodinhas.pt; Thurs.-Tues. noon-10:30pm; €12

Unpretentious Café and Marisqueira O Rodinhas serves seafood delights in a cozy and casual interior.

1: Arrábida Monastery **2:** Café and Marisqueira O Rodinhas

CASA MATEUS

Largo Anselmo Braamcamp 4; tel. 963 650 939; www.casamateus.pt; Tues.-Sun. noon-3:30pm and 7pm-11pm; €15

With its charming worn tile facade and simple wooden tables, acclaimed Bijou Casa Mateus puts all the focus on the seafood. Offerings include *caldeirada* (fish stew) and *arroz de marisco*, along with seafood delicacies such as razor clams, Sesimbra lobster, and cockles.

★ LOBO DO MAR

Av. dos Náufragos, Porto de Abrigo; tel. 212 235 233; www.lobodomar.com; Tues.-Sun. noon-11pm; €15

Simple seaside Lobo do Mar is famous for its grilled fish.

Accommodations

Sesimbra has only a handful of hotels, including newish middle-size units and charming guesthouses.

★ SESIMBRA HOTEL & SPA

Rua Navegador Rodrigues Soromenho; tel. 212 289 800; www.sesimbrahotelspa.com; €200-250 d

Built on a cliff overlooking Califórnia Beach and the Atlantic, modern Sesimbra Hotel & Spa has panoramic views from all rooms as well as from its infinity pool. Its plush interior and stylish seaside décor are relaxing and refreshing.

Information and Services

- **GNR police station:** Rua 4 de Maio; tel. 217 657 700; www.gnr.pt
- **Tourist office:** Rua da Fortaleza; tel. 212 288 500; daily 9am-9pm
- **Main post office:** Av. Padre António Pereira de Almeida 8

Getting There

Sesimbra is 40 kilometers (25 mi) south of **Lisbon,** a 50-minute drive. By car, take the **A2** motorway over the 25 de Abril Bridge and head southwest toward Setúbal. At the junction of the **N378** road, head directly south to Sesimbra. From **Setúbal,** Sesimbra is 30 kilometers (19 mi) west, a 45-minute drive along the **N10** road and **Avenida 25 de Abril.**

SESIMBRA BUS TERMINAL

Avenida da Liberdade

Public transport between Setúbal and Sesimbra is frustratingly sparse, with around a dozen departures a day on weekdays and just four or five on weekends, making a day trip difficult via public transport. The service, **Line 230,** is operated by **Transportes Sul do Tejo** (tel. 707 508 509; www.tsuldotejo.pt; €3.30). Transportes Sul do Tejo also runs an inexpensive express-bus service (Line 207 or 260) between Lisbon's Praça da Espanha and Sesimbra (1 hour; €4.35); tickets can be purchased from the driver. In Sesimbra, the **bus terminal** is just meters from the beach.

CABO ESPICHEL

Wind-battered and rugged, Cabo Espichel is the Setúbal Peninsula's most southwesterly headland, a barren cape with massive cliffs and an eerie, desolate feel. Everything about Cabo Espichel is wild—the waves roar, the scenery is untamed, and there are few modern comforts.

Sights

CABO ESPICHEL PROMONTORY AND LIGHTHOUSE
(Promontório e Farol do Cabo Espichel)

EM 569 Cabo Espichel; open 24/7

Perched on the promontory, this hexagonal lighthouse guards the entire Setúbal Peninsula. The structure stands 32 meters (105 ft) tall but is still dwarfed by the sheer size of the cliffs. On a clear night, sailors can see the powerful beam from the lighthouse 40 kilometers (25 mi) out to sea. The lighthouse is open to the public Wednesday 2pm-5pm only. Entry is free, and visitors can climb to the top to see the lamp.

DINOSAUR FOOTPRINTS
(Pegadas dos Dinossauros)

open 24/7; free

Within walking distance of the lighthouse is a unique sight: dinosaur footprints. Likely made by sauropods, theropods, and ornithopods that inhabited the area millions of years ago, two sets of prints can be clearly seen in the cliffs. Directly above the prehistoric prints, the isolated 15th-century **Chapel of Ermida de Memória** perches perilously close to the cliff's edge. The chapel's interior is clad in traditional tile depicting "The Lady of the Cape"—the Virgin Mary is said to have appeared to an elderly couple in that spot in 1410.

OUR LADY OF THE CAPE SANCTUARY
(Santuário da Nossa Senhora do Cabo)

tel. 212 231 031; Mon.-Fri. 9:30am-1:30pm and 2:30pm-5pm, Sat.-Sun. 9:30am-1:30pm and 2:30pm-6pm; free

Built in 1701, the Baroque Our Lady of the Cape Sanctuary was designed first as a place of defense, then to provide shelter. Two long arms stretching out from either side of the church include rooms that housed pilgrims. The church itself has a simple marble interior.

Food and Accommodations

Most visitors to Cabo Espichel plan on meals and lodging in nearby Sesimbra or Setúbal, though there are a few eateries nearby.

RETIRO DOS AMIGOS

Av. 25 de Abril; tel. 210 847 536; Thurs.-Tues. 8am-midnight; €12

On the main road down toward Cabo Espichel is Retiro dos Amigos, a small and simple little place that serves great seafood at good prices. Friendly and welcoming, this place is a find for anyone wanting to try typical home-cooked Portuguese dishes.

HOTEL DOS ZIMBROS

Facho de Azóia; tel. 210 405 470; www.hotelzimbros. com; €150-200 d

Incongruous with the wild landscape, the sleek 38-room Hotel dos Zimbros is on the main road into Cabo Espichel.

Getting There

Taking public transport to Cabo Espichel is difficult, so most visitors drive. Cabo Espichel is 14 kilometers (8.7 mi) west from **Sesimbra** via the **N379** road (20 minutes) and 40 kilometers (25 mi) west from **Setúbal** via the main **Avenida 25 de Abril** (50 minutes).

A public bus, Line 201, operated by **Transportes Sul do Tejo** (tel. 707 508 509; www.tsuldotejo.pt), runs between Sesimbra's main bus station and Cabo Espichel about eight times on weekdays, less frequently on weekends. The journey takes around 30 minutes and tickets cost about €3 one-way.

Évora and the Alentejo

Making up one-third of Portugal, the vast

Alentejo (ah-len-TAY-zhoo) is underrated. One of Western Europe's poorest and most sparsely populated regions, it makes no apologies for its rustic, unkempt beauty. Situated south of the Tagus River and north of the Algarve, with Spain to the east and the Atlantic to the west, the rusty Alentejo—whose name derives from the Portuguese *além Tejo* (beyond the Tagus)—is deeply traditional and predominantly agricultural.

Life moves more slowly in Portugal's hottest and driest region. During the summer, the golden wheat fields—which give Baixo (lower) Alentejo its nickname "the Breadbasket of Portugal"—are devoid of movement as cows and sheep seek refuge from the relentless sun under

Highlights

Look for ★ to find recommended sights, activities, dining, and lodging.

★ **Chapel of Bones:** This eerie-sounding monument in Évora is the most famous of a handful of Portugal's unique bone chapels. Its walls, arches, and pillars are clad entirely with tightly packed human bones and skulls, making for a chilling but fascinating experience (page 137).

★ **Wineries and Wine-Tasting:** Along with the Douro, the Alentejo is one of Portugal's preeminent wine-producing regions, peppered with excellent wine farms, many of which cater to visitor tastings and even accommodation (page 141).

★ **Elvas:** One of Portugal's few remaining undiscovered treasures, this well-preserved fortified town oozes charm and character (page 158).

★ **Castles:** The Alentejo region is awash with historic relics, boasting some of the most striking castles, formidable fortifications, and loveliest medieval walled villages in the country (page 166).

★ **Beaches of Vila Nova de Milfontes:** With shallow waters that are warmer than others along the coast, this town boasts beautiful swaths of sand (page 176).

Évora and the Alentejo

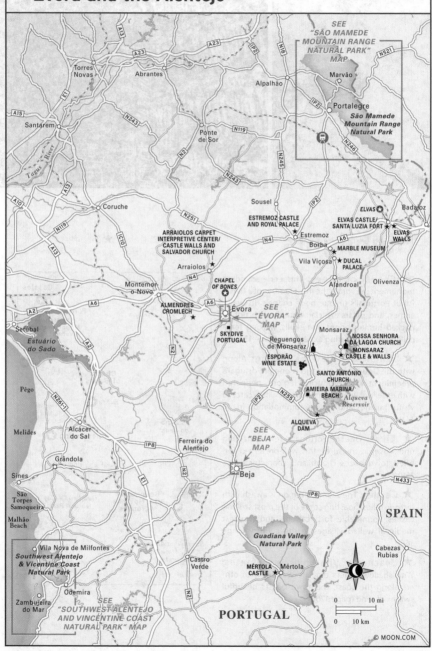

SEE
"SÃO MAMEDE
MOUNTAIN RANGE
NATURAL PARK"
MAP

PORTUGAL

SPAIN

Torres
Novas

Abrantes

Alpalhão

Marvão

Portalegre

São Mamede
Mountain Range
Natural Park

Santarém

Tagus River

Ponte
de Sor

Sousel

ELVAS

Badajoz

Coruche

ESTREMOZ CASTLE
AND ROYAL PALACE

Estremoz

ELVAS CASTLE/
SANTA LUZIA FORT

ELVAS
WALLS

ARRAIOLOS CARPET
INTERPRETIVE CENTER/
CASTLE WALLS AND
SALVADOR CHURCH

Borba

MARBLE MUSEUM

Vila Viçosa

DUCAL
PALACE

Arraiolos

Alandroal

Olivenza

Montemor-
o-Novo

CHAPEL
OF BONES

ALMENDRES
CROMLECH

Évora

SEE
"ÉVORA"
MAP

Setúbal

Estuário
do Sado

SKYDIVE
PORTUGAL

Monsaraz

NOSSA SENHORA
DA LAGOA CHURCH

Reguengos
de Monsaraz

MONSARAZ
CASTLE & WALLS

ESPORÃO
WINE ESTATE

SANTO ANTÓNIO
CHURCH

Pêgo

AMIEIRA MARINA/
BEACH

Alqueva
Reservoir

Melides

Alcácer
do Sal

Ferreira do
Alentejo

SEE
"BEJA"
MAP

ALQUEVA
DAM

Grândola

Sines

Beja

São
Torpes
Samoqueira

Malhão
Beach

Guadiana Valley
Natural Park

Cabezas
Rubias

Vila Nova de Milfontes

Southwest Alentejo
& Vicentine Coast
Natural Park

Castro
Verde

MÉRTOLA
CASTLE

Mértola

0   10 mi

Zambujeira
do Mar

Odemira

SEE
"SOUTHWEST ALENTEJO
AND VICENTINE COAST
NATURAL PARK" MAP

0   10 km

© MOON.COM

the cork oak trees that dot the landscape. In cooler months, green wheat stretches as far as the eye can see. The coast is a string of quaint whitewashed villages and beaches backed by sandy cliffs, rugged and breezy, with a majestic rawness that appeals to surfers and outdoors enthusiasts. In Alto (upper) Alentejo, the landscape darkens to gray as the rolling plains give way to jagged granite hills that border Spain. It's a trove of medieval walled towns and hilltop fortresses off the beaten track. The São Mamede Mountain Range Natural Park, one of few places in the Alentejo where it can snow in winter, spills over the border from Spain, and the Alentejo is also home to the Alqueva Dam, Europe's largest artificial lake.

The Alentejo is an important wine-producing region and the world's largest producer of cork; regional cheeses, cured meats, and olive oil also boost local incomes. Tourism is growing: Several large dams in the region have created reservoirs popular for boating and other sports. Burgeoning wine tourism supports excellent boutique lodgings and wine-pairing menus. Many vineyards welcome visitors to take part in the traditional *vindimas* (grape picking) during the harvest season.

This is a relatively untapped, unexplored region, not as traveled as the Algarve, Porto, or Lisbon despite being home to long, beautiful beaches and Évora, one of the most fascinating historic cities in the region. Its historic hamlets remain unspoiled, hiding fascinating relics of bygone eras. Come here to slow down, enjoy great food and drink, and discover a charming, genuine part of Portugal.

PLANNING YOUR TIME

Vast, sleepy Alentejo varies by region and season. Pleasant times to visit are **spring** and **fall,** warm but without the severe **summer** heat, which can peak above 45°C (113°F). In spring the rolling plains bloom with wildflowers. In autumn the meadows blaze with color and vines are laden with fruit. In the heat of summer days, from 1pm-4pm shops close and locals hide in their homes.

Many people speed through the Alentejo as they travel from Lisbon north to Porto or south to the Algarve, but it's worth extending your trip to linger here for a few days. Plan to spend at least one day in historic Évora (the largest town in the region, a 1.5-hour drive east of Lisbon), exploring the monuments and mazelike cobbled streets. From there, one route would be to make your way south toward the Algarve through atmospheric Beja and the coastal towns of Vila Nova de Milfontes, a popular seaside destination, and quintessentially Alentejan Odemira (allow an additional 2-3 days). For a northbound route, from Évora, visit the enchanting historic walled towns of Elvas, Marvão, and Castelo de Vide (allow another 1-2 days).

The Alentejo is famous for wine, and a self-guided wine tour of the **Alentejo Wine Route** (www.vinhosdoalentejo.pt) is a popular option. Pick the wineries and villages that grab your attention, hit the road, and follow the signs.

The region is vast and public transport can be patchy, so a car is definitely recommended to explore this underrated region. Note that a good road network connects major towns, but roads in rural areas can be narrow, winding, poorly maintained, and sparsely signed.

Previous: Our Lady of Grace Fort; wine tasting in the Alentejo; Chapel of Bones.

Itinerary Ideas

TWO DAYS IN THE ALENTEJO

Day 1: Évora

1 Start your exploration of Évora by enjoying a coffee in the bustling **Giraldo Square.**

2 Head southwest to the creepy **Chapel of Bones,** decorated with the skeletal remains of some 5,000 souls.

3 Afterward, follow the walls northeast to see the quirky sculptures at the **Aldeia da Terra Mini-Village,** a much more lighthearted take on Portuguese village life.

4 Enjoy home-cooked Alentejano specialties at **Chão das Covas Café,** one of Évora's many excellent restaurants.

5 Walk off lunch by following the walls to the well-preserved remains of the **Roman Temple of Évora,** some of the most important ruins in Portugal.

6 Nearby you can also step into the magnificent, medieval **Évora Cathedral.**

7 Wrap up the day with a romantic dinner at **Taberna Típica Quarta Feira.**

Day 2: Wine-Tasting and Medieval Villages

1 On Day 2, make the short trip north outside the city to see the graceful arches of the 16th-century **Água da Prata Aqueduct.**

2 Then, continuing in the same direction, head to the **Cartuxa Estate** for a tour of the vineyards and a spot of lunch.

3 Next, head northeast along the A6 motorway to the historic walled market town of Estremoz (35-minute drive), famous for its marble. Spend a couple of hours exploring on foot; don't miss the beautiful marble Tower of the Three Crowns inside **Estremoz Castle and Royal Palace.**

4 Back in the car, head south toward Reguengos de Monsaraz, gateway to the charming medieval walled town of Reguengos. Don't miss striking **Santo António Church.**

5 Enjoy a typical regional dinner at **O Pingo,** a simple, down-to-earth restaurant where you can indulge in honest home-cooked Alentejo fare, before heading back to your hotel in Évora.

Itinerary Ideas

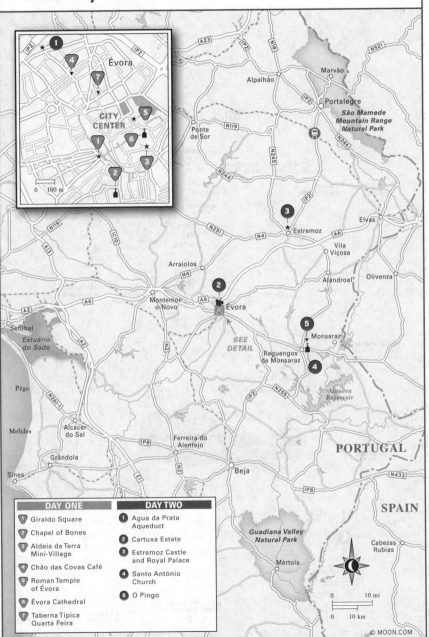

DAY ONE

1. Giraldo Square
2. Chapel of Bones
3. Aldeia da Terra Mini-Village
4. Chão das Covas Café
5. Roman Temple of Évora
6. Évora Cathedral
7. Taberna Típica Quarta Feira

DAY TWO

1. Agua da Prata Aqueduct
2. Cartuxa Estate
3. Estremoz Castle and Royal Palace
4. Santo António Church
5. O Pingo

© MOON.COM

Évora

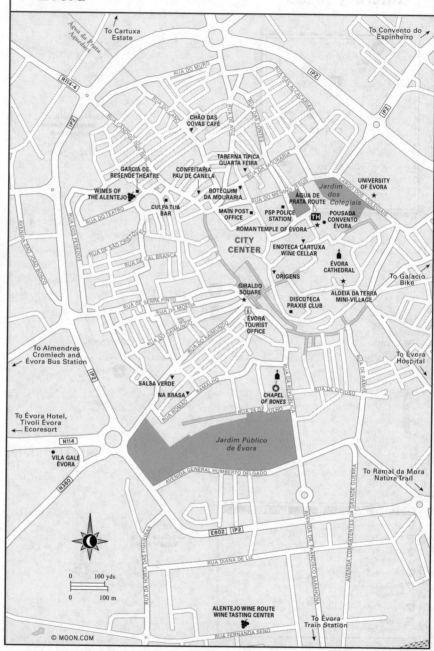

To Cartuxa Estate

To Convento do Espinheiro

Água da Prata Aqueduct

RUA DO MURO

RUA DO CANO

RUA CÂNDIDO DOS REIS

RUA DAS ALCAÇARIAS

RUA DA FLÁ

RUA DAS FONTES

CHÃO DAS COVAS CAFÉ

TABERNA TÍPICA QUARTA FEIRA

GARCIA DE RESENDE THEATRE

CONFEITARIA PAU DE CANELA

RUA DA MOURARIA

UNIVERSITY OF ÉVORA

LARGO DOS COLEGIAIS

WINES OF THE ALENTEJO

BOTEQUIM DA MOURARIA

RUA DO MENINO JESUS

Jardim dos Colegiais

CULPA TUA BAR

MAIN POST OFFICE

ÁGUA DE PRATA ROUTE

PSP POLICE STATION

POUSADA CONVENTO ÉVORA

RUA DO TEATRO

RUA DE SÃO CRISTÓVÃO

ROMAN TEMPLE OF ÉVORA

TH

CITY CENTER

ENOTECA CARTUXA WINE CELLAR

RUA DE CAL BRANCA

ORIGENS

ÉVORA CATHEDRAL

To Galacio Bike

RUA DE SERPA PINTO

GIRALDO SQUARE

ALDEIA DA TERRA MINI-VILLAGE

RUA DA MOEDA

DISCOTECA PRAXIS CLUB

ÉVORA TOURIST OFFICE

To Almendres Cromlech and Évora Bus Station

RUA DO RAIMUNDO

RUA DO RAIMUNDO

To Évora Hospital

SALSA VERDE

RAMALHO

NA BRASA

RUA RAMÃO

RUA DA REPÚBLICA

CHAPEL OF BONES

RUA DE CICIOSO

RUA DE RAMPA

To Évora Hotel, Tivoli Évora Ecoresort

RUA 24 DE JULHO

N114

VILA GALÉ ÉVORA

N380

Jardim Público de Évora

To Ramal da Mora Nature Trail

AVENIDA GENERAL HUMBERTO DELGADO

AVENIDA DE FRANCISCO BARAHONA

AVENIDA COMBATENTES DA GRANDE GUERRA

0   100 yds
0   100 m

E802 IP2

RUA DIANA DE LIZ

RUA DA HORTA DAS FIGUEIRAS

ALENTEJO WINE ROUTE WINE TASTING CENTER

To Évora Train Station

RUA FERNANDA SENO

© MOON.COM

Évora

In the heart of the Alentejo, Évora (EH-voh-rah) is the region's biggest city, built on a small hill under two hours from Lisbon. Wonderfully preserved, Évora is home to unusual historic monuments and leading wine producers, a university city that blends the old with the demands of modern youth.

Often called the megalithic capital of Iberia, Évora, a UNESCO World Heritage Site, has sites that date from prehistory. The most famous is Almendres Cromlech, on the city's outskirts, with menhirs (standing stones) that predate England's Stonehenge. Évora's city center is also well preserved. First inhabited by Celts, the city was conquered by the Romans in the 1st century BC, and relics of their occupancy, such as the Roman Temple, remain, along with surviving architectural influences from the subsequent Moorish occupancy. In the 15th century, Évora was home to Portugal's kings, which brought great wealth, and more prestige came in the 16th century when Évora was elevated to an ecclesiastical city. From its imposing 13th-century Roman-Gothic cathedral, Portugal's largest, to the gruesome Chapel of Bones, whose walls are lined with the bones of thousands of monks, this smorgasbord of monuments forms the foundations for Évora's standing as a cultural-historic heavyweight.

Adding to Évora's touristic prestige, the countryside surrounding the city is dotted by wineries and picturesque historic villages that make for great day trips.

ORIENTATION

Évora is not that big; its main sights can be covered **on foot** in one day. Central **Giraldo Square (Praça do Giraldo)** is the city's main meeting point. Flanked by historic monuments and buildings and lined with elegant cafés and restaurants, it has a grand feel, with a charming church and marble fountain at the northern end. The **Roman Temple of Évora, Évora Cathedral,** and **University of Évora** are all northeast from the square; the **Chapel of Bones** is in the opposite direction, southwest of the square.

Évora's historic center is encircled by strapping 14th-century walls, and the city itself is encircled by the busy **IP2** main ring road. On the northern outskirts of the city is a 16th-century **Água da Prata Aqueduct,** and a little farther in the same direction you can get a taste of the Alentejo Wine Route at the **Cartuxa Estate.** The main **Moorish Quarter,** traversed by Rua da Mouraria, is north of Giraldo Square and the old city walls, and is known today for its great restaurants.

SIGHTS
★ Chapel of Bones
(Capela dos Ossos)

Praça 1 de Maio 4; tel. 266 704 521; www. igrejadesaofrancisco.pt; daily 9am-5pm winter, daily 9am-6:30pm summer; €4

The odd and chilling Chapel of Bones is part of the **Church of Saint Francis** (Igreja de São Francisco) in the heart of the city, a few hundred meters' walk south from Giraldo Square. Small but mesmerizing, it ranks as one of Évora's most visited sights, proof that the macabre is compelling indeed.

Évora's Chapel of Bones dates from the 16th century and is one of just a few in Portugal. The concept of the "Bone Chapel" is thought to have arisen from the need to relocate skeletons exhumed from overflowing medieval cemeteries without forcing the uprooted souls into eternal damnation. Instead of just storing the bones in a crypt, monks put them on display, an opportunity to make a society increasingly preoccupied with the trappings of wealth more conscious of the fleetingness of frivolities. At Évora's Capela dos Ossos the inner walls and pillars are completely clad with the tightly packed bones and skulls of some 5,000 local residents who were exhumed from the overcrowded cemeteries that once sprawled on the city's fringes. Floor-to-ceiling and wall-to-wall, not one centimeter of the chapel is without the empty eye sockets of skulls, femurs, or vertebrae, firmly cemented in strangely organized and almost decorative patterns. Adding to the spectacle, two desiccated corpses are on display in glass cabinets, another warning about the superficiality of materialism and the certainty of death. This is explained in a message above the chapel door that reads: "*Nós ossos que aqui estamos, pelos vossos esperamos,*" or "We bones that are here are awaiting yours."

The Church of St. Francis itself is classified a national monument. Dating back to the 13th century, it predates the Chapel of Bones by a few centuries and has hosted royal weddings. Purported to be the very first Franciscan Order church in Portugal, it retains traces of striking Gothic and Manueline architectural features. Its tremendously opulent interior, with soaring vaulted ceilings, exquisite altars, gilded sculpture-works, Renaissance and Baroque choir stalls, and an 18th-century organ were largely funded by hefty donations from the Portuguese crown, and a thorough restoration in 2015 brought it back to its full luxuriant glory. There is no fee to visit the church.

Évora Cathedral
(Catedral de Évora)

Largo do Marquês de Marialva 809; tel. 266 759 330; www.evoracathedral.com; daily 9am-5pm; cathedral €2, cloister, roof, and museum €4.50

The grand Évora Cathedral, or Sé, is the largest medieval cathedral in Portugal. Similar to Lisbon's monumental cathedral, Évora Cathedral has two massive towers, Gothic cloisters, a Manueline chapel, and a magnificent Baroque chapel. Built on the highest ground in the city, near the Roman Temple, the Gothic structure is an architectural delight, boasting many distinctive features that are characteristic of different eras, from add-ons and repairs carried out over the centuries.

Construction ran from 1280 to 1350 to mark the victory of the Christian Crusaders over the Moors. The cathedral has the look of a fortress with its battlement-encircled terrace. Its main facade is made of rose granite. Inside are ornamental cloisters and beautiful rose windows that give an ethereal feel, a contrast to the simple exterior. Also of note are the striking six-turret lantern-tower, and the main portal, whose huge marble columns have impressive carvings of the apostles.

Évora Cathedral also houses a **museum** (access included with admission) packed with religious art, boasting the only Gothic statue of the pregnant Virgin Mary in Portugal, over a gilded altar inside the church. An added bonus is the view from the rooftop; it's up a narrow 135-step spiral staircase through the bell tower, suitable only for the agile.

Roman Temple of Évora
(Templo Romano de Évora)

Largo do Conde de Vila Flor; tel. 266 769 450; www.cultura-alentejo.pt; 24/7; free

A sacred site dating from the 1st century AD, the Roman Temple of Évora is one of the best-preserved Roman temples on the Iberian Peninsula. A series of Corinthian stone columns on a solid base, the Roman architecture is still evident. Also referred to as the Temple of Diana (incorrectly, as it's thought the temple as actually dedicated to Augustus), it is one of Portugal's most recognizable landmarks. In the historical center, near the cathedral, the temple is on the highest point in the city in front of the manicured public **Garden of Diana** (Jardim de Diana; open 24/7; free), pleasant for a shady stroll and home to a café with glorious views over Évora.

University of Évora
(Universidade de Évora)

Largo dos Colegiais 2; tel. 266 740 800; www.uevora.pt; Mon.-Sat. 9am-8pm; €3, children under 12 free

The University of Évora is overshadowed by

1: the ancient Roman Temple of Évora **2:** Chapel of Bones **3:** fountain in Giraldo Square **4:** cloister of Évora Cathedral

the city's more famous attractions, but it's still monumental. Founded in the 16th century, the university complex is comprised of several restored historical structures dotted around the city, each identified by a dove sculpted into a marble circle above the main entrance. Most of these buildings are small yet grandiose historical buildings; the university's main and most important building, which lies just outside the historic city walls at the address above, is the spectacular square **Espírito Santo College,** a magnificent edifice with an imposing facade of successive grand arches on marble columns, encasing a courtyard and central fountain. The Italian Renaissance-style building was originally a Jesuit college before the Jesuits were expelled by the Marquis of Pombal. Construction took place 1550-1559. Despite being a working university, visitors are welcome to explore the lecture halls on their own, discovering hidden works of art including ancient tile plaques and a mural in the old bookshop.

Aldeia da Terra Mini-Village

Rua de São Manços 15-19; tel. 266 746 049; www. aldeiadaterra.pt; daily 10am-6pm; €3

The quirky Aldeia da Terra Mini-Village is a tongue-in-cheek portrayal of Portuguese village life. Translating to "Village of the Land," it is a colorful collection of pint-size clay sculptures by artist Tiago Cabeça. The collection aims to honor the ancient Portuguese clay-molding tradition while creating laugh-out-loud pieces that show the quirkiness of the Portuguese way of life. Every day new caricatures are added to the village. Opened in 2010, this attraction comprises over 2,000 clay figurines that were relocated in 2017 from the nearby town of Arraiolos to Évora. Clay artisans can often be seen working live, and workshops are also sometimes held here. The funny pieces can also be bought to take home.

Água da Prata Aqueduct
(Aqueduto da Água de Prata)

Rua do Muro 8 (adjacent to city wall); tel. 916 112 655; open 24/7; free

With a total extension of around 18 kilometers (11 mi), this 16th-century stone aqueduct, literally "Silver Water Aqueduct," was a complex and challenging construction project for its era. Massive arches, at points 25 meters (82 ft) high, rise from the ground. The main arches are located outside the city walls, north of Évora near the ring road. In the city's core it blends in seamlessly, fused to houses and shops. Originally, the aqueduct ran from its water source in the countryside to a marble fountain in the main Giraldo Square, with a series of public fountains along the way.

It is possible to follow the route of the aqueduct by foot or bicycle through the city and beyond on the **Água de Prata Route.** Charming little shops have been built beneath some of the arches, and there is a Renaissance-style water box with a dozen Tuscan columns on Rua Nova. Other streets where you can see the aqueduct are Rua do Cano, Rua do Salvador, and Travessa das Nunes.

SPORTS AND RECREATION
Hiking and Cycling

Évora has made concerted efforts to cater to both hikers and cyclists on its trails. To rent a bike for the day, head to **Galacio Bike** (Bairro, Rua do Escoural nº38; tel. 266 785 672; www.galaciobike.com; Mon.-Sat. 10am-7pm; rentals from €15/day), located on the city's outskirts.

ÁGUA DE PRATA ROUTE
(Percurso da Água de Prata)

Hiking Distance: *8.3 kilometers (5.2 mi) (one-way)*
Hiking Time: *2 hours 30 minutes*
Trailhead: *Évora city center by the Roman Temple*
Information and Maps: *www.evora.net/ percursos/folheto_PercursoAguaPrata.pdf*

This hiking trail, which can be walked or cycled, leads from the city through the rural outskirts of Évora (or vice versa), following the centuries-old 18-kilometer (11-mi) aqueduct and its water course. It starts by one of

☆ Wine in the Alentejo

The Alentejo is one of Portugal's primary wine-producing areas, divided into eight DOP (denomination of protected origin) wine-making subregions: Portalegre, Borba, Redondo, Évora, Reguengos, Granja-Amareleja, Vidigueira, and Moura. Wine tourism is a growing trend, and many traditional vineyards have built elegant restaurants and accommodations on-site.

GRAPES AND VARIETALS

Producing smooth, fruity reds and crisp, drinkable whites, Alentejo wines can be found on wine lists, supermarket shelves, and kitchen tables throughout Portugal. With a viticulture reputedly spanning back to the 9th century BC, it is said that wines from the Alentejo were exported to and beloved by the Roman empire.

From grapes grown in the Alentejo's vast sunbaked rolling plains to ones from the mountainous, cooler northeastern corner up near the border with Spain, a general common denominator is that the wines are flavorful and full-bodied. Using techniques from time-honored methods to cutting-edge technology, the region produces many well-known brands, ranging from common table wines to some of the finest wines the country has ever bottled.

In terms of grapes, Alentejo wine production leans on a few core national varieties—**Antão Vaz, Arinto,** and **Roupeiro** being the main bases for whites, and **Aragonez, Alfrocheiro, Castelão,** and **Trincadeira** being the backbones of the reds, along with the French **Alicante Bouschet.** In the new generation wines, these are often blended with other grapes, like international darlings of the grape world such as Syrah and Cabernet Sauvignon. The most typical Alentejo wines are Borba, Évora, Redondo, and Reguengos.

PARTICIPATING IN THE GRAPE HARVEST

The grape harvest, or *vindima,* is usually in September or October. If you visit at this time, you may be able to help with the harvest for a day. Vineyards that participate are listed on the **Alentejo Wine Route** website (www.vinhosdoalentejo.pt). Besides having a hand in making wine, you can also meet local residents. Given the soaring temperatures in late summer, be sure to wear a hat and sturdy shoes and drink plenty of water. And be warned—harvest requires an early start. Some wineries even host mystical-sounding moonlight harvests.

the water reservoirs at the Roman Temple. Following the aqueduct through the city center, it winds through a maze of quaint medieval streets to the historic walls, through a gateway to the fringes of Évora. Through the countryside, the aqueduct is buried in parts, and in other parts it still stands tall on its imposing arches. The route crosses through typical rolling Alentejo fields, cork-oak forests and farmland, and past points of interest like the **Cartuxa Estate.** It culminates in the small hamlet of Nossa Senhora da Graça do Divor, where the original water springs that fed the aqueduct are located.

ÉVORA - RAMAL DA MORA NATURE TRAIL
(Ecopista Évora Ramal da Mora)

Hiking Distance: *21 kilometers (13 mi) one-way*
Hiking Time: *4 hours 30 minutes one-way*
Trailhead: *Chafariz d'El Rei neighborhood*
Information and Maps: *www.evora.net/percursos/ecopista.htm*

Born from the conversion of an old railway track into a walkable or bikeable nature trail, this route takes explorers past points of historical and cultural interest as well as beauty spots and natural attractions in and around Évora. It starts in the city center and rolls out to its very edges.

Wineries and Wine-Tasting

Wine lovers in this region are spoiled for choice. The **Alentejo Wine Route** (Rota dos Vinhos do Alentejo; www.vinhosdoalentejo.pt), with a tasting center in Évora, takes visitors through the region's various wine-growing areas, listing dozens of wineries.

ALENTEJO WINE ROUTE WINE TASTING CENTER (Rota dos Vinhos do Alentejo)

Horta das Figueiras, Rua Fernanda Seno 12, Apartado 498; tel. 266 748 870; www.vinhosdoalentejo.pt; Mon.-Fri. 11am-7pm, Sat. 10am-1pm

This organization just outside the historic city center, between the hospital and the train station, aims to promote regional wine-making as well as other aspects of regional culture. Staff can help organize a trip and winery visits.

WINES OF THE ALENTEJO (Vinhos do Alentejo)

Praça Joaquim António de Aguiar 20; tel. 266 746 498; Mon.-Sat. 11am-7pm

Head to the central Wines of the Alentejo tasting and information center, which harnesses the essence of the region's wines. As well as showcasing two different wines to taste from three different producers, the beautiful center, with vaulted ceilings, stone walls, and windows on a beautiful square, also provides information on what to see in the Alentejo.

CARTUXA ESTATE

Quinta de Valbom; tel. 266 748 383; www.cartuxa.pt; daily 10am-7pm

One of Évora's most iconic vineyards is the Cartuxa Estate, 1.7 kilometers (1.1 mi) from the town center, a 30-minute walk, a 5-minute drive, or €5 by taxi. Producing iconic EA, Foral de Évora, and Pêra-Manca wines, the century-old 15-hectare (37-acre) organic vineyard offers guided tours (1 hour, in English, by appointment only), as well as wine- and olive oil-tasting (€10). Just next door is the Cartuxa Convent, built between 1587 and 1598, which houses monks.

Other Sports and Recreation
SKYDIVE PORTUGAL

Évora Municipal Airdrome; tel. 910 999 991; www. skydiveportugal.pt; from €115

Contact SkyDive Portugal to jump out of a plane over the stunning Alentejo plains.

BALONISSIMO

tel. 935 646 124; www.balonissimo.com; from €140

Enjoy the beauty of the Alentejo from the serenity of a hot-air balloon. Watch the sunrise as you glide over Évora, the aqueduct, and the rolling plains and vineyards with a glass of champagne in hand. Balonissimo offers free pickup from anywhere in Évora. Flights last about an hour, with the full excursion taking 3-4 hours.

ARTS AND ENTERTAINMENT
GARCIA DE RESENDE THEATRE (Teatro Garcia de Resende)

Rua do Teatro 10; tel. 266 777 000; www.cendrev. com

This magnificent century-old building is worth a look if only to admire the simple granite exterior, behind which hides an opulent Italian-style theater. Shaped like a horseshoe, the main concert hall has three tiers of balconies; their deep red lining, gold-trimmed rims, and incredible painted ceiling give the main room a regal, Baroque feel. Inaugurated in 1892, the theater is named for Évora-born poet, designer, and architect Garcia de Resende, an esteemed figure in Renaissance Portugal. The playhouse has a busy year-round program of national and international plays and performances.

FOOD

Évora's food scene spans rustic restaurants to fine dining, centered on hearty, meaty regional dishes, although international cuisine and vegetarian restaurants can be found. Most restaurants in Évora will serve the Alentejo specialty *porco preto* (black pig) and excellent wines. Many of the city's best-known restaurants are in the **Moorish Quarter** *(centro histórico)*.

Alentejo Specialties

The cuisine of the Alentejo is simple and rustic, good food grown from the land made by dexterous hands to age-old recipes. The Alentejo was historically an impoverished region, where life was hard and comforts and resources scarce. Meals were meant for sustenance, with herbs and spices grown on the endless plains thrown in to make the basic ingredients sing. Dishes still reflect this way of life, simple but packed with flavor, many derived from a waste-not want-not mentality. Bread features in many regional dishes, used to fill up and make the meal go further, while pork, especially the local black pig pork, and lamb are key meats.

migas with pork ribs

- **Black pig** *(porco preto)*, also known as Alentejano pig, is a darker-skinned animal traced to wild boars. The black pig is traditionally free-range and feeds on acorns, so the meat is moister, nuttier, more succulent, and more fragrant. Its meat—generally pork chops or thin steaks—is usually served simply grilled, making for delicious but simple meals.

- *Queijada d'Évora* is a small, sweet tart with a thin, crispy pastry crust and a creamy filling made from egg yolks and fresh sheep-milk cheese. It's one of many kinds of *doces conventuais*, traditional Portuguese sweets whose closely guarded recipes come from convents.

- *Açordas* are served either as a bread-soup or a wet bread mash. The most famous is açorda à Alentejana, perhaps the Alentejo's most characteristic dish. Slices of hard Alentejo bread are covered with a hot broth, infused with herbs like cilantro, pennyroyal, oregano, mint, and laurel, and garlic, rock salt, and olive oil. Traditional recipes vary from family to family, but this dish is usually served with a poached egg on top or sometimes with boiled fish. When the *açorda* is made into a wet pasty mash, it might be served with a raw egg on top, which is mixed into the mash and cooks in its heat.

- *Ensopado* (which means soaked bread or soggy bread) is a meaty dish with bread used to soak up the juices. The most common *ensopado* is made with lamb: a rich lamb stew served on top of slices of toasted or fried bread.

- *Sopas* are soups thickened with bread, or dishes in which bread is used to soak up juices and becomes part of the dish, designed by peasant families to make the most of stale leftover bread and create filling meals.

- *Migas*—which translates to "crumbs"—is a bready mash that is usually fried in meat fat or olive oil and garlic until crispy on the outside and, in the case of migas à Alentejana, served with small fried pork ribs.

- *Carne de Porco à Alentejana,* the Alentejo's signature dish and a flavor powerhouse, is found in Portuguese restaurants worldwide. Cubes of pork are cooked in a rich paprika and wine sauce with clams, served with fried potato cubes and topped with chopped pickled vegetables (cauliflower, carrots, and gherkins). It's a unique combination that tantalizes the taste buds.

Regional
CHÃO DAS COVAS CAFÉ

Largo Chão das Covas Évora; tel. 266 706 294; Tues.-Sun. 11am-11pm; €10

Don't be misled by the "café" in the name of Chão das Covas Café; this cute little eatery might be small, but its home-cooked Alentejano dishes and tapas based on fresh seasonal produce are huge in flavor.

★ TABERNA TÍPICA QUARTA FEIRA

Rua do Inverno 18; tel. 266 707 530; Mon. 7:30pm-10pm, Tues.-Sat. 12:30pm-3pm and 7:30pm-10pm; €20

Unpretentious and atmospheric, the family-run Taberna Típica Quarta Feira serves tasty local and regional specialties such as Alentejo-style pork meat and grilled black pork chops.

★ ENOTECA CARTUXA WINE CELLAR

Rua de Vasco da Gama 15; tel. 266 748 348; www. cartuxa.pt; Mon.-Sat. 10am-10pm, Sun. noon-3pm; €20

Cosmopolitan Enoteca Cartuxa Wine Cellar is a polished restaurant by the producers of the famous Cartuxa vineyard wines. The estate's wines are paired with Portuguese regional dishes such as cow tongue, pork cheek, sheep and goat cheese, smoked sausages, and cured meats.

Portuguese
BOTEQUIM DA MOURARIA

Rua da Mouraria 16A; tel. 266 746 775; Mon.-Fri. 12:30pm-3pm and 6:30pm-9:45pm; €15

One of Évora's most popular restaurants, Botequim da Mouraria is small, rustic, and tavern-like, run by a husband-and-wife team who prepare simple, unfussy, traditional Portuguese food. Be sure to try the *presunto* cured ham.

ORIGENS

Rua de Burgos 10; tel. 964 220 790; www. origensrestaurante.com; Tues.-Sat. 12:30pm-3pm and 7pm-10pm; €18

Offering contemporary Portuguese fare, Origens is modern and gleaming, with a sleek menu to match. Don't miss the chilled fresh tomato cream soup with cottage cheese, dried fruit, and honey.

Vegetarian
SALSA VERDE

Rua do Raimundo 93A; tel. 266 743 210; www. salsa-verde.org; Mon.-Fri. 11am-3:30pm and 6pm-9:30pm, Sat. 11am-3:30pm; €10

Vegetarian restaurant Salsa Verde is an airy, colorful setup in a former convent, a true haven for veggie fans in a land of meat lovers. Meat-free twists on traditional Portuguese dishes use fresh local produce and herbs. There are no fixed menus; every day the offerings are fresh and different.

Cafés and Light Bites
CONFEITARIA PAU DE CANELA

Travessa de Lopo Serrão 7A; tel. 266 700 756; http:// confeitariapaudecanela.pt/site; Mon.-Fri. 9am-6pm, Sat. 9am-1:30pm

The best place to try local sweet treat *queijada d'Évora* is straight from the little factory that produces them, confectionary shop Confeitaria Pau de Canela, a few streets north of the Roman Temple.

NIGHTLIFE

Évora has a vibrant alfresco social scene. In summer especially, locals socialize in the cooler temperatures after dark, giving the city a bustling café-culture feel, topped with the energetic vibe of the university students. Many of the city center hotels have upscale wine and cocktail bars, while the other bars around the historic center buzz with students and younger people, particularly on Wednesday night.

Bar
CULPA TUA BAR

Praça Joaquim António de Aguiar 6; tel. 969 533 692; Mon.-Sat. 5pm-3am, Sun. 5pm-midnight

The rustic Culpa Tua Bar is a busy little bar showcasing great local liquor, wine, and fruity cocktails. The bar is in a characterful old building with a vaulted ceiling, brick arches, and a cobbled floor.

Club
DISCOTECA PRAXIS CLUB

Rua Valdevinos 21; tel. 963 937 388; www. praxisevora.wixsite.com; Tues.-Sat. 11pm-6am

Discoteca Praxis Club has four bars and two dance floors popular with the younger crowd. Its packed calendar features resident and guest DJs, live bands, and themed evenings.

ACCOMMODATIONS
€100-200
VILA GALÉ ÉVORA

Av. Túlio Espanca; tel. 266 758 100; www.vilagale. com; €100-200 d

Sleek, modern, four-star Vila Galé Évora is a short walk from the city center, just outside the city walls. It has high-quality rooms, indoor and outdoor pools, a spa, and an on-site restaurant.

ÉVORA HOTEL

Av. Túlio Espanca; tel. 266 748 800; www.evorahotel. pt; from €100-200 d

Sprawling, modern, upscale Évora Hotel, a 5-minute drive from the city center, captures the essence of the Alentejo. Surrounded by quintessential countryside and decorated with tones and textures of the region, it has two outdoor pools and an indoor pool.

TIVOLI ÉVORA ECORESORT

Quinta da Deserta e Malina; tel. 266 738 500; www. ecorkhotel.com; from €100-200

Built using natural materials, refined countryside Tivoli Évora Ecoresort has an eco-friendly ethos with 56 private suites. It's a 10-minute drive from the city center in the rolling Alentejo plains.

★ CONVENTO DO ESPINHEIRO

5.2 kilometers (3.2 mi) north of Évora city center; tel. 266 788 200; www.conventodoespinheiro.com; from €150-250 d

Luxury boutique hotel Convento do Espinheiro, converted from a 15th-century convent, is one of Portugal's most famous and emblematic hotels. Surrounded by gardens, it offers 92 rooms (including 5 suites), divided between sumptuous conventual rooms and a modern wing with midcentury-inspired décor.

Over €200
POUSADA CONVENTO ÉVORA

Largo do Conde de Vila Flor; tel. 266 730 070; www. pousadas.pt/en/hotel/pousada-evora; €200-300 d

The serene 36-room Pousada Convento Évora, with a swimming pool, is in Évora's historic center, converted from a low-rise, white-washed monastery dating to 1487. The luxurious rooms are former monks' cells.

INFORMATION AND SERVICES

- **Évora Tourist Office:** Praça do Giraldo 73; tel. 266 777 071; Mon.-Fri. 9am-6pm, Sat.-Sun. 10am-2pm and 3pm-6pm Nov.-Mar., daily 9am-7pm Apr.-Oct.
- **Main post office:** Rua Olivença; tel. 266 745 480
- **PSP police station:** Rua Francisco Soares Lusitano; tel. 266 760 450; www.psp.pt
- **Évora Hospital:** Largo Senhor da Pobreza; tel. 266 740 100

GETTING THERE

Évora is 1.5 hours' drive east of **Lisbon,** about 140 kilometers (87 mi), following the **A6** motorway.

Train
ÉVORA TRAIN STATION (Largo da Estacão)

The train station in Évora is outside the city walls, 1 kilometer (0.6 mi) south, a 15-minute walk. The station is simple, but look for the old *azulejo* tile murals depicting local life. **CP** (tel. 707 210 220; www.cp.pt) trains run four times daily from Lisbon's Oriente, Sete Rios, and Entrecampos stations (1.5 hours; 2nd class €12.40, 1st class €16.50).

Bus

ÉVORA BUS STATION

Av. Tulio Espanca; tel. 266 738 120

Évora's main bus station is a 10-minute walk west of the walled city center. **Rede Expressos** (tel. 707 223 344; www.rede-expressos.pt) runs air-conditioned buses almost every half hour from Lisbon's Sete Rios bus station (1.5 hours; from €10.60). Tickets can be bought at the station's ticket office or booked online.

There are at least three daily buses from **Faro** in the Algarve; the journey takes around 4 hours and costs €17.50 (www.rede-expressos.pt). There are also direct buses from **Porto** to Évora with Rede Expressos, leaving Porto's Campo 24 Agosto station; the trip takes 5-6 hours and costs €24 one-way.

GETTING AROUND

Most of Évora's sights can be covered **on foot**, but the old cobbled streets can be slippery and uneven. **Horse-drawn carriages** (around €30) can be found outside the cathedral for sightseeing trips.

Car

Rent a car to explore the surrounding wine farms, villages, and Almendres Cromlech. Hotels work with local car rental companies; ask at reception. South of the walled city, between the IP2 road and the Circular de Évora ring road, are a number of car rental offices, including **Europcar Évora** (Estrada de Viana, Lote 10; tel. 266 742 627; www.europcar.pt), **Hertz** (Rua da Revendedora, Lote 7, Bairro da Torregela, Horta das Figueiras; tel. 219 426 300; www.hertz.pt), and **Sadorent** (Rua Manuel Correia Lopes 118; tel. 266 734 526; www.sadorent.pt), all open weekdays 9am-6pm.

Finding **parking** within the city walls can be difficult and must be paid for weekdays 8:30am-7:30pm and Saturday 9am-2pm. There are spacious parking lots outside the walls, usually free; one is on **Rua Cândido dos Reis,** near the aqueduct, north of the city center. It is within walking distance of the center, with no steep hills or stairs.

Bus

Local bus service **TREVO** (www.trevo.com.pt; €1 for 24 hours) serves Évora and its immediate fringes. **Lines 51** and **52** on the Blue Route cover the old city continuously weekdays 8am-8pm and Saturday 8am-2pm.

Taxi

There are plenty of **taxis** near places of interest and the train and bus stations. Local company **Associação de Rádio Táxis de Évora** (Rua dos Altos; tel. 266 735 735) provides service anytime.

Around Évora

The area flanking Évora is the deep heart of the Alentejo, dotted with fascinating little towns that are preserved embodiments of the region's rural, cultural, and historic heritage. Like a chocolate box of different treats, each town is distinct. There's Arraiolos, famous for its wool rugs; marble-town Estremoz; the former European Wine Capital Reguengos de Monsaraz; and unique garrison border town Elvas, all within an hour of Évora city proper. The region east of Évora up to the Spanish border is prime wine territory and home to some of the region's most esteemed wineries.

ARRAIOLOS

Charmingly rustic Arraiolos is a small village north of Évora that is famed for its rugs. Laborious traditional carpet-making, a skilled artisanal craft, dates to Moorish times and produces colorful handmade woolen carpets, tapestries, and cushion covers. Just as colorful is the sloping town itself, quintessentially

The Megalithic Route

Almendres Cromlech

Adding to its collection incredible monuments, Évora is surrounded by the Megalithic Route (www.visitevora.net/circuito-megalitico-evora-alentejo), created by the local council to take visitors to on a tour of the most important **menhirs** (tall, upright stones), **cromlechs** (stone circles), and **dolmens** (stone tombs) on the outskirts of Évora.

It is thought this particular part of the Alentejo is so rich in prehistoric megalithic monuments because it is where the country's three major hydrographic basins—the Tejo, Sado, and Guadiana—meet, which, when coupled with the region's rolling plains, made this spot prime territory for ancient hunter-gatherer communities. There are at least 10 different sites around Évora.

ALMENDRES CROMLECH

Cromeleque dos Almendres; www.cm-evora.pt; open 24/7; free
The finest and largest megalithic site on the Megalithic Route is the Almendres Cromlech, a Neolithic complex just half an hour from Évora. On the gentle slope of Monte dos Almendres, this group of 95 granite standing stones, or menhirs, is arranged in twin rings overlooking the plains. One of the oldest stone circles in Europe, built 6000-3000 BC, the site was discovered in 1966 and is said to predate the world's most famous megaliths, Stonehenge in England. While its purpose is not certain, it is believed to be a ceremonial site for celestial worship or a form of astronomical observatory, constructed over several periods. Look closer and you'll see the stones are engraved with patterns, whose meanings remain unknown.

This is the largest site of such structures on the Iberian Peninsula, which, along with Évora's other smaller sites throughout the region, gives it its nickname "the megalithic capital of Iberia."

Getting There

The Almendres Cromlech is located on the outskirts of Évora (30 minutes, 18 km/11 mi west from Évora), situated off the national roadway (**N114**) from Évora to Montemor-o-Novo, just after the village of Guadalupe. Public transport to the site is sparse, so go by car, but it is open 24/7 and there is no entry fee. Visitors are free to wander and even touch the stones.

Alentejano with its whitewashed houses, red roofs, and a church within the walls of a medieval castle.

Sights
CASTLE WALLS AND SALVADOR CHURCH
(Muralhas do Castelo e Igreja do Salvador)

Paço dos Alcaides, Monte de São Pedro; 24/7; free

Dominating the town's skyline, the 14th-century castle has a long circular wall in a big ring atop St. Peter's Hill (Monte de São Pedro). The area within the castle walls was initially a hive of local activity, but villagers eventually started to head to the plains at the foot of the mound to escape the wind and cold. There's nothing of the actual castle left, but its walls were restored in the 1960s when the fortification was declared a National Monument. On the hill's peak, in the very center of the castle walls, the 16th-century **Salvador Church** is impressive in white with sky-blue trim. From inside the castle walls, views over Arraiolos town are worth the 7-minute climb up the hill.

ARRAIOLOS CARPET INTERPRETIVE CENTER
(Centro Interpretativo do Tapete de Arraiolos)

Praça do Município 19; tel. 266 490 254; www. tapetedearraiolos.pt; Tues.-Sun. 10am-1pm and 2pm-6pm; €1

Most people come to Arraiolos to see the Arraiolos Carpet Interpretive Center, located in a former hospital that's one of the oldest buildings in the village. Get insight into the local craft, believed to have been introduced by the Moors. Carpets were once a status symbol, indicative of wealth, and Arraiolos has been producing carpets since the 16th century. The center has a permanent collection of woven tapestries and carpets on display alongside temporary exhibitions by local artists, with signage in English.

Getting There and Around

Arraiolos is 23 kilometers (14.3 mi) north of **Évora,** a 30-minute drive on the **R114-4** road. **Rodalentejo** (tel. 266 738 120; www. rodalentejo.pt) buses run sporadically between Évora and Arraiolos (1 hour; €6-8), generally a bus in the early morning, one at lunchtime, and one in the afternoon. The bus stops just outside the pedestrianized town center, near a taxi rank and post office.

Arraiolos is a small, easily **walkable** town. There are a number of large free **car parks** within the vicinity of the town center, such as on Travessa dos Moleiros and Largo do Lagar.

REGUENGOS DE MONSARAZ AND MONSARAZ

Small, beautiful Reguengos de Monsaraz is the main gateway to the nearby walled medieval village of Monsaraz. Perched on the banks of the expansive Alqueva reservoir, near the Spanish border, Reguengos de Monsaraz is surrounded by sweeping plains dotted with Neolithic menhirs and dolmens. With interesting architecture, excellent wines, and local arts and crafts, the city has seen its tourism flourish in recent years.

Within castle walls atop a jagged hill that rises from the endless Alentejo plains, the petite medieval village of Monsaraz, 16 kilometers (10 mi) northeast of Reguengos de Monsaraz, sits like a crown. Bookended between the castle tower at one end of the village and an old bell tower at the other, Monsaraz is a cluster of whitewashed houses, restaurants, and guesthouses along steep schist-stone streets, with a statuesque church right in the middle. Bougainvillea provides color along the cobbled streets, and the views from the village over the Alentejo plains to the Alqueva reservoir are stunning. Monsaraz has a whimsical feel but is a down-to-earth village, one of the oldest in Portugal.

Sights

Reguengos de Monsaraz sprawls around the

1: medieval hilltop castle of Arraiolos **2:** tapestry in Arraiolos **3:** church in Monsaraz **4:** Alqueva Dam

main square, **Praça da Liberdade,** in a jig-saw of whitewashed houses and red roofs. Little arts and crafts shops dot the town, many run by working artisans.

At the heart of Monsaraz is the **Largo Dom Nuno Álvares Pereira square** and the striking **Nossa Senhora da Lagoa Church** (Igreja da Nossa Senhora da Lagoa). Leading to the square is the main street, or **Rua Direita,** lined with whitewashed 16th- and 17th-century houses.

SANTO ANTÓNIO CHURCH
(Igreja do Santo António)

Praça da Liberdade, Reguengos de Monsaraz; tel. 926 670 680; Sun. Mass at 11am and 6:30pm

In the middle of Praça da Liberdade, Santo António Church is unusual, with a hexagonal tower front and fanciful Gothic-Manueline style. Its origins date to 1887 when it was commissioned to replace a hermitage on the site, and it was designed by António José Dias da Silva, the architect who created Lisbon's bullring.

ALENTEJO WOOLEN
GOODS FACTORY
(Fábrica Alentejana de Lanifícios)

Rua dos Mendes 79, Reguengos de Monsaraz; tel. 266 502 179; www.mizzete.pt; Mon.-Fri. 9am-5:30pm; free

Ten minutes south of the main square, this factory is one of the country's last remaining traditional handlooms, producing wool blankets, rugs, and carpets, where you can walk around the factory and watch the artisans work.

MONSARAZ CASTLE AND WALLS
(Castelo de Monsaraz e Muralhas)

Largo do Castelo 1, Reguengos de Monsaraz; tel. 963 702 392; www.cm-reguengos-monsaraz.pt; open 24/7; free

It is thought that Monsaraz has been fortified as far back as prehistoric times. The limestone and schist village's high position over the Guadiana River and the Spanish border, made it a desirable and contested location that played a pivotal role in many battles.

Monsaraz Castle, a national monument, was built in the 14th century by King Dinis. After its military functions ended in the 19th century, the castle's main formation square was used as a bullring. Today the arena is used for annual religious celebrations.

The long wall around Monsaraz has four key entrances; the main one, the **Porta da Vila** (Village Door), is flanked by a pair of semi-cylindrical towers, and above its Gothic arch is a memorial stone dedicated to the Immaculate Conception, laid in 1646 by King João IV. On the north side of the wall is the **Porta d'Évora** (Évora Door), another Gothic arch ensconced in a chunky turret. The **Portas d'Alcoba** and **Buraco** have full arches and overlook the splendid Alentejo plains. There are 360-degree views over the countryside, from the vast Alqueva reservoir to Spain.

Wineries and Wine-Tasting
ESPORÃO WINE ESTATE
(Herdade do Esporão)

tel. 266 509 280; www.esporao.com; daily 10am-7pm Apr.-Oct., Tues.-Sun. 10am-7pm Nov.-Mar.

The name Esporão is a heavyweight in wine and olive oil and has placed Reguengos de Monsaraz on the wine map. Founded in 1277, the Esporão Wine Estate, overlooking the Caridade dam 4 kilometers (2.5 mi) south of Reguengos de Monsaraz, a 4-minute drive, opened its doors in 1997. Spanning 1,884 hectares (4,655 acres), the estate is open to the public to explore. It also has a **wine bar and restaurant** (daily 10am-6:30pm Apr.-Oct., daily 10am-6pm Nov.-Mar.) for wine-tastings and lunch; no reservations are necessary.

Esporão Wine Estate's cluster of medieval buildings includes the **Esporão Arch** and the hermitage of **Nossa Senhora dos Remédios.** The **Esporão Tower,** outwardly plain and square, believed to date to the mid-1400s, was built as a symbol of power and today is the symbol of Esporão wines. It houses an archaeological museum and can only be visited as part of a tour.

Guided tours (1 hour, in English 11am

Alqueva Reservoir and Dam

The vast reservoir known as "the Great Lake of Alqueva" (al-KEH-vah) spreads over 250 square kilometers (97 sq mi) on the border of the Alentejo and Spain, located about 30 minutes south of Reguengos de Monsaraz on the N255 (35 km/22 mi) or 45 minutes north of Beja on the IP2 road (63 km/39 mi). The Alqueva Dam (Barragem de Alqueva) was completed in 2002, and the project was controversial, as it completely submerged a local village, Aldeia da Luz. On one of the largest artificial lakes in Europe, the Alqueva Dam irrigates five Alentejo municipalities and provides for water sports and family-friendly leisure. Here are some ways to get out on the water, away from Portugal's Atlantic and Mediterranean coasts.

GO TO THE BEACH

The Alqueva Dam was designed to offer respite from the heat and a place to relax. There are a few artificial beaches around the riverbank.

Mourão Beach
(Praia Fluvial de Mourão)
Mourão parish; open 24/7; free

The popular human-made Mourão Beach is located in the parish of Mourão near the border with Spain, a 20-minute drive east from Reguengos de Monsaraz on the N256. When you get there, you'll be welcomed with all the amenities of a regular coastal beach: grassy and sandy areas, parasols, a small pool, floating pontoon and slides for children, and a car park and snack bar, as well as on-duty lifeguards in summer and a picnic and BBQ area. It's a great spot for a family day out.

Monsaraz Beach
(Praia Fluvial de Monsaraz)
Mourão Nautical Center; daily 9am-7pm; free

Located a 5-minute drive east along the CM1127 from Monsaraz town, Monsaraz beach offers visitors a sandy spot to lay out their towels and stick up a parasol. Facilities include toilets and changing rooms, as well as a snack bar open 10am-10pm.

Amieira Beach
(Praia Fluvial da Amieira)
Portal Parish; https://aquapolis.com.pt/praia-fluvial-de-amieira-portel; open 24/7; free

The most recent dam-beach to open on the banks of the Alqueva, Amieira Beach is the biggest. It's home to 600 curvy meters (2,000 ft) of powdery blond sand, as well as amenities like changing rooms and toilets. It also has equipment like SUP boards and canoes for rent on the beach (from €10/hour), plus parasols for rent (€2.50 half day).

WATER SPORTS

Canoeing, kayaking, boating, water-skiing, wakeboarding, fishing, or lounging on a sun bed on the beaches are possible thanks to outfitters such as **Amieira Marina** (tel. 266 611 173; www.amieiramarina.com; daily 9am-8pm). The marina is the largest infrastructure on the Alqueva, located in the village of Amieira, a 63-kilometer (39-mi), 45-minute drive north of Beja on the IP2 road or a 25-minute drive south of Reguengos de Monsaraz on the N255. You can also rent a houseboat to explore the historic villages around the reservoir's banks, such as the rebuilt Aldeia da Luz and Reguengos de Monsaraz. Rentals from Amieira Marina start from around €200 per night, and piloting a houseboat only requires a regular driver's license.

and 3pm daily; €15) of the wine cellar, vineyards, and olive groves include wine-tasting. Alternatively, skip the tour and head straight to the bar for a wine-tasting (from €8) or an olive oil tasting (from €3) accompanied by local cheeses and cold meats.

Food
O PINGO

Rua de Lisboa 25, Reguengos de Monsaraz; tel. 966 316 263; www.facebook.com/pages/Restaurante-O-Pingo/148121492455630; Mon.-Sat. 7am-midnight; €10

Hearty Alentejo specialties are served here in traditional earthenware pots in a simple, unfussy, down-to-earth dining room. Don't expect fancy trimmings; dishes are simple and home-cooked staples, such as *migas, sopas,* and roasted octopus.

ALOENDRO

Av. do Alentejo 3A, Reguengos de Monsaraz; tel. 266 502 109; www.facebook.com/Restaurante-Aloendro-205279579516708; Wed.-Mon. 10am-midnight; €15

A refined local eatery, Aloendo serves delicious authentic regional cuisine like roast goat and lamb and grilled black pork in a polished setting at good prices.

O BARRIL

Rua do Comércio 17, Reguengos de Monsaraz; tel. 967 953 625, www.facebook.com/pg/restauranteobarril. reguengos/posts; Thurs.-Tues. 11:30am-10pm; €15

Unassuming on the outside and traditional on the inside, with tile-clad walls and vaulted ceilings, O Barril's menu is made up of genuine regional dishes, like Alentejo sausage and goat cheese.

SEM FIM RESTAURANT

Rua das Flores 6, Telheiro, Monsaraz; tel. 266 557 471 or 962 653 711; www.sem-fim.com; Thurs.-Tues. 11am-midnight; €20

Housed in an old olive oil factory, Sem Fim is atmospheric and arty. A tapas bar and restaurant, it serves typical local fare, starting with local bread and olives, homemade pâtés, and cured meats. Mains include regional specialties like lamb *ensopado* and grilled black pork.

TAVERNA OS TEMPLÁRIOS

Rua Direita, no. 22, Monsaraz; tel. 266 557 166; www. facebook.com/tavernaostemplarios; Wed.-Mon. 9am-9:30pm; €15

In a picturesque setting on the edge of the village, the Templários Tavern prides itself on serving patrons fresh, authentic flavors of the Alentejo, like braised pork cheeks and oven-roast lamb. The views from the alfresco terrace are fantastic.

SABORES DE MONSARAZ

Rua de São Bento 2, Monsaraz; tel. 969 217 800; http://saboresdemonsaraz.com; Wed.-Sun. 12:30pm-3:30pm and 7:30pm-10.30pm, Tues. 7:30pm-10:30pm; €25

From a selection of regional starters to mains that include black pork tenderloin, codfish with bread and cilantro, and roasted lamb, everything about this little place screams quality and tradition—not to mention the fantastic views.

Accommodations

If you're undecided when it comes to choosing a home base to explore the region, Reguengos de Monsaraz has slightly more in terms of shops and restaurants, but staying in Monsaraz has old-world whimsical charm.

SOLAR DE ALQUEVA

Rua de São Marcos do Campo 22 A, Reguengos de Monsaraz; tel. 266 502 105; www.solardealqueva. pt; €60

Right in the heart of Reguengos de Monsaraz, Solar de Alqueva is one of the area's newest hotels, housed in a pretty, traditional whitewashed building. It has 25 unpretentious rooms, gleaning floors throughout, and a nice outdoor pool.

ESTALAGEM DE MONSARAZ

Largo de São Bartolomeu 5, Monsaraz; tel. 266 557 019; www.booking.com/hotel/pt/retiro-de-monsaraz. html; €100

A 5-minute walk from Monsaraz Castle, this cheap and clean inn includes basic comforts, like air-conditioning, TVs, and private bathrooms in all rooms. The exposed stonework on walls and floors adds a nice rustic touch. There's a lovely outdoor pool, and its hilltop location provides amazing views in all directions. Convenient and affordable.

Getting There and Around

From **Évora,** Reguengos de Monsaraz is 38.5 kilometers (24 mi) southeast, a 35-minute drive on the **IP2** and **N256** roads. Monsaraz is 16 kilometers (10 mi) northeast of Reguengos de Monsaraz, a 15-minute drive on the **M514** road. A large **car park** just outside the walls helps preserve the village from motorized traffic, and also means visitors can amble the cobbled streets at leisure.

Visitors can also call **Táxis Antral Reguengos Monsaraz** (tel. 266 502 671) for a taxi from Reguengos de Monsaraz to Monsaraz Castle (around €13).

REGUENGOS DE MONSARAZ BUS STATION

Avenida Dr. António José de Almeida
The bus station in Reguengos de Monsaraz is in the town center. **Rede Expressos** (tel. 707 223 344; www.rede-expressos.pt) runs buses almost every half hour between Lisbon's Sete Rios station and Reguengos de Monsaraz (via Évora; 2.5 hours; from €14.30). Rede Expressos runs two other buses between Évora and Reguengos de Monsaraz (35 minutes, 9am and 7:45pm daily; €6.70).

The regional public bus service **Rodalentejo** (tel. 266 738 120; www.rodalentejo.pt) runs four times daily between Évora and Reguengos de Monsaraz (1 hour), two buses in the morning and two in the afternoon during the school year, and three buses a day when school is out. Buses also run 4-5 times a day between Reguengos de Monsaraz and Monsaraz village (Lines 8174 or 8930; 30 minutes; €2-4). The bus drops passengers off just outside the village walls.

ESTREMOZ

Busy, down-to-earth Estremoz is a small walled market town with an authentic feel and dramatic history. The graceful historic center, with tree-shaded streets and picturesque squares, was a key military headquarters and home to Portugal's kings and queens. From afar the town appears piled high on a mound, where the 13th-century castle and walls sit. The fortified architecture is modest, built from regional marble, with 13th-century walls and a 30-meter-high (98-ft-high) solid marble keep within. A second fortified wall runs around Estremoz, which has a newer section, the Vila Nova (New Town), as its lower band. Local blush-pink marble is used liberally for everyday paving and cladding.

Sights

ESTREMOZ CASTLE AND ROYAL PALACE
(Castelo de Estremoz e Paço Real)

Largo do Castelo; tel. 268 332 075, open 24/7, free
Nestled in the heart of the historic town center, Estremoz Castle was built in the 13th century by King Dom Dinis in honor of his wife, Isabel of Aragon. The narrow, winding roads from the compact town surrounding the castle climb up to it. Its centerpiece is the impressive **Tower of the Three Crowns** (Torre das Três Coroas), a keep that stands 30 meters (98 ft) tall, made of local white marble. This tower is widely regarded as one of the most beautiful keeps in Portugal, and its 70 steps can be climbed for 360-degree views over the Alentejo. On a clear day you can see as far as the Serra da Estrela mountain range in central Portugal.

The castle's courtyard, Largo Dom Dinis, houses the former **Royal Palace,** once inhabited by King Dom Dinis and Dona Isabel and today an exclusive luxury hotel, the Pousada Castelo de Estremoz. One of the rooms, where Queen Isabel died in 1336, has been converted into a **chapel** and remains open to the public. The Tower of the Three Crowns is accessed via the hotel.

MUSEUM OF LIVING SCIENCE (Centro Ciência Viva)

Convento das Maltezas; tel. 268 334 285; www. ccvestremoz.uevora.pt; Tues.-Sun. 10am-7pm; adults €9, children 7-17 €5, children 4-6 €3, family €16

Occupying a former 16th-century convent, Estremoz's Museum of Living Science is an interactive setup where science and technology offer insight into the history of the planet, with a particular focus on local geology. Exhibits include a dinosaur skeleton, the Estremoz Yellow Submarine deep-sea experience, and a vast fossil collection. This museum is a great place to keep kids entertained for a few hours if the weather is dreary.

SANTO ANTÓNIO DOORWAY (Porta de Santo António)

Avenida de Santo António

Built into the castle wall, the Santo António Doorway, or Saint Anthony's gate, is one of the main gateways into the city of Estremoz. It is the prettiest of its formal entrances, full of carvings and engravings. Made from creamy-colored chunky stone blocks, it pops out from the whitewashed town walls. With barely enough room for a car to squeeze through, the long tunnel from the doorway is publicly accessible for pedestrians and provides a memorable introduction to the town.

Shopping
SATURDAY MORNING MARKET

Rossio Marquês de Pombal Square; Sat. 8am-1:30pm

Estremoz's fantastic large Saturday morning market has extensive local produce, smoked sausages, and cheeses. Enjoy a *fartura* (like a churro) rolled in sugar and cinnamon, sold fresh from snack vans. A **flea market** usually sets up next to the farmers market; look for local red clay pottery, especially the traditional *bonecos de Estremoz*, colorful pottery figurines, and unique twin-spout stoneware jugs.

1: Estremoz Castle **2:** cobbled street in Estremoz

Food and Accommodations
ALECRIM

Rossio Marquês de Pombal 31 e 32; tel. 268 324 189; http://alecrimestremoz.pt; daily 9am-11pm; €15

With interesting and modern décor along the lines of a modern brasserie, Alecrim takes regional cuisine up a notch. All the staple ingredients—sausage, black pork, *migas,* and cheese—are on the menu, with a contemporary fresh Mediterranean twist. Other more unusual dishes, like pigeon rice, make for interesting alternatives. It's also a wine bar.

POUSADA CASTELO DE ESTREMOZ

Largo Dom Dinis; tel. 268 332 075; www.pousadas. pt; €162

Pousada Castelo de Estremoz is a luxury hotel in the former royal residence adjacent to the Estremoz Castle. It is packed with local historic artifacts and antiques and makes a great base to explore the town.

Information and Services

- **PSP police station:** Rua 31 de Janeiro; tel. 268 338 470; www.psp.pt

- **Main post office:** Rua 5 de Outubro 30; tel. 268 339 190

- **Estremoz Health Center:** Rua Prof. Egas Moniz; tel. 268 337 700

- **Estremoz Tourist Office:** Rossio Marquês de Pombal; tel. 268 339 227; daily 9am-5:30pm

Getting There

Estremoz is 48 kilometers (30 mi) northeast of **Évora** on the **A6** motorway, about a 35-minute drive.

ESTREMOZ BUS STATION

Av. Rainha Santa Isabel; tel. 268 324 266

There are no trains to Estremoz. Estremoz bus station, a short walk east of the city, occupies the disused train station. **Rodalentejo** (tel. 266 738 120; www.rodalentejo.pt) buses runs from Évora to Estremoz (1.25 hours; €4.55) 3-4 times a day, but buses back from Estremoz to Évora are less frequent.

The Marble Route

Estremoz is at the heart of the Alentejo's Marble Route (www.rotadomarmoreae.com), a region pitted with marble quarries and where the rock has been widely used in building and construction. This gives the regional architecture a radiant character, in ethereal iridescent white-gold and pale pink.

The route is designed to take visitors to the towns most representative of the region's marble-extracting heritage, which run about 27 kilometers (17 mi) along the Serra d'Ossa mountain between Estremoz in the north and Redondo to the south. The website offers several different itinerary suggestions; you can make one short trip to a marble hot spot, or spend several days exploring the attractions such as quarries, monuments, and artisan workshops.

SELF-GUIDED TOUR

If you want to do a deep dive into the material that has had such an impact on the region, here's what to look out for on your drive.

Estremoz

There are two marble sights to keep an eye out for in Estremoz. The first is the impressive **Tower of the Three Crowns** in Estremoz Castle, 28 meters (92 ft) high and made of solid marble (page 153). The second is the 16th-century Italian Baroque-style **Congregados Convent** (Rossio Marquês de Pombal; tel. 268 339 200; www.cm-estremoz.pt; Mon.-Fri. 9am-5:30pm; free) whose pink marble facade was only finished in 1967.

Sousel

The tiny town of Sousel has a fine tribute to marble in its **main church** (Igreja Matriz, Praça da República; tel. 268 551 210; mass at noon Sun., 5:30pm Mon.-Fri. Nov.-Mar., and Mon.-Fri. 6:30pm Apr.-Oct.; free), whose staircase is made of solid marble. Sousel is approximately 20 minutes (18 km/11 mi) north of Estremoz.

Borba

Small, traditional, and best known for its eponymous wine (and yearly wine festival in November), Borba (13 km/8 mi southeast of Estremoz; 18 km/11 mi southeast of Sousel) lacks the impressive monuments of neighboring towns. But if you look hard as you wander the quaint narrow streets, you´ll see a rich smattering of marble features, from window frames and doorsteps to street arches and paving, giving the whitewashed town a pearly glow. To honor the importance of those who work in the marble industry, in 2005 the town council commissioned a solid marble **statue** of a quarry worker with an original drill, which takes pride of place on the main roundabout of the EM225 road between Borba and Vila Viçosa. Inside the town, the **Fonte das Bicas,** or Bicas Fountain, is an 18th-century neoclassical monument completely clad in marble.

Vila Viçosa

Nicknamed the "Princess of the Alentejo," Vila Viçosa (20 km/12 mi southeast of Estremoz; 38 km/24 mi southeast of Sousel) is magnificent. Pretty and polished, it's like visiting an open-air museum. The town retains its authentic old-world charm and elegance, and the lands surrounding it are lush and fertile. Made up of various exhibitions showcasing the magnificence of Portuguese marble, the **Marble Museum** is a highlight of the marble route (page 157). Other attractions include the **Marmoris Hotel** (page 158) and the facade of the historic **Ducal Palace** (page 157), veritable celebrations of all things marble.

GUIDED TOURS

Guided tours and visits to quarries are organized by the **Rota Tons de Marmore** (Rua 5 de Outubro 20, Vila Nova de Baronia; tel. 284 475 413; www.rotatonsdemarmore.com) association, set up to promote the region's natural resources. Its headquarters is in Vila Nova de Baronia, 36 kilometers (22 mi) south of Évora on Rua 5 de Outubro. From Évora, it's a 35-minute drive along the N254 road.

Rede Expressos (tel. 707 223 344; www.rede-expressos.pt) express buses run between Évora and Estremoz (40 minutes; €7.60) at least twice a day, mostly in the afternoon, and are quicker than the regular buses. Rede Expressos also operates direct buses between Lisbon's Sete Rios terminal and Estremoz (2.5 hours; €14.70), departing every two hours. Some Lisbon-Estremoz services may require a transfer in Évora; double-check when booking.

VILA VIÇOSA

A short drive southeast of Estremoz is Vila Viçosa (VEE-lah vee-SSOH-sah), which has an aristocratic feel with its own castle and a grand royal palace. A relaxing place to wander along wide boulevards, marble-encased Vila Viçosa is so pretty that it is referred to as the "Princess of the Alentejo" and dubbed an open-air museum. Small but charming, this lush and regal town was the birthplace of famous Portuguese author and poet Florbela Espanca (1894-1930) and is her final resting place. Packed with history and magnificent monuments, it's worth a stop on the way to Estremoz.

Sights
MARBLE MUSEUM
(Museu do Marmore)
Largo da Estação; tel. 268 889 314; Tues.-Sun. 9:30am-1pm and 2:30pm-6pm; €1.50

Small, modern, and unexpectedly fascinating, the local marble museum in Vila Viçosa is a highlight. Housed in a former train station, it showcases many different ways to fashion and use of marble, from contemporary sculptures to decorative pieces. It also explores the history of marble mining in the region, as well as the machinery, equipment, and processes used in its extraction.

DUCAL PALACE
(Paço Ducal)
Terreiro do Paço; tel. 268 980 659; www.fcbragana. pt; Tues. 2pm-6pm, Wed.-Sun. 10am-1pm and 2pm-6pm June-Sept., Tues. 2pm-6pm, Wed.-Sun. 10am-1pm and 2pm-5pm Oct.-May; €7

The magnificent 15th-century Vila Viçosa Ducal Palace has a simple and unique beauty. For centuries it was the seat of the House of Bragança, an important noble family. The palace's mannerist architecture boasts a long symmetrical facade clad in marble from local quarries. Inside, the palace comprises 50 rooms that are open to the public and house collections such as Chinese porcelain, jewelry and gold, armaments, and coaches and carriages. Some of these exhibitions require an additional fee (€2.50-3).

An eerie point of interest is the private quarters of Dom Carlos I, king from 1889 to 1908, and his wife, Marie-Amélia. He left the palace one morning in 1908 for Lisbon and was murdered there that day, the first Portuguese king to be assassinated. His rooms have remained as they were following his last night here, laid out with clothes and toiletries, awaiting his return and untouched since.

Guided **tours** (in English Tues.-Sun. 11am; included in admission) are conducted in various languages.

VILA VIÇOSA CASTLE
(Castelo de Vila Viçosa)
Rua Sacadura Cabral 2; tel. 268 980 128; www.fcbraganca.pt; Tues. 2pm-6pm, Wed.-Sun. 10am-1pm and 2pm-6pm June-Sept., Tues. 2pm-6pm, Wed.-Sun. 10am-1pm and 2pm-5pm Oct.-May; €3

Dating from the 13th century and reconstructed in the 17th century, the intriguing Vila Viçosa Castle houses an archaeology museum; a hunting museum showcasing the collection of Dom Carlos I, with taxidermy animals and skins on display; and an old Gothic chapel. Nearby is the cemetery where renowned Portuguese author Florbela Espanca (1894-1930) is buried. The walled fortress was home to the Bragança dynasty prior to the Ducal Palace being built. Wander the castle and its walls and museums, exploring its hidden tunnels and vaulted ceilings, as well as absorbing the views from the castle walls over pretty Vila Viçosa.

Food

TAVERNA DOS CONJURADOS

Largo 25 de Abril 16; tel. 268 989 530; www.
facebook.com/Tavernadosconjurados; Tues.-Thurs.
7:30pm-10pm, Fri.-Sun. noon-3pm and 7:30pm-10pm;
€20

A family-run eatery just a stone's throw from the Ducal Palace, Taverna dos Conjurados prides itself on serving traditional regional fare made from local farm produce and recipes handed down over generations. Unusual dishes like *cabeça de xara* (head cheese) feature on the menu. The building dates back to 1512 and still retains a number of original features, including the exposed schist walls, brick arches, and domed ceiling.

ADEGA 7160

Rua Cristóvão de Brito Pereira 12; tel. 268 094
862; www.facebook.com/adega7160; Tues.-Sat.
11:30am-1am, Sun. 11:30am-3pm; €20

Adega 7160 showcases the flavors of Vila Viçosa with a modern twist. It's a small restaurant dominated by huge wine barrels, and the menu is limited to a select few regional dishes and a tapas selection, executed beautifully with fresh ingredients. Among the mains are *carne de porco à alentejana,* pork cheeks, *migas,* and regional cheeses and cured meats, complemented by homemade jams and chutneys.

Accommodations

MARMORIS HOTEL

Largo Gago Coutinho no.11; tel. 268 887 010; www.
alentejomarmoris.com; €150-200

Designed to showcase the luxury of Portuguese marble, Marmoris Hotel is a marble masterpiece. This exquisite boutique hotel boasts a sumptuous spa and excellent on-site restaurant. Staying here is a highlight of any visit to the region.

Getting There

Vila Viçosa is 70 kilometers (43 mi) northeast of **Évora** and 27 kilometers (17 mi) southeast of **Estremoz.** As with many of the little towns and villages skirting Évora, the easiest way to

reach Vila Viçosa is by rental car. From Évora, follow the **N245** road for 50 minutes, or take the **N4** and **N255** from Estremoz, around 35 minutes.

Rodalentejo (tel. 266 738 120; www.rodalentejo.pt) buses make at least three journeys a day between Estremoz and Vila Viçosa (30 minutes; €2-4). There are at least two direct daily **Rede Expressos** (tel. 707 223 344; www.rede-expressos.pt) buses from Lisbon's Sete Rios terminal (2.5-3.75 hours; from €14.30), with some trips making more stops. The bus stops in Vila Viçosa on the western fringe of town, a 10-minute walk from the center.

★ ELVAS

The grandly titled Garrison Border Town of Elvas sits on a hilltop above the Guadiana River 15 kilometers (9.3 mi) from Badajoz, Spain. The town is flanked by lush plains and is renowned for olives and plums, brandy, and pottery, as well as for the iconic star-shaped fortified bulwarks that make the area famous. Despite its grandiose title and reputation for being the most fortified town in Portugal, wrapped in moats, bastions, and strapping curtains of walls, Elvas is in fact tranquil and sleepy. Elvas has charming churches, quaint streets, a pretty café-flanked main square, and good restaurants. It's one of Portugal's few remaining undiscovered treasures, but it can get extremely hot in the height of summer.

Sights

ELVAS WALLS
(Muralhas de Elvas)

surrounding Elvas town

A UNESCO World Heritage Site since 2012, Elvas's fortification complex is an outstanding example of *trace italienne* (star fort) military architecture and has a large bulwarked dry-ditch system. The unique star-shaped walls were heavily fortified in the 17th-19th centuries. A solid band of ramparts and

---

1: Santa Luzia Fort seen from over the defensive walls of Elvas **2:** view of the old town of Elvas

moats with gates and bastions protected the historic town. Unlike the residents in other walled towns, Elvas's community remained within the walls rather than relocating outside them. This fortification complex is excellently restored.

ELVAS CASTLE
(Castelo de Elvas)
Rua da Parada do Castelo 4-8; tel. 268 626 403; www.cm-elvas.pt/municipio; Tues.-Sun. 9:30am-5:30pm; €2 to climb castle walls
Peering over Elvas from the highest point in town, this solid and square Moorish castle was rebuilt from a former Roman garrison in the 13th and 14th centuries. The castle itself is small, but the views of the plains surrounding the town are second to none. Take 15 minutes to stroll the castle walls and drink in the views.

AMOREIRA AQUEDUCT
(Aqueduto da Amoreira)
Estrada Nacional No. 4 (EN4)
Towering over Elvas outside the city walls is the massive 16th-century Amoreira Aqueduct, which took over 100 years to complete (1498-1622), designed by architect Francisco de Arruda. The town's water is still delivered by the trellis-like conduit, which in some places looks like an extension of Elvas's walls and at points reaches four stories high, one arch on top of another. Elongating like a chunky knitted ribbon between two hills, the impressive aqueduct has a total of 843 arches, stretching 8 kilometers (5 mi) southwest of the city, and is one of Portugal's five most notable water conduits.

SANTA LUZIA FORT
(Forte de Santa Luzia)
Monte de Santa Luzia; tel. 268 628 357; Tues.-Sun. 10am-6pm; €2
Daintier and prettier than Elvas's other strapping fortifications, this small fort is a short walk south of Elvas town, with fancy star-shaped walls. The fort itself was constructed 1643-1648.

OUR LADY OF GRACE FORT
(Forte da Nossa Senhora da Graça)
tel. 268 625 228; Tues.-Sun. 10am-5:30pm; €5, with guided tour €8
Elvas has two outlying forts on opposite sides of town—the Santa Luzia Fort (Forte de Santa Luzia), within walking distance south of town, and, slightly farther afield on a hilltop to the north, the larger Our Lady of Grace Fort. Built in 1763 and officially known as Conde de Lippe Fort, the Our Lady of Grace Fort is one of Elvas's most distinctive bulwarks, a 10-pointed site in the hamlet of Alcazaba, 1 kilometer (0.6 mi) north of Elvas. Surrounded by a moat, the monumental main entrance to the fort is known as "Dragon's Gate." Even though it's not a long walk from the town to the fort, it might be easier to drive there as it's mostly uphill.

Getting There
Elvas is remote but easily accessible with regular bus services from both Lisbon and Évora. It's is an 84-kilometer (52-mi) drive (1 hour) northeast from **Évora** on the **A6** motorway. From **Estremoz,** it's a 40-kilometer (25-mi) drive (40 minutes) east on the **N4** road.

ELVAS BUS STATION
Rua do Património 1; tel. 268 622 875
Rede Expressos (tel. 707 223 344; www.rede-expressos.pt) runs buses between Évora and Elvas (1.5 hours; €12) around four times daily, usually from 1:45pm. From the Sete Rios bus station in Lisbon, there are seven buses 8:30am-7:30pm daily to Elvas (3.25 hours; €17.50). Buses run between Estremoz and Elvas (45 minutes; €8.50) five times daily. **Rodoviária do Alentejo** (tel. 266 738 120; www.rodalentejo.pt) offers similar service between Estremoz and Elvas (1 hour; €3-6). The bus station is just south of the town, outside the city walls; a taxi costs around €6.

São Mamede Mountain Range Natural Park

Sprawling over 29,694 hectares (115 sq mi) of northeastern Alentejo, the São Mamede Mountain Range Natural Park (Parque Natural da Serra de São Mamede) is a stark contrast to the gentle plains of the region, a mix of bizarrely shaped quartzite peaks scattered with chestnut trees and Pyrenean oaks, cork oaks, Holm oaks, and olive groves. The highest peak south of the Tagus River is here, at 1,025 meters (3,363 ft), and the range has its own microclimate. The park is home to rarely spotted birds of prey such as the vulture, kite, and Bonelli's eagle (symbol of the park); wild boars and deer; and historic whitewashed villages, which serve as the bases for exploring the park. Well-signed hiking trails, many of which can also be done on a mountain bike, are open year-round, and a section of the park is set up for experienced rock climbers; check with the park office.

PORTALEGRE

In the São Mamede Mountain Range Natural Park in northeastern Alentejo, charming whitewashed Portalegre is the biggest city in the region and makes for a good base to explore a cluster of fortified hilltop villages and rural hamlets. as the town also houses the central office for the park. A textile powerhouse in the 15th century and renowned for tapestries, silk cloth, and religious tableaux, faded and humble Portalegre provides glimpses of more affluent times in the once-grand Baroque facades of worn mansions and elegant main streets. Much of the old town is still embraced by city walls, but the newer part of Portalegre and its pretty **Rossio Square** are a more modern hub of transport terminals and apartment blocks.

Sights
PORTALEGRE CATHEDRAL
(Catedral de Portalegre)
Praça do Município; tel. 245 309 480; www. portalegre-castelobranco.pt; Wed.-Sun. 8:15am-noon and 2:30pm-6pm, Tues. 8:15am-noon; free
The majestic little Portalegre Cathedral is on the main square, **Praça do Município.** Construction started in the mid-1500s and took two centuries to complete. Two pointy bell towers, vaulted arches, and exposed brick give the cathedral an austere, almost military look. Inside, it is packed with more than 90 mannerist paintings. As with many religious sites, it is built on the highest point of the city and can be seen from afar.

TAPESTRY MUSEUM
(Museu de Tapeçarias)
Rua da Figueira 9; tel. 245 307 530; Tues.-Sun. 9am-1pm and 2pm-6pm; €2
Tapestry was once a flourishing industry in Portalegre and remains a traditional artisanal craft. The Tapestry Museum is a hidden gem with a marvelous collection of labor-intensive tapestries, explaining the history of the craft and the work. The building is a modern wood and glass structure with exhibits marked in English throughout. A video is available, as is a guided **tour** in English (on request; extra fee).

SANTA CLARA CONVENT
(Convento Santa Clara)
Rua de Elvas 54; tel. 245 307 520; www.biblioteca. cm-portalegre.pt; Mon.-Fri. 10am-1pm and 2pm-6pm, Sat. 3pm-6pm; free
Santa Clara Convent was built on the orders of Queen Leonor Teles in the 14th century, and then added on to over successive centuries. Only the cloister preserves the original features, the centerpiece of which is a

ÉVORA AND THE ALENTEJO
SÃO MAMEDE MOUNTAIN RANGE NATURAL PARK

São Mamede Mountain Range Natural Park

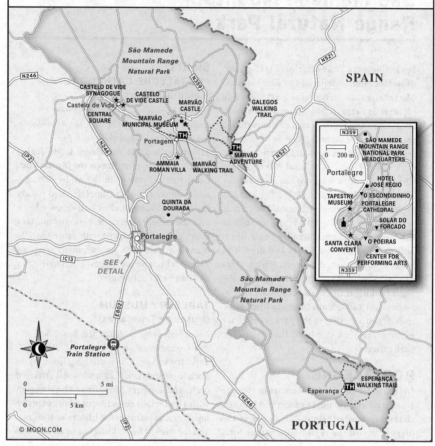

solid-marble Baroque fountain. The convent currently houses the city's library.

Hiking
ESPERANÇA WALKING TRAIL
(PR1 ARR Percurso da Esperança)

Hiking Distance: *16-kilometer (10-mi) loop*
Hiking Time: *5.5 hours round-trip*
Trailhead: *Casario da Esperança (Esperança House), Esperança Parish*
Information and Maps: *www. portuguesetrails.com/en/routes/alentejo-feel-nature/ pr1-arr-percurso-da-esperanca*

This rather long loop trail, located a 40-minute drive south of Pontalegre, showcases the upper Alentejo's wild nature in all its unbridled glory. It sees the landscape transition from smooth rippling plains to the jagged peaks and troughs of the São Mamede mountain range. Going over a stream and through mountains where some of the largest cork oaks in the region are found, it finally snakes its way back around to flatter ground.

Entertainment and Events
CENTER FOR PERFORMING ARTS
(Centro de Artes e Espetáculo de Portalegre)

Praça da República 39; tel. 245 307 498; http:// caeportalegre.blogspot.pt
The city's Center for Performing Arts showcases performances of all types, from fado to rock and jazz.

CONVENTUAL SWEETS FAIR
Throughout Portalegre, 1st or 2nd weekend in Apr.
The annual Conventual Sweets Fair showcases traditional sweets that originated in the country's convents. It is usually staged in some of the city's several convents and monasteries.

Food
SOLAR DO FORCADO
Rua Cândido dos Reis 14; tel. 245 330 866; Mon.-Fri. 12:30pm-3:30pm and 7pm-10:30pm, Sat. 7pm-10:30pm; €10
Cozy and casual Solar do Forcado serves traditional regional dishes that showcase the best of the Alentejo's meats and wines. Dark woods and exposed brick arches add to the rural feel.

O ESCONDIDINHO
Travessa das Cruzes 13; tel. 967 419 084; lunch and dinner; €10
Tucked away on a backstreet in the center of Portalegre, unassuming, cozy little O Escondidinho offers hearty helpings of home-cooked Portuguese fare with local cheeses and desserts, served on traditional earthenware crockery.

★ O POEIRAS
Praça da República 9-15; tel. 245 201 862; Tues.-Sat. 9:30am-9:30pm, Sun. 10am-3.30pm; €10
In the heart of Portalegre's historic center, friendly, upscale tavern O Poeiras serves tasty local and regional specialties, such as pork *à Alentejana* and roast leg of lamb, as well as a range of vegan options.

Accommodations
QUINTA DA DOURADA
Hamlet of Ribeira de Nisa; tel. 937 218 654; www. quintadadourada.pt; €65
Nestled in the heart of the São Mamede Natural Park a few kilometers out of Portalegre, Quinta da Dourada is a delightfully rustic farmhouse-style hotel with a warm and welcoming interior and a refreshing outdoor pool.

HOTEL JOSÉ RÉGIO
Largo António José Lourinho 1-5; tel. 245 009 190; www.hoteljoseregio.com; €70
With one of the best locations in Portalegre, a short walk from all of the city's main sights and overlooking a lovely fountain and gardens, modern-looking Hotel José Régio is practical and plush in equal measures. It is inspired by one of Portalegre's most famous sons, writer José Régio.

Information and Services
SÃO MAMEDE MOUNTAIN RANGE NATURAL PARK HEADQUARTERS
Rua Augusto Cesar Oliveira Tavares 23, Portalegre; tel. 245 309 189; www.icnf.pt
Located in Portalegre, the headquarters for the park's management will be able to provide all information on what to see in the park, its flora and fauna, and which trails to follow. There is good signage and markers throughout the park.

Getting There
By car from **Lisbon**, Portalegre is a 230-kilometer (143-mi), 2.5-hour journey northeast on the **A1** and **A23** motorways. From **Estremoz**, Portalegre is a 57-kilometer (35-mi), 45-minute drive north on the **IP2** road. From **Évora**, it's a 1-hour 15-minute drive (103 km/64 mi) northeast along the **A6** motorway and IP2 road.

There are six **Rede Expressos** (tel. 707 223 344; www.rede-expressos.pt) buses daily between Lisbon's Sete Rios station and Portalegre (3.5-4 hours; €14.70), with stops in other main cities in the region such as Elvas, Évora, and Estremoz. The bus terminal in Portalegre is near Rossio Square in the new town.

PORTALEGRE TRAIN STATION
Portalegre Gare, Urra parish; tel. 707 210 220; www.cp.pt
At least three **CP** (tel. 707 210 220; www.cp.pt)

1

2

trains run daily from Lisbon's Oriente station to Portalegre (3.5-4.25 hours; €13.85-27.40), ranging from the slower regional train to the faster Intercity train. The train station in Portalegre is 12 kilometers (7.4 mi) south of the center, requiring a taxi or bus ride; both serve the station. A taxi (tel. 245 202 375 or 245 201 380 or 245 203 842 or 245 204 694) from the station into Portalegre takes about 10 minutes and should cost no more than €15 one-way. There is one bus a day from Portalegre train station into the city, which leaves around noon, takes about 30 minutes, and costs just a few euros.

MARVÃO

Marvão (mar-VOWN) is a magical little hilltop village on the highest crest of the São Mamede mountain range. Fortified by encircling walls, some of which date to the 13th century, the village is the prettiest in the Alentejo, with tangled narrow streets and typical Alentejano houses with Gothic arches, Manueline windows, and wrought-iron balconies. In summer the village's intrinsic cragginess is cheered up with bright flowers and stunning sunrises and sunsets. Visit Marvão for its **chestnut festival** (www.facebook.com/pages/category/Festival/Feira-da-Castanha-Marvão-397190517017242; usually Nov. 14-15), one of the most authentic chestnut celebrations in the country, when the roasting nuts, smoking chimneys, and winter mist enshroud the village in a mythical aura.

Sights
MARVÃO CASTLE
(Castelo de Marvão)

tel. 245 909 138; www.cm-marvao.pt; 10am-5pm daily; €1.50

The 13th-century Marvão Castle sits atop the 900-meter (2,953-ft) granite peak, with views of the Alentejo plains toward Spain. As Portuguese Nobel laureate writer José Saramago said, "From Marvão one can see the entire land." An austere medieval structure,

---

1: Portalegre Cathedral 2: Marvão Castle

Marvão Castle has thick granite walls that encircle most of the village, except in the east, where the village extends outside. Inside the castle walls are two cisterns and a tall central keep, from which the views are even more astounding. The castle also conceals a cistern chamber that has become a popular wishing well. To the side of the castle are peaceful manicured gardens that add vibrant green and seasonal color to the rocky landscape.

MARVÃO MUNICIPAL MUSEUM
(Museu Municipal de Marvão)

Travessa de Santa Maria; tel. 245 909 132; www.cm-marvao.pt; daily 10am-12:30pm and 1:30pm-5pm; €1.90

Housed inside the whitewashed 14th-century church is the Marvão Municipal Museum. Most of the artifacts on display, from armor to religious art, were donated by locals, giving the exhibition a homegrown feel. In spring the gardens surrounding the church and the castle add color to the mountainous scenery.

AMMAIA ROMAN VILLA
(Cidade Romana de Ammaia)

São Salvador de Aramenha; tel. 245 919 089; Mon.-Fri. 9am-1pm and 2pm-5pm, Sat.-Sun. 10am-1pm and 2pm-5pm; €2

In the heart of the São Mamede mountain range is the Ammaia Roman Villa, the outstanding ruins of a 1st-century town. Among the ruins are a residence, a forum, a temple, parts of a public bath, and the remains of arch doorways and towers. The most interesting artifacts are jewelry, coins, and glassware, displayed in the on-site museum. Ammaia is between Marvão and Castelo de Vide, in São Salvador de Aramenha.

Hiking
MARVÃO WALKING TRAIL
(PR2 MRV Percurso Pedestre de Marvão)

Hiking Distance: *8-kilometer (5-mi) loop*
Hiking Time: *2-3 hours round-trip*
Trailhead: *Almas Square, Portagem parish*
Information and Maps: *www.walkingportugal.*

☆ Castles of The Alentejo

The Alentejo is awash with glorious castles and citadels. Some lie in ruins, just shells of their former selves, others have been given a new purpose, occupied by the likes of boutique hotels, and some stand in their full well-preserved medieval glory.

The Upper Alentejo region, whose eastern outer edge forms a border with neighboring Spain, was prime territory for a natural line of defense, protecting Portugal from invasions. Being more mountainous than the open rolling plains of the lower Alentejo, this corner of the region lent itself perfectly to building castles, high on craggy peaks overlooking the land beyond. Many of Portugal's most magnificent fortresses and fortified towns are in this region, in towns like Castelo de Vide, Marvão, and Monsaraz, whose castles and lands witnessed savage and historic battles.

the climb to Castelo de Vide Castle

IF YOU LIKE...

· **Great views:** Often built at the highest point in a town or village, castles usually boast great views, but **Monsaraz Castle**'s panoramic views take the cake (page 150).

· **Dramatic keeps:** The tower of **Estremoz Castle** is regarded as one of the most impressive in Portugal (page 153).

· **Fascinating history:** The museums and cemetery of **Vila Viçosa Castle** make it especially primed for a history lesson (page 157).

· **Making wishes:** The cistern of **Marvão Castle** has become a well-known wishing well (page 165).

· **Hiking:** It's a healthy climb up to the ruins of **Castelo de Vide Castle** (page 168).

· **Fabulous marble: Beja Castle** showcases the material that made much of the region prosperous (page 170).

· **Moorish culture:** An exhibit on Moorish relics in **Mértola Castle** highlights their cultural impact on this village (page 173).

com/z_distritos_portugal/Portalegre/Marvao/MRV_PR2_Percurso_Pedestre_de_Marvao.html

This nature-rich pedestrian trail takes hikers through the dramatic scenery distinctive of this corner of Portugal, passing escarpments and cliffs, valleys and ravines, and dense forests of oak and chestnut trees. It also passes through narrow cobbled streets of medieval hamlets that time forgot, where the only sounds are the pealing of bells and birdsong.

GALEGOS WALKING TRAIL
(PR2 MRV Percurso Pedestre de Galegos)

Hiking Distance: 11.5-kilometer (7.1-mi) loop

Hiking Time: 4.5 hours round-trip

Trailhead: Galegos Parish, Largo da Ponte Square, near the bus stop

Information and Maps: www.portuguesetrails.com/pt-pt/routes/alentejo-feel-nature/pr2-mrv-percurso-pedestre-de-galegos

As this route alternates between footpaths and dirt roads, the historic walls of Marvão town are a constant companion in the distance. You'll pass through beautiful landscapes dominated by large, rough chunks of granite, in parts swaddled in thick coverings of cork oaks, chestnut trees, oaks, olive trees, and fragrant tufts of lavender and rosemary. There is little shade on this route, which means hats and water are a must if you're planning to walk in hot weather.

Mountain Climbing
MARVÃO ADVENTURE

Monte de Cima - Galegos; tel. 966 496 940; www. marvaoadventure.com; climbing from €28.50

Inject some action and adrenalin into your time in Marvão and contact adventure sports specialists Marvão Adventure for mountain or rock climbing. Expert guides will ensure you enjoy a different side to the region, in safety and comfort.

Getting There

Marvão is 21 kilometers (13 mi) northeast of **Portalegre,** most easily visited by car via the **N359** road, a 30-minute drive.

Public transport to Marvão is unreliable, but there are one or two buses daily from Portalegre (1 hour; €6) with **Rodalentejo** (tel. 245 330 096; www.rodalentejo.pt). **Rede Expressos** (tel. 707 223 344; www.rede-expressos.pt) runs one bus between Portalegre and Marvão (35 minutes, 11:15am daily; €6).

CASTELO DE VIDE

Twenty minutes northwest of Marvão is the enchanting fortified town of Castelo de Vide, unspoiled and charismatic yet not heavily visited. It is famous for the sparkling spring water in the decorative village fountain. Life in Castelo de Vide has changed little over the years. The town covers a sloped foothill in the São Mamede mountain range, a huddle of whitewashed town houses and red roofs with the main church in the middle and more than two dozen other churches among the village's cobbled streets. At the top is a 14th-century castle that overlooks the village and its surroundings. Given the town's overall natural beauty and numinous ambience, it is dubbed the "Sintra of the Alentejo." The imposing castle and the Jewish Quarter are reason enough to spend a few hours in town, which can be comfortably explored on foot.

village fountain in Castelo de Vide

Sights

Wedged between the local market square and the 16th-century marble and granite Renaissance **village fountain** (Fonte de Villa), surrounded by columns and statues, is Castelo de Vide's beautiful **Jewish Quarter** (Judiaria de Castelo de Vide), home to the oldest synagogue in Portugal, with sculpted Jewish symbols on doorposts and Jewish street names.

Contrasting with Castelo de Vide's gentle beauty is the somber 16th-century village pillory (*pelourinho*), a stone column atop four octagonal steps in the middle of a picturesque plaza known as the **Praça Central,** or Praça D. Pedro V, in front of the local prison and clock tower, where offenders were publicly shamed or punished.

CASTELO DE VIDE CASTLE
(Castelo de Castelo de Vide)

Santa Maria da Devassa parish; tel. 245 908 220; www.castelodevide.pt; daily 9am-5pm; free

Clinging to the mountainside, what's left of the once-handsome quadrangular 14th-century medieval fortress Castelo de Vide Castle almost blends in with its surroundings. The strategically important castle was built in 1310 by order of Dom Dinis. To get to the castle from the town, you have to climb many steep steps, along quaint streets lined with historic houses and little shops. Today the castle is in need of repair, but its ruins and battlements are open for exploration. Inside there is also a little exhibit on the Portuguese Inquisition. Panoramic views from the castle extend to the Spanish border.

CASTELO DE VIDE SYNAGOGUE
(Sinagoga de Castelo de Vide)

Rua da Fonte; tel. 245 908 220; daily 9:30am-1pm and 2:30pm-6pm

In the heart of the Jewish Quarter is this former synagogue. The 12th-century home was converted in the 14th century into a temple, which also served as a school and a social meeting point. It reverted to a private residence in the 16th century when the Jews were expelled from Portugal. At the corner of Rua da Judiaria and the fountain street, the synagogue is now an evocative museum of Castelo de Vide's Jewish history and the persecution of Jews by the Inquisition.

Getting There

Castelo de Vide is 12.5 kilometers (7.8 mi) northwest of **Marvão,** a 15-minute drive on the **N246-1** and **N359** roads. **Rede Expressos** (tel. 707 223 344; www.rede-expressos.pt) buses run at least once daily between Marvão and Castelo de Vide (15 minutes, mid-afternoon daily; €5-7).

Beja and Around

Occupying a commanding position on a 277-meter (909-ft) hill, the city of Beja (BAY-zhah) is a rural hub with roots in the fertile plains surrounding it. From its earliest days it has been a strategic, important location. Beja was named Pax Julia by Julius Caesar in 48 BC, when he made peace with the Lusitanians and raised the town to capital status. During the reign of Augustus, the prosperous town, by then an established strategic junction, was renamed Pax Augusta. The largest city in the lower Alentejo, Beja is not as famous, grand, or monument-laden as Évora, but it has countrified simplicity.

From a distance Beja is a whitewashed cluster that looms above the surrounding golden plains, its skyline dominated by a statuesque medieval castle with a large tower. It is also infamously the hottest district capital in Portugal. Great restaurants, boutiques, and pretty squares await in its labyrinth of cobbled streets.

The area surrounding Beja is an immensity

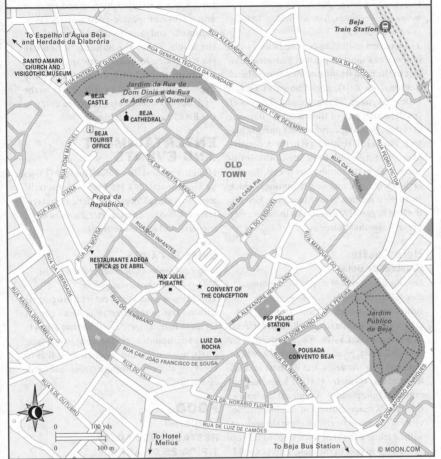

Beja

of flat, rolling plains, peppered with tranquil whitewashed hamlets, grazing cows, and historic towns like medieval Mértola. Unlike the upper Alentejo, attractions here are fewer and farther between, but you'll find plenty of affordable accommodation and excellent coastal towns.

SIGHTS

Most of Beja's monuments are in the historic **Old Town.** A cluster of splendid buildings, including the cathedral and castle, surround the city's main cobbled square, the **Praça da República.**

Beja Cathedral
(Catedral de Beja)

Largo do Lidador 7; tel. 284 388 196; www. diocese-beja.pt; daily 10am-noon and 3pm-7pm; free

Beja Cathedral, known locally as the Sé, was built in 1590 on the site of an earlier church dedicated to Saint James the Great. Mannerist in style and currently the seat of the Diocese of Beja, the cathedral is one of the oldest in the area.

Convent of the Conception
(Convento da Conceição)

Largo da Conceição; tel. 284 323 351; www. museuregionaldebeja.pt; Tues.-Sun. 9:30am-12:30pm and 2pm-5:15pm; €2

The Convent of the Conception houses some of the area's most important historical arti-fact in the **Beja Regional Museum** (Museu Regional de Beja), also known as Queen Leonor Museum (Museu Rainha D. Leonor). Inside, a rich mix of tiled plaques, Baroque carvings, paintings, and statues provide his-tory. The palatial building is in the decorative Manueline style with some late Gothic influ-ences, such as the flamboyant portal, double-arched windows, and lacy trimmings, which mark the transition to the Manueline. Entry to the Beja Regional Museum also includes entry to the Visigothic Museum.

Beja Castle
(Castelo de Beja)

Rua Dom Dinis 3; tel. 284 311 913; www.cm-beja.pt; daily 9:30am-12:30pm and 2pm-6pm; free

Built on the orders of Dom Dinis, a 14th-century king, on the site of a Roman fortress, imposing Beja Castle appears tired even though it is well preserved. Sections have been repaired over the years, but its most famous feature, the 40-meter (131-ft) keep, has re-tained its full splendor. A regional landmark, the keep is made entirely of marble. Inside, visitors can roam freely, ambling the walls at will, or climb a flight of worn steps to the top of the keep to take in the view. This is a solid, old-fashioned castle that is fun to visit.

Santo Amaro Church and Visigothic Museum
(Igreja de Santo Amaro e Museu Visigotico)

Largo de Santo Amaro 26-27; tel. 284 321 465; www. museuregionaldebeja.pt; Tues.-Sun. 9:45am-12:30pm and 2pm-5pm; €2

Adjacent to Beja Castle is 4th-century Santo Amaro Church, one of only a hand-ful of preserved Visigoth churches in the country and one of just four churches in

Portugal that date to the Roman era. A rare example of Paleo-Christian architec-ture, it has a simple whitewashed exterior and a trove of mosaic-tiled walls, carved columns, and motif-covered capitals on the inside. Today the building is home to the Visigothic Museum, with artifacts dat-ing from the 5th-8th centuries, among them tombstones and swords. Entry to the Visigothic Museum also includes entry to the Beja Regional Museum.

ENTERTAINMENT AND EVENTS

Head to the local **Pax Júlia Theater** (Largo de São João; tel. 284 315 090; http://paxjuli-ateatromunicipal.blogspot.pt) for cultural rec-reation, like dance and theater shows, musical concerts, and movie screenings.

OVIBEJA FAIR

Campo da Feira, Rua Cidade de São Paulo, 36; tel. 284 249 024; www.ovibeja.pt; late Apr.

The biggest and most entertaining agri-cultural fair in the country is Beja's annual OviBeja Fair, a five-day event that attracts tens of thousands to see the latest in farm an-imals, machinery, and products as well as to enjoy nightly entertainment, regional food, and drink.

FOOD
Regional
RESTAURANTE ADEGA TÍPICA 25 DE ABRIL

Rua da Moeda 23; tel. 284 325 960; Mon.-Sat. noon-3pm and 7pm-10pm, Sun. noon-3pm; €10

Tavern-style Restaurante Adega Típica 25 de Abril offers traditional local and Portuguese specialties in a cozy, rustic environment. The grilled black pork is delicious.

★ LUIZ DA ROCHA

Rua Capitão João F. Sousa 63; tel. 284 323 179; www.luizdarocha.com; Mon.-Sat. 8am-11pm, Sun. 8am-8pm; €12

In this well-known, century-old restaurant and café in the heart of Beja, art and regional gastronomy go hand in hand. Traditional convent sweets fill the cabinets, while colorful tile murals depicting life in the Alentejo clad the walls. Specialties include Alentejo-style pork, *açorda* (soaked bread with garlic), and *ensopado de borrego* (lamb stew).

ESPELHO D'ÁGUA BEJA
Rua de Lisboa, City Park; tel. 284 325 103; www. espelhodagua.com.sapo.pt; Tues.-Sun. noon-3:30pm and 7:30pm-11pm; €15

Hidden away in the corner of a public park, contemporary Portuguese cuisine restaurant Espelho d'Água Beja overlooks a waterfall and a lake. Modern and light menu items include fresh fish, tapas for sharing, and typical Alentejo specialties.

Fine Dining
CONVENTO BEJA
Largo D. Nuno Alveres Pereira; tel. 284 313 580; www.pousadas.pt; daily 1pm-3pm and 7:30pm-10pm; €25

Inside the luxury Pousada Convento hotel, once a refectory for the Franciscan friars, elegant, airy restaurant Pousada Convento Beja has high walls and vaulted ceilings. It offers a classic fine-dining experience based on fresh seasonal local produce and regional specialties.

ACCOMMODATIONS
Under €100
HOTEL MELIUS
Av. Fialho de Almeida; tel. 284 313 080; www. hotelmelius.pt; €64

The large, clean, and comfortable four-star Hotel Melius, on the edge of the city, has a fitness center and a snack bar.

HERDADE DA DIABRÓRIA
N121; tel. 284 998 177; www.diabroria.com; €70

On the outskirts of Beja, 6 kilometers (3.7 mi) northwest of the center, near the brand-new and largely unused international airport, Herdade da Diabrória is a tranquil, rural Alentejano refuge amid wheat and sunflower fields. This agritourism hotel was converted from a 300-hectare (741-acre) hacienda with an enormous lake at its heart.

€100-200
POUSADA CONVENTO BEJA
Largo D. Nuno Álvares Pereira; tel. 284 313 580; www.pousadas.pt; from €155

Converted from a historic 13th-century convent, the upscale Pousada Convento Beja is set amid extensive manicured grounds in the heart of Beja, a 10-minute walk to the castle.

INFORMATION AND SERVICES

- **Beja Tourist Office:** Largo Dr. Lima Faleiro 1, in the castle square; tel. 284 311 913; daily 9:30am-12:30pm and 2pm-6pm

- **Main post office:** Rua Diogo Gouveia; tel. 284 311 270

- **PSP police station:** Rua Dom Nuno Álvares Pereira; tel. 284 313 150; www.psp.pt

- **Beja Hospital:** Rua Dr. António Fernando Covas Lima; tel. 284 310 200

GETTING THERE

From **Évora,** Beja is 82 kilometers (51 mi) south, under 2 hours on the **IP2** road. It's is 178 kilometers (110 mi) southeast of **Lisbon,** under 2 hours on the **A2** motorway and the **IP8** road. From anywhere in **the Algarve,** take the **A22** motorway to the A2 and the IP2, a 1.5-hour trip.

There is frequent bus and train transport between Beja and Lisbon. Buses are easier, as the train trip requires a transfer.

Train
BEJA TRAIN STATION
Largo da Estação, Largo da Estaçao 17; tel. 707 210 220; www.cp.pt

By train, **CP** (tel. 707 210 220; www.cp.pt) operates four Intercity trains (2 hours, 7:10am, 9:10am, 5:10pm, and 7:10pm daily; 2nd class €14, 1st class €17) between Lisbon's Entrecampos station and the train station in Beja, which is a 10-minute walk east of the city

center. There are four daily trains from Évora to Beja (2.25 hours; €7.40 one-way), two early in the morning and two in the afternoon.

Bus
BEJA BUS STATION
Rua General Humberto Delgado 44; tel. 284 313 620

Rede Expressos (tel. 707 223 344; www.rede-expressos.pt) runs a dozen daily buses between Lisbon's Sete Rios station and Beja (3 hours; €13.30). From Évora, there are nine daily Rede Expressos express buses (1.25 hours; €7.60). The bus station in Beja is a short 600-meter (0.4-mi) walk south of the historic center.

MÉRTOLA

Built on a jagged knoll where the Guadiana River converges with the Oeiras stream, Mértola is situated in the heart of the **Guadiana Valley Natural Park** (Parque Natural do Vale do Guadiana) in the southeastern Alentejo on the border with Spain. The town is a postcard-perfect vision of hodgepodge quaint whitewashed cottages on the rocky mound, with Mértola Castle at its peak. Like many Alentejo border towns, Mértola is ringed by the long arms of its castle. The town's main church was originally a mosque.

Sights
MÉRTOLA CASTLE
(Castelo de Mértola)
Largo da Igreja; tel. 286 610 100; www.museus. cm-mertola.pt; Tues.-Sun. 9:15am-12:30pm and 2pm-5:30pm; castle free, museum €2

The 13th-century medieval Mértola Castle towers over Castro Verde at the highest point, a 600-meter (0.4-mi) walk south from the center. The centerpiece is a 30-meter-high (98-ft-high) keep that houses two exhibitions, one on the castle's history and the other on Moorish relics. From the top of the keep are sweeping views over the Guadiana River.

1: Beja Castle **2:** Church of Our Lady of the Annunciation

CHURCH OF OUR LADY OF THE ANNUNCIATION
(Igreja da Nossa Senhora da Anunciação)
Rua da Igreja; tel. 286 610 100; Tues.-Sun. 9:30am-12:30pm and 2pm-5:30pm Oct.-June, Tues.-Sun. 9:30am-12:30pm and 2pm-6pm July-Sept.; free

Mértola's main church, the Church of Our Lady of the Annunciation, was formerly a mosque, converted to Christianity in the 13th century by the Knights of Saint James. It is believed to be the only church in Portugal that retained its Moorish appearance after conversion. Just 100 meters (328 ft) west of the castle, the dazzling white building is a mix of architectural styles that give it a bit of a frilly wedding cake look. On an isolated spot on a hill below the castle, the church reveals its strong Moorish architectural roots in the keyhole-shaped doors and the mihrab in the wall behind the altar. It has a tiny **museum** in the basement, and the long, low interior is divided into five naves with a bright and airy feel. There is parking at the foot of the hill, but the short cobblestone road up can be challenging.

Getting There

Mértola is 53 kilometers (33 mi) southeast of **Beja,** 50 minutes' drive on the **IC27** road. Mértola is not accessible by train.

From Beja there are three local **Rodalentejo** (tel. 284 313 620; www.rodalentejo.pt) buses (1 hour, daily morning, lunchtime, and afternoon; €6.10) to Mértola. National bus company **Rede Expressos** (tel. 707 223 344; www.rede-expressos.pt) has at least one direct daily bus from Lisbon's Sete Rios station (3.5 hours, 5:15pm daily; €16.60). Rede Expressos has a direct service between the border town of Vila Real de Santo António, in the Algarve, and Mértola (1.25 hours; €10.50). Buses stop at Mertola's main bus station on Av. Aureliano Mira Fernandes (tel. 286 612 157), the main avenue through Mértola center.

Southwest Alentejo and Vicentine Coast Natural Park

Along Portugal's west coast between the Setúbal Peninsula's Sado River and the Algarve, the Alentejo's coastal region has natural beauty that's mostly safeguarded in the Southwest Alentejo and Vicentine Coast Natural Park (Parque Natural do Sudoeste Alentejano e Costa Vicentina). The park crosses into the Algarve, and in the Alentejo, it stretches between Odeceixe in the south and São Torpes in the north.

In summer, the Alentejo coast can get busy as Portuguese holidaymakers flock here in search of a calmer alternative to the frenzied Algarve. Its beauty rivals the Algarve's but is less manicured and less built-up. Outside summer, the pristine beaches backed by golden cliffs and the rugged landscape, dotted with pretty whitewashed villages and the odd wind turbine, offer rare peaceful isolation.

The Southwest Alentejo and Vicentine Coast Natural Park is one of the finest preserved coastlines in Europe. Rugged and wild, it spans 100 kilometers (62 mi) from Burgau in the Algarve to Porto Côvo in the Alentejo and is a magnet for scientists, who are drawn to its unique indigenous flora and fauna, including 700 species of flowers, a dozen of which exist only in the park. Also here are various orchids and unusual plant species such as *Biscutella vicentina, Cistus palhinhae,* and *Plantago almogravensis,* adapted to the limestone terrain and salty breeze. This diverse plant life attracts butterflies and 200 species of birds, including fishing eagles, choughs, and white storks, which nest in the cliffs.

The landscape is sheer, multicolored cliffs carpeted in plant life and bordered by beaches. A network of walking trails and scenic routes, including the **Vicentine Route** (www.rotavicentina.com), a web of designated coastal and countryside walking routes that spans the coast. The **Mira River,** which starts in the Caldeirão mountain range and snakes through Odemira, has a 30-kilometer (19-mi) stretch from Odemira to Vila Nova de Milfontes that has been made navigable for paddleboarding and canoeing.

ODEMIRA

The main point of entry to the Natural Park from the Alentejo is the town of Odemira, a sweet little hilltop town overlooking the Mira River on the edge of the natural park.

Hiking and Cycling

Odemira is a playground for outdoor enthusiasts, with prime terrain for hiking and cycling in the Southwest Alentejo and Vicentine Coast Natural Park. To explore Odemira's understated beauty and the unkempt charm of the Vicentine Coast by normal mountain bike or e-bike, visit **Algarve Bike** (Vale Juncal, Rogil; tel. 932 741 446; www.algarve-bike.com; daily 10am-8pm; from €15/day). Local outdoor activity company **Eco-Trails** (tel. 967 155 383; www.ecotrails.info) offers guided hiking (from €27) and canoe trips (from €20 pp) on the Mira River to explore nature in the gentlest way. A variety of canoe tours are available to suit all ages and energy levels. Horseback treks (€25 per hour), cycling, camping, and fishing trips (€20 pp for 2-3 hours) can also be arranged.

The **Vicentine Route (Rota Vicentina)** is well-marked, with its routes divided into 15- to 25-kilometer (9.3- to 15.5-mi) sections. Spring and autumn are the best times to do these walking trails, as summer is excessively hot and winter can be rainy and blustery.

Southwest Alentejo and Vicentine Coast Natural Park

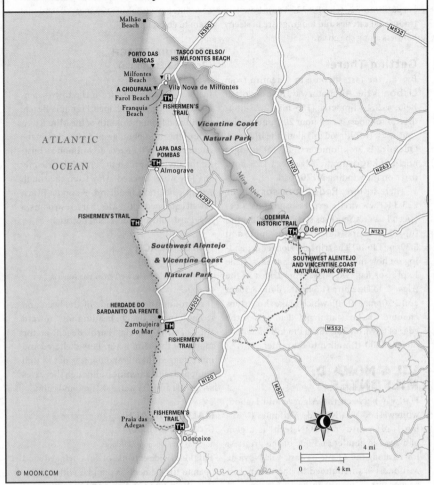

Malhão Beach

PORTO DAS BARCAS

TASCO DO CELSO/ HS MILFONTES BEACH

Milfontes Beach

A CHOUPANA

Vila Nova de Milfontes

Farol Beach

Franquia Beach

FISHERMEN'S TRAIL

Vicentine Coast Natural Park

ATLANTIC

OCEAN

LAPA DAS POMBAS

Almograve

Mira River

FISHERMEN'S TRAIL

ODEMIRA HISTORIC TRAIL

Odemira

Southwest Alentejo & Vicentine Coast Natural Park

SOUTHWEST ALENTEJO AND VICENTINE COAST NATURAL PARK OFFICE

HERDADE DO SARDANITO DA FRENTE

Zambujeira do Mar

FISHERMEN'S TRAIL

FISHERMEN'S TRAIL

Praia das Adegas

Odeceixe

0   4 mi

0   4 km

© MOON.COM

ODEMIRA HISTORIC TRAIL
(Caminho Histórico Odemira – São Teotónio)

Hiking Distance: *19-kilometer (12-mi) loop*
Hiking Time: *6 hours round-trip*
Trailhead: *Odemira gas station*
Information and Maps: *www. portuguesetrails.com/en/routes/rota-vicentina-alentejo-walking/caminho-historico-odemira-s-teotonio*

Feel like you've gone back in time as you explore the history of this tranquil part of the Alentejo, walking from Odemira to neighboring town São Teotónio. Follow the River Mira and the São Teotónio stream, through farming fields and eucalyptus forests, taking in unspoiled countryside as you go. This is one of the more accessible and family-friendly portions of the Rota Vicentina network of hiking routes.

Information and Services

Odemira is home to the **park's office** (Rua Serpa Pinto 32; tel. 283 322 735). Low-key traditional eateries and lodgings are in sleepy hamlets along the coast.

Getting There

By car, the fastest route to Odemira from **Lisbon** is the **A2** motorway, turning off at Beja, a 204-kilometer (126-mi), 2.25-hour drive. From Beja it's a 1-hour 20-minute drive southwest (107 km/66 mi) along the **IP2** road. Odemira is 76 kilometers (47 mi) straight north of **Lagos** in the Algarve, a 1.25-hour drive on the winding **N120** road.

There are three **Rede Expressos** (tel. 707 223 344; www.rede-expressos.pt) buses between Lisbon's Sete Rios station and Odemira (up to 4 hours, daily 7:30am, 3pm, and 5:30pm; €16.10) The trip takes longer depending on how many stops the bus makes. Rede Expressos has two buses from Lagos in the Algarve to Odemira (1.5 hours, daily 8:30am and 3:20pm; €10.50), which make three stops en route. The bus station in Odemira is on the edge of town, on Rua Souza Prado a short 400-meter (1,300-ft) walk into the center.

VILA NOVA DE MILFONTES

Halfway between the Algarve and Lisbon, whitewashed Vila Nova de Milfontes (VEE-lah NOH-vah d' mil-FON-tezh) is a gem of a seaside hamlet and one of the prettiest towns along the Alentejo coast. Vila Nova de Milfontes is surrounded by the distinctive rugged terrain of the Southwest Alentejo and Vicentine Coast Natural Park. Regulations governing the park mean that any development in the area has been kept subtle and in harmony with the landscape. For a place of such striking beauty, Vila Nova is overlooked by foreign visitors, but it is popular among Portuguese holidaymakers and comes to life during the peak July-August vacation season, when the local population soars. In other months it falls back into the region's characteristically unhurried pace.

★ Beaches

Vila Nova has excellent beaches, from small cove-like havens to vast expanses of sand that seem to go on forever.

FRANQUIA BEACH (Praia da Franquia)
Rua dos Medos

Just a 5-minute walk from the town's center is wide, crescent-shaped Franquia Beach, just inland from the mouth of the Mira River. One of the most photographed beaches in the Alentejo, it is Vila Nova de Milfontes's busiest thanks to its proximity and child-friendly shallow water, tucked away from the rough Atlantic behind a headland. Franquia Beach is well equipped with cafés, bars, restrooms, a lifeguard, and a canoe-rental outfitter.

FAROL BEACH (Praia do Farol)
Mira River north bank, west from Vila Nova de Milfontes

Just around the other side of the headland from Franquia Beach, heading west toward the coast, is popular Farol Beach, at the mouth of the Mira River. Less sheltered and more rugged than Franquia, it is not as well equipped with amenities, although the waves are gentle and the water shallow and calm.

MALHÃO BEACH (Praia do Malhão)
north of Vila Nova de Milfontes

This long, wide expanse of dune-fringed sand open to the elements is popular with surfers. It is also a windsurfing and kitesurfing hot spot, although there are no outfitters on the beach to rent equipment. In fact, the beach is unblemished, with zero development—no beachside restaurants or bars—but parking and access have been greatly improved in recent years, though access to the beach is limited to a beaten track with viewing decks and platforms. Malhão Beach is located 10 kilometers (6.2 mi) north of Vila Nova de Milfontes,

1: Vila Nova de Milfontes 2: Malhão Beach

a 15-minute drive on the N390 and CM1072 roads.

Surfing

There are quite a few surf schools in Vila Nova de Milfontes that offer year-round board rentals and lessons.

- **Surfmilfontes Surf School:** Rua António Mantas lote no. 41; tel. 926 900 891; https://surfmilfontes.pt; rentals from €20/day from store or €10/hour at the beach

Hiking
THE FISHERMEN'S TRAIL
(Rota dos Pescadores)
Hiking Distance: *220 kilometers (137 mi) one-way*
Hiking Time: *4 days one-way*
Trailhead: *São Torpes/Lagos*
Information and Maps: *https://rotavicentina.com/en/walking/fishermens-trail*

Sturdy shoes are needed for the demanding Fishermen's Trail, which follows the paths etched into the clifftops by centuries of local fisherfolk. Portuguese fishermen are famed for their fearlessness, and on this route you will understand why. Local anglers perch on jagged cliffs with the Atlantic crashing relentlessly below.

The Fishermen's Trail is a network of tracks that run parallel to the southern half of Portugal's coastline. The most emblematic stretch is the portion that connects São Torpes (Sines) in the north to Lagos (Algarve) in the south—approximately 90 kilometers (56 mi) of trail. It comprises four sections along the Alentejo coastline, plus a number of complementary circuits totaling 120 kilometers (74 mi) of walkable trail through popular and hidden fishing spots. The trail passes through Vila Nova de Milfontes on a 15-kilometer (9.3-mi) trail between Vila Nova and pretty Almograve below it. Go online (www.rotavicentina.com) for an exact map of the route.

LAPA DAS POMBAS
(ODM PR1 Lapa das Pombas)
Hiking Distance: *8.9-kilometer (5.5-mi) loop*
Hiking Time: *3.5 hours round-trip*
Trailhead: *Almograve village center*
Information and Maps: *www.walkingportugal.com/z_distritos_portugal/Beja/Odemira/ODM_PR1_Lapa_das_Pombas.html*

This is a nice coastal walk that runs from Almograve village center along Odemira coastline to the little Lapa das Pombas fishing port. This pleasant seaside walk weaves between cliffs and gazing pastures, the ocean on one hand and green fields on the other, showing off two distinct sides of the region.

Kayaking and Stand-up Paddleboarding

The area around Vila Nova de Milfontes is a great for kayaking and SUP. The translucent, slow-flowing waters of the Mira River are flanked by stunning scenery, making it an evocative and enchanting place to paddle. Another option is to follow the Vila Nova de Milfontes inlet from Franquia Beach up to the Vila Nova de Milfontes bridge.

- **SW SUP:** tel. 963 551 232; https://swsup.pt; from €15/hour

Food
PORTO DAS BARCAS
Estrada Canal; tel. 283 997 160; Wed.-Mon. noon-11pm; €15

On the outskirts of Vila Nova de Milfontes, bright and open, tastefully decorated Porto das Barcas is the place to enjoy creative fresh seafood dishes in classy surroundings with stunning views. It is a 6-minute drive (3 km/1.9 mi) north of town and an excellent spot to enjoy sunset with dinner.

A CHOUPANA
Praia do Farol; tel. 283 996 643; Tues.-Sun. 9am-10pm; €18

A Choupana, a little wooden beach shack on Farol Beach, offers fantastic grilled fresh fish and meats combined with ultimate beach views.

★ TASCO DO CELSO

*Rua dos Aviadores 34; tel. 283 996 753; www.
tascadocelso.com; Tues.-Sun. 11:30am-3pm and
7:30pm-11:30pm; €20*

Popular for its *cataplana* (a seafood stew more commonly associated with the Algarve) and other local and regional specialties, the centrally located, warm, and welcoming tavern Tasco do Celso oozes local flavor. The dining area has solid slabs of wood for tables, a bar propped up on wine barrels, and a cozy area with deep armchairs set out around an open fire for a drink.

Accommodations

Accommodations in this area are for the most part rustic, centering largely on rural estates and decent campsites.

HS MILFONTES BEACH

*Av. Marginal; tel. 283 990 070; http://
hsmilfontesbeach.com; €149*

Four-star HS Milfontes Beach, with simple, unfussy rooms, is in the center of the village overlooking the river mouth. It has three on-site restaurants and an outdoor pool and deck area, and is a short walk to anywhere in town.

★ HERDADE DO AMARELO NATURE & SPA

*EN 532, km 7; tel. 930 520 706; www.
herdadedoamarelo.pt; minimum 2 nights, from €195*

Surrounded by the lush vegetation of the Southwest Alentejo and Vicentine Coast Natural Park, the magical Herdade do Amarelo Nature & Spa farmhouse and estate is both rural and refined, with a large outdoor pool and 10 elegant rooms. It's located 30 minutes south of Vila Nova de Milfontes.

Information and Services

- **Vila Nova de Milfontes Tourist Office:** Rua António Mantas; tel. 283 996 599; daily 9am-1pm and 3pm-6pm

- **Main post office:** Rua Custódio Brás Pacheco 9; tel. 283 990 000

- **GNR police station:** Rua António Mantas 28; tel. 283 990 020; www.gnr.pt

Getting There

By car, Vila Nova de Milfontes is 28 kilometers (17 mi) northwest from **Odemira,** a 30-minute drive on the **N393** road. A **Rede Expressos** (tel. 707 223 344; www.rede-expressos.pt) bus runs twice daily between Odemira and Vila Nova de Milfontes (20 minutes; €6), once in the morning and once in the afternoon. The bus stop in Vila Nova de Milfontes is just north of the town, close to the campsites, a 15-minute walk to the center.

The Algarve and the Southern Beaches

Portugal's southernmost region, the sun- drenched Algarve (al-GARV) is famous for its year-round good weather, heady summer events, golden beaches, and dramatic coastal rock formations in a sparkling sea.

With over 300 days of sunshine per year, the region is a premier destination for tourism and Northern European expats. Over 150 kilometers (93 mi) of coastline are framed by jagged ocher cliffs with golden stretches of sand and sheltered rocky coves. Large tourist towns mix with quaint whitewashed fishing villages, orange groves, and golf courses, and the entire region is peppered with Moorish and Roman ruins.

Portugal's tourism authorities are working to expand the Algarve's

Highlights

Look for ★ to find recommended sights, activities, dining, and lodging.

© MOON.COM

★ **Faro's Old Town:** Encircled by ancient Moorish stone walls in the heart of the city, Faro's Old Town is a warren of quaint cobbled streets and historic buildings, including the medieval Faro Cathedral (page 188).

★ **Ria Formosa Natural Park:** A wonder of nature, this offshore park comprises turquoise lagoons, sandy barrier islets, deserted beaches, and a wealth of flora and fauna (pages 203).

★ **Ferragudo:** This charming little hamlet is the quintessential Algarvian fishermen's village, complete with a picturesque quay, cobbled backstreets, hilltop church, and busy village square (page 225).

★ **Marinha Beach:** Emblematic of the Algarve coast, the award-winning Marinha Beach regularly features on lists of Europe's top beaches but is still a hidden gem (page 228).

★ **Silves Castle:** Perched imposingly above the city of Silves, this impressive medieval fortress is a legacy of the battles the Algarve once endured. Today it is the centerpiece of the city's famous Medieval Festival (page 231).

★ **Fóia Peak:** In the Monchique Mountains, stand on the region's highest point for panoramic views of the Algarve and the Atlantic. The journey up is pretty thrilling, too (page 240).

★ **Cape St. Vincent:** No visit to the Algarve is complete without a trip to the most southwesterly point, once believed to be the world's end, a windswept, desolate area with dramatic cliffs that drop sharply into the tumultuous Atlantic (page 242).

★ **Via Algarviana Hiking Trail:** With over 200 kilometers (124 mi) of rural hiking path, this trans-region trail takes walking enthusiasts through unspoiled nature and rural hamlets (page 244).

The Algarve and the Southern Beaches

Southwest Alentejo and Vicentine Coast Natural Park

Odeceixe Beach
Odeceixe
N120

N266

Monte Clérigo Beach
SERRÃO
Aljezur
FÓIA PEAK
Monchique
N267
908 m ▲
(2,979 ft)
Caldas de Monchique

Arrifana Beach
ALJEZUR CASTLE
ARRIFANA SURF SCHOOL & CAMP

SEE "PORTIMÃO, PRAIA DA ROCHA, AND FERRAGUDO" MAP

N120
Silves
SILVES CASTLE

Bordeira Beach
Carrapateira
Bordeira
SEE "LAGOS" MAP
PENINA HOTEL & GOLF RESORT

N124

Amado Beach

Portimão
Lagoa
ZOOMARINE SEALIFE PARK

VIA ALGARVIANA HIKING TRAIL
Alvor
ALVOR ESTUARY AND WALKWAY
Lagos
Praia da Rocha
Porches
Carvoeiro
Albufeira

N125
Salema
FERRAGUDO
ALGAR SECO
MARINHA BEACH
Fishermen's Beach

CAPE ST. VINCENT

Martinhal Beach
Sagres
SAGRES FORTRESS

THE ALGARVE AND THE SOUTHERN BEACHES

image as more than just a summer beach destination by adding a packed year-round events calendar and wellness tourism to attract visitors in all seasons. In cooler months, the Algarve is a golfing and adventure sports destination, from skydiving to scuba diving, kayaking, and surfing. Beyond tourism, the region is steeped in history. For centuries, the Algarve has been prized and disputed terrain. Having been occupied for long periods by civilizations from the Romans to the Moors, the region is deeply infused with influences from its varied past, seen in its architecture, gastronomy, and music.

ORIENTATION

The Algarve is generally divided into the unspoiled, quiet **Sotavento**—eastern Algarve, which borders Spain, where the sea is warmer than along the rest of the coast, and where you'll find to the **Ria Formosa Natural Park**—and the **Barlavento,** western Algarve, a blend of tourist and traditional, which extends from **Albufeira** to the **Lagos** area.

Previous: the village of Carvoeiro; Faro Cathedral; view from Fóia Peak.

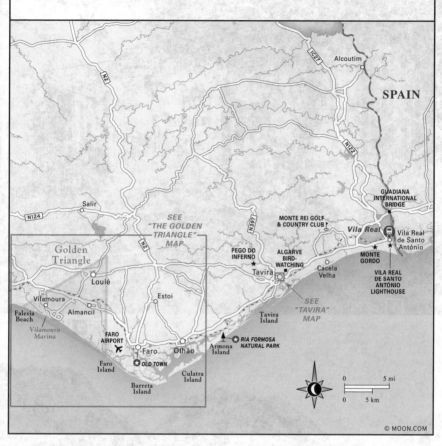

Between the two is glitzy and glamorous central Algarve, home to the affluent **Golden Triangle** and the region's most exclusive hotels, restaurants, and bars. **Faro,** the Algarve's largest city and the main gateway to the region, is nearby, slightly closer to the Spanish border. The **western coast,** in the shadow of the **Monchique Mountains,** is dramatic and untamed, protected by the southern half of the **Southwest Alentejo and Vicentine Coast Natural Park.**

PLANNING YOUR TIME

Portugal's southern coastline spans 155 kilometers (96 mi) and takes 2 hours to drive from end to end, with **Faro International Airport** in the middle. Allow at least a week here to explore the windy, rugged west coast, the lush **Monchique Mountains,** the glitzy **Golden Triangle,** the more traditional, unspoiled east, and the amazing **Ria Formosa Natural Park.** If you only have a few days, spend a night in each area for a quick overview, or settle in one to soak up the local essence.

For a quiet holiday with authentic Algarve flavor and possibly a day trip to Spain, head to the **Sotavento,** the eastern end, home to **Tavira** and **Vila Real de Santo António.** If you appreciate luxury, central Algarve's

Golden Triangle area won't disappoint. For fun in the sun and fantastic beaches with the option of interesting scenery and history, go to the **Barlavento,** or western end. For a break from the beach, head to the Monchique Mountains, the backbone of the Algarve, separating it from the Alentejo region to the north, or to the unspoiled west coast north of **Sagres.**

Beaches in the eastern half of the region are more popular, generally longer with shallower, warmer water. In the west, beaches are windier, better for **surfing** and **kitesurfing.** Most of the Algarve's beaches are accessible, pristine, well-equipped with bars, restaurants, and other facilities, and fly the Blue Flag for quality and environmental standards. **June to September** is beach season; prices and temperatures peak in August, and roads, amenities, and attractions get busy.

Renting a car is the best way to explore the Algarve. The **N125** road and the **A22** motorway run parallel to the coast through the entire region. The A22 has tolls but is faster; the N125 is often under construction, which can cause backups. Many towns and cities in the region are connected via the **Algarve Line,** but be aware that the train station can be quite a way from the town center in some towns. The main bus company in the Algarve is **Eva** (tel. 289 899 760; www.eva-bus.com), for travel around the Algarve and to other regions. Train and bus travel can be cheap and convenient for short distances, if a little unreliable, as delays and cancellations occur with some frequency.

Itinerary Ideas

You'll probably arrive in the Algarve either via Faro airport or the A22 motorway, which terminates near the central city of Albufeira. **Rent a car** and head east to the city of **Faro** first.

DAY 1: FARO AND CARVOEIRO

1 Spend a few hours wandering downtown Faro, the Algarve's largest city. Its **Old Town** is a labyrinth of cobblestoned streets that's a delight to get lost in.

2 After wandering, enjoy a lunch of typical local fare at **Restaurant Dois Irmãos.**

3 Appetite sated, jump in the car and head west toward the quaint and traditional fisherman's village of Carvoeiro, a 50-minute drive. Settle in at your hotel, where you'll be spending the next few nights, and explore the lovely little town: Window shop, stroll the clifftop boardwalk, and enjoy a beachside coffee at **Carvoeiro Beach.**

4 Have dinner at the excellent seafood restaurant **Mar d'Fora** and round off the day with a drink in one of the village's many lively bars.

DAY 2: VILA REAL DE SANTO ANTÓNIO AND TAVIRA

1 The next morning, after breakfast at the hotel, get back into the car and head for Vila Real de Santo António, the Algarve's easternmost town, a drive of just over 1 hour. Park and meander along the leafy riverfront to the main **Praça Marquês do Pombal** square.

2 Enjoy a seafood lunch in cozy **Pisa II** on Vila Real's backstreets.

3 Next, head to the docks to catch a tour with **TransGuadiana River Cruises** and admire neighboring Spain from the Guadiana River.

Itinerary Ideas

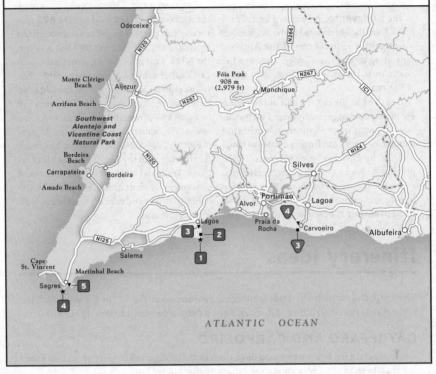

4 En route back to Carvoeiro, stop in historic Tavira, a 25-minute drive from Vila Real. This is another place to stroll and take in the atmosphere. Climb the walls of **Tavira Castle** to get a view of the town's picturesque red roofs.

5 Follow an evening amble along the riverside with dinner at the excellent little restaurant **Copos & Petiscos** before returning to your hotel in Carvoeiro.

DAY 3: LAGOS AND SAGRES

1 Rise early and enjoy a hotel breakfast before setting off along the EN125 for the 40-minute drive west to the city of Lagos. Park along the waterfront and spend the morning seeing Lagos on foot, ending up at the dramatic **Ponta da Piedade** rock formation.

2 Spend a leisurely morning and early afternoon basking on **Dona Ana Beach,** considered among the most beautiful in Europe.

3 Savor local flavors for lunch at the **Casinha do Petisco** tapas restaurant

4 Back in your car, drive farther west along the EN125 to Sagres (32 km/20 mi, 35 minutes). Round off the day exploring this blustery town, and be sure to visit its main attraction, **Sagres Fortress,** one of the Algarve's most imposing monuments.

5 Finish your third day in the Algarve with an extraordinary dinner at **Mum's Restaurant,** which has a refreshingly extensive selection of vegan and vegetarian options.

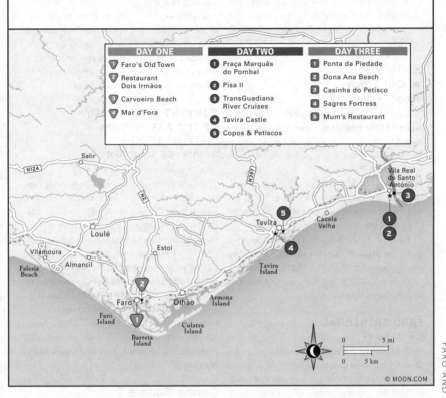

DAY ONE
1. Faro's Old Town
2. Restaurant Dois Irmãos
3. Carveiro Beach
4. Mar d'Fora

DAY TWO
1. Praça Marquês do Pombal
2. Pisa II
3. TransGuadiana River Cruises
4. Tavira Castle
5. Copos & Petiscos

DAY THREE
1. Ponta da Piedade
2. Dona Ana Beach
3. Casinha do Petisco
4. Sagres Fortress
5. Mum's Restaurant

© MOON.COM

Faro and Sotavento

Faro is the largest city in the Algarve and home to the region's only international airport. The city itself is often passed through on the way to beach resorts, but it has a lot to offer. With the exception of some tourist trappings such as the ubiquitous tourist train, Faro has remained largely untouched, despite being packed with historic monuments, cultural events, and genuine local life. With a busy harbor and a large university population, the city is active year-round.

The heart of Faro is its picturesque, well-preserved Old Town and the city's bustling main shopping street, the genteel Rua de Santo António, with cafés and restaurants, all within walking distance of Faro's most popular hotels. Fringing Faro's shoreline is the Ria Formosa Natural Park, a protected coastal lagoon that can be explored by boat.

Farther east, Tavira is one of the eastern Algarve's most popular towns, With the perfect blend of history and beach, it's packed with authentic charm and interesting sights, such as its old Roman Bridge and medieval Moorish center. Occupying the region's southeastern corner is Vila Real de Santo António, on the banks of the Guadiana River, facing Spain. Laid out in a unique grid system, having been completely rebuilt following a massive 18th-century earthquake,

Vila Real de Santo António is an attractive town with a handsome waterfront and noble central square, fringed by long, sweeping beaches.

SIGHTS
★ Old Town
(Cidade Velha)

Just off the harbor front is Faro's **Historic Area (Zona Histórica),** more commonly called the Old Town. Encircled by Moorish stone walls, it's a maze of cobbled streets with historic buildings, mostly dating from the 16th-17th centuries. It's accessed through the 1812 **Arco da Vila** gateway, an ornate monumental archway in the center of downtown.

The hub of the historic center is the spacious **Sé Square (Largo da Sé),** an open, orange-tree-dotted square that is an oasis of calm in a bustling city. This part of town is best explored on foot.

FARO CATHEDRAL
(Sé de Faro)

Largo da Sé 11; tel. 289 823 018; Mon.-Sat. 10am-5:30pm, mass on Sun.; €3

Faro's centerpiece is its Roman Catholic cathedral, a hodgepodge of architectural styles thanks to successive renovations and extensions over the centuries. It was erected in 1251 on the ruins of a 13th-century mosque from the Arab occupation of Portugal. The cathedral's exterior has Romanesque, Gothic, and Renaissance features. Inside are a four-nave church, a Gothic chapel, a presbytery, a museum of sacred art, a remarkable red organ decorated with Chinese motifs, and a narrow staircase that climbs to the top of a medieval tower that has stunning views over the Old Town and the Ria Formosa.

BISHOP'S PALACE
(Paço Episcopal)

Largo da Sé 15; tel. 289 894 040 or 289 823 018

This long, low, whitewashed palace dates to the 16th century, rebuilt after the 1755 earthquake. Its rooms are clad in fabulous late-18th-century *azulejo* plaques; of note is the *azulejo*-clad staircase. Still the official residence of the Bishop of Faro, the building is open to visitors sporadically for art exhibitions (or if a request is made in advance).

CONVENT OF OUR LADY OF THE ASSUMPTION
(Convento da Nossa Senhora da Assunção)

Praça Dom Afonso III; tel. 289 870 829

The Convent of Our Lady of the Assumption is an elegant national monument that was commissioned in 1519 by Queen Leonor. Its distinguishing features include a two-story Renaissance cloister and a Manueline church with a Baroque dome. Since 1973 it has housed the **Faro Municipal Museum (Museu Municipal de Faro)** (Praça Dom Afonso III 14; tel. 289 870 827; Tues.-Fri. 10am-7pm, Sat.-Sun. 11:30am-6pm summer, Tues.-Fri. 10am-6pm, Sat.-Sun. 10:30am-5pm winter; €2), which includes tombstones, mosaics, and 17th- and 18th-century sacred art.

Carmo Square
(Largo do Carmo)

Set back a few streets from the harbor and north of downtown is Carmo Square, opposite Faro's **central post office.** Most people visit this part of town to see a chilling **Chapel of Bones,** of which there are only a handful in Portugal.

CARMO CHURCH
(Igreja do Carmo)

Largo do Carmo; tel. 289 824 490; Mon.-Fri. 9am-5pm, Sat. 9am-1pm Oct.-Mar., Mon.-Fri. 9am-6pm, Sat. 9am-1pm Apr.-Sept., mass on Sun. and holy days 9am; €1

The striking Carmo Church is a fine example of Baroque architecture. It has a simple, quadrangular facade, two distinctive bell towers with resident storks, and elaborate gilded woodwork.

Faro

RUA ABOIM ASCENSÃO

To Faro
Hospital

*Jardim
António
Sérgio*

To Hotel
Afonso III

RUA DA ATALAIA

RUA DA BOAVISTA

CARMO
CHURCH

*Carmo
Square*

BEST WESTERN
HOTEL DOM
BERNARDO

RUA GENERAL TEÓFILO DA TRINDADE

CHAPEL OF BONES

RUA SERPA PINTO

RUA INFANTE DOM HENRIQUE

MAIN
POST OFFICE

LARGO DO CARMO

RUA JARDIM DO CARDEAL

RUA BRITO CABREIRA

HOTEL SOL
ALGARVE

RUA CRUZ DAS MESTRAS

To Faro Train
Station

RUA GIL EANES

RUA DE SÃO PEDRO

TACO Y
TEQUILLA

RUA BAPTISTA LOPES

RUA JOSÉ ESTEVÃO

RUA LETHES

RUA DR. JUSTINO CUMANO

AVENIDA DA REPÚBLICA

PIPERS
IRISH PUB

O CENTENÁRIO

FARO BUS
TERMINAL

APERITIVO
BAR

TV. LETHES

HOTEL EVA

RUA 1 DE MAIO

RESTAURANT
DOIS IRMÃOS

To
Main Tourist
Office

FORMOSAMAR

HOTEL
FARO

NAUTIC BAR

DELGATURIS
TOURIST TRAIN

**HISTORIC
AREA**

PRAÇA ALEXANDRE HERCULANO

PETISQUEIRA
3 EM PIPA

*Jardim
Manuel
Bivar*

COLUMBUS WINE
& COCKTAIL BAR

RUA DA JOÃO DIAS

RUA BRITES
DE ALMEIDA

ZEN SUP

RUA DA MISERICÓRDIA

R. ALEXANDRE HERCULANO

RUA DO ALBERGUE

FARO
BOUTIQUE
HOTEL

ARCO
DA VILA

RUA DO BOCAGE

BISHOP'S
PALACE

⭐ OLD TOWN

RUA RASQUINHO

RUA DONA TERESA RAMALHO ORTIGÃO

To Faro PSP
Police Station

RUA COMANDANTE FRANCISCO MANUEL

ESTRELA DA
RIA FORMOSA

FARO
CATHEDRAL

*Sé
Square*

VILA
ADENTRO

FAZ GOSTOS

CONVENT OF OUR LADY
OF THE ASSUMPTION

RUA DO CASTELO

LARGO DE SÃO FRANCISCO

| 0 | 100 yds |
| 0 | 100 m |

To Faro Island
and Faro Beach

© MOON.COM

CHAPEL OF BONES
(Capela de Ossos)

tel. 289 824 490; Mon.-Fri. 10am-1pm and 3pm-5pm, Sat. 10am-1pm; €1

The bones and skulls in the small chapel are said to be those of Carmelite monks exhumed from a nearby cemetery, displayed to exemplify the brevity of life. It's morbid but fascinating. The chapel is set in a garden just behind the church.

Faro Island
(Ilha de Faro)

Stretching 5 kilometers (3 mi), Faro Island, formally known as the **Ancão Peninsula,** is the westernmost tip of the Ria Formosa in Faro, located just behind Faro airport. This is where you'll find Faro's main beach, the family-friendly **Praia de Faro.** The western end is home to a traditional fishing community with typical huts and boats, and the central and eastern end is a holiday-home hot spot among Portuguese. The island is livelier in summer thanks to its bars, restaurants, and holiday homes, but this means it gets crowded, and parking is limited.

Faro Island is attached to the mainland by a narrow single-lane bridge. To get here, head toward Faro airport and follow signage to Ilha de Faro. Once arrived, you can park along the main drag or in one of the designated parking spots. Or park on the mainland side of the bridge on the outskirts of the airport and walk over to the island. In high season, there is significant traffic congestion and long queues. **Bus 16** (€2.20), operated by Faro's Próximo (www.proximo.pt) service, runs every 30-40 minutes between the main bus terminal on Faro city center's harbor-side, the airport, and Faro Island. The bus doesn't cross the bridge to Faro Island; passengers must walk. This is doable for accessing the central part of the island and its beach, but it's a bit of a walk to the extremities. A taxi between Faro and Faro Island costs around €15.

1: Arco da Vila gateway in Faro's Old Town
2: Carmo Church **3:** Faro Cathedral **4:** Faro's marina

BEACHES

FARO BEACH
(Praia de Faro)

Faro Island

Praia de Faro spans the length of Faro Island, with one long road running alongside it, with more deserted beaches at either end. The water is clean but cold, and the waves can be strong on this long and uninterrupted stretch soft golden sand.

SPORTS AND RECREATION
Surfing

Though not known as a surfing destination like the Algarve's west coast, Faro Island can offer good conditions in winter.

- **Clube de Surf de Faro:** Av. Nascente 107; tel. 963 417 671

Kayaking and Stand-Up Paddleboarding

Glide along the peaceful waters of the Ria Formosa Natural Park or discover the dramatic cliffs, caves, and grottoes of the Algarve coast from a unique vantage point.

- **Faro Beach Nautical Center:** Av. Nascente 25; tel. 289 870 898
- **Zen SUP:** tel. 936 735 778; www.zen-sup.com

Tours
FORMOSAMAR

Faro Harbor, Av. da República, Stand 1; tel. 918 720 002; www.formosamar.com

Formosamar specializes in exploring the Ria Formosa with ecofriendly guided boating, kayaking, biking, hiking, bird-watching, dolphin-spotting, and fishing trips. Guides speak English and operate year-round, although certain activities are weather-dependent. Some activities, such as kayaking (from €30 for 2.5 hours) and cycling (from €6 for 1 hour), can be done independently. Marine wildlife-watching tours (2 hours, Mar.-Oct.; €45) depart regularly from Faro and Olhão.

ESTRELA DA RIA FORMOSA

Faro Marina, in front of McDonald's; tel. 961 129 977; www.estreladariaformosa.com

Catamaran tours depart from the Faro quayside to explore the Ria Formosa, starting from €10, including the popular Four Islands Ria Formosa tour (4 hours, twice daily; from €30), a best-seller. Relax in a comfortable modern catamaran to sail the natural beauty of Armona, Culatra, Deserta, and Farol Islands. Tours are given in several languages, including English.

ENTERTAINMENT AND EVENTS

FARO BIKE MEET

www.motoclubefaro.pt; mid-July

The annual Faro Bike Meet is one of Europe's largest gatherings of motorcycle enthusiasts and one of the biggest events of the Algarve summer, drawing thousands of leather-clad bikers from all over. Held on the outskirts of the city near the airport, over four days in mid-July, it is open to all, welcoming as many curious nonbikers as bikers. The large plot of pine-studded land becomes a makeshift town with campsites, a crafts market, food stalls, and a stage for nightly concerts and colorful entertainment. On the last day, always Sunday, participants mount their motorcycles and rumble through Faro in procession. The locals come out to wave their annual visitors off on their journeys home.

FOOD

Faro has a multitude of restaurants and cafés that are first-rate without being flashy or overpriced. Thanks to its student population, Faro is also home to more international fare, as well as affordable fast food and trendy wine and cocktail bars.

Portuguese

★ RESTAURANT DOIS IRMÃOS

Praça Ferreira de Almeida 15; tel. 289 823 337; www.restaurantedoisirmaos.com; daily 10am-10:30pm; €20

For real character and typical Algarve fare, visit Restaurant Dois Irmãos, where local cuisine meshes with traditional gastronomy. Founded in 1925, it claims to be the oldest restaurant in Faro and one of the oldest in the country. The restaurant features rustic wooden-beam ceilings, brick arches inside, and a leafy courtyard in back, and it has an extensive menu of fresh seafood and a good selection of meat and vegetarian dishes. Specialties include codfish *cataplana* (stew) and baby goat.

VILA ADENTRO

Praça do Afonso III 17; tel. 289 052 173; daily 9am-midnight; €15

At beautiful, elegant Vila Adentro, regional delicacies and traditional flavors are served with panache. In a historic building in the Old Town, the restaurant is a former art gallery clad with hand-painted tile plaques, but brightly laid tables and clean lines give it a contemporary touch. When the weather is warm, enjoy a romantic street-side table.

Seafood

O CENTENÁRIO

Largo do Terreiro do Bispo 4-6; tel. 289 823 343; www.restaurantecentenario.business.site; Mon.-Sat. 12:30pm-3pm and 6:30pm-11:30pm; €12

Exposed brick arches and dark wood tables and chairs give O Centenário seafood restaurant a warm and cozy feel, and the grub is simply divine—an ocean's worth of fresh seafood, including local and Algarvian specialties.

Tapas

PETISQUEIRA 3 EM PIPA

Rua Brites de Almeida 24; tel. 914 841 090; Mon.-Fri. noon-2:30pm and 7pm-11:30pm, Sat. 7pm-midnight; €8

A stone's throw from the Faro Boutique

Algarve Specialties

cataplana

Algarvian cuisine is an interesting palette of recipes and ingredients that range from fresh and fishy along the coast to rich and gamey inland.

From the rolling hills of the mountain ranges that form the backbone along the Algarve's northern border to the golden beaches of the coast, seasonal ingredients coupled with a year-round abundance of fresh fish, farm-raised meats, and heady herbs and spices provide the basis for Algarvian cuisine. These are usually concocted into hearty, flavorful stews in rural inland areas, and simply sizzled on charcoal grills the closer you get to the coast.

With heritage steeped in a colorful history, enjoying ancient Moorish to modern Mediterranean influences, recipes generally vary from region to region and are passed down over family generations. Grilled *piripiri* chicken, barbecue-grilled sardines, and rich seafood *cataplana* are among the Algarve's main specialties.

- **Sardines in Portimão:** Don't be afraid to get your fingers dirty and tuck into the ultimate mouthwatering finger food in Portimão, home of barbequed sardines, a simple feast that attracts visitors in droves.

- *Aguardente de medronho* **in Monchique:** Throat-warming *aguardente de medronho*, also commonly called firewater, is a popular post-meal digestive aid made locally in Monchique from the *medronho* (strawberry tree) fruit.

- **Cured meats and cheeses in Monchique:** Monchique is also known as the place to go to savor delicious cured ham and traditional cheeses. Local eatery Cinzas is a popular place for this (page 242).

- *Piripiri* **chicken:** The town of Guia, near Albufeira, is the place to go to try this famous Algarve specialty: juicy, tasty marinated chicken with a little bit of a kick, served simply with chips and salad. Head to famed Ramires (Rua 25 de Abril 14, Guia; tel. 289 561 232; www.restauranteramires.com; daily 11am-11pm, no reservations in summer; €10), the dish's unofficial home.

- *Cataplana:* Enjoy this flavor-packed meat and seafood stew in the small, family-run A Ria restaurant overlooking the local quay in the traditional fishermen's village of Ferragudo (page 226).

Hotel, Petisqueira 3 em Pipa is a charming, laid-back little restaurant with a tiled facade and floor. *Petiscar* loosely means "to snack" or "to nibble," here meaning delicious tapas like sweet-potato fries, mini-burgers made from *farinheira* (a Portuguese sausage), and excellent homemade desserts.

Fine Dining
FAZ GOSTOS

Rua do Castelo, 13; tel. 289 878 422; www.fazgostos. com; daily noon-3pm and 6:30pm-10pm; €20
Located in Faro's Old Town, Faz Gostos is classy, polished, and Michelin-listed, with rich Portuguese flavors cleverly complemented by international cuisine. Intriguing mains include partridge and mushroom pies served with tropical salad.

Mexican
TACO Y TEQUILA

Rua Filipe Alistão 75; tel. 289 821 844; www. tacoytequilla.pt; daily 7pm-midnight; €10
This warm and colorful little restaurant in Faro city center serves authentic Mexican food as lively as the art on the walls. Offerings include tacos, fajitas, and burritos, plus tequila shots. With great vegetarian options, dining here is a true fiesta.

Snacks
CAIS 73

Av. Nascente 25; tel. 289 037 273; Mon. and Wed.-Fri. 11am-3pm and 6pm-10pm, Sat.-Sun. 11am-10pm; €8
On Faro Island, right on the beach near the campground, Cais 73 is a sand-floored café with surfboards on the walls. Its giant toasted sandwiches are legendary. Be warned—they are huge, enough for two people. Recently renovated, reborn from the famous O Forte café, it is a great place for a light bite on Faro Island.

BARS AND NIGHTLIFE

Given its size, Faro has a relatively compact nightlife scene, but it's energetic and varied thanks to the city's thriving student population. Most bars are along the streets adjacent to the harbor.

COLUMBUS WINE & COCKTAIL BAR

Praça Dom Francisco Gomes; tel. 917 776 222; www. barcolumbus.pt; 2pm-4am daily
A popular hangout, this elegant cocktail lounge is just off the riverside Manuel Bívar garden. Intriguingly set within the arcade of a 16th-century hospital, it has an impressive vaulted brick ceiling and stunning chandeliers.

PIPERS IRISH PUB

Rua do Prior 28; tel. 917 696 643; daily 7pm-4am
They say there's an Irish pub in every city, and Faro has a good one. Expect a great warm welcome, live music, sports on TV, and the obligatory Guinness.

APERITIVO BAR

Rua Conselheiro Bivar 51; tel. 965 410 620; www. aperitivobar.pt; daily 6pm-2am
At contemporary Aperitivo Bar, fashionable drinks are accompanied by tapas. A popular, modern after-work meeting place, it has fabulous cocktails, an extensive wine list, and even a chic cigar room.

NAUTIC BAR

Doca de Faro; tel. 289 090 818; daily 10am-2am
Classy Nautic Bar on Faro harbor is a relaxing place to enjoy a drink and people-watching. It's perfect for a coffee or a cocktail and has a chill-out lounge vibe.

ACCOMMODATIONS

Although not one of the Algarve's busiest resorts, Faro has lodgings to suit various budgets, most within walking distance of the main bus and train terminals. The city has some of the Algarve's better budget and mid-range hotels.

Under €100
HOTEL AFONSO III

Rua Miguel Bombarda 64; tel. 289 803 542; www. hotelafonso.pt; €80
Decent, affordable two-star Hotel Afonso III, 10 minutes from the airport, is near Faro's main train and bus terminals. Around half

of the 41 rooms have been refurbished as part of a gradual overhaul. Rooms are basic but clean.

HOTEL SOL ALGARVE

Rua Infante Dom Henrique 52; tel. 289 895 700; www.hotelsolalgarve.com; €100

Family-run, two-star budget Hotel Sol Algarve is in a central older part of town near the train station. Clean and tidy, it has 38 well-equipped rooms with air-conditioning, en suite baths, TVs, phones, and free Wi-Fi.

€100-200

BEST WESTERN HOTEL DOM BERNARDO

Rua General Teofilo da Trindade 20; tel. 289 889 800; www.bestwestern.pt; €109

Standard chain hotel Best Western Hotel Dom Bernardo is in the heart of Faro overlooking Carmo Square and the church. Modern amenities include free Wi-Fi, and it is good value for money.

FARO BOUTIQUE HOTEL

Rua do Bocage 66; tel. 289 037 300; www.faroboutiquehotel.pt; €123

In downtown Faro, just a stroll from the harbor and Arco da Vila, Faro Boutique Hotel is bright, modern, and comfortable. Rooms are soundproofed but small; some have balconies. Prices are reasonable for the location. The rooftop terrace is a great place for a sunset drink.

HOTEL EVA

Av. da República 1; tel. 289 001 000; www.ap-hotelsresorts.com; €142

Excellently located in the heart of Faro, right on the marina, the 134-room, four-star Hotel Eva offers reasonably priced rooms within walking distance to most attractions. One of Faro's largest and most popular hotels for business and tourism, it has magnificent waterfront views and is adjacent to the bus terminal.

★ HOTEL FARO

Praça Dom Francisco Gomes 2; tel. 289 830 830; www.hotelfaro.pt; 4-night minimum, €171

Overlooking Old Town and the Ria Formosa, modern Hotel Faro boasts a prime location on the doorstep of the main shopping street, Rua de Santo António. Wi-Fi is included, and a rooftop pool and restaurant have panoramic views.

INFORMATION AND SERVICES

- **Faro PSP police station:** Rua da Polícia de Segurança Pública 32; tel. 289 899 899; www.psp.pt

- **Main tourist office:** Av. 5 de Outubro 18-20; tel. 289 800 400; www.visitalgarve.pt; Mon.-Fri. 9am-12:30pm and 2pm-5:30pm

- **Main post office:** Largo do Carmo; tel. 289 892 590

- **Faro State Hospital (Hospital de Faro):** Rua Leao Penedo; tel. 289 891 100

- **Faro Private Hospital (Hospital Particular do Algarve-Gambelas):** Urbanização Casal de Gambelas, Lote 2, Gambelas; tel. 707 282 828; www.grupohpa.com

GETTING THERE

Driving to Faro from outside the Algarve is easy on the **A2** motorway from Lisbon. Faro is 280 kilometers (175 mi) southeast of **Lisbon,** a 2.75-hour drive. Be warned: The roads in and around Faro get busy, especially at rush hour—early morning and late afternoon-early evening.

Air

FARO INTERNATIONAL AIRPORT

FAO; tel. 289 800 800; www.aeroportofaro.pt

Fly to Faro International Airport on daily domestic routes from Lisbon or Porto with TAP or low-cost Ryanair. Flights from Lisbon take 45 minutes (€100 one-way); from Porto, 1 hour (€100-€150 round-trip). European carriers from France, Belgium, Germany, the

Netherlands, and the United Kingdom operate daily routes to Faro.

The airport is 7 kilometers (4.3 mi) southwest of the center, approximately a 10-minute drive along the EN125 road and main airport road. **Car rental companies** with desks at the airport include Goldcar (tel. 707 504 070; www.goldcar.es), Europcar (tel. 289 818 316; www.europcar.com), and Avis (tel. 289 810 120; www.avis.com.pt). Regular bus line **bus 16** (20 minutes, every 30 minutes; €2.25), between Faro's main bus terminal and the airport, is operated by **Próximo** (www.proximo.pt), leaving the airport from outside the arrivals area. Bright yellow signs indicate where to catch it. Buy tickets from the driver. A **taxi** from the airport into the city costs €10-12.

Train
FARO TRAIN STATION
Largo da Estação dos Caminhos de Ferro; tel. 289 830 150; daily 6:20am-10pm

The train station is 300 meters (0.2 mi) west of the main bus terminal, linked to other Algarve towns by the **Algarve Line.**

CP (tel. 707 210 220; www.cp.pt) operates slower Intercity and high-speed Alfa-Pendular trains. The Alfa Pendular train (3 hours; 2nd class €22.60, 1st class €30.30 one-way) runs twice a day between Faro and Lisbon (Oriente, Santa Apolónia, and Entrecampos stations); the Intercity train (3.5 hours; 2nd class €21.60, 1st class €28.30 one-way) runs three times a day. Between Faro and Porto-Campanhã, there are five daily Alfa-Pendular trains (6 hours; 2nd class €52.30, 1st class €71.80) and Intercity trains (6.5 hours; 2nd class €42.40, 1st class €58.60).

Bus
FARO BUS TERMINAL
Av. da República 5; tel. 289 899 760 or 289 899 740; Mon.-Fri. 6am-11pm, Sat.-Sun. 7am-11pm

Faro has a large bus terminal in the heart of the city. Buses run to Faro from most Portuguese cities, including **Rede Expressos** (tel. 213 581 460; www.rede-expressos.pt) buses from Lisbon (3 hours; under €40 round-trip). There

are services to Faro from Porto (7-8 hours; from €30 one-way) with Rede Expressos, but most will require a change at Lisbon's Sete Rios station.

An express Eva bus, the **Transrápido** (tel. 289 899 760; www.eva-bus.com) runs every few hours on weekdays, twice a day on weekends, between Lagos (western Algarve) and Faro bus terminal (2 hours; under €10 one-way), with stops at Portimão and Albufeira.

GETTING AROUND
Most attractions in Faro are in the city center and can be explored on foot.

Car
Faro airport is a hub for car rental companies, with many located at the airport, or ask at your hotel. Driving in Faro is straightforward, but roads can be very busy during rush hour, and the old cobblestone streets in the city center are narrow in places. Expect to pay for **parking** in the downtown and city center. There are free car parks on the outskirts of town—one of the best is **São Francisco Square,** on the eastern side of the Old Town, a short stroll from the main downtown area.

Bus
An easy, reliable, no-frills way to get around Faro is **Próximo Line 16** (tel. 289 899 760; www.proximo.pt), which continuously zips around the busiest spots. Tickets (€0.80-2.30) can be bought on board; daily tickets are also available.

Taxi
Taxi ranks are at the airport, train station, main bus terminal, along the harbor-side, and in the city center. **Táxis Antral de Faro** (tel. 289 827 203) is one of the city's main companies.

Tourist Train
DELGATURIS TOURIST TRAIN
Jardim Manuel Bívar; tel. 289 389 067; www. delgaturis.com; daily 10am-6pm Oct.-May, daily 10am-9pm June-Sept.; €3

For a novel way to see Faro in a short time, jump on the Delgaturis tourist train, which starts and finishes at the city's main harborfront gardens, the Jardim Manuel Bívar. This ride lasts 45 minutes, departing hourly.

TAVIRA

The handsome traditional fishing town of Tavira dates to the Bronze Age and may be one of the first Phoenician settlements in western Iberia. Once an aristocratic town, today a small city, Tavira straddles the Girão River, connected by a photogenic seven-arch bridge known as the Roman Bridge, although it is more likely Moorish in origin.

Amid the closely packed whitewashed houses and red roofs are quaint cobblestone streets, monuments, and sleepy squares. Discover traditional architecture, grand buildings, historic ruins, and over 30 churches—Tavira is nicknamed "the Town of Churches." Unique four-sided hipped roofs, striking red, have a strong Moorish look and are emblematic of the town. The design is thought to allow air to circulate in summer and retain warmth in winter.

Tavira's pretty riverside is lined with cafés and seafood restaurants. Its shoreline, part of the **Ria Formosa Natural Reserve,** is illuminated by white salt pans, from where the Algarve's famous *flor de sal* rock salt is harvested. Neat rows of pristine white salt merge with the turquoise water and golden dunes of the Ria Formosa protected wetlands fronting Tavira. The beach-islands of the Ria Formosa lagoon are easily reached by ferry or water taxi from the town center.

Sights

Tavira's main monuments are clustered in the town center, on the western bank of the **Gilão River.** Here you will find the medieval **Tavira Castle,** the local town hall, and many churches. Straddling the Gilão River in the heart of Tavira is the old **Roman Bridge,** a symbol of the city. The current seven-arch version was built in the 17th century in place of an older, late-12th-century bridge that connected Faro to an important trade route. Such was the bridge's importance at the time that it had protective towers at either end.

TAVIRA CASTLE
(Castelo de Tavira)
Urbanização Tavira Garden; daily 10am-7pm; free

The medieval Tavira Castle, in the southwest part of Tavira near the water tower, overlooks the town and its jumble of bright red roofs and ornate chimneys. On the highest point of the city, the castle is thought to have been built during Moorish rule in the 11th century, although its origins could be older. Castle walls were added in the late 13th century. Despite being partially ruined, two towers and the walls and their battlements are well preserved. Inside are pleasant, well-kept gardens. Walk around the battlements for views over Tavira and the coast.

MISERICÓRDIA CHURCH
(Igreja da Misericórdia)
Rua da Galeria; tel. 289 247 120; Mon. 9am-5pm, Tues.-Sat. 9am-6pm; €2, plus €1 for the bell tower

Misericórdia Church, built 1541-1551, is a fine example of Renaissance architecture in the heart of the Old Town. The striking white and gray facade, with its austere carved archway covered by a canopy with a statue of Our Lady of Mercy, is particularly impressive. The sober exterior belies the church's unique interior, with decorative traditional blue-and-white *azulejo* murals; there's also a gilded altar. Climb the bell tower for great views.

TAVIRA TOWER
(Torre de Tavira)
Calçada da Galeria 12; tel. 281 321 754; www.cdepa. pt; Mon.-Fri. 10am-5pm, Sat.-Sun. 10am-1pm; €4

Converted from a 1931 water tower, Tavira Tower houses the Algarve's first and only **camera obscura.** On an odd-shaped observation platform, from the camera obscura, visitors can observe the city in real time through a series of lenses, mirrors, and magnifying glasses that project images onto

Tavira

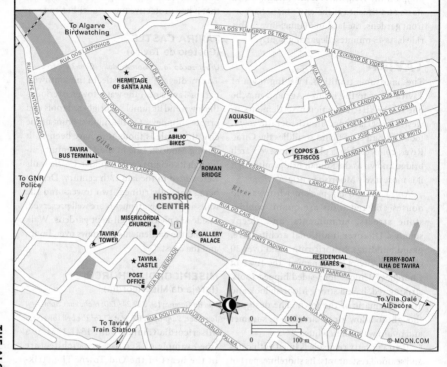

a 2-meter-wide (6.6-ft-wide) screen inside the tower. This gives the extraordinary experience of seeing the city in 360 degrees, almost like hovering above it. A lift and stairs provide access.

GALLERY PALACE
(Palácio da Galeria)

Calçada da Galeria; tel. 281 320 540; www.museumunicipaldetavira.tavira.pt; Tues.-Sat. 9am-4:30pm; €2

Emblematic of Tavira, the elegant 16th-century Gallery Palace is a historic Baroque building that hosts a variety of exhibitions throughout the year on themes such as olive oil production and the Mediterranean diet. On the site of an ancient Phoenician settlement, this Tavira municipal museum was once the home of magistrate João Leal da Gama e Ataíde.

HERMITAGE OF SANTA ANA
(Ermida de Santa Ana)

Largo de Santa Ana; tel. 281 320 540; Tues.-Sat. 9am-12:30pm and 2pm-5pm; free

The Hermitage of Santa Ana is one of the oldest religious buildings in the city. Set in its own little square, it dates from the early 14th century and was completely rebuilt in the 18th century following the devastating 1755 earthquake. From then on, it functioned as a private chapel in the palace of the governor of the Algarve. After a period of abandonment, the building was again renovated and made a museum in 2006. Today it hosts a variety of exhibitions.

PEGO DO INFERNO

M514-2, Santo Estêvão; open 24/7; free

A short drive from town is the breathtaking Pego do Inferno, literally "Hell's Pit," a gorgeous waterfall and a little lake that until recently were a local secret. Now the site is overgrown but captivating in its raw beauty. Folklore has it that a horse-drawn carriage fell into the lake and was never found, and that anyone who falls into it goes straight to hell. As the spot grew in popularity, supporting infrastructure was improved, and today it is a main attraction.

Pego do Inferno can only be accessed by car. From Tavira, take the N270 road and then the M514-2. Pego do Inferno is about 10 kilometers (6.2 mi), a 12-minute drive, northwest of Tavira.

Cycling Tours
ABILIO BIKES
Rua João Vaz Corte Real 23A; tel. 281 323 467; www.abiliobikes.com; from €30
Abilio Bikes has cycling routes for guided tours of Tavira, including the eco-friendly Ria Formosa tour, a Forts and Castles tour, and more.

Food
Tuna, octopus, shellfish, and grilled fish are on the menus of most Tavira restaurants; roast kid is also a local specialty. Sweets are one of Tavira's fortes and are widely available at the many coffee shops and *pastelarias* around town.

COPOS & PETISCOS
Rua Poeta Emiliano da Costa 6; tel. 916 562 645; Mon.-Sat. 11:45am-2:15pm and 6:45pm-10pm; €20
Tavira's finest seafood restaurant is classy Copos & Petiscos, with abundant fresh seafood and excellent wines. It looks unremarkable from outside, but the inside looks smart, with the bottom half of the walls clad in deep green tiles.

AQUASUL
Rua Dr. Augusto da Silva Carvalho 11; tel. 281 325 166; Mon.-Sat. 6:30pm-10pm; €20
Arty Aquasul is a colorfully decorated eatery with an experimental menu that spans the Mediterranean with a heavy Italian accent.

Dutch-owned, this atmospheric restaurant is on a flower-draped backstreet near the riverside in the heart of Tavira.

ACCOMMODATIONS
Tavira lodging ranges from quaint, spotless guesthouses to sprawling, manicured resorts. Absent are high-rise concrete eyesores; all construction conforms with and enhances the town's character.

★ VILA GALÉ ALBACORA
Quatro Águas; tel. 281 380 800; www.vilagale.com; €190
Vila Galé Albacora is a charming beach resort full of character and Portuguese features, sited where the Girão River meets the ocean, 4 kilometers (2.5 mi), a 40-minute walk or a 7-minute drive, south of Tavira center. This 162-room eco-hotel, part of the Vila Galé group, is converted from former fishing houses, workshops, warehouses, and an old chapel—buildings that reflect what was once the local way of life on the Ria Formosa.

RESIDENCIAL MARÉS
Largo Dr. José Pires Padinha 134; tel. 281 325 815; www.residencialmares.com; from €86 d, €346 3-bedroom villa
Residencial Marés is in the heart of Tavira on the riverside, a historic town house transformed into a 24-room lodging with a private villa, within walking distance of anywhere in the city. It has panoramic views over the river and local décor, with polished terra-cotta floor tiles and beachy colors.

Information and Services
- **GNR police:** Rua de Santa Margarida 2; tel. 281 329 030; www.gnr.pt
- **Main tourist office:** Praça da República 5; tel. 281 322 511
- **Post office:** Rua da Liberdade; tel. 707 262 626

Getting There
Tavira is 38 kilometers (24 mi) east of **Faro,**

a 35-minute drive on the **A22** motorway. It's 22 kilometers (13.6 mi) west of **Vila Real de Santo António**, a 30-minute drive on the A22.

TAVIRA BUS TERMINAL
Rua dos Pelames; tel. 281 322 546
A dozen **Eva** (tel. 289 899 760; www.eva-bus.com) buses run from Faro's main bus terminal to Tavira (1 hour, daily 7:15am-7:30pm; €4.45) on weekdays, and about seven buses run on weekends and holidays. Tickets for buses departing from the terminal must be bought at the ticket office, inside the terminal. Eva runs buses slightly more frequently between Tavira and Vila Real de Santo António (1 hour; €4.15). The Tavira Bus Terminal is on the northern edge of town, on the west side of the Gilão River, a short walk to the town center.

TAVIRA TRAIN STATION
Largo de Santo Amaro; tel. 281 326 394; www.cp.pt
Trains to Tavira are slightly faster and cheaper than the bus. **CP** (tel. 707 210 220; www.cp.pt) trains run from Faro to Tavira (40 minutes; €3.20), and there are around a dozen departures a day. CP also runs about a dozen trains daily between Faro and Vila Real de Santo António (1.25 hours; €5.25). The small train station in Tavira is on the southwest side of town, a 10-minute downhill walk to the center.

VILA REAL DE SANTO ANTÓNIO
Vila Real de Santo António is Portugal's southeasternmost city, separated from Spain by the Guadiana River. On a clear day—most days—you can see Spain from the river's edge. Vila Real is easy to explore, built following a neatly organized grid, unlike most Algarve towns. A long, elegant riverside walkway enhances the relaxed, peaceful pace of life. The novelty of being able to cross to Spain never seems to wear

1: Tavira Castle 2: café overlooking the Girão River

off, and with crowd-free beaches, excellent restaurants, and boat trips along the glorious Guadiana, Vila Real may be the last port on the Algarve's coast, but certainly not the least significant.

In the late 19th century Vila Real prospered as a canning center for tuna. Toward the end of the 20th century, as tuna stocks were depleted, the prosperity dried up. The tuna fish's heritage is still celebrated, and most local restaurants feature it on their menus.

As the last stop before Spain, Vila Real de Santo António is also the end of the **Via Algarviana Hiking Trail** (www.viaalgarviana.org), which runs the 240-kilometer (149-mi) length of the Algarve starting (or ending, depending on your point of view) in Vila do Bispo, not far from Sagres on the west coast.

Sights
Running along the eastern side of Vila Real parallel to the Guadiana River, attractive **Avenida da República** is a long cobblestone walkway dotted with palm trees that stretches between the town's port and marina south to manicured gardens and beachfront. The town's **port** (Av. da República; tel. 281 513 769; www.anguadiana.com) is where the Guadiana boat trips and ferry crossings operate from.

A few streets back from the river is the main town square, the **Praça Marquês do Pombal**, fringed with orange trees. The town center is said to be inspired by central Lisbon, and it certainly has a similar feeling of splendor and stateliness.

VILA REAL DE SANTO ANTÓNIO LIGHTHOUSE
(Farol de Vila Real de Santo António)
Av. Min Duarte Pacheco; tel. 281 544 402; Wed. 2pm-5pm; free
South of the city, just before the beach, Vila Real de Santo António Lighthouse, one of the Algarve's largest, is an impressive structure dating from 1923. It's 224 steps or an

elevator up to the 40-meter-high (131-ft-high) viewing platform, with views of the city, the coast, local salt pans, and Spain. A little museum at the base documents the lighthouse's history.

Beaches

As at most beaches in the eastern end of the Algarve, the sands of Vila Real de Santo António are sweeping and golden, and the water shallower and warmer than farther west.

SANTO ANTÓNIO BEACH (Praia de Santo António)

South of the town center
Fronting Vila Real is the vast Santo António Beach, where finding a spot away from other beachgoers is never difficult. Santo António Beach starts at the mouth of the Guadiana River, and its flat creamy sand and tranquil water stretch 12 kilometers (7.4 mi) to the Ria Formosa estuary.

MONTE GORDO

4 kilometers (2.5 mi) west of Vila Real de Santo António, 7-minute drive along EN125 road
A 7-minute drive west from Vila Real de Santo António along the main N125 road is the lesser-known summer resort town of Monte Gordo, with one of the longest and finest beaches in the Algarve, popular with Portuguese families. Monte Gordo's formerly dated beachfront area now has a gorgeous 3-kilometer-long (1.9-mi-long) wooden walkway that will be extended to Vila Real de Santo António.

River Cruises

TRANSGUADIANA RIVER CRUISES

Av. Infante D. Henrique; tel. 966 089 341; www.transguadiana.com; from €47
TransGuadiana River Cruises offers sightseeing, bird-watching, and sunset party cruises on the Guadiana River; joining is a must-do if you're spending any time in the region.

Golf

MONTE REI GOLF & COUNTRY CLUB

tel. 281 950 950; www.monte-rei.com; greens fees from €165
The Monte Rei Golf & Country Club is an exclusive golf development and boasts a stunning Jack Nicklaus signature course. Monte Rei North opened in 2007 and is ranked among the best in Europe by golf publications. This par-72 course is a unique design in the undulating hills north of the A22 motorway; water comes into play on 11 of the 18 holes.

Food

Vila Real's gastronomy is rich and diverse, with strong Roman and Arab influences. Tuna takes center stage, a legacy of the town's canning industry. A local delicacy is ***espinheta de atum,*** tuna and potato stew.

CAVES DO GUADIANA

Av. da República 89; tel. 281 544 498; Fri.-Wed. noon-4pm and 7pm-10:30pm; €15
It might not look like much from the outside, but quaint and traditional Caves do Guadiana, on the riverside, is renowned for fresh fish, particularly tuna. It serves excellently prepared regional and Portuguese classics.

SEM ESPINHAS GUADIANA

Av. da República 51; tel. 281 544 605; www.semespinhas.net; daily noon-midnight; €16
Riverside Sem Espinhas Guadiana ("No Bones") revives age-old traditional cuisine from the eastern Algarve for younger crowds. This trendy, glamorous restaurant is one of four Sem Espinhas restaurants in the area.

★ PISA II

Rua Jornal do Algarve 44; tel. 281 543 157; daily noon-3pm and 6:30pm-10m; €8
Tucked away on one of Vila Real's backstreets is the rustic Pisa II, a husband-and-wife-run restaurant that has been attracting patrons for decades. Nondescript on the outside and snug on the inside, this former tavern is so popular for its seafood that queues form long into the

night. Its reputation hinges on its star dish, fried squid with french fries.

Accommodations

Lodging in Vila Real is limited, but clean and affordable.

ARENILHA GUEST HOUSE

Rua Dom Pedro V 55; tel. 964 722 018; €100

Sleek-looking Arenilha Guest House offers 30 modern rooms and a great central location just off the main square, just a 3-minute walk from the river that overlooks Spain.

HOTEL APOLO

Av. Dos Bombeiros Portugueses; tel. 281 512 448; www.apolo-hotel.com; €144

In the center of town, a couple of streets west of the main square, large and brightly colored three-star Hotel Apolo has 56 rooms, ranging from singles to family size, as well as a pool and a restaurant.

Information and Services

- **GNR police:** Rua Dr. Manuel de Arriaga 19; tel. 281 530 150; www.gnr.pt

- **Tourist information:** Rua 5 de Outubro, António Aleixo Cultural Centre; tel. 281 542 100

- **Post office:** Rua Teófilo de Braga 50; tel. 281 510 450

Getting There

Vila Real de Santo António is 63 kilometers (39 mi) east of **Faro airport,** 1 hour's drive on the **A22** motorway, or longer on the **N125** road, which gets congested in summer. The Guadiana International Bridge connects Vila Real with Ayamonte in Spain and connects to the A22 motorway.

VILA REAL TRAIN STATION

Rua da Estação Velha; tel. 281 543 242

CP (tel. 707 210 220; www.cp.pt) trains and **Eva** (tel. 289 899 760; www.eva-bus.com) buses both run frequently between Faro and Vila Real de Santo António, on the same lines

that pass through Tavira. There are a dozen departures per day of both trains and buses. The train takes 1.25 hours and costs around €5.25; the bus takes under 2 hours and costs €5.60. Buses run slightly more frequently between Tavira and Vila Real de Santo António; the 22-kilometer (13.6-mi) journey takes 1 hour and costs €4.15. The Vila Real de Santo António train station is a 15-minute walk north of the town center. Buses stop in the town center on the riverside, next to where the ferries leave for Ayamonte.

VILA REAL PORT

Avenida da Republica; tel. 218 543 152; www. etrioguadiana.pt

Ferry crossings (15 minutes; adults €1.90, bicycles €1.20, cars €5.50) from Vila Real to Ayamonte in Spain run every half hour throughout the day from Vila Real's port.

★ RIA FORMOSA NATURAL PARK

(Parque Natural da Ria Formosa)

Ria Formosa Natural Park is a protected coastline of sandy barrier islands, swirly lagoon-like canals, and reedy marshlands stretching 60 kilometers (37 mi) along the eastern Algarve, off the coast of Loulé, Faro, Olhão, Tavira, and Vila Real de Santo António. In total it spans 18,000 hectares (44,480 acres) in a patchwork of habitats that include marshes, tidal flats, dunes, salt pans, freshwater lagoons, agricultural areas, and woodlands. A swirl of gold and turquoise when viewed from above, the shifting landscape adapts to the seasons, shaped by the tides. Many of the sandy islets, such as Tavira Island (which serves as the city's main beach), are popular beach destinations accessed by regular boat trips from the mainland.

The Ria Formosa's diverse ecosystems are home to a wealth of flora and fauna, including endangered species like the European chameleon, a large seahorse population, the rare purple swamp hen, and turtles. Farther

out, dolphins can be spotted. It's an important wetland for migrating birds, making it a popular bird-watching spot, and nearly 80 percent of Portuguese clam exports are farmed at its shellfish nurseries.

Sights
ARMONA ISLAND
(Ilha da Armona)

Just off Olhão's coast is Armona Island, one of the barrier islands that make up the Ria Formosa protected wetlands. This vast pile of sand in the calm, shallow ria is considered Olhão's main beach and is hugely popular. Nine kilometers (5.6 mi) long and up to 1 kilometer (0.6 mi) wide, the island has a tiny year-round residential community of fisherfolk. A visit to Armona can offer a deserted-island experience—if you overlook the colorful fishing boats that dot the shoreline and the tons of other visitors in summer. The island is for pedestrians only, and all forms of motor transport are prohibited.

In the busier summer months, the island buzzes with water sports and has all necessary facilities for a relaxing day at the beach, including bars and restaurants, a kids' playground, toilets, sun beds, a mini-market, and even holiday chalets.

Ferries (under €4 round-trip) depart hourly from Olhão harbor and take 15 minutes to reach Armona Island. From arrival it is another 15-minute walk to the main beach area.

TAVIRA ISLAND
(Ilha de Tavira)

Tavira Island is one of the reserve's bigger barrier islands at 11 kilometers (6.8 mi) long and up to 1 kilometer (0.6 mi) wide. In summer, this sandbar is a popular for camping and families taking beach days. Flamingos, among other bird species, are often spotted here, making the island a favorite for bird-watchers. Tavira Island has a campground, bars and restaurants, and a handful of houses.

1: waterfall at Pego do Inferno outside Tavira
2: flamingos on the Ria Formosa **3:** a Kentish plover
4: Ria Formosa

It also has spots for nude sunbathing. Parasols and sun beds are available on the beach.

The island is only reachable by ferry or water taxi from Tavira city center's riverside or the Quatro Águas docks, where the river meets the ocean, a half-hour walk south of Tavira center. Ferries (€1.50 round-trip) run daily year-round, except in poor weather, generally 9am-5pm, although working hours are extended in busy holiday periods. Water taxis operate 24 hours daily in July-August; hours are limited outside this peak season. The taxi is more expensive than the ferry as it runs on demand and is faster.

Hiking

The Ria Formosa is great hiking territory, with enjoyable, flat hikes through bird-rich, salty landscapes offering dazzling scenery from every angle.

SÃO LOURENÇO TRAIL

Hiking Distance: 6.3 kilometers (3.9 mi) one-way
Hiking Time: 2.5 hours one-way
Trailhead: Quinta do Lago resort (cross the wooden bridge to Gigi beach, 16.6 km/10.3 mi east of Vilamoura)
Information and Maps: www.walkalgarve. com/algarve-walking-sightseeing-birding-routes/sao-lourenco-trail-in-quinta-do-lago

Immerse yourself in the serenity of the Ria Formosa's tranquil lagoons and salt pans on this scenic, linear trail, starting in Quinta do Lago and stretching just over 6 kilometers (4 mi) through the Ria Formosa, through sand dunes and crossing romantic wooden bridges, reedy lakes, and ancient Roman relics. Car parks are available; start near Quinta do Lago resort, which has a car park nearby, and head east, ending at the hamlet of Ludo. From here'll you'll either have to walk back or call a taxi.

LUDO TRAIL

Hiking Distance: 7-kilometer (4-mi) loop
Hiking Time: 3.5 hours round-trip
Trailhead: M527 road Ludo/Almancil; from Faro,

the no. 14 or the no. 16 bus operated by Proximo stops here (Ludo stop), or if driving, it's just behind Faro airport, at the western end of the runway, with parking on either side

Information and Maps: *www.walkalgarve. com/algarve-walking-sightseeing-birding-routes/ ludo-trail-in-faro*

One of the Eastern Algarve's most popular hikes is the Ludo trail, which picks its way between salt pans and along the Ria Formosa coastline. It's best visited at sunset and twilight to see the dazzling salt pans in a different light. The almost triangular semi-loop, which is signposted, starts in the hamlet of Ludo, near Quinta do Lago and the São Lourenço stream in Almancil, and takes hikers through countryside to the coastal fringe of the Ria Formosa, eventually convening with the São Lourenço trail. Get your camera ready to snap a huge assortment of waders and long-legged birds, such as the spoonbill, grey heron, and pretty pink flamingo, as well as other types of wildlife, such as turtles.

Bird-Watching

There are a series of prime year-round bird-watching spots along the Algarve coast, but few rival the dazzling salt pans on the Ria Formosa near Tavira. These unique salty marshes and brackish lagoons are home to flamingos, spoonbills, black-winged stilts, Kentish plovers, scores of wader species, waterfowl, and gulls. Portugal's most beautiful and important wetland, the Ria Formosa shelters 30,000 migrating birds every year and is a must for birders. Many types of bird-watching trips, including boat-based trips, are organized from Tavira and other locations such as Faro and Olhão.

- **Algarve Birdwatching:** Urb. Pezinhos, Lote 9 EH; tel. 960 170 789; www.algarve-birdwatching.com; from €50/half day

Tours
FORMOSAMAR
tel. 918 720 002; www.formosamar.com
Formosamar runs ecotourism activities on

the Ria Formosa, including nature sightseeing boat trips (2 hours; €25), seabird-, turtle-, and dolphin-watching boat trips (2 hours; €40), and kayak tours (2 hours; €35).

Boat Trips
SEQUATOURS
tel. 960 170 789; www.sequatours.com
To sunbathe on a beach-island or cruise the Ria Formosa, hire one of the taxi-boats (from €8 per boat, up to 6 people, 1-hour tour from €12 pp). SequaTours runs water taxis from Tavira and Tavira Island.

Accommodations
TAVIRA ISLAND CAMP SITE
Ilha de Tavira; tel. 281 027 430; www.cm-tavira.pt; June-Sept.; €7-80
Pitch up your own tent or rent one from Tavira Island Camp Site, where two types of tents are already set up: a family-size tent, and a fully equipped tent with electricity, rooms, and kitchen. Washing machines, hot water, and lockers are among the services available at the site, along with a snack bar, mini-market, and a children's playground.

ARMONA ISLAND BUNGALOWS
Ilha de Armona; tel. 289 714 173; www.orbitur.pt/en/ destinations/algarve/orbitur-ilha-de-armona; from €100
Run by company Orbitur, Orbitur Ilha de Armona campsite is located just 200 meters (650 ft) from the beach. It offers a range of simple and functional little holiday chalets for 2-5 people, starting from around €100/night, which are equipped with a seating area and a kitchenette with a fridge. Kitchen and bath towels and bed linens are provided; laundry facilities can be found on site.

Getting There
The Ria Formosa can be explored from many points along the 60 kilometers (37 mi) of coastline that stretches between Loulé and Vila Real de Santo António. Some of its attractions, like salt pans and lagoons, are land-based and can be viewed on foot;

the Loulé-Faro stretch of the Ria Formosa is popular for hikes. Other attractions, such as the Ria's islands, are accessible only by boat, mainly from docks along the coasts of Faro, Olhão, and Tavira. The Faro-Tavira section of the Ria is widely regarded as the prime portion, where a number of the islands with the best beaches, like Armona and Tavira, are located. There is no central tourist office, but offices in the main towns along the Ria Formosa (Loulé, Faro, Olhão, Tavira) should be able to provide park-specific information on activities and accommodation.

The Golden Triangle

The Golden Triangle is the Algarve's most affluent and prestigious area, with luxury hotels, Michelin-starred restaurants, pricey real estate, and exquisite gardens and lavish villas. Situated within the municipality of Loulé, it stretches between the traditional town of Almancil at its northern point and widens toward the coast to encompass the up-market resorts of Vale do Lobo and Quinta do Lago. If people-watching and high-end real estate is what floats your boat, then this is the place to come.

LOULÉ

A bustling traditional market town and a large inland residential area, Loulé (LOO-lay) is an attractive city rich in Moorish heritage, with cobblestone streets and petite squares. Known for its markets—Loulé was a major trade center in medieval times—the city is also famous as the home of one of the biggest and oldest Carnival parades in Portugal.

Sights
LOULÉ CASTLE
(Castelo de Loulé)

Rua Dom Paio Peres Correia 17; tel. 289 400 642; www.cm-loule.pt; Tues.-Fri. 10am-1:30pm and 2pm-6pm, Sat. 10am-1:30pm and 2pm-4:30pm; €1.62
Loulé Castle is today an important national monument and one of the city's main attractions. Loulé Castle is unusual in that it has become a part of the city's core: The castle's walls and towers have been incorporated into local buildings. It's free to visit the castle's courtyard, where visitors can see impressive medieval siege artillery.

Built on the site of Roman fortifications, the Moorish castle was expanded in the 13th century under King Afonso III. The remains of the castle comprise four towers and the walls that link them. The views over Loulé's old town from the top of the towers are well worth the small entry fee.

Inside the castle, the **Loulé Municipal Museum** (tel. 289 400 885; www. museudeloule.pt) covers a variety of topics from traditional local gastronomy to fruit drying.

SHRINE OF OUR LADY OF PIETY (Santuário de Nossa Senhora da Piedade)

Mon.-Fri. 9:30am-12:30pm and 2pm-6pm summer, Mon.-Fri. 9:30am-12:30pm and 2pm-5pm winter; free
From afar, the unusually shaped Shrine of Our Lady of Piety, 2 kilometers (1.2 mi) west of Loulé center along the N270 road, looks like a futuristic spaceship. The sanctuary is an important Marian shrine and hosts "the largest religious celebrations south of Fátima." The interior is mostly made of wood and has an eerie candle room. There is also a small chapel at the site, believed to be around 300 years old, with a Baroque altar and lovely frescoes.

The views from the hilltop shrine are superb. The walk from Loulé takes 25 minutes, although it is strenuous, with a climb up a steep cobbled hill. A taxi from Loulé costs around €5; taxis can be found parked in the city center.

The Golden Triangle

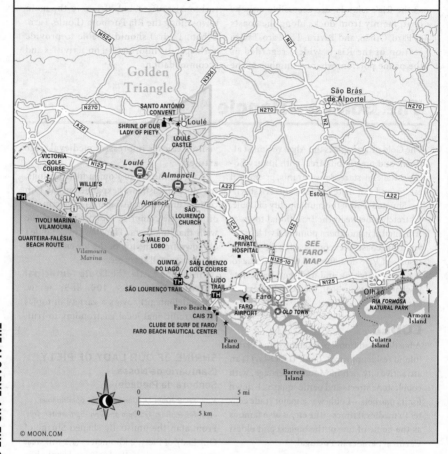

SANTO ANTÓNIO CONVENT
(Convento Capucho de Santo António)

Rua da Nossa Senhora da Piedade, EN270 road;
Tues.-Fri. 10am-6pm, Sat. 9:30am-4pm; free

Located on the outskirts of Loulé, this simple but striking convent as it stands today resulted from restoration and expansion work carried out in the second half of the 17th century. The architecture is in the traditional Portuguese *chão,* or plain style, distinguished by the architectural sobriety characteristic of the Capuchin Franciscan ideals, and shows traces of additions from the 18th century, namely from the post-earthquake period of 1755.

Entertainment and Events
LOULÉ MED FESTIVAL

www.festivalmed.pt; late June

Every year, Loulé hosts one of the country's biggest world music festivals, the Med Festival, a four-day event with concerts around the city. Loulé transforms into a buzzing hive of Mediterranean food and culture with music from around the globe.

CARNIVAL

www.cm-loule.pt; Feb. or early Mar.

Loulé's Carnival celebration is the oldest and one of the most famous in the country, attracting huge crowds for samba-fueled festivities. Not quite as racy as Carnival in Brazil, Portugal's version satirizes political affairs. The allegorical floats usually feature huge papier-mâché puppets and heads parodying government leaders and sports stars. It is nonetheless a vibrant, energetic, exciting affair that goes on for three days, with parades and dancing in the streets. Loulé's main parades take place along the city's central José da Costa Mealha Avenue, which is closed off to the public; spectators must buy a ticket (€2) to enter the main parade area.

Shopping

Along with its famous markets, Loulé has quirky galleries and an array of arts and crafts shops. For traditional handicrafts, venture off the main street and into the backstreets around the castle and city center.

LOULÉ WEEKLY MARKET
(Mercado Semanal de Loulé)

Rua da Nossa Senhora da Piedade; Sat. 8am-1pm

Haggle for a bargain at one of the most famous weekly markets in the Algarve. Held every Saturday morning in front of the Santo António Convent, on the road out of Loulé toward Boliqueime-Albufeira, the Loulé Weekly Market is packed with clothes, handbags, shoes, and sunglasses as well as goods by local artisans such as cork items and pottery.

Food

LOULÉ MUNICIPAL MARKET
(Mercado Municipal de Loulé)

Rua José Fernandes Guerreiro 34; tel. 289 400 600; www.lcglobal.pt; Mon.-Sat. 6am-3pm

With striking red domes and Moorish architecture, Loulé Municipal Market looks more Arab than Portuguese. Inaugurated in 1908, the atmospheric building is busy with vendors selling fresh local produce, jams, preserves, and oils. Stock up on artisanal specialties like cured meats, smoked sausages and cheeses, fresh bread, Algarve liqueurs, and local sweets made from figs and almonds. There are also stalls selling lovely handmade Loulé tablecloths, crocheted items, and cork products. A traditional outdoor farmers market takes place every Saturday morning, adjacent to the municipal market.

CAFÉ Q

Rua Vice Almirante Candido Reis; tel. 289 414 310; www.facebook.com/cosmopolitanfoodcompany.pt; Mon.-Fri. 9:30am-5pm, Sat. 10am-4pm; €10

For a quick snack or a lighter meal, pop into boutique bistro Café Q. It's tucked away on a backstreet near Loulé council in the heart of town, and you can sit in the cozy main dining area or outside in the bougainvillea-covered courtyard. Don't be misled by the name; this superb little hidden gem offers delicious African-inspired treats like prawn and yogurt wrap, Mozambican curry, or a slice of Café Q's famous carrot cake.

BOCAGE

Rua Bocage 14; tel. 289 412 416 or 914 011 482; www.restaurantebocage.com; Mon.-Fri. noon-3pm; €10

In the city center, Bocage is a little corner cottage popular for its traditional Algarvian cuisine, using fresh local products. Specialties include stewed rabbit, Portuguese-style pork, and tuna steak in onions.

Accommodations
HOTEL STAR LOULÉ

Rua Doutor Francisco Sá Carneiro; tel. 933 094 579; www.hotelstarloule.pt; €65

Basic but clean and modern one-star Hotel Star Loulé is within walking distance of the city center. It has free Wi-Fi in all rooms, modern baths, and an excellent central location.

HOTEL LOULÉ JARDIM

Praça Manuel de Arriaga 25; tel. 289 413 094; www.loulejardimhotel.com; €119

Converted from an early-20th-century residence, the stately Hotel Loulé Jardim is in the older part of Loulé, facing a leafy garden. It

has a rooftop pool and is a short walk from the heart of the city.

Information and Services

- **GNR police station:** Travessa Charles Bonnet; tel. 289 410 490; www.gnr.pt
- **Tourist office:** Av. 25 Abril 9; tel. 289 463 900
- **Main post office:** Rua 1 Dezembro; tel. 289 400 500

Getting There

Loulé is 20 kilometers (12.4 mi) northwest of **Faro airport** along the **IC4** and then either the **N125-4** road or **A22** motorway, about a 20-minute drive. The inland city is north of the A22 and the N125, which both run the length of the Algarve region.

LOULÉ BUS TERMINAL

Rua de Nossa Sra. de Fátima; tel. 289 416 655; www.eva-bus.com

Eva (tel. 289 899 760; www.eva-bus.com) buses run every half hour between Loulé's main bus terminal in the city center and Faro (40 minutes; €3.35), on the Loulé-Faro line.

LOULÉ TRAIN STATION

Estação dos Caminhos de Ferro de Loulé; tel. 707 210 220; www.cp.pt

CP (tel. 707 210 220; www.cp.pt) runs trains from Faro to Loulé (10-16 minutes; €3) at least once an hour 7am-8:40pm. The station is 5 kilometers (3.1 mi) out of the town center. There are taxis outside the station, or ask the staff to call one.

Getting Around

Loulé is compact enough to **walk** around. A municipal **shuttle bus** (tel. 289 416 655; www.lcglobal.pt; €1, 48-hour tourist pass €3) runs frequently around the city as well as to the coastal resort of Vilamoura and Loulé's

---

1: Loulé Municipal Market **2:** Loulé's main shopping street **3:** Loulé Castle

train station. There are also plenty of **taxis** in Loulé center.

ALMANCIL

Halfway between Loulé and the coastline, bisected by the busy N125 regional road, Almancil is a bustling town, the beating heart of the Golden Triangle and the gateway to many upscale resorts. Catering more to wealthy holiday homeowners rather than tourists, it's a pleasant, busy town with an excellent selection of restaurants.

Sights
SÃO LOURENÇO CHURCH (Igreja de São Lourenço)

Rua da Igreja; tel. 289 395 451; Mon. 2:15pm-5pm, Tues.-Sat. 10am-1pm and 3pm-5pm, open until 6pm Mon.-Sat. in summer; free

A main attraction but still a hidden gem, São Lourenço Church, a short walk east of the town center, was built during the first half of the 18th century. The exterior of the modest whitewashed church belies its spectacular interior, with an iridescent gilded altar and traditional blue-and-white *azulejo* tiles from 1730.

Food
A QUINTA RESTAURANT

Rua Vale Formoso; tel. 289 393 357; www.aquintarestaurant.com; Tues.-Sat. 12:30pm-2:30pm and 7pm-10pm; €25

On the road heading out of Loulé toward the A22 motorway is polished A Quinta Restaurant, with a sophisticated menu in a refined setting. A firm favorite, A Quinta bases its menu on fresh seasonal produce with a gourmet twist. Fine wines and warm hospitality complement the cuisine, and the restaurant has a beautiful terrace with coastal views.

FIGUEIRAL

Rua Cristovao Pires Norte; tel. 289 395 558; www.figueiral.pt; Wed.-Sat. 12:30pm-2:30pm and 7pm-10pm, Tues. 7pm-10pm; €25

Atmospheric Figueiral specializes in grilled meats, and the famous onion soup and

Portugal's Best Golf Courses

More than 40 acclaimed courses and good winter weather lure thousands of golfers to the Algarve to enjoy challenging and expertly designed greens, concentrated in the Golden Triangle; more than a million rounds are played here annually. Europe's premier golf destination, the Algarve offers wide variety of courses for all levels of skill, from Arnold Palmer's acclaimed **Victoria** championship golf course in Vilamoura (page 213) to the beautiful classic **Penina** course in Portimão, designed by Sir Henry Cotton (page 221). All the region's courses welcome visiting non-members, with some courses offering rounds for less than €50, but prices range widely depending on season and time of day.

VALE DO LOBO
tel. 289 353 000; www.valedolobo.com

Sprawling in fragrant, pine-laden countryside, Vale do Lobo is a large luxury resort founded in 1962, among the first in the Algarve, on 450 hectares (1,112 acres) of beachfront. It is home to two championship golf courses, as well as swimming pools, restaurants and bars, wellness and medical centers, and a tennis academy. All are open to nonguests. Greens fees for visitors for an 18-hole round start from about €190. The resort offers exceptional service and is a destination for the rich and famous who prefer to stay low-key.

It's 6 kilometers (3.7 mi) south of Almancil. **Eva** (tel. 289 899 760; www.eva-bus.com) buses run hourly between Almancil and Vale do Lobo (10 minutes; €2). Alternatively, call **Rádio Táxis de Almancil** (tel. 289 399 998; €7).

QUINTA DO LAGO
tel. 289 390 700; www.quintadolago.com

The exclusive Quinta do Lago is an upscale resort featuring golden-sand beaches and golf courses. The award-winning **San Lorenzo Golf Course** (Quinta do Lago; tel. 289 396 522; www.sanlorenzogolfcourse.com; greens fees from €145 for 18 holes) showcases Quinta do Lago's unique landscape, with beautiful Bermuda-grass greens, saltwater lagoons, and pine woodland. Shaped as a figure eight, the course was designed by Joseph Lee and inaugurated in 1988.

Quinta do Lago is 4 kilometers (2.5 mi) south of Almancil. **Eva** (tel. 289 899 760; www.eva-bus.com) buses run hourly between Almancil and Quinta do Lago (10 minutes; €2). Alternatively, take **Rádio Táxis de Almancil** (tel. 289 399 998; €5).

Brazilian *picanha* (a prized cut of beef) keep patrons coming back. Elegantly laid tables and fresh colors make this restaurant feel classy and airy.

RESTAURANT HENRIQUE LEIS
Estrada Vale Formoso 234; tel. 289 393 438; www. henriqueleis.com; Tues.-Sat. lunch and dinner Sept.-June, Mon.-Sat. dinner July-Aug.; €40

French-inspired Restaurant Henrique Leis has a rich and refined interior, an acclaimed menu, and a wine list showcasing the best Portuguese grapes. It has held a Michelin star since 2000 and is as a benchmark for fine food in the Algarve. Dishes include egg *à la coque*

(soft-boiled) with smoked caviar and lobster from the Algarve Coast with risotto gel.

Getting There

Almancil is 13 kilometers (8.1 mi) northwest of **Faro**, a 15-minute drive via the **IC4** road, and 6 kilometers (3.7 mi) south of **Loulé**, a 10-minute drive via the **M521** road. The main **N125** road runs through the middle of Almancil.

Eva (tel. 289 899 760; www.eva-bus.com) buses run half-hourly from Faro to Almancil (20 minutes; €3.35), passing through on their way to Loulé. The **bus stop** is located close to the main town center.

ALMANCIL TRAIN STATION

Vale Formoso - Apeadeiro CP Almancil; tel. 707 210 220; www.cp.pt

Alternatively, take the **CP** (tel. 707 210 220; www.cp.pt) train from Faro to Almancil (10 minutes; €2). Trains run several times a day between Faro and Almancil. The train station is not in the town center but is within walking distance.

VILAMOURA

Vilamoura, a privately managed resort town, is pleasing to the eye, made up of low-rise resorts, manicured golf courses, and vast artificial lakes. At the heart of the town is its famous marina.

Sights

VILAMOURA MARINA
(Marina de Vilamoura)

www.marinadevilamoura.com

Portugal's Monaco or Marbella, the award-winning Vilamoura Marina is a favorite hangout for the rich and glamorous. The largest marina in Portugal, it has capacity for over 1,000 vessels. Surrounded by elegant restaurants and trendy bars, luxury properties, and smart hotels, the marina is a place to people-watch and be seen, and a great place for a pleasant stroll. It is also home to one of the Algarve's three casinos.

Cycling

For all its pizzazz, Vilamoura is an environmentally conscious and down-to-earth town, and cycling is a popular way to get around, with dozens of pathways for strolling and cycling. The glamorous resort boasts one of the biggest shared bicycle networks in the Algarve, **Vilamoura Public Bikes,** managed by local company **Inframoura** (www.inframoura.pt). The company offers 260 public-use bicycles distributed over 43 stations and 20 kilometers (12 mi) of bike track, although these are only rented for up to 45 minutes. Bikes are widely available to rent through other private companies, including from **MegaSport Travel** (tel. 289 393 044;

www.megasport.pt; €30 per day, €126 per week).

QUARTEIRA-FALÉSIA BEACH ROUTE

Cycling Distance: *5 kilometers (3 mi) one-way*
Cycling Time: *20 minutes one-way*
Trailhead: *Rotunda do Polvo (octopus roundabout, Av. Dr. Carlos Mota Pinto)*
Information and Maps: *www.wikiloc.com/ mountain-biking-trails/ciclovias-do-algarve-ciclovia-de-vilamoura-quarteira-praia-da-falesia-1291522*

One of the most popular cycling routes in Vilamoura, this easy route delimits the outskirts of the town. It follows the Vilamoura cycle path along the busy fringes.

Water Sports

Boats for big-game fishing can be chartered directly from the marina, where visitors will also find facilities for Jet Skis, parasailing, and boat tours.

- **AlgarveXcite:** tel. 289 301 884 or 937 777 913; www.fishingvilamoura.com
- **Watersports Vilamoura:** tel. 289 301 884 or 937 777 913; www.watersportsvilamoura.com

Golf

VICTORIA GOLF COURSE

Urbanização Colinas do Golfe 4; tel. 289 320 100; www.dompedrogolf.com; greens fees from €90

The 18-hole Victoria Golf Course is Arnold Palmer's only signature course in Portugal. With 90 hectares (222 acres) of manicured greens, it is also home to the Portuguese Masters and features extensive gently rolling fairways, smartly placed bunkers, and challenging water hazards that will test even the most accomplished.

Food and Accommodations

THAI BEACH CLUB

Av. Rocha Baixinha, Falésia Beach; tel. 289 322 471; www.thaibeachclub.com; daily 10am-11pm; €30

Located on Falésia Beach, Thai Beach Club is a glamorous beach restaurant with a reputation for serving fine Thai food with some of the most stunning sea views in the Algarve.

WILLIE'S

Rua do Brazil 2; tel. 289 380 849; www.willies-restaurante.com; Thurs.-Tues. 7pm-10:30pm; €35

An institution among the well-heeled locals, Willie's has a solid reputation. Willie Wurger is the chef who dreams up the superlative seasonal menus for his elegant eponymous Michelin-star restaurant. Dishes include Willie's homemade seafood ravioli in a vermouth cream sauce, sautéed sea scallops on truffle risotto, and calf's liver on potato mousse.

TIVOLI MARINA VILAMOURA

Marina de Vilamoura; tel. 289 303 303; www.minorhotels.com; €285

On the water at the mouth of Vilamoura Marina, overlooking the gleaming yachts and bustling bars on one side and the beautiful beach on the other, the Tivoli Marina Vilamoura is glamorous, sophisticated, and contemporary. It comprises several pools and restaurants, a spa, and a summer beach club, and is next door to the casino.

Information and Services

- **Tourist office:** Praça Parlatorio Romano, Edifício Loja 9, Marina Arcadas; tel. 926 066 277

Getting There

Vilamoura is 15 kilometers (9.3 mi) southwest of **Loulé** on the **N396** road, a 25-minute drive. It's 25 kilometers (15.5 mi) west of **Faro** on the **IC4** road, a 30-minute drive.

Eva (tel. 289 899 760; www.eva-bus.com) buses run from Faro's main bus terminal to Vilamoura (45 minutes; €4.10), via Almancil, almost hourly. From Loulé, catch the municipal **shuttle bus** (tel. 289 416 655; www.lcglobal.pt) that runs frequently between Loulé, Vilamoura, and Loulé train station (45 minutes; €1, 48-hour tourist pass €3).

Albufeira and the Barlavento

Albufeira is the Algarve's best-known tourist destination, with everything from fantastic beaches and a quaint Old Town to modern neon-lit bars, a classy marina, and lots of hotels and restaurants for all budgets. It's a magnet for families and young travelers on holiday and can get busy and rowdy in the height of summer.

Albufeira is a town of two halves: the Old Town and the neon-lit Oura area. Two kilometers (1.2 mi) east of Old Town, Oura is home to the neon-lit Strip, the Algarve's ultimate party destination. The charming historic part of Albufeira is worlds away with its large central square fringed with restaurants, quaint cobbled streets with little shops and cafés, and street entertainment in summer. Still, in summer, even Old Town bars stay open until the early hours.

Albfueira's rainbow-colored marina, a short distance west from the old town, is a hub for water sports, boat trips, and a lovely place for a lunch or a few drinks at night, with a small but lively selection of bars, boutiques, and restaurants.

Albufeira is also loosely the starting point of the Barlavento, or western Algarve, which is much busier and more developed compared to the east, and home to some of the western Algarve's most popular towns and attractions, such as the picturesque fishermen's villages of Carvoeiro and Ferragudo, sprawling Portimão, and first-class beach resort Praia da Rocha. Many of the Algarve's most famous beaches can also be found in the western end of the region, including Dona Ana Beach—perhaps one of the most photographed beaches in Europe—in Lagos.

BEACHES

Boasting 25 beaches, Albufeira's coastline has something for everyone, from secret secluded coves to long, shimmering stretches of golden sand that are among the most popular in the Algarve. Many beaches are sought out by Portugal's wealthy and famous for a break from prying eyes. Albufeira's three main beaches, which front the city, are **Fishermen's Beach** and the adjacent **Tunel** and **Inatel** beaches.

FISHERMEN'S BEACH
(Praia dos Pescadores)
off Albufeira Old Town center

Albufeira's main and most central beach, Fishermen's Beach, fronts the Old Town area. Once a hub for fishing, today the colorful little wooden boats have given way to parasols. In summer a range of water sports occupy this beach, while in winter it hosts a big New Year's party. Escalators take beachgoers from the bluff to the Blue Flag-awarded sands.

TUNNEL BEACH
(Praia do Túnel)
West of Fishermen's Beach

Through a tunnel from Albufeira's Old Town, fronting the Old Town area, this buzzing beach is a golden hub of activity. Also known as Praia do Peneco, it's tacked onto the eastern end of Fishermen's Beach. This beach has good access for people with disabilities, with a modern lift at one end, as well as ramps and steps.

INATEL BEACH
East of Fishermen's Beach

A lovely long beach east of Fishermen's Beach, Inatel connects to Fishermen's Beach and Tunel Beach. Pristine and open, it is more spacious than its immediate neighbors, and is a great place to soak up some rays.

SPORTS AND RECREATION

Water sports galore are available on all of Albufeira's main beaches in summer. Beach outfitters tout everything from pedal boats and banana boats, to kayaking and paragliding. Most accept cash only.

Boating
DREAM WAVE ALGARVE
Marina de Albufeira, Passeio dos Oceanos, Lote 5, Loja 31, Fracção A; tel. 962 003 885 or 962 003 801; www.dreamwavealgarve.com; from €22

Dream Wave Algarve has sailing trips on a wooden caravel and the fastest speedboat in the region. Operating from Albufeira Marina, the boating company also offers cave tours and dolphin-watching cruises.

Cycling
ALGARVE BIKE HOLIDAYS
Av. da Liberdade 144; tel. 913 226 954; www.algarvebikeholidays.com; head office daily 9am-8pm

Cycle from Albufeira through gorgeous central Algarve landscapes on a small-group, 4-hour guided bike tour (from €30 pp) with Algarve Bike Holidays. Tours are conducted in English and can be customized.

FOOD
JAIPUR
Rua 1 de Dezembro 28-30; tel. 289 585 707; www.curryclubs.com; daily lunch and dinner; €10

One of Albufeira's most popular restaurants, Jaipur is a spice box of fresh Indian flavors with a garish interior. It's a short walk north of the Old Town center, near the Sineira church and bell tower.

STEWS & MORE
Forte de São João, Rua Almeida Garrett 40; tel. 924 088 166; Tues.-Sun. 5pm-10pm; €15

Cozy and casual Stews & More serves "new-style grandmothers' cooking," old-fashioned home cooking with a contemporary twist, with typical Portuguese one-pot dishes in traditional earthenware. The space is modern-rustic, with wooden finishes and elegant tables. Stew menus are divided into seasonal items and specials.

BEACH BASKET

Praça Miguel Bombarda 7; tel. 289 512 137; daily
noon-midnight; €15

In Albufeira's Old Town, overlooking Peneco Beach, the Beach Basket is a highly recommended beachside restaurant for long, lazy lunches or romantic dinners. Fabulous views are complemented by fresh seafood like stuffed crab, fresh sea bass, and *cataplana.*

THE MARKET RESTAURANT & WINE BAR

Av. Sá Carneiro 1; tel. 289 501 441; daily
5:30pm-11pm; €20

Spacious, modern Market Restaurant & Wine Bar is toward the bottom of Albufeira's main strip heading toward Oura, overlooking the sea. Market has unusual Mediterranean-inspired dishes such as tuna ceviche with coconut, suckling pig croquettes, and a shrimp and chili burger, as well interesting cocktails.

BARS AND NIGHTLIFE

Albufeira is a popular nightlife destination year-round, with live music and shows throughout the town. With a big party scene, Albufeira can get rowdy. Fishermen's Beach hosts one of the biggest New Year's parties in the Algarve, too.

Packed with side-by-side sports bars, Irish bars, tattoo parlors, and restaurants, Albufeira's famous **Strip** is one very long and flashy road with souvenir shops by day and a kaleidoscope of every shade of neon by night. Stretching 2 kilometers (1.2 mi), it is the Algarve's busiest nightlife destination. The Strip can get pretty raucous most nights, especially in summer when it never seems to sleep. Many tourist-oriented international restaurants are also along the Strip.

Not as rowdy as the Strip, Albufeira's **Old Town** hangouts tend to be livelier in summer, although live entertainment is generally put on at least once or twice a week, even in low season. The atmosphere at **Albufeira Marina** is more composed, with reasonably

priced, classy restaurants, plenty of shops and entertainment for the kids, and lovely bars. The marina is a 30-minute clifftop walk west of central Albufeira, or a short taxi ride.

WILD & CO. BAR & STEAKHOUSE

Av. Sá Carneiro 29; tel. 289 583 545 or 911 700 999;
www.wildandcompany.com; Mon.-Sat. 11am-4am,
Sun. 11am-midnight

Upstairs at Wild & Co. Bar & Steakhouse is a steakhouse; downstairs it's one of the wildest bars in Albufeira, with neon flashing, music thumping, dancing on the bar top, and regular live music. Think Irish pub meets American saloon.

KISS DISCO CLUB

Rua Vasco da Gama, Edifício Kiss; tel. 289 515 693;
Wed.-Mon. 1am-7am, Tues. 9am-5pm May.-Oct.,
Fri.-Sat. 11:45pm-7am Nov.-Apr.

Open since 1981, Kiss Disco Club has DJs and live bands with the latest hits to keep the crowd dancing till the early morning. It's a place to go after other bars have closed, but drinks can be pricy. An entry fee may be applied.

CASA DO CERRO

Cerro da Piedade, near Dolphin Roundabout on
the road to the marina; tel. 919 596 665; Tues.-Sun.
8pm-3am

Just a stone's throw from the marina, gorgeously exotic cocktail bar and chill-out lounge Casa do Cerro is adorned with Moroccan-style loungers, throw pillows, and *shisha* pipes, while a warm and spicy color palette and the odd statue of Buddha lend an Indian twist. A hidden gem frequented by the in crowd, it is a relaxing place to see and be seen. Casa do Cerro also serves tapas and has a full restaurant menu.

ACCOMMODATIONS

Albufeira offers scores of lodging, from family-friendly all-inclusive resorts, to self-catering apartments, charming B&Bs, and high-end hotels.

1: Albufeira's Old Town **2:** Fishermen's Beach

HOTEL BRISA SOL

Rua do Município 27; tel. 289 580 420; www. hotelbrisasol.com; €159 d, €179 studio, €249 1-bedroom apartment

On Albufeira's main Avenida dos Descobrimentos, four-star Hotel Brisa Sol is a modern building with a traditional Portuguese interior of polished stone floors and tile-clad walls. This casual apartment-hotel is a 15-minute walk from Fishermen's Beach and a short stroll to the Strip.

HOTEL SOL E MAR

Rua José Bernardino de Sousa; tel. 289 580 080; www.grupofbarata.com; €221

In the middle of Albufeira's Old Town, right on Fishermen's Beach, the four-star Hotel Sol e Mar is massively popular for its location and has 74 rooms on six floors. It dates to 1965 and was refurbished in 2002. Built into the cliff, this distinctive Spanish-looking hotel boasts first-line sea views.

★ EPIC SANA ALGARVE

Aldeia da Falésia; tel. 289 104 300; www.algarve. epic.sanahotels.com; €432

Environmentally conscious low-rise five-star resort Epic Sana Algarve is nestled among Albufeira's characteristic pine trees on the coast overlooking Falésia Beach. Along with 162 rooms, 24 suites, and 43 spacious apartments, it houses a large conference center. This modern and contemporary resort strikes a balance between nature and comfort.

INFORMATION AND SERVICES

- **GNR police station:** Estrada de Vale de Pedras; tel. 289 590 790; www.gnr.pt
- **Tourist office:** Rua 5 de Outubro 4; tel. 289 585 279
- **Main post office:** Rua Alexandre Herculano; tel. 289 580 860

GETTING THERE

Albufeira is 45 kilometers (28 mi) and a 40-minute drive west of **Faro airport** along the **A22** motorway. Following the **N125** road takes 45 minutes. If you arrive at Faro airport at night and want to go straight to Albufeira, arrange a private transfer. A reputable company is **Yellow Fish Transfers** (tel. 289 046 243; www.yellowfishtransfers.com).

Taking the train to Albufeira is not recommended, as the train station (Albufeira-Ferreiras, Largo da Estação; tel. 707 210 220; www.cp.pt) is 7 kilometers (4.3 mi) outside the city center and requires taking a taxi.

ALBUFEIRA BUS STATION

Urbanização Alto dos Caliços; tel. 289 589 055

Eva (tel. 289 899 760; www.eva-bus.com) buses run regularly between Faro and Albufeira, generally via Loulé, or Vilamoura and Quarteira. The regional bus (1.5 hours; €4.85) runs every 30-50 minutes; the Transrápido express coach (1 hour; €6) runs every couple of hours. Albufeira's main bus station is 1.6 kilometers (1 mi) from the city center but is easy to get to on Albufeira's **Próximo** (www.proximo.pt) bus, which stops at the terminal.

GETTING AROUND

It is possible to walk from one end of Albufeira to the other, from the marina or Old Town to the Strip, but it is far, especially at night or in the heat. **Rádio Táxis de Albufeira** (tel. 289 583 230; www.taxis-albufeira.pt) and other taxis are readily available around town and are inexpensive.

The local bus system **Próximo** (www.proximo.pt; €1.10, unlimited 24-hour ticket €5.30) stops at all the city's major attractions, including the main bus terminal. Buy tickets on board; most drivers speak good English.

Giro Bus (www.cm-albufeira.pt; day ticket €4) also runs five circular nonstop lines serving key places such as the main bus terminal, Old Town, Oura, the marina, and the Strip.

ZOOMARINE SEALIFE PARK

N125, km 65, Guia; tel. 289 560 300; www. zoomarine.pt; daily 10am-7:30pm late June-early

Sept., daily 10am-5pm Mar.-late June and early Sept.-Nov.; adults €29 in low season (June 10-June 21 and Sept. 6-Nov. 28), €32 in high season (June 22-Sept. 5), children under 11 €23, discounts online

Zoomarine Sealife Park is one of the Algarve's most exciting theme parks, promoting environmental awareness and ocean conservation. In the town of Guia, 15 kilometers (9.3 mi) west of Albufeira, the park has attractions including dolphin and seal shows, an artificial beach and wave pool, a Ferris wheel, and water rides. You can swim with the dolphins (book in advance, from €126). Don't forget your swimsuit and a towel. The park closes sporadically in quieter months (Mar. and Nov.), so check ahead for open hours.

By car from **Albufeira,** follow the N125 road west to Guia. Zoomarine is just past the town on the N125. A taxi from Albufeira (Rádio Táxis de Albufeira; tel. 289 583 230; www.taxis-albufeira.pt) to Zoomarine costs €12 one-way or €15 on weekends. Organize the return trip with the driver. There is no convenient way to get to Zoomarine by public transport.

PORTIMÃO

In its heyday, Portimão (por-tee-MOWN) was an important fishing and trading port with a thriving sardine and mackerel canning industry. The colorful, iconic designs used on the cans are now considered retro art, seen on modern tins and graffiti and murals around the city, emblems of Portimão's former glory. The award-wining Portimão Museum is dedicated to this era, a glimpse into life in Portimão a century ago.

Today Portimão is a blend of residential and touristy. The riverside is delightful when the weather gets warmer. Families come to stroll the water's edge and enjoy ice cream in the gentle breeze from the sea. Delimited to the south by Praia da Rocha, a well-known holiday hot spot, and the Arade River to the east, the once-impoverished city is bouncing back as a cool place to visit. And just 15 minutes west of Portimão is Alvor, one of the trendiest little villages in the region.

Sights

The main **Manuel Teixeira Gomes Square** is the heart of Portimão, a good place to enjoy the sunshine and watch the world go by. It's also known as **Casa Inglesa Square** for the century-old café Casa Inglesa. Along riverfront **Largo do Dique,** visitors will find plenty of convenient metered parking as well as stalls touting boat trips and bicycle hires.

PORTIMÃO MUSEUM
(Museu de Portimão)

Rua D. Carlos I; tel. 282 405 230 or 282 405 265; www.museudeportimao.pt; Tues. 2:30pm-6pm, Wed.-Sun. 10am-6pm Sept.-July, Tues. 7:30pm-11pm, Wed.-Sun. 3pm-11pm Aug., adults €3, children under 16 free

Toward the south end of Portimão's riverside and Praia da Rocha, the Portimão Museum has breathed new life into the site of a once-thriving cannery building. Inaugurated in 2008, the museum has won awards for its insight into fishing and canning traditions. An interactive re-creation of the entire process, from landing catches to production lines and canning, uses state-of-the-art effects.

Also on display are local artifacts from prehistoric, Roman, and Islamic times. Part of the museum is dedicated to Portimão's most famous son, Manuel Teixeira Gomes, an acclaimed writer, diplomat, and president of Portugal 1923-1925. English translations on exhibits are scarce, although staff will try to answer questions in English. The documentary videos in the interactive experience have English subtitles.

Cycling

Both Portimão and Praia da Rocha have many bike hire outlets, such as **Motorent** (http://motorent.pt), **Europcar** (www.rentbikescooters.com), and **Scooters and Bikes to Rent** (https://scootersandbikes.pt), which offer regular and eclectic bike rentals with delivery if necessary.

Portimão, Praia da Rocha, and Ferragudo

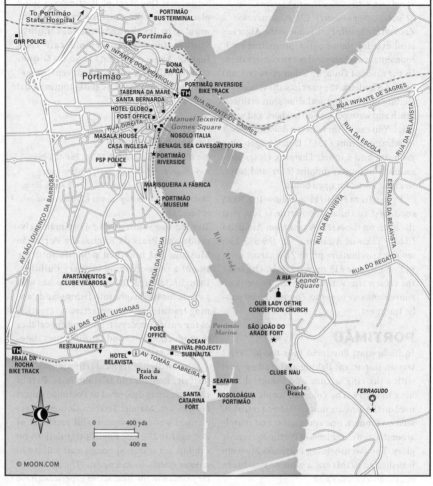

PORTIMÃO RIVERSIDE BIKE TRACK

Cycling Distance: 1.3 kilometers (0.8 mi) one-way

Cycling Time: 15 minutes one-way

Trailhead: Under Old Bridge

Information and Maps: www.ciclovia.pt/ciclovias/5algarve/2faro/portimao/pzribeirinha.php

The riverside's bike track is popular with cyclists and joggers. It runs from under the iconic old bridge at one end to the Portimão Museum at the other, along the entire stretch of the riverfront.

PRAIA DA ROCHA BIKE TRACK

Cycling Distance: 1.4 kilometers (0.9 mi) one-way

Cycling Time: 20 minutes one-way

Trailhead: Rua da Falésia, near old Post Office

Information and Maps: www.ciclovia.pt/ciclovias/5algarve/2faro/portimao/pprocha.php

Ending near Praia da Rocha's Santa Catarina

Fortress overlooking the marina, this pleasant and flat track stretches along the entire beachfront.

Golf

PENINA HOTEL & GOLF RESORT

N125, Penina; tel. 282 420 200; www.penina.com; greens fees from €45, 2 players plus cart €105

Built on a former rice field, the Penina Hotel & Golf Resort was the first 18-hole golf resort in the Algarve, designed by Sir Henry Cotton, who described it as his greatest achievement; it also has the Resort Course and the Academy Course. Inaugurated in 1966 by Portugal's president, it is one of the few true championship golf courses in Southern Europe.

Boating

SANTA BERNARDA

Rua Júdice Fialho 4; tel. 282 422 791 or 967 023 84; www.santa-bernarda.com

A large wooden "pirate ship"-style caravel, the Santa Bernarda is one of the most boats recognizable on the Algarve, with half-day and full-day trips (from €35) along the coast to explore caves, with options such as a barbecue lunch on the beach.

BENAGIL SEA CAVEBOAT TOURS

Rua Júdice Fialho; tel. 914 983 967; www.benagilseacavetour.com

This hugely popular 2-hour trip takes visitors from Portimão east along the Lagoa coastline, past some of the region's best-loved beaches, to the famous Benagil sea caves, cavernous grotto and chimney rock-formations in soaring cliffs that require skill and knowledge to navigate. Trips depart from Portimão riverfront at least twice daily, at 11:30am and 3pm; other times on a traditional sailing boat are available. Prices from €30. The same company also operates cruises up the Arade River to the historic city of Silves, allowing 1.5 hours to visit the city.

Entertainment and Events

PORTIMÃO SARDINE FESTIVAL

tel. 282 470 700; www.cm-portimao.pt; early Aug.

Portimão is home to the popular summer Sardine Festival. Held since 1985, the festival runs for five days, accompanied by nightly concerts. Entry is free, and for around €6, visitors can enjoy a plateful of sardines and a drink.

SAINT MARTIN (SÃO MARTINHO) FAIR

Portimão Arena Fair and Exhibition Grounds; early Nov.

Every fall, Portimão welcomes the Saint Martin Fair, once a celebration of the saint and now a celebration of the harvest, with roasted chestnuts and *farturas* (sugar- and cinnamon-coated doughnuts) in abundance. One of the most popular festivals in the region, it runs for 10 days before November 11, the Day of Saint Martin (São Martinho). Held annually since 1662, the fair is open from morning till midnight near the train station at the Park for Fairs and Exhibitions, with hundreds of stalls selling food, kitchenware, clothes, shoes, trinkets, and fairground rides.

Food

Besides sardines, other Portimão specialties include the **cataplana** fish stew cooked in a clam-like copper pan and served directly onto the plate by a waiter. The traditional Algarvian *cataplana* is made with clams, monkfish, potato, garlic, onion, tomatoes, green pepper, and olive oil, producing a sauce that is deep red, rich, and aromatic.

CASA INGLESA

Praça Manuel Teixeira Gomes; tel. 282 416 290; daily 8am-8pm

Enjoy coffee, a cool beverage, and a sweet pastry treat at this historic café, which takes price of place in the city's main square and is an institution among the locals.

NOSOLO ITALIA

Praça Manuel Teixeira Gomes; tel. 282 427 024; www.nosoloitalia.com; daily 10am-11pm; €8

The ice cream parlor Nosolo Italia, renowned for its huge and varied sundaes, is a must.

MASALA HOUSE

14 Rua Carlos da Maia; tel. 282 412 020; daily 10am-11pm; €9

Masala House, in the center of Portimão, has a reputation for being one of the best Indian restaurants in the region. Located opposite the striking city hall building, this small restaurant serves up fresh Indian specialties and a range of vegetarian options.

★ DONA BARCA

Largo da Barca 22; tel. 282 484 189; daily noon-3pm and 6pm-10pm; €15

Tucked away under Portimão's bridge is Dona Barca, a favorite among locals with a festive interior that reflects the colorful characters who frequent it. The menu is all about fresh seafood, including, of course, sardines.

TABERNA DA MARÉ

Travessa da Barca 9; tel. 282 414 614; Tues.-Sun. noon-3pm and 7pm-10pm; €15

Just up the road from Dona Barca is the traditional Taberna da Maré, a quaint place with wooden benches and a tiled counter on the bar, adding to the authenticity. On the menu are no-frills traditional dishes like grilled meats, cuttlefish, and freshly grilled catch of the day.

Accommodations
HOTEL GLOBO

Rua 5 de Outubro 26; tel. 282 490 160; www. hotel-globo.portimao.hotelsalgarve.org; €70

Hotel Globo is one of the few in the heart of Portimão city. Its glass-clad top-floor restaurant is an illuminated landmark seen for miles, offering diners stunning views. After a full refurbishment, this modern, three-star hotel now offers a boutique feel. It is within walking distance of Portimão riverside and the main shopping street.

1: an exhibit in the Portimão Museum **2:** Santa Catarina Fort, Praia da Rocha **3:** promenade along the beach in Praia da Rocha

APARTAMENTOS CLUBE VILAROSA

Rua da Vila Rosa, Lote 1; tel. 282 430 100; www. clubevilarosa.com; €165

This holiday apartment complex is halfway between Portimão and Praia da Rocha and within walking distance of both. A well-kept, pretty pink resort, it has a large pool, tennis courts, and plenty of entertainment in summer.

Information and Services

- **PSP police:** Av. Miguel Bombarda 16; tel. 282 417 717; www.psp.pt

- **GNR police:** Av. São Lourenço da Barrosa; tel. 282 420 750; www.gnr.pt

- **Main tourist office:** Largo 1° de Dezembro; tel. 282 430 165

- **Post office:** Praça Manuel Teixeira Gomes, near the riverfront; tel. 282 420 150

- **Portimão State Hospital:** Estrada do Poço Seco; tel. 282 450 300

Getting There and Around

Portimão is 72 kilometers (45 mi) west, a 45-minute drive, from **Faro airport** on the **A22** motorway. Take the Portimão turnoff, which leads into the north of the city. Buses and trains run to Portimão from Faro and other major Algarve towns.

One of the best ways to get around Portimão is on the city's nifty **Vai-e-Vem shuttle bus** (www.cm-portimao.pt; €1.50, day tickets €3.50), which runs from early morning to late night and covers a comprehensive network within the city and its fringes. The Vai-e-Vem's hub is in Portimão main square, Largo do Dique; there are 10 lines around Portimão, and 7 to and around the village of Alvor. Buy tickets from the driver.

PORTIMÃO TRAIN STATION

Largo Engenheiro Serra Prado; tel. 707 210 220; www.cp.pt

CP (tel. 707 210 220; www.cp.pt) trains run almost hourly between Faro and Portimão (1.5

hours; €6.10-15.55). The train station is in a seedy part of town, 2 kilometers (1.2 mi) from the riverfront, but there are usually taxis on the doorstep.

PORTIMÃO BUS TERMINAL

Rua da Abicada; tel. 282 415 104; www.eva-bus.com

Portimão has two main bus terminals: Local buses to neighboring towns and destinations like Praia da Rocha, Alvor, Lagoa, and Lagos run from along the riverfront, while the likes of long-distance Eva and Rede Expressos coaches from places such as Faro and Lisbon stop at a new terminal inaugurated in 2017 on Rua da Abicada, on the outskirts of the city, near the train station and the arena fair and exhibition grounds. An express Eva bus, the **Transrápido** (tel. 289 899 760; www.eva-bus.com), runs between Faro bus terminal and Portimão (1.75 hours, Mon.-Fri. every 2 hours 8am-7:40pm, Sat.-Sun. 12:30pm and 5:35pm; under €10), with stops at Albufeira.

PRAIA DA ROCHA

Praia da Rocha, 3 kilometers (1.9 mi) south of Portimão, is a premier holiday destination and one of the western Algarve's most popular tourist spots, with a stunning beach and vibrant nightlife year-round. Spanning 1 kilometer (0.6 mi), the long golden strip of sand is backed by cliffs, with the town's main hotels, restaurants, bars, and shops on a road running along the clifftops parallel to the beach. In summer, the beach is packed with families and young people on school holidays. A wooden walkway runs the length of the beach along the foot of the cliffs, punctuated with restaurants selling snacks, meals, ice cream, and cocktails. Water sports concessionaires also dot the beach, touting pedal boats, Jet Skis, and kayaks.

With 300 berths, **Portimão Marina** accommodates some of the sleekest yachts in the Algarve, lending a sophisticated atmosphere to this part of town. The marina is fringed by buildings painted bright terra-cotta, yellow,

and red. A number of bars and restaurants can also be found along the water.

Sights

SANTA CATARINA FORT
(Fortaleza de Santa Catarina)

tel. 282 402 487; open 24/7; free

At the eastern end of Praia da Rocha, overlooking Portimão Marina and the Arade River mouth, the 17th-century Santa Catarina Fort is a small medieval stronghold built to defend the town from pirates and maritime invasions. It is mirrored on the opposite side of the river by the São João do Arade Fort in Ferragudo. Inside are cafés and a courtyard with panoramic views over Praia da Rocha and Ferragudo. Take a steep flight of steps down to Praia da Rocha Marina and the beach. The fortress is right off the main road, Avenida Tomás Cabreira.

Scuba Diving

Rich in shipwrecks and marine life, the Portimão area is a hub for diving, with several PADI schools. With the growing interest in diving and a wealth of subaquatic attractions, the **Ocean Revival Project** (Rua Engenheiro José de Bívar, Edifício Scorpius, Praia da Rocha; tel. 935 577 000; www.oceanrevival. org) seeks to create a world-class diving destination. Four decommissioned warships were sunk to create an underwater park, the Ocean Park Revival, and act as an artificial reef.

SUBNAUTA

Rua Engenheiro José de Bívar, Edifício Scorpius, Loja B, Praia da Rocha; tel. 935 577 000; www.subnauta. pt; daily 8:30am-6pm

Subnauta is a well-established dive center with a highly qualified team that organizes dives (from €50) and courses.

Boating

Dolphin-watching excursions depart Praia da Rocha's marina, from where big-game fishing trips, sunset cruises, and private charters can also be arranged.

SEAFARIS

Portimão Marina; tel. 913 222 275; www.seafaris.net

Boat trips from Portimão's riverside and marina include scenic voyages along the Arade River (from €25), fishing trips (€30-50), coastal sightseeing cruises (€35-70), sunset cruises (€30), and dolphin-watching trips (€40).

Food and Bars

Praia da Rocha, along with Albufeira, is one of the most popular nighttime spots in the western Algarve, drawing crowds year-round. As well as a colorful selection of bars, many of Praia da Rocha's hotels put on live music events open to nonguests in summer. Praia da Rocha is also home to one of the Algarve's three casinos.

Not quite as long as Albufeira's Strip but almost as flashy, Praia da Rocha's main strip, **Avenida Tomás Cabreira,** stretches the length of the beach along the clifftops and has most of the resort's main hotels, restaurants, Irish pubs, sports bars, discos, and karaoke bars. It's busy year-round and has a more family-oriented feel than Albufeira's Strip.

★ RESTAURANTE F

Av. Tomás Cabreira, Edifício Falésia; tel. 919 115 512 or 282 483 014; www.restaurante-fe.negocio.site; Mon.-Sat. 3pm-10:30pm; €20

For a special occasion, head to F Restaurante, which offers excellent service. The creative menu, inspired by seasonal local produce and traditional recipes with a contemporary twist, is outshone only by the stunning views of Praia da Rocha beach.

NOSOLOÁGUA PORTIMÃO POOL AND BEACH CLUB

Portimão Marina; tel. 282 498 180; www.nosoloagua. com; daily 10am-2am Mar.-Oct.

In the upscale marina, the ultra-cool NoSoloÁgua is a chic place to be seen on sun loungers during the day, and in summer it becomes a premier venue for night events such as regular live music and dance, guest DJs, and huge parties hosted by the likes of MTV.

Accommodations

★ HOTEL BELAVISTA

Av. Tomas Cabreira; tel. 282 460 280; www. hotelbelavista.net; €378

Imposingly on the cliff edge, overlooking the beach, the historic Hotel Belavista has been voted one of the most beautiful hotels in Europe. Converted from a 1918 mansion, this gorgeous boutique hotel was one of the first hotels opened in the Algarve. It boasts stunning gardens, direct access to Praia da Rocha beach, and a fabulous spa.

Information and Services

- **Main tourist office:** In front of Hotel Jupiter, Av. Tomás Cabreira; tel. 282 419 132
- **Post office:** Rua Engenheiro José de Bívar, Edifício Plaza, LJ 2; tel. 282 416 532

Getting There

Praia da Rocha is on the southern fringe of **Portimão,** 3 kilometers (1.9 mi) south of the city center. Take a **taxi** to Praia da Rocha from Portimão (€5) or jump onto one of the handy **Vai-e-Vem shuttle buses** (www.cm-portimao.pt; €1.50) that dart around the city. The main lines that run between Portimão's main Largo do Dique riverfront square and Praia da Rocha are numbers 33 and 11. Buy tickets on board. It is possible to walk from Portimão to Praia da Rocha in 45-60 minutes.

★ FERRAGUDO

At the mouth of the Arade River, across from Portimão, Ferragudo is a stunning 14th-century hamlet, the quintessential Algarve fishing village. Less touristy than other spots in the Algarve, it's a maze of bougainvillea-framed cobblestone streets lined with traditional whitewashed cottages cascading down the hillside, with the main church at the top.

An opportunity to see traditional fishing work, the village's pretty harbor is also the setting for breathtaking sunsets and postcard-perfect pictures, with small wooden fishing vessels bobbing on silken water. The harbor is particularly striking at night, as the village lights twinkle in the background.

It may be small and quaint, but Ferragudo has a lot to offer, from the Praia Grande main beach to art and antiques shops, artisans' workshops, and laid-back café life. Ferragudo has a popular monthly **flea and antiques market** (along the main central canal; 2nd Sun. Sept.-July) and a sweet **Christmas market** (1st weekend of Dec.).

Sights

Ferragudo's main **Queen Leonor Square (Praça Rainha Leonor)** is the core of village life, fringed by restaurants, cafés, bakeries, and ice cream parlors; in summer there is nightly live entertainment. Just beyond the square, near the Our Lady of the Conception Church, is the striking, privately owned **São João do Arade Fort,** opposite the Santa Catarina Fort, across the river in Praia da Rocha (Portimão).

OUR LADY OF THE CONCEPTION CHURCH (Igreja Nossa Senhora da Conceição)
Rua da Igreja 10; tel. 282 461 962; daily 10am-noon and 3pm-5pm; free

The 16th-century Our Lady of the Conception Church sits high above the harbor of Ferragudo. Those who make it up the steep streets and flights of stairs to the pretty church are rewarded with stunning panoramic views over the Arade River to the city of Portimão. The church's exterior is bright and simple, with large whitewashed walls and sunny yellow trim. Inside, the church has a richly gilded rococo altarpiece and a number of religious works of art.

Beaches

Ferragudo's **Praia Grande** beach is a hub of activity. The long stretch of sand has lovely water and is great for a brisk walk. In summer, beach outfitters provide plenty of activities, from pedal boats to kayaks.

GRANDE BEACH (Praia Grande)
South of the village center

Stretching along the southern side of Ferragudo, a short walk up some steep hills from the village center, Praia Grande is worth the effort. A long, golden stretch of sand that opens onto a lagoon-like body of water that is the Arade River mouth, this beach is known for being quiet and spacious, with cool but calm water. If you're lucky, you might even see dolphins playing in the bay. Toilets and showers are available at the top of the flight of stairs leading down to the beach, where there is also a small car park. More parking is available within walking distance.

Food and Bars

In summer, the village square comes to life with nightly entertainment, including live music.

A RIA
Rua Infante Santo; tel. 282 461 790; Tues.-Sun. 6:30pm-10pm; €20

On Ferragudo's picturesque quayside, A Ria specializes in traditional Algarvian seafood. Specials at the quaint and cozy family-run restaurant include razor clam rice and *caldeirada* (fish stew).

CLUBE NAU
Praia Grande; tel. 282 484 414; www.club-nau.com; daily 10am-midnight

On the beach is the fabulous Clube Nau, a shack-like wooden bar and restaurant that is one of the coolest hangouts in the Algarve. Sundays are legendary, with a live band, drinks, dinner, and dancing. With an eclectic menu heavily focused on fish and cocktails, it is so popular that reservations are recommended if you want a table for dinner.

Getting There

Ferragudo is 5 kilometers (3.1 mi) east of **Portimão,** across the Arade River; it's a 10-minute drive along the **M530** road. **Eva** (tel. 282 341 301; www.eva-bus.com) buses run hourly between Portimão and Ferragudo (10 minutes; €3).

The **Carvoeiro Tourist Train** (tel. 914 906 599), operated by **Turistrem** (tel. 965 135 466; www.turistrem.com), runs twice a week from Carvoeiro to Ferragudo (30 minutes, Tues. and Fri.; €10 round-trip), where it stops in the village center. Tickets can be bought from the driver.

A handy **water taxi** (tel. 927 272 784; Mar.-Nov.) between Ferragudo and Portimão (5 minutes; €4 one-way, €6 round-trip) crosses the Arade River on demand. It takes passengers to the museum and marina in Portimão and also stops at Ferragudo's Praia Grande beach. The water taxi stop in Ferragudo is at the far end of the riverfront quay, by the lifeboat station. Beneath a large umbrella is a little manned desk—staff there can answer questions and sell tickets.

ALVOR

Alvor has managed to flourish from a simple fishing village into a hugely popular seaside resort without sacrificing any of its original character. With the village's smart riverfront area dotted with trendy wooden café-bars, a main street that's busy without being brash, and plentiful fish restaurants along the harbor, it's easy to see why people flock here. It is a place to enjoy a walk, the scenery, a meal, and a cocktail or two.

The picturesque village is fringed to the south by a pretty harbor and wetlands with uninterrupted views of Lagos to the west and rugged coast to the east. Water sports are a major draw, with kayaking, kitesurfing, and boat trips available.

Hiking
ALVOR ESTUARY AND WALKWAY
Hiking Distance: *6 kilometers (3.7 mi) one-way*
Hiking Time: *1.5 hours one-way*
Trailhead: *Near the Alvor municipal swimming pool, on the waterfront*
Information and Maps: *https://webapp. algarvefantastic.com/en/listings/699585-passadico-de-alvor-slash-alvor-walkway*

A wooden boardwalk is built on the dunes that separate Alvor's waterfront from the beach, providing a serene walk through the scenic *ria* (estuary). Benches along the walkway allow you to enjoy the view. It starts by the harbor and winds through dunes and marshes, a tapestry of green and gold with abundant birdlife. Visit in the evening for a spectacular sunset.

Boating
ALVOR BOAT TRIPS
Alvor harbor-front; tel. 962 091 551; www. alvorboattrips.com; from €15
Alvor Boat Trips operates tours and charters along the coastline as well as down the Arade River to Silves, in a number of different vessels, among them a solar-powered boat.

Skydiving
SKY DIVE ALGARVE
Aeródromo Municipal de Portimão; tel. 282 496 581; www.skydivealgarve.com; from €235
The Algarve is a top winter skydiving destination thanks to excellent weather conditions. A number of companies organize packages that cover everything from airport transport to lodging. One of these is Sky Dive Algarve, certified and experienced, operating 365 days a year. Be wowed by the stunning Algarve from a unique vantage point.

Food and Accommodations
★ CHURRASQUEIRA MERCADO
Largo Castelo, Loja 2; tel. 282 458 248; Tues.-Sun. lunch and dinner Feb.-Nov.; €8
Alvor's main Rua Dr. Frederico Ramos Mendes, a steep cobblestone street that runs from the top of the village to Alvor Bay, has the right mix of bars, restaurants, and shops. At the top is a municipal market, selling produce and fish and at night transforming into a popular restaurant, Churrasqueira Mercado. Basic pine tables and benches enhance the simplicity of the menu, which features grilled fish and chicken, so delicious, fresh, and cheap that the restaurant attracts queues from the

moment it opens. Phone ahead to reserve a table.

CANIÇO RESTAURANT
AND BEACH BAR

tel. 282 458 503; www.canicorestaurante.com; daily noon-5pm and 6pm-midnight

Popular among trendsetters, Caniço Restaurant and Beach Bar is famous for its summer parties. Sandwiched between two cliffs and perched over Caniço Beach, it's a good place to enjoy a sundowner followed by a great meal of Portuguese Mediterranean fare, and then join the after-dinner party as it spills onto the beach, where a DJ plays until dawn. It can only be accessed via an elevator within the Prainha Resort (Praia dos Três Irmãos; www.prainha.net), 4 kilometers (2.5 mi) east of Alvor village.

PESTANA ALVOR SOUTH BEACH

Praceta do Barinel 1; tel. 282 243 000; www.pestana. com; €226

Contemporary four-star beachside Pestana Alvor South Beach has a Miami vibe with a sleek contemporary design, art deco-inspired rooms, and palm tree-fringed infinity pools. Set on the gorgeous Três Irmãos Beach, it is a 20-minute, 2.5-kilometer (1.6-mi) walk southeast of Alvor village center.

Information and Services

- **HPA Private Hospital:** Estrada de Alvor; tel. 707 282 828; www.grupohpa.com
- **Main tourist office:** Rua Dr. Afonso Costa 51; tel. 282 457 540

Getting There

Alvor is 6 kilometers (3.7 mi) east of **Portimão** and **Praia da Rocha.** It can be reached in 10 minutes by taxi from Portimão or Praia da Rocha (about €10). Or jump on one of the many **Vai-e-Vem shuttle buses** (www.cm-portimao.pt; €1.50) that run among the three. Line 14 is one of the main routes between Portimão's main Largo do Dique riverside square and Alvor waterfront.

Tickets can be bought on board. By car, take the main **M531-1** road between Portimão and Alvor.

CARVOEIRO

A small fishing village turned tourist hot spot, Carvoeiro (CAR-voo-AY-roo) is big fun in a petite package. The heart of the town is its main beach, nestled between two steep hills blanketed in whitewashed apartments and town houses. It is a popular settlement for expats and has a lively café culture, with a selection of restaurants and bars that are busy year-round.

Sights
ALGAR SECO ROCK FORMATION

A 10-minute walk up a steep hill east of Carvoeiro village center, Algar Seco is a remarkable cliffside rock formation, carved out by the tide. A long wooden walkway runs along the clifftops with views of the ocean. Accessed via a flight of stairs from the top, the unusual rock formation contains a network of sinkholes, pools, and spouts. In a large pinnacle is a grotto named **A Boneca** (The Doll), with two windows to the Atlantic (the doll's eyes). Nestled in the groove of the rock formation is a popular café-restaurant, **Restaurant Boneca Bar** (tel. 282 358 391; daily 10am-midnight). For a breathtaking treat, visit at sunset.

Beaches
CARVOEIRO BEACH

Carvoeiro village front

A small but perfectly formed wedge of sand, Carvoeiro Beach is bookended by high cliffs and can get quite busy in summer. Beachside cafés and restaurants and toilet and changing facilities with showers are available.

★ MARINHA BEACH
(Praia da Marinha)

This award-winning beach is one of the most famous and beautiful in the country. Emblematic of the Algarve and its natural splendor, Marinha Beach has been used in many advertising campaigns and frequently appears on must-see lists. Encased by sheer ocher cliffs, the beach has craggy rock formations that stretch out over the soft golden sand to a calm, translucent sea. Accessible by car or bus, this popular beach can be very busy in summer. It is accessed from the clifftop car park by a long staircase down to the sand, which can be a challenge for the less agile. The view from the car park and a photo of Portugal's most famous beach are worth the trip.

Marinha Beach is in the hamlet of Caramujeira, 10 kilometers (6.2 mi) and 15 minutes' drive east of **Carvoeiro.**

Golf
PESTANA CARVOEIRO GOLF RESORT
tel. 282 340 900; www.pestanagolf.com; greens fees from €73 June-Aug. and Dec.-Jan., €110 Feb., Apr.-May, Sept., and Nov., €120 Mar. and Oct.
Built on flat terrain, 10 minutes' drive northwest of Carvoeiro, the Pestana Carvoeiro Golf Resort offers the playable 18-hole Gramacho course and the challenging and stunning 18-hole Vale da Pinta. Inaugurated in 1991, Gramacho was designed by Ronald Fream and former world champion Nick Price. Fream also designed Pinta, inaugurated in 1992. Both courses highlight the region's natural countryside, combining olive and carob trees with ornamental sculpted lakes.

Boat Trips
CARVOEIRO CAVES
left side of Carvoeiro Beach square, near changing rooms; tel. 965 041 785; www.carvoeirocaves.com; daily 9am-7pm daily; from €25
This part of the Algarve's coast is studded with caves and dramatic rock formations. Carvoeiro Caves specializes in tours (1-1.5 hours) guided by experienced sailors to the stunning caves, including the popular **Benagil sea caves.**

Entertainment and Events
BLACK & WHITE NIGHT
throughout Carvoeiro; tel. 202 380 400 (Lagoa councilwww.facebook.com/carvoeironoite; mid-June
Don't miss Carvoeiro's famous Black & White Night, when the village is flooded with visitors to enjoy the bands on various stages set up throughout town, and to dance on the beach until dawn.

Food
MAR D'FORA
Rua do Paraíso 522; tel. 282 180 735; Tues.-Sun. noon-10:30pm; €25
No fishing village would be complete without an awesome fish restaurant. Mar d'Fora, halfway down the western hill of the two hills that encase Carvoeiro village square, has ocean views as a backdrop. The beach shack-chic restaurant overlooks the beach, so you can expect wonderful sunsets to complement tasty fish dishes.

TASTE RESTAURANT
Rua do Barranco; tel. 282 358 092; www. tastecarvoeiro.com; Wed.-Sat. and Mon. 4pm-11pm, Sun. noon-11pm; €30
At the very top of the road into Carvoeiro, colorful Taste is hard to miss. Popular and usually very busy, it's also hard to forget once you've eaten the tasty tapas, excellent steaks, and fresh seafood.

BON BON
Rua do Cabeço de Pias; tel. 282 341 496; www. bonbon.pt; Mon. and Thurs.-Fri. 6:30pm-9:30pm; Sat.-Sun. noon-2:30pm and 6:30pm-9:30pm; 4-course tasting menu from €98
In 2015 Carvoeiro welcomed its first Michelin-star restaurant, the gracefully understated Bon Bon, about 4 kilometers (2.5 mi) northwest of Carvoeiro village, near the Pestana Golf Resort. Seasonal specialties are gastronomic masterpieces, with a focus on Portuguese ingredients and locally sourced seafood, meat, and vegetables.

Accommodations
★ O CASTELO GUEST HOUSE
Rua do Casino 59-63; tel. 282 083 518; www.
ocastelo.net; €113

Perfectly appointed boutique B&B O Castelo Guest House overlooks Carvoeiro Beach from high up on one of its hills. Its 12 rooms are bright and spacious, and it offers privileged sea views from all rooms.

TIVOLI CARVOEIRO
Vale do Covo, Praia do Carvoeiro; tel. 282 351 100;
www.minorhotels.com; €225

Toward the top eastern end of Carvoeiro village is the Tivoli Carvoeiro, thoroughly refurbished and reopened as a deluxe, modern five-star hotel in 2017. It boasts 248 tastefully decorated rooms, most with stunning sea views, and Sky Bar, one of the hippest bars in the village.

Information and Services
- **GNR police:** Rampa Sra. da Encarnação 15; tel. 282 356 460; www.gnr.pt
- **Main tourist office:** Carvoeiro main beachfront square; tel. 282 357 728

Getting There and Around
Carvoeiro is 10 kilometers (6 mi) east from **Portimão**, a 20-minute drive along the **EN125** road. There is a permanent **taxi rank** just off Carvoeiro's main village square, Carvoeiro can be covered easily **on foot,** but it does have some steep hills.

The **Cliffs Route** (Rota das Falésias; 24-hour ticket adults €10, children €8, 48-hour ticket adults €15, children €12) is a new hop-on hop-off round-trip service operated by **Turistrem** (tel. 965 135 466; www.turistrem.com) in an air-conditioned minibus that departs Carvoeiro and drops passengers at some of the region's most popular beaches, coastal beauty spots, the village of Ferragudo, Marinha Beach, and the Algar

1: Marinha Beach near Carvoeiro **2:** a bougainvillea-covered street in Ferragudo **3:** Silves Castle **4:** Algar Seco in Carvoeiro

Seco rock formation and boardwalk. Buy tickets on board.

CARVOEIRO TOURIST TRAIN
Main Village Square; tel. 914 906 599

The Carvoeiro Tourist Train, operated by **Turistrem** (tel. 965 135 466; www.turistrem.com), departs regularly daily from the main village square and does 40-minute round-trips of the village (€3-5). The train also does round-trips to **Ferragudo** (Tues. and Fri.; €10 round-trip), where it stops for a few hours for passengers to wander around before coming back. More information is at Carvoeiro's tourist office on the main beachfront square. Tickets can be bought from the driver.

SILVES
The city of Silves (SIL-vesh) is an impressive sight on approach, with its imposing castle and cathedral on the hill, a crown atop a cascade of whitewashed houses and bright-red roofs staggering down to the Arade River through the middle of town. The capital of the Algarve in Moorish times and now the self-proclaimed Orange Capital of the Algarve, due to the orange groves surrounding the town, Silves is of historic and archaeological importance. Few signs of mainstream tourism are evident, but it is host to one of the biggest events of the Algarve summer, the famous Medieval Festival. Silves is an easy day trip from Portimão.

Sights
★ SILVES CASTLE
(Castelo de Silves)
Rua da Cruz de Portugal; tel. 282 440 800; www.
cm-silves.pt; daily 9am-8pm; €2.80

Besides being one of the best-preserved castles in the Algarve, Silves Castle has extraordinary medieval military architecture inherited from the Moors, who once occupied the region. Excavations suggest the first fortress was built by the Romans or Visigoths on the remnants of a Lusitanian military camp. Circa 716, the citadel was conquered by the Moors, who bolstered the existing fortifications with

Porches Pottery

The town of Porches (POR-shezh) is synonymous with pottery. Charming yet unassuming, it is overshadowed by its bigger, touristy neighbors. A smattering of pottery shops still produce ceramics using traditional artisanal methods. If handicrafts are your thing, spend a few hours browsing the colorful ceramics, have lunch, and walk around town.

A piece of Porches pottery makes a unique souvenir of the Algarve. Once a flourishing trade, the art in Porches had started to wane until Irish artist Patrick Swift and renowned Portuguese ceramicist Lima de Freitas collaborated to establish the famous Porches Pottery workshop in 1968. With increased tourism in the Algarve, Porches's pottery gained renewed interest and can now be found in first-class restaurants and hotels and homes around the world.

Pottery shops line both sides of the N125 road, which delimits the northern boundary of Porches, and the shop fronts are clad with the typically colorful hand-painted designs on bright-red handmade clay pots. Traditionally, Algarvian ceramics are painted blue and white, but designs today use a variety of colors and patterns.

The **Porches Pottery Shop and Atelier** (N125; tel. 282 352 858; www.porchespottery. com; Mon.-Fri. 9am-6pm, Sat. 10am-2pm) produces the famous original Porches pottery. Founded in 1968, the shop produces pieces in the traditional way, handmade and then hand-painted and glazed with the region's distinctive patterns and colors, often blue and white. From mugs to salt-shakers to plates, all are painted freehand. Prices range from around €8 for a small souvenir like a coaster, to several hundred euros for larger personalized items like *azulejo* murals and plaques.

Porches is located on the main EN125 road, a 17-kilometer (11-mi), 20-minute drive east from **Portimão.**

new walls, including extensive ramparts to the west. Silves was later captured by the Spaniards and again by the Moors, then taken by King Sancho I of Portugal in 1189 with the help of Crusaders, and again captured by the Moors in 1191. The fortress was finally regained by Afonso III of Portugal in the 13th century during the reconquests. After reconstruction following earthquakes, including the catastrophic earthquake of 1755, Silves Castle was restored to its current glory in the 1940s.

Today, as well as being home to an interactive visitors center, in summer the solid-red castle also hosts **Sunset Secret** (Thurs. 6:30pm-11pm June-Aug.; €5) cocktail events, where food and wine are served within the castle walls, with live fado singers and chill-out music.

It's a 20-minute climb from the riverside to the castle on Silves's steep cobbled streets. At the top, the views of the surrounding countryside, blanketed with orange and lemon groves, are a reward. Walk around the castle walls, admire the excavations, and relax in the courtyard with a cocktail or a meal. Exhibitions located in the turrets and in below-ground cisterns showcase artifacts unearthed during on-site excavations; descriptions are available in English. You could spend a couple of hours in Silves Castle; bring the camera.

Entertainment and Events
MEDIEVAL FESTIVAL
tel. 282 440 800; www.visitportugal.com; mid-Aug.
Silves's main yearly attraction is the Medieval Festival, nine days when the entire city is closed to traffic and transformed into a medieval marketplace, complete with hog roasts, jousters, hay bales, belly dancers, snake charmers, and fire jugglers. It's a remarkable experience. Costumes are also available to rent for those who want to get into the spirit of things.

Food
On the river, the delicious scents of grilled chicken and fish waft from simple water's-edge restaurants. Hidden in the rolling hills

surrounding the city are a number of *maris-queiras* (seafood restaurants) and typical Portuguese restaurants offering hearty home-cooked dishes and local specialties.

★ CHURRASQUEIRA VALDEMAR

Mercado Municipal 11; tel. 282 443 138; Mon.-Sat. lunch and dinner; €7

In the riverside municipal market, vibrant and friendly no-frills Churrasqueira Valdemar specializes in grilled *piripiri* chicken. Regulars don't bother with a menu and go for the staple garlicky barbecue chicken (*piripiri* optional), homemade bread, fresh salad, and crunchy fries; other meats are also available. The food is basic but fabulous.

Ú MONCHIQUEIRO

Av. Marginal; tel. 282 182 046; Thurs.-Tues. lunch and dinner; €8

Ú Monchiqueiro is a long-established typically Portuguese restaurant along the Arade River, popular for its fresh grilled fish and meats and renowned for its tasty *cozido à Portuguesa* (Portuguese stew), a rustic dish for sharing that includes boiled pork, *choriço* sausage, cabbage, carrots, and potatoes.

★ CAFÉ INGLÊS

Rua do Castelo 11; tel. 282 442 585; www.cafeingles.com.pt; Tues.-Sun. 10am-11:30pm; €12

For fantastic international food, Café Inglês is one of the most charismatic café-restaurants in the Algarve. Popular and trendy, it has an exceptional location high above the town along the castle walls, with incredible views. The menu ranges from international classics like beef tenderloin, lamb chops, and roast duck to artisanal pizzas. Live music, from jazz to world music to pop, is also available regularly.

Getting There

Silves is 63 kilometers (39 mi) west of **Faro**, a 45-minute drive via the **A22** motorway. It's 16.5 kilometers (10.2 mi) northeast of **Portimão**, a 25-minute drive via **N124-1**. Silves is easiest to visit by car and offers ample parking in large free car parks along the riverside.

SILVES TRAIN STATION

tel. 707 210 220; www.cp.pt

There are six **CP** trains between Portimão and Silves (20 minutes, daily 11:30am-9:30pm; €2). Trains depart every few hours from Faro (1 hour; €5.20). The train station is on a steep hill 2 kilometers (1.2 mi) south of Silves. There are sometimes taxis outside the station, or call a taxi from the neighboring café.

ALGARVE SUN BOAT TRIPS

tel. 919 919 450; www.algarvesunboat.com

A novel way to get to Silves from Portimão is by boat up the Arade River. Algarve Sun Boat Trips operates solar-powered boats that depart Portimão's riverside year-round for Silves (1.5 hours; €30). The boats stop in Silves for three hours for passengers to wander around before they are brought back to Portimão by road. Refreshments on the boat are included.

LAGOS

At the mouth of the Bensafrim River, Lagos (LAH-goosh) has long been a favorite for backpackers and surfers thanks to its beaches, tourist-friendly attitude, laid-back vibes, and genuine Portuguese character. Add an Old Town, cool nightlife, and a variety of places to eat and drink, and Lagos pulls visitors in droves.

Lagos played an important role in the Age of Discoveries, as Prince Henry the Navigator lived and built his ships here, having founded a navigation school in nearby Sagres. Other Portuguese explorers set sail from Lagos and helped establish the city as a prosperous trading point.

Lagos's economy is tightly linked to the sea and to tourism. As one of the Algarve's most popular destinations, it is a good base for exploring the western Algarve, with proximity to Sagres, Aljezur, and Luz for day trips.

Sights

Lagos's Old Town Center (Centro Histórico)

Lagos

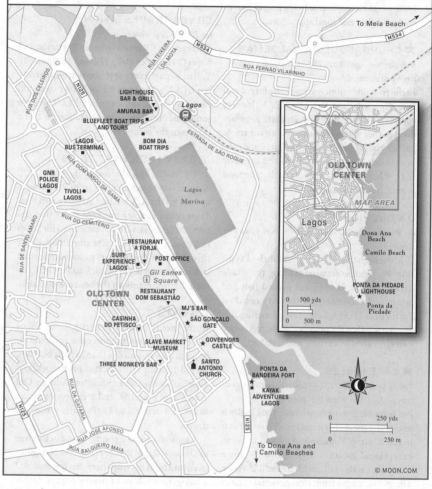

is a place to appreciate the city's history and lounge at one of the many pretty cafés. Sixteenth-century stone walls from Lagos's castle encircle the Old Town, explored by passing through the impressive **São Gonçalo Gate,** flanked on either side by watchtowers. The Old Town Center is a tangle of cobbled streets, picturesque squares, shops, simple whitewashed cottages, and tile-clad town houses. Also within the Old Town is the **Gil Eanes Square (Praça Gil Eanes),** named

after another Portuguese navigator, where locals meet for a *café*. It's most vibrant after dusk.

SANTO ANTÓNIO CHURCH (Igreja de Santo António)

Rua General Alberto da Silveira; tel. 282 762 301; Tues.-Sun. 10am-12:30pm and 2pm-5:30pm; church and museum €3

A highlight of the Old Town is the tiny 18th-century national monument Santo António

Church, whose plain limestone exterior belies its lavish Baroque interior, a single aisle with no side chapels, clad with ornate gilded wooden carvings and *azulejo* plaques. The centerpiece is an opulent golden altar. No photography is allowed inside, and explanatory notes are in English. Adjacent to the church is the **Dr. José Formosinho Museum,** packed with a random—bordering on bizarre—collection of local artifacts, from coins to model ships, doll houses, and Roman relics.

SLAVE MARKET MUSEUM
(Mercado de Escravos)

Praca Infante Dom Henrique; tel. 282 762 301;
Tues.-Sun. 10:30am-12:30pm and 2pm-5:30pm; €3

Lagos was home to the first market for enslaved Africans in Europe. The historic building, today housing the Slave Market Museum, was built in the 17th century, first to house the Royal Overseer's office and later the local customs house. The museum is on two floors, the upper floor accessed via a staircase on a side street. The museum offers a sobering look at the history of slavery in Lagos and throughout the Algarve, from the arrival of the first boatload of enslaved Africans in 1444. Artifacts include weapons, manacles, and maps used during the slave trading era.

GOVERNORS CASTLE
(Castelo dos Governadores)

Jardim da Constituição; open 24/7; free

Lagos's most prominent feature is the impressive 17th-century Governors Castle. In its heyday, it housed kings and explorers and was the seat of the region's governors. The entrance to the stout stone fort is guarded by chunky towers, and many parts of the pentagonal medieval city walls are well preserved. There's not much to see inside, but the castle is an excellent photo opportunity. Follow the castle walls around the city for excellent views. The pretty gardens to the front and side of the castle are also worth a visit.

PONTA DA BANDEIRA FORT
(Forte da Ponta da Bandeira)

Cais da Solaria; tel. 282 761 410; Tues.-Sun.
9:30am-12:30pm and 2pm-5pm; €2

The squat quadrangular Ponta da Bandeira Fort dates from the late 17th century, completing Lagos's defense system and one of the last strongholds built here. It is also the city's best-preserved monument. Cross a little drawbridge to find a small 18th-century chapel, barracks converted into art exhibitions, a restaurant, and views over the sea and the city.

LAGOS MARINA
(Marina de Lagos)

www.marlagos.pt

On the Bensafrim River, across from Lagos's riverfront promenade, Lagos Marina separates the city of Lagos from Meia Praia and the local train station. Opened in 1994, it hosts hundreds of vessels and charter boat trips. Connected to Lagos city center with a bridge, the petite marina houses a number of good bars and restaurants, too.

PONTA DA PIEDADE

Piedade Point, south of city center

At the southernmost tip of Lagos, 3.5 kilometers (2.2 mi) south of the center, is Ponta da Piedade (Piety Point), a vast headland that juts into the Atlantic with a lighthouse. Centuries of tides and gales have weathered the cliffs into extraordinary formations: tunnels, arcs, caves, and pillars. The 1913 **Ponta da Piedade Lighthouse** (Farol da Ponta da Piedade; Estrada da Ponta da Piedade; open 24/7; free) is dwarfed by the 50-meter (164-ft) promontory. Just over an hour's walk from Lagos, it is now decommissioned and closed, but the views from the headland are phenomenal. A web of pathways spans the area. Lovely beaches, including the popular Praia do Camilo (accessed down a flight of 200 steps), flank the headland.

Boat trips to explore this awesome feat of nature run year-round from Lagos Marina as well as from the base of the promontory, weather and sea conditions permitting. Little boats can be found at the foot of the outcrop, accessed down a flight of 200 steps. The

smaller the boat, the more grottoes and narrow passages it can squeeze into. A 15-minute boat trip into the caves costs around €20 pp.

Beaches

Lagos boasts a healthy selection of beaches, from long stretches of sand to small cove-like hideaways.

MEIA PRAIA BEACH
(Meia Praia)

Just east of Lagos Marina, between Lagos and Alvor

Meia Beach is a sweeping 4-kilometer (2.5-mi) crescent of soft golden sand that stretches from Lagos to Alvor, starting on the east side of Lagos Marina, offering ample space even in the height of summer. Development is low-rise and sparse in places, so it can feel quiet and secluded. The western end, a 40-minute walk (7 km/4.3 mi) from Lagos city center, over the bridge to the marina and past the train station, tends to be the busiest section, but a bit farther along is all the space and peace you could want. The sea tends to be shallow and calm, albeit cooler than in the eastern Algarve. Beach beds and parasols are provided by outfitters (from €10 per day), along with equipment for windsurfing, kitesurfing, and Jet Skiing.

DONA ANA BEACH
(Praia Dona Ana)

South of city center, before Piedade Point

A 2-kilometer (1.2-mi), 25-minute walk south of the city center, postcard-perfect Dona Ana Beach has recently been praised as one of the most beautiful beaches in the world. Bigger than the average cove-type beach, it doesn't feel crowded but offers a romantic feel. Golden cliffs surround the soft golden sand fronting cool crystalline water. Be warned that it gets busy on weekends and throughout summer, so parking around the area might be harder to find at those times.

1: square in Old Town Lagos **2:** boat tour near Ponta da Piedade **3:** Praia Dona Ana

CAMILO BEACH
(Praia do Camilo)

just after Praia Dona Ana

Camilo Beach is a sensational little sheltered cove-beach between Dona Ana Beach and Ponta da Piedade, on the outcrop's western face. Its 200 wooden steps lead down from the cliffs. Just around the corner, west of the Piedade headland, is **Porto de Mós Beach,** the second longest in Lagos after Meia Beach. Camilo Beach is 2.2 kilometers (1.4 mi) south of Lagos center, a 30-minute walk.

Surfing

The most popular pastime in Lagos is surfing, and a number of surf schools and camps have popped up in recent years. Many instructors are foreigners, and all speak good English.

- **Surf Experience Lagos:** Rua dos Ferreiros 21; tel. 282 086 012, 919 830 591, or 916 137 082; www.surfexperience.com; weeklong surf camps from €428
- **Filsurf:** tel. 917 127 517; www.filsurf.com; surf lessons from €50

Kayaking
KAYAK ADVENTURE LAGOS

Av. dos Descobrimentos, Cais da Solaria, Lugar 2; tel. 913 262 200; www.kayakadventureslagos.com; from €29 pp

Explore iconic Lagos coastal spots from the water with Kayak Adventure Lagos and its English-speaking guides. Paddle through caves and grottoes and find deserted beaches at sunrise or sunset, or try a kayak and snorkel trip.

Boating

A variety of boat trips and charters are run from Lagos Marina, including dolphin-watching trips and grotto exploring. Stroll around the shops and stalls to see what takes your fancy.

- **Bom Dia Boat Trips:** Lagos Marina, Shop 10; tel. 282 087 587; www.bomdia-boattrips.com; €20-55

- **BlueFleet Boat Trips and Tours:** Lagos Marina; tel. 911 963 309; www.bluefleet.pt

Hiking

WEST COAST ADVENTURE COMPANY

tel. 918 903 899; www.westcoastlagos.com

Don your comfiest walking shoes for trekking with West Coast Adventure Company. Led by an experienced English-speaking guide, tailor-made group adventure hikes (from €69 pp) show off secret beauty spots, with sunset picnics.

Food

Lagos has an eclectic mix of dining options, from warehouse-like cantinas to food trucks and international restaurants.

THE LIGHTHOUSE BAR & GRILL

Marina de Lagos; tel. 282 762 115; daily 4:30pm-11:30pm; €8

On Lagos Marina, British pub-style The Lighthouse Bar & Grill is a top spot for a comfortable beer and a bite. With a laid-back atmosphere, it serves pub grub like fish-and-chips, chili, and a Sunday roast. There's live music and karaoke during the week.

RESTAURANT DOM SEBASTIÃO

Rua 25 de Abril 20-22; tel. 282 780 480; www.restaurantedonsebastiao.com; daily noon-10:30pm; €12

Just back from the river, Restaurant Dom Sebastião is a classically rustic Portuguese restaurant with polished cobblestone floors and dark wood tables and chairs, making it feel cozy and intimate. With a dedicated following since opening in 1979 and a vast underground wine cellar, it provides fine dining with accomplished dishes from local ingredients.

CASINHA DO PETISCO

Rua da Oliveira 51; tel. 282 084 285; Mon-Sat 5"30pm-10pm; €12

Casinha do Petisco, which means "Little House of Snacks," offers tapas-size dishes of local and regional specialties, made for sharing with beer or wine and good company.

RESTAURANT A FORJA

Rua dos Ferreiros 17; tel. 282 768 588; Sun.-Fri. noon-3pm and 6:30pm-10pm; €14

A few streets back from the river is Restaurant A Forja, from the outside little more than an unremarkable doorway. But inside, this typical *adega* (wine cellar) has a strong local feel, serving generous portions of home-cooked, unfussy Portuguese food, including grilled fish and steaks.

Bars and Nightlife

Lagos has vibrant, easygoing nightlife for surfers, backpackers, and the more discerning. The city center has an eclectic assortment of bars and nightclubs, many in historic buildings on the city's cobbled backstreets. The marina boasts classy upmarket bars, while Meia Beach is for a chilled cocktail and a beach party that goes until daybreak.

MJ'S BAR

Travessa de Sra. de Graça 2; tel. 969 923 639; daily 7:30pm-2am

One of Lagos's top nighttime haunts, just off the waterfront, colorful MJ's Bar is a cool little place serving great cocktails and playing old-school music (requests taken).

THREE MONKEYS BAR

Rua Lancarote de Freitas 26; tel. 282 762 995; www.3monkeys.me.uk; daily 1pm-2am

One place where the party always gets started, Three Monkeys Bar is close to hostels and draws a young and energetic crowd fueled by shots, happy hours, dancing, and a great variety of music.

AMURAS BAR

Marina de Lagos, Shop 4; tel. 282 792 112; daily 9am-2am

Comfortable, laid-back Amuras Bar on Lagos Marina has a friendly, lively atmosphere, televised sports, and live music most evenings. A popular meeting place for locals, it attracts a more demure clientele and serves pub grub.

Accommodations
TIVOLI LAGOS
Rua António Crisógono dos Santos; tel. 282 790 079; www.minorhotels.com; €134

Relaxed, whitewashed Tivoli Lagos hotel has three restaurants and three pools and is at the entrance to Lagos, within walking distance of the town center and a short walk to the train station and marina.

Information and Services

- **GNR police:** Largo d'Armas 28; tel. 282 770 010; www.gnr.pt
- **Main tourist office:** Praça Gil Eanes 17; tel. 282 764 111
- **Post office:** Rua da Porta de Portugal 25; tel. 282 770 251

Getting There

Lagos is 90 kilometers (56 mi) west of **Faro,** 1 hour's drive on the **A22** motorway from Faro airport, or follow the **N125** road west to Lagos. It's 23 kilometers (14.3 mi) west of **Portimão,** a 25-minute drive along the N125 road.

LAGOS BUS TERMINAL
Largo do Rossio de São João; tel. 282 762 944

An express Eva bus, the **Transrápido** (tel. 289 899 760; www.eva-bus.com), runs between Faro bus terminal and Lagos (2 hours, every 2 hours Mon.-Fri. 8am-7:40pm, Sat.-Sun. 12:30pm and 5:35pm; under €10), with stops at Albufeira and Portimão. Eva also operates a half-dozen buses on Interurbanos (Intercity) and Litoral (Coastal) lines between Portimão and Lagos (35 minutes; €4). The Lagos Bus Terminal is in the city center.

LAGOS STATION
Estação de São Roque; tel.7070 210 220; www.cp.pt

The Lagos train station is the Algarve Line's westernmost terminus. **CP** (tel. 707 210 220; www.cp.pt) trains run between Faro's main station and Lagos Station (1.75 hours, every 2 hours; €7.50-16.05). Trains run almost hourly between Portimão and Lagos (20 minutes, 8:30am-10pm; €2.05). Lagos Station is opposite the waterway, behind the Lagos Marina, a 15-minute walk from the city center.

Getting Around

The best way to explore Lagos is **on foot,** but to go beyond the center, the **Onda** (www.aonda.pt; €1.20-1.60, day pass €3.60) bus network runs nine color-coded lines from the center to all attractions as well as popular villages in the suburbs. The Red and Turquoise Lines circulate in the city center. Tickets can be bought from the driver or at the **main bus station.**

Taxis (tel. 282 763 587) are readily available in Lagos and can be found along the waterfront.

Monchique and the West Coast

The mountainside farming town of Monchique (MON-sheek) is part of the Serra de Monchique mountain range, which parallels the coast as the backbone of the western Algarve. Swaddled in eucalyptus, pine, and cork-oak trees, this part of the Algarve is a fragrant escape from the bustle of the coast and home to the highest point in the Algarve, Fóia Peak. Lush and cool, Monchique's landscape changes with the seasons, emerald green in winter, a kaleidoscope of color in spring, golden in summer, and red in autumn. Monchique can be done as a day trip from Portimão but also warrants staying a night or two.

Monchique is famous for its ultra-strong liquor *(aguardente),* a potent alcoholic drink made from the strawberry-like *medronho* fruit. It is also famous for its spring water and traditionally made smoked meats and sausages, the centerpiece of an annual festival. Monchique is a town still steeped in tradition, where shops along winding cobbled streets display local handicrafts and artisans open their doors to anyone passing by.

The west coast resides under the protection of the **Southwest Alentejo and Vicentine Coast Natural Park,** which extends north into the Alentejo. One of the finest preserved stretches of coast in Europe, the park covers 100 kilometers (62 mi) from Porto Covo in the Alentejo to the village of Burgau, 23 kilometers (14.3 mi) east of Sagres. The dramatic cliffs and beaches are home to hundreds of unique plant and animal species. Coupled with Sagres's water-sports beaches, it is the perfect place for active tourists, with unlimited hiking, trekking, and surfing.

SIGHTS

Caldas de Monchique

Along N266 road up to Monchique town
The Caldas de Monchique natural springs and spa village are a magical place to spend a few hours, or stay a night at the **Villa Termal Caldas de Monchique Spa Resort,** which has a hot-spring spa where you can enjoy the famous warm spring water massages or soak in the pool, said to have therapeutic benefits (single entry for pool is €15 for hotel guests, €20 for nonguests).

Made up of a handful of mini palace-like properties, the hamlet is a lovely mountainside place for an invigorating walk in the mountain air, with tall trees framing the running spring. Amid the trees are ancient stone tables and benches for picnics. On balmy summer nights, open-air movies and other events are held, while colorful lights are hung in the trees to add extra wonder to this unique spot.

The Caldas are just off the main road up to Monchique, 8 kilometers (5 mi) south of the town center.

HIKING

★ HIKING FÓIA PEAK

Hiking Distance: *8-kilometer (5-mi) loop*
Hiking Time: *1.5-2 hours round-trip*
Trailhead: *Fóia Peak*
Information and Maps: *www.alltrails.com/ trail/portugal/algarve/alto-da-foia-trail*

At 908 meters (2,979 ft), Fóia Peak is the highest point in the Algarve. The drive up is gentle and winding and can be hair-raising at points, although the roads and safety barriers are in good condition. Visitors who don't have a car can make the journey from the town center by bus, taxi, or the 8-kilometer (5-mi) hike (which is much easier coming down than going up). Near the peak is a viewpoint with a spring-water fountain. At the peak, it's like standing on top of the world: On a clear day, the view stretches to Cape St. Vincent in the west and Faro in the east—a breathtaking experience.

Admire the vast, rugged Monchique mountain range on this scenic loop, taking in lake and mountain views as you walk clockwise (fewer steep inclines) through the peaks and troughs of Monchique's highest points. Stunning scenery, good signage, and parking and services are available at the start/end of trail.

If you're not hiking, Fóia Peak is 8 kilometers (5 mi) west of Monchique on the N266-3 road. The drive up takes 15 minutes. There is no public transport to Fóia, but a taxi from Monchique town costs around €8. Try local company **Táxis Ginjeira Martins Unipessoal** (tel. 282 913 157).

ENTERTAINMENT AND EVENTS

FEIRA DOS ENCHIDOS

early Mar.
In March, Monchique throws its popular Feira dos Enchidos (stuffed meats fair), showcasing the region's tasty cured and smoked *choriça* sausage and *presunto* ham as well as cheeses,

1: Fóia Peak near Monchique **2:** Caldas de Monchique **3:** Cape St. Vincent Lighthouse **4:** Sagres Fortress

honey, and *aguardente*. It takes place over two days, usually the first weekend in March. Other local specialties, such as roast kid with plums, black pig cheeks, cabbage Monchique-style, and honey cake, are also available.

FOOD AND ACCOMMODATIONS

Monchique's gastronomy is literally from plot to plate. Meat, especially pork, is popular in Monchique, renowned for its traditional cured hams and smoked sausages. Monchique's rural essence comes to the fore in its gastronomy, with restaurants offering hearty meals at reasonable prices. Local specialties include stews incorporating cabbage, pork, and beans. Platters of cured or smoked meats and cheeses, warm rustic bread, and big jugs of wine are staples. An added bonus is that many restaurants are on the mountainside and offer gorgeous views to the coast.

CINZAS

Pocilgais; tel. 282 912 221; daily lunch and dinner; €10
Established in 1958, Cinzas restaurant is a well-known family-run eatery on the winding road up to the town, just before the Caldas. As well as serving hearty home-cooked local specialties like eel stew, Cinzas also serves platters of traditional Monchique products, like wafer-thin slices of dry-cured ham *(presunto)* and regional cheeses. Much of the food comes from the family's own farm. This place is a must to sample the real flavors of Monchique.

VILLA TERMAL CALDAS DE MONCHIQUE SPA RESORT

Rua de Caldas de Monchique; tel. 282 910 910; www. monchiquetermas.com; €107
The historic Villa Termal Caldas de Monchique Spa Resort is in five small, ancient hotel buildings. The resort also has a wine bar, a restaurant, a convenience store, and a hot-spring spa that nonguests can also enjoy.

GETTING THERE

Monchique is 32 kilometers (20 mi) and a 30-minute drive north of **Portimão.** From the **A22** motorway, take the Monchique turn-off near Portimão and follow the signs. It's a short drive from Portimão to the base of the mountain. You can also take the main **N125** road to Portimão, then head north toward the A22, following the **N266** road.

Buses operated by **Frota Azul** (tel. 282 400 610; www.frotazul-algarve.pt) run almost hourly between Portimão and Monchique (45 minutes, daily 7:50am-8:30pm; €4). Buses depart Portimão from Avenida Guarané, on the riverfront, at Stop 5, and drop passengers in Monchique town center.

SAGRES

Windswept and rugged, Sagres (SAH-grezh) is a surfer's paradise at the western tip of the Algarve, 33 kilometers (20 mi) west of Lagos, on a remote headland. The dune-like terrain, combined with dramatic cliffs, tumultuous sea, and sweeping beaches, incites adventure. Intrepid Portuguese explorer Prince Henry the Navigator founded his famous navigation school here, and Sagres remains adventurous. With long beaches, a sweet fishing port, Cape St. Vincent, and Sagres Fortress, Sagres is a great day trip from Lagos or a weekend stay. The town is small and sleepy, but the region is expansive, with much to see and do, so pack sturdy hiking boots.

Sights

★ CAPE ST. VINCENT
(Cabo de São Vicente)

Wind-battered Cape St. Vincent headland is Europe's most southwesterly point, jutting into the Atlantic some 60 meters (197 ft) above the sea, with dramatic cliffs topped by the commanding **Cape St. Vincent Lighthouse (Farol do Cabo de São Vicente)** (N268; tel. 282 624 234; Tues.-Sun. 10am-6pm; €3), the second brightest in Europe, built around the turn of the 20th century and perched close to the cliff edge. The lighthouse itself is closed to the public, but it's part of a larger complex that includes a cafeteria, a gift shop, and a little museum with information on the lighthouse.

Standing on these blustery cliffs at the tip

of Europe feels like teetering on the edge of the world—Europeans believed that Cape St. Vincent was literally the edge of the world prior to the 15th century. On Cape St. Vincent, where the lighthouse stands today, Prince Henry the Navigator had his private residence, and he set up a school for explorers in nearby Sagres town, making it a launching point for exploration in the Age of Discoveries.

Cape St. Vincent is located on the **Vicentine Coast,** a belt of wild protected natural park that stretches from the western tip of the Algarve north to the Alentejo. The winding road from Cape St. Vincent, 7 kilometers (4.3 mi) west of sleepy Sagres, snakes through rugged, remote, boulder-littered landscape, with captivating and eerie desolation.

SAGRES FORTRESS
(Fortaleza de Sagres)

tel. 282 620 140; www.monumentosdoalgarve.pt; daily 9:30am-8pm May-Sept., daily 9:30am-5:30pm Oct.-Apr., last admission 30 minutes before closing; €3

Sprawling, imposing Sagres Fortress was built in the 1400s where the prosperous Mediterranean and Atlantic maritime routes crossed. It played a key role in Portugal's strategic defenses, protecting the coast from North African invaders. Just south of Sagres town, this vast, squat fort has an impressive arched entrance, a restored 15th-century church, a 16th-century monastery, and the remnants of a 43-meter-wide (141-ft-wide) cobbled compass, the Compass Rose, one of the first of its kind in the country. It was here in the fortress that Henry the Navigator spent much of his time planning voyages. He died in the fortress in 1460.

Spend a few hours strolling the perimeter of the fortress, punctuated by cannons, and taking in the ocean views. It can be windy, so go prepared with warm clothes or at least a windbreaker, even in summer. There are restrooms inside, and free parking in front of the fortress.

Sagres Fortress is 1.4 kilometers (0.9 mi) south of Sagres town, a 5-minute drive. The regular Lagos-Sagres buses (tel. 282 762 944; www.eva-bus.com; €3) also stop here.

Beaches

Given the unique weather on the southwestern tip of the Algarve, the beaches are more frequented by surfers and kite-surfers. Despite usually being a few degrees cooler and breezier than the rest of the region, on a good day, Sagres's beaches offer a chance to escape the crowds and enjoy tranquil, unspoiled sand without a banana boat in sight. Also popular for surfing are Bordeira and Amado Beaches in **Carrapateira,** the ultimate unspoiled west coast community about 20 kilometers (12 mi) to the north. They're a 20-minute drive via the N268 road, or a €25 taxi ride.

MARTINHAL BEACH
(Praia do Martinhal)

Fringed by reedy dunes, Martinhal Beach is a bay-like stretch of sand that sweeps around to Baleeira Port and the Sagres promontory and its fortress. In summer, outfitters operate for surfing, body-boarding, kitesurfing, and windsurfing, with rental equipment and English-speaking instructors. Off-season, the hardy can take a bracing walk on the beach. Conveniently, a large free car park borders the beach.

BORDEIRA BEACH
(Praia da Bordeira)

Flanked by rugged untamed countryside, Bordeira Beach is a long creamy swath of sand that offers large waves year-round, a 20-minute walk north of Carrapateira. At low tide the beach increases in size, making it one of the largest in the Algarve. A stream also flows into the sea, sometimes forming a shallow lagoon that children love to play in.

AMADO BEACH
(Praia do Amado)

A 30-minute walk south of Carrapateira, Amado Beach is one of the best surfing spots in the region. It is a long sandy strip of beach with great year-round waves and a wooden hiking trail around it. The spot is usually occupied by a good-looking surf crowd and is also popular among campers. **Amado Beach Rentals** (tel. 913 810 449; www.amadobeachrentals.com) has a large range of surf equipment for hire, right on the beach.

Surfing

With rough Atlantic waves, Sagres is a top spot for surfing and has decent conditions most of the year. The west coast's beaches, including the western tip of the southern coast, are generally windier and the water much cooler than east along the southern coast—which means they're also less crowded, even in the height of summer.

- **Casa Azul Sagres:** tel. 282 624 856; www.casaazulsagres.com

Boating
CAPE CRUISER

Porto da Baleeira; tel. 919 751 175; www.capecruiser.org

Dolphin-, whale-, and seabird-watching excursions (from adults €35, children under 12 €25) sail from Baleeira Port with Cape Cruiser, which also does fishing trips and coastal exploration, narrated in English. Trips depart three times a day October-March, and four times a day April-September. If you're lucky, you might even spot a shark.

Hiking

The town of Sagres is on a headland bordered by one of Portugal's natural parks, **Southwest Alentejo and Vicentine Coast Natural Park (Parque Natural do Sudoeste Alentejano e Costa Vicentina).**

★ VIA ALGARVIANA HIKING TRAIL

Hiking Distance: *300 kilometers (185 mi) one-way*
Hiking Time: *14 days one-way*
Trailhead: *Guadiana River bank, Alcoutim (east), or Cape St. Vincent Lighthouse, Sagres (west)*

Information and Maps: *www.viaalgarviana.org*

The Via Algarviana Hiking Trail is an old pilgrims' path that runs 300 kilometers (185 mi) from Cape St. Vincent to the Spanish border. It is the backbone of the region's popular hiking routes, launched in 1995 to promote walking, ecotourism, and sustainable development. The Via Algarviana offers a landscape starkly different from that along the coast, and it changes with the seasons, passing through rural hamlets, lush countryside, historic sites, and natural beauty spots.

Those who hike the trail from one end to the other take a couple of weeks to do so, hiking between 20-40 kilometers each day. The Via Algarviana website offers information on specific stretches, with advice on accommodations, viewpoints, and where to stop for drinks and food.

Shorter **themed routes** have been drawn up for a few hours' or a day's hiking. These include the intriguing Contraband Route, the Water Route, the Monumental Trees Route, and the Geology Route. See the trail's website. The **main office** (Association Almargem, Project Via Algarviana, Rua de S. Domingos 65, Loulé; tel. 289 412 959) is in Loulé.

Food

Fresh seafood is the dish in Sagres, and local delicacies hard to find elsewhere are gooseneck barnacles, sea urchins, and cuttlefish. Local fisherfolk sometimes risk their lives to collect these animals, often in rough conditions.

An eclectic cross-section of restaurants varies from typical Portuguese to vegetarian and international.

A SAGRES RESTAURANT

Ecovia do Litoral; tel. 282 624 171; www.a-sagres.com; Mon.-Tues. and Thurs.-Fri. 11am-5pm, Sat.-Sun. 11am-10:30pm; €12

The cozy and casual A Sagres Restaurant is warm and rustic, reflected in its menu, which showcases interesting seafood creations such as seafood pasta stew and octopus rice.

TELHEIRO DO INFANTE RESTAURANT

Praia da Mareta; tel. 282 624 179; www.
telheirodoinfante.com; Wed.-Mon. 10am-10pm; €15

For the freshest seafood, head to Telheiro do Infante Restaurant, overlooking Mareta Beach. What started as a small factory around 1910 has evolved into Sagres's finest eatery, where specialties include monkfish *cataplana* and a lobster rice pot.

★ MUM'S RESTAURANT

Rua Comandante Matoso; tel. 968 210 411; www.
mums-sagres.com; Tues.-Sat. 7pm-2am; €15

Mum's Restaurant promotes slow-cooking based on organic produce, with a variety of vegan and vegetarian options. The highly creative menu includes dishes such as purple rain soup, made with red cabbage, and cod-fish cappuccino.

Accommodations

CASA AZUL SAGRES, ROOMS & APARTMENTS

Rua Dom Sebastião; tel. 282 624 856; www.
casaazulsagres.com; €175 d, €240 2-bedroom
apartment

Homey and spotless, this pretty little bed-and-breakfast is finished to high levels of comfort. Anywhere in Sagres is a 10-minute walk, and Casa Azul runs its own surf school. Weekend barbecues are the main attraction. Double or twin rooms have en suite baths, and there are self-contained studio and one- and two-bedroom apartments.

★ MARTINHAL SAGRES BEACH FAMILY RESORT HOTEL

Quinta do Martinhal; tel. 282 240 200; www.
martinhal.com; €362

Eco-conscious Martinhal Sagres Beach Family Resort Hotel is among Europe's finest luxury family resorts. Overlooking the bay-like Martinhal Beach, which sweeps to the pretty Baleeira Port, the hotel has lodging in rooms, apartments, houses, and luxury villas. The restaurant uses fresh local ingredients, and the design complements the surrounding landscape. Among its facilities are a sumptuous spa, a kids' club, heated swimming pools, sports facilities, and a village square where guests can meet and socialize.

Information and Services

- **GNR police:** Rua de Santa Fé; tel. 282 630 010; www.gnr.pt
- **Main tourist office:** Rua Comandante Matoso 75; tel. 282 624 873
- **Post office:** Rua Comandante Matoso s/n; tel. 282 624 890

Getting There

Sagres is 33 kilometers (20 mi) west of **Lagos,** 30 minutes' drive on the **N125** road. Head west after Sagres for Cape St. Vincent. **Eva** (tel. 282 762 944; www.eva-bus.com) buses run from Lagos bus terminal to Sagres (1 hour, almost hourly daily 7:15am-8:30pm; €4), stopping at the fortress in Sagres as well as in the town center.

ALJEZUR

Sleepy Aljezur (al-zheh-ZOOR), the main town on the Algarve's west coast, has stunning countryside beaches. Untamed and unpretentious, the Algarve's west coast is one of the region's best-kept secrets.

Aljezur is a small town built on a valley plain about 30 kilometers (19 mi) north of Lagos. The drive from Lagos is relaxing and scenic, following a winding road through shaded countryside dotted with farmhouses and cottages. The easygoing town straddles a pretty river, its older and newer halves connected by an old Moorish bridge. Local folklore has it that the new part of Aljezur emerged when an outbreak of malaria struck the older part in the 18th century, and the Algarve bishop moved inhabitants away from the disease to the other side of the river.

The nearest beaches are 10 kilometers (6.2 mi) away on the rugged western Vicentine coastline and are among the best in the Algarve for surfing, which adds to the town's laid-back feel.

Sights
ALJEZUR CASTLE
(Castelo de Aljezur)

Rua do Castelo; tel. 282 990 010; open 24/7; free

Aljezur's skyline is dominated by the ruins of the once-imposing medieval Aljezur Castle, on a hill above the town. Excavations indicate the site could date to the Bronze Age. The castle was likely built by the Moors in the 10th century. Its distinctive circular stone tower can be seen from afar, and the steep 10-minute walk up to the castle is a challenging 300 meters (984 ft); it's also possible to drive up. There are views of the countryside from the top, and interesting relics inside the ruins have explanatory boards in English.

Beaches

Popular beaches for surfing include Arrifana and Monte Clérigo, both within Southwest Alentejo and Vicentine Coast Natural Park. The west coast beaches are best accessed by car or taxi, as public transport is unreliable. The popular beaches of Carrapateira, Bordeira, and Amado are also accessible from Sagres, a 20-minute (22 km/14 mi) drive south on the N268 road, a €25 minute taxi ride.

ARRIFANA BEACH
(Praia da Arrifana)

The views from the cliffs above medium-size Arrifana Beach are mesmerizing. The secluded beach is protected by the cliffs and is off the tourist track but is very popular among locals. Constant unintimidating waves are great for beginner surfers. Parking at the top of the cliffs is scarce in summer, and the walk down to the beach is steep. Off-season it is a tranquil hideaway for strolls and sunsets. Arrifana fishing village is along the top of the cliffs above the beach and has a cluster of cafés, snack bars, and restaurants. Arrifana is 10 kilometers (6.2 mi) west of Aljezur town; a taxi from Aljezur (tel. 282 991 176 or 917 574 630; www.taxiluis.com) is around €13 one-way.

MONTE CLÉRIGO BEACH
(Praia de Monte Clérigo)

Monte Clérigo Beach is low and open, flanked by hills on either side, scattered with cottages and topped with sandy dunes. This beach is great for families, with rock pools and restaurants, plenty of parking, and easy access, although it is a 10-minute walk from the car park to the beach below. A 10-minute, 8-kilometer (5-mi) drive northwest of Aljezur,

surfers at Arrifana Beach

this is one of the west coast's quieter beaches, even in summer.

Surfing

With great surfing conditions almost year-round, Aljezur has numerous surf trips and schools.

- **Arrifana Surf School & Camp:** Urbanização Vale da Telha 31; tel. 927 310 441 or 961 690 249; www.arrifanasurfschool.com; lessons from €35

Other Sports and Recreation

ALGARVE HORSE RIDING

tel. 967 607 840; www.algarvehorseriding.com

With often deserted beaches and luxuriant terrain, Aljezur is prime riding country. Algarve Horse Riding has safe trails (from €25 for a beginner's walk) throughout the Southwest Alentejo and Vicentine Coast Natural Park on beaches and rugged terrain; all levels of riders can be accommodated.

SANDY TOES ALGARVE

tel. 282 998 063; www.sandytoes-algarve.com

Explore the remote terrain of the western Algarve on a customized, family-friendly 4WD jeep safari (6 hours; from €70) with Sandy Toes Algarve, taking in hidden hamlets and unspoiled secret spots. Safaris are mindful of the environment and include a picnic of local produce. Local sights such as Aljezur Castle can be incorporated, along with lake swims, sand-boarding, and off-roading.

Food

Aljezur's gastronomy is a mix of land and sea, with abundant fresh fish, game, and produce. Local specialties include sweet potato cake and sweet potato pasties.

PONT' A PÉ RESTAURANT AND BAR

Largo da Liberdade 12; tel. 282 998 104; www.pontape.pt; Mon.-Sat. noon-10pm; €10

In a quaint, rustic, whitewashed cottage with blue-framed windows, the Pont' a Pé Restaurant and Bar is one of the oldest in town, specializing in the genuine flavors of Aljezur like beans, cabbage, sweet potato, and whelk stew.

RESTAURANT-BAR A LAREIRA

Rua 13 de Janeiro; tel. 282 998 440; daily noon-4pm; €10

Warm and welcoming Restaurant-Bar A Lareira ("The Fireplace") showcases authentic Portuguese cuisine, with a focus on local specialties and products. The unfussy dishes include fish *cataplana*, pork loin, and specials like duck rice. There's also a guesthouse with rooms above the restaurant.

Accommodations

Lodging in Aljezur tends to be cozy guesthouses or private rental cottages and villas. The surf companies also have their own lodging. **Camping** in the Southwest Alentejo and Vicentine Coast Natural Park is also an option.

AMAZIGH DESIGN HOSTEL

Rua da Ladeira 5; tel. 282 997 502; www.amazighostel.com; €29 dorm, €109 d

In a prime location in the heart of Aljezur is this hostel, nestled amid historic walls and picturesque alleys. Clean and unfussy shared dorms and private doubles are complemented by well-equipped social areas and a decorative courtyard.

VICENTINA

Av. General Humberto Delgado; tel. 282 990 030; www.vicentinahotel.com; from €120

In town, the small but well-equipped Vicentina is a great base for exploring the Vicentine Coast. A short stroll to the river and town center, it comprises 26 rooms and apartments, and has a pool and an on-site restaurant and bar.

SERRÃO CAMPGROUND

Herdade do Serrão; tel. 282 990 220; www.campingserrao.com; adults €5.50, children €2.75, plus €5-9 per tent, €7-9 per RV, cottages from €75

The Serrão campground is on the edge of the stunning west coast, swaddled by the protected Southwest Alentejo and Vicentine Coast Natural Park, just a few minutes' drive from the town of Aljezur and within walking distance to the Monte Clérigo and Arrifana Beaches. It is superbly equipped with clean communal shower and toilet facilities, a swimming pool, a sports field and tennis courts, summer entertainment, an on-site minimarket, a bar and restaurant, and even a crepe and waffle shop. Shared bungalow dorms with bunk beds and one-bedroom cottages with a kitchen and bath are available.

Information and Services

- **GNR police:** Rua da Escola 3; tel. 282 998 130; www.gnr.pt

- **Post office:** Rua 25 de Abril 75; tel. 282 997 275

Getting There

Aljezur is 30 kilometers (19 mi) north of **Lagos,** a 40-minute drive north on the twisty **N120** road. Heading west on the A22 motorway, take the last exit north on the N120 road for 20 minutes.

Alternatively, take a train from Faro or elsewhere to Lagos, then catch a **Rede Expressos** (www.rede-expressos.pt) bus to Aljezur (30 minutes, twice daily, 3 daily summer; €6-8). **Eva** (tel. 282 762 944; www.eva-bus.com) buses run more frequently but take longer from Lagos to Aljezur (50 minutes, every few hours Mon.-Fri., 1 bus Sat.; €4). Aljezur doesn't have a train station.

Coimbra and the Centro

In the heart of Portugal, between Lisbon and

the Alentejo to the south and Porto to the north, the Centro is a vast region of history and extraordinary landscapes. Towns like medieval Óbidos, the holy site Fátima, and the Templar city Tomar are infused with tradition and legend.

The Silver Coast (Costa da Prata), one of the Iberian Peninsula's lesser-known *costas*, stretches the length of the central coast between Lisbon and Porto, offering long, pristine beaches that aren't crowded, even in high season. Development is sparse, so the increasingly elusive unspoiled beach can still be found. Move inland and explore the remarkably preserved historic cities like Coimbra and Santarém, which played a key role in shaping the country, as well as hidden caves and

Highlights

Look for ★ to find recommended sights, activities, dining, and lodging.

★ **Óbidos:** One of Portugal's most historic and well-preserved medieval villages, beautiful Óbidos is famous for its castle walls and *ginja* cherry liqueur, served in a chocolate cup (page 254).

★ **Surfing in Nazaré:** The monster waves that roll into Nazaré have catapulted the formerly sleepy fishing town to global fame as one of the top big-wave surf spots on the planet (page 264).

★ **Convent of Christ:** Looming over the historic town of Tomar, this 12th-century complex is one of Portugal's greatest works of Renaissance architecture, famous as the local headquarters of the Knights Templar (page 271).

★ **Sanctuary of Our Lady of Fátima:** Spellbinding Fátima is an important pilgrimage site and a hub of mysteries, miracles, and monuments (page 277).

★ **Coimbra University:** The beautiful old buildings of Coimbra's university complex crown its historic hill, encapsulating the elegance and prestige of learning in times gone by and buzzing with the energy of today's youth (page 282).

★ **Schist Villages:** Hidden away in deepest

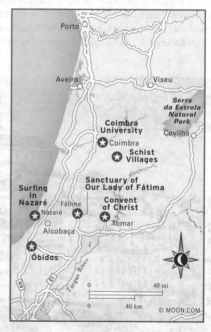

Central Portugal is a string of unique fairy-tale villages built entirely from schist stone (page 290).

Coimbra and Central Portugal

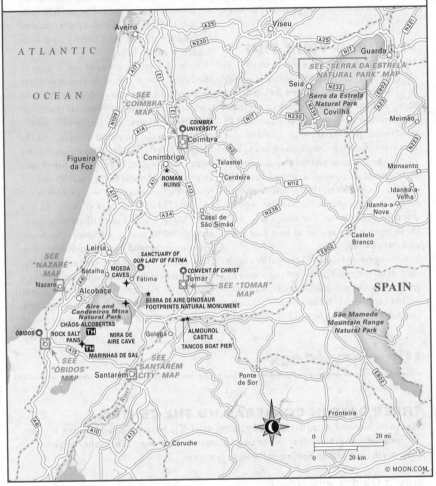

schist villages. The majestic Serra da Estrela mountain range are home to Portugal's only ski slopes.

Discover welcoming hospitality, hearty meals, awesome sights, and enthralling tales around every bend.

ORIENTATION

The expansive Centro comprises four key areas: the **Oeste,** the lower portion of the Silver Coast, just north of Lisbon and home to the medieval village of Óbidos and the surfing town of Nazaré; **Santarém,** home to momentous cities such as Tomar and Fátima;

Previous: the city of Coimbra; surfing in Nazaré; Santa Maria Church, Óbidos.

the famed ancient university city **Coimbra;** and in the northwest, the emblematic **Serra da Estrela** mountain range and its gateway town, Covilhã.

PLANNING YOUR TIME

Most people visit the Oeste region while traveling between **Lisbon** and **Porto,** stopping in its lovely towns and villages for lunch or a sunny stroll before jumping back on the main A1 motorway to the north. You can start in the **Oeste,** passing through **Óbidos** and **Nazaré** before traveling inland to explore **Fátima** and **Tomar,** and then heading north to **Coimbra** and the snowcapped **Serra da Estrela.** Or, do this trip from Porto in reverse. Nazaré, Óbidos, and Tomar are also popular day trips from Lisbon. The easiest way to do these tours is by **car** over at least four days and up to a week.

Getting around Central Portugal by road is easy, as all the main towns are connected by good roads and motorways. Public transport within big towns is relatively good, but getting farther afield can be difficult. The main routes through Central Portugal are the **A1** motorway between Porto and Lisbon, the **A8** between Lisbon and Leiria, the **A13** from Setúbal to Santarém, the **A14** from Coimbra to Figueira da Foz, and the **A15** between Santarém and Peniche.

Central Portugal is one of few regions in the country best visited in **summer** (May or June-Oct.), as winters can be bitterly cold and wet. Exceptions are perhaps the medieval stone villages, which take on a mystical charm in the hazy autumn light, and the Serra da Estrela mountain range, famous for being the only place in Portugal where it reliably snows and home to the county's sole ski resort. You should book well in advance if you would like to stay there in **snow season** (Dec.-Mar.). Another place where some planning could be useful is Óbidos, due to its year-round demand from tourists, and especially during its most popular **festivals,** the International Chocolate Festival (late Apr.-early May), Medieval Fair (July-Aug.), and Christmas Village (Dec.). Accommodations sell out fast during these peak times.

Itinerary Ideas

THREE DAYS IN COIMBRA AND THE CENTRO

Take in the best the Centro has to offer by basing yourself in Nazaré, Tomar, Coimbra, or some combination of the three; all are about an hour apart. This itinerary can also be completed en route north from Lisbon heading to Porto, or vice versa.

Day 1: Óbidos and Nazaré

1 Start your day in Óbidos, parking in the lots outside of town. Be sure to admire the traditional tiling on the vaulted **Porta da Vila** on the way into the town.

2 Have a late lunch at **A Nova Casa De Ramiro,** in the backstreets far from the crowds.

3 Make your way to the well-preserved **Óbidos Castle,** now a hotel, passing Santa Maria Square, with church and town pillory, en route.

4 Back in your car, drive another 30 minutes north to Nazaré on the coast, where you can enjoy the local specialty of octopus with olive oil for dinner at **Pangeia Restaurante.**

5 At the northern end of the beach, take the **funicular** up to the Sítio headland.

6 Enjoy the views of the town and coast at night from the **Suberco viewpoint,** before heading to your hotel for the night.

Day 2: Tomar

1 In the morning, take a surf lesson or enjoy some sunbathing on **Nazaré Beach.**

2 An hour inland on the IC9, in Tomar, head straight to the **Convent of Christ** and allow a good couple of hours to explore its nooks and crannies.

3 Make your way to the center of Tomar and enjoy lunch and a *queijada* at **Café Estrelas de Tomar.**

4 Walk off lunch with a stroll through Tomar's quaint streets, to the Nabão River and **Mouchão Park.**

5 Explore the quirky **Matchbox Museum** before dinner.

6 In the evening, enjoy perfectly prepared Portuguese food at **O Alpendre.** You can spend the night in historic Tomar, or head back to Nazaré for another night.

Day 3: Coimbra and the Schist Villages

1 The bustling university city of Coimbra is under an hour from Tomar, and just over an hour from Nazaré. As soon as you arrive, make a beeline for the university campus, perched at the top of the towering hill. Work your way down, making sure to see the fairy-tale **Joanina Library.**

2 As you start nearing the Baixa neighborhood at the bottom of the hill, you'll pass the **Old Cathedral,** whose Romanesque interior is worth a stop.

3 To learn more about Portuguese art, you should also visit the nearby **Machado de Castro National Museum,** filled with sculptures, *azulejo* tiles, and other artistic masterpieces.

4 For lunch, try a meaty dish at quirky local restaurant **Zé Manel dos Ossos.**

5 Walk off lunch wandering the atmospheric streets of the Baixa's historic center, crossing the Mondego River to see the stark gothic ruins of the **Santa Clara-a-Velha Monastery.**

6 Spend the remainder of your afternoon on a scenic drive through the **Schist Villages Route,** where ancient and ethereal villages such as Cerdeira, Talasnal, and Casal de São Simão stand mostly untouched by time. Return to either Coimbra, Tomar, or Nazaré for dinner and a good night's sleep.

Oeste

Formerly known as Estremadura Province, the Oeste (West) region of Central Portugal loosely refers to the lower Silver Coast, which runs north from Lisbon. This region is home to some spectacular seaside towns, like the surfing mecca Nazaré, the renowned medieval village Óbidos, and history-drenched Alcobaça with its colossal monastery.

Often referred to as "the land of vineyards and sea," the Oeste is a popular destination for a balance between rural and coastal. Castles and aqueducts sit alongside beaches, spas, and golf courses, all with the area's lovely weather.

★ ÓBIDOS

Not to be missed, enchanting Óbidos (AW-bee-doosh) is a pretty fortified town and a quintessential Portuguese village, with white-washed houses that exude undiluted charm huddled within the walls of the castle, now a hotel. One of Portugal's best-preserved medieval towns, its parking lot is usually packed with tour buses from dawn till dark.

Over the centuries Óbidos's beauty has made it a favorite among royals. In the 13th century, King Dom Dinis gifted the village to his wife, Queen Isabel, starting a tradition; centuries later, in 1441, King Afonso V famously wed his cousin, Princess Isabella of Coimbra, here when they were age 9 and 10, respectively. The regal favoritism gave the village its nickname "Village of Queens," a legacy that makes the town treasured and well looked after by its residents.

Home to festivals that take over the entire town, some of the country's biggest and best-known, including a Medieval Fair and Chocolate Festival, Óbidos is always buzzing. Walk through the main archway, the ancient tile-clad Porta da Vila, into a maze of cobblestone streets lined with flowers and cute craft shops touting souvenirs, including *ginja*, Óbidos's famous cherry liqueur. For a special view of the town (if you can handle heights),

circumnavigate the historic center on the elevated battlements.

Authentic and magical, Óbidos is the archetypal fortified Portuguese town, referred to locally as the "wedding gift town." Its classic beauty and layers of history make it a top destination for a day trip from Lisbon. High numbers of visitors, especially during popular annual events, mean narrow streets are often crowded. Allow at least a few hours to explore the town's attractions, or spend a night to enjoy the less busy hours before 9am and after 8pm, when the tour buses leave.

Orientation

Parking is limited in Óbidos, and most visitors will be required to leave their cars in one of the parking lots located on the village doorstep. Tour buses also stop just outside the town walls. Entry to Óbidos is made via the **Porta da Vila** gateway. Flights of steps are found regularly along the battlements, allowing visitors to climb the walls. Óbidos's main street, **Rua Direita,** stretches between the Porta da Vila and the historic **Pousada Castelo Óbidos** castle, now a hotel. It is along this street that most of the town's main attractions and little craft shops are found. But venture off the thoroughfare to see some of Óbidos's more picturesque backstreets and colorful little houses. At the top end of Rua Direita is Óbidos Castle and the area where its famous events, such as the **Medieval Fair** and **Christmas Village,** are set up. The **aqueduct** is located outside the town walls, opposite the main parking lot.

Sights
SANTA MARIA CHURCH
(Igreja de Santa Maria)
Praça de Santa Maria; tel. 262 959 633; daily 9:30am-12:30pm and 2:30pm-5pm Oct.-Mar., daily 9:30am-12:30pm and 2:30pm-7pm Apr.-Sept.; free
In the middle of town, in a little square along

Óbidos

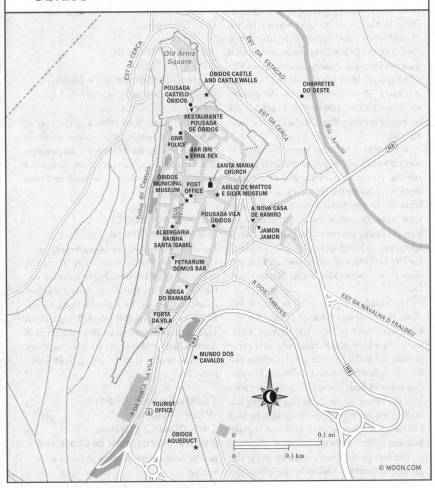

the main Rua Direita, is this pretty 12th-century church with its striking white bell tower and fancy Renaissance portal. Inside, the walls are clad from the floor to the painted wooden ceiling in 18th-century *azulejos*. The church also houses the tomb of Dom João de Noronha, a 16th-century commander of Óbidos. In front of the church is the 15th-century **town pillory,** decorated with fishing nets in homage to the fishermen who recovered the body of Afonso, son of Queen Leonor

and King João II, who died in a riding accident by the Tagus River.

ÓBIDOS CASTLE AND CASTLE WALLS (Castelo de Óbidos)

Pousada Castelo Óbidos hotel www.pousadas.pt/en/ hotel/pousada-obidos; walls open 24/7; walls free
Originating from the 12th century, Óbidos's excellently preserved medieval castle dominates the village. The main part, including the

keep, is today an outstanding luxury *pousada* (hotel), the **Pousada Castelo Óbidos**. The castle was a wedding present from King Dom Dinis to his new wife, Queen Santa Isabel, in 1282 when they were married here. From then until 1834, the village was owned by each queen of Portugal, earning its nicknames Vila de Rainhas (Village of Queens) and "wedding gift town." Over the centuries, the queens spent much time in Óbidos, and each left her influence on the village, including the local aqueduct.

The castle remains an impressive and romantic feature of Óbidos, protectively guarding the village. The castle was extensively reinforced during the 14th century, so most of what can be seen today is from that era, with little surviving evidence of its earlier incarnation. A visually interesting structure, it blends four main architectural styles that characterize the centuries of its origins and expansion: Romanesque, Manueline, Baroque, and Gothic.

The sturdy **castle walls,** accessible via stony flights of stairs dotted around the village, were built in the 14th century when the castle's keep and battlements were reinforced; the walls encircle Óbidos and make for a unique stroll around the town. The circuit takes an hour and offers bird's-eye views over the village center. Note that walking the walls is not for everyone—the height, lack of railings, and unevenness underfoot require balance, agility, and a tolerance for heights.

The hub of the town's main events is the grounds adjacent to the castle, the **Old Arms Square.**

ÓBIDOS MUNICIPAL MUSEUM
(Museu Municipal de Óbidos)

Rua Direita 97 - Solar da Praça de Santa Maria; tel. 262 955 500; www.obidos.pt; Tues.-Sun. 10am-1pm and 2pm-5pm; free

Pop into the small but well-formed Óbidos Municipal Museum to learn more about the town's devout religious history through the permanent artwork collection. There are 16th- and 17th-century paintings by

influential artists Josefa de Obidos and André Reinoso, Portugal's first Baroque painter. There's also a little bookshop and clean bathrooms.

ABÍLIO DE MATTOS E
SILVA MUSEUM
(Museu Abílio de Mattos e Silva)

Santa Maria Square; tel. 262 955 500; Tues.-Sun. 10am-1pm and 2pm to 5pm; free

Located just off Rua Direita at the rear of Santa Maria Square, this curious museum is worth a look, showcasing old marionettes and artwork by Óbidos resident, renowned painter, and set and costume designer Abílio de Mattos e Silva.

ÓBIDOS AQUEDUCT
(Aqueduto de Óbidos)

Across from the main parking lot and Porta da Vila

On the town's outskirts, across from the main parking lot and Porta da Vila entrance, the long, spindly Óbidos Aqueduct is also known as the Aqueduct of Usseira. Slender and remarkably intact, it was built in 1573 at the order of Queen Dona Catarina of Austria, wife of Dom João III, to bring water from the nearby Usseira spring to Óbidos's fountains.

Festivals and Events
INTERNATIONAL
CHOCOLATE FESTIVAL
(Festival Internacional de Chocolate)

www.festivalchocolate.cm-obidos.pt; Feb., Mar., or Apr.; €4

A 12-day event over a series of weekends in February, March, or April, the International Chocolate Festival is staged in the Old Arms Square, next to the castle, where small shacks emit the glorious, sweet scent of warm chocolate. The festival showcases cocoa-based goodies from traditional Portuguese sweets to contemporary concoctions, plus hot

---

1: Óbidos village 2: the Porta da Vila gateway 3: café in Óbidos village 4: Bar Ibn Errik Rex in Óbidos

chocolate or *ginja* liqueur served in a chocolate cup. Guests can also take cocoa-making classes for all ages.

MEDIEVAL FAIR
(Feira Medieval)

www.mercadomedievalobidos.pt; July-Aug.; €7

Every year from a Thursday in mid-July to the Sunday in the first week of August, Óbidos's quaint streets are transformed into a medieval village, complete with colorful bunting, fire-eaters, wizards, court jesters, jousting knights on horseback, falconry, and medieval gastronomy. The hub of activity is the Old Arms Square, adjacent to the castle, where little shacks form a medieval marketplace selling food and handicrafts typical of the era. A costume shop rents outfits for just €5 if you want to get into the theatrical spirit of the fair. This is one of Portugal's most famous events and well worth a visit.

CHRISTMAS VILLAGE
(Óbidos Vila Natal)

www.obidosvilanatal.pt; Dec.

Every year during December, Óbidos becomes a real-life snow globe, full of festive spirit and sparkly trimmings, when it hosts its famous annual Christmas Village. Hundreds of stalls sell gifts and hot chocolate, and fairground rides, shows, and entertainment fill the quaint streets. Dress warmly; this open-air event has an authentic winter chill.

Food
JAMON JAMON

Rua da Biquinha; tel. 916 208 162; Tues.-Sat. noon-3pm and 7pm-midnight, Sun. noon-3pm; €15

Traditional Portuguese cuisine is served with a generous helping of warm hospitality at this popular little tavern. Highly recommended are the chef's duck rice special and pork cheeks.

A NOVA CASA DE RAMIRO

Rua Porta do Vale 12; tel. 967 265 945; Mon. 7pm-11pm, Tues.-Thurs. noon-3pm and 7pm-11pm, Fri. 1pm-4pm and 7pm-11pm; €18

Located away from the throngs, just outside the city walls, this theatrically glamorous restaurant with chandeliers and an open fireplace is highly regarded by locals and highly rated by visitors. It serves luscious Mediterranean cuisine; fresh fish and seafood are menu staples.

ADEGA DO RAMADA

Travessa Nossa Sra. do Rosario 3; tel. 964 606 711; www.adegadoramada.com; Mon. noon-10pm, Tues.-Sat. noon-4pm and 6:30pm-9:30pm, Sun. noon-4:30pm; €20

Tucked away on one of Óbidos's quaint cobbled backstreets just off the main drag, Adega do Ramada is a simple tavern with stepped outdoor seating. It serves tasty grilled meat and fish dishes on traditional clay crockery from its streetside open grill; local specialties include a black pig grilled skewer with hand-cut chips. There's good house wine to boot.

RESTAURANTE POUSADA DE ÓBIDOS

Pousada Castelo de Óbidos hotel, Paço Real s/n; tel. 262 955 080; www.pousadas.pt/en/hotel/pousada-obidos; daily 1pm-3pm and 7:30pm-10pm; €45

For fine dining with a difference, head to the Pousada Castelo de Óbidos castle hotel and enjoy a romantic meal in a historic setting. The menu features traditional gourmet fare, inspired by regional ingredients and recipes.

Accommodations
ALBERGARIA RAINHA SANTA ISABEL

Rua Direita 63; tel. 262 959 323; www.obidoshotel.com; €50-100 d

Inside the town walls on the main street, the charming and casual three-star Albergaria Rainha Santa Isabel is in a historic white-washed building, with 20 simple old-fashioned rooms and a cozy guest lounge. Breakfast is included.

Ginja: Óbidos's Own Cherry Liquor

Like many of Portugal's most famous sweet treats, history has it that this popular drink, an infusion of macerated morello cherries in *aguardente* alcohol, originates from the country's convents. Dating to the 17th century, its original recipe is to this day a closely guarded secret, known only to a privileged few. That recipe is thought to have been first brewed by a friar—possibly with medicinal purposes, as *ginja* is a renowned digestive aid—and later local families would compete to see who could best replicate the recipe. Its popularity skyrocketed hand-in-hand with Óbidos's tourism. Thanks to its specific microclimate, the Óbidos region produces some of the finest cherries in Europe.

Try *ginja* for yourself at either of the following bars, or at any of the many other shops that sell it along **Rua Direita.**

BAR IBN ERRIK REX

Rua Direita 100; tel. 262 959 193; daily 10am-2am

Don't miss Bar Ibn Errik Rex, one of the oldest and best *ginja* bars in town, open since 1956. This medieval-style, family-run bar has more than 1,800 dusty, miniature bottles hanging from the ceiling.

PETRARUM DOMUS BAR

Rua Direita 38; tel. 262 959 620; www.petrarumdomus.com; daily 10am-10:30pm

This historic bar and restaurant with natural stone and wood décor transforms traditional *ginja* into delicious cocktails.

POUSADA VILA ÓBIDOS

Largo Dr. João Lourenço; tel. 210 407 635; www. pousadas.pt; €100-200 d

Opened in 2018, the Pousada Vila Óbidos is one of the most recent of the Pestana Group's fascinating conversions of local historic buildings, this time of Óbidos's old town hospital. Providing a "home-tel" experience, this lovely little building offers a tranquil and comfortable refuge with 17 rooms of modern and stylish décor and a pretty courtyard, conveniently located inside the walls of the bustling town.

★ POUSADA CASTELO ÓBIDOS

Paço Real; tel. 210 407 630; www.pousadas.pt/en/ hotel/pousada-obidos; €250-350 d

Spend a night in the heart of Óbidos town in the imposing 700-year-old Castelo Óbidos, which is today a luxury *pousada* (hotel). Each of the 11 rooms, 3 of which are in the castle keep, is individually decorated, while the adjacent 8-room Casa do Castelo cottage offers authentic yet comfortable medieval lodging.

Information and Services

- **Tourist office:** Rua da Porta da Vila, ground floor; tel. 262 959 231; www. obidos.pt; Mon.-Fri. 9:30am-6pm, Sat.-Sun. 9:30am-12:30pm and 1:30pm-5:30pm

- **Post office:** Praça Santa Maria; tel. 262 955 041; www.ctt.pt; Mon.-Fri. 9am-12:30pm and 2:30pm-6pm

- **GNR police:** Rua Direita; tel. 262 955 000; www.gnr.pt

Getting There

Óbidos is 80 kilometers (50 mi) north of **Lisbon,** a fast and easy drive on the **A8** motorway (tolls apply) that takes just over 1 hour. Cars can be parked in a large **car park** (€2 for 1.5 hours) just outside the Porta da Vila gate, opposite the tourist information center. When it gets full, which is especially common in summer, there is a large overflow car park just across the road, by the aqueduct.

An express-bus service named the Rápida Verde (1 hour, Mon.-Fri. hourly, less frequently Sat.-Sun. and holidays; €7.70), operated by bus company **Rodoviária do Tejo** (tel. 249 787 878; www.rodotejo.pt), runs between Lisbon's Campo Grande station, near Alvalade stadium, and Óbidos's parking lot, just outside the city walls near the Porta da Vila gate. The same service also runs to Alcobaça and Nazaré.

Getting Around

Óbidos is easily seen in one day and can be explored comfortably **on foot.** Cars are not allowed within the historic center and must park in the **parking lot** just outside the city walls, a 2-minute walk south of the Porta da Vila gate.

Take a step back in time and rumble along the cobbled streets in an old-fashioned horse and carriage (30 minutes; 4 adults from €30 outside the walls, €65 inside the walls). **Charretes do Oeste** (tel. 262 835 562; www.charretesdooeste.com) and **Mundo dos Cavalos** (tel. 968 881 805 or 918 509 521; www.mundodoscavalos.pt) operate year-round, awaiting passengers in the main car park, but rides are subject to weather conditions.

NAZARÉ

Before becoming a monster-wave surfing hot spot, Nazaré was a fishing town and popular traditional seaside resort. Today the town's charming main seafront avenue is flanked by dense construction. Famed for its excellent fresh seafood as much as for incredible surfing conditions, Nazaré can feel overrun, especially in peak season, and modern development has taken the shine off its fishing-town charm. Nonetheless, authentic traits and traditions persevere.

Watch the laden dragnets brought in to the shouts of local fisherwomen, who still wear the traditional seven skirts and headscarves. Along the beachfront, you'll see boards of butterflied fish left to cure in the open air, sold by the fisherwomen as a local delicacy. You can also enjoy the fresh catch at one of the many local beachfront seafood restaurants.

Orientation

Nazaré's main landmarks are mostly located along its **beachfront** and up on the **Sítio headland** that towers over the town. Fantastic fresh fish restaurants line the vast crescent moon of golden sand that is Nazaré's famous beach. The **funicular** up to Sítio is located at the north end of the beachfront, along which there is a pleasant seafront promenade and main avenue, **Avenida da República**. An interesting part of Nazaré town is the **fishermen's quarters,** located between **Manuel de Arriaga square** and **Avenida Vieira Guimarães.** The **lighthouse, Suberco viewpoint,** and **Memorial Hermitage** are all located up on the Sítio headland, which is where the older part of Nazaré is situated. From up here in winter, visitors can watch surfers ride the monster waves.

Sights
NAZARÉ FUNICULAR
(Ascensor da Nazaré)

Rua de São Lázaro; tel. 262 550 010; www.cm-nazare.pt; daily 7:30am-8:30pm Oct.-May, daily 7:30am-midnight June-mid-July and late Sept., daily 7:30am-2am mid-July-mid-Sept.; €1.20

The dizzying Nazaré Funicular takes passengers from the urban beachfront up to **Sítio,** an older extension of the town on a headland atop cliffs to the north. Modern funicular cabs climb a historic track, ascending 318 meters (1,043 ft) in 15 minutes, between residential buildings at the bottom, through a tunnel, offering astounding views of Nazaré as they ascend to the top. This fun, easy, and cheap experience is a short trip and a good way to get to Sítio without a car—parking at the top can be hard to find, especially on weekends. The funicular runs every 15 minutes or so.

SUBERCO VIEWPOINT
(Miradouro do Suberco)

Sítio promontory, just beyond the funicular exit

Soar up the vertiginous rock face on Nazaré's famed funicular to the elevated part of town, on cliffs to the north of Nazaré main beach,

Nazaré

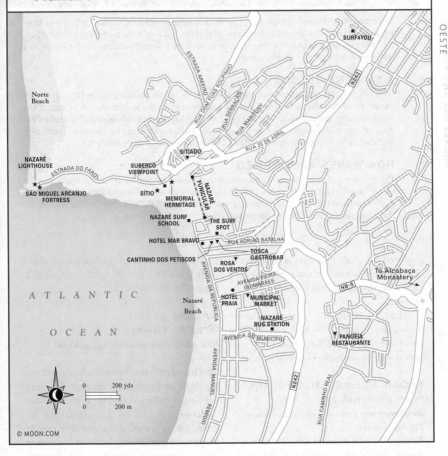

© MOON.COM

known as Sítio. Sítio comprises a lovely large square flanked by stunning views, quaint shops and restaurants, a large sanctuary, and a chapel. In summer, Sítio can offer some respite from the throngs in the main part of town. Make sure to stop at the Suberco viewpoint for breathtaking vistas of Nazaré and the beach.

MEMORIAL HERMITAGE
(Ermida da Memória)

Rua 25 de Abril; open 24/7; free

Once upon a time, the Sítio promontory

teemed with deer. According to local legend, in 1182 a nobleman was hunting in dense fog when his deer vanished near the edge of the cliff. Just as he was about to fall to his death, he cried out to Our Lady of Nazaré, who appeared before him and stopped his horse. The rider ordered this chapel just off Sítio's main square built in honor of this miracle.

This piece of folklore is depicted in the traditional 17th-century *azulejos* that completely clad the interior of the small, square chapel, with its pyramidlike roof. Supposedly, the **hoofprint** of the nobleman's horse is

Nazaré's Big Wave

Since the 1960s, Nazaré has been a popular place among experienced surfers looking for a challenge—but recently it gained a whole new level of fame as one of the planet's top spots for extreme big-wave surfing. Once a year, typically in November, Nazaré's underwater canyon creates perfect conditions for enormous waves.

A SURFING RECORD

In November 2011, US professional big-wave surfer Garrett McNamara conquered a monstrous 24-meter (79-ft) wave in Nazaré, setting a world record for the largest wave ever surfed. His name is now synonymous with Nazaré's surf scene, having almost singlehandedly catapulted the once-sleepy coastal resort onto the must-surf map. (McNamara's record has since been broken by Brazilian surfer Rodrigo Koxa, who surfed a 24.4-m/80-ft wave in November 2017.)

HOW WAVES ARE FORMED

The monster waves are formed by a unique underwater canyon off Nazaré, a finger-shaped crevice pointing toward the town. The colossal waves create a year-round attraction, as visitors hope to witness Mother Nature's full fury unleashed—especially in winter. Outside November, the waves can still be big but nowhere near as spectacularly fearsome.

engraved in a stone in the crypt beneath the chapel. Other folktales claim explorer Vasco da Gama prayed here before setting off on his voyages.

A bizarre contemporary **statue** of a surfer with a deer's head, which stands halfway down the road to the São Miguel Fortress, pays tribute to the locale's blended history.

SÃO MIGUEL ARCANJO FORTRESS

Estrada do Farol; tel. 938 013 587; https:// praiadonorte.com.pt/sobre/forte-s-miguel-arcanjo; daily 10am-6pm; €1

Built in 1577 by order of King Sebastian of Portugal and later expanded in 1644 by D. João VI, the fortress of São Miguel Arcanjo sits in a privileged position on a jagged promontory. Surrounded by the fearsome Atlantic, it has become one of Nazaré's top attractions and is the ultimate viewpoint for big-wave surfing competitions. Open year-round, the fortress also houses an interpretive center on the underwater Nazaré Canyon as well as surf-related exhibitions.

Beaches

While the main **Nazaré Beach** is surfable,

particularly in winter, the famous big-wave surfing is a little farther north, off wild and windy **Norte Beach.**

NAZARÉ BEACH (Praia da Nazaré)

Nazaré beachfront, República Avenue; limited parking

This huge crescent-moon stretch of glimmering blond sand favored for fishing and surfing is Nazaré's calling card. Due to the offshore underwater formation that creates the famously huge waves, the water here can be choppy and cool, although calmer in summer when the beach is packed with holidaymakers. Strong undercurrents are something to watch out for, but the main beach is sheltered by the Sítio headland and therefore calmer and less breezy than just around the corner, on Norte Beach (Praia do Norte).

Nazaré's main beach is fringed by a long seafront avenue and the main avenue, **Avenida da República,** with its end-to-end shops, bars, and restaurants.

1: a Nazaré fisherwoman selling dried fish 2: half-man, half-deer statue paying tribute to Nazaré's surfers 3: Nazaré Funicular

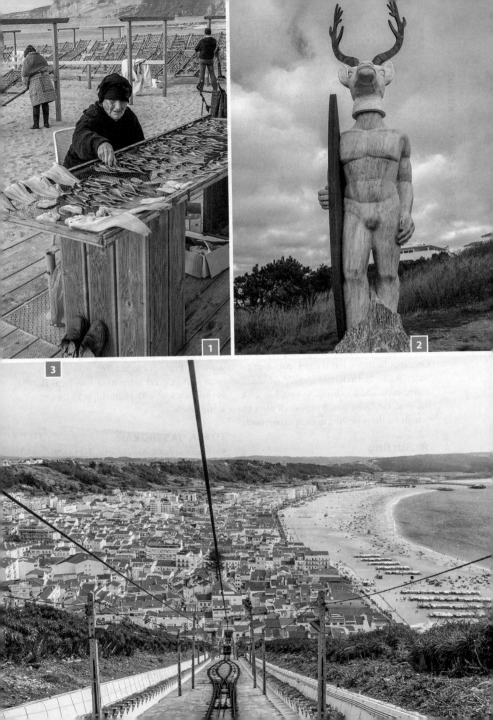

Octopus with Olive Oil

Given the town's seafront location, Nazaré's local gastronomy is based on fresh seafood. A typical dish is *polvo á lagareiro* (octopus cooked in a pressure cooker and served with hot olive oil). The octopus should be soft, not chewy, and is usually served with small baked potatoes and lots of garlic.

Two top places to try this local delicacy are:

- ★ **Pangeia Restaurante** (Rua Abel da Silva 50; tel. 917 934 726; www.pangeiarestaurante.com; Thurs.-Tues. noon-3pm and 7pm-10pm, Wed. noon-3pm; €20)

- **Cantinho dos Petiscos** (Rua Alexandre Herculano; tel. 915 064 325; Wed.-Mon. 10:30am-2am; €20).

NORTE BEACH
(Praia do Norte)

Rua Praia do Norte; parking available

This hot spot for extreme surfing is just after the Sítio headland, where a deep finger-shaped underwater canyon off the shore channels colossal swells. It's not really a swimming beach, as the water can quite often be tumultuous, but it is a surfing magnet and real spectacle of nature when the waves are fiercest. The beach has a wild, solitary feel, backed by reedy dunes and devoid of facilities, but is enjoyable when the water is calm. Not as family-friendly as Nazaré's main beach, and it's also quite a walk to get to the sand, but Norte Beach provides a great antithesis for those looking to escape the crowds.

★ Surfing

Nazaré, particularly **Norte Beach,** is known as a surfing mecca, whether you want to try some of the legendary waves yourself or watch the pros. Given the size of the waves, swells generated by the canyon, and local underwater currents, Nazaré's beaches, especially Norte Beach, are best suited to experienced surfers during big-wave season (Oct.-Mar.).

- **Surf4you:** Rua Fernando Ybarra 21; tel. 926 384 594; www.surf4-you.com
- **Nazaré Surf School:** Avenida da Republica, edificio S.Miguel s/n (basement); tel. 916 386 907; www.nazaresurfschool.pt
- **The Surf Spot:** Rua Mouzinho de Albuquerque 5; tel. 916 966 328; daily 10am-11pm

Food
MUNICIPAL MARKET
(Mercado Municipal)

Av. Vieira Guimarães; tel. 262 550 010; Tues.-Sun. 8am-1pm

Get up close and personal with the locals at the lively Nazaré Municipal Market. Sellers' benches are piled high with colorful fresh fruit and veggies, sweets, and local delicacies, as they noisily go about their business as they have for decades. This place is an authentic working Portuguese market with genuine local soul. A great place to sample local flavor and stock up with picnic supplies for a day at the beach.

TOSCA GASTROBAR

Rua Mouzinho de Albuquerque 4; tel. 262 562 261; Thurs.-Tues. noon-3pm and 7pm-10pm; €15

Local products meet international favorites at Tosca Gastrobar, a small, trendy gastropub where creative snack-size dishes take center stage. Baked camembert with walnuts and red fruit coulis, shrimp pasta, and spinach, apple, and cheese strudel are on the innovative menu. Reservations are recommended.

SITIADO

Rua Amadeu Guadêncio; tel. 262 087 512; Mon.-Fri. 6pm-10:30pm, Sat.-Sun. noon-3pm and 7pm-10:30pm; €15

The quirky vintage décor at Sitiado, a colorful, petite restaurant (note the bicycle hanging on the wall), does little to convey the traditionally Portuguese essence of its menu. Simple salads, juicy grilled tuna steaks, beef steaks, and a range of tasty tapas (try the *casquinhas*, potato skins) make up the menu.

ROSA DOS VENTOS
Rua Gil Vicente 88; tel. 918 267 127; Fri.-Wed. noon-3:15pm and 7pm-9:30pm; €18

It might not be a beachfront place, but the seafood at Rosa dos Ventos is second to none. Set back from the beach on the main road through the top end of town, near the funicular, Rosa dos Ventos serves fresh fish and shellfish, simply boiled or grilled. Tasty fish stews and homemade desserts round out the offerings.

Accommodations
HOTEL MAR BRAVO
Praca Sousa Oliveira 71; tel. 262 569 160; www. marbravo.com; €100-200 d

This fantastic little 16-room hotel is at the northern end of Nazaré's main beach. Hotel Mar Bravo's clean and contemporary décor enhances the summery vibes of the dazzling white sands and deep blue sea of its beachfront location.

HOTEL PRAIA
Av. Vieira Guimarães 39; tel. 262 569 200; www. hotelpraia.com; €100-200 d

Located in the center of Nazaré, just 2 minutes' walk from the beachfront, this hotel blends great location, comfort, and modern style. Family apartments are available, it has a pool, and parking costs an extra €5/day.

Getting There
By car, Nazaré is 122 kilometers (76 mi) north of **Lisbon,** a 1.5-hour drive, following the **A8** motorway (tolls apply). From **Óbidos,** Nazaré is a 40-kilometer (25-mi), 30-minute drive north along the A8.

NAZARÉ BUS STATION
Av. do Município 2450

The main bus station is on Avenida do Município, a few streets back from the beachfront, about a 10-minute walk. **Rodoviária do Tejo** (tel. 249 787 878; www.rodotejo.pt) operates the Rápida Verde express-bus service between Lisbon's Campo Grande station and Nazaré (1.75 hours, Mon.-Fri. hourly, less frequently Sat.-Sun. and holidays; €9.85). **Rede Expressos** (tel. 707 223 344; www. rede-expressos.pt) operates a similar bus service from its main Lisbon hub, Sete Rios (1.75 hours; €10.90).

Rodoviária do Oeste (tel. 262 767 676; www.rodoviariadooeste.pt) operates buses three times a day between **Óbidos** and Nazaré (1.25 hours; €4), and there is an evening **Rápida Verde** bus between the towns.

GETTING AROUND
Most of Nazaré can be easily covered **on foot.** The main beachfront drag, **Avenida da República,** between the little port to the south and the funicular at the northern end of the main **Praia da Nazaré,** is about 1.5 kilometers (1 mi), a 20-minute walk from one end to the other. The funicular is the best way to get from the main town to Sítio, although there are stairs. You could also drive, but **parking** is at a premium in Nazaré, especially up in Sítio and during holidays and on weekends.

Santarém

Santarém (San-tah-RAYN), a sprawling district of flat, fertile, cattle-rich farmland along the north bank of the Tagus River, encompasses much of the former Ribatejo Province. The region is known for bullfighting, the famous *sopa da pedra* (stone soup), and a number of Portugal's most important religious and historic landmarks, among them the Sanctuary of Our Lady of Fátima; Tomar, seat of the Knights Templar; and the fabled Almourol Castle.

SANTARÉM CITY

Despite its formidable history as one of the most strategically important strongholds in Portugal, Santarém city, an hour's drive northeast of Lisbon, is a lesser-known and untouristed city. Built atop a large plateau on the northern bank of the Tagus River, it was hotly disputed by several civilizations who settled there, including the Romans, Visigoths, and Moors. Santarém's advantageous position also made it a desirable location during the 11th- and 12th-century *reconquistas,* with Afonso Henrique I ultimately reclaiming the country from the Moors. Afonso Henriques's reconquest of Santarém on March 15, 1147—along with regaining Lisbon later that year—unlocked the *reconquista* of Portugal as a whole and its foundation as an independent nation.

Santarém is not usually high on the list of tourists' must-see places, but it does have a lot to offer, from captivating historic buildings to staggering vistas. The traditional town center is architecturally rich and atmospheric, if a tad worn. Belvederes throughout the city offer bird's-eye views over the Tagus River and the marshy wetlands that flank it.

Sights
PORTAS DO SOL CASTLE AND GARDENS
(Portas do Sol Castelo e Jardins)

Largo das Alcaçovas; tel. 243 304 437; daily 8:30am-9pm June-Sept., daily 9am-8pm Oct.-May; free

Within the citadel of the town's old castle, the Portas do Sol Castle and Gardens have sun-dappled lawns, huge trees, and a picturesque bridge crossing a blue lake. Within these grounds, Dom Afonso Henriques, first king of Portugal, and his soldiers ambushed the occupying Moors at night, and consequently conquered the land in 1147. The Portas do Sol (Doors of the Sun) are two imposing old gateways built into the toothy citadel walls. With views over the Tagus River and the region's distinctive *lezírias* (low-lying, lush meadows), this small park is a lovely place to wander and enjoy a coffee at the little on-site cafeteria. Within the gardens are children's play areas and the **Urbi Scallabis Interpretation Center and Museum** (Largo das Alcaçovas; tel. 243 357 288; Wed.-Sun. 9:15am-12:30pm and 2pm-5:30pm; free), offering insight to the city's history and local relics.

Festivals and Events
NATIONAL GASTRONOMY FESTIVAL
(Festival Nacional de Gastronomia)

www.festivalnacionaldegastronomia.pt; Oct.; €2

Every year for 11 days in late October, Santarém hosts the National Gastronomy Festival, celebrating Portugal's gastronomic heritage through regional foods and drink (think amazing cheese, meat, and wine). Since 1981 it has attracted the region's top restaurants, chefs, and producers, usually in the city's exhibition and trade center, **Casa do Campino** (Campo Emílio Infante da Câmara; tel. 918 638 507). The festival makes for a unique opportunity to indulge in regional cuisine with the locals.

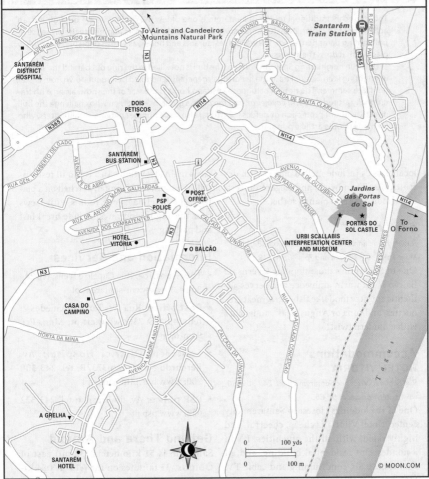

Santarém City

To Aires and Candeeiros Mountains Natural Park

SANTARÉM DISTRICT HOSPITAL

DOIS PETISCOS

Santarém Train Station

SANTARÉM BUS STATION

POST OFFICE

PSP POLICE

HOTEL VITÓRIA

O BALÇÃO

CASA DO CAMPINO

A GRELHA

SANTARÉM HOTEL

Jardins das Portas do Sol

PORTAS DO SOL CASTLE

To O Forno

URBI SCALLABIS INTERPRETATION CENTER AND MUSEUM

Tagus

0 100 yds
0 100 m

© MOON.COM

Food
A GRELHA

Rua do Ateneu Comercial de Santarém, ground floor left; tel. 243 333 348; www.grelhasantarem.blogspot. pt; Tues.-Wed. and Fri.-Sat. 11am-11pm, Sun. 11am-3pm and 7pm-11pm; €15

A swanky little place with contrasting dark and bleached woods on the outskirts of town, A Grelha serves typical Portuguese food—lots of it grilled, as the name (The Grill) suggests—in generous portions. Smoked hams

and cheeses, octopus salad, seafood rice, meat kebabs, and grilled veal ribs are favorites.

DOIS PETISCOS

Cerca da Mecheira 20; tel. 243 095 552; daily noon-3pm and 7pm-10:30pm; €15

At minimalistic Dois Petiscos, the food is as fresh and clean as the brilliant-white and bleached-wood interior, with a creative menu based on the concept of taking regional *petiscos* (snacks) to a new level. Modern twists on

Bullfighting in Portugal

The staunchly traditional region of Santarém is one of few in Portugal where bullfighting, an activity not to everyone's taste, remains widely appreciated. Visitors might note the presence of bullfighting paraphernalia on the walls of restaurants and hotels, as well as depictions on *azulejo* plaques that dress the streets.

Unlike in neighboring Spain, in Portugal the bull is not killed in the ring but behind the scenes. Bullfighting is an age-old tradition in Portugal, generally scheduled before sundown from Easter until late summer. The noble Portuguese Lusitano horse is the star of the show, along with traditionally attired riders, or *cavaleiros*, and *forcados*, a group of eight men who challenge the bull directly without protection or defense. Portugal also has a number of female bullfighters, who for many people are like pop stars.

local classics include melted cheese with dry fruits, oxtail sandwich, and elegant desserts like lemon cake and mango sorbet.

O BALCÃO

Rua Pedro de Santarém 223; tel. 243 055 883; Mon.-Sat. noon-3:30pm and 7pm-10pm; €18

One of Santarém's most popular taverns, O Balcão has a warm ambience and serves authentic country food like fishcakes, meat croquettes, and tuna or Angus steak sandwiches with a modern twist.

Accommodations
HOTEL VITÓRIA

Rua Segundo Visconde Santarém 21; tel. 243 309 130; www.hotelvitoria.com.pt; €55

One of the lodgings closest to Santarém city center, Hotel Vitória is cheap, cheerful, and highly rated, with all the amenities. It's in a nondescript residential building, and all rooms have air-conditioning and cable TV. Décor is slightly dated, but it's a clean and comfortable place to stay, a 15-minute stroll to the riverside Portas do Sol Gardens.

SANTARÉM HOTEL

Av. Madre Andaluz; tel. 243 330 800; www.santaremhotel.net; €65

Equipped with pools, terraces, and a fitness center, the smart, bright, airy, and clean four-star Santarém Hotel is on the outskirts of Santarém center, a 6-minute drive to the

city's main attractions. In a tranquil residential area south of the center, perched on a plateau, the hotel has some rooms with views over the Tagus, and rates include breakfast and parking.

Information and Services

- **Tourist office:** Rua Capelo e Ivens; tel. 243 304 437; www.cm-santarem.pt

- **Post office:** Rua Dr. Teixeira Guedes 2; tel. 243 309 730; www.ctt.pt; Mon.-Fri. 9am-6pm

- **Santarém District Hospital:** Av. Bernardo Santareno 3737B; tel. 243 300 200; www.hds.min-saude.pt

- **PSP police:** Av. do Brasil 1; tel. 243 322 022; www.psp.pt

Getting There and Around

Santarém is 51 kilometers (32 mi) east of **Óbidos,** 35 minutes on the **A15.** It's 84 kilometers (52 mi) northeast of **Lisbon** on the **A1** (tolls apply), a 1-hour drive, and 135 kilometers (84 mi) south of **Coimbra,** a 1.25-hour drive also on the A1.

The town is walkable, but there is a handy local bus in summer operated by municipal company **Scala Bus** (www.scalabus.pt), which runs a free tourist circuit (*circuito turistico*) July-September, covering the city's main sights.

Monasteries of Oeste

Portugal's Oeste region is a trove of magnificent monastic buildings; the three finest are Alcobaça, Batalha, and Tomar (page 271). These exceptional and well-preserved examples of religious buildings were constructed by the various orders that once thrived in this region, among them the Cistercians and the Benedictines, dating back to the 12th century. Following a civil war in the 1800s, many of these monasteries were disbanded and fell into disrepair. But the legacy left by the monks of those bygone eras lives on, not only through the surviving buildings, but also in centuries-old recipes for sweets and liqueurs that continue to delight today.

A combined ticket to the Alcobaça Monastery, Batalha Monastery, and Tomar Convent of Christ (€15) is valid for seven days.

ALCOBAÇA MONASTERY

Mosteiro da Alcobaça, Praça 25 de Abril; tel. 262 505 120; www.mosteiroalcobaca.
pt; daily 9am-6pm Oct.-Mar., daily 9am-7pm Apr.-Sept.; €6

Understated Alcobaça (al-koh-BAH-ssah)'s staggering focal monument, the Alcobaça Monastery, was founded by the Order of Cistercians in 1153. Also known as the Royal Abbey of Santa Maria, it's a masterpiece of Gothic architecture classified by UNESCO as a World Heritage Site. It was Portugal's first truly Gothic building, constructed by Afonso Henrique I after victory over the Moors at Santarém in 1147.

Construction began in 1178, with the main central church—the largest in Portugal at the time—completed in the mid-13th century. Behind the lavish Baroque facade, a soaring ribbed ceiling lets light flood in. Added to the monastery in the late 13th century, the Cloister of Silence (Claustro do Silencio) is one of the largest medieval Cistercian cloisters in Europe, named for the silent monks who inhabited it. In the Kings Room (Sala dos Reis), sculptures of Portuguese kings peer down on visitors.

Alcobaça is a 1.5-hour drive via the A8 motorway and 16 kilometers (10 mi) east from coastal Nazaré, a 15-minute drive via the IC9 road. There is also direct bus service from Lisbon and Nazaré provided by Rodoviária do Tejo (Campo Grande, Lisbon; tel. 249 787 878; www.rodotejo. pt; 2 hours; €9.85) and Rede Expressos (Sete Rios; tel. 707 223 344; www.rede-expressos.pt; 2 hours; €10.90). Rodoviária do Tejo (tel. 249 787 878; www.rodotejo.pt; 20 minutes; €2.30) also operates over a dozen daily services between Nazaré and Alcobaça. The bus station in Alcobaça is on Avenida Manuel da Silva Carolino, a 10-minute walk east of the monastery.

BATALHA MONASTERY

Mosteiro da Batalha, Largo Infante Dom Henrique; tel. 244 765 497; www.mosteirobatalha.gov.
pt; daily 9am-5:30pm mid-Oct.-Mar., daily 9am-6:30pm Apr.-mid-Oct.; €6, includes audio guide

A few kilometers north of Alcobaça, the lovely old town of Batalha (bah-TAL-yah) is home to this masterpiece of intricate ornamental late Gothic-Manueline architecture. The Batalha Monastery, a Dominican convent, was constructed to celebrate victory in the 1385 Battle of Aljubarrota, when Dom João I defeated the Castilians, ensuring two centuries of independence from Castilian invaders.

The main church is free to visit. Paid sections include the Founders Chapel (Capela do Fundador), Portugal's first royal pantheon, whose unique octagonal chamber contains the combined tomb of John I and his wife, Queen Philippa; the fancy Gothic-Manueline Royal Cloister (Claustro Real); and the austerely medieval King Afonso V Cloister (Claustro de Dom Afonso V).

Batalha is 22 kilometers (13.6 mi) north of Alcobaça, a 25-minute drive along the IC9 and IC2 roads. From Lisbon, Rede Expressos (tel. 707 223 344; www.rede-expressos.pt) operates buses six times daily from its main Lisbon hub, Sete Rios (under 2 hours; €10.90). Rodoviária do Tejo (tel. 249 787 878; www.rodotejo.pt) and Rodoviária do Oeste (tel. 262 767 676; www. rodoviariadooeste.pt) operate 10 daily connections between Alcobaça and Batalha (25 minutes; €3.30). The main bus stop in Batalha is in Largo 14 de Agosto, next to the parish church.

O Forno and Stone Soup

In the small village of **Almeirim,** a 20-minute drive from Santarém city, is one of the most famous restaurants in the whole district, O Forno, famous for its *sopa da pedra* (stone soup), a Portuguese peasant soup with a fascinating fable. The traditional version includes beans, potato, pig ears, pork ribs, *chouriço* sausage, *morçela* (black blood) sausage, *farinheira* (flour) sausage, bay leaves, coriander, and mint.

sopa da pedra (stone soup)

THE LEGEND

The story goes that a poor, famished friar on a pilgrimage stopped in the village. He asked around for donations to buy food, but no one had any to spare, so he announced he was going to make a marvelous soup from just a stone and water. Enthralled, the villagers gathered round.

Having borrowed an old pan, he got water boiling and threw in a stone. Tasting the water, he commented that it might need seasoning, which the villagers happily provided. Then he said it might benefit from some spicy *chouriço* sausage or pork belly to add more flavor; the curious villagers obligingly supplied them. Then the friar asked for some vegetables like beans or potato to add substance, and these were also promptly provided.

By the time the soup was finished, the villagers agreed the scent from it was indeed mouthwatering. After his meal, the friar took the stone from the bottom of the pan, washed it off, and put it back in his pocket, ready for the next time.

WHERE TO TRY IT

★ **O Forno** (Largo Praça Touros 23, Almeirim; tel. 243 241 163; www.restauranteoforno.pt; Wed.-Mon. 11:30am-3:30pm and 6:30pm-10:30pm; €12) a famed restaurant in the heart of Almeirim town, is the ultimate place to enjoy real *sopa da pedra*. Most days, queues form around the door to eat at this unassuming traditional restaurant. Though many other restaurants in the area that serve *sopa da pedra*, O Forno boasts a cult following. Reserve a table well in advance to avoid a long wait.

GETTING THERE

Almeirim is a 20-minute, 13.7-kilometer (8.5-mi) drive south of Santarém city along the **N3** and **N114** roads. **Ribatejana** (tel. 707 201 371; www.ribatejana.pt) runs a half-dozen buses daily between Santarém's main bus station (Av. do Brasil) and Almeirim (€2.10), more frequently in the afternoon than in the morning. **Rodoviária do Tejo** (tel. 249 787 878; www.rodotejo.pt) operates almost hourly buses between the towns (15 minutes; €2.10).

SANTARÉM BUS STATION

Av. do Brasil 41

Two bus companies run regular services between Lisbon and Santarém city center: **Rede Expressos** (from the Sete Rios station in Lisbon; tel. 707 223 344; www.rede-expressos. pt; 1 hour; €7.60) and **Rodoviária do Tejo**'s Rápida Laranja line (Campo Grande station; tel. 249 787 878; www.rodotejo.pt; 1 hour; €7.65). Both operate about six buses daily, every few hours. From Coimbra to Santarém, Rede Expressos runs three daily buses (2-4 hours; €14), which take longer if there is a transfer in Lisbon. From Santarém's main bus station (Av. do Brasil), it is a 15-minute walk west to the town center.

SANTARÉM TRAIN STATION

Estrada da Estação de Caminhos de Ferro

From Coimbra, **CP** (tel. 707 210 220; www. cp.pt) trains run almost hourly to Santarém (high-speed train 1.5 hours; 2nd class €19, 1st class €26.70; regional train 2.5 hours; €10.75). CP also runs trains between Lisbon and Santarém (1 hour; €7.50-18.30). Santarém train station is 2 kilometers (1.2 mi) north of the city, a 45-minute uphill walk into town. Taxis are available outside the station, or call **Taxis Santarém** (tel. 243 102 500; www. taxis-santarem.net); the trip into the town center should cost under €5.

TOMAR

A sense of history and grandeur pervades Tomar, which straddles the pretty Nabão River. Shrouded in mystery and packed with fascinating sights and ruins, the town was a key pillar in the formation of Portugal. During the 13th century, Tomar was a powerful town as the seat of the Knights Templar, a Catholic military order founded in 1119.

For at least 130 years Tomar's Convent of Christ was the hub of the Templars in Portugal as they fought to free the country from Moorish control. In 1190 a Moorish invasion crossed the Tagus River and attacked Tomar, capturing nearby castles, but the Templars withstood a six-day siege and eventually claimed victory. With this and similar conquests in the region, the Templars gradually started the reconquest of Portugal from the Moors. The Knights Templar order came to an abrupt end in the early 14th century when Philip IV of France, allegedly jealous of their conquests, convinced the pope to extinguish the order. Most Templars had their wealth and land repossessed, but in Portugal they were spared that fate, instead renamed the Order of Christ. A century later, Tomar was restored to its full glory as their headquarters by Prince Henry the Navigator, an exceptional figure who played a pivotal role in the Age of Discoveries.

In addition to intriguing history, Tomar offers leisurely, picturesque walks along the Nabão River, traditional cafés in the sleepy town center, and a variety of typical, indulgent cakes.

Orientation

The **Nabão River** flows tranquilly through the middle of Tomar; the town's main square, **Praça da República**, the **train station**, and other attractions such as the **Matchbox Museum** and the fascinating **Convent of Christ** are all on the western side of the river. The Convent complex is a 10-minute uphill hike from the main square, or a 15-minute walk from the train station, and the vistas en route are fantastic. Or take one of the *tuk-tuks* that can be found zipping around.

Sights

★ CONVENT OF CHRIST
(Convento de Cristo)

Igreja do Castelo Templário; tel. 249 315 089 or 249 313 434; www.conventocristo.gov.pt; daily 9am-5:30pm Oct.-May, daily 9am-6:30pm June-Sept.; €6

The 12th-century Convent of Christ is a great work of Renaissance architecture, blending Romanesque, Gothic, and Manueline features in its remodeling over the centuries. The compound is on a hill overlooking Tomar, its lofty location dominating the skyline and enhancing the feeling of power and secrecy that cloaked the Order of the Knights Templar.

The Templars settled in Portugal in the early 12th century and built what is today the Convent of Christ in 1160 under the leadership of Gualdim Pais, provincial master of the order in Portugal. In the early days the convent was a symbol of the Templars' privacy and their desire to recapture the kingdom, but later, having been occupied by Henry the Navigator in the 15th century, it became an emblem for Portugal opening to the world.

The Convent of Christ complex is a mix of a 12th-century castle and eight cloisters that were added in the 15th and 16th centuries, plus vast gardens. The sumptuous interior is even more opulent than the striking exterior. The centerpiece is

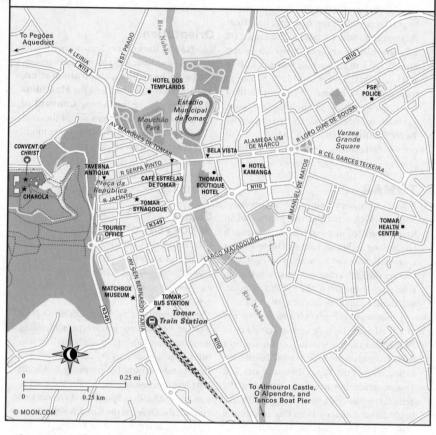

Tomar

the unusual **Charola,** the oratory of the Templars, an exuberantly decorated, light-filled church built by the first great master of the Templars and inspired by the architecture of the Holy Land, with lavish décor and floor-to-ceiling paintings.

It's possible to spend hours wandering this incredibly beautiful complex. Construction began in the 12th century on land donated by King Afonso Henriques to thank the Templars for their role in the *reconquistas*. It evolved into an impressive military complex. Henry the Navigator added a palace in the 15th century, when he was grand master of the order. He extended the monastic premises by adding two new cloisters and transformed the military house into a convent to be used by the clergy. The complex was completely remodeled in the 16th century by Manuel I, who also became master of the order. Classified a UNESCO World Heritage Site in 1983, it has intricate details and surprises around every corner, such as the many masons' inscriptions that linger from its days as the seat of the Templars.

Audio guides are available. A combined ticket to the Convent of Christ, Alcobaça Monastery, and Batalha Monastery (€15) is valid for seven days. Note that there are narrow, uneven passages, cobbled floors, and lots of worn stairs, potentially problematic for people with limited mobility.

TOMAR SYNAGOGUE
(Sinagoga de Tomar)

Rua Dr. Joaquim Jacinto 73; tel. 249 329 823; www. cm-tomar.pt; Tues.-Sun. 10am-1pm and 2pm-6pm Oct.-Apr., Tues.-Sun. 10am-1pm and 3pm-7pm May-Sept.; free

Built in the 15th century in Tomar's historic center, the Tomar Synagogue is a rare example of a medieval Jewish temple in Portugal, the best preserved in the country. Tomar's Jewish community thrived until the late 15th century, when the Jews were forced to convert to Roman Catholicism or leave the country. Subsequently, the synagogue served as a prison, a Christian chapel, a hay storehouse, and a grocery warehouse. From the outside, it blends in with the simple whitewashed houses on the street, distinguished by the blue Star of David above the door. Inside, Gothic vaulted ceilings connecting to the floor with spindly stone columns are impressive. The synagogue's present-day north-facing entrance is not an original feature; the pointy Gothic east-facing arch was the main entrance in the Middle Ages. In 1921 the building was classified a National Monument, and it also houses a small Jewish **museum.**

MATCHBOX MUSEUM
(Museu dos Fosforos)

Av. Gen. Bernardo Faria; tel. 249 329 814; Tues.-Sun. 10am-1pm and 3pm-6pm; free

The quirky, colorful Matchbox Museum, located in the São Francisco convent, houses an extraordinary collection of 43,000 matchboxes, collected over 27 years from 127 countries and dating back to 1827, filling cabinets and creating a striking visual effect. The collection was started by local man Aquiles da Mota Lima and donated to the municipality in 1980. His fascination with matchboxes started when he traveled to the United Kingdom to attend the coronation of Queen Elizabeth II in 1953, and his first box features the British monarch.

PEGÕES AQUEDUCT
(Aqueduto de Pegões)

Looming above the Ribeira dos Pegões valley, on the northwestern outskirts of Tomar, the 16th-century Pegões Aqueduct was originally built to supply the Convent of Christ with water. Like a caterpillar on long legs, the colossal water channel with its succession of lofty double-tiered arches winds around the hills for over 6 kilometers (3.7 mi). Its highest point is 30 meters (98 ft). Construction started in 1593 by Italian architect and engineer Filipe Terzi and was completed in 1641 by Portuguese architect Pedro Fernandes Torres.

Entertainment and Events
TRAY FESTIVAL
(Festa dos Tabuleiros)

June or July every 4 years

One of Tomar's most ancient local traditions, the Tray Festival is a spectacle like no other. Staged every four years in June or July (there was one in 2019), it takes its name from the festival's high point: a procession of local girls wearing headdresses made from bread piled staggeringly high, parading through the streets with male partners as attendants. The headdresses, called *tabuleiros*, are decorated with colorful flowers and topped off with a white dove, symbolizing Christianity's Holy Spirit. The day after the procession, the *pêza* takes place, when bread and meat are shared among the local people. The festival is believed to have originated in rituals dating to the 13th century. Almost the entire local population—thousands of men, women, and children—takes part in this event.

KNIGHTS TEMPLAR FESTIVAL
(Festival dos Templários)

tel. 249 310 040; www.templarknights.eu; July

The annual Knights Templar Festival is a series of celebrations dedicated to the Templars, held over four days in early July. These include a torchlit Knights Parade, medieval banquets, and a reenactment of the 1190 Moorish siege of Tomar. The festival dates to 2013, when Tomar was chosen to be world headquarters

Almourol Castle

Set on a solitary islet that juts out into the Tagus River, in a parish known as Praia do Ribatejo (Ribatejo Beach), the Almourol Castle (Castelo de Almourol, Ilhota do Rio Tejo, Praia do Ribatejo, Vila Nova da Barquinha; tel. 249 720 358; www.igespar.pt; daily 10am-1pm and 2:30pm-5pm Nov.-Feb., daily 10am-1pm and 2:30pm-7pm Mar.-Oct.; €2.50 includes boat trip) rises from a rocky outcrop. The castle dates to the 12th century, and its origins are shrouded in mystery. It is believed to have been built on the site of an ancient Lusitanian *castro* (a pre-Roman fortification) that was conquered by the Romans in the 1st century BC and later held by invading Visigoths and Moors. It remains unclear when the structure was founded, although an inscription on the main entrance suggests it was circa 1171.

Enigmatic and powerful, Almourol is symbolic of the Christian reconquest, distinguished by its riverside location on land that once fell under the protection of the Knights Templar. Almourol Castle forms part of a protective belt that was a frontline of defense along the Tagus River in the Middle Ages, along with the castles of Tomar, Zêzere, and Cardiga. It was abandoned with the extinction of the Knights Templar in Portugal, but rediscovered in the 19th century, and in the 20th century was used by the government to host many important meetings.

GETTING THERE

Reach the castle from the nearby **Tancos boat pier,** in the parish of Vila Nova da Barquinha, sailing across the Tagus on a little boat to the islet. Boats depart hourly and allow visitors 40 minutes to wander the castle before the return trip. The castle is a magnificent fairy tale sight as the boat approaches. The views from the castle are phenomenal.

Vila Nova da Barquinha and Almourol Castle is a 25-minute, 22-kilometer (13.6-mi) drive northeast from **Tomar** on the **N110** and **A13** roads. **CP** (tel. 707 210 220; www.cp.pt) trains run six times daily from Tomar to Tancos train station (1-2 hours; €3.15); the journey may require a transfer at Entroncamento. Tancos train station is a 10-minute walk east of the boat pier.

of the International Order of the Knights Templar (OSMTH)—the oldest Knights Templar organization in the world. The entire town dresses in its best medieval finery to recreate the mysticism and magic of the bygone era, with costumes, arts and crafts, and food and drink galore.

Sports and Recreation
MOUCHÃO PARK
(Parque do Mouchão)

Rua do Parque; tel. 249 313 326; open 24/7; free

Straddling the heart of Tomar town and a sliver of land called Mouchão Island in the Nabão River, Mouchão Park is a shady public park providing tranquility on hot days. Stroll the lovely gardens and hear the river running nearby. An old wooden waterwheel stands guard near one of the park's entrances. The park is divided into two areas, with a playground, a sports field, and pavilion on one side and the verdant island on the other, connected by a bridge.

Food

Tomar is famed for its local sweets, such as the almond and squash *queijadas* (sticky cakes) or the *fatias de Tomar* (Tomar slices), which are made with egg yolks, sugar, and water slowly cooked in a special pan invented by a local tinsmith in the mid-20th century. As the locals say, the secret is in the pan.

★ CAFÉ ESTRELAS DE TOMAR

R. Serpa Pinto 12; tel. 249 313 275; www. estrelasdetomar.pt; daily 8am-8pm; €5

Established in 1960, this riverfront café and bakery is one of the oldest and most celebrated in Tomar, producing fresh local sweets and "conventual" confectionary (traditional recipes from the country's convents), including Tomar's famous *queijadas* and *fatias,* every day. It's located on the west bank, near the Rua Marquês de Pombal Bridge.

TAVERNA ANTIQUA

Praça da República 23-25; tel. 249 311 236; www. tavernaantiqua.com; Tues.-Sun. noon-11pm; €15

Fitting for a town so closely linked to knights, this medieval-themed restaurant, on the main Praça da República square, offers a unique dining experience with food, crockery, and entertainment of the era. Think banquet vibes, heavy wood tables, rock walls, and candlelight.

O ALPENDRE

Rua Principal 13; tel. 919 562 990; daily 9am-midnight; €15

Portuguese food doesn't get any better than at O Alpendre, a homey, inexpensive eatery on the Nabão's east bank, with rich regional favorites including excellent beef dishes and homemade desserts.

BELA VISTA

Rua Marquês de Pombal No. 68; tel. 249 312 870; http://abelavista.pt; Wed.-Sun. noon-3pm and 7pm-9:30pm, Mon. noon-3pm; €15

Sitting pretty on the Nabão riverbank, Bela Vista serves authentic regional meat and fish dishes like octopus rice and roast kid. Founded in 1922, it boasts stunning views over the river, Mouchão Park, and the convent hill.

Accommodations
HOTEL KAMANGA

Rua Major Ferreira do Amaral 16; tel. 249 311 555; www.hotelkamanga.com; €55 d

In a good location on the east side of the Nabão River, within walking distance of Tomar's attractions and an 11-minute walk to the train station, Hotel Kamanga is budget lodging at its best. Rooms are clean, with simple wood furnishings and colorful, crafty quilts; some offer views of the convent.

THOMAR BOUTIQUE HOTEL

Rua Santa Iria 14; tel. 249 323 210; www. thomarboutiquehotel.com; €63 d

This chic and contemporary urban boutique hotel is within walking distance of Tomar's main sights. Located on the Nabão riverside, it has a nice rooftop with great views over the historic town center.

★ HOTEL DOS TEMPLÁRIOS

Largo Candido dos Reis 1; tel. 249 310 100; www. hoteldostemplarios.com; €92 d

Overlooking the Nabão River, at the foot of the Convent of Christ hill, the central, four-star Hotel dos Templários has spacious rooms and sizable indoor and outdoor pools. Its great location makes a good base for exploring the region.

Information and Services

- **Tourist office:** Av. Dr. Cândido Madureira 531; tel. 249 329 800; www.cm-tomar.pt; daily 8am-6pm
- **Tomar Health Center:** Rua Nabância 14; tel. 249 329 710; Mon.-Fri. 9am-12:30pm and 2pm-5:30pm
- **PSP police:** Rua Dom Lopo Dias de Sousa 8D; tel. 249 328 040; www.psp.pt

Getting There

Tomar is a 1.5-hour, 140-kilometer (87-mi) drive north from **Lisbon** on the **A1** motorway; a 45-minute, 70-kilometer (43-mi) drive north of **Santarém** city on the A1; and a 35-minute, 39-kilometer (24-mi) drive east from **Fátima** on the **IC9.** There is plenty of **parking** in Tomar, such as the free parking lot in the Varzea Grande square in front of Tomar Station and an underground parking garage on the opposite side of the river.

TOMAR BUS STATION

Rede Expressos (tel. 707 223 344; www. rede-expressos.pt) runs four daily buses between Lisbon's Sete Rios hub and Tomar (1.75 hours; €9.50). **Rodoviária do Tejo** (tel. 249 810 700; www.rodotejo.pt) has seasonal buses

(May-Sept.) that connect Santarém's main destinations (Tomar, Fátima, and Nazaré, stopping at the monasteries of Batalha and Alcobaça) along the IC9 road, including Fátima to Tomar (€4 one-way). Tomar's bus station is located on the west side of the Nabão river, a 10-minute walk south of the Convent of Christ.

TOMAR TRAIN STATION

CP (tel. 707 210 220; www.cp.pt) trains run from Lisbon's Santa Apolónia and Oriente stations to Tomar (2 hours; €10.10) roughly every couple of hours. Tomar's railway station is a short walk from the historic city center.

Getting Around

Tomar is easy to navigate, with most of the main sights and transport terminals being packed into town on the west side of the river. The town is easily (and best) covered **on foot.** However, seeing as the Covent is somewhat of an uphill hike (albeit a relatively short one), driving up or even getting a local *tuk-tuk* is also an option (Tuk Lovers; Praça da República main square; tel. 918 541 229 or 918 350 329; www.tuklovers.com; from €10).

FÁTIMA

This once sleepy rural backwater is today one of Europe's top Marian shrines and pilgrimage spots. It's hard not to be gripped by the sheer scale of the town's main sanctuary or by the devotion of the pilgrims, crawling on their knees along the sanctuary's stone strip to the Chapel of Apparitions. Nearly every street, hotel, and restaurant has a religious reference in its name. Formerly inhabited by sheep farmers, Fátima had a change of fate in 1917, when three children claimed to have witnessed an apparition of the Virgin Mary, who gave them important messages to convey over several months. The Roman Catholic Church's belief in these apparitions brought the faithful flocking to the hamlet.

1: Convent of Christ in Tomar 2: Alcobaça Monastery 3: Almourol Castle 4: Sanctuary of Our Lady of Fátima

The millions of visitors have fed the emergence of tourist shops around the sanctuary, laden with religious souvenirs, including candles to be lit at the sanctuary, plus glow-in-the-dark Virgins and fridge magnets.

Sights
★ SANCTUARY OF OUR LADY OF FÁTIMA
(Santuário de Fátima)

tel. 249 539 600; www.fatima.pt; open 24/7; free
In the center of Fátima, the expansive Sanctuary of Our Lady of Fátima is a cluster of religious buildings constructed after the 1917 apparition. It's one of the most famous Marian shrines in the world, and five million people pass through annually.

Central to the sanctuary is the main plaza, a large, paved esplanade flanked by the neo-Baroque **Basilica of Our Lady of the Rosary** (Basílica de Nossa Senhora de Fátima; daily 7:30am-6:30pm; free) at one end, built 1928-1953, and the contrasting contemporary **Basilica of the Most Holy Trinity** (Basílica da Santíssima Trindade; daily 7:30am-6:30pm; free) at the other. The three shepherd children, siblings Francisco and Jacinta and their cousin Lúcia, are buried in tombs inside the Basilica of Our Lady of the Rosary, where mass is still held. The Holy Trinity Basilica, inaugurated in 2007 to accommodate growing visitor numbers, is a minimalistic sleek round structure of ghostly pale stone that borders on the sterile. It is one of the largest churches in Europe and an award-winning feat of structural engineering that also hosts mass. In the middle of the main central esplanade is a fountain with holy water, where visitors can fill containers. Tiny empty flasks are sold at the many souvenir stalls around the site.

The heart of the sanctuary is the **Chapel of Apparitions (Capelinha das Aparições),** marking the spot of the apparition. Enclosed by a modern structure of glass panels, it was built to fulfill one of the last instructions from the Virgin Mary to the children. The modern outer building is simple; inside, a statue of the Virgin and the original tiny white chapel are flanked by rows of benches, where many sit in silent prayer. From the top of the central esplanade to the little chapel is a long strip of polished stone, named the Penitential Path, which the devout shuffle along painfully slowly on their knees.

Daily masses are held in Portuguese at the two basilicas (daily various times 7:30am-6:30pm), and in English at the Chapel of Apparitions (Mon.-Fri. 3:30pm; free). Visitors are free to explore, although group selfies and loudness are discouraged. May 13 and October 13 are the main dates for international pilgrimages, mass vigils, and special services.

WAX MUSEUM
(Museu da Cera)

Rua Jacinta Marto; tel. 249 539 300; www.mucefa. pt; daily 9am-6pm; adults €7.50, children 7-12 €4.50

There's an interesting Wax Museum in the middle of town that tells the story of the shepherd children and the apparitions, along with other town history, through 30 well-made sequential wax scenes. It's an enjoyable stop on a bad-weather day.

Food
CASA PLÁTANO

Av. Dom José Alves Correia da Silva 218; tel. 249 148 316; www.casaplatano.pt; daily 10am-5pm; €20

Situated right next to the sanctuary, Casa Plátano is elegant, with light-wood ceilings and features, streamline furniture, huge floor-to-ceiling windows, and smartly presented dishes. The restaurant has a light and clean air of sophistication. The menu is based on Portuguese classics with a contemporary twist, like slow-cooked duck leg served with traditional duck rice and lamb shank with a chickpea and fresh spinach stew. Light meals like sandwiches and salads are also available.

A TASQUINHA

Rua Monfortinos; tel. 249 533 446 or 918 955 357; www.tasquinhafatima.com; Thurs.-Tues. noon-3pm and 7pm-10pm; €20

A Tasquinha serves a smorgasbord of authentic Portuguese dishes in full and half portions. Centrally located inside a small shopping center, the restaurant is spacious and serves favorites like oven-roasted octopus, codfish, monkfish rice, Portuguese-style beef steak, grilled black pork, and veal chops. Chef's special suggestions change daily.

O CRISPIM

Rua de São João Eudes 23; tel. 249 532 781 or 915 426 464; www.ocrispim.com; Mon.-Fri. noon-3:30pm and 7pm-10:30pm, Sat. noon-1pm; €25

Warm and cozy with wood- and stone-clad walls, like a rustic hunting lodge, O Crispim showcases regional flavors. Starters include a local cured meats and cheese platter, while mains offer a choice of fish and meat dishes, like fresh fish skewers and stew, Mirandese veal, lamb chops, and grilled black pork meat. Specialty game dishes are available by order, and desserts are a rainbow of homemade regional delights.

Accommodations
HOTEL CASA DAS IRMÃS DOMINICANAS

Rua Francisco Marto 50; tel. 249 533 317; www. hoteldominicanas.pt; €55

The Hotel Casa das Irmãs Dominicanas (House of the Dominican Sisters) is a large convent-like building fronted by well-kept lawns and palm trees. This simple white-washed hotel with wood accents is a 10-minute walk from the sanctuary.

★ HOTEL DOM GONÇALO & SPA

Rua Jacinta Marto 100; tel. 249 539 330; www. hoteldg.com; €85

On the outskirts of Fátima center, the large four-star Hotel Dom Gonçalo & Spa is comfortable, with a well-equipped spa, a modern renovated wing, and an older wing. It's about a 25-minute walk to the sanctuary.

Getting There

A popular day-trip destination halfway between Lisbon and Porto, Fátima benefits from easy motorway access and regular public transport. By car, Fátima is 125 kilometers (78 mi) north of **Lisbon,** a 1.5-hour drive on the **A1** motorway (tolls apply). Fátima is 195 kilometers (121 mi) south of **Porto,** a 1.75-hour drive via the A1 motorway. From **Tomar,** Fátima is 40 kilometers (25 mi) west, a 35-minute drive on the **IC9** road.

There are a number of large **car parks** in Fátima, but they can be busy and crowded on major religious holidays.

FÁTIMA BUS STATION

Av. de Dom José Alves Correia da Silva

Fátima's bus station is a 10-minute walk west of the sanctuary. **Rede Expressos** (tel. 707 223 344; www.rede-expressos.pt) operates up to two dozen buses daily to Fátima from Lisbon's Sete Rios station (1.5 hours; €11.90). Rede Expressos also has regular daytime buses from Porto's Campo 24 Agosto station (2 hours, 2 buses hourly 5:30am-5:30pm daily; €17.10), plus a few at night. Tickets can be booked online in advance. From Tomar, Rede Expressos has one round-trip bus daily (40 minutes; €6.80 one-way, €13.60 round-trip), leaving at 7am and returning at 4:55pm.

Rodoviária do Tejo (tel. 249 810 700; www.rodotejo.pt) has seasonal buses (May-Sept.) that connect Santarém's main destinations (Tomar, Fátima, and Nazaré, stopping at the monasteries of Batalha and Alcobaça) along the IC9 road, including Fátima to Tomar (€4 one-way). There are a few daily connections on Rodoviária do Tejo's regular service between Tomar and Fátima (40 minutes; €4)—one early morning, one at noon, and one in the afternoon.

AIRE AND CANDEEIROS MOUNTAINS NATURAL PARK
(Parque Natural das Serras de Aire e Candeeiros)

Comprising the mountain ranges of Aires and Candeeiros, the sprawling Aire and Candeeiros Natural Park covers 40,000 hectares (154 sq mi) of hilly terrain between Santarém and Leiria, a natural limestone barrier between the coast and the interior. The park's most famous features are an eerie web of cool caves and grottoes, fissures, and rock formations. The caves shelter 18 species of bats, the symbol of the park. Several of the larger caves have steps, elevators, and arty lighting so visitors can explore their innards.

Among other features in the park are Portugal's only inland rock salt pans, in the village of Rio Maior, on the southern tip of the Aires and Candeeiros Mountains Natural Park, and a web of 16 well-mapped hiking trails spanning 2-15 kilometers (1.2-9.3 mi).

Sights
MIRA DE AIRE CAVES
(Grutas Mira de Aire)

Av. Dr. Luciano Justo Ramos 470, Mira de Aire village; tel. 244 440 322; www.grutasmiradaire.com; daily 9:30am-5:30pm Oct.-Mar., daily 9:30am-6pm Apr.-May, daily 9:30am-7pm June and Sept., daily 9:30am-8pm July-Aug.; adults €6.80, children €4

About 15 kilometers (9.3 mi) south of Fátima, the Mira de Aire Cave is the biggest, stretching 11 kilometers (6.8 mi), although only the first few hundred meters are accessible. Visits are in groups accompanied by a guide and descend 110 meters (361 ft) on stairs to the deepest part of the cave, where natural water features, rock formations, and lighting transform the gaping cavern into a magical kaleidoscopic Middle-earth. An elevator takes visitors back to the surface. Tours depart every 20 minutes. The cave's complex comprises a water park, windmills, and a restaurant.

MOEDA CAVES
(Grutas da Moeda)

Rua das Grutas da Moeda, São Mamede; tel. 244 703 838; www.grutasmoeda.com; daily 9am-5pm mid-Oct.-mid-Mar., daily 9am-6pm mid-Mar.-mid-July and mid-Sept.-mid-Oct., daily 9am-7pm mid-July-mid-Sept.; €7

Just a few kilometers west of Fátima in the parish of São Mamede are the dramatic underground Moeda Caves, spectacular caverns of immense natural beauty, with areas packed with stunning limestone formations, lighted lagoons, and moisture that drips off stalactites like sparkly diamonds. Legend has it the caves were discovered in 1971 by two hunters chasing a fox. At 45 meters (148 ft) below the entrance level, the caves' various sections have been given romantic titles like Lake of Happiness, Flawed Chapel, and Spring of Tears. Visits are in group tours (30-40 minutes, every 20 minutes) accompanied by guides, who provide information in various languages.

SERRA DE AIRE DINOSAUR FOOTPRINTS NATURAL MONUMENT
(Monumento Natural das Pegadas dos Dinossáurios da Serra de Aire)

Bairro village; tel. 249 530 160; www. pegadasdedinossaurios.org; Tues.-Sun. 10am-12:30pm and 2pm-6pm; €3

The park is also home to the Serra de Aire Dinosaur Footprints Natural Monument, the world's largest and most important collection of sauropod dinosaur footprints from the mid-Jurassic period, making them over 175 million years old. They are in the eastern flank of the park in the village of Bairro, about 10 kilometers (6.2 mi) south of Fátima. This unassuming patch of Portugal offers the unique chance to walk among dinosaur footprints. Wander solo at this low-key, unspoiled site or take a guided tour (1 hour; minimum 10 people, booked at least 8 days in advance).

ROCK SALT PANS
(Salinas de Rio Maior)

Estr. das Salinas; tel. 962 286 600; www. turismoriomaior.pt; open 24/7; free

Portugal's only inland salt pans, the Rio Maior pans are a curious phenomenon. Located at the foot of the Serra dos Candeeiros mountain range, surrounded by trees and farmland, they are considered a natural wonder, as the sea is some 30 kilometers (19 mi) away. A tiny village of rustic stone streets and wooden houses surround the salt pans, former salt warehouses now turned into little arts and crafts shops. The buildings are positioned higgledy-piggledy around pans and tanks, which fill with very salty spring water that gives rise to sparkling mounds of salt. History has it that these pans have been in use for over 900 years, founded in 1173 and allegedly once run by the business-savvy Knights Templar. Salt is produced in summer, but the site is open year-round.

Hiking
PR1 RMR MARINHAS DE SAL
Hiking Distance: *3.5-kilometer (2.2-mi) loop*
Hiking Time: *1.5 hours round-trip*
Trailhead: *Rio Maior Salt Pans*
Information and Maps: *https://natural. pt/protected-areas/parque-natural-serras-aire-candeeiros/pathways/pr1-rmr-marinhas-sal?locale=en*

Located at the southern end of the Aire and Candeeiros Natural Park, the Rio Maior Salt Pans make for an interesting and unusual walk. This easy and short circular hike takes walkers around the centuries-old dazzling pans and salty ponds, through pretty, hilly countryside before coming back to the salt pans.

PR2 RMR - CHÃOS-ALCOBERTAS
Hiking Distance: *16-kilometer (10-mi) loop*
Hiking Time: *6-7 hours round-trip*
Trailhead: *Artisanal Weaving Center (Largo do Centro Cultural de Chãos; building next to the old ForestRanger's House, in the square of Chãos's Cultural Center), Chãos parish*
Information and Maps: *www.walkingportugal. com/z_distritos_portugal/Santarem/Rio_Maior/ RMR_PR2_Chaos_Alcobertas.html*

Starting from the Chãos Artisanal Weaving Center, this invigorating and somewhat challenging hike passes through countryside and villages, where farming is still a mainstay. After enjoying scenic tranquility, prepare for an energetic ascent, along which the spotted kestrel often makes an appearance. Cross a picturesque valley, shaped into farming terraces, to where the route climaxes at the Serra dos Candeeiros peak (487 m/1,600 ft).

Shopping
TERRA CHÃ WEAVING WORKSHOP
Largo do Centro Cultural de Chãos No. 1; tel. 243
405 292 or 968 889 287; www.cooperativaterracha.
pt and on Facebook; Sat.-Sun. 10am-5pm

The Terra Chã Weaving Workshop is part of the wider Terra Chã Cooperative project, which also comprises a restaurant showcasing typical local dishes and local agricultural products. The project aims to preserve and develop the Serra dos Candeeiros handicraft heritage through innovative components, which involves creating a traditional product line adapted to modern demands. At the workshop you can see local artisans working on traditional looms weaving local wool, you can and take home a colorful carpet or handbag as a souvenir.

Information and Services
SERRAS DE AIRE E CANDEEIROS INTERPRETATION CENTER
(Centro de Interpretação do Parque Natural das Serras de Aire e Candeeiros)
Rua Dr. Augusto César Silva Ferreira, Apartado 190,
Rio Maior; tel. 243 999 480; www2.icnf.pt; Mon.-Fri,
9am-1pm and 2pm-6pm, closed holidays

Housed in a former elementary school, the Aire and Candeeiros Mountains Natural Park Interpretation Center and headquarters are located in the county of Rio Maior. There's an auditorium for 50 people, an interpretative space featuring exhibitions, a documentation center, and administrative services inherent to the running and management of the park.

This venue aims to provide visitors with information on the park, its flora and fauna, hiking trails, and main attractions. Its other main mission is to promote and protect the natural values of the park.

Getting There and Around
From **Fátima,** the Mira de Aire Caves, Moedas Caves, and Serra de Aire Dinosaur Footprints Natural Monument are all just a short drive away; the Mira de Aire Caves are a 20-minute drive south, into the Natural Park, along the **N360** road; the Moedas Caves are a shorter 10-minute (6.4-km/2.9-mi) drive west along the **Irmã Lúcia de Jesus** avenue, and the Serra de Aire Dinosaur Footprints Natural Monument is a 10-minute drive southeast, along the **N357.** The Rio Maior Salt Pans, situated in the very southern tip of the Aire and Candeeiros Mountains Natural Park, are about a 50-minute J-shape drive southwest from Fátima; it is from here that the PR1 RMR Marinhas de Sal hike starts. Chãos parish and the weaving center, starting point for hike PR2 RMR - Chãos-Alcobertas, is about an hour's drive southwest from Fátima along the **IC9** and **IC2** roads, or a 10-minute drive north from the Rio Maior Salt Pans, up Rua Principal.

The park is best explored by car. While there is some public transport between the various hamlets and villages, it can be inconsistent. Taking a **taxi** from Fátima to the Serra de Aire Dinosaur Footprints Natural Monument or to the Moeda Caves should cost under €15 one-way.

Coimbra

Piled on a large hill and the banks of the Mondego River, halfway between Lisbon and Porto, is the charming city of Coimbra (koo-WEEM-brah), a trove of history and home to the country's oldest university. Dubbed "the City of Students," Coimbra exudes white-washed splendor and was Portugal's capital in the 12th and 13th centuries. Divided into the older uptown and the newer downtown, Coimbra is the country's third most-populous city.

In the late medieval period, the city became a hub of culture and learning, propelled by sprawling Coimbra University. Coimbra's well-preserved medieval center pumps with a youthful vivacity and a blend of ancient and modern. Surrounded by mountains, the densely constructed urban sprawl is famous for nightlife and its own type of fado.

Orientation

Bathed by the **Mondego River,** Coimbra is a steeply heaped pile of handsome buildings, topped off by the revered university complex. Upper Coimbra (the **Alta**), on the east bank of the Mondego, is the oldest part of the city, where visitors will find many main attractions, including the imposing **Coimbra University,** which sits like a crown atop the splendid mount; the **Machado de Castro National Museum;** and the **Old Cathedral.** It's an atmospheric tangle of narrow, steep streets and historic buildings, which buzz with the youthful vibrancy of students. All roads lead to the top of the hill, and there are plenty of scenic **viewpoints** along the way.

The downtown (**Baixa**), north of the Alta, is also known as Coimbra's Historic Center and centers around the **Praça da República** square, the "heart" of the Baixa. Traditionally, the city's wealthy, clergy, and later students lived in the Alta, while the Baixa was dominated by services and trade. Today the two are more blended, but the Baixa is still the main area for commerce, hotels, and restaurants, on avenues like **Rua Ferreira Borges,** the main shopping street. The Baixa lost some of its allure with the construction of large malls outside the city center, but an ambitious regeneration plan is bringing back some of its pull. The **Santa Clara-a-Velha Monastery** is on the Mondego's west bank.

SIGHTS
★ Coimbra University
(Universidade de Coimbra)

Pátio das Escolas; tel. 239 859 900; www.uc.pt; daily 9am-7pm

Coimbra University is the oldest in the Portuguese-speaking world, founded by King Dinis in Lisbon in 1290 and moved to Coimbra in 1537. For 300 years it was the only university in Portugal. Currently spread over several campuses throughout the city, it has an ancient core, mostly the **Royal Palace,** which has housed the university since 1537, and the **College of Jesus,** the oldest Jesuit college in the world, which dates from the 16th century. Classified a World Heritage Site by UNESCO in 2013, Coimbra University is today a cosmopolitan place to study, with many international students.

The historic core of the vast university complex has a hilltop location and astounding architectural treasures, such as the 12th-century Manueline **São Miguel Chapel (Capela de São Miguel),** with its 18th-century Baroque organ centerpiece, and the gorgeous 18th-century Baroque **Joanina Library,** also known as the Book House. Many of the campus's main attractions, such as the Joanina Library, the **Great Hall of Acts (Sala dos Capelos)** that hosted academic ceremonies, and the **Arms Room (Sala das Armas)** with its unique collection of the Royal Academic Guard halberds, are inside the Royal Palace. There's also an **academic prison** beneath the Joanina Library, believed to be the only

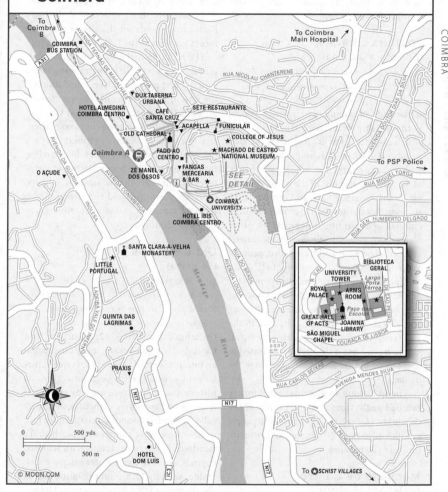

Coimbra

existing medieval prison in Portugal. The university had its own court, and the prison held unruly students. Don't miss a trip up to the **University Tower** (daily 10:30am-7pm; €2), which affords the best views in the city.

To visit the university, take a taxi to the top of Coimbra's steep hill and walk back down through the labyrinth of cobbled streets. **Guided campus tours** (tel. 239 242 744; 1.5-2 hours; €20 pp) run by the university run twice daily (depending on guide availability)

at 11am and 2:30pm. Book at least three days in advance, indicating preference of language and timing. Audio guides and leaflets are also available on-site, at the ticket office in the university's main library, the **Geral Library** (Biblioteca Geral; Largo Porta Férrea; tel. 239 247 280; www.uc.pt/bguc; Mon.-Fri. 9am-12:30pm and 2pm-5:30pm). There are also four **self-guided tours,** from a simple trip up University Tower (program 4; €4 pp) to an all-encompassing journey (program

1, includes São Miguel Chapel, Great Hall of Acts, Arms Room, Joanina Library, and College of Jesus; €12 pp).

JOANINA LIBRARY
(Biblioteca Joanina)

Largo da Porta Férrea; tel. 239 859 841; Mon.-Fri. 9am-5:30pm, Sat.-Sun. 10am-4pm Nov.-mid-Mar., daily 8:30am-7pm mid-Mar.-Oct.; €12

In the midst of Coimbra's university complex is the lavishly decorated Joanina Library, which radiates a warm glow from the rich woodwork. Amazing Baroque architecture with elaborate carpentry and ancient books make this arguably one of the world's grandest libraries, named for João V, who in 1717 sponsored its construction to promote artistic, cultural, and scientific endeavors. The ornamental bookshelves, made from exotic materials from all over the world, are gilded, painted, and engraved, and covered by an elaborate trompe l'oeil ceiling to lend the room extra height. The shelves house 250,000 books on subjects such as medicine, science, philosophy, and theology, spanning the 15th to the 19th centuries; some are written by hand. Urban legend has it that bats are released at night to eat any bugs that might damage the books.

Timed tickets to the Joanina Library can be bought from the ticket office at the **Biblioteca Geral.** Groups of up to 60 people are allowed in every 20 minutes, and visits are limited to 20 minutes.

Machado de Castro National Museum
(Museu Nacional Machado de Castro)

Largo Dr. José Rodrigues; tel. 239 853 070; www. museumachadocastro.gov.pt; Tues. 2pm-6pm, Wed.-Sun. 10am-6pm; €6, cryptoporticus only €3

Named after the renowned Portuguese sculptor Joaquim Machado de Castro (1731-1822), most famous for the statue of Dom José I on horseback in the center of Lisbon's Comércio Square, the Machado de Castro National Museum houses a fine collection of Roman relics and classical Portuguese art.

The building, near Coimbra University and within walking distance of the Old Cathedral, was converted from a 12th-century Bishop's Palace and stands on the site of a Roman forum founded by the Emperor Augustus.

The building includes a remarkable 1st-century cryptoporticus (subterranean vaulted galleries that provided a level foundation for the forum) in the museum's basement and a restored 16th-century church that stood on the original site. A 16th-century veranda teeters on a series of columns so spindly they are practically transparent. Besides Roman relics, the museum houses a large collection of sculptures as well as traditional *azulejos,* carpets, ceramics, furniture, gold and silver objects, medieval tapestries, and 16th- to 18th-century religious paintings.

Old Cathedral
(Sé Velha)

Largo da Sé Velha; tel. 239 825 273; www. sevelha-coimbra.org; Mon.-Fri. 10am-5:30pm, Sat. 10am-6:30pm, Sun. 11am-5pm, no entry during religious ceremonies; €2.50

Coimbra's handsome 12th-century Old Cathedral is a grand example of Romanesque architecture, one of the few to survive the turbulent Christian reconquests unscathed. Its history and architecture are why many call it the most Portuguese cathedral. While its solid, blocky facade and crenellated walls give it the austere air of a fortress, the cathedral's hundreds of interior columns with sculpted capitals are true to its Romanesque roots. Inside, an early 13th-century cloister marks the transition from Romanesque to Gothic, and in the main chapel a beautiful gilded altarpiece in elaborate late-Gothic style steals the show. A number of 13th- and 14th-century tombs also pay homage to the Gothic era.

Santa Clara-a-Velha Monastery
(Mosteiro de Santa Clara-a-Velha)

1: Old Cathedral cloister 2: interior at Coimbra University 3: Little Portugal 4: Joanina Library

Rua das Parreiras; tel. 239 801 160; www. santaclaraavelha.drcc.pt; daily 10am-7pm May-Sept., daily 10am-5pm Oct.-Apr.; €4

On the left bank of the Mondego River across from central Coimbra are the well-preserved Gothic ruins of the Santa Clara-a-Velha Monastery. Built in the 13th century, the monastery was abandoned by the resident nuns in the 17th century due to persistent flooding. After three centuries of neglect, it was excavated and gradually restored over 12 years, reopening in 2009. The building's design is believed to have been influenced by the Alcobaça Monastery. During the excavations, so many archaeological vestiges were unearthed that a modern interpretive center was built, housing a **museum.**

Little Portugal
(Portugal dos Pequenitos)

Largo Rossio de Santa Clara; tel. 239 801 170; www. portugaldospequenitos.pt; daily 10am-5pm Jan.-Feb. and mid-Oct.-Dec., daily 10am-7pm Mar.-May and mid-Sept.-mid-Oct., daily 9am-8pm June-mid-Sept.; adults €9.95, children 3-13 €5.95

Imagine an entire nation's cultural heritage shrunk to miniature size. Little Portugal offers miniature replicas of traditional Portuguese houses and famous monuments as well as pavilions dedicated to Portugal's former colonies. Established in 1938 on the left bank of the Mondego River across from downtown Coimbra, close to the Santa Clara-a-Velha Monastery, this small theme park is a favorite attraction among Portuguese families.

FESTIVALS AND EVENTS
BURNING OF THE RIBBONS
(Queima das Fitas)

www.facebook.com/pg/queimadasfitascoimbra; first Fri. of May

The Burning of the Ribbons is one of Coimbra's best-known student rituals, today replicated across the country. Starting every year on the first Friday in May and running for a week, it celebrates graduation with the symbolic burning of ribbons that represent each faculty.

FOOD
FANGAS MERCEARIA & BAR

Rua de Fernandes Thomas 45-49; tel. 934 093 636; Thurs.-Tues. noon-3:30pm and 7pm-11pm; €12

Fangas Mercearia & Bar merges a traditional grocery store with a bar, meaning clients can buy and try. On the menu of this atmospheric little backstreet tavern, a former grocery store, are regional delicacies like smoked sausages and cured meats, cheeses, tinned products, wines, and sweets.

★ ZÉ MANEL DOS OSSOS

Beco do Forno 12; tel. 239 823 790; Mon.-Fri. 12:30pm-3pm and 7:30pm-10pm, Sat. 12:30pm-3pm; €12.50, cash only

Hidden deep in the backstreets of central Coimbra is the local gastronomic institution Zé Manel dos Ossos opened in 1942. The walls of this eccentric, snug restaurant, which has just a half-dozen tables, are plastered thick with notes penned by patrons. People queue just to say they have eaten here and tried some of Zé's famous boiled pork knuckles, roast goat, or wild boar and bean stew. It's the kind of place where finger-licking is encouraged.

O AÇUDE

Av. da Guarda Inglesa 63; tel. 239 441 638; Mon.-Sat. noon-3pm and 7pm-11pm, Sun. noon-3pm; €15

An excellent spot to enjoy fine regional cheeses and wines on the west bank of the Mondego River, O Açude is a low-key little restaurant that takes authentic Portuguese cuisine up a notch, with classic dishes such as Lagareiro-style octopus and codfish skewers. An extensive wine list is available.

DUX TABERNA URBANA

Rua Dr. Manuel Rodrigues 59; tel. 239 093 723; www. duxrestaurante.com; daily noon-3pm and 7pm-11pm; €20

In the heart of Coimbra, this refined, trendy restaurant boasts a rainbow of snack-size *petiscos* (snacks) from land and sea, along with

The Roman Ruins of Conímbriga

A national monument since 1910, Conímbriga (tel. 239 941 177 or 239 949 110; www.conimbriga.pt; daily 10am-7pm Mar.-Oct., daily 10am-6pm Nov.-Feb.; €4) is a large walled Roman settlement believed to be among the biggest on the Iberian Peninsula. The site embodies Roman Portugal, with a wealth of relics from that era, including parts of an amphitheater, an aqueduct, water gardens, and thermal baths that have survived 2,000 years. The centerpiece is the beautiful **House of Fountains.** The **Conímbriga Monographic Museum** (tel. 239 941 177 or 239 949 110; www.conimbriga.pt), a gift shop, and a café-restaurant are also on-site.

THE HISTORY

Conímbriga has many layers built up by the civilizations that occupied it over the centuries. The Romans arrived circa 139 BC, seizing the settlement from its Celtic inhabitants, and under Roman rule the town quickly prospered. Given the size of the amphitheater, archaeologists believe the population at that time was more than 10,000. As it evolved, Conímbriga became an important stop for those traveling between Olisipo (Lisbon) and Bracara Augusta (Braga).

After a number of attempted incursions by invaders, the Romans built a massive defensive wall through the middle of the city, made from stones from residential houses that were taken apart, sacrificed for the city's protection. But it was to no avail—circa AD 468, the city came under attack by the Suebi people, and the Romans were defeated, fleeing to nearby Coimbra.

GETTING THERE

The Roman Ruins of Conímbriga are a large site in the parish of Condeixa-a-Velha, 16 kilometers (9.9 mi) south of **Coimbra** along the **IC2** and **IC3** roads. Explanatory signs in Portuguese and English dot the site. Allow a couple of hours to absorb this spectacular attraction. The site is exposed to the elements and can get very hot in summer and wet in winter, so dress accordingly. There's free **parking** on-site.

A regular **Transdev** (tel. 255 100 100; www.transdev.pt) bus runs the scenic route from Coimbra to nearby Condeixa-a-Nova's bus terminal (40 minutes, every half hour Mon.-Fri., less frequently Sat.-Sun.; €2.55), which is 1.6 kilometers (1 mi) from the Conímbriga ruins; from the terminal it is possible to walk to the ruins or catch a taxi. Buses that go directly to Conímbriga; are marked with a "C" on the timetable.

a more limited number of main dishes, from matured steaks to tuna steak with avocado mayonnaise.

SETE RESTAURANTE

Rua Martins de Carvalho 8; tel. 239 060 065; www.seterestaurante.wixsite.com; daily 12:30pm-3pm and 7pm-11pm; €20

Opened in 2017, Sete Restaurante hasn't taken long to establish itself as a serious contender on the local gastronomic scene. In downtown Coimbra next to the famous Café Santa Cruz, Sete elevates traditional regional favorites and national ingredients into refined dishes like crunchy sardines, traditional "Bairrada" suckling pig patty with pineapple chutney, and a selection of vegetarian offerings.

BARS AND NIGHTLIFE

Coimbra has a good nightlife scene, with lively bars and nightclubs and more sedate hangouts for a quiet drink.

Bars
PRAXIS

Rua António Augusto Gonçalves, Lote 28-29; tel. 239 440 207 or 911 922 162; www.beerpraxis.com; Mon.-Sat. 10:30am-2am, Sun. 10:30am-1am

If you like beer, you'll love Praxis, a unique brewpub and beer museum on the left-hand side of the Mondego River, just over the bridge from central Coimbra. An established gastro-brewery, it produces its own beer, the secret to which is the natural brewing process and Coimbra water.

A covered, heated terrace makes for year-round enjoyment.

Fado

For something more cultural, Coimbra is known as the home of the "other" fado. While Lisbon fado tends to be melancholic, the Coimbra version is slightly less forlorn. Closely associated with academic traditions, Coimbra's fado is sung exclusively by men dressed all in black in an ensemble akin to university cloaks. Performances take place as darkness falls, traditionally in public places such as alleys, streets, and the staircases of monuments, adding to the intensity and mystique. Tradition also has it that while in Lisbon people applaud fado, in Coimbra one coughs as if clearing the throat. Make sure to see a fado performance while you're here.

CAFÉ SANTA CRUZ

Praça 8 de Maio; tel. 239 833 617; www. cafesantacruz.com; café Mon.-Sat. 8am-midnight, Sun. 8am-8pm

Café Santa Cruz is the place to people-watch and eavesdrop. Established in 1929, the historic café has welcomed some of Portugal's leading academics and intellectuals over the decades and still witnesses debates at its marble-top tables. This lovely converted 16th-century church includes a lofty vaulted ceiling and stained-glass windows. It is as famous for its prized egg and almond *crúzios* sweets, for a slice of history with your coffee.

Café Santa Cruz is equally famous for its fado. Pop in to take in one of its nightly free fado sessions (Mon.-Sat. 6pm and 10pm, Sun. 6pm).

FADO AO CENTRO

Rua de Quebra Costas 7; tel. 239 837 060; www. fadoaocentro.com; center daily 10am-8pm; fado show €10

Live fado shows (daily 6pm) take place at cultural center Fado ao Centro, created to promote the fado of Coimbra, showcasing some of the city's finest musicians. Reservations are advised because of the limited space.

ACAPELLA

Rua do Corpo de Deus, Largo da Vitoria, Nossa Sra da Vitória chapel; tel. 962 205 564; www.acapella. com.pt; daily 7pm-2am; cover €10 pp, includes 1 drink

An atmospheric converted 14th-century chapel, aCapella offers tapas complemented with a bar and fado sessions (daily from 9:30pm). It's a popular place where culture and gastronomy merge over dinner or drinks and a show with a difference.

ACCOMMODATIONS

HOTEL ALMEDINA COIMBRA CENTRO

Av. Fernão de Magalhães 199; tel. 239 855 500; www. almedinacoimbra.com; €55

Large, centrally located, three-star Hotel Almedina Coimbra Centro has good value for the money. Rooms have balconies, and there is free Wi-Fi throughout.

HOTEL IBIS COIMBRA CENTRO

Av. Emídio Navarro 70, Edifício Topazio; tel. 239 852 130; www.accorhotels.com; €65

With views over the Mondego River, and located just 300 meters (0.2 mi) from the railway station, Hotel Ibis Coimbra Centro is central and offers the cheap and cheerful, clean comfort for which the budget Ibis chain is known.

HOTEL DOM LUÍS

Rotunda Ponte Rainha Santa Isabel; tel. 239 802 120; www.hoteldluis.pt; €75

Providing panoramic views over Coimbra, the smart three-star Hotel Dom Luís, on the western outskirts of the city on the Mondego's left bank, across the bridge from downtown Coimbra, has spacious rooms, some with balconies, and an on-site restaurant. The hotel provides a free shuttle bus into Coimbra for guests.

★ QUINTA DAS LÁGRIMAS

Rua António Augusto Gonçalves; tel. 239 802 380; www.quintadaslagrimas.pt; €200

Quinta das Lágrimas is a romantic retreat in an 18th-century palace surrounded by 4 hectares (10 acres) of lush gardens. It's on the left bank of the Mondego River, close to attractions like Little Portugal.

INFORMATION AND SERVICES

- **Tourist office:** Av. Emídio Navarro 35; tel. 239 488 120; www.turismodocentro. pt; Mon.-Fri. 9am-6pm, Sat.-Sun. 9:30am-5:30pm

- **Coimbra Main Hospital:** Centro Hospitalar e Universitário de Coimbra, Praceta Prof. Mota Pinto; tel. 239 400 400; www.chuc.min-saude.pt

- **PSP police:** Av. Elísio de Moura 155; tel. 239 797 640; www.psp.pt

GETTING THERE

Coimbra is 200 kilometers (124 mi) north of **Lisbon,** a 2-hour drive on the **A1** motorway. From **Porto,** it's a 130-kilometer (81-mi) drive south, a 1.5-hour journey along the A1 motorway.

Train
COIMBRA A
Largo da Ameias; tel. 707 210 220; www.cp.pt

COIMBRA B
Rua do Padrão–Eiras; tel. 707 210 220; www.cp.pt; services run daily 6:15am-12:15am

Coimbra has two train stations. Coimbra A is more central, on the riverfront between the Alta and the Baixa. Coimbra B is located about 1 kilometer (0.6 mi) north of the city center, but is the main hub for national intercity and inter-regional trains and a connecting point for local trains; there is a free connecting train to Coimbra A, which takes about 5 minutes.

Taking the train from Lisbon or Porto to Coimbra is the fastest method, but it's more expensive than the bus. **CP** (tel. 707 210 220; www.cp.pt) runs the high-speed Alfa Pendular train (AP; 1.5 hours,;2nd class €23.20, 1st class €33.30) and the slower and cheaper Intercity train (IC; 2 hours; 2nd class €19.50, 1st class €24.70) hourly to Coimbra B

station, the main station on the Porto-Lisbon line, from Lisbon's Oriente Station, and most also stop at the Santa Apolónia station. Trains run hourly from Porto's main Campanhã station to Coimbra B station; the AP train (2nd class €17, 1st class €22.10) takes just under an hour, while the IC train (2nd class €13.40, 1st class €17.50) takes a little over an hour. The cheaper Regional train from Porto (€9) takes two hours.

Once in Coimbra, take a free CP shuttle train from Coimbra B station to Coimbra A. To avoid a steep uphill walk from Coimbra A station to the city center, take a short taxi trip from Coimbra B station to downtown Coimbra (€5).

Bus
COIMBRA BUS STATION
Av. Fernão de Magalhães 667, 3000-178 Coimbra, Portugal

Rede Expressos (tel. 707 223 344, www. rede-expressos.pt) operates buses hourly and sometimes every half hour from Lisbon (2.5 hours, €13.80) and Porto (1.5 hours, €11.90). The bus station in Coimbra is on Avenida Fernão de Magalhães. From the station, it's a 15-minute walk to the city center. There is a taxi rank outside.

GETTING AROUND

Coimbra is easily covered **on foot,** and the main attractions are within comfortable walking distance of each other. Most of the bars and restaurants are in the downtown area and along the riverfront. However, Coimbra is built on a steep hill that can involve strenuous uphill treks, especially to the hilltop university and the old uptown neighborhood.

Given its hills and maze of steep, narrow streets, Coimbra can be a challenge to navigate by car, and **parking** is hard to find. Leave your car on the outskirts of town, on the left bank of the river, where there is plenty of designated parking. There is also free parking in the side streets flanking the university for those lucky enough to find a spot.

☆ Schist Villages

Hidden deep in Central Portugal, peppering the mountains that stretch east from Coimbra, a string of villages built entirely from schist stone (*aldeias do xisto*) draws visitors with their one-of-a-kind architecture, heritage, traditions, and gastronomy.

Schist is a type of rock formed from mudstone or shale. It was found in abundance in this part of Portugal and was used to create unique abodes that glint in the sunlight. Large, flat flints are interspersed with larger rocks, packed tight to create the prehistoric-looking houses.

This unique side of Portugal is about as far off the beaten track as you can get, but thanks to eye-catching promotion, it's attracting a growing number of visitors, who are enthralled by rural life that goes on as it has for centuries. Comprising a total of 27 villages, some better known than others, the **Schist Villages Route (Rota das Aldeias do Xisto)** (tel. 275 647 700; www.aldeiasdoxisto.pt) was devised by local authorities and outlines various routes to follow, what to see in each village, and where to eat and stay.

Talasnal

Casal de São Simão, Talasnal, and **Cerdeira,** all in the Lousã mountain range, are among the prettiest schist hamlets and are closest to Coimbra.

CASAL DE SÃO SIMÃO

A tiny hamlet formed around a single street, picturesque Casal de São Simão (kah-ZAL d' SOWN see-MOWN) stretches along a ridge that runs almost parallel to the Ribeira de Alge watercourse. With a little chapel and a river beach, this gorgeous little stone village, with its string of rocky cottages set against a forest backdrop, offers the ultimate photo op.

Casal de São Simão is 47 kilometers (29 mi) south of Coimbra, a 30-minute drive on the **A13** motorway.

CERDEIRA

Wedged between green slopes and often misty skies is Cerdeira (ser-DAY-rah), whose schist houses cling to the rocky hillside. The main bridge leads to a brook that passes through the heart of the village. Cerdeira is known as a hub of artistic creativity, home to artisans who run lodgings, ateliers, and retreats. The annual July **Art Meets Nature** festival transforms the village into an open-air gallery.

Cerdeira is 36 kilometers (22 mi) southeast of Coimbra, a 50-minute drive on the **N17** road. It's 13 kilometers (8.1 mi) east from neighboring Talasnal, about a 30-minute drive along the winding **N236** road.

TALASNAL

Characterful Talasnal (tah-lazh-NAL) is a unique village teeming with verdant vegetation, deer, and wild boar. The pre-17th-century vine-covered stone cottages ooze charm. Houses and streets are well-preserved, and local crafts can be found in abundance. In the village center is a natural spring offering drinking water.

Talasnal is 40 kilometers (25 mi) south of Coimbra, a 55-minute drive on the **N17** road.

Bus

Coimbra's bus system is the **SMTUC** (www. smtuc.pt). Lines 27, 28, and 29 run between the main bus station, Coimbra B train station, and the main Praça da República square every 15-30 minutes. A single-trip ticket costs €1.60; it's €3.50 for a day ticket. SMTUC tickets can be bought from kiosks, newsagents, or directly from the driver.

The Pantufinhas electric mini-buses, or **Blue Line** (Mon.-Fri. 8:45am-1pm and 2:45pm-7pm, Sat. 9:15am-1:15pm), are another way of getting around Coimbra's historic heart and between its uptown and downtown; the same tickets are accepted as on the SMTUC buses.

Taxi

Using a taxi to get around Coimbra city center and from one side of the river to the other is an option. The main taxi company is **Politaxis** (Rua do Padrão, Kiosk A; tel. 239 499 090; www.politaxis.pt; open 24/7). A taxi from the Little Portugal theme park, on the left bank of the river, to the university costs about €5; from Coimbra B train station to the university costs €6. There is a fare calculator on Politaxis's website.

Serra da Estrela Natural Park

One of Portugal's most famous mountain ranges, the snow-topped Serra da Estrela (Star Mountain Range) boasts the country's only ski resort. The most popular parts of the Serra are near the city of **Covilhã**, a convenient gateway.

Sprawling 1,000 square kilometers (386 sq mi), more than half of which is above 700 meters (2,297 ft), the Serra da Estrela Natural Park (Parque Natural da Serra da Estrela) has majestic mountains, boulder-littered meadows, rocky glacial valleys, and dramatic lakes. It was the first natural park in Portugal and remains the largest. It's home to the highest point on mainland Portugal, the Torre summit, the country's only ski resort and the source of the Mondego and Zêzere Rivers. It's inhabited by a wealth of wildlife, including wolves, foxes, wild boars, otters, golden eagles, falcons, and owls. It even has an indigenous breed of dog, the Estrela mountain dog, used by local shepherds for centuries.

Once famed for its traditional woolen products, in recent decades, flocks of sheep have given way to visitors, especially in winter to enjoy the snow. Highlights include the mirror-like Vale do Rossim Lake—surrounded by mountains, it is a top hiking spot—and the sleepy mountain town of Manteigas, known as the heart of Serra da Estrela.

Over 100 kilometers (62 mi) long, 30 kilometers (19 mi) wide, and 300 million years old, the Serra da Estrela mountain range can be explored on marked walking routes, off-road mountain bike routes, or by car, although the weather can hamper visits and should be taken into account. The scenery changes with the seasons, from flower-peppered meadows in spring to snowcapped peaks in winter. Spring and summer have the best temperatures and clear skies for hiking or cycling, although the summer sun can be fierce, and many treks have little shade. Fall can bring rain, especially toward the end of the season, while December-February is prime time for snow sports.

ORIENTATION

Serra da Estrela Natural Park is made up of dramatic valleys and majestic mountains flanked by interesting towns and villages. With **Torre** summit and its **ski resort** as a central point within the park, the town of **Covilhã**, the unofficial gateway, lies southeast, while **Manteigas** town is northeast. The **Zêzere Glacial Valley** runs almost

Serra da Estrela Natural Park

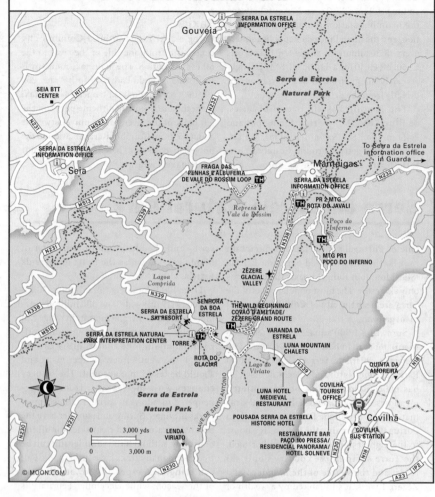

SIGHTS
N339 ROAD TO TORRE

parallel to the main **N338** road between Manteigas and the foot of the mountain range; the **N339** road is the main road up to Torre peak from the south. Main attractions within the park include the **Poço do Inferno** waterfall, which is located almost halfway along the N338, just off the main road, and the **Covão d'Ametade** scenic beauty spot, which is also along the N338 but closer to the foot of the mountain.

First, visitors should see **Torre,** the highest point on mainland Portugal at 1,993 meters (6,539 ft), usually easy to reach by car. Torre is marked by a simple stone point in the middle of a roundabout, reached by following the N339 road that cuts straight across Serra da Estrela from Covilhã to Seia. The drive up is scenic and the views from the top are breathtaking. Visit the little mountaintop shops that sell local cheese, ham, and trinkets. There are also restrooms. Torre is a 23-kilometer (14.3-mi), 35-minute drive west from Covilhã, and a 28-kilometer (17-mi), 40-minute drive east from Seia.

COVÃO D'AMETADE
N338 road; open 24/7
Covão d'Ametade is a gorgeous little picnic area. Verdant, peaceful, and quiet, it's worth having a quick stop here on your way up the mountain for a photo and some fragrant mountain air.

SENHORA DA BOA ESTRELA
In the heart of the Serra da Estrela range, on the way from Covilhã to Torre on the N339 road, 21 kilometers (13 mi) or 35 minutes' drive from Covilhã, **Covão do Boi** is a remarkable section of mountain with huge eroded stone blocks affectionately referred to by locals as "cheeses." Stop here to see the 7-meter-tall (23-ft-tall) Senhora da Boa Estrela rock sculpture, created by Portuguese sculptor António Duarte in 1946 when a local priest wanted to pay tribute to the Senhora da Boa Estrela, patron saint of

shepherds, whose flocks are a familiar sight in the rugged terrain.

ZÊZERE GLACIAL VALLEY
Thirty minutes' drive north from Torre, 20 kilometers (12.4 mi) along the N339 and then N338 roads toward the town of Manteigas, is the 13-kilometer-long (8-mi-long) Zêzere Glacial Valley, a dramatic gorge of imposing granite. The valley can also be reached from Seia, 50 minutes on the N232 road, or Covilhã, 40 minutes on the N18 and N232 roads, before heading south, up to Torre peak. The views are best when heading down from Torre to Manteigas. The Zêzere Glacial Valley is a unique landscape in Portugal—immense, U-shaped, and ice-clad in winter, the valley is sandwiched between soaring, barren mountains of rock-strewn pastures peppered with tiny stone-built farmhouses typical of the region. The Zêzere River gushes through the valley. The valley is very popular among hikers for its easy walking.

POÇO DO INFERNO
One of the Serra's best-kept secrets is Poço do Inferno (Hell's Well), a 10-meter (33-ft) waterfall considered one of the most beautiful in the country. Despite its name, the spot is

Serra da Estrela Natural Park

beautiful and can be explored by **hike,** with a clear pool at the bottom that can run dry in summer. By car from Manteigas, drive along the N232 road for about 8 kilometers (5 mi) to the signed turnoff, then follow a narrow, winding road through the forest for another 5 kilometers (3.1 mi) to a spacious car park and an information board.

VALE DO ROSSIM LAKE

One of the Serra da Estrela's most scenic attractions, people visit the park to walk around this enchanting lake, resulting from a human-made dam and located in the heart of the Serra da Estrela mountain range at an altitude of 1,437 meters (4,715 ft). In summer, its banks provide spots for locals and visitors to enjoy a refreshing dip in the clean waters and cool off from the heat.

SPORTS AND RECREATION

Various hiking and mountain bike trails traverse the park, although signage can be sketchy, so ask for a map at one of the park's information offices. Opportunities abound for canyoneering and mountaineering. Join a guided tour with experienced local companies such as **Trans Serrano** (tel. 235 778 938; www.transserrano.com) for riverbed hikes (4-5 hours; €17.50), canyoneering (4-5 hours; from €25), climbing, and rappelling in hidden nooks and crannies.

Hiking

FRAGA DAS PENHAS E ALBUFEIRA DE VALE DO ROSSIM LOOP

Hiking Distance: *11.7-kilometer (7.3-mi) loop*
Hiking Time: *3.5 hours round-trip*
Trailhead: *Casa das Penhas Douradas Hotel, Penhas Douradas hamlet, Manteigas*
Information and Maps: *www.alltrails.com/ trail/portugal/center-region--2/fraga-das-penhas-e-albufeira-de-vale-do-rossim*
This mostly easy hike forms a loop around the Vale do Rossim Lake. The scenery is stunning and the trail mountainous and quiet. Start and finish near the Casa das Penhas Douradas

Hotel (a 22-minute drive from Manteigas), or closer down to the lake so you can enjoy a dip if the weather is warm.

PR 2 MTG ROTA DO JAVALI

Hiking Distance: *11-kilometer (7-mi) loop*
Hiking Time: *5 hours round-trip*
Trailhead: *Casa das Penhas Douradas Hotel, Penhas Douradas hamlet, Manteigas*
Information and Maps: *www.alltrails.com/ trail/portugal/center-region--2/fraga-das-penhas-e-albufeira-de-vale-do-rossim*
The Rota do Javali (Route of the Wild Boar) showcases the rich Serra da Estrela countryside in all its glory. The magical and highly scenic hike offers panoramic views over the village of Manteigas, passes through magnificent forests, carves its way through cliffs and valleys, and weaves around the stunning, 10-meter-high (33-ft-high) Poço do Inferno waterfall.

MTG PR6 - ROTA DO GLACIAR

Hiking Distance: *17.2 kilometers (10.7 mi) one-way*
Hiking Time: *6 hours one-way*
Trailhead: *Manteigas town or Torre Peak*
Information and Maps: *www.walkingportugal. com/z_distritos_portugal/Guarda/Manteigas/MTG_PR6_Rota_do_Glaciar.html*
Set off on this exciting trek along rural mountain trails to explore the captivating sights of the Serra da Estrela Natural Park. The trail starts from Manteigas town and ends at the most important landmark of the Serra da Estrela range, Torre peak, which, at 1,993 meters (6,539 ft), is the highest point on mainland Portugal. The route snakes along a wide, steep, U-shaped glacial valley, sandwiched between verdant pastures dotted with sheep, and bright blue skies. As this is a linear route, a good suggestion is to start from Torre and hike to Manteigas, due to a lack of public transport near Torre peak to take you back to your starting point.

MTG PR1 - POÇO DO INFERNO

Hiking Distance: *2.5-kilometer (1.5-mi) loop*

Hiking Time: *1.5 hours round-trip*

Trailhead: *Poço do Inferno waterfall*

Information and Maps: *www.walkingportugal. com/z_distritos_portugal/Guarda/Manteigas/MTG_ pr1_rota_do_poco_do_inferno_folheto.pdf*

This moderately challenging circular hike is short and scenic. It takes trekkers around the Poço do Inferno waterfall, one of the park's main attractions. The 10-meter-high (33-ft-hight) waterfall turns into ice in harsher winters, making an unusual glacier feature. This hike has stunning vistas over the Zêzere Glacial Valley, leafy forests, and unusual rock formations. The first half is the more challenging portion.

Biking

The rugged, mountainous terrain of the Serra da Estrela park can be challenging for those more comfortable with biking on flat ground. As many of the routes take riders off-road, some of them are best suited to those who enjoy all-terrain mountain biking or have a good level of fitness and cycling experience. That said, a guided tour is a great way to find routes through the park to suit all levels of experience. Six kilometers (3.7 mi) north of Seia, the **Seia BTT Center** (Rua Domingos Gonçalves Santiago, parish of Santa Comba; tel. 238 317 762; www.aldeiasdemontanha.pt; daily 9am-7pm June-Sept., daily 9am-4pm Oct.-May), part of the Portuguese Cycling Federation network, can provide information on mountain bike routes and rentals.

ZÊZERE GRAND ROUTE
(Grande Rota do Zêzero)

Cycling Distance: *370 kilometers (230 mi)*

Cycling Time: *approx. 20 hous*

Trailhead: *Zêzere River source (Covão d'Ametade park and picnic area)*

Information and Maps: *www. portuguesetrails.com/en/routes/grande-rota-do-zezere-cycling*

Covering 370 kilometers (230 mi) through 13 districts, the Zêzere Grand Route involves some serious cycling. It starts from Serra da Estrela and follows the Zêzere River all the

way from its source near the Covão d'Ametade park (a 15-minute drive east of Torre, Serrada Estrela's highest point, along the N339 and N338 roads), to its mouth near Santarém, where it merges with the Tagus River. En route it passes some of Central Portugal's appealing schist villages. The good news is the route can also be chopped up into portions, with 13 support stations along the way.

THE WILD BEGINNING
(O Selvagem Inicio)

Cycling Distance: *64 kilometers (40 mi)*

Cycling Time: *2 hours*

Trailhead: *Zêzere River source (Covão d'Ametade park and picnic area)*

Information and Maps: *www. portuguesetrails.com/en/routes/grande-rota-do-zezere-cycling/o-selvagem-inicio*

Starting at the source of the Zêzere River, this highly interesting and engaging route is a good mix of demanding climbs and enjoyable descents and excellent scenery. The first stage of the Zêzere Grand Route, it drops down along the soaring sides of Covão d'Ametade and tapers through the untamed and unspoiled rugged beauty of the Zêzere Glacial Valley, culminating in the village of Valhelhas (20 minutes' drive, 16.3 km/10.1 mi west of Manteigas on the N232 road).

Skiing

Serra da Estrela is the only place in Portugal for snow sports. Skiing, sledding, and snowboarding are all available at the resort. Off-season, there are artificial ski slopes.

SERRA DA ESTRELA SKI RESORT
(Estância de Ski da Serra da Estrela)

N339 road; tel. 238 031 940; www.skiserradaestrela. com; daily 9am-5pm; adults €22, children €15, rentals from €25, snowboards €15

The Serra da Estrela Ski Resort has just four ski lifts and nine trails, best for beginners and families, but some sections are advanced. When the weather is bad, many roads are closed, meaning access is limited.

FOOD

Most of the little villages and hamlets in the park will have a restaurant or at least a café; a wider range of eateries can be found in larger towns like Covilhã and Manteigas. Visitors can expect rustic, traditional restaurants that serve typical local fare and excellent cured meats and cheeses.

LUNA HOTEL MEDIEVAL RESTAURANT

Penhas da Saúde parish; tel. 275 310 300; www.lunahoteis.com; daily 12:30pm-3pm and 7:30pm-10pm; €14-20

For a real treat, head to the Luna Hotel Medieval Restaurant, on the N339 road 13 kilometers (8.1 mi) west of Covilhã, for a medieval feast. With old world, tavern-style décor, the restaurant puts on a banquet-like buffet of regional food.

QUINTA DA AMOREIRA

Rua da Amoreiras 4, Canhoso; tel. 275 084 892 or 919 884 684; www.quintadaamoreira.pt; Wed.-Sun. 12:30pm-4pm and 7:30pm-11:30pm; €18

Famous for its matured local beef, the magnificent Quinta da Amoreira restaurant is in a typical Serra da Estrela farmhouse, in the parish of Canhoso, a 5-minute drive north of Covilhã city center. The rustic-chic interior fits with the accomplished menu of mountain specialties, many of which are cooked in a traditional wood oven.

VARANDA DA ESTRELA

Penhas da Saúde parish; tel. 963 447 873; www. varandadaestrela.pt; Thurs.-Tues. 10am-midnight; €20

Mountaintop eatery Varanda da Estrela, 13 kilometers (8.1 mi) west of Covilhã, specializes in pure and simple Portuguese cuisine, with good-size portions, lots of flavor, a cozy atmosphere and incredible views. Try the *arroz de zimbro* (juniper berry rice), a regional specialty.

RESTAURANTE BAR PAÇO 100 PRESSA

Travessa Sao Tiago 3, Colvihã; tel. 925 868 877; www. paco100pressa.com; Mon.-Sat. noon-midnight, Sun. noon-3:30pm; €20

In a lovely old stone town house, the gorgeously moody, sophisticated-looking little Restaurante Bar Paço 100 Pressa has wrought-iron furniture, bringing a twist of trendy to the rustic mountain scene. Specialties include local wines, octopus, and codfish dishes, and bed-and-breakfast lodgings are available.

★ LENDA VIRIATO

Rua Santo Aleixo 16; tel. 275 971 252; www. lendaviriato.pt; Tues.-Fri. 7:30pm-10pm, Sat.-Sun. 12:30pm-4pm and 7:30pm-10pm; €25

In Unhais da Serra parish, 23 kilometers (14.3 mi) west of Covilhã, behind the church, this rustic stone-built restaurant is known for traditional mountain food. Staff dress in old-fashioned costumes and the local meats and wines are outstanding.

ACCOMMODATIONS

Serra da Estrela is full of cozy mountain inns and chalets that are cheap and cheerful. There is a great selection of places to stay in this region; in the main towns there are larger hotels, while a number of older buildings throughout the region have been converted into comfortable, modern, and in some cases high-end, tourist accommodation.

RESIDENCIAL PANORAMA

Rua dos Bombeiros Voluntários 7-9; tel. 275 323 952; www.residencialpanorama.pt; €40

Housed in a traditional stone building dating from the 1940s, the cozy, typical mountain inn Residencial Panorama is a great place to stay for authentic local atmosphere. In the historic center of Covilhã, the inn boasts wonderful views over the mountains, and all of the 25 comfortable, elegantly furnished rooms have private baths.

HOTEL SOLNEVE

Rua Visconde de Coriscada 126; tel. 275 323 001; www.solneve.pt; €48

In Covilhã's historic center, housed in a fancy old building in the main square opposite the city hall, this affordable hotel is 1 kilometer (0.6 mi) northwest of the train station. Inside are spacious rooms, an indoor pool, and a good restaurant.

★ LUNA MOUNTAIN CHALETS

Penhas da Saúde parish; tel. 275 310 300; www. lunahoteis.com; €140

Chalets always sound cozy, and modern alpine Luna Mountain Chalets are no exception. At 1,500 meters (4,921 ft) within Serra da Estrela Natural Park, this warm wooden cluster of chalets is 11 kilometers (6.8 mi) east of the ski resort, with two on-site restaurants (one with a medieval theme) as well as a rustic bar, a romantic log fire-warmed lounge, and a spa. They're 13 kilometers (8.1 mi) west of Covilhã on the N339 road, sort of halfway between Covilhã and Torre summit.

★ POUSADA SERRA DA ESTRELA HISTORIC HOTEL

Penhas da Saúde parish; tel. 210 407 660; www. pousadas.pt; €142

Pousada Serra da Estrela Historic Hotel has a fascinating history. With distinct turrets and an imposing facade, it was converted from an old sanatorium, built here for the pure mountain air believed to cure chronic ailments. On a hilltop on the edge of the Serra da Estrela mountain range, it is 14 kilometers (8.7 mi) from the Serra da Estrela Ski Resort and 13 kilometers (8.1 mi) west of Covilhã on the N339 road. Most of the rooms have balconies with mountain views. The hotel has a spa and indoor and outdoor pools.

INFORMATION AND SERVICES

The park also has a number of **information offices,** including:

- **Manteigas** (Rua 1º de Maio 2; tel. 275 980 060 or 275 980 061), in the center of the park; **Seia** (Praça da República 28; tel. 238 310 440), along the northern edge of the park.

- **Gouveia** (Casa da Torre, Av. Bombeiros Voluntários 8; tel. 238 492 411), along the northern edge of the park, northeast of Seia.

- **Guarda** (Rua D. Sancho I 3; tel. 271 225 454), northeast of the park.

COVILHÃ TOURIST OFFICE

Av. Frei Heitor Pinto; tel. 275 319 560; www. turismodocentro.pt; daily 9am-12:30pm and 2pm-5:30pm

The Covilhã tourist office provides information on Serra da Estrela as well as useful maps.

SERRA DA ESTRELA NATURAL PARK INTERPRETATION CENTER (Centro de Interpretação da Serra da Estrela)

Praceta os Doze de Inglaterra 11, Seia; tel. 238 320 300; www.cise.pt; Tues.-Sun. 10am-6pm; €4

The Serra da Estrela Natural Park Interpretation Center is a good place to learn more about the park's sights and routes, flora, and fauna. It's in Seia, on the opposite side of the mountain range from Covilhã, the main gateway to the park. Seia is 50 kilometers (31 mi) west of Covilhã, across the mountain range, a 1.25-hour drive on the hilly N339 road.

GETTING THERE AND AROUND

The easiest way to get to Serra da Estrela is through its main gateway, **Covilhã.** Behind the Serra da Estrela range in a remote part of the country, Covilhã is surprisingly easy to reach. It's 212 kilometers (131 mi) southeast of **Porto,** a 2.5-hour drive on the **A25** motorway, and 278 kilometers (175 mi) northeast of **Lisbon,** a 2.75-hour drive on the **A1** and **A23** motorways. From **Coimbra,** Covilhã is a 191-kilometer (118-mi), 2-hour drive along the **IC8** and A23 roads. The ski resort is 24 kilometers (15 mi) west of Covilhã, a 30-minute drive along the **N339** road.

Bus

COVILHÃ BUS STATION

N230 27

Rede Expressos (tel. 707 223 344; www.rede-expressos.pt) direct buses run daily between Covilhã and major neighboring cities as well as from Lisbon and Porto. From Porto, Rede Expressos buses (1.5 hours, daily 6am-9pm; €11.90) run hourly, not always on the hour. From Lisbon (2.5 hours, daily 6am-10:30pm; €13.30), buses depart almost hourly, sometimes twice an hour. The easiest way to get from Coimbra to Covilhã by bus is **Rodonorte** (tel. 259 340 710; www.rodonorte.pt) buses from Coimbra to Viseu (1 hour, 4 buses daily; €8.30); change in Viseu for Covilhã. From Viseu there are six daily buses (2 hours; €12.20) operated by Rede Expressos and **Citi Express** (tel. 707 223 344; www.citiexpress.eu).

The main bus terminal is on a plain below the city, 1.5 kilometers (0.9 mi) east of the center, at the foot of a steep hill. The main bus station is about 450 meters (0.3 mi), a 5-minute walk, south from the train station. Covilhã's local bus service, **Covibus** (tel. 275 098 097; www.covibus.com, €1.30), runs every 35 minutes between the main bus station (Central de Camionagem) and the city center. There are also **taxi** ranks outside the main bus station and the train station (Covilhã Taxis; tel. 275 323 653); a trip into the city center costs €5-7.

Train

COVILHÃ TRAIN STATION

Largo da Estação dos Caminhos de Ferro; tel. 808 208 208; www.cp.pt

National rail company CP operates trains to Covilhã but there are no direct routes from Porto. From Lisbon, all trains to Covilhã depart from the Santa Apolónia station and pass through Oriente; there are three direct intercity trains per day, the journey takes around 3.5 hours, and tickets cost €17.50 one-way. From Porto Campanhã station via Entroncamento, the journey to Covilhã can take 5-6 hours. The train and bus stations are at the foot of a very steep hill in Covilhã; be prepared for a steep climb up to the old town.

GETTING THERE AND AROUND

The best way to explore the park is by **car**, as public transport is limited. If you don't have a car, opt for an organized tour, for example from **Trans Serrano** (www.transserrano.com) or the **Seia BTT Center** (www.aldeiasdemontanha.pt). A **taxi** from Covilhã to the Serra da Estrela Ski Resort costs around €20.

The road network across Serra da Estrela, unlike that of some mountain ranges, is decent and well signed. Even the highest summit, Torre, is accessible by car. The park is open 24 hours daily, except when heavy snowfall closes roads. The **Roads of Portugal** (Estradas de Portugal) website (www.estradas.pt) provides current information on all road incidents and closures. There's also information on the Serra da Estrela Ski Resort's website (www.skiserradaestrela.com/acessos). Police are posted at closed roads to inform drivers of detours.

Porto and the Norte

With verdant landscapes, medieval villages, and majestic mountains, Northern Portugal is invigorating. Its defining feature is the Douro River, flowing westward through the rugged landscape to the Atlantic at its biggest city, Porto. Portugal's second-largest city after Lisbon is a hardworking metropolis with newfound fame as a getaway among budget travelers. Flanked by terraced vineyards and charming wine estates and guesthouses, the river reflects the emerald tranquility of the Douro Valley, which yields the grapes that have made the region's port wines famous. They owe their distinctive flavor to the valley's schist terrain.

The north is home to around one-third of the country's people, and this region is where the Portuguese trace their origins as a people and

Highlights

Look for ★ to find recommended sights, activities, dining, and lodging.

★ **Clérigos Tower:** Climb to the top of this spindly landmark for fantastic views of Porto (page 308).

★ **Porto's Riverfront:** Walk the Ribeira, a hive of activity with distinctive bustling cafés and haphazardly arranged houses (page 309).

★ **Port-Tasting in Vila Nova de Gaia:** Visit famous winemakers to learn more about the history of the tipple, and round it off with a tasting or two (page 312).

★ **Boat Tours on the Douro River:** Drink in the breathtaking Douro Valley on a gentle cruise up the river (page 314).

★ **Côa Valley Archaeological Park:** This mysterious open-air gallery of Paleolithic art runs for 17 kilometers (10.5 mi) along the Portuguese-Spanish border (page 332).

★ **Peneda-Gerês National Park:** Portugal's only national park teems with wildlife as well as Roman roads and medieval castles (page 338).

★ **Guimarães:** The town's well-preserved center is an architectural jewelry box with gems that span centuries (page 342).

Porto

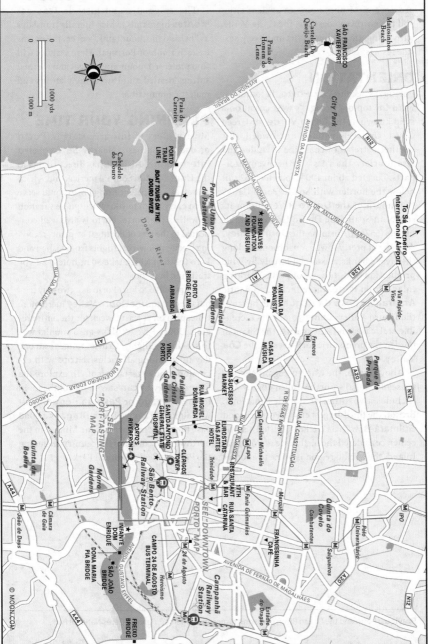

a nation. It is said that Portugal was founded here in the 12th century in the picturesque province of Minho, home to ancient cities and the northern coastline, the Costa Verde, with authentic fishing towns and lively seaside resorts.

ORIENTATION

Portugal's second city, **Porto,** is found toward the top of Portugal's west coast, on a strip known as the **Costa Verde,** or Green Coast. Undeveloped and uncrowded, this northern stretch of coastline is wilder and less touristy than its southern counterparts. Located about 100 kilometers (62 mi) below the border with Spain, Porto flanks the mouth of the **Douro River.** From its source in Spain, the Douro flows 897 kilometers (557 mi), forming the **Douro Valley.** A string of pretty towns mushroomed along the river's banks, sustained largely by wine production and, today, tourism. Working inland from Porto, these include romantic **Amarante; Peso da Régua,** the heart of the Douro Valley; **Lamego** and its incredible staircase; and, up against the Spanish border, the prehistoric rock-art site, the **Côa Valley.**

Above Porto, the **Minho** region encompasses Portugal's northwestern corner and includes two other major destinations: **Braga,** the third-largest city in Portugal, and **Guimarães,** with its UNESCO-listed historic center, considered the birthplace of Portugal. Inland, the Minho region is home to another region of great natural beauty, **Peneda-Gerês National Park.**

The enigmatic and historic **Trás-os-Montes** highlands, which literally translates as "behind the mountains," covers the northeastern flank of Portugal. Here visitors will find preserved mountain villages and thermal springs nestled amid sweeping plateaus and majestic mountains.

PLANNING YOUR TIME

Most visitors to this area start in **Porto** or use it as a base. Nearby **Sá Carneiro International Airport** has direct flights to the United States, South America, and Africa as well as Europe, meaning Porto could serve as an entry point to your Portuguese vacation as well as the Norte. Porto is also well connected to the rest of Portugal by plane, receiving frequent, low-cost flights from Lisbon and Faro (both of which take 50 minutes), and by train and bus, too.

It's possible to visit Porto as a two-day trip, but the city and the **Douro Valley** merit more time; plan on at least a week for the entire region. Douro River **cruises** are a popular way to see the highlights. Cruises range from one day to weeklong all-inclusive trips with excursions and entertainment. To explore the Douro Valley by **car,** stay in one of the main towns, **Lamego** or **Peso da Régua,** halfway along the Douro River. **Braga** is a good base for exploring picturesque Minho, in the northwestern corner of the country, including the Peneda-Gerês National Park.

Previous: Porto and the Douro River; port wine tasting at Sandeman; Peneda-Gerês National Park.

Porto Itinerary Ideas

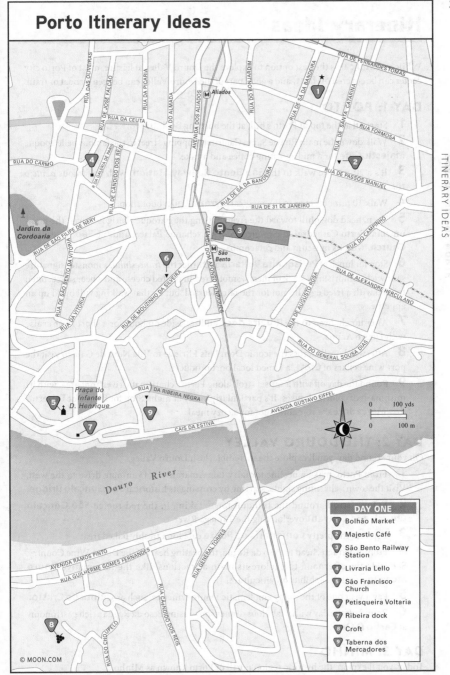

© MOON.COM

DAY ONE

1. Bolhão Market
2. Majestic Café
3. São Bento Railway Station
4. Livraria Lello
5. São Francisco Church
6. Petisqueira Voltaria
7. Ribeira dock
8. Croft
9. Taberna dos Mercadores

Itinerary Ideas

While a **rental car** is the best option to explore the Douro Valley at leisure, most of Porto city center can be covered **on foot,** and a good part of the Douro Valley can be seen by boat or train.

DAY 1: PORTO

1 Start off at the top of Porto's hill, at the bustling **Bolhão Market.**

2 Walk down the main Rua de Santa Catarina shopping street to the famous belle epoque **Majestic Café** for a mid-morning coffee and a cake.

3 It's a 20-minute walk to the **São Bento Railway Station,** with its famous *azulejo* tiles.

4 Walk 10 minutes over to the magical **Livraria Lello** bookshop.

5 Then, head downhill toward the river, passing the baroque Clérigos Tower, the monumental Porto Cathedral, the opulent Stock Exchange Palace, and the **São Francisco Church,** with its museum and catacombs.

6 Stop for lunch at **Petisqueira Voltaria** and order the *francesinha,* a monster signature sandwich comprising a stack of meats, smothered in melted cheese and a beer sauce, often topped with a fried egg. It's not for the fainthearted, but all that walking will build up an appetite.

7 After lunch, head to the **Ribeira dock** and set aside an hour for a short river cruise with Douro Acima.

8 Afterward, walk across the iconic Dom Luís I Bridge to Vila Nova de Gaia to visit the port wine cellars of **Croft,** a famed local port producer.

9 Round the day off with a sunset stroll along Porto's charismatic riverfront area, with its mishmash of colorful houses. It's particularly lovely at night. Stop for dinner at **Taberna dos Mercadores,** a romantic spot for a cozy meal.

DAY 2: THE DOURO VALLEY

On your second day, you'll explore the incredible, lush Douro Valley.

1 From Porto, make a beeline for fairy-tale Amarante, a 45-minute drive to the west. Visit the town's charming sights, starting by crossing its historical **São Gonçalo Bridge.**

2 Enjoy a stroll around the tranquil town, taking in the red-roofed **São Gonçalo Church and Convent** overlooking the Tâmega River.

3 Pop into the pretty **Confeitaria da Ponte** café for a freshly baked treat.

4 From Amarante, head to Peso da Régua, the beating heart of the Douro Wine Country. Set aside the afternoon to explore its main attractions, like the informative **Douro Museum,** with its exhibits on viticulture.

5 Pay a visit one of the many emblematic Douro wineries, such as **Quinta do Crasto.**

6 Round off the day with a fabulous dinner showcasing Peso da Régua's rich gastronomy at **Cacho D'Oiro.**

DAY 3: MINHO

Today, you'll explore the historic region north of Porto known as Minho.

Douro Valley and Minho Itinerary Ideas

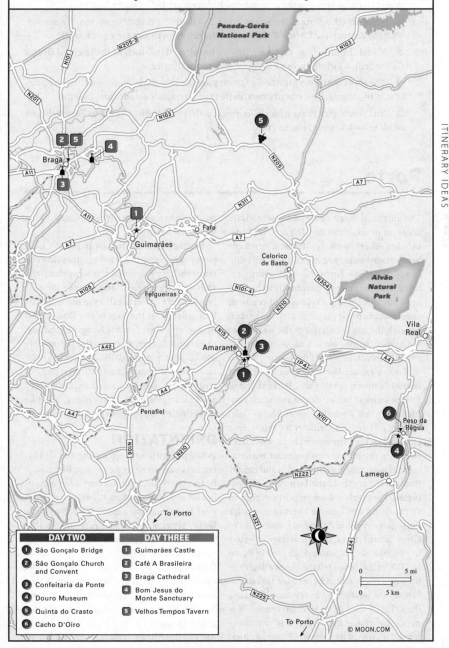

DAY TWO	DAY THREE
1 São Gonçalo Bridge	**1** Guimarães Castle
2 São Gonçalo Church and Convent	**2** Café A Brasileira
3 Confeitaria da Ponte	**3** Braga Cathedral
4 Douro Museum	**4** Bom Jesus do Monte Sanctuary
5 Quinta do Crasto	**5** Velhos Tempos Tavern
6 Cacho D'Oiro	

© MOON.COM

1 Start in the well-preserved medieval city Guimarães, known as the "Cradle of Portugal," a 45-minute drive north of Porto. Wander its historic town center, a UNESCO World Heritage Site, and the atmospheric 10th-century **Guimarães Castle.**

2 From here, keep heading north to Braga, less than a 30-minute drive from Guimarães. Visit the century-old **Café A Brasileira** in Braga's main square for a quick lunch.

3 Spend the afternoon exploring Braga's top attractions, such as the splendid **Braga Cathedral,** which features a medley of architectural styles.

4 The **Bom Jesus do Monte Sanctuary** and its incredible white, multilayered staircase, a 10-minute drive east of Braga, more than warrants a detour from the city.

5 End your day in Braga with a filling meal at the rustic **Velhos Tempos Tavern** before heading back to your hotel in Porto.

Porto

The unrefined charm of Portugal's second city is part of its allure. Shabby in parts, sophisticated in others, with significant investment being made to upgrade its infrastructure and image, as a whole Porto is down-to-earth, relaxed, and endearingly genuine. Northerners are known for using expletives liberally in conversation, but if they lack airs and graces, beneath the gritty exterior is the warmth of the *tripeiros* (tripe eaters), a nickname derived from the local tradition of tripe-based dishes.

Known among Portuguese as the Cidade Invicta (Unvanquished City), Porto is one of Europe's oldest nuclei, dating to the 1st century BC, when it was known as Portus Cale. Evidence of ancient Celtic and Proto-Celtic citadels has been uncovered here, and under Roman occupation Porto flourished as a commercial port, trading with Lisbon and nearby Braga to the north. In the 14th and 15th centuries, Porto played an important role in shipbuilding and became a seat of power for Portuguese royalty. Porto has historic ties to Great Britain through the marriage of João I to Philippa of Lancaster, celebrated in Porto in 1387, which cemented the oldest alliance in the world that is still in force today. Indeed, locals say the weather here is closer to Britain's than that of the balmy Mediterranean—it is noticeably cooler than the rest of the country and it's one of the wettest European cities, but occasional gray drizzle rarely dampens the local vivacity.

Visitors looking for great photos have plenty of opportunities. For breathtaking vistas of the city's jumbled rooftops, climb the 18th-century Clérigos Tower, once the tallest structure in Portugal. Take the Guindais Funicular from the foot of the Dom Luís I Bridge, one of six famous bridges in the city, to Batalha Square, or climb the remarkably contemporary Arrábida Bridge. Porto's best-known export, port wine, is reason enough to visit the city. Despite its centuries of history and culture, Porto still feels young, and like port wine, it only seems to get better with age.

ORIENTATION

While not without steep streets and climbs, Porto is easy to navigate on foot or by public transport. It's built out over a large granite hill above the **Douro River,** across from port wine making center **Vila Nova de Gaia.** Houses, bars, and restaurants line the **Ribeira,** or riverside district. A number of medieval neighborhoods form Porto's **Downtown,** a UNESCO World Heritage Site, which also includes the main **Avenida dos Aliados.** The **historic electrified trams,** buses, and a modern subway system provide easy access to the fringes. At the foot of Avenida dos Aliados is the famous **São Bento**

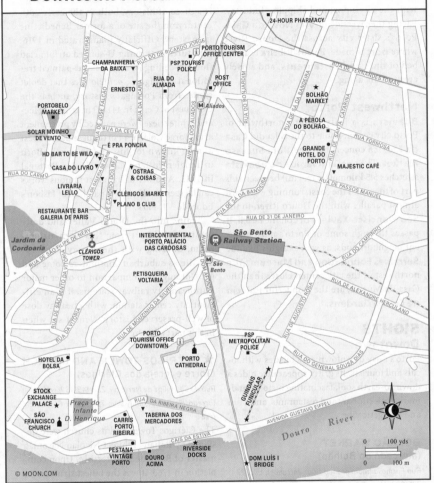

Downtown Porto

Map labels:
24-HOUR PHARMACY
PORTO TOURISM OFFICE CENTER
PSP TOURIST POLICE
RUA DO DR RICARDO JORGE
CHAMPANHERIA DA BAIXA
RUA DO ALMADA
POST OFFICE
RUA DE FERNANDES TOMÁS
ERNESTO
RUA DAS OLIVEIRAS
RUA DA PICARIA
Aliados
RUA DO BONJARDIM
BOLHÃO MARKET
RUA DE SÁ DA BANDEIRA
PORTOBELO MARKET
RUA DE JOSÉ FALCÃO
A PÉROLA DO BOLHÃO
RUA DE SANTA CATARINA
SOLAR MOINHO DE VENTO
RUA DA CEUTA
É PRA PONCHA
AVENIDA DOS ALIADOS
RUA FORMOSA
HD BAR TO BE WILD
GRANDE HOTEL DO PORTO
MAJESTIC CAFÉ
CASA DO LIVRO
RUA DA GALERIA DE PARIS
RUA DO ALMADA
RUA DE PASSOS MANUEL
RUA DO CARMO
OSTRAS & COISAS
LIVRARIA LELLO
RUA DE CÂNDIDO DOS REIS
CLÉRIGOS MARKET
PLANO B CLUB
RUA DE SÁ DA BANDEIRA
RESTAURANTE BAR GALERIA DE PARIS
RUA DE 31 DE JANEIRO
Jardim da Cordoaria
INTERCONTINENTAL PORTO PALÁCIO DAS CARDOSAS
São Bento Railway Station
RUA DE SÃO FILIPE DE NERY
CLÉRIGOS TOWER
AVENIDA DOM AFONSO HENRIQUES
São Bento
RUA DO CAMPINHO
PETISQUEIRA VOLTARIA
RUA DE ALEXANDRE HERCULANO
RUA DE SÃO BENTO DA VITÓRIA
RUA DA VITÓRIA
RUA DE MOUZINHO DA SILVEIRA
RUA DE AUGUSTO ROSA
PORTO TOURISM OFFICE DOWNTOWN
PSP METROPOLITAN POLICE
HOTEL DA BOLSA
PORTO CATHEDRAL
RUA DO GENERAL SOUSA DIAS
STOCK EXCHANGE PALACE
Praça do Infante D. Henrique
RUA DA RIBEIRA NEGRA
GUINDAIS FUNICULAR
SÃO FRANCISCO CHURCH
CARRIS PORTO RIBEIRA
TABERNA DOS MERCADORES
AVENIDA GUSTAVO EIFFEL
Douro River
PESTANA VINTAGE PORTO
DOURO ACIMA
CAIS DA ESTIVA
RIVERSIDE DOCKS
DOM LUÍS I BRIDGE
0   100 yds
0   100 m

© MOON.COM

Railway Station, and behind this, the noble, historical **Batalha Square,** a local transport hub. Northwest of the city's historic hub is **Boavista,** home to several cultural and historical landmarks.

Downtown

Downtown Porto is where most of the city's key sights, such as the main **Avenida dos Aliados** plaza, **Rua de Santa Catarina** shopping street, **Clérigos Tower and**

Church, Bolhão Market, Stock Exchange Palace, Porto Cathedral, and **São Bento Railway Station,** are found. This dense jumble of mismatched-size buildings is busy by day and buzzing by night. All of its narrow, cobbled streets flow toward the iconic Ribeira riverside.

Riverfront

Porto's Ribeira riverfront is perhaps the city's most iconic vista. A row of higgledy-piggledy historic buildings, it is one of the oldest parts of Porto, its illustrious history intertwined with the city's port and shipping industry. Facing the riverside of **Vila Nova da Gaia,** Porto's sister city across the Douro River where **port** is made, Porto's Ribeira is a hotbed of **bars and restaurants,** and a lively area to walk along.

Northwest Porto

Boavista is a leafy suburb northwest of Porto city center, home to the splendid **Casa da Música** concert hall and **Bom Sucesso Market.** The elegant **Avenida da Boavista** stretches 5.5 kilometers (3.4 mi) between this part of town and the coast, running westward almost parallel with the Douro River, to the **São Francisco Xavier Fort** on the beach. It passes through some of Porto's most affluent neighborhoods, as well as sights like the **Serralves Foundation and Museum.** Also northwest of the city center, closer than the Casa da Música, are the wonderful **Palácio de Cristal Gardens.**

SIGHTS
Downtown

Porto's busy downtown area bustles with locals and tourists. Its gritty appearance hides a down-to-earth soul, fascinating historic landmarks, eclectic bars and restaurants, and a fun and energetic vibe.

BOLHÃO MARKET
(Mercado do Bolhão)

Rua Formosa (main ground floor entrance); tel. 223 326 024; Mon.-Fri. 8am-8pm, Sat. 8am-6pm

Inside an impressive neoclassical building, the loud and lively Bolhão Market is packed with stalls run by farmers, butchers, and fisherfolk, roaring with trade each morning. Browsing shoppers can indulge in a real taste of Porto in the cafés on the ground floor. The market is currently undergoing renovations and is set to reopen May 2021.

SÃO BENTO RAILWAY STATION
(Estação de São Bento)

Praça Almeida Garrett; tel. 707 210 220; www.cp.pt

More than just a railway station, São Bento is a piece of history, built in the early 20th century on the site of a former Benedictine monastery. Officially inaugurated in 1916, it features a stunning U-shaped atrium clad floor-to-ceiling in 20,000 hand-painted traditional Portuguese *azulejo* tiles that depict scenes from Portugal's history, such as the Conquest of Ceuta in 1415. The oversize blue-and-white friezes were painted by preeminent artist Jorge Colaço, a Portuguese painter best known known for his *azulejo* panels. Born in Tangiers in 1868, Colaço died in Portugal in 1942. Another of his most famous works can be seen on the sports pavilion of Lisbon's Eduardo VII Park.

Trains into the Douro Valley and daily commuters depart from this open-air museum, buzzing with the energy of everyday life as suburban commuters come and go. Not huge by comparison to other major European city railway stations, it is an efficient city center station, with a healthy dose of well-preserved history. A must-see when in this part of town.

★ CLÉRIGOS TOWER AND CHURCH
(Torre e Igreja dos Clérigos)

Rua de São Filipe de Nery; tel. 220 145 489; www. torredosclerigos.pt; daily 9am-7pm; tower €6, church free

The Clérigos Tower and its church were designed by Italian architect Nicolau Nasoni, a master of Baroque architecture. Upon completion in 1763, it was the tallest structure in Portugal at 75 meters (246 ft). Spanning the late 17th and 18th centuries, the Baroque movement arrived later in Portugal than it did the rest of Europe, but it flourished with the wealth of the era. Nasoni left an extensive portfolio of Baroque works in Portugal, typically elaborate and opulent outside and in. Construction of the church was initiated in 1732 to be the headquarters of the Brotherhood of Clerics, whose mission was to help members of the clergy who were sick, poor, or dying. Completed around 1750, the church's spindly, highly decorative bell tower—a masterpiece of motifs, delicate spires, and carvings—was added on a few years later. Over the centuries, the tower has had various uses: In the 19th century, mortars were fired from the tower to mark noon, when merchants would stop for lunch; it also served as a guiding landmark for vessels sailing on the Douro.

Though no longer Porto's tallest structure, the tower still dominates the skyline and is visible almost everywhere in the city. For an extra-special panorama, climb the 225 stone steps of the inner spiral for amazing 360-degree views of the city.

Despite living in the shadows of its monumental tower, Clérigos Church itself is also worth a look. Its elegant facade is supported by two pairs of Tuscan columns; a dome above the main door boasts the coat of arms of the Brotherhood of the Clerics, in faux granite, and rests on six pillars. Inside, the spacious chapel is embellished with a marble altar and a Rococo-inspired altarpiece, flanked by painted wooden sculptures of the co-patron saints of the Brotherhood of Clerics, St. Peter ad Vincula and St. Philip Neri. The main chapel also houses two pipe organs dating from the late 1770s.

PORTO CATHEDRAL
(Sé do Porto)
Terreiro da Sé; tel. 222 059 028; free

Built on the highest spot in the city, Porto Cathedral was constructed in the 12th-13th centuries in a Romanesque style, but was successively enlarged and extended, adding new styles to its mixed heritage. The fortified church has a simple whitewashed extension. Inside are a gold-leaf altar, cloisters, and a Gothic funerary chapel. The sweeping views of Porto's jumble of rusty roofs rambling down toward the Ribeira make it worth a visit.

The church is open Monday-Saturday 9am-7pm, Sunday and holy days 9am-12:30pm and 2:30pm-7pm April-October, Monday-Saturday 9am-6pm, Sunday and holy days 9am-12:30pm and 2:30pm-7pm November-March. The cloisters are open Monday-Saturday 9am-6:30pm, Sunday and holy days 2:30pm-6:30pm April-October, Monday-Saturday 9am-5:30pm, Sunday and holy days 2:30pm-5:30pm November-March.

STOCK EXCHANGE PALACE
(Palácio da Bolsa)
Rua de Ferreira Borges; tel. 223 399 090; www. palaciodabolsa.com; daily 9am-6:30pm Apr.-Oct., daily 9am-1pm and 2pm-5:30pm Nov.-Mar.; €11

This imposing neoclassical building once housed Porto's stock exchange. Built 1842-1910 on the ruins of an old convent, it was meant to impress visiting businesspeople, dignitaries, and heads of state with the city's economic vitality. Beyond its stately facade are the even more impressive glass-domed Hall of Nations and the opulent Arabian Hall, with Moorish nuances and floor-to-ceiling gilding. Guided tours run regularly throughout the day.

SÃO FRANCISCO CHURCH
(Igreja de São Francisco)
Rua do Infante D. Henrique; tel. 222 062 125; www. ordemsaofrancisco.pt; daily 9am-5:30pm Nov.-Feb., daily 9am-7pm Mar.-Oct., daily 9am-8pm July-Sept.; €7.50

Facing the riverside, the 14th-century São Francisco Church is full of surprises. Its austere gray Gothic exterior hides a mind-blowing Baroque interior. Construction began in 1245 but was disrupted by a huge fire that destroyed the old cloister. Over 300 kilograms (660 lbs) of gold dust clad the lavish new interior, radiating a golden glow and dripping with cherubs and animals, vaulted pillars and marble columns, and soaring ogival (pointed) arches. Distinguished citizens are interred in the catacombs.

★ Riverfront
(Ribeira)

One of Porto's oldest and most typical areas, the Ribeira is most tourists' first port of call, to soak up the genuine atmosphere of the city,

Six Bridges

Known as the City of Bridges, Porto has six bridges that unite it with Vila Nova de Gaia across the Douro River. Counting inward from the *foz* (river mouth), the bridges are the Arrábida, Dom Luís I, Infante Dom Henrique, Dona Maria Pia, São João, and Freixo.

The two most famous, standing side by side, are named after husband and wife King Luís I and Maria Pia of Savoy. The **Dona Maria Pia Bridge** was designed by Gustave Eiffel, famous for the tower that bears his name in Paris. The 142-meter (466-ft) double-deck **Dom Luís I Bridge**, built 1881-1886 and designed by Eiffel's disciple, Théophile Seyrig, is a symbol of the city. Both the Dom Luís I Bridge's decks are open to pedestrians, with the views from the upper platform 60 meters (200 ft) above water level worth the vertigo.

The other four Douro bridges are built from concrete with more streamlined silhouettes. Inaugurated in 2003, the modern **Infante Dom Henrique Bridge** was the last of the six to be built and boasts the longest single-platform arch in the world.

enjoy a river cruise, or cross one of its iconic bridges on foot to Gaia.

You can't say you've been to Porto until you've walked the riverside, the lively **Riverside Docks** (Cais da Ribeira), which date to medieval times. Disorderly narrow pastel buildings of mismatched heights, sizes, and colors seem to teeter into each other. Their fronts are adorned with tiny wrought-iron balconies and freshly washed laundry as well as more modern trappings like satellite dishes. Traditional flat-bottomed *rabelo* bob up and down on the Douro, adding to the romantic ambience. Used for centuries to ferry barrels of port and other cargo on the river, the boats are today mostly decorative. At ground level, a series of busy restaurants and tourist shops run along the river. Have refreshments or a relaxed meal in one of the myriad establishments, most enjoyable during and after sunset.

ARRÁBIDA BRIDGE

Douro Rivermouth

Of Lisbon's six bridges, the Arrábida Bridge is closest to the Douro River mouth, where it stands triumphant, sweeping over the outlet into the Atlantic. Built 1957-1963, the symmetrical reinforced concrete structure is remarkably contemporary in its look. At the time of its inauguration, it was considered an extraordinary feat of engineering and architecture: the biggest single concrete arch bridge in the world. It links Porto and Gaia's main roads, carrying six lanes of traffic over the Douro River. It also plays host to one of Porto's most unique tourist attractions, to Porto Bridge Climb.

Ascend to the tip of the landmark Arrábida Bridge's sweeping inner arch on the **Porto Bridge Climb** (Rua do Ouro 680; tel. 929 207 117; www.portobridgeclimb.com; climbs leave every 45 minutes daily 2:30pm-8:30pm; €15-16.5; the climb itself takes around 30 minutes), in which experienced guides lead you up the 262 steps to the peak of the sleek cement arch. Once the longest single cement arch in the world, it reopened in 2016 for the first time since the 1960s. One of Porto's best-kept secrets, these tours run for groups of five or more people, minimum age 12. Full-moon and sunrise climbs are also available. Reservations are required.

GUINDAIS FUNICULAR

R. da Ribeira Negra 314; tel. 808 205 060; www. metrodoporto.pt; Sun.-Thurs. 8am-8pm, Fri.-Sat. 8am-10pm Nov.-Mar., Sun.-Thurs. 8am-10pm, Fri.-Sat. 8am-midnight Apr.-Oct.; €2.50

The Guindais Funicular runs between Batalha Square, near Porto Cathedral, and

---

1: Dom Luís I Bridge over the Douro River
2: Clérigos Tower **3:** São Bento Railway Station
4: Stock Exchange Palace

☆ Port-Tasting in Vila Nova de Gaia

Deep, rich, fortified port wine has become an ambassador for Portugal as a whole. Port wine must be produced in northern Portugal, and authentic port is produced exclusively in vineyards in the Douro Region, demarcated in 1756, with mostly native grape varieties. It is transported downriver and aged in barrels stored in cellars such as those in **Vila Nova de Gaia,** just over the Douro River from Porto.

Generally enjoyed as a dessert drink, the best-known port is typically ruby red in color. **Ruby** is the younger, lighter, fruitier variety, while **tawny** varieties are older and nuttier. Exceptional **vintage** port is produced only from the finest harvests and aged for long periods in oak casks. **Rosé** and **white** varieties have recently given the wine a trendy makeover as an ingredient of white port and tonic, a popular summer cocktail. The essence of the north in a bottle, port wine is the quintessential Porto souvenir.

Some of Portugal's oldest port companies were founded by British mercantile families in the 17th and 18th centuries and are still run by their descendants. Most of the lodges offer **guided**

the riverside far below. Inaugurated in 1891, it has been successively upgraded for a short and swift journey, and the views over the river are phenomenal.

Northwest Porto
PALÁCIO DE CRISTAL GARDENS
(Jardim do Palácio de Cristal)

Rua de D. Manuel II; tel. 225 320 080; www. cm-porto.pt/jardins-e-parques/palacio-de-cristal_33; daily 8am-9pm Apr.-Sept., daily 8am-7pm Oct.-Mar.; free

Occupying 8 hectares (20 acres) in the center of Porto, the Palácio de Cristal Gardens are a jigsaw of manicured lawns, colorful flowerbeds, and beautiful water features, divided

by walkways and inhabited by peacocks. The garden's terraces are called the "verandas of the Douro" for their views of the river and its bridges. Although the gardens were designed by a German landscape architect for a 19th-century exhibition, little remains of the original crystal palace, replaced in the 1950s by a modern pavilion, now slightly run-down. The gardens are about 30 minutes' walk west of the city center.

SERRALVES FOUNDATION
AND MUSEUM
(Fundação e Museu de Serralves)

Rua D. João de Castro 210; tel. 226 156 500; www.serralves.pt; Mon.-Fri. 10am-7pm, Sat.-Sun.

tours in multiple languages, including English, culminating in a tasting session. Basic tours of the cellars (€10-12, including tasting) last about an hour. All the lodges listed below are open daily 10am-6pm year-round. **Porto Walkers** (tel. 918 291 519; www.portowalkers.pt; from €27) takes groups on half-day walking tours that include a trio of different lodges. Knowledgeable guides teach you about the origins of port, and even how to sample the drink properly.

Vila Nova de Gaia is a short walk across the **Dom Luís I Bridge** from Porto's riverside. Take the lower deck for the riverside and port cellars. Alternatively, Porto's Metro (tel. 225 081 000; www.metrodoporto.pt; €1.20 one-way) light-rail system runs regularly between the two cities; take the **D Line** to **Santo Ovidio** from the São Bento station, stopping at Jardim do Morro. This line crosses the Dom Luís I Bridge's upper deck. Metro trains run every six minutes weekdays 6am-1am, every 15 minutes on the weekend.

CÁLEM
Av. Diogo Leite 344; tel. 916 113 451; https://tour.calem.pt; from €13

Founded in 1859, Cálem is one of Portugal's signature ports. Tour options include tastings, food, and even fado performances.

SANDEMAN
Largo Miguel Bombarda 47; tel. 223 740 534; www.sandeman.com; from €14

Globally renowned since 1790, tours of the magnificent 200-year-old cellars include a 1970 vintage tour and a 100-Year-Old Tawnies tour.

CROFT
Rua Barão Forrester 412; tel. 220 109 825; www.croftport.com; from €14

Founded in 1588, Croft is the oldest active port producer. A visit to Croft's cellars includes a guided tour and tasting of three ports.

TAYLOR'S
Rua do Choupelo 250; tel. 223 772 973; www.taylor.pt; €15

Producing port since 1692, Taylor's is among Portugal's oldest port houses. Audio-guided tours provide information in 11 languages.

10am-8pm Apr.-Sept., Mon.-Fri. 10am-6pm, Sat.-Sun. 10am-7pm Oct.-Mar.; general ticket (access to all areas) €20, museum only €12, art deco villa only €12, park only €12

The Serralves Foundation and Museum seeks to promote contemporary art, thought, architecture, and landscape. The **Serralves Museum (Museu Serralves)** features contemporary art in a building designed by distinguished architect Álvaro Siza. **Casa de Serralves,** a pink art deco villa built in the 1930s, offers insight into the architectural and decorative details of the era; it also serves as the foundation's office. Both are surrounded by the 18-hectare (45-acre) **Parque de Serralves,** with its sprawling gardens, woodland, and a farm. Serralves is 5.5 kilometers (3.4 mi) west of the city center.

SÃO FRANCISCO XAVIER FORT (Forte de São Francisco Xavier)
Praça de Gonçalves Zarco 20

Perched on a cliff jutting out between the Douro and Matosinhos River mouths, the São Francisco Xavier Fort offers lovely ocean views. Built in the 17th century to protect the city from attack, it's commonly called the Castelo do Queijo, "Castle of Cheese," because it was built on a rotund granite rock that looks like a cheese round. The trapezoidal walls are built from chunky granite blocks that give the small fortress a robust look, enforced by a dry moat and drawbridge, turreted watchtowers, and cannons. Inside is an exhibition of military paraphernalia. Two of Porto's most popular beaches are on either side of the fort: Praia Internacional, on the larger Matosinhos Beach, to the north, and Castelo do Queijo Beach, to the south. The fort is located approximately 8 kilometers (5 mi) west of the city center at the end of Porto's main Avenida da Boavista, which links the city center to the coast. Nearby is the idyllic **City Park,** nice for a relaxing walk.

SPORTS AND RECREATION
Parks
CITY PARK
(Parque da Cidade)
Estrada Interior da Circunvalação; tel. 225 320 080; Tues.-Sun. 7am-midnight, Mon. 9am-11pm; free

Sprawling over 83 hectares (205 acres), Porto's City Park is the largest urban park in the country, an oasis of tranquil greenery covering the northwest tip of the city's outskirts. A large lake in the middle of the park is a lovely centerpiece to walk or cycle around. There are also a children's play areas, sports fields, and little coffee shops dotting the park. Parking is relatively easy to find, with the roads around the eastern flank offering free street parking. The western end of the park leads on to **Matosinhos Beach,** near the **São Francisco Xavier Fort.**

Beaches
MATOSINHOS BEACH
(Praia de Matosinhos)
Matosinhos; open 24/7; free

On the north bank of the Douro, facing the Atlantic, sandy Matosinhos Beach is wide, long, and windy, popular among sunbathers and surfers. Stretching northward from the São Francisco Xavier Fort to Matosinhos port, it fronts the town of Matosinhos, a short Metro ride from Porto city center. It's conveniently close to Porto, and in summer all sorts of facilities can be found on the beach, including sun bed and surfboard rentals.

CASTELO DO QUEIJO BEACH
(Praia do Castelo do Queijo)
São Francisco Xavier Fort; open 24/7; free

This small beach is adjacent to the São Francisco Xavier Fort. There are plenty of rock pools to explore, as well as nice portions of sand, but beware; the rocky parts can be sharp on feet. The views of the fort standing guard in the background are impressive. A row of restaurants and cafés sits across the road.

★ Boat Tours
One of Porto's most popular excursions is a cruise on the river, with options ranging from hour-long trips to multiday cruises that explore the Douro Valley. Each of Porto's bridges has a story to tell, and a cruise along the Douro is the best way to hear them.

- **Douro Acima:** Ribeira dock; tel. 222 080 677; www.douroacima.pt; daily every 30 minutes 10am-6pm Apr.-Oct., daily hourly 10am-4pm Nov.-Mar.; from €15

- **Douro Azul:** Rua de Miragaia 103, departs from Gaia docks; tel. 223 402 500; www.douroazul.com; every 30 minutes 9:30am-5:30pm summer, every 60 minutes 9:30am-4:30pm winter; 50-minute bridge cruises from €14

- **Cruzeiros Douro:** tel. 226 191 090; www.cruzeiros-douro.pt; 10-hour Douro Valley tour €60

ENTERTAINMENT AND EVENTS
The Arts
CASA DA MÚSICA
Av. da Boavista 604-610; tel. 220 120 220; www.casadamusica.com; Mon.-Sat. 9:30am-7pm, Sun. 9:30am-6pm

Northwest of the city's historic hub, the Casa da Música stages year-round concerts and events ranging from classical to contemporary. Its striking modern building, designed

1: São João Festival **2:** inside Livraria Lello bookshop **3:** Cálem port cellar **4:** bridge over the Douro River

by Dutch architect Rem Koolhaas, has a fluid, sleek look, in stark contrast with the rugged city surrounding it. Private tours of the building (€10) are available in English twice daily.

Festivals and Events
SÃO JOÃO FESTIVAL
throughout Porto; June 23

This 600-year-old festival, honoring Saint John, patron saint of lovers, is one of the most raucous street parties in Portugal. Every year, thousands flock to Porto for the 24-hour-long *festa* that starts on the eve of June 23.

Thousands of floating lanterns are launched, creating a dazzling picture in the night sky overhead. One of São João's quirky traditions is to bash and be bashed over the head with leeks, which in recent times have given way to squeaky plastic hammers. Even though this bashing can get quite vigorous, it's all good-natured, a wish for luck in love and fertility. Almost every home in the city is draped in cheery bunting. Stalls selling beer, sangria, grilled sardines, and kale soups spring up all over the city.

The party bubbles until a gigantic fireworks display over the Douro River at midnight, when the city's main squares and avenues become dance floors as live bands and DJs play until dawn. The day after is a much-needed local holiday.

SHOPPING

Rua de Santa Catarina is lined with a mixture of international chain stores such as Mango, Zara, and H&M along with boutiques that give it a cool, cosmopolitan feel. Major brands can also be found along the **Avenida da Boavista**, while **Rua do Almada** is a hub of alternative shops. Peruse the chic window displays along **Rua Miguel Bombarda,** interspersed with arty galleries.

Markets
CLERIGOS MARKET
(Mercadinho dos Clérigos)
Rua Cândido dos Reis; 2nd and last Sat. of each month 10am-8pm

On the second and last Saturday of every month, Rua Cândido dos Reis hosts Mercadinho dos Clérigos, a marketplace bursting with crafts, antiques, music, and even gastronomy.

PORTOBELO MARKET
(Mercado Portobelo)
Praça Carlos Alberto; Sat. noon-7pm

Vintage clothing, antiques, and decorative objects are found alongside local produce in Mercado Porto Belo.

Books
LIVRARIA LELLO
Rua das Carmelitas 144; tel. 222 002 037; www. livrarialello.pt; daily 9:30am-7pm; entry €5, fully deductible from any book purchase from the store

A frontrunner for the title of most beautiful bookshop in the world, Livraria Lello inspired author J. K. Rowling, who lived in Porto in the 1990s: The shop served as the basis for the Flourish & Blotts bookshop in her Harry Potter novels. Close to the Clérigos Tower, the bookshop dates to 1881 and is housed in a 1906 building with a magical feel, with a ghostly-white facade of neo-Gothic and art nouveau architecture, a sweeping crimson central staircase, and a spectacular stained-glass skylight. Outside, the front is embellished with two figurines, painted by José Bielman, symbolizing science and art, while inside, the stained-glass ceiling bears detailing of Lello's motto, *Vecus in Labore* (Dignity in Work). Besides books in several languages, the shop has a **café** upstairs that sells coffee, port wine, and cigars. The small shop is so popular, especially with Harry Potter fans, that long queues form at the door. It's worth braving the crowds. Tickets can be bought online or from a shop just around the corner.

FOOD

Offal is a staple in Porto's regional cuisine, as are rice and beans. Classic dishes include chicken *cabidela* (chicken stewed with giblets, blood, and rice) and Porto-style **tripe,** with various meats, sausages, and beans in a rich, seasoned sauce that led to the nickname *tripeiros* (tripe eaters) for the locals. No trip to Porto would be complete without trying a meaty *francesinha* sandwich—covered in thick sauce—at least once, but it's so filling you may never eat again. Rounding off a meal with a glass of **port** is virtually compulsory.

Downtown
A PÉROLA DO BOLHÃO
Rua Formosa 279; tel. 222 004 009; Mon.-Fri. 9:30am-7:30pm, Sat. 9am-1pm
Opened in 1917, A Pérola do Bolhão is a gorgeous grocery and delicatessen with an eye-catching art nouveau facade. Inside, it's stuffed to the rafters with colorful traditional products, including sweets, nuts, dried fruits, cookies, local cheeses, cured meats, and, of course, port wines. It's near the busy Bolhão Market.

FRANCESINHA CAFÉ
Rua da Alegria 946; tel. 912 653 883; Mon.-Sat. 12:30pm-3pm and 7pm-11pm; €8
A definite contender for the best *francesinha* is found on the edge of downtown at the Francesinha Café. It looks unremarkable, but the huge picture of the namesake sandwich in the window gives its secret away.

CHAMPANHERIA DA BAIXA
Largo Mompilher 1-2; tel. 223 235 254; www. champanheriadabaixa.com; Mon.-Thurs. noon-12:30am, Fri.-Sat. noon-2:30am; €8
If you like finger food and fancy drinks, you'll love sophisticated Champanheria da Baixa downtown. The décor is bohemian and atmospheric, and the tapas are delicious. Wash it all down with cocktails, sangria, or champagne.

★ PETISQUEIRA VOLTARIA
Rua Afonso Martins Alho 109; tel. 223 256 593 or 913 885 252; Thurs.-Tues. noon-10pm; €12
If you can get a table at Petisqueira Voltaria, a narrow tapas place near the São Bento Railway Station, thank your lucky stars. Sharing platters are creatively conjured with local delicacies in sample-size portions, a great way to

savor the scope of local gastronomy in one sitting. Also on the menu is the ubiquitous *francesinha*.

SOLAR MOINHO DE VENTO
Rua de Sá de Noronha 81; tel. 222 051 158; www. solarmoinhodevento.com; Mon.-Sat. noon-3:30pm and 6:30pm-10:30pm, Sun. noon-3:30pm; €13
Cozy Solar do Moinho de Vento serves hearty portions of quality home-cooked local dishes, such as octopus with tomato rice, Porto-style tripe, and chicken *cabidela* rice.

★ ERNESTO
Rua da Picaria 85; tel. 222 002 600; www.oernesto. pt; Mon. noon-3pm, Tues.-Sat. noon-3pm and 7:15pm-10:30pm; €15
Ernesto is a local family favorite. Dishes include Alheira sausage with fries and *marmota frita,* fish fried whole with its tail in its mouth. Inside, the exposed stone walls and gleaming crockery provide a fresh, warm feel.

★ MAJESTIC CAFÉ
Rua de Santa Catarina 112; tel. 222 003 887; www. cafemajestic.com; Mon.-Sat. 9:30am-11:30pm; €15
Opened in the 1920s to cater to high society, glittering Majestic Café has carried its splendor across the decades. Decked out with distinctive belle epoque furnishings, including elegant chandeliers and oversize mirrors, Majestic is perfect for a refined afternoon tea, a snack, a light meal, or to try the famous *fracesinha*. Fame comes at a price; be prepared to pay more (a regular coffee is around €5) and wait in a queue to get in, unless you reserve ahead online.

TABERNA DOS MERCADORES
Rua dos Mercadores 36; tel. 222 010 510; Tues.-Fri. and Sun. 12:30pm-11pm, Sat. 12:30pm-3:30pm and 7pm-11pm; €20
Busy Taberna dos Mercadores is hidden behind heavy wooden doors on a narrow street near the riverside. The rustic and romantic interior is complemented by tasty traditional dishes and local specialties.

All About *Francesinhas*

the *francesinha* sandwich

It might sound elegant, but there's nothing petite about the *francesinha*, which translates literally as "little Frenchie." Porto's ubiquitous monster sandwich with a cult following is less a snack and more a gut-busting meal. This mound of a sandwich comprises cured and cold meats, such as *chouriço* sausage and bacon, piled on top of slices of roast pork or beefsteak and fresh sausage, wedged between two slices of bread, covered first in melted cheese, then in a hot beer and tomato sauce, and served with fries and a fried egg on top for good measure. Variations include hamburger patties instead of pork or beef, and a spicier sauce made with *piripiri*.

ORIGINS

The *francesinha* is believed to derive from its daintier French cousin, the *croque monsieur* (a fried or grilled sandwich with cheese and ham). A local tale pinpoints its origins to a man named Daniel David Silva, who, after living in France and Belgium, brought the *croque monsieur* back to Porto and transformed it into today's *francesinha*. He called the sandwich "little Frenchie" because, he said, French women were the sauciest he had ever met. Silva made his name serving his creation at the A Regaleira restaurant, established in 1953 in Porto, arguably the home of the *francesinha* (it closed in 2018). Legend has it that the recipe for Silva's sauce was a fiercely guarded secret until an employee passed it on to a rival restaurant across the river in Vila Nova de Gaia.

Another theory about the *francesinha's* origins dates to the early-19th-century Peninsular War, when Napoleonic troops would eat all sorts of meats and heaps of cheese in bread as sustenance. The sauce was Porto's contribution later on.

Whatever its origins, this classic Porto dish is now served at eateries throughout the country.

THE BEST *FRANCESINHA*

It's generally agreed that the *francesinha* sandwich, stuffed with meats and covered in rich tomato and beer sauce, should be washed down with an ice-cold beer. However, the best *francesinha* in town remains hotly debated; visit any of the following restaurants to decide for yourself.

- **Francesinha Café** (page 317)
- **Petisqueira Voltaria** (page 317)
- **Majestic Café** (page 317)

★ OSTRAS & COISAS

Rua da Fábrica 73; tel. 918 854 709; www.
ostrasecoisas.pt; Sun.-Fri. 7pm-10:30pm, Sat.
noon-2:30pm and 7pm-10:30pm; €30

Trendy Ostras & Coisas serves fresh seafood straight from the docks. Indulge in
Mozambican-style shrimp, clams Bulhão
Pato-style, or, as the restaurant's name suggests, go for the oysters. Mixed platters for two
are a specialty.

★ 17TH

Rua do Bolhão 223; tel. 223 401 617; www.
decimosetimo.pt; Sun.-Thurs. 12:30pm-3pm and
7:30pm-10:30pm, Fri.-Sat. 12:30pm-3pm and
7:30pm-11pm; €30

On the top two floors of Porto's Dom
Henrique Hotel, the elegant 17 Restaurant
& Bar offers a fabulous gastronomic expe-
rience alongside bird's-eye city views. The
menu fuses traditional Portuguese dishes with
Mediterranean flavors.

Northwest Porto
BOM SUCESSO MARKET

Praça Bom Sucesso 74-90; tel. 226 056 610; www.
mercadobomsucesso.pt; daily 10am-8pm

Tantalize your taste buds at Bom Sucesso
Market, browsing the 40-plus stalls serving
myriad gastronomic treats, from traditional
savory snacks to handmade chocolates and
Portuguese wines and gin.

BARS AND NIGHTLIFE

Porto's colorful nightlife is consistent with
the city's work-hard, play-hard ethos. The
city's most popular bar street is **Rua Galeria
de Paris.** If one full street of bars does not
suffice, try the parallel **Rua Cândido dos
Reis.** Both are in the historic area, just off
the Clérigos Tower. Nightlife doesn't get into
full swing until after 11pm, although most
bars are open earlier. Be prepared to stay up
late.

Downtown
HD BAR TO BE WILD

Rua Galeria de Paris 113; tel. 222 032 514; daily
6pm-late

Decorated with Harley Davidson memorabilia, laid-back biker bar HD Bar to Be Wild
has an American jukebox and an energizing
road-trip soundtrack.

É PRA PONCHA BAR

Rua Galeria de Paris 99; tel. 969 472 546; Mon.-Sat.
5pm-1am

É Pra Poncha Bar, a narrow cave-like space

Majestic Café

with a wavy multicolored ceiling, is the setting for great punch-based cocktails like Madeira Poncha.

CASA DO LIVRO
Rua Galeria de Paris 85; tel. 222 025 101; Tues.-Thurs. 9pm-3am, Fri.-Sat. 9pm-4am

Once upon a time, Casa do Livro was a bookshop, but now it's a nightlife classic, with diverse music from DJs and live musicians. Its walls are decorated with the bookshelves of its former life, while gleaming polished wood and low-lit lamps provide a warm glow, contributing to the intimate drawing-room atmosphere.

GALERIA DE PARIS
Rua Galeria de Paris 56; tel. 222 016 218; daily 10am-3am

Housed in a former warehouse, Galeria de Paris is packed with vintage paraphernalia: old toys, musical instruments, and even bicycles hanging from the ceilings. Enjoy eclectic live acts, from jazz bands to trapeze artists and belly dancers. Candlelit tables add a touch of romance. Galeria also serves breakfast, lunch, and dinner.

PLANO B CLUB
Rua de Cândido dos Reis 30; tel. 222 012 500; http://planobporto.com; Thurs.-Sat 10pm-6am

One of Porto's best dance venues, boho-chic Plano B offers an interesting mashup of music and art, design and culture, and a regular lineup of DJs and live acts playing everything from R&B and techno to hip-hop.

ACCOMMODATIONS

Porto offers a wide range of options, from basic to high-end historic conversions, all with central locations.

Downtown
HOTEL DA BOLSA
Rua de Ferreira Borges 101; tel. 222 026 768; www.hoteldabolsa.com; €100

Just 100 meters (300 ft) from the Palácio da Bolsa, three-star Hotel da Bolsa offers 34 comfortable rooms, a good buffet breakfast, an on-site bar, and a great location.

★ GRANDE HOTEL DO PORTO
Rua de Santa Catarina 197; tel. 222 076 690; www.grandehotelporto.com; €171

Just around the corner from the iconic Majestic Café on busy Rua de Santa Catarina, Grande Hotel do Porto is a stately 94-room retreat on the doorstep of the city's best monuments, theaters, and shops. Established in 1880, it embodies the grandeur of bygone eras, brought up to date with modern comforts.

★ INTERCONTINENTAL PORTO PALÁCIO DAS CARDOSAS
Praça da Liberdade 25; tel. 220 035 600; www.ihg.com; €256

Feel like royalty at the opulent five-star Intercontinental Porto Palácio das Cardosas, a beautiful 18th-century palace reborn. Think grand chandeliers, polished marble floors, and Romanesque columns. It's just a short stroll from the São Bento Railway Station and the Livraria Lello bookshop.

Riverfront
CARRIS PORTO RIBEIRA
Rua do Infante D. Henrique 1; tel. 220 965 786; www.carrisportoribeira.com; €120

A few streets back from the riverfront in the old Ribeira, four-star Carris Porto Ribeira occupies a refurbished 17th-century building with chic rooms, a cozy tapas bar, and views across the Douro.

★ PESTANA VINTAGE PORTO
Praça da Ribeira 1; tel. 223 402 300; www.pestanacollection.com; €227

On the romantic riverfront, five-star Pestana Vintage Porto was created from a set of 18 pastel-color historic buildings emblematic of Porto's cityscape. Some date to the 16th century. Inside, it's plush and comfortable, and the on-site restaurant, Rib Beef & Wine, is excellent.

Northwest Porto

★ EUROSTARS DAS ARTES HOTEL

Rua do Rosário 160-165; tel. 222 071 250; www.

eurostarshotels.com.pt; €138

In central Porto, Eurostars das Artes Hotel is an art lover's dream. In an area surrounded by galleries and museums, it features boutique accommodations, with rotating exhibitions inside the hotel and a peaceful outdoor deck. It straddles two structures: a palatial older building with a sky-blue tiled facade and its contemporary sibling.

★ VINCCI PORTO

Alameda de Basílio Teles 29; tel. 220 439 620; www.

vincciporto.com; from €171 d

Four-star Vincci Porto is a stylish retreat in a renovation of the landmark Bolsa do Pescado fish market. It has a big, bright, and airy glass-brick atrium, distinctive avant-garde décor, and a terrace with views over the Douro.

INFORMATION AND SERVICES

- **Porto Tourism Office Downtown:** Calçada Dom Pedro Pitões 15; tel. 300 501 920; www.visitporto.travel; daily 9am-7pm

- **Porto Tourism Office Center:** Rua Clube dos Fenianos 25; tel. 300 501 920; www. visitporto.travel; daily 9am-7pm

- **Post office (main downtown branch):** Allied Post Office, Praça General Humberto Delgado; www.ctt.pt; Mon.-Fri. 8am-9pm, Sat. 9am-6pm

- **PSP Tourist Police:** Rua Clube dos Fenianos 19; tel. 222 081 833

- **PSP Metropolitan Police:** Largo 1º de Dezembro 3; tel. 222 092 000; www.psp.pt

- **Santo António General State Hospital (Centro Hospitalar do Porto):** Largo do Professor Abel Salazar; tel. 222 077 500; www.chporto.pt

- **Santa Maria Private Hospital:** Rua de Camões 906; tel. 225 082 000; www. hsmporto.pt

- **24-hour pharmacy:** Farmácia Antunes, Rua do Bonjardim 485; tel. 222 007 936

GETTING THERE

Porto is northern Portugal's major transport hub and is easily accessed from all over the country. Bus and train connections run from all major towns and cities and are cost-efficient; road routes are straightforward and in good condition; and short domestic flights link the north to Lisbon, the Algarve, and the islands. From the Algarve, it can often be cheaper to fly to Porto than to go by car or public transport.

Porto is 300 kilometers (185 mi) north of **Lisbon.** It's served by an excellent network of motorways, although it can be costly as tolls apply to most A-roads. The main **A1** motorway links Lisbon to Porto in under 3 hours. There is plenty of **parking** in Porto, mostly metered street parking, car parks, and garages. Hourly prices vary widely—the closer to the center, the more expensive parking becomes. Average prices range from €0.80-2.60/hour; daily rates can cost up to €30.

Air

SÁ CARNEIRO INTERNATIONAL AIRPORT

tel. 229 432 400; www.aeroportoporto.pt

Porto's Sá Carneiro International Airport (OPO) has daily flights from dozens of European destinations year-round as well as regular direct flights from Canada, the United States, South America, and Africa. Daily domestic flights operate to the Azores; there's also an hourly express flight between Porto and Lisbon. From Lisbon, the hourly express flight operated by regional **TAP Express** takes 1 hour and costs around €70 one-way; **Ryanair** also offers less frequent flights.

Porto's airport is in Maia, 10 kilometers (6 mi) north of Porto city center and served by the **Metro** (tel. 225 081 000 or 808 205 060; www.metrodoporto.pt) light rail and tram system to central Porto, every 20 minutes Monday-Friday, less frequently on weekends and holidays. It takes around 30 minutes to reach Porto by Metro, and a one-way ticket costs €2.55. Tickets can be purchased from ticket machines or the airport's tourist information office.

There is little to no public transport midnight-6am (a late-night bus service runs hourly between the airport and the downtown Aliados area), so a **taxi** might be necessary. Both conventional taxis and Uber operate in Porto. From the airport, the trip costs €20-30. Rental companies at the airport include **Sixt** (Francisco Sá Carneiro Airport; tel. 255 788 199; www.sixt.pt) and **Europcar** (Av. do Aeroporto 322; tel. 229 482 452; www. europcar.pt). Most rental car depots are near the airport. A free **shuttle** takes passengers from arrivals to the depot, and most are open 7am-midnight daily.

Train

When traveling to Porto by train from outside the city, all trains will stop at **Porto Campanhã** station, on the eastern outskirts. From here there are regular services to the **São Bento** urban station in the heart of Porto city center, which are usually included on train ticket fares, but will likely require a change of platform.

CAMPANHÃ STATION

Rua Pinheiro de Campanhã, Largo da Estação
CP (tel. 707 210 220; www.cp.pt) operates high-speed Alfa-Pendular trains and slightly slower Intercidades (Intercity) trains that connect **Lisbon** and the **Algarve** to Porto's Campanhã station daily. Campanhã station is 5 kilometers (3 mi) east of Porto's downtown. From Lisbon, the Alfa-Pendular runs almost hourly from the Santa Apolónia and Oriente stations and takes 3 hours to reach Porto. Tickets cost €31.60 one-way for second class, €43.70 first class. Book tickets online (www. cp.pt), as they are often cheaper if bought in advance. A few car-rental offices are based at the station.

Bus

Porto doesn't have a main bus terminal, but rather has several hubs for long-distance buses located around the city. The main intercity bus company between Lisbon and Porto is **Rede Expressos** (tel. 707 223 344; www. rede-expressos.pt; 8am-9pm daily), whose buses are modern, comfortable, and air-conditioned. Bus travel is cheaper than rail but takes longer. Dozens of buses depart daily between **Lisbon** and Porto (3.5-4 hours; €19); Rede Expressos buses depart Lisbon's Oriente station (in the Park of Nations area) every few hours, and hourly from the Sete Rios hub (near the zoo). Buses arrive at Porto's main bus hub, **Campo 24 Agosto** (Campo 24 de Agosto 125), about 1 kilometer (0.6 mi) east of Bolhão Market; it has a nearby Metro station with the same name.

International bus lines, such as **AVIC, Internorte,** and **Resende,** stop at the **Casa da Música,** while many urban buses drop off and depart from the **São João Hospital** (Alameda Professor Hernâni Monteiro), north of the city center, and the **Camelias Park** (Rua de Augusto Rosa) in downtown Porto, just before Batalha Square. **Eurolines** (www. eurolines.com) operates regular international bus services between Porto and London, Madrid, and Paris. **Internorte** (tel. 707 200 512; www.internorte.pt) is another option.

GETTING AROUND

Getting around Porto is easy, with several efficient forms of transport. The historic center is compact and easy to cover **on foot,** but the cobbled streets can be very steep. Bus, car, or Metro travel is required to see sights on the outskirts, such as the São Francisco Xavier Fort and the Serralves Foundation and Museum. There's no need for cars in Porto, though they can be useful to explore neighboring cities and the northern region. Traffic can be dense and chaotic, especially on weekdays during rush hour, and parking can be hard to find.

An all-encompassing multimodal travel card called the **Andante Tour Card** (tel. 225 071 000; www.stcp.pt) covers bus, tram, Metro, and urban train lines between the

Espinho, Valongo, and Travagem stations. It is great for getting around stress-free and comes in two versions: Andante Tour 1 (€7) is valid for 24 hours after first validation. Andante Tour 3 (€15) is valid for 72 hours. Andante tickets can be purchased from all bus and Metro ticket machines and booths, or from tourism offices. The rechargeable card costs €0.60.

If passengers are caught traveling without a valid ticket on any form of Porto's public transport, fines range from €120-350. Be sure to hold onto your ticket to avoid getting fined, whichever type of public transit you're using.

Car

The traffic on Porto's narrow roads can be intense, especially at peak rush hour and on weekends. It may make the most sense to drop off your rental car or park it for the duration of your time in the city; inquire with your hotel to see if they provide parking. The best **car parks** for visiting the center are Trindade Park on Rua Fernandes Tomás at the top end of the city (open 24/7), and Alfandega Park, which is best located for visiting the Ribeira riverside and Vila Nova de Gaia's wine cellars. The best option is probably to park on the outskirts of the city and commute by public transport as Porto has a very good public transport system. Once in the city center, it is easily covered on foot.

Bus

Porto's transport company **STCP** (tel. 225 071 000; www.stcp.pt) runs wide-ranging bus service, including less extensive late-night bus service in the main Aliados and airport areas 12:30am-5:30am. Late-night service operates hourly. Most single-journey tickets cost €1.95.

Tram

Porto has gorgeous vintage 1920s wooden trams (tel. 225 071 000; www.stcp.pt) that rattle around the city. The three main tram lines are **Line 1,** along the riverfront area between Porto's historic area and the Passeio Alegre garden; **Line 18,** between Massarelos and Carmos; and **Line 22,** a circular route through downtown. Tickets (€3) can be bought on board. A 48-hour tram pass (adults €10, children €5) can also be bought on board as well as from most hotels and tour agencies. Trams come along every 20 minutes daily 8am-8pm.

Metro

Porto's Metro (tel. 225 081 000; www.metrodoporto.pt) is a light-rail network that runs above ground in the suburbs and underground in the city center. Trains run every 10-20 minutes daily 6am-midnight. Scenic **Line D** runs across the Douro River over a bridge to Gaia. Metro also runs to the **airport** in Maia. Trips are priced by zones and cost just over €1 for a two-zone single trip; cards are rechargeable.

Taxi

Local taxi companies include **Taxis Invicta** (Rua de Cunha Júnior 41B; tel. 225 076 400; www.taxisinvicta.com), **Taxis Porto** (Rua da Constituição 823; tel. 220 997 336; www.taxisporto.pt), and **Taxis do Porto** (Av. da Boavista 1002; tel. 223 206 059; www.taxisporto.pt). Getting a taxi is easy; taxi ranks can be found at the airport and bus and train stations, outside shopping centers and hospitals, near the riverside, and along the main Avenida dos Aliados. Taxis can also be hailed in the street.

The Douro Valley

Curvaceous landscapes unfold as the Douro (DOH-roo) River carves through rolling hills and forested mountains, extending over 200 kilometers (124 mi) from coastal Porto to the border with Spain. The breathtaking scenery around every bend changes with the seasons, from luxuriant greens in spring to gold and copper in autumn. Vine-clad terraces zigzag down hillsides in one of the world's oldest demarcated wine regions.

The river's banks are studded with towns and villages where farming is the way of life and historic ruins pepper the landscape. The renowned Alto Douro wine region is steeped in tradition, packed with restored historic villages and home to standout towns like Peso da Régua and Vila Nova de Foz Côa. Farther east still is the dramatic Côa Valley, with its prehistoric rock art.

PLANNING YOUR TIME

The best times to visit the Douro Valley are September, for the harvest, or any time in **autumn**, when the valley is ablaze with color. Main stops include fairy-tale **Amarante,** the valley's "capital" **Peso da Régua, Lamego** and its famous hilltop chapel, and the **Côa Valley Archaeological Park,** home of prehistoric rock art.

GETTING THERE

The most scenic ways to explore the Douro Valley are by boat or by train. Both depart regularly from Porto. The valley can be toured by car, but sharp bends and steep inclines mean that the designated driver will miss out on much of the scenery, not to mention wine-tastings.

Cruises

Splashing out on a peaceful cruise upstream is a memorable way to explore the gorgeous scenery of the Douro Valley. Nowadays a series of locks keeps the once-formidable river calm enough to navigate. Cruises departing from Porto, Vila Nova de Gaia, and Peso da Régua range from a day to a week. The daylong cruises from Porto (€60-125) range 10-18 hours and often involve one leg by train, either upriver or downriver. Longer cruises run April-October and frequently include excursions, meals, and entertainment.

Prices range from €200 for a two-day cruise to €2,000 for an eight-day cruise. The number of towns the boat stops at depends on the length of the cruise. Cruise operators include **Cruzeiros Douro** (tel. 226 191 090; www.cruzeiros-douro.pt) and **Douro Azul** (tel. 223 402 500; www.douroazul.com). Douro Azul's fleet of boats includes historic British river barge *Spirit of Chartwell.*

Train

The Douro Valley is one of Europe's best rail journeys. The national rail service, **CP** (tel. 707 210 220; www.cp.pt), operates the **Linha do Douro (Douro Line),** which connects Porto in the west to Pocinho in the east, hugging the river's edge through tunnels and past vineyards and picturesque towns. The full journey takes around 3.5 hours and costs €14 one-way. The Douro Line train runs several times a day, starting from Porto's São Bento or Campanhã stations, and less frequently on weekends and holidays.

The handsome 1925 **Douro Historic Steam Train** (tel. 707 210 220; www.cp.pt) runs from Peso da Régua and Tua on a one-day round-trip (3 hours, varying afternoons late May-Oct.; adults €42.50, children 4-12 €19). Tickets can be bought at CP ticket offices or online.

Car

Exploring the Douro Valley by car offers the freedom of impromptu pullovers at scenic viewpoints. Drive any of three **port wine routes** passing through the Baixa Corgo

The Douro Valley

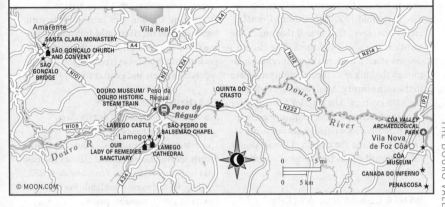

(below the Corgo River), Cima Corgo (above the Corgo), and Douro Superior (Upper Douro); see www.dourovalley.eu. The N222 road between Régua and Pinhão has been voted one of the best drives in the world and promises incredible scenery at every bend.

Wine Tours

A number of wine tours in the Douro Valley offer a range of organized excursions (day tours from €100) to wine- and port-producing farms, with pickups and drop-offs at hotels in Porto and Vila Nova de Gaia. They can even put together tailor-made packages with the estates of your choice, transport, and accommodations. For more information, see **EFun Tours** (tel. 220 945 375; www.efungpstours.com) or **Lab Portugal Tours** (tel. 916 119 101; www.labportugaltours.com).

AMARANTE

Thriving Amarante straddles a gentle bend on the Tâmega River (a tributary of the Douro, on its north bank), the town's storybook buildings reflected in the glassy river. The striking São Gonçalo Bridge unites the town, with the Serra do Marão mountain range rising magnificently in the background. Tall whitewashed buildings with balconies and wrought-iron grills flank the riverbank.

The town is named after a Roman centurion, Amarantus, while the bridge takes its name from the town's patron saint, who made a pilgrimage to Italy and Jerusalem and went on to cure the sick and pair lovers. A grand church and convent named for São Gonçalo, a main highlight of Amarante, is across the river.

Most of Amarante's sights are along the river and in the town center. The busy local **market** takes place every Wednesday and Saturday.

Sights
SÃO GONÇALO BRIDGE
(Ponte de São Gonçalo)

Over the glassy Tâmega River, the 18th-century São Gonçalo Bridge is simple and sturdy, named after the town's patron saint, a traveling Benedictine monk. Portuguese forces fended off an attack by the French here in 1809. Ornate pylons flank its extremities, its trio of arches framing the scenery beyond. At one side of the bridge is an image of Our Lady of Pity; at the other is an image of Christ crucified.

SÃO GONÇALO CHURCH AND CONVENT
(Igreja e Convento de São Gonçalo)

Praça da República; tel. 255 437 425; daily 8am-6pm; free

Small São Gonçalo Church has a handsome and complex tiered portico, a 17th-century organ case, and the tomb of São Gonçalo, who died in the mid-1200s. According to local legend, visitors will find love if they touch the saint's statue above the tomb. The church's origins stretch back to the 13th century, although the bulk of its construction took place in the 16th century. A bell tower was added in the 18th century. The interior is notable for its gilded Baroque altar, exquisite ceilings, and wood-clad sacristies adorned with sacred art. Behind the church, a lovely, peaceful courtyard boasts fabulous stonework clad with moss.

SANTA CLARA MONASTERY (Mosteiro de Santa Clara)

Largo de Santa Clara; tel. 255 420 236; Mon.-Sat. 10am-12:30pm and 2pm-6:30pm; free

Founded in the 13th century, sprawling Santa Clara Monastery was rebuilt and expanded in 1560, accommodating a large community of nuns for the next two centuries. In 1809 it was mostly destroyed in a fire, which tore through the village during the Napoleonic battles with Anglo-Portuguese troops; today just part of the original chapel and a gateway survive. During the late 20th century, archaeological digs uncovered the original outline of the monastery, with four distinct wings, a cloister, and a bell tower. The existing building is currently the municipal library and archive, and the original chapel has been repaired and restored.

Food

Amarante is famous for its **traditional cakes and sweets,** conceived by the nuns at the Santa Clara convent. Pastry recipes emerging from convents were common from the 15th century in Portugal. Conventual sweets *(doçaria conventual)* are based on sugar and egg yolk. Amarante specialties include almond *lérias* and eggy *foguetes.* Most cafés and cake shops in town sell them. Authentic savory dishes include oven-roasted goat *(cabrito serrano assado)* and Maronesa-bred beef.

CONFEITARIA DA PONTE

Rua 31 de Janeiro; tel. 255 432 034; www. confeitariadaponte.pt; daily 8:30am-8pm; €6

Occupying a prime spot in Amarante with lovely views of the river, cathedral, and bridge, the Confeitaria da Ponte is a charming café packed with local sweet treats, regional cakes, specialty pasties, and great coffee.

TASQUINHA DA PONTE

Rua 31 de Janeiro 193; tel. 255 433 715; daily noon-3pm and 7pm-11pm; €15

Unpretentious Tasquinha da Ponte is a rustic tavern serving home-cooked classics such as wild boar and bean stew *(feijoada de javali),* fried squid, and oven-roast lamb. Portions are hearty at very reasonable prices.

Getting There

From **Porto,** Amarante is a 45-minute drive, 60 kilometers (37 mi) east along the **A4** motorway, which has tolls. Trains no longer run to Amarante, but northern bus company **Rodonorte** (tel. 259 340 710; www.rodonorte. pt) runs a direct bus hourly between Porto's Hospital São João stop and Amarante (€7-11). The bus station in Amarante is on the south side of the river, a short 1.5-kilometer (0.9-mi), 20-minute stroll from the town center.

PESO DA RÉGUA

Surrounded by stepped terraces covered in lacy vines, Peso da Régua (PAY-zoo dah RAY-gwah), commonly abbreviated to just Régua, is at the center of wine country, equidistant between Porto and the Spanish border to the east. Régua is the largest town along the Douro River, so many cruises either stop here midway or finish here. Not as picturesque as nearby towns, hardworking Régua is important in the port wine trade as a crossroads for shipping. The riverfront lacks charm, but if you wander a few streets back, you'll find a quaint, authentic town.

1: Santa Clara Monastery **2:** Amarante **3:** Our Lady of Remedies Sanctuary **4:** Douro River cruise near Peso da Régua

Sights
DOURO HISTORIC STEAM TRAIN
tel. 707 210 220; www.cp.pt; one-day round-trip 3 hours, varying afternoons late May-Oct.; adults €42.50, children 4-12 €19

Take a trip back in time on the 1925 vintage Douro Historic Steam Train as it crosses rickety bridges, passes through atmospheric countryside and provincial villages, and stops in ornate old stations. It runs through one of the most scenic stretches along the Douro, between Peso da Régua and the town of Tua. Tickets can be bought at CP ticket offices or online. Trips include onboard entertainment courtesy of local folk singers as well as a glass of port wine.

DOURO MUSEUM
(Museum do Douro)
Rua Marquês de Pombal; tel. 254 310 190; www.museudodouro.pt; daily 10am-5:30pm; €7.50, includes a glass of port

To get a feel for local winemaking culture and history, spend an hour or so at the Douro Museum, where exhibits take you through the process, from growing and harvesting to fermenting and shipping. Short films, vintage photos, and even a *rabelo* boat add some interest. The building, 18th-century Casa da Companhia Velha, was once the headquarters of the Royal Company of Vine-Growers from the Alto Douro Region, the oldest company in Portugal.

Wineries and Wine-Tasting
QUINTA DO VALLADO
Vilarinho dos Freires; tel. 254 323 147; www.quintadovallado.com; daily 9am-7pm

Established in 1716, Quinta do Vallado is one of the oldest wine estates in the Douro Valley, producing reds, whites, rosés, and port wines. The historic estate comprises a manor house built in 1733, with a new wing built from locally sourced slate, and handsome grounds. Day visitors enjoy tours (1.5 hours, in English 11am and 2:45pm daily; €15) that include the working vineyards, state-of-the-art winery, and cellars, and end with a wine-tasting.

The on-site **restaurant** offers lovely views over the Douro River. The refurbished **hotel** (from €210) has 13 rooms, all equipped with modern conveniences like air-conditioning. The estate can organize activities such as walks, bicycle rides, boat trips, fishing, picnics, and wine-tastings. Quinta do Vallado is 3.5 kilometers (2 mi) north of Régua town center. It's about a 1-hour walk or a 5-minute ride in a taxi (€5).

QUINTA DO CRASTO
Gouvinhas; tel. 254 920 020; www.quintadocrasto.pt; Mon.-Fri. 9am-1pm and 2pm-6pm; from €20

Quinta do Crasto has roots stretching back to 1615. The vast estate comprises 135 hectares (334 acres)—74 hectares (183 acres) of which are vineyards—and produces 1.4 million bottles of wine and port per year. At its heart is a century-old farmhouse. Visits include guided tours (available in English, must be reserved in advance) with wine-tastings, which can also include lunch or dinner and boat trips on the Douro River. Guests are invited to enjoy a dip in Quinta do Crasto's famous infinity pool, designed by Portuguese architect Eduardo Souto de Moura, or just take in the stunning view over the valley from the poolside. Prebooking a visit is mandatory.

Quinta do Castro is 32 kilometers (20 mi) east of Régua, a 50-minute drive along the N313-2 road. It can also be reached by train from Régua to the Ferrão station (15 minutes, 5 trains daily 9:10am-7:10pm; €2.15). Ferrão train station is a 45-minute walk from Quinta do Castro, but the Quinta can pick up visitors.

Food
Its role as a crossroads makes Peso da Régua's regional gastronomy diverse. Typical dishes include onion soup with red beans, oven-roasted rice with kid and potatoes, and *feijoada á transmontana*, a robust, intense stew.

★ CACHO D'OIRO
Rua Branca Martinho 5050; tel. 254 321 455; www.restaurantecachodoiro.pt; daily noon-3pm and 7pm-10:30pm; €15

Hidden at the end of a small dead-end street, unpretentious Cacho D'Oiro is worth looking for. Its traditional menu is packed with local and regional specialties complemented by a vast selection of Douro wines.

TASCA DA QUINTA

Rua do Marquês de Pombal 42, ground floor; tel. 918 754 102; Tues.-Fri. 7pm-10pm, Sat. 12:30pm-2:30pm and 7pm-10pm, Sun. 12:30pm-2:30pm; €15

Behind the Douro Museum, gorgeous Tasca da Quinta serves authentic Portuguese tapas at just six tables. The crepes with homemade jams are a must. Make a reservation; it's hugely popular with both visitors and locals.

Getting There

Peso da Régua is an easy day trip from **Porto;** take a boat cruise to get there and travel back on the train, which runs along the river. Combined tickets are available via many Douro Valley Cruise organized excursion providers, such as **Cruzeiro Porto** (tel. 925 675 253; www.cruzeiroporto.com; from €60).

From **Porto** by car, Peso da Régua is 118 kilometers (73 mi) east, a 1.5-hour drive on the **A4** motorway, which has tolls. From **Amarante,** Régua is a 40-minute, 61-kilometer (38-mi) drive southeast on the **A24** and A4.

PESO DA RÉGUA TRAIN STATION

Largo da Estação

CP (tel. 707 210 220; www.cp.pt) runs trains every 2 hours from Porto's Campanhã station (2 hours; €7-14). Peso da Régua's train station is a 20-minute walk east of the town center.

PESO DA RÉGUA BUS STATION

Avenida da Galiza, 134

Rodonorte (tel. 259 340 710; www. rodonorte.pt) runs buses hourly from Porto's main terminal to Peso da Régua (2.5 hours; 7am, 8am, noon, and 2:30pm; €9.50), with a transfer in Vila Real in Trás-os-Montes. The bus and train stations in Régua are close to each other, on the riverside, about 20 minutes' walk east of the main town center.

LAMEGO

Between two hills, Lamego (lah-MEH-goo) sits primly on the banks of the Balsemão River, a small tributary of the Douro. It's drenched in Baroque and Renaissance influences, seen in the remnants of its 12th-century castle on a hill and in the fabulous Our Lady of Remedies Sanctuary. Lamego has long walks, both in and out of the city. Explore its Baroque landmarks, tangle of narrow streets, or the lofty terraces that crisscross the surrounding hills.

Home to Raposeira sparkling wine, Lamego flourished in the 18th century thanks to its production of port, but its origins predate the Roman era. It is also believed that the first Portuguese *cortes*—medieval assemblies of nobles, clergy, and commoners summoned by the king—were held here in 1143.

Sights

OUR LADY OF REMEDIES SANCTUARY

(Santuário Nossa Senhora dos Remedios)

Monte de Santo Estevão; tel. 254 614 392; daily 7:30am-6pm Oct.-Apr., daily 7:30am-8pm May-Sept.; free

Perched gracefully on a hill, this sanctuary is a triumph of Baroque architecture, flanked by a pair of elaborate bell towers and with a grandiose facade. Construction began circa 1750 but was completed two centuries later. Inside, an intricate gilded altar has a statue of Our Lady of Remedies at its heart. But outside is the most impressive part, with a monumental staircase zigzagging down the hillside to the town below. The various levels of the 686-step stone staircase include decorative fountains, tiled friezes, and sculptures as well as benches and picnic spots that take advantage of the views. September 6-8, faithful pilgrims climb the sanctuary's stairs to ask Our Lady for miracles. The three-day festival culminates in a procession on September 8. There is a road to drive up to the sanctuary if you don't want to climb the steps.

The Wines of the Douro Valley

The beating heart of Portuguese viticulture, the Douro Valley's deep valleys are flanked by steep terraced vineyards that step prettily down the hillsides toward the languid Douro River, which carves its way through the region. Covering close to 250,000 hectares (620,000 acres), the distinctive landscape is stunning, protected from the humid Atlantic winds by the mountainous topography. Winters can be bitterly cold, while summers are arid and hot, climactic extremes beneficial for grape-growing. The soil here is made up mostly of slate-like schist rock, rich in nutrients and an excellent humidity-retainer.

The region is a UNESCO World Heritage Site, and the 1-2 hour drive (depending on which town you visit) inland from Porto through the scenic and peaceful Douro Valley along the EN222 road is said to be one of the most beautiful in Portugal. Or, to get the best of the scenery, take the **train** or a **cruise** from Porto.

HISTORY

Wine production in the Douro Valley stretches back centuries. It was one of the first regions in the world to become a regulated, demarcated winemaking region. The Romans were among the earliest producers, and production flourished with the establishment of the Kingdom of Portugal in the 12th century. The signing of the Treaty of Windsor between Portugal and England in 1386 really consolidated its importance as a major and quality wine producer, boosting trade between the two countries.

GRAPES AND WINE VARIETALS

The Douro Valley is home to scores of different grapes, more than 80 indigenous varieties, chosen

LAMEGO CASTLE
(Castelo de Lamego)

Rua do Castelo; tel. 254 612 005; Tues.-Thurs. 10am-6pm; free

Standing high on the hill opposite the Our Lady of Remedies Sanctuary, the 12th-century Lamego Castle holds a tangle of quaint alleys and narrow streets within its walls. Its square 13th-century tower has thick stone walls. Little of the castle remains, but it's worth the hike for the views from the top.

LAMEGO CATHEDRAL
(Sé de Lamego)

Largo da Sé; tel. 254 612 766; daily 8am-1pm and 3pm-7pm; free

Built in the 12th century by Portugal's first king, Afonso Henriques, Lamego Cathedral is believed to be one of the oldest in Portugal, although little remains of the original building. Its longest-surviving original features are the Romanesque tower's windows with their dexterously carved capitals. The cathedral underwent major renovation in the 16th and 18th centuries, resulting in an unharmonious blend of frilly Gothic, Manueline, and Renaissance styles. A floor-to-ceiling blue-and-white 18th-century tile mural depicting the life of Saint Nicholas adds some interest to the interior, which—thanks to a large skylight—is bright and airy.

SÃO PEDRO DE BALSEMÃO CHAPEL
(Capela de São Pedro de Balsemão)

tel. 254 600 230; Tues.-Sun. 10am-1pm and 2pm-6pm; free

In the nearby hamlet of Sé, the tiny 7th-century São Pedro de Balsemão Chapel is believed to be the oldest Visigothic chapel in Portugal. Its well-preserved features include Corinthian columns, enigmatic symbols carved into the walls, a painted ceiling, and a statue of the pregnant Virgin Mary.

to suit the varying types of terrain and exposures. As a general rule, port wine grapes are thicker-skinned and hardier than other varieties, better suited to the valley's dry conditions. While the Douro's whites can be a lovely surprise, the region is best known for its reds, the most famous of which is, of course, port wine.

The most popular red grape varieties are the Touriga Nacional, Touriga Francesa, Tinta Roriz, Tinta Barroca, and Tinto Cão. These varieties are renowned for being intense and robust, often blended with other national and international varieties. Port grapes provide depth, a strong tannin structure, and rich, fruity, or floral aromas. Rabigato, Gouveio, Viosinho, and Malvasia Fina are the most common whites.

BEST WINERIES

The Douro Valley is full of renowned wine estates; many are also centers of gastronomy and architecture.

- **Quinta da Pacheca:** Located a few kilometers from Peso da Régua, this preeminent 18th-century manor wine estate overlooks the Douro River and was one of the first to bottle its own brand of wine (page 331).

- **Quinta do Crasto:** With idyllic vistas over the Douro River, family-run Quinta do Crasto is a centuries-old estate whose name sits alongside regional heavyweights and embodies the essence of Douro winemaking (page 328).

- **Quinta do Vallado:** Another of the best-known names in Douro wine production, Quinta do Vallado is a historic estate with a contemporary look and feel (page 328).

The chapel is 5 kilometers (3 mi) northeast of Lamego, a 14-minute drive along the N226 road, which involves navigating winding rural roads and narrow streets. Walking takes an hour, a scenic downhill stroll from Lamego, but a steep hike coming back. Lamego tourist office (Av. Visconde Guedes Teixeira; tel. 254 099 000; Mon.-Sat. 8am-6pm) can provide a map.

Wineries and Wine-Tasting
QUINTA DA PACHECA

Rua do Relógio do Sol 261; tel. 254 331 229; www.quintadapacheca.com; daily 10am-7pm

Prestigious Quinta da Pacheca is one of the Douro's finest wine estates, its origins stretching back to the 1730s. It was also one of the first to bottle wine under its own label. Spread over 140 hectares (346 acres) that step toward the river, it comprises a winery, a posh wine hotel, and quirky cabins in the shape of wine barrels. Eight granite winepresses *(lagares)*,

constructed in 1916, are still in use today. Guided tours (daily 10:30am-5:30pm; €9) include a wine-tasting.

Quinta da Pacheca is a 10-kilometer (6.2-mi), 20-minute drive north of Lamego on the N226-1 road. Alternatively, take a **Rodonorte** (tel. 259 340 710; www.rodonorte.pt) bus from Lamego to Peso da Régua (25 minutes, daily 12:45pm and 6:15pm; €5.90), then get a taxi (5 minutes; €6) from Régua to the estate. Quinta da Pacheca is a 50-minute walk south of Régua town center, across the river.

Entertainment and Events
DOURO GASTRONOMIC TOURISM FESTIVAL

tel. 254 609 600; www.cm-lamego.pt; late Oct.-early Dec.

Lamego hosts one of the Douro Valley's biggest annual events, the Douro Gastronomic Tourism Festival, which showcases the region's fabulous wines along with its rich and

☆ Côa Valley Archaeological Park

Nestled in a crook of the Douro River near the Spanish border, far-flung Vila Nova de Foz Côa (VEE-lah NOH-vah d' FOZH KOH-wah) became an archaeological hot spot in the 1990s with the discovery of thousands of mystifying rock engravings along the Côa Valley, depicting animals, hunters, weapons, and abstract images. The Côa Valley Archaeological Park was created to manage and protect the most important Paleolithic art collection in the world, with more than 60 sites in 17 kilometers (10.5 mi) of the valley. The earliest drawings in the Côa Valley are believed to date back more than 20,000 years.

HIGHLIGHTS

Guided **tours** (€15) are offered of the three main sites—**Canada do Inferno, Ribeira de Piscos/Fariseu,** and **Penascosa**—via all-terrain vehicles. Each stop includes a guided walk; Penascosa can also be toured in the evening. Reservations are required.

At the gateway to the park, on one of the slopes where the Douro and the Côa Rivers meet, the state-of-the-art **Côa Museum** (Museu do Côa, Rua do Museu, Parque Arqueológico do Vale do Côa; tel. 279 768 260 or 279 768 261; Tues.-Sun. 10am-1:30pm and 2pm-5:30pm; museum €6) offers more detailed insight into prehistoric artwork. Over four floors, exhibits explore the valley through multimedia, photography, and images of the engravings. Objects unearthed during excavations in the valley are also showcased. Inside the museum, **Aldeia Douro** is a classy modern restaurant and wine bar that brings together the regional cuisine and wines, along with some international dishes.

GETTING THERE

From **Porto,** Vila Nova de Foz Côa is a 2.5-hour, 198-kilometer (123-mi) drive east on the **A4** motorway, crossing almost all of northern Portugal. Vila Nova de Foz Côa is best explored as part of a Douro Valley trip.

---

varied cuisine. Around 20,000 people attend the 40-day event. Participating restaurants, hotels, and wineries offer special rates.

Food

Local specialties include wild rabbit, lamb or goat *chafana* stew, and *bolas de lamego* (buns stuffed with a savory filling like ham or tuna).

MERCADO MUNICIPAL

Av. 5 de Outubro; tel. 254 609 651; Mon.-Sat. 7:30am-6:45pm

To taste genuine local products, head to Mercado Municipal, where all sorts of food and drink are sold to go.

RESTAURANTE CASA FILIPE

Rua Virgílio Correia 58; tel. 254 612 428; Sat.-Thurs. 8:30am-9pm; €10

You'll find down-to-earth regional cooking at family-run Restaurante Casa Filipe, behind

Lamego Cathedral. Specialties include the local *bola de Lamego,* beans and tripe stew, and a typical Lamego tart for dessert.

RESTAURANTE VINDOURO

Rua Macário de Castro; tel. 961 422 784; www. restaurantevindouro.com; Tues.-Sun. noon-2:45pm and 7pm-10:45pm; €20

Located in the town center, stylish Restaurante Vindouro has a creative menu showcasing contemporary cuisine based on traditional recipes. Reservations are advised.

★ DOURO EXCELLENCE

Rua Macario de Castro Largo da Vitoria; tel. 969 686 787; www.facebook.com/Douro-Excellence-2091264167636023, Wed.-Thurs. noon-3pm, Fri. noon-3pm and 7pm-11pm, Sat. 7pm-11pm; €25

With Lamego cathedral in view, Douro Excellence is a wine and tapas restaurant showcasing fine and tasty local produce. Local cheeses, cured meats, honeys, and olives are all on the smorgasbord of delicious regional ingredients, accompanied by the Douro's renowned wines.

Accommodations
IMPÉRIO HOTEL
Rua José Vasques Osório 8; tel. 254 320 120; www.imperiohotel.com; €55

The two-star Império Hotel has 33 bright and basic rooms and serves a decent breakfast. It's a good no-frills base for exploring the region.

QUINTA DE CASALDRONHO HOTEL
Quinta de Casaldronho; tel. 254 318 331; www.quintadecasaldronho.com; €157

Located on a wine estate, luxurious four-star Quinta de Casaldronho Hotel has an avant-garde contemporary design, an à la carte restaurant, and an outdoor swimming pool. The scenery around the hotel is amazing.

★ QUINTA DA PACHECA WINE HOUSE HOTEL
Quinta da Pacheca, Cambres; tel. 254 331 229; www.quintadapacheca.com; €315

Four-star Quinta da Pacheca Wine House Hotel is a charming, atmospheric retreat in a restored 18th-century house surrounded by vineyards. Enjoy gourmet dining and river views. For a unique experience, stay in one of its wine barrel-shaped luxury cabins.

Getting There
Lamego is 130 kilometers (81 mi) east of **Porto.** By car, the most direct route is the **A4** motorway, which takes 1.5 hours but incurs tolls. Lamego is 16 kilometers (9.9 mi) south of **Régua,** a 20-minute drive on the A24 road.

The easiest and most scenic way to get to Lamego without a car is by taking the train from Porto to Peso da Régua, then catching a **Rodonorte** (tel. 259 340 710; www.rodonorte.pt) bus from Régua to Lamego (20 minutes, daily 10:25am and 4:25pm; €5.90), although this is a limited option with only two buses per day. The bus stop is in the city center, on Avenida Visconde Guedes Teixeira, between the castle and the church.

Minho

In the picturesque northwestern province of Minho (MEEN-yoo), the soil is rich, the rain abundant, and the vegetation luxuriant. Deep green blankets the valleys. Even Minho's most famous product—*vinho verde* (green wine), a young, fizzy white wine—is green in name if not in color. The coast is flanked by long sand dunes called the Costa Verde (Green Coast) and punctuated with captivating villages, an enticing mix of authentic fishing towns and lively seaside resorts.

Considered the birthplace of Portugal, Minho is home to ancient cities steeped in history, evident not only in the architecture and well-preserved landmarks but also in the customs that are part of daily life. Baroque Braga and historic Guimarães are two of the major cities in this part of Portugal; both have played significant roles in the country's history. Along the coast, Viana do Castelo, aka "the last town before Spain," is one of the region's most popular seaside resorts. With pristine natural beauty, rich gastronomy, and monuments steeped in history and folklore, Minho's trump card is Peneda-Gerês National Park, the only national park in Portugal, a veritable playground for fresh-air lovers.

BRAGA
Founded over 2,000 years ago by the Romans, who called it Bracara Augusta, Braga is the country's fourth-largest city and often referred to as the "capital" of Minho. It's also known as the "City of

Minho

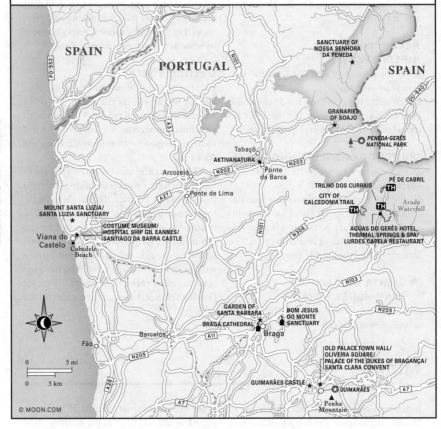

Archbishops," its religious standing reflected in its many churches, chapels, and monasteries and its vibrant celebration of Semana Santa, the Holy Week leading up to Easter. Braga is lively despite its age. Amid the Roman ruins, churches, and quaint lanes in the town center are trendy bars and restaurants. The student population at Minho University keeps the city fun and oriented toward the future.

Sights
BRAGA CATHEDRAL
(Sé de Braga)

Rua Dom Paio Mendes; tel. 253 263 317; www.

se-braga.pt; daily 9am-6:30pm Oct.-Mar., daily 9am-7pm Apr.-Sept.; cathedral €2, museum €3

The twin-towered Romanesque Braga Cathedral is the oldest in Portugal, dating to the 12th century. It was built by the first king of Portugal, Afonso Henriques, and houses the tombs of his parents, Henrique and Teresa. Inside are a beautiful altar, elaborate choir stalls, exquisite gilded woodwork, and tile murals. Spectacular painted ceilings depict Braga's history. The lower floor houses the main Manueline chapel, a cloister lined with Gothic side chapels, and two huge Baroque organs still in playing condition. Upstairs, a museum exhibits sacred art, including a statue of the breast-feeding Virgin Mary, and an iron cross used by Frei Henrique of Coimbra to celebrate the first mass in Brazil.

GARDEN OF SANTA BARBARA
(Jardim da Santa Barbara)

Rua Dr. Justino Cruz; tel. 253 262 550; open 24/7; free

The manicured municipal Garden of Santa Barbara, with its box-hedged borders and bright flower beds, is a lovely place for a peaceful stroll. Sandwiched between modern city buildings on one side and the medieval Archbishop's Palace on the other, it represents the harmonious balance struck by Braga's two halves.

BOM JESUS DO MONTE SANCTUARY
(Monte do Bom Jesus)

Estrada do Bom Jesus; tel. 253 676 636; www. bomjesus.pt, daily 8am-7pm June-Sept., daily 9am-6pm Oct.-May; free

Five kilometers (3 mi) northeast of the city center is the stunning Bom Jesus do Monte Sanctuary. The first stone of the neoclassical basilica was laid in 1784 atop the magnificent Baroque staircase known as the Sacred Way. Flanked by dense forest and lined with little chapels, the chalk-white staircase climbs 116 meters (381 ft) with 600 steps. Made from granite, it is divided into sections devoted to the five senses and the three virtues, represented by fountains and statues, with a different surprise at each landing. At the top, you're rewarded with a lovely garden laced with streams and a magical hidden grotto, as well as vertiginous views. A funicular train (€1.20 one-way, €2 round-trip), inaugurated in 1882, makes a quicker—albeit less eventful—ascent.

A bus marked "Bom Jesus" (€2) leaves every 20 minutes from Braga's train station and the central bus station. Buy tickets from the driver. Bom Jesus is the last stop, and the bus stops at the bottom of the staircase.

Entertainment and Events
HOLY WEEK
(Semana Santa)

www.semanasantabraga.com; Mar. or Apr.

In March or April, starting the Friday before Palm Sunday and ending Easter Sunday, Braga's Holy Week attracts as many as 100,000 people, who flock to the city to participate in colorful, energetic celebrations whose origins date to the 4th century. The city is bedecked with flowers and lanterns, its streets flooded with processions. A highlight is the

Braga Cathedral

Holy Thursday parade of the *farricocos:* barefoot men dressed in hooded purple tunics and carrying torches, reminiscent of the reconciliation of public penitents that took place until the 15th century.

BRAGA ROMANA FESTIVAL

bragaromana.cm-braga.pt; late May-early June

Once a year, over five days in late May-early June, Braga transforms into a living reenactment of the Roman Empire in Braga Romana, as the city celebrates its origins. Visitors can sample Roman delicacies and drinks, learn ancient dances and games, and browse handicrafts.

Food

★ CAFÉ A BRASILEIRA

Largo Barão de São Martinho 17; tel. 253 262 104; daily 8am-midnight; €5

Don't leave Braga without having a coffee and a cake at Café A Brasileira, on a corner of the main Barão de São Martinho square. A striking *azulejo* tile facade fronts this busy hive of activity, established in 1907.

RESTAURANT ANJO VERDE

Largo da Praça Velha 21; tel. 253 264 010; Mon.-Sat. noon-3pm and 7:30pm-10:30pm; €10

At Restaurant Anjo Verde, the keywords are innovation and variety. This excellent vegetarian and vegan restaurant is located in a small square next to a pillar of the Porta Nova archway, the gateway to the city. It also hosts art exhibitions and monthly classical concerts.

VELHOS TEMPOS TAVERN

Rua do Carmo 7; tel. 253 214 368; Mon.-Fri. 10am-8pm, Sat. 10am-11pm, Sun. 10am-2pm; €15

A warren of rooms and staircases, Velhos Tempos Tavern feels like a step back to a bygone era. The food is old-fashioned home-cooked Portuguese fare like *rojões* (chunks of pork loin), served in heaping portions. Don't miss the *alheira* sausage starter or the *abade de priscos* pudding dessert, made with bacon and port.

RESTAURANTE CENTURIUM

Av. Central 134; tel. 253 206 260; www.centurium. bracaraaugusta.com; Mon.-Sat. 12:30pm-3pm and 7:30pm-10pm; €20

In a historic 19th-century building, elegant Restaurante Centurium centers its menu on the finest seasonal produce. Octopus carpaccio, creamy codfish, and slices of grilled black pork are on the menu. Charming features include a classy bar and a private garden.

Accommodations

IBIS BUDGET BRAGA CENTRO

Av. da Liberdade 96; tel. 253 614 500; www. accorhotels.com; €37

Clean and comfortable Ibis Budget Braga Centro is a good budget option a short distance from Braga's main sights.

★ HOTEL DO LAGO

Largo do Santuário do Bom Jesus; tel. 253 603 020; www.hoteisbomjesus.pt; €79

With 53 modern rooms, three-star Hotel do Lago boasts stunning views of the beautiful Serra do Gerês mountains.

★ HOTEL DO PARQUE

Bom Jesus do Monte; tel. 253 603 470; www. hoteisbomjesus.pt; €100

Nestled amid romantic gardens, Hotel do Parque is in a restored 19th-century mansion. Features include a spa and a piano bar, and rooms are equipped with modern amenities.

Information and Services

- **PSP police station:** Rua dos Falcões; tel. 253 200 420; www.psp.pt
- **Braga Hospital:** Rua das Sete Fontes; tel. 253 027 000; www.hospitaldebraga.pt
- **Tourism office:** Av. da Liberdade 1; tel. 253 262 550; www.cm-braga.pt; Mon.-Fri. 9am-6:30pm, Sat.-Sun. 9:30am-1pm and 2pm-5:30pm
- **Post office (nearest to center):** Rua do Raio; tel. 253 200 361; www.ctt.pt

Highlights of Trás-os-Montes

The name Trás-os-Montes (TRAZH-oosh-MON-tesh) translates as "Behind the Mountains," an indication of this region's hidden splendor. Steeped in history, the Trás-os-Montes highlands have sweeping flowered plateaus and majestic mountains as well as historic villages. Age-old traditions thrive in this well-preserved alcove, still relatively off the tourist track, giving visitors a sense of the Portugal of old.

CHAVES

On the banks of the Tâmega River, Chaves (SHAH-vezh) is a far-flung fortified settlement whose name, Portuguese for "keys," reflects its strategic position along the Spanish border. Nestled in a fertile valley, Chaves started as a Roman military outpost known as Aquae Flaviae.

Wandering the streets, you'll see antiquated buildings with colored doors and wrought-iron balconies draped in fresh flowers. Visit the excellently preserved **Roman Bridge,** a city landmark also known as Trajan's Bridge, where construction began during the reign of Emperor Vespasian circa AD 78 and was concluded during Trajan's reign in 104. The heart of the medieval center is **Camões Square (Praça de Camões),** with a statue of the Duke of Bragança. This ancient neighborhood contains churches, temples, and monumental old buildings which enhance the medieval ambience.

Finally, have a hot soak in restorative **Chaves Hot Springs** (Termas de Chaves, Alameda do Tabolado; tel. 276 332 445; www.termasdechaves.com, Mon.-Sat. 9am-7pm, Sun. 9am-1pm; from €4), which bubble up at a lovely 73°C (163°F) year-round. The hot springs has both medical therapies and indulgent massage and spa services.

In Chaves, you can sample authentic regional Transmontana cuisine. It's famous for delights such as cured ham and minced meat-stuffed pasties, *folar* (sweet dough stuffed with sausage), meaty stews, and stuffed trout. To try it, head to **Pensão Flávia Flávia** (Travessa Cândido dos Reis 12; tel. 961 693 890; Wed.-Mon. 12:30pm-2:30pm and 7:30pm-10:30pm; €15), housed in a traditional guesthouse. The restaurant has no menu; ask the waitstaff for recommendations, sit back, and enjoy tasty tapas-size local cuisine.

Chaves is about 160 kilometers (99 mi) northeast of **Porto,** 1.75 hours via the **A7** motorway.

BRAGANÇA

Time appears to stand still in remote Bragança (brah-GAN-ssah), on the doorstep of untamed Montesinho Natural Park (Parque Natural de Montesinho, Forest Park; tel. 273 329 135; www. montesinho.com), with a long fortified medieval wall that embraces the city and its ancient citadel. Beyond the city center, modern museums and new buildings adjoin quaint whitewashed town houses and medieval monuments, surrounded by the plains that stretch as far as the eye can see. Keep an eye out for the granite pig statues, symbols of power or fertility, depending on which folktale you prefer.

The town's main **Sé Square** has a distinctive cross in the middle and a church to one side. Bragança's stocky **castle** is a well-preserved relic of Portugal's turbulent past, its 13th-century citadel protected by a 2-meter-thick (6.6-ft-thick) fortified wall. This stronghold was key to maintaining the region's sovereignty from Spain and stands intact today.

Rustic and unfussy, Bragança's gastronomy features locally raised meat and seasonal vegetables, simply cooked in the oven or on open fires. Chestnut honey is a local specialty.

Bragança is 208 kilometers (129 mi) northeast of **Porto,** 2.5 hours on the **A3** motorway (tolls apply).

Getting There

Braga is 55 kilometers (34 mi) north of **Porto,** 45 minutes on the **A3** motorway.

BRAGA BUS STATION

Av. General Norton de Matos

The **Getbus** (tel. 253 262 371; www.getbus. eu) airport shuttle bus operates a dozen direct buses (50 minutes, daily 4am-12:45am; €8) between Porto Airport and Braga's main bus station, with fewer services on weekends and holidays. The bus terminal is close to the center, walking distance to sights such as the cathedral.

Long-distance bus company **Rede Expressos** (tel. 707 223 344; www.rede-expressos.pt) also operates regular buses between Porto's Campo 24 Agosto bus station and Braga (1 hour, hourly daily 10am-11pm; €6). There are also a couple of late-night buses daily at 1am and 4am.

BRAGA TRAIN STATION

Largo da Estação

From Porto's Campanhã station, there are frequent **CP** (tel. 707 210 220; www.cp.pt; 1 hour, hourly daily 6am-1am; €3.20-16.25) trains to Braga, with trains running more frequently at peak times. Faster direct services (the high-speed Alfa Pendular train), with two stops en route, take just 40 minutes and are more expensive than the regular Urbano trains.

The train station is on the western fringe of the center. Taxis and local buses (www.tub. pt) can be found outside the train station and main bus terminal.

Getting Around

Braga's main historic center is easily covered on foot, but transport is required to get to the Bom Jesus do Monte Sanctuary. Braga's local **bus routes** (www.tub.pt) are comprehensive and easy to navigate. A 24-hour tourist ticket to ride all buses costs €3.35 and can be purchased on board.

★ PENEDA-GERÊS NATIONAL PARK

(Parque Nacional da Peneda-Gerês)

www2.icnf.pt/portal/ap/pnpg, www.natural.pt

In the far north of Portugal, hugging a C-shaped swath of the Portuguese-Spanish border, the rambling and resplendent Peneda-Gerês National Park, known more commonly to locals as simply "the Gerês," hides stony spa villages, medieval castles, megalithic monuments, and Roman roads amid rugged mountainous terrain. A vast natural amphitheater shaped by wind and water, the Peneda-Gerês, Portugal's only national park, covers over 70,000 hectares (270 sq mi), sprawled across four mountain ranges—Peneda, Soajo, Amarela, and Gerês. It is, in a word, huge, with hundreds of charming little hamlets and villages within it. The dramatic, unspoiled landscape ranges from dense forest to bald hilltops, deep ravines, natural pools, streams, and waterfalls, and the park is home to roe deer, Iberian wolves, wild Garrano ponies, Barrosã cattle, boars, badgers, otters, and Castro Laboreiro cattle dogs.

The park's main points of interest include the quirky collection of *espigueiros* (stone granaries on stilts) in the village of Lindoso; the **Geira Roman Road,** which once connected Braga to Astorga in Spain; the **Arado Waterfall and bridge,** near Gerês village; and the **Pitões das Júnias** stone village, with the remnants of a 9th-century Benedictine monastery, about 12 kilometers (7.4 mi) northwest of the Montalegre entrance.

Exploring the park is difficult without an organized tour or your own vehicle. A good option is to travel to Braga and sign up for an organized excursion to the park with a company that includes hotel transfers.

Orientation

There are five main gateways to the park; each has an information office as well as services such as bathrooms. Among the main sights within the park are the **Sanctuary of**

Nossa Senhora da Peneda and the Vale da Peneda viewpoint (in the northern part of the park, most easily reached via the Lamas de Mouro or Mezio Gates), the Granaries of Soajo (Mezio Gate), and the Arado Waterfall (Campo de Gerês Gate). The impressive Pé de Cabril mountain, a popular hiking site, is situated near the Campo do Gerês Gate. There are lots of scenic and rewarding hikes to be enjoyed here, and there is a decent road infrastructure lining the villages within the park, so most of the main sights and attractions are reachable by car. But be warned, though, some of the roads can be pretty winding and narrow.

Entrances

There are five main entrances to the park:

- **Lamas de Mouro Gate** (Melgaço municipality), at the northern tip of the park.

- **Mezio Gate** (Arcos de Valdevez municipality), on the western flank of the park.

- **Lindoso Gate** (Ponte da Barca municipality), on the western flank of the park.

- **Campo do Gerês Gate** (Terras de Bouro municipality), about 6.6 kilometers (4.1 mi) west of Gerês village, the closest entrance to Braga, the best base for exploring the park.

- **Montalegre Gate** (Montalegre municipality), at the eastern tip of the park.

Each entrance has a visitors office with guidance on the terrain and activities in that area. There is also an **education and activities center** (Lugar do Vidoeiro 99; tel. 253 390 110; Mon.-Fri. 9am-12:30pm and 2pm-5:30pm; free) near the Vidoeiro Gate, 15 kilometers (9.3 mi) southeast of Montalegre.

Tours

Peneda-Gerês is prime terrain for adventure activities such as canyoneering, kayaking, and hiking. Guided tours and self-guided signposted routes are available throughout the park. Contact the **park's head office** (Av. António Macedo; tel. 253 203 480) in Braga.

- **Keen Tours:** tel. 938 690 513; www. keentours.com

- **Tobogã Canyoning Tours:** Rua dos Prados 21, ground floor; tel. 915 707 938; www.portal.toboga.pt

- **AktivaNatura:** Largo de São João 13; tel. 916 336 628; www.aktivanatura.com

Sights

SANCTUARY OF NOSSA SENHORA DA PENEDA (Santuario de Nossa Senhora da Peneda)

EN202215, Lugar de Peneda, Gavieira parish, Arcos de Valdevez; www.arcostour.net/peneda; open 24/7; free

A catholic sanctuary dedicated to the Virgin Mary, the Sanctuary of Nossa Senhora da Peneda is located in Lugar da Peneda, Gavieira parish, a 1-hour drive from Arcos de Valdevez. It is set in a dramatic and remote location, high in a mountain valley in the northern part of the Peneda-Gerês park with a big rocky peak towering dramatically over it. Symmetric staircases plait their way up to the main sanctuary building, with its twin bell towers and pretty gardens. Every year in early September, pilgrims make their way to the sanctuary, where a huge street party is held.

VALE DA PENEDA VIEWPOINT (Miradouro do Vale da Peneda)

Arcos de Valdevez, EM503 road between Tibo and Soajo parishes; open 24/7; free

Close to Peneda and the village of Soajo, the Vale da Peneda viewpoint (a 20-minute drive north of Soajo) boasts some of the most breathtaking views of the park, over forest-covered mountain peaks, valley villages, the river separating Portugal from Spain, and the Sanctuary of Nossa Senhora da Peneda. Access the viewpoint by turning off the main road from Gerês (the N-308-1, it's signposted) in the north part of town.

GRANARIES OF SOAJO (Espigueiros do Soajo)

www.arcostour.net/espigueirosdesoajo

Set in the striking landscape of Peneda-Gerês National Park, in the quaint hamlet of Soajo, this unique, historic attraction draws visitors for its cluster of little buildings on stilts. A short drive from the Mezio Gate, these traditional granite granaries were used for storing crops and are raised from the ground to protect the cereals from rats and rodents. The communal *espigueiros,* the oldest of which date back to 1782, have become a unique attraction in the Peneda-Gerês.

ARADO WATERFALL (Cascata do Arado)

open 24/7

In the southern foot of the Peneda-Gerês, close to the Campo do Gerês Gate near Terras do Bouro, the cascading Arado Waterfall is nestled amid tranquil forest and surrounded by a scenic swimming hole. An idyllic beauty spot with a little river and bridge running through it, it's reached via a 20-minute hike along a dirt path and down Roman steps, from a parking lot at the end of a paved road.

Hiking

Peneda-Gerês National Park is crossed by dozens of hiking trails, ranging from easy and short to long, challenging hikes. All of the park's information centers provide information on routes and maps. In addition to marked, maintained trails, there are also unmarked trails, such as old shepherds' pathways. Visit http://adere-pg.pt/trilhos for more information.

TBR PR3 - TRILHO DOS CURRAIS

Hiking Distance: *10-kilometer (6-mi) loop*
Hiking Time: *4-5 hours round-trip*
Trailhead: *Vidoeiro parish*
Information and Maps: *www.walkingportugal. com/z_distritos_portugal/Braga/Terras_do_Bouro/ TBR_PR3_Trilho_dos_Currais.html*

This fairly easy loop through pine forests and rocky countryside shows the boulder-strewn mountainous terrain in all its splendor. Sweeping views of the rugged landscape can be enjoyed as you walk through traditional

communities of farmers and their flocks, massive granite rock formations, wild horses, and the odd farmhouse built into the hillside. There are some steep climbs involved in this walk. This trail is the easiest to access without a car from Gerês.

TBR PR1 - CITY OF CALCEDONIA TRAIL

Hiking Distance: *7-kilometer (4-mi) loop*
Hiking Time: *4 hours round-trip*
Trailhead: *Lugar do Calvário, Covide village*
Information and Maps: *www.walkingportugal. com/z_distritos_portugal/Braga/Terras_do_Bouro/ TBR_PR1_Trilho_da_Cidade_da_Calcedonia.html*

One of the Peneda-Gerês's most challenging and emblematic hikes, the City of Calcedonia trail takes walkers through traditional communities and ancient geological spots in the rural Covide valley. The loop explores areas where the earliest inhabitants are believed to date back to the Iron Age, and you'll see Roman roads and unusual rock formations.

PÉ DE CABRIL

Hiking Distance: *12-kilometer (7-mi) loop*
Hiking Time: *5 hours round-trip*
Trailhead: *Near old forest ranger's house, Junceda, Portela de Leonte parish*
Information and Maps: *http://adere-pg.pt/ trilhos/percursos2.php*

This engaging hike explorers the imposing Pé de Cabril mountain, located in the municipality of Terras do Bouro. This mound of rock is one of the most recognizable and characteristic sights of Peneda-Gerês National Park, protruding above the other mountaintops. Standing at 1,236 meters (4,055 ft) high, the 360-degree views from the summit are unforgettable.

Food and Accommodations

There are plenty of little hotels, guesthouses, and restaurants sprinkled thorough

---

1: Sanctuary of Nossa Senhora da Peneda **2:** cows on the road in the Peneda-Gerês National Park **3:** Arado Waterfall **4:** Palace of the Dukes of Bragança in Guimarães

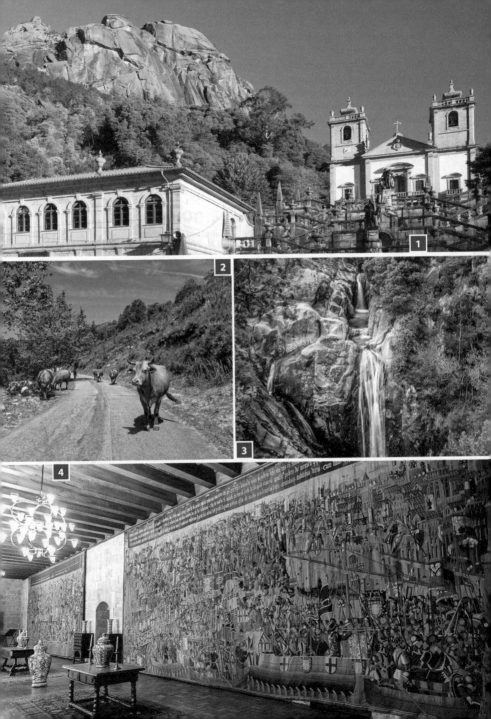

Peneda-Gerês National Park, as well as campsites, though they are mainly located in the areas surrounding the main gates and bigger villages. Much of the accommodations are converted from historic stone-built houses and have a charming rustic feel, and some have their own restaurants. For private lodging, see **Gerês Holidays** (tel. 253 352 803; www.gerescasas.com) for a range of chalets and cottages in Peneda-Gerês.

LURDES CAPELA RESTAURANT
Av. Manuel Gomes de Almeida 77; tel. 253 391 208; Mon.-Sat. 11:30am-2:45pm and 6:30pm-9:45pm, Sun. 11:30am-3pm; €10

The Lurdes Capela restaurant, in the heart of Gerês village, is one of the best in the region, serving local fare such as wild boar and slow-cooked kid. A simple, countrified restaurant that might look either dated or charmingly antiquated, it has been handed down in the family for generations.

AGÚAS DO GERÊS HOTEL, THERMAL SPRINGS & SPA
Av. Manuel Francisco da Costa 136; tel. 253 390 190; www.aguasdogeres.pt; €86

For travelers with a car, there is no shortage of quality local hotels, cozy inns, and family-run farmhouses in Peneda-Gerês. Agúas do Gerês Hotel, Thermal Springs & Spa is a grand 54-room, three-star hotel in the picturesque village of Gerês, near one of the park's main entrances.

Information and Services
HEAD OFFICE
Avenida António Macedo, Braga; tel. 253 203 480; Mon.-Fri. 9am-12:30pm and 2pm-5:30pm

In addition to the information centers at every park entrance, the park's main headquarters are located in Braga.

Getting There and Around
The best way to get to the Peneda-Gerês National Park is by car from **Braga,** a 40-minute drive. Roads inside the park are good. Follow the **A3** motorway from Porto to Braga, then the **N103** road from Braga to the park's nearest border.

By public transport, take the bus or train to Braga, the best base for exploring the park; from Braga, local **Empresa Hoteleira do Gerês** (www.ehgeres.com) or **Transdev** (www.transdev.pt) buses run to the closest main entrance, the Campo do Gerês Gate in Gerês village, also referred to as Caldas do Gerês. The buses (1.5 hours; €6) run every few hours weekdays 7am-7pm, but on Saturday-Sunday there are only about four buses.

★ GUIMARÃES
Guimarães (gee-mah-RAYNZH) is often referred to as the "Cradle of Portugal," where the first king, Afonso Henriques, was born in the early 12th century. Guimarães was the first capital of the new kingdom. The city's well-preserved historic features are its main allure. Wander the narrow streets of the quaint UNESCO-listed historic center and head north to Largo Hill (Monte do Largo) to see the castle and the palace.

Wandering Guimarães's excellently preserved buildings, whose styles span several centuries, is a trip back in time. The city's past is showcased in the evolution of techniques, materials, and tastes. The center covers 16 hectares (39.5 acres) with 14th- and 15th-century fortress styles giving way to Renaissance and neoclassical buildings and colorful bourgeois homes. A labyrinth of medieval backstreets frames the main **Oliveira Square** and its 14th-century freestanding arch. The **Old Palace Town Hall** is a 16th-century Manueline building with a ribbed-arch gallery. The 16th-century **Santa Clara Convent** today houses the city council.

Sights
GUIMARÃES CASTLE
(Castelo de Guimarães)
Rua Conde Dom Henrique; tel. 253 412 273; www. cm-guimaraes.pt; daily 10am-6pm; €2

Ten minutes' walk north of the center, the town's 10th-century castle is said to be the birthplace of Afonso Henriques, first king of

Portugal, in 1112. Guimarães Castle towers above the city atop a granite hill, Monte Latito, with forested gardens and pedestrian trails around it. It was built in late Romanesque style with Gothic touches, its walls forming a pentagram that contains eight towers, a square, and a central keep, added in the 13th century. Inside, visitors can trek around the castle walls, visit the Chapel of São Miguel, and take in sweeping views of the city.

PALACE OF THE DUKES OF BRAGANÇA (Paço dos Duques de Bragança)

Rua Conde Dom Henrique; tel. 253 412 273; http://pduques.culturanorte.pt; daily 10am-6pm; palace €5, with castle €6

Amid the forested gardens of Monte Latito, a stone's throw from Guimarães Castle, the sprawling medieval Palace of the Dukes of Bragança is a fine example of austere late-medieval construction. The rectangular building is laid out around a central courtyard. Inside, explore multiple rooms featuring ancient furniture, tapestries, and weapons. A stunning chapel has a soaring ceiling, a huge chandelier, and a beautiful stained-glass window. There's also an impressive bronze statue of King Afonso, created in 1874 by renowned Portuguese sculptor Soares dos Reis.

PENHA MOUNTAIN (Montanha da Penha)

Montanha da Penha; tel. 253 414 114; www.penhaguimaraes.com

Penha Mountain, also known as Monte da Santa Catarina, 6.5 kilometers (4 mi) south of the city center and rising to 586 meters (1,923 ft), is the highest point in Guimarães. It includes enchanting green woodlands, a network of caves, and many magnificent viewpoints. The mountain also offers a diverse range of activities, includes hiking, camping, horseback riding, and miniature golf. There are picnic areas, restaurants, bars, and coffee shops. A scenic **cable car** (Rua Aristides de Sousa Mendes; tel. 253 515 085; www.turipenha.pt; daily 10am-8pm June-Sept.,

daily 10am-6:30pm Apr.-May and Oct., daily 10am-5:30pm Nov.-Mar.; €5 round-trip) takes around 10 minutes.

Food

The nuns of the local Santa Clara Convent had a huge influence on local cuisine, as evidenced by the number of traditional *conventual* sweets like *tortas de Guimarães* (a glazed croissant-like pie stuffed with a sweet concoction of squash, egg, and almond) and *touchino do céu* (a cake made with lard). Another staple is the meat cake, pizza-like dough topped with pork, sardines, and other unusual ingredients.

CANTINHO DOS SABORES

Rua Francisco Agra 33; tel. 253 095 645; Mon.-Sat. 10am-10pm; set menu €5-8

Simple little Cantinho dos Sabores serves fantastic regional food at low prices. Simple grilled meats, stuffed codfish, codfish with bread, and grilled octopus are all on the limited but well-considered menu.

TABERNA TROVADOR

Largo do Trovador 10; tel. 913 205 263; Wed.-Mon. noon-3pm and 7pm-late; €10

Charming Taberna Trovador matches tasty tapas made from fresh local products with an extensive wine list. Tongues in spicy sauce, chicken gizzards, and fish salad are some of the intriguing dishes.

MANJAR DOS DOCES

Rua do Salgueiral, Edificio Principe Real Loja A; tel. 253 528 298; Tues.-Sun. 8am-10pm; €5

Posh *pastelaria* Manjar dos Doces offers a huge range of traditional sweets and cakes, along with a selection of sandwiches on fresh-made bread.

Getting There

Guimarães is 55 kilometers (34 mi) northeast of **Porto** (45 minutes on the **A3** and **A7** motorways, with tolls) and 25 kilometers (15.5 mi) southeast of **Braga** (25 minutes on the **A11** motorway).

GUIMARÃES BUS TERMINAL

Alameda Doutor Mariano Felgueiras

The **Getbus** (tel. 253 262 371; www.getbus.eu) airport shuttle bus runs a dozen direct buses (50 minutes, daily 4am-12:45am, fewer on weekends and holidays; €8) between Porto's Sá Carneiro Airport and Guimarães's main bus terminal, a 20-minute walk west of the city center.

Rede Expressos (tel. 707 223 344; www. rede-expressos.pt) operates four buses (25 minutes, 1 bus at 9am, 3 buses in the afternoon; €6) daily between Braga and Guimarães. **Rodonorte** (tel. 259 340 710; www.rodonorte.pt) also runs buses (25 minutes; €5.90) between Braga and Guimarães, five times a day.

GUIMARÃES TRAIN STATION

Avenida Dom João IV

Direct **CP** (tel. 707 210 220; www.cp.pt) trains run almost hourly between Porto's main Campanhã station and Guimarães, with slower Urbano service (1.25 hours; €3.20 round-trip) and the direct high-speed Alfa Pendular train (53 minutes; €14.50), which makes just two stops. CP trains also run hourly between Braga and Guimarães (1-3 hours; €3.50-17.15). The train station is south of the city center.

VIANA DO CASTELO

Sprawling across the River Lima, Viana do Castelo (vee-AH-nah doo kash-TEH-loo) is a medieval city with beautiful seaside suburbs. In the historic city center, old buildings line tree-shaded avenues and quaint backstreets. The plethora of architectural styles show the city's history and evolution: Romanesque, Manueline, Renaissance, Baroque, and art deco blend with modern structures.

Water is the backbone of the city's history; on the docks of the Lima's mouth, the *Gil Eannes* ship museum covers maritime heritage from the Age of Discoveries to the

---

1: Guimarães Castle **2:** Santa Luzia Sanctuary at Viana do Castelo

modern cod-fishing industry. Local beaches make water the focus of recreation, including surfing and kitesurfing.

Sights
COSTUME MUSEUM
(Museu do Traje)

Praça da República; tel. 258 809 306; www. cm-viana-castelo.pt; Tues.-Sun. 10am-1pm and 3pm-6pm, open until 7pm June and Sept.; €2

Located on the main Praça da República square in the city's historic center, the Costume Museum hosts a splendid array of traditional regional and local costumes. Housed in a mid-20th-century bank building and spread over three floors, it displays colorful outfits that range from working clothes to wedding garments, many exquisitely embellished and embroidered, all carefully preserved. Among the outfits on display are traditional costumes worn during local festivals.

HOSPITAL SHIP *GIL EANNES*
(Navio *Gil Eannes*)

Doca Comercial; tel. 258 809 710; www. fundacaogileannes.pt; daily 9:30am-8pm; €4

Moored on the commercial docks is the Hospital Ship *Gil Eannes,* a restored mid-20th-century vessel built in local shipyards. The *Gil Eannes* was a state-of-the-art floating medical facility at the time of its launch in 1955. This pride of Portugal's White Fleet assisted cod-fishing vessels in the seas of Newfoundland and Greenland. Now permanently moored, it's a museum and occasional youth hostel. Wander the decks, explore the compartments, and view the original equipment, such as the operating theater and X-ray machine.

SANTIAGO DA BARRA CASTLE
(Forte de Santiago da Barra)

Campo de Castelo; tel. 258 820 270; Mon.-Fri. 9am-5pm; free

On the edge of the Lima River's mouth, peering over the sea, Santiago da Barra Castle is likely the first castle built along the Lima.

Fortification may have existed on this site as long ago as the 13th century; this building was completed under King Manuel I in the 16th century and enlarged a century later to protect the prospering city against pirate attacks. Cross the drawbridge over a moat to wander the castle walls and admire its distinctive Manueline-style Roqueta Tower. A busy Friday market takes place outside its walls.

SANTA LUZIA SANCTUARY (Santuário de Santa Luzia)

Monte de Santa Luzia; tel. 258 823 173 or 961 660 300; www.templosantaluzia.org; daily 8am-7pm Apr.-Sept., daily 8am-5pm Oct.-Mar.; free

Few churches are as dramatic as the Santa Luzia Sanctuary, also known as Templo do Sagrado Coração de Jesus (Temple of the Sacred Heart of Jesus). This 20th-century Byzantine Revival building is gracefully poised on top of **Mount Santa Luzia,** 228 meters (748 ft) above the estuary in the suburb of Santa Maria Maior. It can be reached from the city on the country's longest **funicular tram** (€2 one-way, €3 round-trip), which departs every 15 minutes from the local train station. The panoramic views of the coastline are worth the 7-minute journey. Once inside Santa Luzia, visitors can ascend to the domed roof by lift (€0.80), then walk up a narrow stairway to enjoy still more impressive views. The church can also be reached by car or taxi, 3.5 kilometers (2.2 mi) from the center, or a steep 2-kilometer (1.2-mi) hike that is only for the fit. Mass (weekdays 4pm, Sun. 11am and 4pm) is held here.

The hill behind the sanctuary, with eucalyptus trees, is peppered with stony ruins, thought to be a **fortified Celtiberian settlement** from the 4th century BC.

Food

Viana do Castelo's local cuisine is about fish, particularly *bacalhau* (cod). For dessert, try a **Viana Half Moon,** a sweet pastry stuffed with cassava paste, ground almonds, egg yolks, and sugar, and dusted with icing sugar.

O LARANJEIRA

Rua Manuel Espregueira 24; tel. 258 822 258; www. olaranjeira.com; daily 9:30am-11pm; €15

Located in the city center, poised and polished O Laranjeira is a charismatic restaurant and guesthouse that first opened in the 1940s. The funky flowered wallpaper is just one talking point; authentic local fare served with finesse is another.

TASCA A LINDA

Rua dos Mareantes A8; tel. 258 847 900; www. tasquinhadalinda.com; Mon.-Sat. 12:15pm-3pm and 7:15pm-10:30pm; €25

Near the Santiago da Barra Castle, Tasca a Linda is tavern-chic, with an elegantly simple interior, nice views, and delicious seafood, including stuffed crab and seafood *cataplana.*

Entertainment and Events
PILGRIMAGE OF OUR LADY OF AGONY

Romaria da Senhora da Agonia; http://vianafestas. com; Aug.

Famous for the women's bright multicolored costumes and gold jewelry, the city's biggest event, the four-day Pilgrimage of Our Lady of Agony, has been held each August since 1783. Processions, exhibitions, and concerts are staged in key spots around town.

Beaches
CABEDELO BEACH (Praia do Cabedelo)

Darque, Viana do Castelo

Stroll along lovely Praia do Cabedelo, a stretch of pristine sand lined by reedy dunes and a few beach shacks. Its rolling waves attract surfers in droves, along with summer crowds of kitesurfers, windsurfers, and body-boarders. Contact **Sports Center Feelviana** (tel. 258 249 841; http://hotelfeelviana.com) and **Vianalocals** (tel. 258 325 168 or 914 193 535; www.vianalocals.com) for surfing lessons, trips, and rentals. **Ondimar** (tel. 912 274 244) rents Jet Skis.

May to October, a **ferry** (5 minutes; €1.50) crosses the estuary to connect the city to the beach; it leaves every 30 minutes daily 9am-6pm from the quay south of Praça 5 Outubro square. A **bus** to the beach also departs the local bus station frequently (10 minutes; €2).

Getting There

Viana do Castelo is 80 kilometers (50 mi) north of **Porto,** an hour by car on the **A28** motorway, and 62 kilometers (38 mi) north of **Braga,** a 45-minute drive on the **A11** and A28 motorways.

VIANA DO CASTELO TRAIN STATION

Largo da Estação

You can easily get to Viana do Castelo on public transport, both by train and by bus. **CP** (tel. 707 210 220; www.cp.pt) runs Regional trains (1-3 hours; €6.85-16) every couple of hours from Porto's Campanhã station. The slower Urbano train is cheaper but stops often and may require a transfer in the town of Nine; direct Inter-regional trains are faster and more expensive. Trains run every half hour between Braga and Viana do Castelo (1.5 hours; €6-16). The train station is near the city center, at the far end of Avenida dos Combatentes da Grade Guerra, a straight walk down to the riverfront.

VIANA DO CASTELO BUS STATION

Avenida 25 de Abril, 5

Rede Expressos (tel. 707 223 344; www.rede-expressos.pt) buses travel direct between Porto and Viana do Castelo (1 hour; €7.60), departing hourly from Porto's Campo 24 Agosto. Viana do Castelo has a new bus station, just outside the center next to the railway station and a large shopping center called Estação Viana.

Madeira

Off the coast of western Africa, 970 kilometers

(600 mi) southwest of mainland Portugal, Madeira (mah-DAY-rah) is one of Portugal's two autonomous archipelagos.

Lush, low-key, laid-back, and majestic, Madeira is known for sunny, warm weather and is rapidly growing in popularity as a winter escape for Northern Europeans. Comprising Madeira Island, smaller Porto Santo, and two clusters of uninhabited islands, the Desertas and the Savage Islands Natural Reserve, the subtropical archipelago is one of the European Union's farthest outposts has soared in popularity thanks to its balmy year-round climate and gorgeous scenery.

Semiautonomous since 1976, the colorful archipelago, in the same time zone as mainland Portugal, is today driven by tourism, with most

Highlights

Look for ★ to find recommended sights, activities, dining, and lodging.

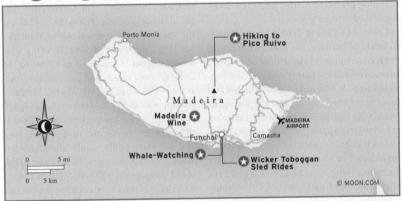

Porto Moniz

★ Hiking to
Pico Ruivo

Madeira

Madeira
Wine ★

★ MADEIRA
AIRPORT

Funchal
Camacha

★ Whale-Watching

★ Wicker Toboggan
Sled Rides

0   5 mi

0   5 km

© MOON.COM

★ **Wicker Toboggan Sled Rides:** Hold your breath as you whiz down Funchal's steep mountainsides on Madeira's novel answer to Venice's gondolas (page 361).

★ **Whale-Watching:** Gaze in awe as these majestic creatures surface from the deep to greet visitors (page 362).

★ **Madeira Wine:** Make sure to try Madeira wine in its birthplace. Often thought of as a dessert wine, the unique drink is in fact so versatile it can be paired with anything from fish to chocolate (page 366).

★ **Hiking to Pico Ruivo:** Feel on top of the world as you stand on Madeira's highest peak, with the island—or clouds, depending on the weather—spread out at your feet (page 370).

visitors staying on Madeira Island. The island is also a popular stop for Mediterranean and transatlantic cruises. A daily ferry between Madeira Island and neighboring Porto Santo Island has seen the number of visitors to tiny Porto Santo grow as well. Just a short hop from the mainland, Madeira is a great short-break destination any time of year.

THE ISLANDS

The Madeira archipelago consists of two inhabited islands, Madeira and Porto Santo, and two clusters of uninhabited islets, the **Desertas,** just south of Funchal, and the **Savage Islands,** or Selvagens, 230 kilometers (143 mi) south of Funchal, halfway between Madeira and the Canary Islands just off the coast of Morocco. Barren, inhospitable, and without regular transport, few other than passing sailors ever visit these remote isles, currently protected nature reserves belonging to the Portuguese state.

Created in 1982 to defend the archipelago's natural heritage, the **Madeira Natural Park** covers around two-thirds of Madeira Island, comprising nature reserves and protected areas. It also encompasses the Natural Reserves of the Desertas and the Selvagens Islands. Its legislations safeguard a number of endangered species, including global rarities such as Zino's petrel, as well as the indigenous laurel, or laurissilva forests. This makes the habitats within the Madeira Natural Park important breeding grounds for thousands of nesting and migrating birds, as well as extraordinary marine biodiversity.

Madeira Island

Called the "pearl" or the "floating garden" of the Atlantic, Madeira Island is a botanical bonanza, known for its unusual fruit, including the Madeira banana and banana passion fruit; for Madeira wine and amazing New Year's fireworks; and as the birthplace of soccer megastar Cristiano Ronaldo.

Inhabited since shortly after being discovered in July 1419 by Portuguese explorers João Gonçalves Zarco and Tristão Vaz Teixeira, subtropical Madeira Island is latticed by a network of small irrigation channels *(levadas)* that once watered the terraces created for farming in the precipitous terrain, but nowadays serve mainly as landmarks on popular **hiking routes.**

Dotted with **lakes, waterfalls,** and dramatic precipices, Madeira is a tranquil haven. The weather is generally warm and breezy but can be temperamental; visitors may experience four seasons in one day as they travel around the island. The entire island is skirted by **beaches** and **seawater pools;** most of Madeira's beaches are pebbly and lack soft sand.

Funchal, the main city, with its scenic cable cars and glorious botanical gardens, is on the southeast coast, with the main international airport and seaport. On the east coast is the town of **Caniçal,** the center of Madeira's whaling industry until 1982. Heading west from Funchal is the town of **Câmara de Lobos,** home to unusual gastronomy, such as the Nikita, a baffling mix of wine, beer, and pineapple ice cream, and famous hanging kebabs. On the northwestern tip of Madeira is charming **Porto Moniz,** with inviting natural saltwater pools, sandwiched between mountains and the ocean. In the heart of the island is cloudy **Pico Ruivo,** Madeira's highest peak, flanked by incredible vistas and challenging hikes.

Porto Santo Island

A short 15-minute flight or a 2-hour ferry ride from Madeira Island, paradisiacal Porto Santo Island is like the Caribbean with its year-round balmy weather, warm turquoise water, and 9 kilometers (5.6 mi) of soft **white-sand beaches.** Drier than Madeira Island and just under 15 kilometers (9.3 mi) from one end to the other, Porto Santo is a

---

Previous: view from Pico Ruivo; dolphin off the coast of Madeira; wicker tobaggan sled ride in Funchal.

Madeira

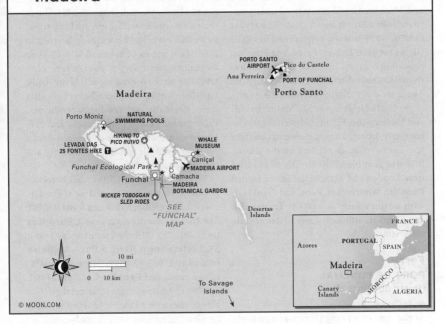

PORTO SANTO
AIRPORT
Pico do Castelo
Ana Ferreira
PORT OF FUNCHAL

Madeira
Porto Santo

Porto Moniz
NATURAL
SWIMMING POOLS

HIKING TO
PICO RUIVO
LEVADA DAS
25 FONTES HIKE
WHALE
MUSEUM
Caniçal
Funchal Ecological Park
MADEIRA AIRPORT
Funchal
Camacha
MADEIRA
BOTANICAL GARDEN
WICKER TOBOGGAN
SLED RIDES
SEE
"FUNCHAL"
MAP
Desertas
Islands

0   10 mi
0   10 km

To Savage
Islands

FRANCE
Azores
PORTUGAL
SPAIN
Madeira
MOROCCO
Canary
Islands
ALGERIA

© MOON.COM

MADEIRA

first-rate beach resort, the ultimate getaway for rest and relaxation. Tourism development has been regulated in harmony with the size and spirit of the island. Equipped with an international airport, Porto Santo also offers excellent diving conditions and spectacular **mountainside trekking.** Dubbed the "Golden Island," it is one of Europe's last undiscovered treasures.

GETTING THERE

The fastest, easiest way to get to Madeira is on one of the daily **flights** from Porto and Lisbon; frequency varies depending on the season, from several a day in winter to over a dozen a day in peak season. A growing number of tourists opt to stop at Madeira on a **cruise,** but the seasonal summer **ferry** from Portimão in the Algarve only accounts for a nominal number of visitors. Be it by air or sea, most travelers will arrive in the main city on Madeira Island, **Funchal.**

Air

There are many daily flights between Porto and Lisbon on mainland Portugal and Funchal on Madeira Island.

MADEIRA AIRPORT
(Aeroporto da Madeira)

FNC; Santa Cruz; tel. 291 520 700; www.
aeroportomadeira.pt

Funchal's airport is famous for its intriguing runway and dramatic setting. Surrounded by sheer mountains on one side and the Atlantic on the other, often battered by breezy conditions, the runway has a reputation for being challenging, and is an innovative feat of engineering, a long platform over the ocean on 180 cement stilts. In 2017 the airport, also known as Funchal Airport, was officially rebranded Cristiano Ronaldo Madeira International Airport in honor of the island's most famous son. The airport is 20 minutes west of Funchal, connected to the city center by good roads and **buses.**

TAP Air Portugal (tel. 707 205 700; www. flytap.com) operates flights between Lisbon and Madeira Island every few hours year-round, while British low-cost carrier **easyJet** (tel. 707 500 176; www.easyjet.com) has daily flights between Lisbon, Porto, and Funchal, providing competitive fares, sometimes less than €100 round-trip for the 1.5-hour trip. There are direct flights between the Azores (from Ponta Delgada, on São Miguel Island) and Madeira, too. Flights between the two islands take around 3 hours 15 minutes and cost €50-150 one-way, depending on the season. It is also possible to fly directly to Madeira from London and Manchester in the United Kingdom, Amsterdam, Paris, and Frankfurt, with airlines such as easyJet, **Transavia,** and **Condor,** although some routes operate seasonally.

Ferry
PORT OF FUNCHAL
(Porto do Funchal)
Av. Sá Carneiro 3

At the time of writing there was a summer ferry between the Algarve (**Naviera Armas,** Rua do Convento, Portimão; tel. 269 860 600; www.madeira-ferry.pt; 24 hours; from €85 one-way), which continues to the Canary Islands.

GETTING AROUND

A **car** is the best way to explore Madeira Island. Generally, **public bus services** between the main towns and villages are frequent, cheap, and punctual, but they can be slow and bumpy. **Taxis** on Madeira Island are reasonable and plentiful.

Car

For a short stay in Madeira, book a **rental car** in advance to pick up at the airport for exploring the island. For a longer stay, visit one of the numerous local car rental companies in Funchal and get a vehicle for a day or two.

The island's main route is the **ER101** coastal road, which runs around the island's edge; main regional roads are denominated

ER1, while complementary roads start with ER2. The island is connected by a good, modern road network with long tunnels through the mountainous landscape, making travel swift and easy. But be warned: Driving in Madeira is not to be taken lightly. Outside the major routes, traveling short distances can take time on the winding roads. Many roads, especially within towns, can be vertiginously steep. Rockfalls, wet and foggy conditions, sheer exposed cliffs, long tunnels, and narrow roads are a few of the challenges. Rent a good car with a decent engine and drive at a sensible speed.

Vehicles can be hired through hotels or at offices in Funchal as well as at the airport. Companies include **Auto Rent** (tel. 291 634 463; www.autorentacar.net), **Europcar** (tel. 291 765 116; www.europcar.com), **Statusflamingo Rent a Car - Madeira Island** (tel. 963 424 149; https://statusflamingo.com), and **Express Car Rental** (tel. 966 890 639; https://expresscarrental.pt). Car hire is cheap on Madeira, making it worth considering even for a one-day adventure.

Bus

Public bus service on Madeira is generally useful and efficient. As a rule of thumb, the nearer to Funchal the destination is, the greater the frequency of service. The distinctive yellow buses of Funchal's main bus company, **Horários do Funchal** (tel. 291 705 555,; www.horariosdofunchal.pt), serve the city center and its urban fringes. Information in English is available on the website. **SAM** (tel. 291 201 151; www.sam.pt) operates the main routes between Funchal, the airport, and the neighboring towns of Caniço, Machico, Caniçal, Porto da Cruz, and Santo da Serra. **Rodoeste** (tel. 291 220 148; www.rodoeste. com.pt) covers the north and west, while **EACL** (tel. 291 222 558; www.eacl.pt) serves the east.

PLANNING YOUR TIME

Traveling to Madeira is quick and easy from mainland Portugal, with daily 1.5-hour flights from **Lisbon** and **Porto.** There are also a few direct flights between Madeira and **the Azores,** if you want to do some island-hopping. In addition, there are direct flights to Madeira from European destinations outside Portugal, including **London, Amsterdam,** and **Paris.** It's also possible to fly directly to **Porto Santo Island** from mainland Portugal, and from some cities in Europe in the summer.

If your primary destination is mainland Portugal, a long weekend in Madeira is plenty of time. The main destination is **Funchal,** the capital city, on Madeira Island's south coast and a great base for exploring. In a rush, most of the island can be seen in a day, especially if you **rent a car.** It's better, though, to spend 2-3 days, with a day at either end of the island.

Nearby Porto Santo Island is an unspoiled beach destination a short 2-hour **ferry** trip from Funchal; the ferry generally makes one daily round-trip, though the crossing can be hampered by Madeira's infamously temperamental weather. If you have the time, spend a night on Porto Santo, especially if visiting in summer.

Madeira is at its best in **late spring** and **early summer,** when flowers bloom and just before peak season. It's generally dry April-September and is rainiest in winter (Nov.-Mar.), although much of the rain falls on the northern side of the island (meaning Funchal is often drier). Outside summer (July-Aug.), Funchal gets very busy for two of the island's main events: **New Year's** and the annual **Flower Festival** in May. To visit around these times, book flights and lodging well in advance.

Itinerary Ideas

DAY 1: FUNCHAL

1 Start the morning by walking the **Lido Promenade** into downtown Funchal.

2 Set a few hours aside to explore the Old Town's top sights and quaint cobbled streets, starting with the wonderful **Funchal Cathedral.**

3 While in the Old Town, choose quaint, typical restaurant **o Avô** for lunch; make sure to try a sandwich made with *bolo de caco* bread, washed down with a Coral beer.

4 It's a short walk from here to the waterfront, where you'll find the modern **Funchal Cable Car** that whizzes you up to the neighboring mountainside town of Monte.

5 In Monte, explore the beautiful **Madeira Botanical Garden.**

6 To get back to Funchal, take a thrilling ride down the hill on a **wicker toboggan.**

7 Start making your way back to your hotel, stopping in at the **CR7 Museum** on the waterfront to celebrate Cristiano Ronaldo.

8 Finish the day off with a lovely meal at **Casa Velha Restaurant Funchal** in the heart of the hotel district.

DAY 2: PORTO MONIZ AND CÂMARA DE LOBOS

1 After having breakfast at your hotel, jump in your car and head north and then west, toward Porto Moniz, via the VR1 and VE2 roads, where you'll spend the morning lounging at the **Porto Moniz Natural Swimming Pools,** for which the area is famed.

2 Have a light lunch with a fantastic sea view at **Conchinha.**

3 Jump in the car and start slowly winding your way counter-clockwise around the island along the ER101 back toward Funchal, taking in lovely hamlets and dramatic, rugged scenery. Make a pit stop at the famed **Pukiki** cocktail bar in Calheta for a tiki drink.

4 Keep heading toward Câmara de Lobos. Hopefully you've saved room for dinner, so you can enjoy a traditional *espetada* hanging kebab at **Restaurante Viola.**

5 Afterward, spend a little time wandering the picturesque village of Câmara de Lobos, which is particularly appealing at night. Wash dinner down with a Nikita at **Casa do Farol** bar. Head back to Funchal for a good night's sleep.

DAY 3: CANIÇAL AND *LEVADA* HIKE

1 Rise bright and early, have breakfast at the hotel, and make your way to the incredibly colorful and exotic **Lavradores Market,** where you'll buy supplies for a picnic lunch while drinking in the sights, sounds, and scents of this hive of activity.

2 From here, make a beeline for the east, toward the fishing town of Caniçal along the VR1. After you park, walk around to admire the fishing boats and seafront, and visit the acclaimed **Madeira Whale Museum.**

3 From Caniçal, keep heading counter-clockwise along the island's edge to the parish of São Vicente, where you'll turn inland and head south to the start of the **Levada das 25 Fontes hike.** Spend the afternoon enjoying one of Madeira Island's most famous *levada* hikes, eating your packed lunch along the way.

4 After the hike, make your way back to Funchal, scrub up, and wrap up your stay in style at the **Casino da Madeira.** Enjoy dinner, a cabaret show, and a little bet at the tables.

Funchal

Madeira's capital is an awesome sight, a sloping mountainside covered in tiny houses down to the waterfront, where sheer escarpments end abruptly in the sea. From afar, the slope appears gentle, but up close the vertiginous angles of the steep ridges and narrow roads become apparent. Clumps of tropical foliage sprout between chalky white facades and red roofs.

Funchal (fun-SHALL) is the largest and most populous city in the archipelago, its name said to derive from the fennel *(funcho)* in dense forests that once covered the shores. Forests were replaced with profitable sugarcane plantations, the main export for many years; famous products made from sugarcane include *bolo de mel* (honey cake, made with sugarcane molasses) and *mel de cana* (sugarcane honey). Clean and cosmopolitan

yet steeped in culture and history, Funchal is the island's main destination year-round. The annual Flower Festival, summer season, and New Year's Eve are peak times. It is also Portugal's leading cruise destination, with huge liners docking at the port on a regular basis.

In the hills over Funchal, 6 kilometers (3.7 mi) north of the city center, Monte (MONT, with a silent *e*) is a small mountainside town where the famous, exhilarating wicker toboggans can be found. Easily accessed by a scenic cable car from Funchal's waterfront near the old town, this village was formerly a well-being retreat for wealthy Europeans.

Funchal is an enthralling place to explore, with its stunning scenery and unusual attractions, and is particularly enchanting by night, when the slope of houses becomes a blanket

Funchal

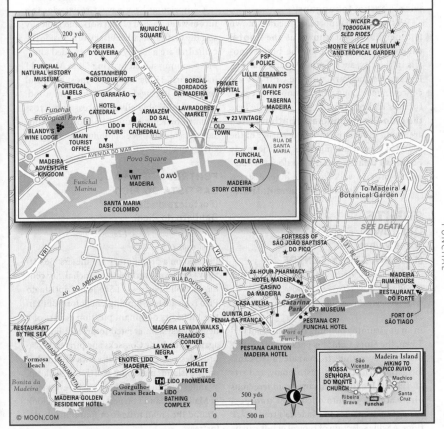

of lights twinkling in the inky black of the Atlantic.

ORIENTATION

Funchal's main downtown district centers on the **Avenida do Mar** main waterfront avenue, which extends between Funchal port (where it starts off as Avenida de Sá Carneiro) and Funchal Marina.

The historic center, the **Old Town (Zona Velha),** at the eastern extremity of the Avenida do Mar, is an idyllic maze of picturesque streets, old houses, colorfully painted doors, and traditional restaurants. The oldest buildings in Old Town date to the 15th

century. **Rua de Santa Maria** is one of the oldest streets in this area, a narrow, cobbled cavalcade of quaint old shops, restaurants, and old-fashioned streetlights. Easily covered on foot, this area is where you'll find the colorful **Lavradores Market** and its weird and wonderful fruits and flowers, and the noble main **Municipal Square** (Praça do Município), with its striking chessboard-like black-and-white cobbling.

Just south of Old Town, the **Port of Funchal** and **marina** bustle, with Cristiano Ronaldo's **CR7 Museum** and Hotel pulling in sports fans. A short **cable car** ride north from waterfront **Povo Square** (Praça do

Povo) is **Monte,** a peaceful suburb with one of Madeira's most famous trademarks, the **wicker basket toboggans.**

West of Funchal port and the downtown is a neighborhood known as the **"hotel district"** where some of the biggest hotels in the city, such as the Pestana Carlton, Pestana Casino Park, and the Cliff Bay are concentrated, along with a rainbow of colorful bars and restaurants. This is also where the **Lido Promenade and bathing area** are found. Rounding this little corner of the island, a short walk northwest, is the lovely **Formosa Beach,** about a 4-kilometer (2.5-mi) 50-minute walk from the hotel district, along the main **Estrada Monumental road.**

SIGHTS

Old Town
(Zona Velha)
MADEIRA STORY CENTRE
Rua D. Carlos 27-29; tel. 291 639 081, museum tel. 291 639 081 or 291 639 082; www. madeirastorycentre.com; daily 10am-7pm; adults €5, children €3

In an unassuming building in the heart of Old Town, the Story Centre is packed with information on everything from Madeira's volcanic formation to its culture, gastronomy, and arts and crafts. It explores history from ferocious pirate attacks to outmoded local transport such as hydroplanes to Madeira's trademark flora. A wide selection of typical goods can be purchased from the well-stocked **gift shop.** The rooftop **restaurant** has gorgeous views and traditional island cuisine.

FUNCHAL CATHEDRAL
(Sé Catedral do Funchal)
Rua do Aljube 3; tel. 291 228 155; www.sefunchal. com; daily 7am-noon and 3pm-7pm; free

Just west of the Old Town in its own cobblestone square, Funchal Cathedral is a beautiful blend of Gothic and Manueline, built in the late 15th century entirely from volcanic stone blocks, one of few surviving structures from colonial times. The archipelago's most

important church, it has been classified a National Monument since 1910.

Comprising three naves, its exterior is a mix of whitewashed plasterwork and typically spindly Gothic detailed brickwork. Inside the cathedral are a highly elaborate gilded altarpiece commissioned by King Dom Manuel I in the early 1500s; one of the most beautiful ceilings in Portugal, made with island wood; and a remarkable silver processional cross donated by King Manuel I of Portugal, considered a masterpiece of Manueline liturgical silverwork.

FORTRESS OF SÃO JOÃO BAPTISTA DO PICO
(Fortaleza de São João Baptista do Pico)
Calçada do Pico 7; tel. 291 231 502; Tues.-Sat. 10am-6pm; free

Perched on a promontory 111 meters (364 ft) above sea level overlooking Funchal city center, the solid Fortress of São João Baptista do Pico is an austere-looking, squat fort. Built in the 1600s, its dominant position is part of a defensive system created to protect Funchal against attacks by Cossacks and pirates. It also provides some of the best views of Funchal on the island, making it worth the walk up. Wander the fort's walls for bird's-eye views of Madeira Island's biggest city, or have a look around the small **museum** found inside the fortress.

FUNCHAL NATURAL HISTORY MUSEUM
(Museu de Historia Natural do Funchal)
Rua da Mouraria 31; tel. 291 229 761; https://cultura. madeira.gov.pt/museu-de-hist%C3%B3ria-natural-do-funchal.html; Tues.-Sun. 10am-6pm; €3.91

Housed in a former palace widely considered of the most important examples of mid-18th-century civil architecture, Funchal's Natural History Museum houses permanent and changing exhibitions

1: Funchal's charming historic downtown
2: Funchal Cable Car 3: Madeira Botanical Garden
4: Fort of São Tiago

dedicated to local natural history. Housing tens of thousands of examples of flora, fauna, and fossils found in Madeira, it is Madeira's oldest museum, inaugurated in 1933. It houses a scientific library and the municipal aquarium, as well as 560 square meters (5,000 sq ft) of gardens.

Waterfront

Located in a sheltered nook of Funchal waterfront, the **Funchal Marina** (tel. 291 232 717; www.marinadofunchal.pt; open 24/7) is a pleasant area for a stroll, to admire the bobbing yachts and stop for a coffee. With 210 berths, it is lined with attractive restaurants, shops, and bars, while Funchal city center is just across the other side of the main waterfront avenue, **Avenida do Mar.** The marina provides 24-hour surveillance, boat support services, and key amenities and supplies.

CR7 MUSEUM
(Museu CR7)

Av. Sá Carneiro 27; tel. 291 639 880; www.museucr7.com; daily 10am-6pm; €5

To understand the fuss regarding soccer star Cristiano Ronaldo and his connection to the island, this is the place to go. Packed with gleaming trophies, photos, a huge assortment of personal memorabilia, the CR7 Museum—named for Ronaldo's initials, plus his jersey number—maps his ascension from a humble islander who played soccer in the streets to an international superstar, philanthropist, and Madeira's biggest ambassador. Ronaldo's career achievements, including his Ballon d'Or, Golden Shoes, and club trophies, are in glass cabinets that fill the ground-floor show area. Outside, a full-size bronze statue of Ronaldo welcomes streams of cruise-ship passengers. The museum, run by the icon's family members, is in the same building as a hotel, partly designed by the player. If you're not really a soccer fan, you can skip the museum and its artifacts, although the interactive features are interesting.

FUNCHAL CABLE CAR
(Teleférico do Funchal)

Caminho das Babosas 8; tel. 291 780 280; www.madeiracablecar.com; daily 9am-6pm; €11 one-way

To get the most phenomenal views of Funchal and really appreciate its dramatic landscape, take the Funchal Cable Car from **Povo Square** on the waterfront to **Monte,** soaring high over streets, roads, and dramatic ridges, and through misty clouds on the 15-minute journey. At the top, enjoy the stunning **Monte Palace Tropical Garden,** within walking distance, as well as the **Madeira Botanical Garden,** reached by a second cable car (www.telefericojardimbotanico.com; €8.25 one-way); the cable car terminals in Monte are a minute's walk from each other. Later, you can whizz all the way back down to the city center on one of the famous wicker basket **toboggans.**

FORT OF SÃO TIAGO
(Forte de São Tiago)

Rua do Portão de São Tiago; tel. 291 213 340; www.visitfunchal.pt; Mon.-Fri. 9am-12:30pm and 2pm-5:30pm, closed public holidays; €3

Perched right on water's edge just east of Funchal Marina, this bright yellow fort is hard to miss. Its construction spanned over a century, completed in two phases: the first was started by Royal Master Builder Jerónimo Jorge in the mid-17th century, years later taken over by his son Bartolomeu João. Phase two was completed in the mid-18th century. The fort's original purpose was to defend Funchal from sea enemies, and it has since been used to accommodate flood victims and troops. Inside the fort is a luxury upscale restaurant, the **Restaurant do Forte** (Rua do Portão de São Tiago, Forte de São Tiago; tel. 291 215 580 or 919 581 326; Tues.-Sun. 10am-3pm and 6pm-11pm; €30), a contemporary art exhibition, and a small exhibition of old photos, but its ramparts offer outstanding views of the Old Town, mountains, and waterfront.

Monte
MADEIRA BOTANICAL GARDEN
(Jardim Botânico da Madeira)

Caminho do Meio, Bom Sucesso; tel. 291 211 200;
www.ifcn.madeira.gov.pt; daily 9am-7pm; €5.50

The Madeira Botanical Garden is an exquisite, fragrant oasis of peace and tranquility with rare and exotic flora worth an hour or two of strolling. Three thousand plants from all over the world cover 8 hectares (20 acres) on several levels, with views of Funchal. Once a private estate, the garden has been open to the public since 1960, though it suffered extensive damage in the 2016 wildfires that swept Funchal. Replanted, it is slowly recovering. Facilities include toilets, a **museum,** and a **café.** Steep, unleveled pathways can be inaccessible for people with disabilities.

The gardens, in the rugged hills 3 kilometers (1.9 mi) northeast of Funchal center, are reached most cheaply by **bus 31** or **31A** from Funchal seafront (€1.95), by **taxi** (€5-8 one-way), or by **cable car** from Funchal to Monte and then a shorter cable car ride from Monte to the gardens. It is possible to **walk** up to the gardens, but the roads are steep and busy, and it's a long walk (approx. 1 hour). Ride up and walk back down, or jump on one of the thrilling **wicker toboggans** in Monte.

MONTE PALACE MUSEUM
AND TROPICAL GARDEN
(Jardim Tropical Monte Palace)

Caminho do Monte 174; tel. 291 780 800; www.
montepalace.com; daily 9:30am-6pm; €12.50

Covering 70,000 square meters (17 acres), the Monte Palace Tropical Garden houses formal gardens, lakes and ponds, and rich flora and fauna, including swans. On three floors, the funky-looking museum is well organized, with two floors showcasing African sculptures and the third housing a unique mineral collection. The sparkling centerpiece is an exhibition of 300 semiprecious and precious gems, among them rough and cut diamonds.

Throughout the lovely gardens are statues and sculptures in stone and metal, creating an intriguing open-air art collection hidden among lush exotic flora. The property was originally purchased by English consul Charles Murray in the 18th century, then sold to a Portuguese merchant who, inspired by the palaces along the banks of the Rhine River, converted it into a fine hotel, which attracted wealthy nationals and foreigners. Following his death, the property was taken over by a local financial institution, and later purchased by prominent Portuguese businessman, investor, and art collector, José Berardo, who elevated it from a state of abandonment to one of the most important artistic and botanical hubs on the island.

NOSSA SENHORA DO
MONTE CHURCH
(Igreja Paroquial de Nossa
Senhora do Monte)

Rampa da Sacristia 1; tel. 291 783 877; www.
freguesiadomonte.com/freguesia/historia/nossa-
senhora-do-monte; Tues.-Sat. 9am-7pm, Sun.-Mon.
9am-6pm; free

Widely regarded as the most important place of worship on the island and the main church in picturesque Monte parish, the Our Lady of Monte church is a short uphill walk from the Monte cable car station, then about 60 steps up to the main entrance. It was built on the spot of a primitive 15th-century church later completely razed by an earthquake in 1748. The church that stands high above Funchal today was finished in 1818.

Inside are gorgeous chandeliers, important 17th- and 18th-century silverwork, and a statue of Our Lady that dates back to the island's settlement. It is also the final resting place of Charles I of Habsburg, the last emperor of Austria, who went into exile in Madeira in 1921. This little gem is a peaceful haven with breathtaking views from the front door; climb the church towers for even better views. Pretty gardens surround the foot of the church. Every year on August 15, colorful processions from across the city make their way to the church to honor Our Lady of Monte, patron saint of Funchal.

SPORTS AND RECREATION
Parks
SANTA CATARINA PARK
(Parque de Santa Catarina)

Avenida Sá Carneiro 3; www.visitfunchal.pt; daily 7am-7pm; free

Sprawled over 36,000 square meters (9 acres), Santa Catarina Park is a well-manicured, verdant oasis just off the waterfront, backing the CR7 Museum. It has a lovely lake inhabited by ducks and swans, attractive fountains, a children's play area, a cute little chapel, and sweeping views. The garden is planted with eye-catching flora from around the globe and provides welcome tranquility from the bustle of downtown Funchal. Follow one of the walking paths through the park for a relaxing stroll.

POVO SQUARE
(Praça do Povo)

Avenida do Mar; open 24/7; free

Fronting the main waterfront avenue, **Avenida do Mar,** adjacent to the marina, the Praça do Povo (People's Square) is a historic meeting point and a vibrant, bustling spot, with a garden, a harbor, and little stalls touting an array of goodies, from farmers' produce to souvenirs. With sea views to one side and mountain views to the other, it's a lovely place to sit and take a moment to rest on a park bench, amid carpets of colorful flowers, palm trees, and locals hurrying by.

FUNCHAL ECOLOGICAL PARK
(Parque Ecológico do Funchal)

Reception Center, Estrada Regional 103, No. 259; tel. 291 784 700; daily 9am-5pm; park entry free

Created in 1994, the vast hilly terrain of the Funchal Ecological Park, 12 kilometers (7.4 mi) north of Funchal, is preserved to promote environmental education and provide recreational opportunities such as picnic areas, hiking, mountain biking, canyoneering, and camping. Covering 1,000 hectares (2,471 acres), it is home to rare native tree species such as the mountain ash, lily of the valley

tree, and canary laurel. The park also has a landing strip for paragliders and hang gliders as well as an igloo-like reservoir where snow was stored before being transported to hotels and hospitals in Funchal. More information on hiking, bicycle rentals, and even donkey rides is available at the Reception Center.

Hiking
LIDO PROMENADE

Hiking Distance: *3-4 kilometers (2-2.5 mi) one-way*
Hiking Time: *1 hour one-way*
Trailhead: *Car park on Rua do Gorgulho*
Information and Maps: *www.visitfunchal.pt*

Funchal's Lido Promenade is one long waterfront boulevard, lined with manicured gardens, leafy palm trees, and benches, enjoyed by locals and tourists alike. Also known as the Passeio Publico Marítimo, this safe and pleasant seaside promenade extends about 4 kilometers (2.5 mi) along the sea ront between the Lido area in the east, to Praia Formosa t the west. It's hugely popular for early-morning and evening strolls, when a pleasant and invigorating breeze blows in from the sea.

If you fancy a dip, the Lido gives access to two large seawater pools—the **Lido Bathing Complex** (daily 8:30am-8pm; €6) and **Ponta Gorda Pool** (daily 9:30am-5:30pm; €5), a 15-minute walk west from the Lido complex along the Lido Promenade. Both of have excellent facilities—and the Lido Promenade is dotted by scenic cafés and restaurants along the way. Another extension (about 6.5 km/4 mi) of the walkway from Praia Formosa goes all the way to Câmara de Lobos. To start from Câmara de Lobos, take the No. 1 bus there from downtown Funchal (about €2 one-way); it's a mostly downhill walk back into town.

Beaches and Pools

The Funchal coastline is a mix of sandy beaches and well-kept pools built into the rocky island edge, with cement decks and facilities like sun beds, changing rooms, and children's pools. There's usually a small fee, typically less than €10.

☆ Funchal's Wicker Toboggans

Whiz down the steep, winding roads of Funchal from Monte back toward downtown on the famous wicker toboggans run by **Associação dos Carreiros do Monte** (Caminho do Monte, Entrata 151, Porta 4; tel. 291 783 919; www.carreirosdomonte.com; Mon.-Sat. 9am-6pm; €30 per basket). Madeira's answer to Venice's gondolas, the toboggans are an exhilarating, unique way to get around arising from the region's traditional basket-weaving craft. A ride in the handmade two-seater *carros de cesto* (basket cars) is one of Madeira's most popular experiences.

THE HISTORY

Dating to the 1850s, these sleds were originally used to transport people and goods from the hills to downtown. The baskets are still handcrafted by expert artisans from local wicker and mounted on wooden runners, just like the earliest sleds.

Funchal's wicker toboggans

Madeiran wicker craft also dates back to the mid-1800s, but it's a dying tradition. While travelling around the island, you'll notice the odd interior decoration piece, chairs, hats, and baskets made from wicker. The wicker is made from willow grown on the island, then cut, boiled, and treated.

Nowadays, there are few wicker artisans still practicing the artform. One of the best places to see artisans at work and maybe buy some genuine items is in the town of Camacha (in the mountainous interior of the island, some 7 km/4 mi northeast of Funchal), at the renowned **Camacha Wicker Factory** (Largo Conselheiro Aires de Ornelas 12; tel. 291 922 777/114; daily 9am-8pm).

THE RIDE

The sled baskets are big enough for two people and travel on runners, pushed and steered by two smartly dressed men called *carreiros*, who have only the thick rubber soles of their shoes as brakes. These 2-kilometer (1.2-mi), 5-minute runs reach 48 km/h (30 mph) and are an art form as well as one of Madeira's must-do attractions.

Get on the toboggans in Monte, at the bottom of the **Nossa Senhora do Monte Church** stairs. You'll end up halfway down the hill back to Funchal, in the parish of Livramento. From there, you can either walk (a steep 40-minute walk), catch a cab (about €10, make sure you agree the price first), or take the No. 19 bus. Both taxis and buses can be found where the toboggans stop, along with a refreshment and souvenir stand for the obligatory photo purchase.

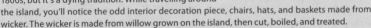

LIDO BATHING COMPLEX

Rua do Gorgulho 11; tel. 291 105 163; www. frentemarfunchal.com; daily 8:30am-8pm; €6 (includes sun bed)

Set in a cement jetty jutting out in the blue ocean, the Lido Bathing Complex is Funchal's best-known and most popular pool area. It comprises a big adult pool as well as a children's swimming pool and has direct access into the sea. Other facilities include sun loungers and parasols, lockers and changing rooms, toilets, and a snack bar. Frequented by tourists and locals alike, the complex boasts fantastic sea views and is a lovely alternative to lounging on the beach.

GORGULHO-GAVINAS BEACH
(Praia do Gorgulho-Gavinas)

Lido Promenade; tel. 291 706 950; www. frentemarfunchal.com; open 24/7; free

This typical Madeiran pebble-stone beach, topped with a cement sun deck situated straight off the **Lido Promenade,** is free and open to the public 24/7. It has showers, restrooms, and is monitored by lifeguards in the summer months.

FORMOSA BEACH (Praia Formosa)

Lido Promenade; open 24/7; free

West of Funchal in the city's hotel district, Funchal's preeminent beach plays a key role in Madeira's history: It was via this beach that pirates ransacked the city in 1508. Stretching out over 2 kilometers (1.2 mi) between Funchal and Câmara de Lobos, it is a black-sand beach, pebbly in spots, that has been divided into four portions known locally as Nova, Formosa, Namorados, and Areeiro Beaches. It is accessible to people with disabilities, including the visually impaired, with general information displayed on the beach also available in Braille, and plenty of parking on the doorstep.

★ Dolphin- and Whale-Watching

Due to its mid-Atlantic position, Madeira enjoys regular visits from whales, some of whom take up residence June-September, though there's a good chance of sighting one any time of year. Among the species here are fin, sei, pilot, sperm, beaked, and humpback whales, along with dolphins and rare seabirds. Various companies operate whale- and dolphin-watching trips, mostly from Funchal's marina. Trips operate year-round except in poor weather.

- **VMT Madeira:** Shop 9, Funchal Marina; tel. 291 224 900; www.vmtmadeira.com; 3 hours, daily 10:30am and 3pm; adults €35, children 5-12 €17.50
- **Santa Maria de Colombo:** Shop 3, Funchal Marina; tel. 291 220 327, 291 225 695, or 965 010 180; www. santamariadecolombo.com; 3 hours, daily 10:30am and 3pm; adults €35, children 6-11 €17.50
- ***Bonita da Madeira:*** Estrada Monumental 187; tel. 291 762 218 or 919 183 829; www. bonita-da-madeira.com; 3 hours, Wed. and Sun. 10:30am and 3pm; adults €33, children 5-12 €16.50

Entertainment and Events
FLOWER FESTIVAL

www.visitportugal.com/en/node/155972; 4 weeks after Easter

A tribute to the arrival of spring, Madeira's weeklong Flower Festival is one of Portugal's most famous celebrations. Funchal bursts into fragrant bloom with flower-decked floats and parades. Folk dancing, singing, and flowers stimulate every sense and bring the "floating garden" to life. Fresh flowers create the famous floral carpets along central Avenida Arriaga. One of the most poignant moments is the Wall of Hope ceremony, staged for over three decades, where hundreds of local schoolchildren, flower in hand, march toward the Municipal Square to place flowers into a wall as a call for world peace. Madeira Island is like a tropical garden on any given day of the year, but when the Flower Festival takes over, it is absolutely stunning.

NEW YEAR'S

throughout Funchal; Dec. 31

The island's New Year's celebrations are the legendary highlight of the holiday season, and hotels often sell out months in advance. Madeira's fireworks display is one of the most dazzling in the world, the biggest in Europe, making it one of the continent's leading New Year's destinations. Funchal's waterfront is the epicenter of the fireworks displays, in inky skies over the dark sea. Anywhere with an unobstructed view of the waterfront is a good place to watch; the higher you go, the better the view. Hotels and restaurants in Funchal fill up quick for New Year's Eve, so if you want to visit at this time of year, book well in advance. Over this festive period, Funchal becomes a natural amphitheater of color and sound, trimmed with colorful Christmas lights and decorations, festival food stalls, and joyous carols.

SHOPPING

LILLIE CERAMICS

Armazém do Mercado, Rua Latino Coelho; tel. 914 486 951; https://lillieceramics.com; Mon.-Fri. 10am-5pm

For a beautiful locally made gift, pop into the Lillie Ceramics shop and studio. Admire lovely, colorful handmade pieces inspired by the subtropical sights and scents of Madeira Island. Located on the narrow streets of the Old Town, this is a great place to look for a souvenir.

BORDAL-BORDADOS DA MADEIRA

Rua Doutor Fernão Ornelas 77; Mon.-Fri. 9am-7pm, Sat. 9:30am-1pm

Bordal showcases the laborious traditional art of Madeira hand embroidery. Founded in 1962, the little store is replete with over 40,000 embroidered designs and strives to keep the ancient art alive. Here, you can watch the artisans embroider, learn more about the craft's importance to the island, and take home a tablecloth, pillowcase, or tea towel as a memento.

PORTUGAL LABELS

Rua da Carreira 92; tel. 291 222 632; www.facebook. com/PortugalLabels; Mon.-Sat. 10am-8pm, Sun. 11am-5pm

This funky little shop located right on the waterfront is packed with cool local mementos. Everything sold here is made exclusively in Portugal, from shoes to soaps to sunglasses. It's a port-of-call for original and authentic gifts.

FOOD

The island's gastronomy is simple and unfussy. *Prego no Bolo do Caco* (beef steak on the traditional Madeiran *caco* bread, made with sweet-potato flour) is a popular snack, best accompanied with an ice-cold **Coral beer.** Look for little **limpets** (*lapas*), the local seafood of choice, and huge **hanging kebabs** (*espetadas da Madeira*), big, juicy chunks of island-reared meat grilled on long skewers that hang over the tables. Fruits unique to Madeira include the **Madeira banana** and the **banana passion fruit.** Distinctive, wonderful signature drinks include **Madeiran *poncha*** (a potent punch), *laranjada,* a refreshing fizzy orange drink produced on the island, often mixed with sangria; and the fabled **Nikita** (a mix of wine, beer, and homemade pineapple ice cream, indigenous to Câmara de Lobos).

Markets

LAVRADORES MARKET (Mercado dos Lavradores)

Rua Latino Coelho 38; tel. 291 214 080; Mon.-Thurs. 8am-7pm, Fri. 7am-7pm, Sat. 7am-2pm

This busy and colorful traditional market in the heart of Funchal is a great place to sample Madeira's unique local produce.

Regional

TABERNA MADEIRA

Travessa João Caetano 16; tel. 291 221 789; www. tabernamadeira.com; Mon.-Wed. 6pm-10pm, Thurs.-Fri. 11:30am-3pm and 6pm-11pm, Sat. 11am-3pm; €15

Trendy little Taberna Madeira takes typical Madeira produce and makes it cool, serving delicacies like cod fritters, tuna belly, and calf liver, with side servings of cabbage and sweet potato. Reservations are recommended.

★ O GARRAFÃO

Rua da Queimada de Baixo 25; tel. 291 635 328; Mon.-Sat. 11am-10pm; €15

On Funchal's quirky backstreets, O Garrafão serves authentic cuisine at a good value. Homemade soups and traditional mains in a cozy setting make this eatery highly recommended. Don't miss the passion fruit pudding for dessert.

CHALET VICENT

Estrada Monumental 238; tel. 291 765 818; daily noon-11pm; €20

A century-old chalet in the heart of Funchal, Chalet Vicent has classic Madeiran cuisine such as *espetadas* (hanging kebabs) skewered on bay-leaf sticks, oven-roasted goat, old-fashioned tuna dishes, and huge veal cutlets.

CASA VELHA RESTAURANT FUNCHAL

Rua Imperatriz D. Amelia 69; tel. 291 205 607; www.casavelharestaurant.com; daily noon-3pm and 6:30pm-11pm; €20

Situated in Funchal's hotel district, Casa Velha is a time-honored local restaurant with a tropical feel. It has a tranquil garden setting surrounded by lush vegetation, with bamboo furniture and crisp table linen. Its menu is an elegant selection of fine classics, like seafood risottos, steaks, and grilled fresh fish, using quality local ingredients.

Fine Dining
FRANCO'S CORNER

Rua da Casa Branca 82; tel. 291 782 005; https://francos-corner-restaurant.business.site; daily noon-11pm; €25

With a lovely alfresco dining terrace, Franco's Corner serves refined haute cuisine with polished service. Indulgent mains include lobster and prawn risotto, scallops with citrus risotto, and classic favorites like chateaubriand and duck breast.

ARMAZÉM DO SAL

Rua da Alfândega 135; tel. 291 241 285; www.armazemdosal.com; Mon.-Fri. noon-3pm and 6:30pm-11pm, Sat. 6:30pm-11pm; €30

Pricey but unique, swanky Armazém do Sal has a clever and accomplished fusion of traditional Portuguese gastronomy with typical Madeiran influence and strong international nuances. It is in a historic 200-year-old salt warehouse.

Seafood
RESTAURANT BY THE SEA

Estrada da Praia Formosa; tel. 291 763 120; daily 10am-11pm; €15

Overflowing with the freshest seafood, Restaurant by the Sea is off the beaten track, its idyllic waterfront location making this hidden gem a great place to try scabbard-fish eggs, squid, and limpets.

fruit stand at Lavradores Market

The Hanging Kebabs of Câmara de Lobos

To enjoy one of Madeira's best-known specialties, hanging kebabs, or *espetadas* (which literally translates as "skewered"), take a scenic, hilly drive to the quaint fishermen's village of Câmara de Lobos, 10 kilometers (6.2 mi) west of Funchal along the VR1 road.

Beef cubes are marinated in salt, pepper, garlic, and bay leaf, strung on long metal skewers or, traditionally, bay-leaf sticks, and slowly grilled over coals. Slices of onion, green pepper, and *chouriço* sausage are wedged between the cubes for extra flavor. These kebabs are then brought to the table on tall hooks that hang over plates, so all you have to do is slide your juicy hunks of meat off the skewers and onto the plate. They're usually served with sides of fries, fried polenta, or rice, to mop up the meaty juices, and salad.

the Nikita, another specialty of Câmara de Lobos

The *espetadas* is a traditional dish of Madeira Island that was once reserved for special festivals and celebrations, where the kebabs would be cooked over open fires and which at any other time would be a privilege accessible only to wealthier islanders. Câmara de Lobos has been a magnet for *espetada*-lovers ever since the very first dedicated *espetada* restaurant on the island opened there in the mid-1950s.

While you're in Câmara de Lobos, you should also sample the unique **Nikita,** a mixture of white wine, beer, and pineapple ice cream. The original Nikita has been served since 1985 at **Casa do Farol** (Rua da Nossa Senhora da Conceição 11, Câmara de Lobos; tel. 291 945 413; daily 9am-4am; €5), recently reinvented into a swanky tapas bar and restaurant. The Nikita is said to have been the creation of a local man who had lived in Brazil, hence the drink's tropical twist, and loved the 1985 Elton John hit by the same name. This unusual alcoholic milkshake is best suited to those with a sweet tooth. The unusual concoction won't appeal to everyone, but when in Madeira…

RESTAURANTE SANTO ANTÓNIO

Estrada João Gonçalves Zarco, Estreito de Câmara de Lobos; tel. 291 910 360; www. restaurantesantoantonio.com; daily noon-midnight; €18
Established in 1966, traditional, unpretentious Restaurante Santo António has become an institution specializing in espetadas. Savor the best local cuisine, including caco bread, washed down with a poncha.

★ RESTAURANTE VIOLA

Estrada João Gonçalves Zarco 594, Estreito de Câmara de Lobos; tel. 291 945 601; Tues.-Sun. noon-midnight; €18
Seek out authentic, down-to-earth little Restaurante Viola, with cork-clad walls; a huge guitar above the door gives it away. Inside are succulent espetadas and the traditional accompaniments: salad, chunks of fried cornbread, poncha, sangria, and beer.

☆ Madeira Wine

You can't leave Madeira without sampling Madeira wine. To Madeira what port is to Porto, this robust fortified wine is produced exclusively on the Madeira Islands, with a history that dates back to the end of the 15th century. During the era of exploration and colonization, wine suppliers found the beverage had intensified in flavor when unsold shipments were brought back to the islands after long periods at sea in the heat of ships' holds. This slow baking at high temperatures, over extended periods, called *estufagem*, is what gives Madeira wine its unique caramelized flavor. Today it's replicated in modern, technologically acclimatized warehouses, and most of the liquid is stored in big stainless steel or cement vats, as opposed to wooden barrels. Higher quality Madeira wines are "baked" for longer and stored in wooden casks.

To be true Madeira wine, the grapes must be grown on Madeira Island or neighboring Porto Santo. On Porto Santo, they are grown flat along the sandy fringes of the beach, said to give the wine an even more distinctive taste. Most of the harvest is shipped to Madeira Island, but some Porto Santo locals produce their own homemade varieties, more akin to a rosé in color and strong in flavor.

During the 18th century, the popularity of Madeira wine grew; Thomas Jefferson even toasted with it at the signing of the Declaration of Independence. Madeira wine was severely compromised by a mid-19th-century outbreak of powdery mildew that destroyed crops; in the 20th century, the Russian Revolution and Prohibition in the United States saw two of its biggest markets shrunk. Still, Madeira wine's reputation as little more than a cooking wine improved toward the end of the 20th century, and it is enjoying fresh popularity in new markets.

Ranging from dry to sweet, it's usually consumed as an aperitif or dessert accompaniment, although its versatility and acidic nuance mean it can be paired with everything from meats to sushi, while cheaper versions are used for culinary purposes.

BLANDY'S WINE LODGE

Av. Arriaga 28; tel. 291 228 978; www.blandyswinelodge.com; Mon.-Fri. 10am-6:30pm, Sat. 10am-1pm

In the heart of Funchal, Blandy's Wine Lodge provides an opportunity to explore the history of Madeira wine. Acquired by the Blandy family in 1840, it is home to 650 barrels of the famous fortified wine. The comprehensive **Premium Tour** (45 minutes; €5.90) covers two centuries of winemaking history in the cool warehouse with its thick stone walls, as well as the **museum**, which contains artifacts such as letters from Sir Winston Churchill; the revered Vintage Room,

Steak Houses
LA VACA NEGRA

Rua Velha da Ajuda 10-12; tel. 291 764 491; Tues.-Fri. 12:30pm-3:30pm and 6pm-9:30pm, Sat.-Sun. 12:30pm-4:30pm; €22

Characterful La Vaca Negra is highly rated for its steaks. Small and busy, it's a must for meat lovers; reservations advised.

Snack Bars
O AVÔ

Rua da Praia 49A; tel. 291 632 651; www.baroavo. weebly.com; Mon.-Fri. 8:30am-11pm, Sat.-Sun. 11am-11pm; €10

Hundreds of soccer scarves hang from the rafters of quirky little snack bar O Avô, owned by larger-than-life Ricardo. A great selection of beer and wine accompanies the typical menu, making this a great stop for a light lunch.

BARS AND NIGHTLIFE

Funchal has varied but contained nightlife, leaning toward trendy places rather than the rowdy scenes of other holiday islands. Nightlife areas are along the **Lido waterfront boardwalk, Rua Santa Maria** in the Old Town, and just behind the Pestana Carlton Madeira hotel. The clubs open only on weekends.

which houses Blandy's rarest and oldest Madeira wines; and a tasting. The **Vintage Tour** (1 hour; €16.50) adds the opportunity to see the aging process, access to the Blandy family's private collection of vintage Madeiras, and a tasting in the Vintage Room. Both tours are available in various languages, including English.

PEREIRA D'OLIVEIRA

Rua Dos Ferreiros 107; tel. 291 220 784; www.doliveiras.pt; Mon.-Fri. 9am-6pm, Sat. 9:30am-1pm; tastings free

Central and easily accessible, this Funchal wine cellar is fun and free to visit, like a countryside vineyard in the heart of town. It's housed in a century-old building with shelf after shelf lined with hundreds of bottles, from historic and vintage through to modern-day mainstream Madeiras. You can enjoy as many samples of wine as you like, accompanied by other local specialties like traditional Madeira honey cake.

bottles at Blandy's Wine Lodge

BARBEITO MADEIRA

Estrada Ribeira Garcia Parque Empresarial Camara de Lobos, Lote 8, Camara De Lobos parish; tel. 291 761 829; www.vinhosbarbeito.com; Mon.-Fri. 9am-5:30pm; tours and tastings free if you purchase products

Located in Câmara de Lobos (11 km/7 mi west of Funchal along the VR1), this family-run wine plant, named after founder Mário Barbeito, specializes in handcrafted artisan wines, produced in a modern plant on a large scale. Informative guided **tours** of the facilities explain the wine-maturing process, accompanied by a tasting of different Madeira wines. Enjoy the scents of Madeira wines being stored, the flavors of the robust wines, and the stunning views of the countryside surrounding the picturesque fishing village of Câmara de Lobos. It's highly recommended to book your tour in advance.

CASINO DA MADEIRA

Av. Do Infante; tel. 291 140 424; www. casinodamadeira.com; daily 3pm-3am

At the Casino da Madeira, have dinner and enjoy a cabaret show before gambling in the flashy Games Room. It's worth stopping by the casino just to admire its unusual space-age-looking architecture, which seems to stretch up from the ground. Inside, the décor's a little dated, but there are plenty of cards tables and slot machines to keep the excitement levels high.

MADEIRA RUM HOUSE

Rua Portao de Sao Tiago 19c; tel. 291 611 303; www. facebook.com/madeirarumhouse; daily 6pm-midnight

The ultimate island rum bar, the Madeira Rum House serves the potent drink in traditional and new styles. Sample different types of Madeira's famous *poncha* freshly made to order, as well as inventive cocktails, rum tastings, and food pairings.

DASH

Rua da Alfândega 1B; tel. 961 014 423; Tues.-Sat. 8pm-2am

With a trendy backlit shelving unit lined with row after row of bottles of colorful spirits, Dash is cool and creative, as are its craft cocktails. The bar uses only fresh ingredients and homemade infusions in their drinks. Dash's excellent cocktail list has earned the venue quite a following, and it's fascinating to watch the bartender make them.

23 VINTAGE

Rua de Santa Maria, no. 23; tel. 914 758 975; www. facebook.com/23VintageBar; Tues.-Sun. 6pm-2am

Tucked away at the end of a row of restaurants, just back from the waterfront, 23 Vintage bar has a good selection of cocktails and wines, and a great atmosphere. Warm and welcoming, it is one of Funchal's most popular meeting places for both locals and tourists, with a fantastic playlist of Golden Oldies played from a retro jukebox and visiting DJs.

ACCOMMODATIONS

Accommodations in Funchal are plentiful and varied, from grand, old-school-glamour hotels to charming boutique guesthouses. Prices vary accordingly, from high-end travel to budget accommodations. While there are many different types of accommodations scattered through the city center, the biggest and best known hotels are found in an area known as the **Hotel District.** Set west of the main town, this area has a real holiday vibe about it, with large hotels, busy bars and restaurants, and a glitzy casino, and is close to the Lido Promenade and Praia Formosa Beach. There's plenty of fun to be had on the doorstep in this area, which is still only a 10-15-minute walk to Funchal downtown.

Under €100
HOTEL CATEDRAL FUNCHAL

Rua do Aljube 13; tel. 291 230 091; www. catedral-funchal.madeirahotels.net; €61

In the heart of historic Old Town, overlooking the main cathedral, three-star Hotel Catedral Funchal has elegant rooms and an extensive breakfast buffet. Founded in 1972, it's just a short walk from city center attractions.

HOTEL MADEIRA

Rua Ivens 21; tel. 291 230 071; http://hotelmadeira. com; €80

Laid-back, affordably priced, central Hotel

Madeira has clean and cozy rooms and a rooftop pool.

MADEIRA GOLDEN RESIDENCE HOTEL

Rua do Cabrestante 25; tel. 291 710 100; www. goldenresidencehotel.com.pt; €85

Sleek, modern, low-rise four-star Madeira Golden Residence Hotel, on the cliffs on the western outskirts of Funchal center, is a 2-minute walk to Praia Formosa, Madeira's largest beach.

€100-200
★ QUINTA DA PENHA DA FRANÇA

Rua Imperatriz D. Amelia 85; tel. 291 204 650; www. penhafrancahotels.com; €117

A splendid manor house plus a newer wing form the Quinta da Penha da França, with pretty private gardens, two saltwater pools (one heated in winter), and ocean or garden views from all 109 rooms. This family-run hotel is an oasis of tranquility.

★ PESTANA CARLTON MADEIRA HOTEL

Largo António Nobre 1; tel. 291 239 500; www. pestana.com; €152

Pestana Carlton Madeira Hotel was one of Madeira's first five-star hotels, combining old-school glamour with impeccable service, with views from every room and a gorgeous infinity pool overlooking the Atlantic.

★ PESTANA CR7 FUNCHAL HOTEL

Av. Sá Carneiro; tel. 291 140 480; www.pestanacr7. com; €167

For a tiny taste of how sports stars live, spend a night at Pestana CR7 Funchal Hotel, a small industrial-chic hotel on Funchal's marina that is a partnership between Pestana hotels and soccer legend Cristiano Ronaldo. Ronaldo is said to have had a hand in the interior design, which includes banana-print throw pillows, plush carpets, novel doorknobs, and fake-grass walls. The unusual open-plan kitchen-bar-reception lobby has a sleek feel, while rooms are plush and swank. Guests wake to splendid views of mountains on one side and huge cruise ships on the other. The **CR7 Museum** is right beneath.

CASTANHEIRO BOUTIQUE HOTEL
Rua do Castanheiro 31; tel. 291 200 100; www. castanheiroboutiquehotel.com; €180

Formed from five historic buildings, trendy, singular Castanheiro Boutique Hotel is a short walk from the heart of downtown, with 81 polished rooms and a lap pool on the roof deck, with panoramic views of Funchal Bay.

ENOTEL LIDO MADEIRA
Rua Simplício dos Passos Gouveia 29; tel. 291 702 000; www.enotel-lido-madeira.com; €200

Perched above the Lido open-air pool complex and promenade, the contemporary Enotel Lido Madeira is a gorgeous glass-fronted all-inclusive hotel a short walk from the casino. It has a variety of on-site bars and restaurants.

Information and Services

Madeira is well equipped, with good health centers and hospitals, English-speaking medical and police services, well-stocked pharmacies, supermarkets, banks, post offices, and plenty of ATMs all over the island, especially in Funchal. You will also find helpful tourist bureaus in Funchal and most other larger towns.

- **Main tourist office:** Av. Arriaga 16; tel. 291 211 902; www.visitmadeira.pt; Mon.-Fri. 9am-8pm, Sat.-Sun. 9am-3:30pm

- **PSP police:** main squadron, Rua Conde Carvalhal; tel. 291 208 400; www.psp.pt

- **Main hospital:** Hospital Dr. Nélio Mendonça, Av. Luís de Camões; tel. 291 705 600, emergency tel. 808 201 414; www.sesaram.pt

- **Private hospital:** Madeira Medical Center, Rua do Hospital Velho 23ª; tel. 291 003 300; www.madeiramedicalcenter.pt

- **24-hour pharmacy:** La Vie shopping center, just back from the marina, Rua Dr. Brito Câmara; tel. 291 231 174

- **Main post office:** Mercado, near the Lavradores Market and Madeira Story Center, Rua Acipreste, 9A; Mon.-Fri. 9am-6pm

GETTING THERE

Parking in Funchal center is not a problem, as there are a number of designated car parks.

MADEIRA AIRPORT (Aeroporto da Madeira)
FNC; Santa Cruz; tel. 291 520 700; www. aeroportomadeira.pt

Madeira Airport is 23 kilometers (14.3 mi) east of the city center, a 20-minute drive on the VR1 road. Many car rental companies, including Europcar (tel. 291 524 633; www. europcar.pt) and Sixt (tel. 255 788 199; www. sixt.pt), can be found inside the airport terminal as well as in the immediate vicinity of the airport. **SAM** (tel. 291 201 151; www.sam.pt) operates a shuttle between Funchal center and the airport (30 minutes, hourly daily; €5); buy tickets from the driver. A **taxi** from Funchal airport to the city center will cost €30; a taxi rank with Madeira's distinctive yellow cabs is located right outside the airport.

GETTING AROUND

Funchal's lower city area, along the riverside, is easily explored **on foot,** but farther inland the hills are steep: In places the grade of the roads can be quite intimidating, even for experienced drivers, and they can also be congested. With good bus service and the cable cars, it's easy to reach all of Funchal's main sights with minimal effort and without a car.

A distinctive bright yellow color with blue stripes, **taxis** are widely available in Funchal and are a reasonable way to get around town. Flag them down in the street or go to one of the taxi ranks found throughout the city. Fares should be displayed on the meter, but don't hesitate to ask roughly how much a journey will cost before setting off.

The easiest way to get to **Monte** is the cable car (departs from Campo do Almirante Reis; tel. 291 780 280; www.madeiracablecar.com; 15 minutes, daily 9am-5:45pm; €11) from

Funchal's Old Town. Horários do Funchal (tel. 291 705 555; www.horariosdofunchal.pt) also runs buses 20 and 21 (20 minutes; €1.60 plus €0.50 bus card), from Rua 31 Janeiro, the main road through Funchal center to Monte. The buses run about hourly, sometimes more frequently (Mon.-Fri.about 6am-midnight, Sat.-Sun. about 6am-8pm). A taxi from Funchal to Monte costs around €20.

Bus

Bus company **Horários do Funchal** (tel. 291 705 555; www.horariosdofunchal.pt) has a useful guide to Funchal's public bus services and networks in English that can be downloaded (www.horariosdofunchal.pt/guia-en/ mobile). Their easily recognizable yellow buses serve the city center and its urban fringes. Fares start from €1.95; tickets can be bought from the driver. Rechargeable cards, which cost €0.50, can be purchased from newsagents, post offices, and tourist offices, and can be credited with prepaid single journeys. At €1.35 for a single journey, it works out cheaper than buying from the driver. A 24-hour pass for unlimited bus travel is €4.50; three-, five-, and seven-day passes are also available. There is a decent bus network between Funchal and other main points on Madeira Island, but it is limited elsewhere.

Funchal doesn't have a main bus terminal; most buses depart near the **waterfront.**

Around Funchal

Beyond Funchal, Madeira's landscapes get even more dramatic, with oversized crags, swooping hillsides, gnarly cliffs topped with ancient laurissilva forests, sheer roadside drops, and stretches so high up that you're literally above the clouds. Mist closes in around Madeira's higher grounds in the blink of an eye; one minute you're admiring breathtaking vistas, the next you're engulfed by a curtain of white fog. Parts of the island are wild and haphazard, while others are farmed, with stepped terraces.

Porto Moniz on the western coast is renowned for its natural lava pools; the east coast is known for its charming historic towns and fishing villages; and the center is home to the island's highest peaks.

CENTRAL MADEIRA ISLAND

Near the center of the island is Madeira's highest peak, Pico Ruivo, at 1,862 meters (6,109 ft), the third-highest point in Portugal. On a clear day, the summit affords views of the entire island. There are two main hiking routes up to the peak, one of which begins at Pico do Areeiro, Madeira's third-highest mountain.

Not far from the Pico do Areeiro trailhead is the small village of Ribeira Frio, 15 kilometers (9.3 mi) north of Funchal center and the start of another great hike.

To the west is one of Mother Nature's great achievements, Rabaçal (rah-bah-SSAL), a spectacular amphitheater of natural springs, mountains, waterfalls, and laurissilva forest, a botanical rarity that covers around 20 percent of the island and dates back 20 million years. The forest is classified by UNESCO as Natural World Heritage and is best discovered on foot. Pack a waterproof raincoat and comfy boots, maybe a swimsuit, and a camera, and take a popular *levada* hike.

★ Hiking to Pico Ruivo

Of the two main hiking routes to the top of Pico Ruivo, the more popular and more challenging is the Vereda do Areeiro (footpath PR1), from the peak of nearby Pico do Areeiro, which is accessible by car and home to a NATO radar unit.

Both hikes are challenging and should never be attempted in the dark. The weather is famously temperamental, up in the heights even more so. Be prepared and take warm

Caniçal and the Madeiran Whaling industry

A 30-minute drive up the coast from Funchal past the airport, to Madeira's easternmost tip, is Caniçal (kah-nee-SSAL), famous for fishing, shipping, and, until 1982, whaling, before conservation became the focus. The town's port was extensively developed in the mid-1990s and mid-2000s as Madeira's biggest cargo port and is now home to boats of all size; on a clear day, the nearby island of Porto Santo can be seen. You'll see reminders of Caniçal's whaling history in the modern and interactive whaling museum, with a life-size whale monument suspended inside, and photos and posters on the streets. Today Madeira's whales aren't hunted anymore, but are instead a tourism draw.

MADEIRA WHALE MUSEUM
(Museu da Baleia)

Rua Garcia Moniz 1; tel. 291 961 858; www.museudabaleia.org; Tues.-Sun. 10:30am-6pm; adults €10, children 12-17 €8.50, children 6-11 €5

The Madeira Whale Museum is a large and innovative exploration of the island's short whaling history, from 1941 until 1982, when commercial whaling dried up as the international conservation movement gained force. In an unexpectedly modern building on a hillside overlooking the sea, the museum houses interesting interactive exhibitions, 3-D movies, life-size statues, scale examples of whaling boats, and historic whaling paraphernalia, all of which provide insight into how Madeirans hunted the huge mammals and their uses. The museum is on three floors, divided into the island's whaling history and whale species and conservation. While many exhibits are child-friendly, some are graphic; special tours for children are available. The institution that runs the museum conducts scientific research projects and collects and catalogs Madeiran marine life.

GETTING THERE

Caniçal is 32 kilometers (20 mi) and 30 minutes' drive from **Funchal** along the main **VR1** coastal road, east past the airport. Regular public transport is on **SAM** (tel. 291 201 151; www.sam.pt) bus 113 (45 minutes; €3.35), departing from near the park on Funchal's main Avenida do Mar. The bus runs about hourly on weekdays, less frequently on weekends.

MADEIRA
AROUND FUNCHAL

clothes, a flashlight (particularly for the Pico do Areeiro route), and plenty of drinking water. There are shelters along the walks in the event of a sudden change in weather.

VEREDA DO AREEIRO HIKE (PR1)
Hiking Distance: *11 kilometers (6.8 mi) round-trip*
Hiking Time: *4 hours round-trip*
Trailhead: *Areeiro Peak Viewpoint (Miradouro do Pico do Areeiro)*
Information and Maps: *www.visitmadeira. pt/en-gb/what-to-do/activities/search/pr1-vereda-do-areeiro*

Not for those with vertigo, this route passes sheer ridges, narrow ledges, steep slopes, and dark tunnels, stringing together the three highest peaks on Madeira. Moderate physical fitness and stamina are required.

VEREDA DO PICO RUIVO HIKE (PR1.2)
Hiking Distance: *6 kilometers (3.7 mi) round-trip*
Hiking Time: *3 hours round-trip*
Trailhead: *Achada do Teixeira village*
Information and Maps: *www.visitmadeira. pt/en-gb/what-to-do/activities/search/pr1-2-vereda-do-pico-ruivo*

The second and more moderate route is the Vereda do Pico Ruivo (footpath PR1.2), starting from the village of Achada do Teixeira, east of Pico Ruivo. This trail snakes along the ridgeline from the village's car park to the summit. At the end of the hike is a flight of steps to the summit of Pico Ruivo, a 10-minute climb.

Other Hikes
LEVADA DO FURADO HIKE
Hiking Distance: *12 kilometers (7.4 mi) one-way*
Hiking Time: *5 hours one-way*
Trailhead: *Ribeiro Frio parish*
Information and Maps: *www.visitmadeira.pt/en-gb/what-to-do/activities/search/pr10-levada-do-furado*

The island's unique *levada* irrigation channels offer an invigorating way to absorb Madeira's natural beauty. One of the island's most popular and prettiest walks is the Levada do Furado, also known as the Ribeiro Frio-Portela Walk. This moderately challenging full-day trek goes through forested terrain between Ribeiro Frio and the neighboring village of Portela. The sun-dappled path is covered by heather and laurel trees, and trout swim in the *levada* alongside. The route, one of few *levadas* that can be reached by public transport, can become crowded at times.

Take **Horários do Funchal** (tel. 291 705 555; www.horariosdofunchal.pt) bus 56 or 103 from Funchal toward Santana, getting off at Ribeiro Frio (40 minutes; €3.35). The route ends in Portela, from where bus 78 can be taken back to Funchal.

LEVADA DAS 25 FONTES HIKE
Hiking Distance: *4.5 kilometers (2.8 mi) one-way*
Hiking Time: *3-4 hours one-way*
Trailhead: *Rabaçal forest shelter house on ER110 regional road*
Information and Maps: *www.visitmadeira.pt/en-gb/what-to-do/activities/search/pr-6-and-6-1-levada-das-25-fontes-(rabacal-25-fontes)*

Arguably the most popular *levada* walk on the island, the Levada das 25 Fontes (25 Fountains) trail is well marked and zigzags through spectacular landscape, starting at the car park on the main ER110 road on the Paúl da Serra plateau in Rabaçal. It takes its name from the number of pretty waterfalls and fountains along the way. From the Paul da Serra car park, through a gate, a signed road leads down a gentle 2-kilometer (1.2-mi) walk to a forest ranger's station. A **minibus** runs at regular intervals between the car park and the shelter (€3 one-way, €5 round-trip). This makes the trek easier on the return. There are toilet facilities at the forestry house but nowhere else on the route.

From the forestry house, the 25 Fontes *levada* leads to the mesmerizing **Risco Waterfall,** passing through the Rabaçal valley and the picturesque cascading waterfalls from which the *levada* takes its name. Construction on the 25 Fontes *levada* started

hiking to Pico Ruivo

Madeira's *Levada* Hikes

Madeira is laced with 2,100 kilometers (1,300 mi) of *levadas* (**irrigation channels**), mini aqueducts that were used to irrigate the island's farmed terraces and supply drinking water. Today they are an extraordinary network of walking paths through breathtaking countryside. You can walk for kilometers on narrow dirt tracks that run alongside the extensive *levadas*, a unique way of exploring the island specific to Madeira.

PLANNING YOUR *LEVADA* HIKE

Do your homework when deciding which *levada* to follow. Some provide relaxing, scenic strolls and others can be challenging, with tunnels and vertigo-inducing sheer cliffs. Two popular routes are **Levada do Furado,** starting in the inland village of Ribeiro Frio, and the waterfall-laced **Levada das 25 Fontes,** in Rabaçal. Sturdy, comfortable hiking boots, waterproof clothes, a flashlight, sunscreen, and drinking water are advised for embarking on a *levada* trek, and if the weather is poor, be prepared for wet, muddy conditions.

The *levada* irrigation channels make for unusual and often challenging treks.

LEVADA TOURS AND GUIDES

A guided tour can be a great way to explore these unique paths. Another great resource is the **WalkMe mobile guide** (www.walkmeguide.com), which was created by local hikers and offers a multitude of information, maps, guides, tips, and a downloadable app to help trekkers in Madeira see the best of the island in a safe and enjoyable way.

- **Lido Tours:** Estrada Monumental 284, Monumental Lido shopping center, Shop 18, Funchal; tel. 291 635 505; www.lido-tours.com; €27-37

- **Madeira Levada Walks:** Monumental Lido shopping center, Shop 23, 1stfloor, Funchal; tel. 291 763 701; www.madeira-levada-walks.com; half-day €27, full-day €37

- **Madeira Adventure Kingdom:** Estrada da Eira do Serrado 38B; tel. 968 101 870; www.madeira-adventure-kingdom.com; from €25

in 1835 and took 20 years. The trail also passes through astonishing tunnels of tree heather, shaded woodland, fragrant laurel trees, and forest to Risco, a beauty spot famed for its magnificent cascade pouring into a crystalline, half-moon-shaped lagoon. As the trail climbs to 1,290 meters (4,232 ft) elevation, a number of stone staircases are involved, and the trail can get very crowded with large tour groups, so try to get here before 9:30am to enjoy it at its most peaceful.

Getting There

Pico Ruivo is 20 kilometers (12.4 mi) north of Funchal. Public transport to either trailhead, Pico do Areeiro or Achada do Teixeira, from Funchal is intermittent and scarce; the easiest way is by car. To get to Achada do Teixeira, drive around the eastern edge of the island to Santana, along the **VR1** and **VE1** roads, and then head inland along a winding road to the car park near the village, from where it is a short hike to the summit. The drive from Funchal via Santana takes an hour. Driving to Pico do Areeiro is a much shorter 20-kilometer (12.4-mi), 40-minute trip along the **ER103** road, north from Funchal.

Rabaçal and the 25 Fontes *levada* are 30

kilometers (19 mi) west of **Funchal** on the **VR1** road and north on the **VE4** road to Encumeada; then, head west again on the **ER110** road toward Gazebo Rabaçal. The route and parking are well signed. Follow signs on foot to the Rabaçal shelter house and the start of the 25 Fontes *levada*. The drive from Funchal takes an hour. A round-trip by **taxi** from Funchal to the 25 Fontes *levada* costs around €90. There is no public transport.

A great option for less experienced hikers is to join an organized **tour;** inquire at your hotel or the tourist office.

THE WEST COAST

With dramatic mountains and ocean as a backdrop, Porto Moniz (POR-too moo-NEEZH) is famous for natural saltwater pools, created from lava and filled with seawater by the tide. The journey here is gripping, skirting around the edge of the island through a series of tunnels and along steep hillsides before arriving at the island's northwesternmost point.

Beaches and Pools
PORTO MONIZ NATURAL SWIMMING POOLS
Off Lyra Square (Praça do Lyra), Porto Moniz village
Made from lava that trickled into the ocean to create jagged black formations, the famous, beautiful natural swimming pools of Porto Moniz, on the northwest tip of Madeira Island, fill with seawater. Surrounded by the Atlantic, they make the ultimate infinity pool and are particularly enticing when the weather is hot. Many locals have an invigorating dip as part of their daily routine.

Near the entrance to the town of Porto Moniz are the wild-feeling **Cachelote natural pools** (24 hours daily; free), and a short walk from these are the **managed pools** (Rue do Forte de São João Baptista 7A; tel. 291 850 190; www.portomoniz.pt; daily 9am-7pm; €1.50), which also have a children's swimming pool, a children's play area, sun beds and parasols, lifeguards, changing facilities, a snack bar, and disabled access.

Food and Bars
CONCHINHA
Rua dos Emigrantes 4; tel. 291 615 510; www. facebook.com/ConchinhaSnackBar; daily 9am-7pm
Pop into Conchinha for a coffee and a freshly made cake or a light lunch like a toastie or a delicious sandwich made with island beef and *bolo de caco* bread.

PUKIKI
Rua das Furnas 77, Calheta; tel. 967 560 948; www. pukikibar.com; Wed.-Sat. 4pm-11pm, Sun. 3pm-10pm
On Madeira Island's southwestern coast, on the way back from Porto Moniz to Funchal, soak up some chilled subtropical island vibes at this laid-back bar. It's about 40 minutes from Porto Moniz and 45 minutes west of Funchal in the town of Calheta, but it's worth a visit, as the island's first and so far only Tiki Bar. It celebrates the historic links between Hawaii and Madeira and offers a huge selection of delicious rum and tiki cocktails, as well as spectacular views.

Getting There
Porto Moniz is 50 kilometers (31 mi) and 1.5 hours from **Funchal** by car on the main **VR1** road west from Funchal to Ribeira Brava, then through the middle of the island along the **VE4** road to the north coast, and then west along the **VE2** road from São Vicente to Porto Moniz.

By public transport, **Rodoeste** (tel. 291 220 148; www.rodoeste.com.pt) operates bus 139 (3 hours, daily morning and afternoon; €12 round-trip) to Santa-Porto Moniz, via São Vicente village, and bus 80 (3 hours, daily 9am, arriving at noon; €12 round-trip) to Porto Moniz (return bus departing daily 4pm), via Calheta village, both departing from Funchal and passing through lovely villages and around the rugged rim of the island. Bus 139 has fewer stops. Tickets can be purchased at the kiosk on the main Avenida do Mar in Funchal.

Porto Santo Island

A 2-hour ferry journey or a short flight from Madeira is the much smaller island of Porto Santo, an unspoiled haven of golden sand, tranquil water, and a smaller range of activities, attractions, bars, restaurants, and hotels. Stretching 43 kilometers (27 mi), Porto Santo is the northernmost and easternmost island of the Madeira archipelago, famed for year-round mild weather and Porto Santo Beach—a 9-kilometer (5.6-mi) crescent of pristine sand and warm turquoise water. Dubbed the "Golden Island," it has a Caribbean feel, with the rugged ocher landscape and architecture of Portugal.

Porto Santo's tourism has recently taken off, with a few good hotels and elegant, four-star, all-inclusive resorts. But it is not being overrun or overbuilt, as construction has been regulated, in harmony with the island's character. The southwest shore is one long, glorious beach, and its northeastern shore is rocky and rugged, spiked with mountain peaks. This makes the southern part popular among sun lovers and the northern coast popular among adventure seekers, although neither becomes crowded. Stretch out on the warm sand, dive, hike, or try stand-up paddleboarding.

The biggest town is Vila Baleira, on the south side, the island's first settlement and active year-round. Home to most of the island's residents and action, as well as the port for ferries arriving from Madeira Island, Vila Baleira is charming, low-key, unspoiled, and unhurried, except on weekends and summer when visitor numbers are higher.

GETTING THERE

There are direct **flights** between Porto Santo and mainland Portugal; and the daily **ferry** from Madeira Island takes 2 hours.

Air
PORTO SANTO AIRPORT
(Aeroporto do Porto Santo)

PXO; tel. 291 520 700; www.aeroportoportosanto.pt
Two kilometers (1.2 mi) north of Vila Baleira, Porto Santo Airport is a small but modern terminal and a 3,000-meter (9.843-ft) runway that receives just a couple of daily flights in winter, growing to a handful in summer.

There are a few direct flights between mainland Portugal and Porto Santo. **TAP Air Portugal** (tel. 707 205 700; www.flytap.com) flies from Lisbon to Porto Santo weekly in low season (Oct.-May) and more frequently in high season (June-Sept.). Regional airline **SATA Azores Airlines** (tel. 707 227 282; www.azoresairlines.pt) operates a direct flight from Lisbon to Porto Santo. Airfares start from €200 round-trip, and the flight takes 1.5 hours.

Porto Santo is more easily reached from Madeira Island. Regional airline **Sevenair** (tel. 214 444 545; www.sevenair.com) is the main carrier to Porto Santo, operating daily flights from Funchal. At the time of writing, Spanish airline **Binter Canarias** (tel. +34 902 391 392; www.bintercanarias.com), based in the Canary Islands, was offering cheap direct flights between Funchal and Porto Santo (15 minutes; from €66 one-way) twice daily in summer high season.

Porto Santo Airport is 5 minutes north of Vila Baleira. It's easiest to take a **taxi** (€10-15) from the taxi rank right outside.

Ferry
PORT OF PORTO SANTO
(Porto do Porto Santo)

Porto de Abrigo do Porto Santo - ER233, Vila Baleira; tel. 291 980 080; www.apram.pt/site/index.php/en/ports/caracteristicas/port-of-porto-santo
By sea, Porto Santo Line's **Lobo Marinho ferry** (tel. 291 210 300; www.portosantoline.pt) runs daily between Madeira and Porto Santo (2 hours; €47-72 adults Oct.-Mar., €58-81 Apr.-Sept.), weather permitting; the ferry departs from Funchal in the early morning

and departs Porto Santo in the late afternoon or evening. Passengers enjoy a number of bars, restaurants, and even a cinema on board. Cars (€93-121), bicycles, and motorbikes can be transported. First- and second-class tickets can be purchased online, from a ticket office (Av. do Mar e das Comunidades Madeirenses 20, Funchal; tel. 291 210 300; Mon.-Fri. 8:30am-6pm, Sat. 9am-12:30pm and 2pm-5pm; Estrada Monumental 175C, Funchal; tel. 291 210 300; daily 9am-12:30pm and 2pm-8pm), or from the passengers' terminal at either port, up to one hour before departure.

GETTING AROUND

Given Porto Santo's small size, **taxis** are a good option, and they are widely available. The best way to explore Vila Baleira is **on foot.** In summer, **horse-drawn carriages** (tel. 964 682 937; up to 6 people, €15 for 15 minutes, €30 for 30 minutes, €50 for 1 hour) are usually available around the ferry terminal or the main promenade, the Promenada do Porto Santo.

Taxi

There are plenty of taxis on Porto Santo, a reasonable option, as distances on the island are short. The island's main taxi rank is next to the gas station on Avenida Dr. Manuel Gregório Pestana Júnior, at the end of Rua João Gonçalves Zarco, in Vila Baleira. You can also call **Vila Baleira taxis** (tel. 291 982 334). A half-day taxi tour of the island costs around €30.

Car

By car, the entire island can be covered in a day. The roads are easy and safe, much quieter and flatter than Madeira's, and rented cars can be brought here on the ferry from Funchal. A number of car rental companies operate on Porto Santo, mostly at the airport and in the main town center. If you're staying

for a short time, book ahead to get the car at the airport.

Bus

Porto Santo has a public bus service, but due to the island's limited size, the routes are not extensive; buses run the same route around the coast and inland. Its main hub is next to the petrol station at the beach end of Rua João Gonçalves Zarco. Six daily buses, leaving hourly, run the same route around the coast and inland; costs vary depending on destination. One-way bus fares to anywhere on the island will rarely exceed a few euros; the bus (Line 1) between Vila Baleira and the airport costs €2 one-way. There will always be a bus, operated by **Moinho Rent-a-Car** (tel. 291 982 141 or 966 066 389; www.moinhorentacar. com; €1) waiting for the ferry to take passengers from the terminal to the main town, Vila Baleira.

A local **tour bus,** operated by **Lazermar** (tel. 963 501 488; www.lazermar.com), departs from the city's main taxi rank daily at 10am and 3pm and makes a 2-hour tour of the island (adults €20, children 6-12 €10).

Tours

Plenty of tours, which can be booked through your hotel, take you to more remote attractions. Top companies include **Porto Santo Destination Tours** (tel. 911 798 989, www. lisbondestinationtours.com/porto-santo) and **Lazermar** (tel. 963 501 488, www.lazermar. com). **Dunas Travel** (tel. 291 983 088, www. dunastravel.com)offers jeep tours.

SIGHTS
CHAPEL OF THE HOLY SPIRIT
(Capela do Espirito Santo)

Estrada Regional 120, Campo de Baixo; tel. 291 982 215; open for mass only, Sun. 10am, Sat. 5:30pm Oct.-May, Sat. 6:30pm June-Sept.; free

Small, simple, and perfectly formed, this 17th-century chapel in the village of Campo de Baixo, 2.4 kilometers (1.5 mi) southwest from Vila Baleira, was built in the mannerist style and extensively refurbished during the 19th

---

1: Porto Moniz Natural Swimming Pools **2:** Porto Santo Beach

century. A short walk from Vila Baleira, this pretty little chapel has a simple facade with a bell tower. Inside it features 17th-century Flemish paintings of the Last Supper. It is a 2.5-kilometer (1.6-mi), 30-minute walk southwest from Vila Baleira.

CHRISTOPHER COLUMBUS HOUSE MUSEUM
(Casa de Colombo)

Travessa da Sacristia 2-4, Vila Baleira; tel. 291 983 405; Tues.-Sat. 10am-12:30pm and 2pm-5:30pm, Sun. 10am-1pm; €2

Famed explorer and navigator Christopher Columbus is said to have lived on Porto Santo while planning his voyages. The house in which he is believed to have spent several years with his wife has been transformed into the Christopher Columbus House Museum. The small 15th-century stone house is in an alley behind the main church. Spread over several rooms, it houses artifacts relating to Columbus and his expeditions, including a portrait and replicas of 15th- and 16th-century maps, as well as large panels tracing Portuguese maritime history. A separate room showcases artifacts recovered from a Spanish galleon that sank off Porto Santo in 1724. The museum, inaugurated in 1989, also has a lovely little courtyard.

SPORTS AND RECREATION
Beaches and Pools
PORTO SANTO BEACH
(Praia Porto Santo)

Porto Santo south coast

Porto Santo Beach is an uncrowded 9-kilometer (5.6-mi) strip of pristine soft sand and warm turquoise water for tranquil beach days and long strolls. Hugging most of the island's south coast, it stretches southwest along the main strip of hotel resorts between Vila Baleira and Calheta Point, the southwestern tip of the island. Widely believed to have therapeutic properties, the fine volcanic sand mixed with particles of ancient coral reefs gives the beach a yellow-and-gray hue.

Flanked by snack bars, restaurants, and elegant resorts, Porto Santo is the ultimate beach paradise, one of Europe's best-kept secrets.

Stand-up paddleboards can be rented from outfitters and hotels along the beach, including **On Water Academy** (tel. 964 838 535; www.onwateracademy.com; from €25 for 1.5 hours).

PORTO DOS FRADES BEACH
(Praia do Porto dos Frades)

Porto Santo east coast

Around the corner from Porto Santo Beach, on the island's eastern fringe, Porto dos Frades is a tiny beach ensconced in rocky cliffs. It is a popular spot for snorkeling and a peaceful, tranquil haven away from the busy main tourist area.

ZIMBRALINHO BEACH
(Praia do Zimbralinho)

Porto Santo southern tip, Ponta da Calheta

Nestled between steep cliffs on the southern tip of Porto Santo known as Ponta da Calheta, the hidden Zimbralinho Beach is secluded, rugged, unspoiled, and pebbly, with exceptionally translucent waters.

Hiking
CASTELO PEAK HIKE – PS PR2
(Pico do Castelo)

Hiking Distance: *3.2-kilometer (2-mi) loop or 4.6-kilometer (2.9-miles) loop*
Hiking Time: *1.5 or 2 hours round-trip*
Trailhead: *Sítio do Moledo, off ER regional road*
Information and Maps: *www.visitmadeira.pt/en-gb/what-to-do/walking-routes/ps-pr2-vereda-do-pico-castelo*

Shaped like a volcano, Castelo Peak, in the very middle of the northeastern portion of the island, has precipitous sides but good conditions for walking. The hiking trail starts in the hamlet of Moledo, just off the Regional Road (Estrada Regional), about a 15-minute, 3.5-kilometer (2.2-mi) drive north from Vila Baleira. The trail passes Facho Peak, the highest point on the island, and winds through forested hillsides with native flora and fauna before reaching a legendary viewpoint at 437 meters (1,434 ft) elevation. The trailhead is signposted and easy to find. Two trails can be followed: one a shorter and easier 3.2-kilometer (2-mi) loop around the north side of the peak that takes 1.5 hours, and a longer and tougher 4.6-kilometer (2.9-mi) loop on the south side, which takes 2 hours and is the longest pedestrian trail on the island.

Despite its name, there is no castle; in the 15th century there was a fort here where residents took refuge from invaders. The viewpoint looks out over the airport and the ocean; on a clear day you can see the Desertas and Madeira Islands.

ANA FERREIRA PEAK HIKE
(Pico de Ana Ferreira)

Hiking Distance: *1.3 kilometers (0.8 mi) there and back*
Hiking Time: *1 hour there and back*
Trailhead: *Regional Road ER111*
Information and Maps: www.wikiloc.com/hiking-trails/pico-ana-ferreira-18161090

Ana Ferreira Peak is unique for its unusual summit, which erupts in an oddly ridged rim of pentagonal basalt rock columns like bizarrely shaped teeth. Nicknamed "the Organ," these peculiar pipes—similar to the famous Giant's Causeway in Northern Ireland, only bigger—were shaped millions of years ago by volcanic activity, when thick lava flows cooled and cracked. Also named the "Piano Quarry," this unusual formation is a fantastic viewpoint, at 283 meters (928 ft) elevation, with views over Porto Santo. The hike to Ana Ferreira Peak, whose trailhead starts near the Porto Santo golf course, is easy and short on a road or on dirt tracks, southwest from Vila Baleira.

An exciting way to explore the peak is to take a 4WD Jeep excursion, such as those operated by **Lazermar** (Rua João Gonçalves Zarco 66, Vila Baleira; tel. 963 501 488; www.lazermar.com; 3.5 hours; €25) on a bumpy off-road round-trip, passing through hidden beauty spots and geological places of interest.

Snorkeling and Scuba Diving

Porto Santo is a world-class diving spot thanks to its unspoiled water with a rare high level of visibility. Impressive dive sites include the *Madeirense,* a purposely sunk ship that attracts fish.

RHEA DIVE CENTER

Hotel Pestana; tel. 969 333 777; www.rheadive.com; daily 9am-6pm

Rhea Dive Center has taken divers and snorkelers to Porto Santo's best spots since 2007.

FOOD

Porto Santo shares typical dishes with big sister Madeira. Signature fare includes *fragateira,* a fish stew for sharing, as well as *gaiado,* sun-dried skipjack tuna. Most of Porto Santo's restaurants and bars are in the main town, Vila Baleira.

★ CASINHA DO BOLO DO CACO

Praça do Barqueiro, Porto Santo quay, Vila Baleira; tel. 291 645 852; Mon.-Sat. 9am-7pm; €5

Casinha do Bolo do Caco is a little beach shack specializing in sandwiches and snacks made with typical fresh-baked *bolo do caco* bread rolls. These include *bolo do caco* smeared with chocolate spread or stuffed with spicy sausage or bacon and cheese. This is a great place to grab a quick bite during a day at the beach: street food with a smile.

★ MERCADO VELHO

Rua João Gonçalves Zarco, Vila Baleira; tel. 291 984 205; Mon.-Sat. 8am-midnight; €10

Quirky little Mercado Velho is in the island's fish market. Patrons perch on little stools at cement tables as unfussy traditional fare, including *lapas,* grilled fish, *bolo do caco* sandwiches, and a great *poncho,* is served at cheap prices.

CASA D'AVO

Campo de Baixo; tel. 291 982 037; Mon.-Sat. 5pm-2am; €20

Casa d'Avo, 2.5 kilometers (1.6 mi) southwest of Vila Baleira, off the main ER111 road, is an elegant little restaurant in a lovely setting that serves flavorful traditional Madeiran dishes, nicely presented with local ingredients. Madeiran staple *lapas* are on the menu, as are steak with shrimp sauce and other regional favorites such as the *espetada* kebabs.

ACCOMMODATIONS

Porto Santo has some excellent hotels, especially all-inclusive beachfront resorts to enhance the holiday vibe.

VILA BALEIRA RESORT

Sitio do Cabeço da Ponta; tel. 291 980 800; www. vilabaleira.com; €150

An idyllic, family-friendly all-inclusive resort, Vila Baleira Resort Porto Santo is a beautiful beachfront hotel about 4 kilometers (2.5 mi) south of the main town Vila Baleira. Sprawled spaciously over the sandy island, it has great amenities for adults and children, including swimming pools and free bicycles, and it's also near the island's golf course.

PESTANA PORTO SANTO

Estrada Regional 163 Sitio do Campo de Baixo; tel. 291 144 000; www.pestana.com; €150

Right on Porto Santo Beach, the Pestana Porto Santo all-inclusive resort is a lovely low-rise, upscale resort, offering large rooms, a spa, indoor and outdoor pools, and a garden. It also comprises several restaurants and bars onsite, with an exotic and exciting vibe. A little slice of tropical on a subtropical island.

INFORMATION AND SERVICES

Porto Santo has the services and amenities to make a stay on the island comfortable, though emergencies will likely be transferred to Madeira Island or to the mainland; there is no hospital on the island.

- **Health Center:** Rua Dr José Diamantino Lima; tel. 291 980 060
- **PSP police:** tel. 291 980 010
- **Tourist bureau:** Av. Dr. Manuel Gregório Pestana Junior; tel. 291 985 244; Mon.-Fri. 9am-5:30pm, Sat.-Sun. and holidays 10am-12:30pm; tourist helpline tel. 966 765 802 or 966 765 718, available daily 9am-8pm
- **Pharmacy:** Rua João Gonçalves Zarco, 50; tel. 291 980 420; Mon.-Fri. 9am-8pm, Sat. 9am-7pm, Sun. 9am-1pm

The Azores

It's hard to describe the breathtaking natural mystique of the volcanic Azores, nine lush islands scattered like emeralds in the middle of the Atlantic. Tourism has started to take off on the main island, São Miguel, in recent years, and low-cost and charter flights from all over Europe now visit this Edenic oasis. But the islands are still far from being a mainstream destination, and traveling to a relatively uncharted place of idyllic beauty and friendliness makes the Azores alluring. The archipelago's famously changeable weather, which swings from sunny and warm to cool with low-hanging clouds in the blink of an eye, adds to its mystical aura. A short hop from the mainland, luxuriant gardens, soothing hot springs, quaint villages, and dramatic landscapes make the Azores a world away from the everyday.

Highlights

Look for ★ to find recommended sights, activities, dining, and lodging.

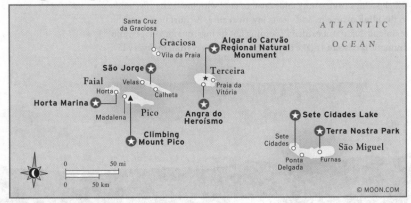

ATLANTIC OCEAN

Santa Cruz da Graciosa
Graciosa
Vila da Praia
★ Algar do Carvão Regional Natural Monument
São Jorge ★
Faial
Horta
Velos
Calheta
Terceira
★ Praia da Vitória
Horta Marina ★
Madalena
Pico
★ Angra do Heroísmo
★ Climbing Mount Pico
★ Sete Cidades Lake
★ Terra Nostra Park
Sete Cidades
São Miguel
Ponta Delgada
Furnas

0   50 mi
0   50 km

© MOON.COM

★ **Sete Cidades Lake:** This stunning Azorean landmark is infused with local legend (page 396).

★ **Terra Nostra Park:** Stroll through a paradisiacal Eden packed with beautiful flora before dipping into a relaxing hot-spring pool (page 399).

★ **Angra do Heroísmo:** History pervades port town Angra do Heroísmo, whose staunch maritime tradition and unique architecture have seen it classified a UNESCO World Heritage Site (page 404).

★ **Algar do Carvão Regional Natural Monument:** Descend to the depths of this ancient volcanic vent in the heart of Terceira Island (page 410).

★ **Horta Marina:** No trip to the Azores is complete without passing through this place of swashbuckling seafaring legend (page 413).

★ **Climbing Mount Pico:** Stand high over the Atlantic by climbing the Azores' most iconic volcano (page 425).

★ **São Jorge:** The least-visited of the islands covered in this book is well worth the trek (page 426).

Bubbling fumaroles, hissing hot-water geysers, and soothing springs are some of the island's main attractions.

The Azores were discovered circa 1427 and colonized by the Portuguese from the 1430s. Legend has it that sheep were the first inhabitants, let loose on the islands ahead of human occupation to sustain future settlers. Settlement to such a far-flung location was slow, but eventually the first colonizers came, mostly from the Algarve, Alentejo, Central Portugal, and Madeira. This intermittent settlement influenced local dialects and gastronomy, which vary remarkably, as do the landscapes and climates of the islands. Interestingly, the Azores also had a large Flemish settlement whose influences are noticeable to this day, most visibly in the many little windmills that pepper the islands.

THE ISLANDS

A 2-hour flight west from mainland Portugal, roughly a quarter of the Atlantic Ocean toward the United States, the Azores spread over 600 kilometers (370 mi). This group of nine volcanic islands (actually the tips of some of the biggest underwater mountains on the planet) is divided into three groups: São Miguel and Santa Maria make up the **Eastern Group;** Graciosa, Terceira, São Jorge, Pico, and Faial form the **Central Group,** with the close-knit São Jorge, Pico, and Faial forming the **Azores Triangle;** and far-flung Flores and Corvo comprise the **Western Group.** The time zone in the Azores is one hour earlier than on the mainland. This book covers the most accessible islands.

São Miguel

Locally dubbed the "Green Island," São Miguel is the biggest and most populous island in the Azores. Its main city and the Azores' capital, **Ponta Delgada,** is densely populated, but just 10 minutes out of town, sprawling green fields dotted with sheep and cattle and a rainbow of colorful flowers justify the island's nickname. Among the highlights of long, whale-shaped São Miguel are the incredible **Sete Cidades crater lakes** and soothing **hot springs** in the town of **Furnas.**

Terceira

An almost perfectly round island, Terceira means "third," as it was the third island to be inhabited and is also the third largest in the archipelago; it's the second-most populous. Terceira is nicknamed the "Lilac Island" for its stunning sunsets as well as an abundance of purple hydrangea. The main port, **Angra do Heroísmo,** is the oldest city in the Azores and the historical capital, a UNESCO World Heritage Site. The island also boasts the extensive **Algar do Carvão** caves.

The Azores Triangle
FAIAL

Faial is best known for its main town, **Horta,** a popular transatlantic **port** that gives the town an international and cosmopolitan feel and boasts stunning views of nearby Pico. Faial's nickname, the "Blue Island," derives from the vast ocean surrounding it and the blue hydrangeas that cover it. The island slopes gently upward toward a central volcano before dropping into the 400-meter-deep (1,312-ft-deep) **Faial Caldera.**

PICO

Pico's snowcapped summit, **Mount Pico,** is the highest point in all of Portugal at 2,351 meters (7,713 ft), dominating the second-largest island in the Azores, often referred to as the "Black Island" due to its dark volcanic terrain. The island's main town, **Madalena,** spreads along the foot of Mount Pico, facing Faial Island, 7 kilometers (4 mi) away. One of the last islands to be inhabited, Pico is today one of the most popular, with a unique and successful **wine** industry.

Previous: Sete Cidades Lake; Terra Nostra's hot springs; natural pool on São Jorge.

The Azores

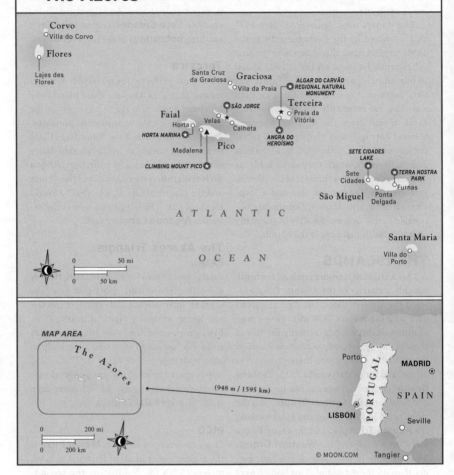

SÃO JORGE

A long slither of soaring volcanic ridge, São Jorge is an island of food and **fajãs,** or lava plateaus. Famed for its excellent **cheeses** and local lagoon **clams,** São Jorge is 54 kilometers (34 mi) long and 7 kilometers (4 mi) at its widest. Breathtaking vistas of neighboring Pico's summit can be enjoyed from almost every part of the island. São Jorge is an island to be explored on foot, with a fantastic network of scenic **hikes;** many of the *fajãs* are pedestrian-access only.

GETTING THERE

The only way to get to the Azores is **by air.** All nine islands have an airfield for interisland transportation, but only three (São Miguel, Faial, and Terceira) have international airports. Flights from major airports throughout Europe are frequent, usually between 2-3 hours, and can typically be found for around €100 round-trip.

- **Ponta Delgada Airport** (Aeroporto de Ponta Delgada; PDL; tel. 296 205 400;

www.aeroportopontadelgada.pt), on São Miguel, is the Azores' main airport and receives the vast majority of international flights, including from **North America** (Boston, Toronto, and less frequently from Montreal, Canada, and Oakland, California). Transatlantic flights range from 4-6 hours and typically cost €500-600 round-trip.

- **Lajes Airport,** also known as Lajes Civil Air Base (Aeroporto das Lajes/Aerogare Civil das Lajes; TER; tel. 295 545 454; www.aerogarelajes.azores.gov.pt), on Terceira, is both a civilian airport and a military airbase, managed by the Portuguese with a US presence. It also has direct international flights, primarily from Europe.

- **Horta Airport** (Aeroporto da Horta; HOR; tel. 292 943 511; www.aeroportohorta.pt), on Faial, receives direct international flights mainly from Europe.

From mainland Portugal, the Azores are a short and cheap (usually around €100 round-trip) 2-hour flight. The main airlines are national flag-carrier **TAP Air Portugal** (tel. 707 205 700; www.flytap.com), regional carrier **SATA Azores Airlines** (tel. 707 227 282; www.sata.pt), and Irish low-cost airline **Ryanair** (tel. +44 871 246 0002; www.ryanair.com). The majority of flights leave from **Lisbon Portela Airport** (Aeroporto de Lisboa; LIS; tel. 121 841 3500; www.aeroportolisboa.pt) and Porto's **Francisco Sá Carniero Airport** (Aeroporto Francisco Sá Carniero; OPO; 122 943 2400; www.aeroportolisboa.pt).

SATA provides a **free onward service** from Porto, Lisbon, or Funchal via Ponta Delgada, meaning you can request a free connecting flight to any other Azorean island. The flight must be taken within 24 hours of landing in Ponta Delgada.

GETTING AROUND

For travel between the islands, interisland flights are the most reliable, with the exception of the Azores Triangle islands of Pico, Faial, and São Jorge, which are connected by frequent ferries. On the islands themselves, renting a car usually provides the most convenience and flexibility, though guided tours, taxis, motorbikes, and scooters can also be good options. Public bus services, when present, are usually geared more toward island residents than tourists.

Between the Islands

The general rule is that except for the quick, frequent, year-round, and relatively cheap **ferries** (Atlânticoline; main cruise terminal on Ponta Delgada harbor, Av. Infante Dom Henrique; tel. 707 201 572; www.atlanticoline.pt) between the Azores Triangle islands, **interisland flights** (run by SATA Air Azores; tel. 707 227 282, www.sata.pt) are usually the best way to travel between the Azores, even if they are more expensive. Other ferries could make sense for those with a sense of adventure, or with more time, but they can be slow and unreliable and often run infrequently (or not at all in the winter months). Flights between all the islands are generally frequent (more so in summer than in winter) and quick (usually clocking in at around an hour). Round-trip tickets can usually be found for around €100.

On the Islands

Renting a **car** is the way to go for the bigger islands (São Miguel, Terceira, and Pico), particularly if you're going to be spending a few days. Faial and São Jorge, smaller islands, can be explored on a rental **scooter.** Car rentals are cheap and are more flexible than booking often costly excursions. Fuel is cheaper than on the mainland, and the roads are generally quiet and well maintained. **Taxis** are practical and are reasonably priced; **public transport,** however, is designed for locals, and even on the bigger islands service is infrequent, particularly on weekends. The bigger islands do have cheap public transport, although buses tend to follow the main coastal roads, and few travel inland.

PLANNING YOUR TIME

If your primary destination is mainland Portugal, a **long weekend** provides time to visit one island—**São Miguel** tends to be the number-one destination. If you intend to see more than one island, take at least four days. **Terceira** is a great island to tack on to São Miguel, and the **Azores Triangle** of São Jorge, Pico, and Faial could take up a week in themselves.

The Azores are busier in **summer,** but they experience nothing near the mass tourism of Madeira or the mainland. While winter can get rainy, the rest of the year is generally mild and pleasant, bearing in mind that all the Azores islands are prone to **"four seasons in one day"** weather at any time of year.

Make sure to book hotels and rental vehicles in advance for the best prices, especially if visiting smaller islands or during busier times such as summer, **Christmas,** and **Holy Festivals.**

São Miguel

The Azores' biggest island, São Miguel (sown mee-GELL), is fun and stimulating. With pools of rusty-red hot spring water and wild flora interspersed with pretty towns and fishing villages, the volcanic island's landscape is vastly diverse. Blanketed by verdant woodland and meadows, São Miguel is home to capital city Ponta Delgada and the main international airport, though it shows few signs of pandering to mainstream tourism: Life moves at an unhurried, laid-back pace. São Miguel is also where many of the Azores' most famous sights can be found, like Sete Cidades Lake and the geothermal mecca of Furnas, plus evocative landscapes and excellent gastronomy far off the beaten track.

GETTING THERE

Though it's possible to fly to Terceira, Pico, and Faial from mainland Portugal, and some international flights fly in and out of Terceira's airport as well, the majority of travelers will likely start their trip on São Miguel, which boasts the Azores' largest airport. It's also possible to travel by ferry to São Miguel from Terceira during the summer months (May-Sept.), but it's not recommended as it tends to be slow and unreliable.

A growing number of transatlantic and European **cruises** now also stop in Ponta Delgada, including cruises operated by companies MSC Cruises, Royal Caribbean, P&O Cruises, AIDA Cruises, and Holland America Line.

Air

Ponta Delgada Airport, on São Miguel, is the Azores' main airport, also called João Paulo II Airport for Pope John Paul II. It's just a 10-minute drive from the center of Ponta Delgada, the island's main city. It receives the vast majority of international flights to the islands; most travelers to the Azores will start here. There are **interisland flights** to Ponta Delgada Airport from every island in the Azores except Corvo and Graciosa.

Ferry
**PONTA DELGADA
FERRY TERMINAL**

Portas do Mar; tel. 296 629 424; open 24/7

São Miguel can be reached by seasonal ferry operated by **Atlanticoline** (tel. 707 201 572; www.atlanticoline.pt), from **Terceira** (Praia da Vitória harbor, Cabo da Praia; tel. 295 540 000; 6 hours; €70 one-way) and **Santa Maria** (Vila do Porto harbor, Cais de Ilha de Santa Maria; tel. 296 882 782; 2.5-3 hours; €50 one-way), but only from **mid-May to late September.** There are at least two weekly departures from these islands to São Miguel during this period, all arriving in Ponta Delgada. Note ferry service is often slow and unreliable due to rough Atlantic waters.

ORIENTATION

São Miguel is long and slender. **Ponta Delgada,** the main city and home to the international airport, is on the southern coast, toward the western side of the island. The hot spring village of **Furnas** is located inland, to the eastern part of the island; the stunning **Sete Cidades Lake** is located on its western tip. Crossing the island from south to north across its skinniest point in the middle takes just 20 minutes, whereas traversing from west to east (or vice versa) across its 64-kilometer (40-mi) longitude would take around 1.5 hours. The main **EN1-1A** road runs around the rim of the island. Follow this road and eventually (4-5 hours for the full loop) you will come full circle.

PLANNING YOUR TIME

In a rush, the island could be visited in a day, but a weekend or more is better. São Miguel's western half, home to **Sete Cidades Lake** and **Ponta Delgada,** makes for one great day; the hot springs of **Furnas,** in the island's center, could easily fill another. **Renting a car** is the best way to get around. Most sights are a short drive from Ponta Delgada, making it a good base; on the rest of the island, accommodations are fewer and more remote.

Thanks to its year-round mild weather, São Miguel is great in any season, but there are a few things to bear in mind when planning: **ferries** to other islands only run seasonally (May-Sept.); **winter** (Nov.-Feb.) is rainiest and coolest; the **whale-watching** season runs roughly from April to September; and the **busiest months** are July and August, reflecting the summer holidays on the mainland. It's wise to book **hotels** well in advance for the busier months, and make reservations for the most popular **restaurants,** particularly those selling the typical *cozido das Furnas* in Furnas village.

On São Miguel, make sure you always have a swimsuit and a towel with you, as jumping into steaming hot springs is tempting whatever the weather—but make sure it's an old swimsuit, as the iron-rich waters can turn clothes orange.

Tours

If the comfort and security of an organized tour is your preferred way of exploring a new destination, there are plenty to choose from on São Miguel.

- **Pure Azores:** tel. 932 532 200; www. pureazores.com; walking tours €30 pp, van tours from €59 pp
- **Greenzone Azores:** tel. 962 770 410; https://greenzoneazores.com; jeep tours from €35

PONTA DELGADA

The gateway to the Azores, Ponta Delgada is quaint yet polished, a cosmopolitan city that retains its small-town feel. Its architecture is distinctively two-toned, with whitewashed walls and black basalt trim. Centuries-old churches, the grand Portas da Cidade old City Gates, and the imposing Fort of São Brás evoke Ponta Delgada's days as a trading port. It's still a great spot for whale-watching, with trips departing from the marina at the far eastern end of the harbor promenade. The streets throughout Ponta Delgada are an attraction in themselves, boasting fancy black-and-white cobblestone designs in stripes, stars, chains, and other eye-catching symmetrical patterns. Tourists mingle with locals in elegant gardens, and while the city largely escapes the trappings of tourism, it does cater well to visitors, with plenty of hotels and restaurants, a large, well-equipped hospital, good roads, a modern shopping center, and clean streets.

Avenida Infante Dom Henrique, a beautiful harborside promenade, is a pleasant stroll from the formidable 16th-century **Fort of São Brás** on the western tip of a cosmopolitan marina, with chic restaurants and trendy bars. Opposite the fort is Ponta Delgada's main squares, the pretty **5 de Outubro Square** (Praça 5 de Outubro); the **Convent of Nossa Senhora da Esperança**

São Miguel

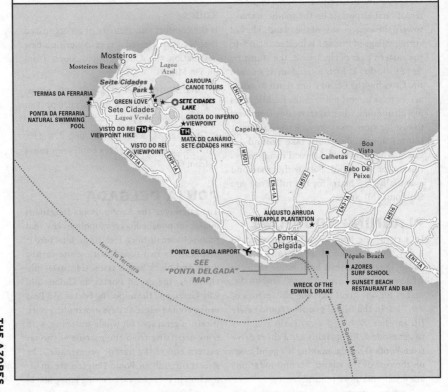

is also just across the road from the fort. A little farther down are the imposing old **City Gates,** historic stone archways with the decorative **Gonçalo Velho Square** stretching before them.

Sights
CHURCH OF SÃO SEBASTIÃO
(Igreja de São Sebastião)

Largo da Matriz 62; tel. 296 285 321; Mon.-Sat. 7:30am-7pm, Sun. 7:30am-1pm and 4pm-6pm; free

Rising from its starry cobblestone base like the centerpiece on a fancy cake, the magnificent São Sebastião church, also referred to as the city's Mother Church (or main church), is a wonderful example of 16th-century Manueline architecture, with the Azores'

trademark white with black trim. It was built on the site of a small chapel and expanded following extensions in the 18th century. The inside of the church is lavish, with intricate carvings, paintings from the 17th and 18th centuries, and swaths of opulent gilding. It also has the distinction of hosting the only tall clock tower in the city.

CONVENT OF NOSSA SENHORA DA ESPERANÇA
(Convento de Nossa Senhora da Esperança)

Campo de São Francisco; tel. 296 284 453; daily 11am-noon and 5:30pm-6:30pm; free

On the main **5 de Outubro Square,** this 16th-century convent still houses nuns of

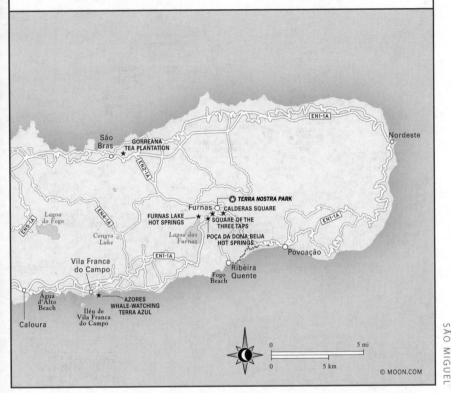

the order of St. Francis. The adjacent **Chapel of Senhor Santo Cristo dos Milagres** (Santuário do Senhor Santo Cristo dos Milagres) is closely linked to the worship of the Christ of the Miracles, a spectacularly embellished statue said to have been brought to the island in the 16th century. This statue, often hidden away in a sanctuary for safekeeping, can only be viewed at specific times (usually daily 5:30pm-6:30pm in winter, and 11am-noon and daily 5:30pm-6:30pm in summer), when the nuns allow visitors.

The Convent and Chapel of Our Lady of Hope is one of the main pillars of the extravagant **Cult of the Lord Holy Christ of the Miracles Festival** (Festa do Senhor Santo Cristo dos Milagres; starting 5th Saturday after Easter) celebrations, when the building is dressed top-to-toe in lights. It's the most popular festival in the Azores and one of the oldest, venerating an ornate wooden statue of Christ. Once a year the statue is brought out of the sanctuary and gleefully paraded through the main streets of Ponta Delgada, feted and festooned in bejeweled flowers and colorful garlands.

FORT OF SÃO BRÁS
(Forte de São Brás)

Rua Engenheiro Abel Ferin Coutinho 10; tel. 296 304 920; www.monumentos.gov.pt; Mon.-Fri. 10am-6pm; €3

Situated on a promontory on the western tip of the marina, this formidable, historic 16th-century Renaissance fort is today occupied by the Portuguese Navy and houses a **museum**

Ponta Delgada

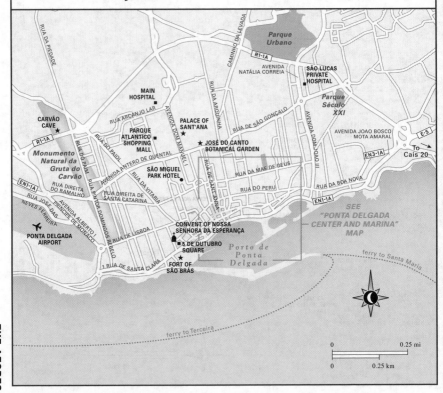

RUA DA PIEDADE

CAMINHO DA LEVADA

Parque
Urbano

R1-1A

AVENIDA
NATÁLIA CORREIA

SÃO LUCAS
PRIVATE
HOSPITAL

MAIN
HOSPITAL

RUA DA ARQUINHA

Parque
Século
XXI

CARVÃO
CAVE

RUA ARCANJO LAR

AVENIDA DOM MANUEL I

PALACE OF
SANT'ANA
★

RUA DE SÃO GONÇALO

AVENIDA DOM JOAO II

AVENIDA JOAO BOSCO
MOTA AMARAL

E-5

R1-1A

RUA DO PAIM

RUA DO PAIM

PARQUE
ATLANTICO
SHOPPING
MALL

★ JOSÉ DO CANTO
BOTANICAL GARDEN

EN3-1A

To
Cais 20

Monumento
Natural da
Gruta do
Carvão

AVENIDA ANTERO DE QUENTAL

SÃO MIGUEL
PARK HOTEL

RUA DA VITÓRIA

RUA DA SANT'ANA

RUA DA MAE DE DEUS

RUA DA BOA NOVA

EN1-1A

RUA DIREITA
DO RAMALHO

RUA PINTOR DOMINGOS REBELO

RUA DIREITA DE
SANTA CATARINA

RUA DO PERU

EN1-1A

RUA JOSÉ DAS
NEVES FERREIRA

AVENIDA PRÍNCIPE DE MÓNACO

AVENIDA ALBERTO I

RUA DE LISBOA

SEE
"PONTA DELGADA
CENTER AND MARINA"
MAP

PONTA DELGADA
AIRPORT

✈

CONVENT OF NOSSA
SENHORA DA ESPERANÇA

Porto de
Ponta
Delgada

ferry to Santa Maria

1 RUA DE SANTA CLARA

5 DE OUTUBRO
SQUARE

FORT OF
SÃO BRÁS
★

ferry to Terceira

0   0.25 mi

0   0.25 km

dedicated to Azorean military paraphernalia, a treat for anyone interested in military history. The most powerful fortification on the island, the squat, bulky quadrangular fort was built to defend the city against pirate attacks that were once a regular occurrence in this part of the Atlantic Ocean.

JOSÉ DO CANTO
BOTANICAL GARDEN
(Jardim Botânico José do Canto)

Rua José do Canto; tel. 296 650 310; www.
josedocanto.com; daily 9am-5pm Oct.-Mar., daily
9am-7pm Apr.-Sept.; free

North of the city center, the José do Canto Botanical Garden is a peaceful floral oasis. Comprising colorful flowerbeds, exotic trees, a large lake, this area is also home to the

Palace of Sant'Ana (Palácio de Sant'Ana; Rua José Jácome Correia; tel. 296 301 000, www.azores.gov.pt, Tues.-Sun. 10am-5pm; €2), an impressive salmon-colored palace. Also known as the Palácios da Presidência, today it's the seat of the office of the Presidency of the Regional Government. Built in the second half of the 19th century, it remained a family home until 1977, when it was purchased by the government. It's a lovely little refuge providing peace and tranquility, plus cooling shade on hotter days.

CARVÃO CAVE
(Gruta do Carvão)

Rua do Paim - 2ª Circular; tel. 961 397 080 or 296
284 155; http://grutadocarvao.amigosdosacores.pt;
daily 10am-12:30pm and 2pm-6pm; €5

Ponta Delgada Center and Marina

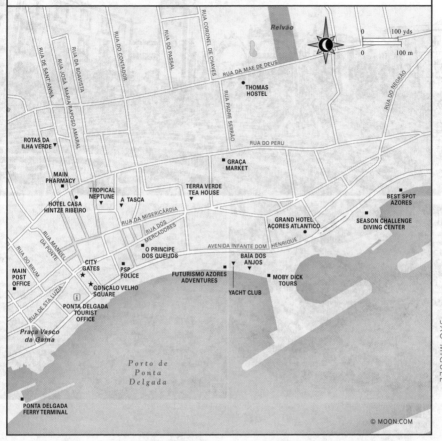

On the northern outskirts of Ponta Delgada, the Carvão (coal) Cave is actually a 5,000-12,000-year-old lava tube, and is classified as a Natural Monument. The volcanically formed cave's walls are covered in spectacular speleological structures such as lava stalactites and stalagmites, balconies, benches, bridges, and ribbed walls. It is the biggest such formation on the island at nearly 2 kilometers (1 mi) in length. One of São Miguel's top attractions, it attracts some 15,000 visitors annually. Start at the little **visitor center,** which is packed with information. Pay at the ticket counter,

then follow a long, narrow passage to a flight of stairs that leads to the belly of the pit. This is not an experience for the claustrophobic or less able-bodied. Good walking boots or sneakers are recommended with thick, non-slip soles.

Two **tours** are available: a shorter 30-minute tour (€5), and a 3-hour tour for 2-4 people (€20), which goes deeper into the cave and should be booked in advance to avoid disappointment. The smaller main cavity is open to visitors unguided.

AUGUSTO ARRUDA PINEAPPLE PLANTATION
(Plantação de Ananases Augusto Arruda)

Rua Doutor Augusto Arruda; tel. 296 384 438; www. ananasesarruda.com; daily 9am-6pm; free

Delve into the sticky-sweet joy of the famous Azores pineapples with a trip to this historic plantation, which has a history spanning over 100 years and is open and free for the public to visit. Learn how pineapples are grown and harvested, understand their importance to the local economy, explore the greenhouses, and, of course, sample the delicious fruit. An on-site **gift shop** sells all kinds of pineapple souvenirs, from jams and liqueurs to actual pineapples.

Diving and Snorkeling

São Miguel has some great spots for divers and snorkelers, found away from the shoreline, including the famous **wreck of the *Edwin L. Drake*** and the hydrothermal vents off the **Vila Franca do Campo Islet.** Various companies, such as those listed below, run snorkeling and dive excursions to these spots from Ponta Delgada. Joining one of these tours is the easiest and safest way to explore São Miguel's best dive spots, some of which are quite remote.

- **Season Challenge Diving Center:** Av. Dr. João Bosco Mota Amaral; tel. 914 464 511; www.seasonchallenge.pt; daily 8am-8pm; from €40
- **Best Spot Azores Dive Center:** Marina Pero de Teive, Kiosk B; tel. 963 469 932 or 912 108 658; www.bestspotazores.com; daily 8am-7pm; from €50

Dolphin- and Whale-Watching

The Azores' deep waters are home to one of the largest whale populations on the planet, with both resident and migrating species

---

1: Ponta Delgada's old City Gates **2:** grilled *lapas* (limpets) **3:** a whale- and dolphin-watching tour **4:** Ponta Delgada's waterfront avenue and the Fort of São Brás

roaming the royal blue depths. Dolphin- and whale-watching trips run year-round, although generally the best time to see the graceful giants is spring, in **April and May,** when the seas are busiest with migrating species. Numerous companies operating on São Miguel specialize in these tours; a sighting is almost guaranteed on every trip.

- **Azores Whale Watching Terra Azul:** tel. 296 581 361; www.azoreswhalewatch.com; daily 8:30am and 12:30pm; €55-60 for 2.5 hours
- **Moby Dick Tours:** Av. Infante Dom Henrique; tel. 919 942 831; www.mobydick-tours.com; 9am and 2pm; €40

Food

Rustic, rich, and hearty, Azorean cuisine is bolstered by **homegrown cheeses,** of which many islands have their own varieties; try São Miguel's at O Príncipe dos Queijos. Here, typical Azorean fare is accompanied by fresh **pineapples** from the Augusto Arruda Pineapple Plantation and local **tea** from the Gorreana Tea Plantation.

GRAÇA MARKET
(Mercado da Graça)

Rua do Mercado; tel. 296 282 663; Mon.-Wed. 7:30am-6:30pm, Thurs. 7:30am-7pm, Fri.-Sat. 7am-2pm

The local market, Mercado da Graça, is an opportunity to get up close with the island's intriguing local produce. Products to take home include cheeses and honey, hand-rolled cigars, and, of course, the island's famous Gorreana tea.

O PRÍNCIPE DOS QUEIJOS

Rua dos Mercadores 50; tel. 916 531 433; www. oprincipedosqueijos.pt; daily 8am-8pm

The ultimate cheese deli, O Príncipe dos Queijos (Prince of Cheese in Portuguese) is practically a temple of cheese. Packed with local cheeses in rounds of all sizes, a vast range of wines, and other local products to complement the cheeses, this little shop is a brilliant place to pop into for a souvenir or trappings for a picnic.

TERRA VERDE TEA HOUSE
Rua de São João 16; tel. 296 628 264; https://terra-verde-tea-house.negocio.site; Mon.-Sat. 10am-6pm, Sun. 10am-7pm; tea from €5

This pretty little teahouse serves delicious Portuguese pastries, freshly baked local sweets, and a large selection of teas.

★ A TASCA
Rua do Alijube 16; tel. 296 288 880 Mon.-Sat. 11am-1am; €12

Big portions of traditional Azorean food are served up at A Tasca, an unassuming backstreet tavern with rustic wooden tables that are usually full due to its reputation as the island's best place to eat. Local fare is given a creative twist without being pretentious, and it's cheap. Due to demand, reservations are necessary.

★ CAIS 20
Rua do Terreiro 41, São Roque; tel. 296 384 811; www.restaurantecais20.pt; daily noon-5am; €12

This simple, understated restaurant with amazing sea views serves an array of intriguing dishes and tapas, including the freshest island-caught shellfish, are barnacles and limpets, tuna kebabs, and whelk salad. Meat options include the local snack known as *pregos* (beef sandwiches). The restaurant is open late in the parish of São Roque, 2 kilometers (1 mi) east of Ponta Delgada. It's a 30-minute walk or a 4-minute drive east from Ponta Delgada's marina.

ROTAS DA ILHA VERDE
Rua de Pedro Homem 49; tel. 296 628 560; www.rotasilha.blogspot.pt; Mon.-Fri. noon-3pm and 7pm-11pm, Sat. 7pm-11pm; €12

As its name, "Routes of the Green Island," suggests, highly regarded Rotas da Ilha Verde takes diners on a vegetarian gastronomic journey through the island's cuisine. This small, charming restaurant has a wide and creative range of delicious vegetarian and gluten-free meals made from fresh local produce. Reservations are advised.

YACHT CLUB
Av. Infante Dom Henrique 111; tel. 296 284 231; www.grupoanjos.pt; daily 11am-midnight; €20

On the main marina at the newer end of the waterfront, the Yacht Club restaurant overlooks the pretty docks. Its waterfront location is the perfect place to enjoy fresh seafood and quality meats in a polished cosmopolitan environment.

Bars and Nightlife
There are a number of trendy bars toward the end of the marina. In addition, many little cafés and taverns that stay open late—some even hosting open-air karaoke—are scattered throughout the waterfront area.

TROPICAL NEPTUNE
Rua Manuel Inácio Correia 50; tel. 296 283 141; https://tropicalneptune.com; Tues.-Thurs. 8:30am-6:30pm, Fri. 8:30am-11:45pm, Sat. and Mon. 8:30am-6:30pm and 8:30pm-11:45pm

Tropical Neptune bar is an oasis of thirst-quenching natural juices, smoothies, and cool cocktails. Accommodating staff, chill-out music, and relaxed vibes make this lively haunt popular with the cool crowd.

BAÍA DOS ANJOS
Portas do Mar, Loja 22; tel. 296 284 231; www.grupoanjos.pt; daily 11am-4am

One of the biggest and busiest waterfront bars, Baía dos Anjos enjoys a lovely location overlooking the harbor. Stop for a drink or dinner, with a menu comprising a number of traditional Azorean dishes. For a pre-dinner cocktail, try the unusual and refreshing pineapple gin and tonic. There is also live music some nights.

Accommodations
THOMAS HOSTEL
Rua da Mãe de Deus 20; tel. 296 653 921; https://thomas-place.business.site; €80

Located walking distance to the town center,

small and friendly Thomas Hostel is bright, clean, and budget-friendly. Basic but spacious rooms, from basic doubles to family rooms, some with sea views, are serviced daily.

SÃO MIGUEL PARK HOTEL

Rua Manuel Augusto Amaral s/n; tel. 296 306 000; www.bensaude.pt; €144 d

Back from the western end of the waterfront, São Miguel Park Hotel is in a quiet part of town near a large supermarket. Modern, welcoming, and well-presented, it has an outdoor pool, a heated indoor pool, and very friendly, helpful staff.

HOTEL CASA HINTZE RIBEIRO

Rua Hintze Ribeiro 62; tel. 296 304 340; www.casahintzeribeiro.com; €150 d

On one of the main streets leading to the town center, family-friendly Hotel Casa Hintze Ribeiro is packed with charming details that nod to local heritage, like *azulejo* tiles and overtones of deep blue and white. It also has a nice rooftop pool.

★ GRAND HOTEL AÇORES ATLANTICO

Av. Infante Dom Henrique 113; tel. 296 302 200; www.grandhotelacoresatlantico.com; €250 d

The grand dame of São Miguel hotels, the Grand Hotel Açores Atlantico is as impressive as it is imposing. Right on the waterfront with superb sea views, this classic hotel is a short walk to the town center. Immaculate rooms, impeccable service, and stylishly elegant modern-retro décor make staying at this hotel a special and enjoyable experience.

Information and Services

Ponta Delgada is well equipped with basic amenities, such as pharmacies and post offices, and to deal with medical emergencies. **ATMs** are easily found; there are several along Ponta Delgada's waterfront, throughout the main town, in all banks and most gas stations and large supermarkets, and also in the **Parque Atlantico shopping mall** (Rua da Juventude; tel. 296 307 550; www.parqueatlanticoshopping.pt; Sun.-Thurs. 8:30am-10pm, Fri.-Sat. 8am-11pm).

- **Tourist office:** Av. Infante Dom Henrique; tel. 296 308 625; www.visitazores.com; daily 9am-6pm fall-spring, daily 9am-7pm summer
- **PSP police:** Rua da Alfândega 1; tel. 296 205 500; www.psp.pt
- **Main hospital:** Hospital do Divino Espírito Santo, Matriz, Av. D. Manuel I; tel. 296 203 000; www.hdes.pt
- **Private hospital:** São Lucas Private Hospital, Rua Bento José Morais 23, 1st Norte Direito; tel. 296 650 740; www.hpsl.pt
- **Main pharmacy:** Farmácia Popular, Rua Machado dos Santos 34; tel. 296 205 530
- **Main post office:** Rua Conselheiro Doutor Luís de Bettencourt Câmara; tel. 296 304 071; Mon.-Fri. 8:30am-6:30pm

Getting There

Ponta Delgada Airport's small single terminal is 3 kilometers (2 mi) west of Ponta Delgada center on the **EN1-1A road,** a 5-minute drive. A shuttle bus operated by **MiniBus** (tel. 967 995 536) runs hourly, every day of the week, 5am-midnight, between the airport and Ponta Delgada. Tickets are available from the airport kiosk on weekdays (7am-midnight), as well as on board from the driver. Tickets cost €4.50 one-way and the trip takes about 20 minutes.

There are plenty of **taxis** outside the airport's arrivals area (€10 into the city); **Associação Taxis Ponta Delgada** (tel. 296 302 530, 296 382 000, or 938 346 759; www.taxispdl.com) offers 24-hour service. Taxis are also found widely throughout the city. Fares vary depending on the time of day and whether you have luggage.

Ponta Delgada has plenty of **parking,** paid and free, although the waterfront area can get full, especially on weekends. Most roadside parking is free at night; the farther from the city center, the easier it is to park.

Getting Around

It's easy to get around Ponta Delgada **on foot,** especially its historic center and waterfront area, where most of the main attractions are found. A city-run **mini-bus service** (www. cm-pontadelgada.pt/pages/16) runs to the fringes of Ponta Delgada on four lines: Yellow, Green, Blue, and Orange. Single-trip tickets bought from the driver cost €0.50. Collective transport on São Miguel is operated by **Auto Viação Micaelense** (tel. 296 301 358), **Caetano Raposo & Pereiras (CRP)** (tel. 296 304 260), and **Varela & Ca.** (tel. 296 301 800). Visit http://horarios.visitazores.de/smiAVM. pdf for timetables.

TOP EXPERIENCE

★ SETE CIDADES LAKE AND AROUND

EN9-1A; tel. 296 249 016; open 24/7; free

The Azores' most famous vista is postcard-perfect Sete Cidades (Seven Cities) Lake (Lagoa das Sete Cidades). Twelve kilometers (7 mi) around, the largest freshwater lake in the Azores is technically two large twin lakes in the crater of a giant dormant volcano, surrounded by vibrant vegetation. Connected by a narrow, bridged strait, the lakes are locally called "Green Lake" and "Blue Lake," differing in how they reflect the sun. Folklore has it that the lakes were formed by the tears of a young princess and a local shepherd who fell in love but were forbidden from seeing each other by the king.

The natural area surrounding the lake is **Sete Cidades Park;** helpful information on the area can be found at the park's **visitor center** (Arruamento da Lago das Sete Cidades; tel. 296 249 016; http:// parquesnaturais.azores.gov.pt; Tues.-Fri. 10am-1pm and 1:30pm-5pm, Sat.-Sun. 2pm-5:30pm). **Trails** surround the lake so hikers can appreciate it from various angles. The **Vista Do Rei Viewpoint** (Miradouro da Vista do Rei. Road 9-1 142; tel. 917 189 250; open 24/7; free) and **Grota do Inferno Viewpoint** (Miradouro da Grota do Inferno,

Rua Ribeira do Ferreiro 117, Candelaria; http://parquesnaturais.azores.gov.pt; open 24/7; free) offer some of the Azores' most famous vistas.

On the shore in **Vila das Sete Cidades,** or Sete Cidades village, enjoy lunch at **Green Love** (9-1 23, Sete Cidades; tel. 296 915 214 or 914 229 699; Mon.-Thurs. 9:30am-6pm, Fri.-Sun. 9:30am-9:30pm; €15) or rent a kayak from **Garoupa Canoe Tours** (Lagoa das Sete Cidades, Sete Cidades; tel. 917 158 701; www. garoupa.pt; open 24/7; from €10).

Beaches and Pools

Bathing sites along São Miguel's western coast are predominantly natural tidal pools rather than sandy beaches.

PÓPULO BEACH (Praia do Pópulo)

Estrada Regional do Pópulo, São Roque; open 24/7; free

Pópulo Beach is one of the best beaches on the island for a swim and a sundowner. It has plenty of free parking in the immediate surroundings and a fantastic beach bar, the **Sunset Beach Restaurant & Bar** (Canada do Borralho, Pópulo Beach; tel. 911 050 309; Thurs.-Fri. 8am-2am, Sat.-Wed. 8am-1am; €15), for a snack and a drink with a view. You can also take surf lessons and rent equipment from nearby **Azores Surf School** (Canada do Borralho 26; tel. 914 012 978; http://azoressurfschool.com; Tues.-Sat. 8:30am-10:30pm, Sun.-Mon. 8am-10:30pm; lessons from €30, board rentals from €20/day), founded in 2004 by national big rider and coach José Seabra. It's a 10-minute (4-km/2-mi) drive east along the coast from Ponta Delgada

PONTA DA FERRARIA NATURAL SWIMMING POOL (Piscina Natural da Ponta da Ferraria)

Rua Padre Fernando Vieira Gomes; open 24/7; free

The Ponta da Ferraria pool is formed by the island's far southwesternmost edge sitting in the sea, which on the one hand receives hot spring water from São Miguel's innards, and on the other is mixed with bursts of cool seawater that come and go with waves from the ocean, making the water consistently lukewarm, more pleasant than the nearby Atlantic.

Small ladders lead down to the pool, crisscrossed with rope for swimmers to hang onto as they bob about in the surf, which at times can get pretty rough. Take care if it is choppy, as the rocks are jagged and quite sharp. If you want to dry off afterward, spread your towel out on the black basalt rock and soak up some rays. A little thermal spa nearby, **Termas da Ferraria** (Rua Ilha Sabrina; tel. 296 295 669; http://termasdaferraria.com; Tues.-Sun. 11am-7pm; massages from €35), harnesses hot water from another local spring for its spa and treatments, and has restrooms and a café. Ponta da Ferraria natural pool is a 35-minute (26 km/16 mi) drive west from Ponta Delgada along the EN1-1A road, at the end of a rather steep, hairpin road.

Hiking
VISTO DO REI VIEWPOINT HIKE (PR3SMI)
Hiking Distance: *15.4 kilometers (9.6 mi) round-trip*
Hiking Time: *4-5 hours round-trip*
Trailhead: *Visto do Rei viewpoint*
Information and Maps: *http://trails. visitazores.com; maps also available from tourist offices*

An easy, though lengthy, walk exploring the verdant slopes of the southwest Sete Cidades ridges, this hike takes in the interior of the volcano's crater and incredible twin lakes and views of Mosteiros village, and ends in Sete Cidades village. It goes through scenic protected landscape and is also a popular birdwatching trail.

Getting There and Around
Sete Cidades Lake is 25 kilometers (16 mi) northwest of **Ponta Delgada**, a 30-minute drive on the **EN1-1A** and **9-1** roads. It is possible to get to Sete Cidades village by local **bus**; the **205** line runs between Ponta Delgada's

Bairro do Ramalho stop and drops off near the São Nicolau church in Sete Cidades. This takes around an hour, but costs just €3. Be aware, though, there are only a couple of direct services every day, one at around 8:30am and the other just before 7pm. Alternatively, a **taxi** will cost between €30 and €40, oneway, and takes 30 minutes. You can also get here by guided tour, like a kayak excursion from Ponta Delgada with **Futurismo Azores Adventures** (www.futurismo.pt).

FURNAS
Furnas and its eponymous nearby lake are under an hour's drive from Ponta Delgada, almost in the island's center. This inland hamlet is a spa resort, a busy tourist attraction, and a gastronomic outpost, all fueled by simmering geothermal activity. Geysers and fumaroles hiss and splutter with boiling water; steaming springs form popular thermal pools, and the island's signature dish, *cozido das Furnas,* is cooked underground on the shores of Furnas Lake. A whole day or two can be spent in this exhilarating community. It's a beautiful place for a romantic break for two.

Throughout Furnas, especially in the center of town, hot and cold geothermal spring water flows from public taps known as *caldeiras*. See and sample the water in an area known as **Calderas Square** (Largo das Caldeiras): The high iron content in the water gives it a bitter taste that fizzes on the tongue. Little stalls sell **corncobs** cooked in the steaming geysers. There's also the **Square of the Three Taps** (Largo das Três Bicas), on the ER1-1 road, with a century-old public fountain.

Sights
FURNAS LAKE AND HOT SPRINGS (Caldeiras da Lagoa das Furnas)
Furnas Lake shore; tel. 296 588 019; open 24/7; €2

A 10-minute drive southwest of Furnas village, Furnas Lake is the second-largest lake on São Miguel. It lacks the breathtaking beauty of Sete Cidades but is still compelling with its intense heat and sulfurous smell. The northern

swath of the Furnas Lake shore is occupied by bubbling fumaroles where the local specialty, *cozido das Furnas*, is cooked. Visitors can follow a wooden **walkway** that snakes safely through the hissing, spitting geysers and bubbling mud pools.

In the early morning, huge steel pots of local stew are lowered into the ground and covered, left to cook until they're removed around midday, loaded into waiting vans, and zipped off to nearby restaurants. This culinary curiosity has taken place for decades, having started as a local delicacy. Some of the fumaroles are allocated to specific local restaurants, while others belong to locals, who bring their own pots and pans and ingredients to cook *cozido*. Visit around noon, when the large metal pots are lifted out.

The Caldeiras have ample **parking** on-site, included in the €2 entry fee.

★ TERRA NOSTRA PARK
(Parque Terra Nostra)

Rua Padre Jose Jacinto Botelho; tel. 296 549 090; www.parqueterranostra.com; daily 10am-6pm; adults €8, children 3-10 €4

Paradise on earth might look like this park, an Eden of sprawling gardens, secret grottoes, shady tree-covered walkways, babbling streams, lily-covered ponds, and a big pool of hot, rusty-red spring water that soothes aching muscles and joints. The park is decorated with exotic plant life from around the world, including more than 2,000 different types of trees.

This sublime botanical park was the brainchild of wealthy American consul Thomas Hickling, who had a summer house on the site nicknamed **Yankee Hall** and started shaping the gardens in 1775. Yankee Hall today overlooks the gardens' famous **thermal pool** (Rua Padre Jose Jacinto Botelho; tel. 296 549 090; www.parqueterranostra.com; daily 10am-6pm; adults €8, children 3-10 €4), built in 1780 and extended in later years. The

1: Sete Cidades Lake **2:** Ponta da Ferraria natural swimming pool **3:** Poça da Dona Beija Hot Springs **4:** Terra Nostra Park

volcanic water that feeds the pool ranges 35-40°C (95-104°F) and is an uninviting, murky dark-orange color due to its iron content, but is perfect for a dip after walking around the gardens (so long as you don't mind the rust-colored water staining your bathing suit!). Admission to the gardens also grants you access to the pool, which also has good changing facilities with hot showers.

POÇA DA DONA BEIJA HOT SPRINGS

Lomba das Barracas; tel. 296 584 256; www. pocadadonabeija.com; daily 7am-11pm; €4

Take a soothing, invigorating soak in the Poça da Dona Beija hot springs, one of São Miguel's best-known attractions. Deep tanks of steaming crystalline water transform this former wild spring into an indulgent open-air spa. Construction began in 1988 following an influx of visitors seeking the site's restorative properties. Public access was regulated in 2007 due to the growing number of visitors. Nowadays the site is equipped with a small parking lot (though finding parking can still be a challenge due to the spa's popularity), a ticket office, and changing rooms. The several large tanks were redesigned by a group of architects in 2015 to blend in with the surrounding lush greenery, stone walls, and stone-block houses, particularly lovely at night. Or, enter the steaming water when it's rainy and cold—a pleasant novelty.

Food
CHALET DA TIA MERCÊS

Rua das Caldeiras s/n; tel. 914 295 470; https:// azores-essentials-lda.business.site; Sat.-Sun. 10am-10pm; €10

Excellent Azorean foods and drinks are served at this homey, emblematic restaurant. With a large selection of delicious foods from across the archipelago, all made from quality regional ingredients, this charming chalet-like teahouse (originally a 19th-century public bath) overlooks bubbling calderas and offers some of the best views of Furnas. It's a great choice for tea and a light lunch—tuck into delicacies like local pastries, cheeses and pâtés, seaweed patties, and fresh bruschetta.

★ RESTAURANTE MIROMA

Rua Dr. Frederico Moniz Pereira 15; tel. 296 584 422; daily 10am-9pm; €15

This simple and traditional, yet large and lofty restaurant is one of the top places to go in town for the traditional *cozido das Furnas* and is usually always buzzing with tourists and local families. Waiters place heaped servings of the famed stew on the table, along with bread, rice, and other trimmings. Other dishes like fried ribs, grilled chicken, and tuna steak are also available. You should be able to walk in and enjoy *cozido* most days, even without a reservation, but book ahead to make sure. You wouldn't want to miss this must-do experience.

ESPINHA.COME

Av. Pereira Atayde no. 11; tel. 296 588 204; www.facebook.com/espinha.come; Fri.-Wed. noon-3pm and 6:30pm-9:30pm; €10

Simple and quirky Espinha.Come serves sticky chicken wings, deep-fried prawns, sandwiches on the local *lêvedo* bread, salads, burgers, and more substantial meals like meat and tuna steaks that can be enjoyed in this laid-back, casual eatery.

Accommodations

TERRA NOSTRA GARDEN HOTEL

Rua Padre José Jacinto Botelho 5; tel. 296 549 090; www.bensaudehotels.com; €160 d

One of the Azores' most iconic hotels and the Bensaude group's flagship unit, the Terra Nostra Garden Hotel is ensconced in the leafy grounds of the incredible Terra Nostra Gardens. It's refined, exotic, and has an art-deco style that sits in harmony with its luxuriant surroundings. Guests enjoy privileged access to the 18th-century Terra Nostra Park.

★ FURNAS BOUTIQUE HOTEL & SPA

Av. Dr. Manuel de Arriaga; tel. 296 249 200; www.furnasboutiquehotel.com; €306 d

THE AZORES
SÃO MIGUEL

The Gorreana Tea Plantation

Plantações de Chá Gorreana; just off EN1-1A road, Maia; tel. 296 442 349; www.gorreana.pt; Mon.-Fri. 8am-7pm, Sat.-Sun. 9am-7pm; free

The only tea plantation in Europe is on São Miguel. Since 1883 the family-run Gorreana Tea Plantation has been producing world-class organic green and black teas.

Located 33 kilometers (20 mi) northeast of Ponta Delgada, a 30-minute drive along the EN1-1A road, the 32 hectares (79 acres) of vivid green fields blend perfectly with the rest of the island's emerald tapestry and contrast with the sea. A boutique souvenir **store, café,** and **museum** are on the site, along with the **factory,** to offer insight on how the tea came to the island, how it is produced, and its evolution. Gorreana currently produces 33 metric tons (36 tons) of tea per year, although only a small portion is destined for the Azorean market, with the rest exported to mainland Portugal and other countries. Visitors can stroll at leisure among the fields along the Atlantic, a sight to behold and the perfect place to enjoy a cup of fresh tea.

A visit to the plantation and museum, self-guided or guided, is free, as is a tea-tasting offered at the end. A box of Gorreana tea makes a great souvenir.

The Furnas Boutique Hotel embodies the serenity and beauty of Furnas with a hip bar, an outdoor hot-spring pool, and minimalist-modern rooms with distant mountain views. It is just a 10-minute walk to the gorgeous Terra Nostra Park.

This hotel's large **spa** (daily 9am-6pm, pools and gym open 24/7; treatments from €45) is the ultimate retreat; it has 10 treatment rooms and promises a unique sensorial experience based on the properties of famous local hot spring waters, as well as a range of indulgent massages and treatments by experienced therapists.

Getting There and Around

Furnas is 46 kilometers (29 mi) east of **Ponta Delgada,** a 40-minute drive on the **EN1-1A** road. There's plenty of **parking** throughout the town, roadside, and in a number of large parking lots near the Terra Nostra Park and the town springs.

A **bus** (lines **318** or **110;** www. smigueltransportes.com) to Furnas village (1.5 hours; €3-5) departs roughly every two hours from Ponta Delgada's main waterfront avenue 7am-6pm. Ask the **Ponta Delgada Tourist Office** for timetables.

Furnas is a **walkable** town; it takes roughly 15 minutes to cross the town from the main springs to the Terra Nostra Park. The streets are well sign-posted and the locals are used to helping out lost tourists.

Terceira

Packed with fascinating volcanic attractions, from basalt-walled vineyards to underground lava tubes, Terceira Island is approximately 220 kilometers (140 mi) northwest of São Miguel. It's the archipelago's second largest island in terms of population (after São Miguel) and third largest in size (after São Miguel and Pico).

Quieter and less touristy than São Miguel, but modern enough to cater to creature comforts, Terceira is known as the "Lilac Island," due to the number of purple hydrangeas that blanket it in spring. It's home to the Azores' oldest city, Angra do Heroísmo, a UNESCO World Heritage Site, and to a strategic international air base, Lajes.

The island has a cheery, colorful vibe, with its colorful Divino Espírito Santo chapels, or *impérios;* at least 70 of these quirky little chapels dedicated to the Holy Spirit (or Holy Ghost) dot the island. Finally, there's the island's distinctive Verdelho wine, produced near the charming village of Biscoitos on the island's northwestern coast.

GETTING THERE

Traveling to Terceira Island is almost as easy as getting to São Miguel, the Azores' main island. **By air** is easiest and quickest, both from the mainland and other islands. Terceira is the only other island in the archipelago to receive direct flights from mainland Portugal, as well as some international flights (though these are mostly seasonal charter flights).

You can also get to Terceira on direct flights from every other island in the archipelago except Santa Maria, or by **ferry,** operated May-September, though flying is quicker and can be just as cheap.

Air

The main airport on Terceira is **Lajes Airport,** also known as Lajes Civil Air Base (Aerogare Civil das Lajes), in Praia da Vitória, on the northeastern tip of Terceira, 24 kilometers (15 mi) from Angra do Heroísmo, the island's main city. There are direct flights to Lajes almost daily from Lisbon, and at least three times a week from Porto. Flight time from both Lisbon and Porto is around 2.5 hours, and round-trip flights can often be found for less than €100, depending on the season.

Interisland flights on smaller propeller planes are operated exclusively by **SATA** (www.azoresairlines.pt); you can fly to and from Terceira via every island in the archipelago except Santa Maria.

Ferry
PRAIA DA VITÓRIA PORT

Cabo da Praia Industrial Area, Praia da Vitória; tel. 295 105 134; www.amn.pt

Praia da Vitória Port, on Terceira's east coast, receives the seasonal **interisland ferry** (www.atlanticoline.pt); from May-September, you can take the ferry from Terceira to Ponta Delgada on São Miguel (4 hours 30 minutes;

Terceira

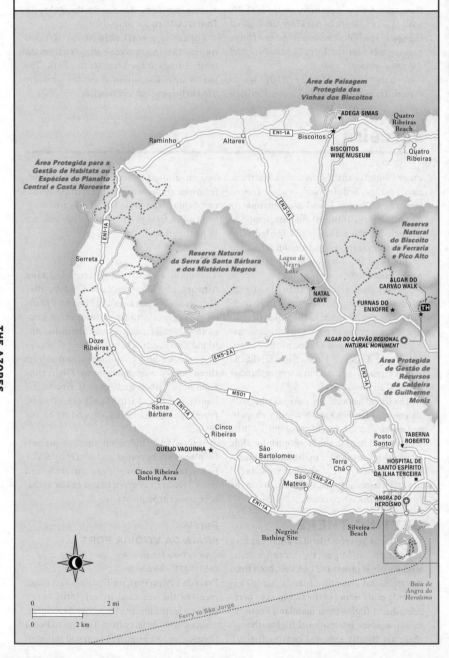

Área de Paisagem Protegida das Vinhas dos Biscoitos

ADEGA SIMAS ▼

Quatro Ribeiras Beach

Quatro Ribeiras

BISCOITOS WINE MUSEUM

Biscoitos ★

Altares

Raminho

ENI-1A

ENI-1A

Área Protegida para a Gestão de Habitats ou Espécies do Planalto Central e Costa Noroeste

Serreta

EN3-1A

Reserva Natural do Biscoito da Ferraria e Pico Alto

Reserva Natural da Serra de Santa Bárbara e dos Mistérios Negros

Lagoa do Negro Lake

NATAL CAVE ★

FURNAS DO ENXOFRE ★

ALGAR DO CARVÃO WALK

TH

ALGAR DO CARVÃO REGIONAL NATURAL MONUMENT

Doze Ribeiras

EN5-2A

Área Protegida de Gestão de Recursos da Caldeira de Guilherme Moniz

EN3-1A

M501

Santa Bárbara

ENT-1A

Cinco Ribeiras

São Bartolomeu

Posto Santo

TABERNA ROBERTO

QUEIJO VAQUINHA ★

Terra Chã

HOSPITAL DE SANTO ESPÍRITO DA ILHA TERCEIRA ■

São Mateus

EN6-2A

Cinco Ribeiras Bathing Area

ENI-1A

ANGRA DO HEROÍSMO

Silveira Beach

Negrito Bathing Site

0   2 mi

0   2 km

Ferry to São Jorge

Baía de Angra do Heroísmo

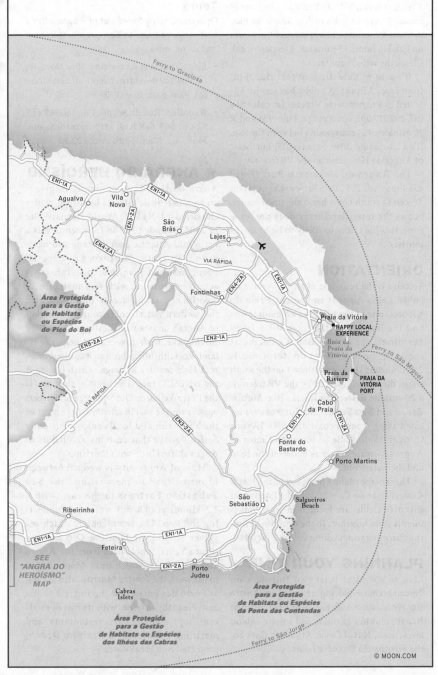

Ferry to Graciosa

Agualva

Vila Nova

São Brás

Lajes

EN1-1A

EN1-1A

EN3-2A

EN4-2A

VIA RÁPIDA

Fontinhas

EN4-2A

EN1-1A

Área Protegida para a Gestão de Habitats ou Espécies do Pico do Boi

EN5-2A

Praia da Vitória

■ HAPPY LOCAL EXPERIENCE

Baía da Praia da Vitória

Ferry to São Miguel

EN2-1A

Praia da Riviera

■ PRAIA DA VITÓRIA PORT

VIA RÁPIDA

EN3-2A

Cabo da Praia

EN1-1A

EN1-2A

Fonte do Bastardo

Porto Martins

Ribeirinha

São Sebastião

Salgueiros Beach

EN1-1A

Feteira

EN1-1A

EN1-2A

Porto Judeu

SEE "ANGRA DO HEROÍSMO" MAP

Cabras Islets

Área Protegida para a Gestão de Espécies da Ponta das Contendas

Área Protegida para a Gestão de Habitats ou Espécies dos Ilhéus das Cabras

Ferry to São Jorge

© MOON.COM

4 ferries/week), Vila da Praia on Graciosa (3 hours; 3 ferries/week), or São Roque on Pico (6 hours 45 minutes; 10 ferries/week), or Horta on Faial (8 hours 15 minutes; 4 ferries/week). Check the website for fares.

It's a 10-minute drive or taxi ride (€10) from Lajes Airport. A public bus service operated by **Empresa de Viação Terceirense** (tel. 295 217 001; www.evt.pt; Lines 151 and 3; 10 minutes; €2) runs hourly between the two. It's a 20-minute drive or taxi (€25) northeast of Angra do Heroísmo on the **VR** freeway.

The **Angra do Heroísmo Port** (Porto das Pipas; tel. 295 204 570; www.amn.pt) on Terceira's south coast hems the town center, but as the interisland ferry does not leave from this port, it is unlikely to be of use to tourists.

ORIENTATION

Terceira is the roundest of all the Azores islands. **Lajes Airport** and beachy **Praia da Vitória,** one of the island's two main towns and the location of the interisland **ferry terminal,** are on the island's northeast coast. The capital, **Angra do Heroísmo,** is 23 kilometers (14 mi) southwest on the south coast, directly connected by the **VR** freeway, a 20-minute drive. Landmarks like **Mount Brasil** and **São Sebastião Fortress** are located along Angra's coast; the **EN1-1A** runs through the middle of town, and most of Angra's historic center is between the road and the waterfront.

Three of the island's main sights, the **Natal Cave, Algar do Carvão,** and the **Furnas do Enxofre** fields, are located inland, conveniently close together. To the west, you'll find the charming winemaking village **Biscoitos.**

PLANNING YOUR TIME

Plan to spend at least two full days on Terceira: One exploring its main city **Angra do Heroísmo** and the beautiful **Mount Brasil;** another at the island's main inland attractions, **Natal Cave, Algar do Carvão,** the **Furnas do Enxofre** fields.

Tours

Operators, many based out of Angra, offer a vast range of tours to Terceira's best-known and secret spots.

- **Spot Tourism Activities:** Rua Nova 19; tel. 964 242 969; https://spottours.pt; Mon.-Sat. 9am-6am; from €37

- **AzorBus:** Rua da Sé, no. 190; tel. 969 668 829 or 969 668 839; http://azorbus.com; Mon.-Sat. 10am-6pm; from €22.50

★ ANGRA DO HEROÍSMO

Angra do Heroísmo, or simply Angra, is an exquisite little city, its historical center classified a UNESCO World Heritage Site in 1983. Founded in the 15th century as a main mid-Atlantic port of trade and navigation, an exotic coexistence of imperial Portuguese and Spanish architecture characterizes the town, with well-maintained, colorful houses and streets contrasting with the modern waterfront. Around 70 percent of Angra's houses were destroyed in a 1980 earthquake; with government help, the island was faithfully rebuilt to its unique original 15th-century heritage, which landed it the UNESCO title. The heart of the town is the Praça Velha, or Old Square, a few streets back from the marina, from where most of the buses run and locals enjoy their daily coffee—a sign that customs and habits in Angra shifted little with tourism.

Most of Angra city is wedged between **Mount Brasil** to the west and the **São Sebastião Fortress** to the east, with a 1.3-kilometer (0.8-mi) **walkway** connecting the two. The town center, which revolves around the bustling **Old Square** (Praça Velha), pools back from the **Angra Bay** waterfront, which links Mount Brasil in the west, the **Angra Marina,** also known as Porto das Pipas, and the fortress to the east. Near the marina, with its row of modern shops housing bars, restaurants, and maritime businesses, is **Prainha Beach,** protected by a breakwater.

Angra do Heroísmo

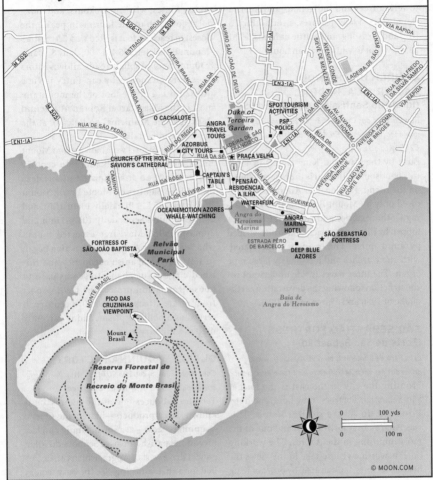

Sights

You could spend a whole day soaking up the colorful streets and sounds of cheery, culture-packed Angra city center. If you want more of the history behind Angra, or to boil it down into a shorter time, **Angra Travel Tours** (Rua Direita 155; tel. 295 206 900; www.angratravel.net; Mon.-Fri. 9am-6pm; from €35) offers half- and full-day historic city walking tours.

DUKE OF TERCEIRA GARDEN (Jardim Duque da Terceira)

Rua Direita 130; tel. 295 401 700; daily 8am-6pm; free

The impressively manicured Duke of Terceira Garden, dating from the late 19th century, is a shining example of a municipal garden. Located in Angra's historic center, just off the main square and down the road from the cathedral, the garden features a pretty central bandstand in the heart of the green oasis, flanked by an intricate design of landscaped lawns, ponds, and a compelling diversity of towering trees and indigenous and international flora. Water features, a soundtrack of frog and birdsong, and a little café make this a lovely spot to while away an hour.

CHURCH OF THE HOLY SAVIOR'S CATHEDRAL
(Igreja do Santíssimo Salvador da Sé)

Rua Carreira dos Cavalos 53; tel. 295 216 670; www. igrejaacores.pt; Mon.-Fri. 10am-6pm, mass Sat.-Sun.; €2 (free to attend mass)

Built by the Cardinal-King Henry in 1568, this handsome cathedral is the biggest church on the island. Peering over Angra, overshadowed only by Mount Brasil, with an imposing Gothic exterior and twin bell towers, it's topped by distinctive black-and-white-striped pyramid spires. The inside is understated, with stone arches and a famously large pipe organ. The three naves inside underwent reconstruction following the devastating earthquake of 1980 and a large fire in 1983.

SÃO SEBASTIÃO FORTRESS
(Forte de São Sebastião)

Estr. Pero de Barcelos 1; tel. 295 403 560; www. pousadas.pt; open 24/7; free to visit for a look around

Fronting the city to the east is the former São Sebastião Fortress, now boutique hotel **Pousada de Angra do Heroísmo.** This was Angra's first fortification and one of the most imposing in the Azores. The working hotel is worth a visit to take in the views the historic fortress, built in 1580 by order of King D. Sebastião. In its heyday, the São Sebastião Fortress worked together with the Fortress of São João Baptista on Mount Brasil to shield Angra from attacks and invasions.

MOUNT BRASIL
(Monte Brasil)

Sé parish; open 24/7; free

For the best views, climb this attraction-packed remnant of a mostly submerged crater. A government-managed **nature reserve** (Terceiraís Forestry Service; tel. 295 206 310;

daily sunrise-sunset; free), Mount Brasil is scattered with picnic spots, well-maintained hiking routes, whaling lookouts, and viewpoints on each of the four main peaks; the closest to reach on foot is **Pico das Cruzinhas** (Mount Brasil; tel. 295 401 700; daily 8:30am-8:30pm; free). Asphalt roads allow visitors to explore on foot or by car. Entry is via a **guardhouse** at the foot of the mountain; most of the hikes start at **Relvão Municipal Park** (Parque Municipal do Relvão), at the foot of the mountain.

A number of forts were built around Mount Brasil, including the elaborate 16th-century **Fortress of São João Baptista** (Fortaleza de São João Baptista do Monte Brasil; Mount Brasil; tel. 295 214 011; daily 10am-11am and 2pm-6pm June-Sept., daily 10am-11am and 2pm-5pm Oct.-May; free escorted tours), which looks over Angra. Construction began in 1593 during Spanish occupancy and finished circa 1640. The fortress was used to house troops and protect the trading port from pirate attacks. In the 20th century, it served as a political prison and is currently used as a military base.

QUEIJO VAQUINHA FACTORY

Canada do Pilar, 5; tel. 295 907 138; https:// queijovaquinha.pt; daily 10am-10pm; free

Terceira produces one of the Azores' best-known dairy products—handmade Queijo Vaquinha cheese—at a small, family-run factory in the parish of Nossa Senhora do Pilar, a short drive west of Angra, which can be visited for a cheese-tasting. See the busy factory in full swing, get up close and personal with the cows and calves, and pop into the gift shop and coffee shop for snacks and souvenirs.

Another way to experience Terceira's dairy heritage and cattle raising is with a quirky farming and milking excursion. Totally unique, authentic, and fun, the **Happy Local Experience** (Circular Interna; tel. 916 592 283; https://happylocalexperience.

1: Angra do Heroísmo and Mount Brasil **2:** entrance to Algar do Carvão Cave **3:** fountain in the Duke of Terceira Garden **4:** Angra do Heroísmo

pt; tours daily at 9am and 4pm; €32 pp) involves a 2-hour tour to the Terceira countryside to visit a typical Terceira farm and find out exactly why Azores' cows are known as happy cows.

Diving and Snorkeling

The waters surrounding Terceira Island house some of the Azores' most intriguing and iconic dive sites. The unique **Underwater Archaeological Park of the Bay of Angra do Heroísmo** (http://dive.visitazores.com/en/divespots/cemiterio-das-ancoras) comprises various spots of archeological interest to divers, mapped out with underwater signposts and markers, the **Cemetery of Anchors** being its most popular and famous.

- **Deep Blue Azores:** Porto das Pipas; tel. 962 772 199; www.deepblueazores.com; daily 8:30am-6pm; scuba diving from €55

Dolphin- and Whale-Watching

Terceira is one of the Azores' top islands for whale- and dolphin-watching, with plenty of companies running tours daily. The odds of spotting one of these majestic mammals from Terceira are high, particularly along the south coast. Between spring and autumn, you might be lucky enough to spot the majestic blue whale as it swims between Terceira and São Jorge.

- **OceanEmotion Azores Whale Watching:** Angra Marina; tel. 295 098 119 or 967 806 964; www.oceanemotion.pt; daily 9am-6pm; from €50
- **Water4Fun:** Angra Marina, kiosk 5; tel. 969 296 485 or 295 212 017; www.water4fun.pt; daily 9am-noon and 1:30pm-6pm; from €50

Food

Terceira's gastronomy is closely related to that of the northern Trás-os-Montes region on the mainland, as people from that area were among the first settlers. Typical local dishes are *alcatra* (a melt-in-the-mouth

stew made with beef rump, red wine, and black peppercorns) served with *massa sovada* (a slightly sweet puffed-pastry bread), Holy Ghost soups (*sopas de espírito santo,* hearty soups made from dry bread and the stock from boiled meats), and the sweet **cornucópias** (pastry cones stuffed with fruits and flowers).

★ CAPTAIN'S TABLE

Rua da Rocha 14; tel. 295 216 358; https://captainstabledangra.negocio.site; Tues.-Sat. 6pm-11pm; €10

A small, bright restaurant with colorful checkered tablecloths, Captain's Table excels in fresh Mediterranean cuisine. Offering the freshest farm-to-table ingredients, the menu is a fusion of Portuguese, Turkish, and Italian cuisine using local Azorean ingredients. Popular specials include slow-cooked dishes, grilled tuna steaks, seafood pasta, and a family secret crunchy pumpkin dessert with a delicious passion fruit ice cream. It's fancy but with a laid-back atmosphere.

TABERNA ROBERTO

EN3-1A 3; tel. 966 431 126; www.facebook.com/tabernadoroberto; Tues.-Sat. 11:30am-3:30pm and 6:30pm-10:30pm, Sun. 10am-3pm; €15

This exceptional, lively little restaurant looks a bit like a wine shop when you walk in, with shelves loaded with hundreds of bottles. The menu includes local fish and meats all cooked in a traditional wood oven. Taberna Roberto is renowned for specialties such as its wood-oven-baked ribs, roast octopus, and homemade cinnamon ice cream.

★ O CACHALOTE

Rua do Rego 14; tel. 914 237 459, Mon.-Sat. 6:30pm-10pm; €20

How much more quintessentially Azorean can you get than excellent beef cooked on a sizzling lava rock? That's what O Cachalote specializes in. Ignore the garish red-and-green color scheme and enjoy the best steak for miles.

Wine-Tasting in Biscoitos

The peaceful and character-packed village of Biscoitos is known for its winemaking heritage, wine museum, traditional architecture, and colorful *império* chapels. Vine fields here are still hemmed in by distinctive basalt-rock stone walls, shaping little squares called **curraletas,** built centuries ago to protect the vines from the Atlantic's strong, salty winds.

Thanks to this unique convergence of natural attributes, Biscoitos's wines have a unique composition and flavor, with a deep golden straw color and a taste that is dry, crisp, and, some say, with a distinct hint of saltiness from the volcanic island terrain and Atlantic sea breeze. Made from **Verdelho** grapes, the wine has been protected and promoted since 1993 by the Vinho Verdelho dos Biscoitos Fraternity. Here are a few places to try it.

BISCOITOS WINE MUSEUM

Museu do Vinho dos Biscoitos; Canada do Caldeiro 3; tel. 965 667 324; https://pt.azoresguide. net/servicos/museu-do-vinho-dos-biscoitos; Tues.-Sat. 10:30am-5:30pm; free

For a small space, this charming, atmospheric wine museum packs a lot of information on the history of local wines, in addition to tastings. A family-run estate since 1890, now in its fifth generation, the Biscoitos winery was one of the first producers of local wines.

ADEGA SIMAS

Canada Tenente Coronel 5; tel. 961 329 139; https://adega-simas.webnode. pt; Mon.-Sat. 2pm-5pm, call two days ahead to book; €5 pp

For a taste of locally produced wines, jams, and preserves, head to the family-run Adega Simas winery. Enjoy a unique wine-tasting of the famous island Verdelho and stay for a home-cooked regional-inspired lunch or dinner in their on-site **restaurant,** which features the famous island-reared beef rump (*alcatra*).

Accommodations

PENSÃO RESIDENCIAL A ILHA

Rua Direita 24; tel. 295 628 180; €55 d

Budget 12-room inn Pensão Residencial A Ilha is in a great city-center location 100 meters (300 ft) from the marina and the beach. Rooms are clean and simple and breakfast is included, but there's no elevator.

★ ANGRA MARINA HOTEL

Estrada Pero de Barcelos, Porto de Pipas; tel. 295 204 700; www.angramarinahotel.com; €154 d

Large and imposing, modern five-star Angra Marina Hotel is cut right into the cliff face that hems Angra do Heroísmo. All 157 gleaming rooms have sea views and aquamarine accents. There is a panoramic rooftop restaurant, a spa, and an outdoor pool. It is on the marina side, a 10-minute walk east from the city center.

Information and Services

- **Tourist Office:** Rua Direita 70-74; tel. 295 404 810; www.visitazores.com; Mon.-Sat. 9am-7pm
- **PSP Police:** Praça Doutor Sousa Júnior 1; tel. 295 212 022; www.psp.pt
- **Main hospital:** Hospital de Santo Espírito da Ilha Terceira, Canada do Briado; tel. 295 403 200; www.hseit.pt

Getting There and Around

Lajes Airport (Aeroporto das Lajes) is located in Praia da Vitória, on the northeastern tip of Terceira, 24 kilometers (15 mi) from Angra do Heroísmo. The drive from Angra to Lajes Airport takes 20 minutes on the VR freeway. A number of local and international car rental desks. The drive from Angra to Lajes Airport takes 20 minutes on the **VR** freeway. There is a limited, roughly hourly bus service between Angra and Lajes operated by Empresa de Viação Terceirense (tel. 295 217 001; www.evt.pt; 1hour; €5). Taxis (about €25-30 to Angra) are available outside the terminal.

Angra do Heroísmo is easily covered on foot; parking is extremely limited. Most taxi companies are small and privately run, but fairly affordable and can generally be found waiting around main attractions. Try Taxi Amigos (tel. 963 729 390).

★ ALGAR DO CARVÃO REGIONAL NATURAL MONUMENT

With a wealth of volcanic attractions and peculiarities, the area flanking the Algar do Carvão Cave has been declared a Regional Natural Monument, covering 40 hectares (100 acres) of fascinating landscapes showcasing the variety made possible by geology. It is a fabulous place for compelling hikes and seemingly infinite volcanic vistas.

Sights

ALGAR DO CARVÃO CAVE

EN5-2A, Algar do Carvão Regional Natural Monument; tel. 295 212 992; www.montanheiros. com/algarCarvao; daily 2:30pm-5:15pm Mar. 25-May 31, daily 2pm-6pm June 1-Oct. 15, Tues.-Wed. and Fri.-Sat. 2:30pm-5:15pm Oct. 17-Mar. 23; €6, €9 combined ticket with Natal Cave

Vast and mesmerizing Algar do Carvão Cave takes its name ("coal pit") from its black volcanic walls. Descend into the depths of an extinct volcano with formidable features including a huge chimney and spectacular chambers, created in an eruption some 2,000 years ago. Beautiful milky-white stalactites and stalagmites cover the cavern; the walls change color as you descend through the layers of earth, a mysterious world revealed on a series of staircases (at least 250 steps, some quite steep) and tunnels. Dim, modern spotlights that enhance the natural light from the chimney.

You'll find a guide or two on a landing at the bottom of stairs offering information upon request. The local conservation association, Os Montanheiros (tel. 295 212 992 or 961 362 215; www.montanheiros.com), manages the caves.

The caves are 11 kilometers (7 mi) north of Angra do Heroísmo, a 15-minute drive on the EN3-1A road. There's a designated parking lot. A combined €9 ticket provides access to the smaller Natal Cave, 6 kilometers (4 mi) away.

NATAL CAVE (Gruta do Natal)

tel. 295 212 992; www.montanheiros.com; Tues.-Wed. and Fri.-Sat. 2:30pm-5pm; €6, €9 combined ticket with Algar do Carvão Cave

Amateur geologists will be delighted by the array of craggy rock formations that line the Natal Cave. The 700-meter-long (2,000-ft-long) lava tube was formed by naturally cooled lava in the earth's belly. Hard hats are supplied at the entry, as you'll have to stoop to pass through certain parts. The Gruta do Natal (Christmas Cave) takes its name from the fact that Christmas mass and other special ceremonies, such as christenings and weddings, are celebrated in the grotto. Entry to the cave is via a traditional stone house, unassuming from the outside, but with an informative interpretive center inside.

FURNAS DO ENXOFRE

off the EN5-2A road, follow signs between the Algar do Carvão and Gruta do Natal; http:// parquesnaturais.azores.gov.pt/pt/terceira/o-que-visitar/areas-protegidas/monumento-natural/furnas-do-enxofre; open 24/7; free

Another unique (and free) attraction, the Furnas do Enxofre sulfur field, located between the Algar do Carvão Cave and the Natal Cave, is extraordinary. A raised wooden walkway allows visitors to walk around an area pitted with underground fumaroles. Sulfurous vapor rises in steamy plumes from perforations in the ground, giving the area a steamy, almost ethereal feel. Take 15-20 minutes to wander around in the smelly steam.

Hiking

ALGAR DO CARVÃO WALK

Hiking Distance: *6.1 kilometers (3.8 mi) one-way*

Hiking Time: *1 hour 20 minutes one-way*

Trailhead: *Algar do Carvão Cave*

Information and Maps: *Follow signs, or ask for directions at Algar do Carvão Cave or Gruta do Natal Cave visitor centers*

Instead of making the short drive, it's possible to walk between the Algar do Carvão Cave and Natal Cave, a 1-hour 20-minute walk east to west, following the **EN5-2A** and **EN3-1A** roads across the very heart of the island. En route, take a right turn following the road sign toward the **Furnas do Enxofre** fields. Spend 15-20 minutes here following the wooden walkway through the steamy, smelly landscape, before continuing to the Natal Cave. The scenery is lush and green, vast and volcanic. You'll either have to walk back again or call for a taxi.

Getting There and Around

Rent a **car** or **scooter** to explore Algar do Carvão, with attractions a short drive, or a longer (but enjoyable) walk, apart. Getting to this area is tricky by public transport (except by **taxi**); you could opt for an organized excursion from **Angra Travel Tours** (Rua Direita 155; tel. 295 206 900; www.angratravel.net; Mon.-Fri. 9am-6pm; from €45) or **AzorBus City Tours** (Rua da Sé, no. 190; tel. 969 668 829 or 969 668 839; http://azorbus.com; Mon.-Sat. 10am-6pm; from €46).

The Azores Triangle

A cluster of three distinct islands in the middle of the archipelago, the Azores Triangle makes for a fascinating and compelling alternative or an enthralling complement to the better-known islands of Terceira and São Miguel. The "Triangle" of São Jorge, Faial, and Pico is part of the Central Group of islands, along with Terceira and Graciosa, located roughly 100 kilometers (62 mi) southwest of their peers. São Jorge is known as the island of *fajãs* (lava plateaus) and the Azores' preeminent cheese and tinned tuna producer; Pico boasts snow-capped Mount Pico, the highest point in Portugal, one of Europe's epic hikes; and Faial's famous port town Horta is a major meeting point for transatlantic yachtsmen.

ORIENTATION

Faial, the smallest of the three islands, forms the top-western tip of a downward-pointing triangle. Closest to Faial, slightly larger **Pico** would be the bottom tip of the triangle, with an 8.3-kilometers (5.2-mi) strait, called the Faial Channel, between their main towns, **Horta** (southeast Faial) and **Madalena**

(northwest Pico), crossed by regular ferries; this crossing takes around 30 minutes. East of Faial and Pico is **São Jorge,** roughly a 1.5-hour ferry crossing from them both.

PLANNING YOUR TIME

Allow at least five days to explore these stunning islands. Despite being the smallest island, cosmopolitan **Faial** is possibly the best base, due to its transport links by sea to the other islands and by air to Terceira, São Miguel, and (sporadically) to the Lisbon. Spend a night or two in Faial before heading over to **Pico;** spend at least one night there and try to climb Mount Pico if possible. From Pico, head to **São Jorge** for one night and return to Faial for departure.

FAIAL

Unspoiled and unique, Faial is bursts with character and charm. The lively little island is *the* meeting place for Atlantic-crossing sailors and is home to volcanic attractions such as the gaping Faial Caldera and the extraordinary Capelinhos Volcano. Known as the "Blue Island" due to the bright blue hydrangeas that cover the island in summer, Faial is closest to Pico, separated by an 8.3-kilometer (5.2-mi) strait with stunning views over its neighbor from almost every angle.

Faial sort of resembles a pentagon, albeit a crooked one, measuring 21 kilometers (13 mi) in length and 14 kilometers (9 mi) wide at its fattest. A 54-kilometer (34-mi) ring road, the **EN1-1A,** encircles the island, hemming the coast. Faial's main attraction, the **Caldera,** is bang in the middle of the island, while the main port town, **Horta,** is down on the southeast end, facing Pico. The almost crescent-shaped **Monte da Guia** protrudes south from Horta, with **Horta Marina** to the east. The island's other main attraction, the **Capelo Volcanic Complex,** is on the opposite side of the island.

Getting There

Fly direct to Faial's **Horta Airport** from Lisbon, or take an interisland flight from São Miguel or Terceira. Faial is also well connected by **ferry** to the other two "triangle" islands, Pico and São Jorge. It's possible to take the ferry to Faial from São Miguel in the summer, but the rough Atlantic makes this crossing long and unreliable.

A **taxi** (Taxi – Horta Açores, tel. 925 863 592) from the airport into Horta town takes around 10 minutes will cost €10-15. **Buses** run past the airport four times a day (7:40am, 8:30am, 1:15pm, and 4pm; €1.50 one-way) and take 15 minutes to get into Horta. There is just one bus on Saturdays (8:30am), and none on Sundays or bank holidays. The buses stop on the main ER regional road, 150 meters (500 ft) from the terminal. By **rental car,** from the airport to Horta it's about 9 kilometers (6 mi), heading east along the EN1-1A and EN2-2A roads.

HORTA FERRY TERMINAL

Avenida 25 de Abril; tel. 292 292 132; https:// portosdosacores.pt

Faial benefits from year-round ferries

between the Azores Triangle islands, especially from Pico, its closest neighbor. All connections are operated by Azores ferry company **Atlanticoline** (tel. 707 201 572; www.atlanticoline.pt). **Horta's Ferry Terminal** is a pleasant 15-minute walk along the waterfront from the town center.

From **Pico,** ferries leave from both **São Roque do Pico** (Gare Marítima de São Roque; tel. 292 642 482; www.atlanticoline. pt) and **Madalena** (Rua dona Maria da Glória Duarte; tel. 292 623 340; www.atlanticoline. pt). The São Roque do Pico ferry (1 hour 20 minutes, €10-15) sails twice a week. The Madalena ferry (30 minutes, €4) is much more frequent, sailing daily and around every four hours. There is currently only one route between **São Jorge** and Faial, between **Velas** (Cais Velas; tel. 295 412 047; 1 hour 40 minutes; €20 one-way).

Getting Around

A **rental car** is the best way to explore here: You can drive around the island in about 2 hours via the 54-kilometer (34-mi) ring road that encircles the island, the **EN1-1A.** Rental companies operate from the airport or Horta harbor or town center.

Public transport is limited. **Farias** (tel. 292 292 482; www.farias.pt) covers **Horta** as well as the coast, but there are only two or three services a day. Buses run to the airport four times a day (7:40am, 8:30am, 1:15pm, and 4pm) a 15-minute journey (€1.50 one-way). There is just one bus on Saturdays (8:30am), and none on Sundays or bank holidays.

Taxis are not as widely available on Faial as on other islands, but there are a handful of small taxi firms in Horta, such as **Rádio Táxis da Horta** (tel. 292 391 500) or **Associação de Taxistas do Faial** (tel. 292 391 300). In addition to quick trips around Horta, you could also consider a half-day taxi tour taking in the main sights. This will cost around €55.

Sights

★ HORTA MARINA

Cais de Santa Cruz; tel. 292 391 693; http://turismo.cmhorta.pt/index.php/pt/oquevisitar/marina-da-horta; open 24/7

For centuries, the colorful little town of Horta has been a meeting point for transatlantic sailors, a hub of enthralling seafaring tales recounted over a beer by the yachters who pass through every year. It's among the top five most-visited ports in the world, a legendary Atlantic port of call. Its **Jetty Murals,** colorful pictures that visiting sailors leave along the marina walls and pavement, are famous.

Horta Marina is also where keen sailors will find the iconic **Peter Café Sport Bar,** the ultimate mariners haunt. It dates back to the early 1900s, when the venue originally opened as a handicraft shop, later incorporating a bar to quench the thirst of weary sailors. It's a lively place to enjoy a beer or one of the bar's renowned gin and tonics; every inch inside the bar is covered with nautical paraphernalia. It is also home to a **Scrimshaw Museum,** idely considered the world's largest and most beautiful private collection of scrimshaw, or engraving bone or ivory (especially whale bone).

MONTE DA GUIA

An amalgamation of two volcanoes (one formed at sea, the other on land) forms a sort of peninsula connected to the mainland by a sandy isthmus a short stroll south of Horta center. It affords amazing views over Porto Pim Bay to the west, and Horta Bay and Horta's historic center to the east, as well as over neighboring islands. A little chapel, the **Chapel of Nossa Senhora da Guia,** patron saint of fishermen, is located on the summit of the hill and dominates the landscape.

A number of *vigias* (lookouts linked to whaling) still dot the mount, as well as the **Porto Pim Whaling Station Museum** (Museu da Baleia; Monte da Guia; tel. 292 292 140; www.oma.pt; Mon.-Fri. 10am-5pm Nov. 1-Mar. 31, daily 10am-6pm Apr. 1-Oct. 31; €4), a tour of a former sperm-whale-processing factory. Learn more about whaling on the **Monte da Guia Whaling Route** (tel. 292 292 140; geral@oma.pt, http://oma.centrosciencia.azores.gov.pt/actividade/percurso-tem%C3%A1tico-roteiro-baleeiro-do-monte-da-guia; Mon. and Thurs.), run by the **Azores Sea Observatory** (http://oma.centrosciencia.azores.gov.pt). Register by phone or email up to the day before the walk.

FAIAL CALDERA VOLCANIC COMPLEX AND NATURE RESERVE (Reserva Natural da Caldeira do Faial)

http://parquesnaturais.azores.gov.pt/pt/faial/oquevisitar/areasprotegidas/reservanatural1/caldeirafaial; open 24/7; free

Covering 313 hectares (749 acres) in the very middle of Faial, this complex is unique, one of the last remaining havens for the Azores' natural laurissilva forest, home to many species of rare and endemic flora, and practically untouched by human hands. The real showstopper is the monumental caldera, like a Hawaiian Grand Canyon. It's immense, 2 kilometers wide (1-mi-wide) and 400 meters deep (1,300-ft-deep), carpeted in varying shades of green fuzz, a breathtaking, almost prehistoric, scene. Various outdoor activity companies, such as **Our Island** (tel. 967 172 754; https://ourisland-azores.com; from €115 pp), organize the popular descents, which usually take around 1.5 hours.

CAPELO VOLCANIC COMPLEX AND CAPELINHOS VOLCANO

Ponta dos Capelinhos, west coast; open 24/7; free

The Capelo Volcanic Complex, part of which is formed by the Capelinhos Volcano, is a geographical wonder, the "newest" piece of land in Portugal. The submerged Capelinhos Volcano exploded in 1957 and rumbled on for 13 months before going dormant. Spewing white-hot sand, rock, and ashes, along with molten lava, destroyed swaths of the surrounding area, triggering mass evacuations. After streaming into the sea and cooling, the disgorged lava formed a stark, dark volcanic landscape: an isthmus, rugged in some places,

Faial

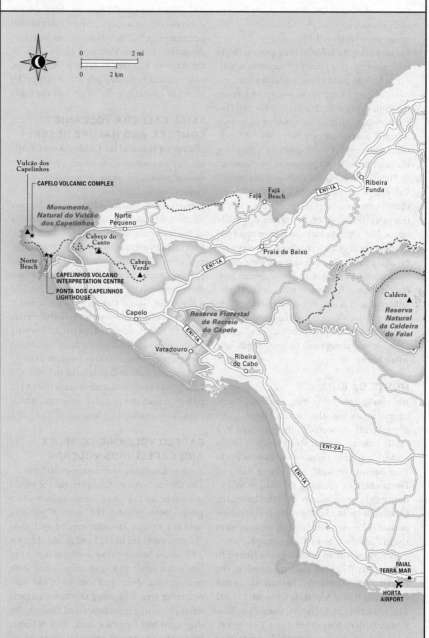

Vulcão dos
Capelinhos

CAPELO VOLCANIC COMPLEX

*Monumento
Natural do Vulcão
dos Capelinhos*

Norte
Pequeno

Cabeço do
Canto

Cabeço
Verde

Norte
Beach

**CAPELINHOS VOLCANO
INTERPRETATION CENTRE**

**PONTA DOS CAPELINHOS
LIGHTHOUSE**

Capelo

*Reserva Florestal
de Recreio
do Capelo*

Varadouro

Ribeira
do Cabo

Fajã   Fajã
       Beach

Ribeira
Funda

ENI-1A

Praia de Baixo

ENI-1A

Caldera

*Reserva
Natural
da Caldeira
do Faial*

ENI-2A

ENI-1A

FAIAL
TERRA MAR

HORTA
AIRPORT

0   2 mi

0   2 km

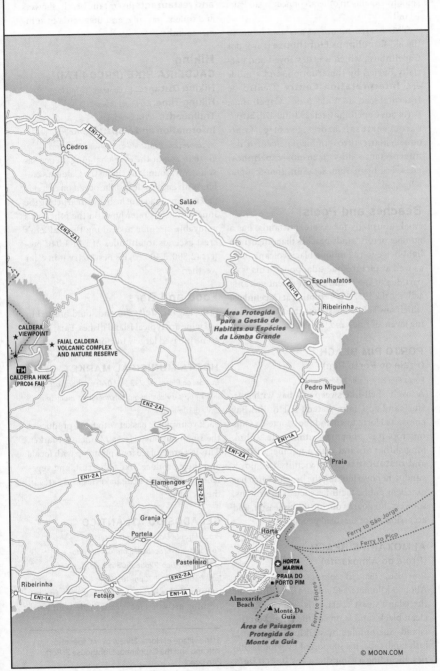

smooth-flowing in others, connecting to Faial Island.

This barren moonscape is also home to the old **Capelinhos Lighthouse** (Farol dos Capelinhos), which was destroyed and partially buried by the eruption, and a modern **Interpretation Centre** (Centro de Interpretaçao do Vulcão dos Capelinhos; Farol dos Capelinhos; tel. 292 200 470; http:// parquesnaturais.azores.gov.pt/pt/faial/ oquevisitar/centros-ambientais/centro-de-interpretacao-do-vulcao-dos-capelinhos; Tues.-Fri. 10am-5pm, Sat.-Sun. 2pm-5:30pm; €9).

Beaches and Pools

Faial, unusually for Azorean islands, has a number of soft, sandy beaches that range from light beige to the unique black volcanic hue, as well as picturesque tidal pools. This is in part due to the island's most recent volcanic activity, the 1957-1958 eruption at Capelinhos, which saw Faial's coast drenched in ash, adding layers of fine sand to the beaches.

PORTO PIM BEACH
(Praia do Porto Pim)

Porto Pim Bay; open 24/4; free

A lovely shell-like sweep of a bay with soft, fine sand and calm waters, Porto Pim Bay connects Horta town and the Monte da Guia outcrop. It is a popular bathing site, a thin, long slither of sand with a number of **bars** and **restaurants** in the vicinity to enjoy a sundowner overlooking the beach. It also has excellent public facilities such as restrooms, showers, lifeguards during beach season, and accessibility for disabled people.

ALMOXARIFE BEACH
(Praia do Almoxarife)

Conceição parish, east coast; open 24/7; free

About 3 kilometers (2 mi) north of Horta on the island's east coast, this stretch of soft, clean black sand is one of the largest on the island. Surrounded by strikingly beautiful, lush landscape, it's supported by good facilities, including a campsite, a few **beach bars**

and **restaurants** just off the beach, showers and toilets, parking, and lifeguards in summer months.

Hiking
CALDEIRA HIKE (PRCO4 FAI)

Hiking Distance: *8 kilometers (5 mi) loop*
Hiking Time: *2.5 hours round-trip*
Trailhead: *Caldera viewpoint*
Information and Maps: *http://trails. visitazores.com/en/trails-azores/faial/caldeira*

Gaze in awe at the ever-changing scenery as you stroll around the rim of the Caldera's crater. With endless deep-blue ocean on one side and varying shades of lush green carpeting the innards of the crater bowl on the other, this enjoyable circular hike along the Caldera's crest ascends to altitudes of 840-1,040 meters (2,800-3,400 ft); it's best to try it in clear weather.

Food and Bars

Fish stew (*caldeirada*) and squid braised in red wine are typical island dishes. Faial's food scene is based largely in Horta.

HORTA MUNICIPAL MARKET

Rua Serpa Pinto; tel. 292 202 074; www.cmhorta.pt/ index.php/servicos-municipais/mercado-municipal; daily 6:30am-7pm

Pack your picnic basket with fresh produce at the small but busy Horta Municipal Market. This is a great place for a photo op with locals and their produce, like fish, fruit, and vegetables, with great little bakeries and cafés in the vicinity.

GELADOS DO ATLÂNTICO

Praça Infante Dom Henrique 2; tel. 925 460 688; www.facebook.com/Gelados-do-Atl%C3%A2ntico-996585803693228; Tues.-Sun. 1pm-7:30pm and 8:30pm-10:30pm; €5

Indulge with a scoop or two of unique and refreshing artisanal ice cream made with local

---

1: the village of Horta **2:** view over Capelinhos Volcano and the Capelinhos Lighthouse **3:** Porto Pim beach

fruity flavors like pineapple, guava, passion fruit, cherry, papaya, and cardamom and green apple, and unusual daily specials like chili chocolate or kefir. Homemade wafer cones perfectly complement the ice cream, and waffles and crepes are also delicious on cooler days, all to be savored slowly while enjoying lovely waterfront views over Pico. Bruch menus are also available.

★ RESTAURANT GENUÍNO

Rua Nova; tel. 292 701 542; www.genuino.pt; Thurs.-Tues. noon-3pm and 6:30pm-10pm; €20

With gorgeous views over Porto Pim Bay, this is a great little restaurant to enjoy the finest flavors of the sea. Meat dishes are also available, but ocean delights straight from the ocean to the table, like simple grilled fish, fish soups, stews, and more unusual feasts like tuna meatballs, burgers, and rice dishes, are the specialty here. This authentic gem of a restaurant brings the ocean theme inside—it looks a little like a ship, with warm wooden cladding, sails on the ceiling, and simple wooden bench-tables—and its popularity has attracted the likes of visiting dignitaries. The restaurant's charismatic owner, Genuíno Madruga, is himself an avid sailor and has circumnavigated the globe by boat more than once.

PETER CAFÉ SPORT

Rua José Azevedo 9; tel. 292 392 027; www. petercafesport.com; daily 9am-midnight

Soak up the vibe at the most famous sailors' bar in the world. Swap swashbuckling stories with the regulars or simply enjoy the unique atmosphere with a refreshing local beer or a trademark gin and tonic as the sun sets over Horta harbor.

Accommodations

Most of Faial's bigger hotel units and guesthouses are located in Horta.

★ AZORIS FAIAL GARDEN

Rua Consul Dabney; tel. 292 207 400; www. azorishotels.com; €84 d

Azoris Faial Garden combines the tranquility of nature with a great location. Offering incredible views over Pico, this four-star hotel is within walking distance of Horta's main attractions, a 5-minute stroll to the marina. Accommodation is in the form of rooms that range from classic singles to deluxe suites.

INTERNATIONAL AZORES BOUTIQUE

Rua Conselheiro Medeiros 1; tel. 292 292 216; http:// internacionalazores.com/home; €100

A gorgeous boutique townhouse with a distinctive turquoise facade, eclectic art deco features, and tasteful interior décor, rooms are clean, bright, elegant, and spacious, ranging from high-quality dorms to VIP sea-view rooms, all equipped with mod cons. Located right on Horta Marina, the building is intrinsically linked to the early hydro-aviation period.

Information and Services

Horta has good public services including banks, ATMs, pharmacies, and dental clinics. Faial also has one of the region's three modern and well-equipped hospitals (the other two being on Terceira Island, and the main hospital on São Miguel). Faial Hospital underwent remodeling works in 2019 and the first brick was laid for a new health center, but urgent or more complex cases will likely be transferred to the bigger units on Terceira or São Miguel, or back to the mainland.

- **Tourist Office:** Rua Comendador Ernesto Rebelo 14, Horta; tel. 292 200 500; www. visitazores.com; daily 10am-10pm
- **PSP Police:** Av. Gago Coutinho e Sacadura Cabral s/n, Horta; tel. 292 208 510; www. psp.pt
- **Main hospital:** Rua Comendador Ernesto Rebelo 14, Horta; tel. 292 200 500; www. visitazores.com, daily 10am-10pm
- **Pharmacy Ayres Pinheiro:** Rua Serpa Pinto 26, close to ferry terminal; tel. 292 292 749; Mon.-Fri. 9am-7pm, Sat. 9am-1pm

PICO

Pico is as famous for its majestic eponymous volcano, the highest point in Portugal, as it is for the volcanic wines that come from its unique vineyards. Also one of the best islands in the Azores for whale-watching, Pico is nicknamed the "Gray Island" due to the amount of exposed lava rock that makes the scenery so unmistakably volcanic. Scarcely populated, peaceful, and shaped a bit like a whale, Pico Island covers some 447 square kilometers (173 sq mi). It is the second biggest island in the Azores archipelago after São Miguel, and it is around 50 kilometers (30 mi) long, east to west.

Both of Pico's two biggest towns, **Madalena** and **São Roque do Pico** (often called just São Roque) are located on the northern half of the island, along with the **Landscape of the Pico Island Vineyard Culture.** Otherwise, most of Pico's sights are in the western half of the island, including **Mount Pico.** One exception is **Lajes do Pico,** which is on the south coast, the main point of departure for whale-watching trips and home to Pico's fascinating **Whaling Industry Museum.**

The **ER1** road traces the island's coast; driving around the entire island would take around 3 hours. The **EN2** winds through the middle of the island, north-south, dividing the island more or less and half. Make sure to drive the **EN3** road, also known as the Longitudinal, which links Madalena to São Roque or Lajes.

Getting There

Pico can be reached via interisland **flight** from São Miguel or nearer-by **Terceira** Island; by **ferry,** year-round from São Jorge and Faial (the closest islands, part of the Azores Triangle with Pico); or by seasonal ferry from São Miguel (May-Sept.), although the journey takes close to 14 hours and stops at other islands, too.

PICO AIRPORT
PIX; Bandeiras; tel. 292 628 380

To reach Pico, an interisland flight from **São Miguel** (50 minutes) or **Terceira** (35 minutes) is usually necessary, though **Azores Airlines** (www.azoresairlines.pt) runs a seasonal direct flight (June-Sept.) between **Lisbon** and Pico three times a week (2 hours 45 minutes). Pico Airport is located on the north coast, 15 minutes (8 km/5 mi) east of the island's main city, **Madalena,** on the ER1 road, which circumscribes the entire island. You can **rent a car**

Mount Pico

Pico

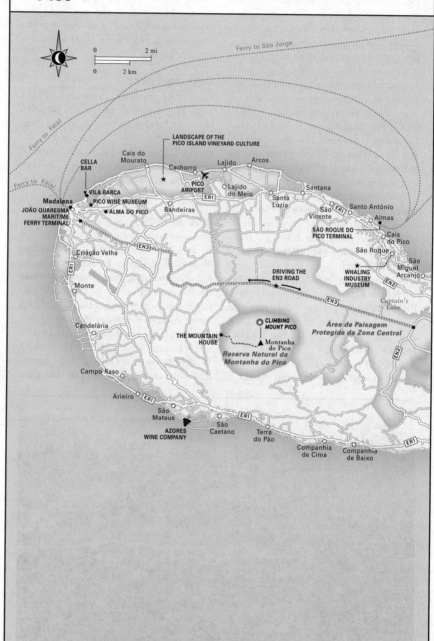

Ferry to São Jorge

Ferry to Faial

Ferry to Faial

0   2 mi
0   2 km

LANDSCAPE OF THE
PICO ISLAND VINEYARD CULTURE

CELLA
BAR

Cais do
Mourato

Cachorro

Lajido

Arcos

VILA BARCA
PICO WINE MUSEUM

PICO
AIRPORT

Lajido
do Meio

Santana

Madalena

JOÃO QUARESMA
MARITIME
FERRY TERMINAL

ALMA DO PICO

Bandeiras

Santa
Luzia

São
Vicente

Santo António

Almas

SÃO ROQUE DO
PICO TERMINAL

Criação Velha

EN3

Cais
do Pico

São Roque

Monte

DRIVING THE
EN3 ROAD

WHALING
INDUSTRY
MUSEUM

São
Miguel
Arcanjo

EN2

EN3

Captain's
Lake

Candelária

CLIMBING
MOUNT PICO

Área de Paisagem
Protegida da Zona Central

THE MOUNTAIN
HOUSE

Montanha
do Pico

Reserva Natural da
Montanha do Pico

EN2

Campo Raso

Arieiro

ER1

São
Mateus

São
Caetano

ER1

Terra
do Pão

AZORES
WINE COMPANY

Companhia
de Cima

Companhia
de Baixo

ER1

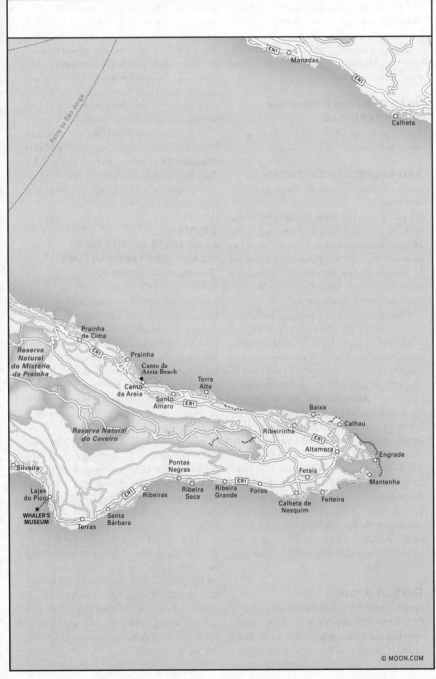

from the airport, catch the local **Carreira do Norte** (North Line; https://cristianolimitada.pt/horarios_cristiano_limitada.html) bus, which takes around 20 minutes and costs €2, or catch a **taxi** for around €13. There is a taxi rank outside arrivals.

JOÃO QUARESMA MARITIME FERRY TERMINAL

Rua dona Maria da Glória Duarte; tel. 292 623 340; www.atlanticoline.pt

SÃO ROQUE DO PICO TERMINAL

Gare Marítima de São Roque; tel. 292 642 482; www.atlanticoline.pt

It's pretty easy and cheap to reach Pico from both São Jorge and Faial, its closest neighbors, by ferry. Ferries from São Jorge and Faial sail to João Quaresma Maritime Ferry Terminal in Madalena, Pico's main town, on the island's northwestern tip, or to São Roque do Pico Terminal, on its northwestern flank.

There are around half a dozen weekly ferry links between the **Velas ferry terminal** (Cais Velas; tel. 295 412 047) on São Jorge to both Madalena (1 hour 40 minutes) and São Roque (1 hour). Tickets prices range €10-16 one-way. The daily ferry, the **Green Line,** is operated by **Atlanticoline** (tel. 707 201 572; www.atlanticoline.pt). Sailings to Pico on the **Blue Line** or the **Green Line** are more frequent from Faial's main town, **Horta** (Avenida 25 de Abril; tel. 292 292 132; https://portosdosacores.pt), with around 50 ferry links a week. The ferry from Horta to **São Roque** runs four times per week and takes around 1 hour 20 minutes; the ferry between Horta and **Madalena** sails about six times daily and takes 30 minutes. One-way prices between Faial and both ports on Pico are usually under €5.

Getting Around

Limited **public transportation,** operated by **Cristiano Limitada** (tel. 292 622 126; https://cristianolimitada.pt/horarios_cristiano_limitada.html), revolves around the island's main town, Madalena, and along the coast;

public transport inland is practically non-existent. Like with the rest of the Azores, **renting a car** gives you the most flexibility. For a small island, there are a good number of car rental companies like **Europcar** (www.europcar.com) and **Rent-a-Car Oásis** (www.rentacaroasis.com). You can collect at the airport, or ask for the vehicle to be dropped off and picked up from your hotel.

In addition to providing rides within Pico's main towns, taxi companies like **Taxis Madalena do Pico** (tel. 962 400 120) and **E'z Taxi Pico Island** (tel. 918 268 183) will provide quotes for half- and full-day tours and trips around the island.

Sights

LANDSCAPE OF THE PICO ISLAND VINEYARD CULTURE (Paisagem da Cultura da Vinha da Ilha do Pico)

Northern coast of Pico Island; open 24/7; free

Pico Island's viticulture dates back to the 15th century. Vast swaths of the island are covered with woven grids of basalt rock walls, forming pens called *currais* within which the island vines grow. The *currais* are designed to protect the vines from harsh sea air as well as release heat overnight to regulate the grapes' temperatures. So unique and characteristic is this lattice-like landscape that it has been classified a UNESCO World Heritage Site since 2004. The designated Landscape of the Pico Island Vineyard Culture covers over 3 hectares (7 acres) of the northwestern flank of the island, an excellent example of historic farming practices being preserved and continued today.

Drive around or park to wander the *currais,* taking in one of the most unique and exquisitely preserved winemaking traditions on the planet. Visit the Vineyard Culture Interpretation Center, enjoy a tasting of local wines, and see other historic artifacts linked to winemaking, such as the old stone manor houses, wine cellars, warehouses, churches, and wells.

Start your visit to the Landscape of the

The Basalt Wines of Pico

The first vines on Pico were reputedly planted by 15th-century Franciscan friars, who were among the first settlers on the island. Battling extreme elements like blasts of salty winds from the open Atlantic, mineral-rich volcanic soil, humidity, and proximity to the sea, the vines thrive in the most remarkable conditions, grown in ancient basalt-walled pens known as *currais,* producing equally distinct flavors. Learn more about island winemaking at the **Pico Wine Museum** (Rua dos Baleiros 13, Madalena; tel. 292 672 276; www.museu-pico.azores.gov.pt/museu/museu-do-vinho; Tues.-Fri. 9am-12:30pm and 2pm-5:30pm, Sat.-Sun. 9am-12:30pm; €2).

WINES TO TRY

Pico's wines are mostly produced from three varietals of grape: **Verdelho, Arinto dos Açores,** and **Terrantez do Pico.** Once most famous for the production of its *licoroso* fortified wine, still sometimes available from Pico's wineries, the island's forte today is without doubt its **white wines:** crisp, citrusy, and some with an oddly salty, minerally note.

Frei Gigante, Terras de Lava, and Basalto brands, produced by the Pico Island Wine Cooperative, are among the top wines to look out for, as well as **Curral Atlantis, Arinto dos Açores,** and **Cancela do Porco.** You may also encounter *vinho de cheiro,* a light red wine with a perfume-like fragrance. And make sure to try the **Lajido** or **Czar** *licoroso* fortified wines.

WHERE TO TRY THEM

In addition to the Landscape of the **Pico Island Vineyard Culture,** wineries dot the island.

Pico Island Wine Cooperative

Cooperativa Vitivinícola da Ilha do Pico; Av. Padre Nunes Rosa 29, Madalena; tel. 292 622 262 or 912 533 243; www.picowines.com; Mon.-Fri. 8am-8pm, Sat. 3pm-8pm

Pico's largest and oldest wine cooperative, the Pico Island Wine Cooperative is responsible for some of the island's most famous brands. They offer several **tour** options (from €6 pp); check the website for times and to book ahead, and pop into the **gift shop** to stock up on wine on your way out!

Azores Wine Company

Rua dos Biscoitos, 3, São Mateus; tel. 912 530 237; http://azoreswinecompany. com; Mon.-Fri. 11am-12:30pm and 4pm-5:30pm

Founded in 2014 to produce and promote Pico's unique wines, the privately run Azores Wine Company has recovered about 40 hectares (100 acres) on the island of Pico for its own production, and is on track to become the largest private producer in the Azores. **Themed tastings** with catchy names like Volcanic Wines, Salt & Spices, and Crazy About Whites are available four times a day, every day of the week (prices upon request; call or email to inquire or reserve).

Pico Island Vineyard Culture by learning more about the fascinating history of Pico's winemaking at the **Interpretation Center** (Centro de Interpretação da Paisagem da Cultura da Vinha da Ilha do Pico; Rua do Lajido Santa Luzia; tel. 965 896 313; http://parquesnaturais.azores.gov.pt/pt/pico/o-que-visitar/centros-de-interpretacao/centro-de-interpretacao-da-paisagem-da-cultura-da-vinha; Tues.-Sat. 10am-1pm and 1:30pm-5pm Nov. 1-Mar. 31, daily 10am-1pm and 2pm-6pm Apr. 1-Oct. 31; €3). Enjoy a wine-tasting and guided tour of the beautiful vineyards and volcanic *currais* (€5 pp by appointment, request 48 hours in advance).

Dolphin- and Whale-Watching

Being far less developed than many other main islands means whales come within close proximity of Pico, and the pristine waters around the island are a natural haven for many species of both whales and dolphins.

Various companies run trips offering the magical experience of seeing these majestic

From Whaling to Whale-Watching

The Azores unreservedly showcases its whaling tradition, warts and all. While the activity has long been eradicated in this part of the world, its heritage remains ingrained in the region: Most islands have statues or monuments alluding to the islands' former lifeblood; former whaling factories have been converted into modern museums; *vigias* (lookouts) once used by whalers to spot their prey dot the coast; and old wooden boats have been proudly kept since whaling came to a staggered end in the 1980s, after being officially banned in 1982.

As tourism crept into the Azores, the region gradually established itself as one of the foremost whale-spotting sites on the globe. Tourism has thrived hand in hand with marine conservation, with preservation replacing profitability. Today, the Azores' waters provide a safe haven for over 20 species of whales that can be spotted year-round, one of the most magical experiences on offer in the Azores.

LEARNING ABOUT AZOREAN WHALING HERITAGE TODAY

Remnants of the whaling industry can be seen all over Pico, especially in the *vigias* (lookouts) dotting the island's coasts that were once used by whalers to spot their prey. But a visit to the excellent museums dedicated to the history of whaling, followed by seeing the majestic animals up close on a whale-watching tour, will provide the best education.

- **Whaling Industry Museum:** This former factory in São Roque do Pico teaches visitors all about how whales were processed into the products that made them so valuable (Rua do Poço; tel. 292 642 096; www.museu-pico.azores.gov.pt/museu/museu-da-industria-baleeira; Tues.-Sun. 10am-5:30pm; €2).

- **Whaler's Museum:** This museum in Lajes do Pico focuses on the heritage and culture of the former Azorean whaling industry (Rua dos Baleeiros, 13; tel. 292 679 340; www.museu-pico.azores.gov.pt/museu/museu-dos-baleeiros; Tues.-Fri. 9am-12:30pm and 2pm-5:30pm, Sat.-Sun. 2pm-5:30pm; €2).

- **Whale-Watching:** Pico's relative lack of development, even by Azorean standards, means it is perhaps the best island in the archipelago for whale-watching. Set off on your expedition from Lajes do Pico, the island's whale-watching center.

beasts up close, mostly during peak season (Apr.-Oct.), although whales can be seen year-round. The species spotted vary from season to season, but may include sperm whales, bottlenose and Risso's dolphins, and more rarely blue whales, fin whales, sei whales, and humpback whales, among others. Your best bet to see blue whales is in the spring.

Most whale-watching trips depart from **Lajes do Pico,** on the south coast of the island, and last 3-4 hours (half-day trips). Some companies also run full-day trips (7-8 hours).

- **Aqua Açores:** Rua Manuel Paulino de Azevedo e Castro 9; tel. 917 569 453; www.aquaacores.com.pt; daily 8am-8pm; from €50 pp

- **Espaço Talassa:** Lajes do Pico; tel. 292 672 010; www.espacotalassa.com; daily 8am-8pm; from €39

★ Hiking Mount Pico

It might not quite be in the same category as climbing Everest or Kilimanjaro, but Pico is by no means a walk in the park. At 2,351 meters (7,713 ft), it is the highest point not only in the Azores, but the whole of Portugal. It requires some degree of fitness to reach the top, which is roughly 3-4 hours up at a relaxed pace, and the same again back down. Just when you think you've reached the top, there's another little summit—**Piquinho,** or Pico Pequenho—to scale, if you still have the

---

1: view from Mount Pico **2:** dolphins off the coast of Pico Island **3:** Pico Island Vineyard Culture

☆ The Tip of the Triangle: São Jorge

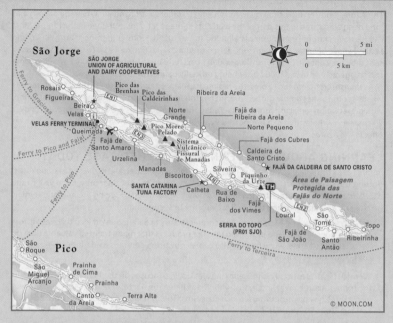

Long, slender, and shaped like a knife, pristine São Jorge is arguably one of the Azores' most beautiful islands, rising strikingly from the sea. A compelling combination of sculpted nature and well-preserved heritage, the famous Queijo da Ilha cheese is still produced to time-honored recipes; the island is home to the Azores' most famous fish-canning factory; and it also boasts the only coffee plantations in Europe.

FAJÃ DA CALDEIRA DE SANTO CRISTO

São Jorge is hemmed by unique coastal formations known as **fajãs,** flat tongues of terrain formed

energy. It's a full day's effort and is very steep in parts, meaning appropriate footwear and gloves are essential. Also, plan ahead for the Azores' notorious ever-changing weather, which reduces visibility and swings from pleasant to cool in the blink of an eye, and try to avoid hiking in the hottest hours in summer by starting early.

All climbers are required to check in and out at the **Mountain House information center** (Caminho Florestal 9, Candelária; tel. 967 303 519; http://parquesnaturais. azores.gov.pt/pt/pico/o-que-visitar/

centros-de-interpretacao/casa-da-montanha; open 24/7 May 1-Sept. 30, Mon.-Thurs. 8am-8pm, Fri. 8am-Sun. 8pm uninterrupted Apr. and Oct., daily 8am-6pm Nov. 1-Mar. 31). The number of climbers is limited to 160 at any given time, or a daily load of 320, to protect the mountain. Only 32 people are allowed to spend the night on the mountain, which is why booking ahead via a tour company is recommended.

Pack some **snacks** and **water,** and **layer up,** as the Azorean weather can change rapidly. If hiking during summer, don't forget the

by lava flows that pooled and cooled by the sea, creating unique geological plains that are usually rich and fertile. These lava plateaus are what give São Jorge its nickname, the "Brown Island" or the "Island of the Fajãs." The most famous, Fajã da Caldeira de Santo Cristo, is a surfers' haven, only accessible by the **Serra do Topo-Caldeira de Santo Cristo-Fajã dos Cubres (PR01 SJO) hike** (http://trails.visitazores.com; 10 kilometers/6 mi one-way; 2.5 hours one-way; trailhead: Serra do Topo car park, off the EN2, 30 kilometers/19 mi east of Velas).

CHEESE, TUNA, AND COFFEE

The distinctive, semi-hard, tangy São Jorge cheese is produced at the **São Jorge Union of São Jorge Union of Agricultural and Dairy Cooperatives** (União de Cooperativas Agrícolas de Lacticínios de São Jorge, Canadinha Nova, Beira (4 km/2 mi north of Velas); tel. 295 438 274 or 295 438 275; www.lactacores.pt; Mon.-Fri. 9am-5:30pm; €1.50). Call ahead for a guided **tour** around the pungent-smelling factory, or just pop in on any day to sample the cheese and buy some straight from the source.

The **Santa Catarina Tuna Factory** (Santa Catarina Indústria Conserveira, Rua do Roque, 9, Calheta; tel. 295 416 220; www.atumsantacatarina.com; Mon.-Fri. 8:30am-5pm; €3.90) produces one of the archipelago's most revered and renowned products: canned Azores tuna. The tins are lovely little mementos of the island, with a retro, vintage look, and this busy factory welcomes visitors.

Finally, at Europe's only coffee plantation, **Café Nunes** (M 1-2a, Fajã dos Vimes, Ribeira Seca parish; tel. 295 416 717; daily 7am-midnight; free), unique, organic coffee can be sampled and bought along with homemade local pastries.

GETTING THERE AND AROUND

Arriving on São Jorge requires some planning; you will likely need to fly there via São Miguel or Terceira Island, or hop over on a ferry from Pico or Faial. **São Jorge Airport** (SJZ; Queimada; tel. 295 430 360; www.sata.pt/pt-pt/sata/sata-aerodromos) is located about 6 kilometers (4 mi) southeast of main town **Velas**, a 10-minute drive. **Atlanticoline Ferries** (tel. 707 201 572 or 965 995 002; www.atlanticoline.pt) sail year-round between Velas Ferry Terminal (tel. 295 432 225; http://marinas.visitazores.com/marinas/velas) and nearby Faial and Pico.

Renting a car here is not strictly necessary; as hiking is often the main purpose for visiting, São Jorge's **taxis** have fixed fares for dropping off and picking up at most trailheads. For more information on visiting São Jorge, contact the **tourist office** (Rua Conselheiro Dr. José Pereira no. 1 r/c; tel. 295 412 440; www.visitportugal.com; daily 9am-1pm and 3pm-7pm).

sunscreen, a hat, and more water! There are no toilets on the route. To reach the mountain, head southwest from **Madalena** following the signs that, appropriately, say "Mountain." The official trail starts at the Mountain House, a 25-minute drive from Madalena. A one-way **taxi** trip should cost around €25. A few good tour guides in the area include:

- **Tripix Azores:** Madalena Docks; tel. 912 087 199; www.tripixazores.com; open 24/7; from €65 pp (day climb)

- **Atipico:** Rua Eng. Falcão s/n, Lajes do Pico; tel. 915 340 487 or 919 991 776; http://atipicoazores.com; from €50 pp

Food

On Pico, look for bright ruby-red **figs,** often turned into a brandy, soft fresh **cheeses,** cured sausages like **morçela** (blood sausage) and **linguiça** (a type of thin *chouriço* sausage), and the local **corn bread.** Mains feature rich stews, fish soup, and octopus and squid stewed in wine. Most of the restaurants on the island are in Madalena.

MERCADO BIO

Rua Carlos Dabney no. 6 r/c; tel. 292 623 778; Mon.-Fri. 8am-10pm, Sat. 9am-10pm, Sun. 10am-10pm; €15

Packed with fresh, quality produce made into tasty dishes, Mercado Bio (Bio Market) is a warm and surprisingly chic eatery where healthy eating meets local cuisine. Make the most of your visit by stocking up on produce to take home.

TASCA O PETISCA

Avenida Padre Nunes da Rosa; tel. 292 622 357; www. facebook.com/tascapetisca; Mon.-Sat. 10am-3pm and 6:30pm-midnight; €15

Specializing in traditional regional tapas, or snack dishes (*petiscos*), O Petisca was the first restaurant of its kind on the island. Seafood, island beef, local breads, and homemade desserts are among the specialties at this busy and popular eatery.

★ CELLA BAR

Rua Da Barca; tel. 292 623 654; www.cellabar.pt; Mon.-Fri. 4pm-11pm, Sat.-Sun. noon-late; €20

Housed within a futuristic-looking, award-winning wooden building attached to a traditional stone house, this bar is unique not only for its striking architecture, but also for its magnificent beachside setting and views. Seafood soup, pork ribs, and tuna steaks all feature on the menu. It's also a great place for some delectable tapas and a sunset cocktail.

Accommodations

VILA BARCA

Caminho da Barca; tel. 915 457 152; https://vilabarca. com; €85

Resembling an elegant boathouse, Vila Barca stylishly blends the old with new. Comprising five apartments and four rooms, the aparthotel is a 15-minute walk to the center of Madalena. With mountain or sea views from all rooms, which are equipped with mod cons, there is also a natural swimming pool a short stroll away.

★ ALMA DO PICO

Rua dos Biscoitos 34; tel. 914 232 760; www. almadopico.com; two-person bungalow €95

An enchanting and serene place set in a hectare (2 acres) of stunning woodland, Alma do Pico is a 5-minute drive (€5 taxi ride) from Madalena harbor. The décor takes inspiration from nature, with cozy accommodation in refined wooden houses.

Information and Services

Pico has good facilities and amenities. It has a decent primary health care network with well-equipped centers in larger towns (including Madalena and São Roque), pharmacies in most towns and villages, and an acute medical emergency response service (INEM; tel. 112) that covers the island. Emergency and critical health cases will be transferred to hospitals on bigger islands, namely São Miguel, or back to the mainland if necessary.

There are **ATMs** available across the island, on main streets and at the port and airport terminals.

- **Tourist Office:** Rua Dona Maria da Glória Duarte - Gare Marítimo da Madalena; tel. 292 623 524; www.visitazores.travel; Mon.-Fri. 10am-6pm, or by appointment
- **PSP Police:** Engenheiro Álvaro de Freitas, s/n; tel. 292 622 860; www.psp.pt
- **Madalena Health Center:** Praça Dr. Caetano Mendonça, Alto da Cruz; tel. 292 628 800
- **Pharmacy:** Avenida Machado Serpa, 1; tel. 292 622 159

Background

The Landscape

Portugal is a coastal country whose landscape varies greatly by region, from the rugged mountain valleys of the north to the wooded mounts of Central Portugal and the rolling plains and sunny beaches of the south. Portugal's coastline is characterized by sheer cliffs alternating with golden beaches and coves. Inland, vegetation is predominantly European species in the north and shrubby Mediterranean in the south. The southern region is particularly beautiful in spring, dusted with white almond blossoms and the exotic fragrance of orange blossoms on the air.

Across the middle of Portugal is the Tagus River, and the Douro River crosses the country's width in the north. All of Portugal's main watercourses—the Tagus, Douro, Minho, Mondego, and Guadiana—have their sources in Spain and traverse the country to the Atlantic. Wedged between the Douro and the Tagus is Portugal's Central Region, with the snowcapped Serra da Estrela mountain range and the mainland's highest peak, Torre.

While the landscape inland is predominantly pastoral, dry in summer and vibrant green in winter, the coastline is cosmopolitan and touristy. The two archipelagos—Madeira and the Azores—are subtropical and lush year-round, although their location in the Atlantic means that the mild climates can be unpredictable. The beaches of these volcanic islands are mostly black and pebbly, in stark contrast to the mainland's famous soft golden sands.

GEOGRAPHY

On the southwestern flank of the Iberian Peninsula, encased by Spain to the north and east and the Atlantic Ocean to the west and south, Portugal is Europe's westernmost country. Portugal occupies a total landmass of 92,391 square kilometers (35,672 sq mi), and the mainland has 943 kilometers (580 mi) of coastline. Situated on the tectonic Eurasian Plate near its southern boundary with the African Plate, mainland Portugal, especially the Algarve, is a hotbed of seismic activity, but most of the tremors are relatively small and generally go unnoticed. The Azores, located on the junction of three tectonic plates—the North American, Eurasian, and African—also sees frequent quakes and tremors, mostly of low and moderate intensity, that go unnoticed.

CLIMATE

Mainland Portugal has one of the mildest year-round climates in Europe, and its more than 3,300 hours of sunshine per year make it a popular winter-sun destination. Notwithstanding, it does have distinct seasons, with mild springs (sunny days but cool nights), hot and dry summers, warm and sunny autumns (a popular time to visit Portugal, along with spring), and bright but chilly and wet winters.

Winter is generally December to February, and summer is June to late September, although some years have seen summer reach well into October. Traditionally, the hottest months are July and August, when temperatures can exceed 40°C (104°F) in some places; the wettest month is November, and the coldest January. But it is not unusual in Portugal to have downpours in April and heat waves in June or October. Overall, the consensus is that the best times to visit are June and September-October, with pleasant weather and when the popular resorts are not yet in full-throttle peak summer.

Northern Portugal is generally wetter and cooler than the rest of the country, while the south is warmer and drier. Rural inland areas, particularly in the central region, suffer from extremes, being blisteringly hot in summer and bitterly cold in winter. It also snows in winter, but only on the Serra da Estrela mountain range in Central Portugal. Other high-lying areas like Fóia peak in the Monchique mountain range, the highest point in the Algarve, can sometimes see light smatterings of snow. Largely influenced by the Atlantic, coastal areas usually benefit from a pleasant sea breeze, even in the scorching throes of summer. There are also distinct microclimates within the country, with the weather in Northern Portugal resembling that of Northern Europe, the south taking on an increasingly North African feel, and inland areas reflecting the climes of Central Europe.

ENVIRONMENTAL ISSUES

In recent years, Portugal has been increasingly afflicted by sporadic climate change-related environmental issues such as flash floods, tornadoes, more ferocious and widespread wildfires, and coastal erosion, examples of growing extreme and atypical climatic phenomena. Portugal also battles the palm weevil, a beetle from Asia that kills palm trees. Tough there are no major pollution issues, although large forest fires and growing cities have caused alerts for air quality. Significant investment is being made in Portugal to combat air pollution, especially in Lisbon, where new regulations governing vehicles and new data collection systems were implemented in 2017.

Plants and Animals

Portugal's diverse array of flora and fauna come from around the globe. Almost identical to the flora and fauna of neighboring Spain, it is a mix of Atlantic, European, Mediterranean, and North African. The distribution of Portugal's vegetation reflects varying regional climates, denser and leafier to the north and sparser and shrubbier to the south. Simply put, the farther south, the more Mediterranean the vegetation becomes. The country has a number of indigenous species of plants and animals, and several native breeds of dogs, cows, donkeys, horses, pigs, and chickens. The countryside is home to an abundance of wild animals, including wolves, foxes, deer, hares, goats, boars, and lynx. The Iberian lynx has been brought back from the brink of extinction thanks to a proactive conservation and reintroduction program.

Portugal also teems with birdlife as it is on a major winter migration route for western and central European species. It has rich fish stocks off the coast as well as a rapidly expanding number of exotic plant species, particularly invasive species. The Azores can claim the peculiarity of having only small wild mammals, such as rabbits, ferrets, rats, mice, and bats, while Madeira's Desertas Islands are home to the endangered Mediterranean monk seal. In terms of poisonous insects and reptiles, Portugal is one of the countries with the lowest number of dangerous species.

VEGETATION ZONES

Vegetation varies from the predominantly European vegetation of the north to the Mediterranean vegetation of the south. Thick pine and chestnut forests characterize the north, where deciduous trees blanket the landscape. Portugal's central ridge is distinguished by oak and eucalyptus, as is the Alentejo, where, farther south, symbolic cork and holm oaks take over the undulating plains. Farther south still, in the Algarve, the landscape takes on a shrubbier look with predominantly Mediterranean vegetation such as olive, almond, orange, and carob trees as well as vineyards. The lush Azores and Madeira islands abound with mosses and ferns, and throughout the mainland there are a number of protected natural parks established to defend regional natural heritage.

TREES

Not so long ago, most of Portugal was clad in forests. Due to deforestation and, more recently, wildfires, just over one-third of the country remains wooded. Vast swaths of the country, particularly Central Portugal, are blanketed by dense holm and cork oak woodlands (the cork oak is Portugal's national tree), which cover approximately 1.2 million hectares (almost 3 million acres) between Central Portugal and the Alentejo region. Portugal is a leading producer of paper and is the world's leading producer of cork, exporting close to 200,000 tonnes (more than 440 million pounds) every year. Corks found in some of the finest bottles of champagne on the planet derive from Portugal. Mountainous and sandy areas are covered in fragrant eucalyptus and pines as well as ancient olive trees and, farther south, almond trees. Palm trees are a common sight, particularly in popular coastal areas. While many of the common palm species are native, many are foreign, introduced by humans.

FLOWERS AND OTHER PLANTLIFE

You would be hard-pressed to travel around Portugal and not notice the national flower, lavender, growing wild and in gardens It is also a popular ingredient in soaps and teas. Thanks to Portugal's year-round mild climate, a stunning range of colorful flora includes orchids, azaleas, proteas, water lilies, the lovely bougainvillea that grows on seemingly every street, jacarandas, and gerberas, as well as the birds-of-paradise that are synonymous with the island of Madeira. Among the flowers native to Portugal are daffodil, thyme, and sweet marjoram. Portugal's landscape comes to life in spring.

MAMMALS

Portugal's diverse countryside is home to over 100 mammal species, the most common being wild boars, goats, deer, foxes, rabbits, and the Iberian hare. Wolves still live wild in remote parts of the far north and northeast, and the endangered Iberian lynx is gradually being reintroduced into its natural habitat, the Malcata Mountains and the Algarve-Alentejo border regions, after being brought back from the brink of extinction by a successful breeding program implemented in Portugal and Spain. Driven out of its native territories by dwindling food resources, loss and degradation of habitat, urban development, and illegal hunting, Iberia's largest wild cat is once again roaming the hills of its home. Smaller rodents, such as water voles, dormice, rats, and hedgehogs can also be found throughout the country, while Iberian badgers, otters, common genets, and mongooses are also found in central and northern thickets but are rarely sighted.

SEA LIFE

The waters off Portugal's coast teem with life, from tiny sardines to huge tuna, and fishing is an important economic activity. Dolphins can be spotted off the south coast, where dolphin-watching trips are popular, while the Sado Estuary, near Lisbon, is home to a resident pod of bottlenose dolphins unique in Europe. Turtles can be found in the tranquil waters of the Algarve's Ria Formosa, as well as in the waters off the Azores. Whale- and dolphin-watching can be enjoyed on the Azores and Madeira, and Portugal has a plethora of interesting dive sites off its shores and islands. The most common fish caught off the coast and staples in the national diet are sardines, mackerel, and tuna, while the craggy coastline is also a source of shellfish such as clams, cockles, crabs, and oysters.

BIRDS

Positioned on a major migration route between Europe and Africa, Portugal hosts common European species that reside here year-round as well as exotic transients. Over 600 species of birds have been logged in Portugal, with at least one new species recorded every year. Due to their unique geographical location, the Azores and Madeira are particularly interesting to bird-watchers, as they host North American species rarely found elsewhere in Europe. Mainland Portugal's many *rias* (lagoons), marshes, estuaries, and salt pans attract beautiful species like flamingos, which can often be seen standing one-legged. Another common sight is the cattle egret, which likes to pick mites off the backs of livestock or eat insects that emerge from soil disturbed by the animals' hooves.

The elegant stork is a protected species in Portugal and has become symbolic of the south, even though they can be found throughout the mainland. Their huge nests, which withstand even the most ferocious weather, crown pylons, pillars, and buildings in cities and the countryside, a captivating sight. The soaring Iberian white stork *(Ciconia ciconia)* is revered in Portugal as it eats insects that blight crops. It is also illegal to move a stork's nest in Portugal, so many new buildings, especially those converted from old factories, have to retain the original brick chimneys if they have a nest on top.

REPTILES

When the weather is hot, tiny chameleons, lizards, and geckos come out to bask in the sun and to feast on the insects that come out in warmer months. Small reptiles are common throughout Portugal, particularly in arid southern areas, to the delight of some people and the disgust of others. Portugal is home to several species of snakes, but few are venomous and none are deadly. The most common snakes in Portugal are the ladder snake, the false smooth snake, the grass snake, the Montpellier snake, the viperine snake, the Lataste's viper (the only species thought to be harmful to humans), the southern smooth snake, and the horseshoe snake.

AMPHIBIANS

Portugal's sandy dunes and lagoons are a haven for amphibians including terrapins, toads, frogs, newts, and salamanders. The natterjack toad *(Bufo calamita)* is commonly found, even though it is very rare in other European countries.

INSECTS AND ARACHNIDS

Unlike its snake population, Portugal has many biting spiders, several of which are poisonous, the most common being the *armadeira* (wandering spider). The *armadeira* is light brown, is slightly furry, and has long legs. Its bite can be painful and cause dizziness, vomiting, and muscle spasms. The *armadeira* generally comes out in cooler weather, growing up to 5 centimeters (2 inches). If bitten, seek immediate medical attention. If left unattended, the bite can cause serious wounds or even loss of a limb. The *armadeira* is not native to Portugal but was brought from South America in banana boxes. Portugal is also home to the Mediterranean black widow spider, distinctively black with a red spot on its back, the brown recluse spider (also known as the violin spider), and tarantulas, which are less common. But all will bite if provoked. Sound advice is to never handle a spider.

Much more common is the dreaded mosquito, prevalent in areas with still water, such as lagoons and canals, and more so during warmer months. There is no risk of malaria in Portugal, although the island of Madeira has had cases of dengue fever. Besides being itchy, a mosquito bite seldom turns into anything more than a nuisance.

Thanks to its wealth of flowers, Portugal also has bees and wasps, which can give a nasty sting, as well as many butterflies and moths, with common species including the swallowtail butterfly *(Papilio machaon)* and the monarch, most often seen in the Algarve.

One of Portugal's more unusual insects is the pine processionary caterpillar, which turns into a moth and lives in pine trees. These toxic caterpillars can often be seen shuffling along in formation, nose-to-tail, in long lines. They have long hairs that make them look cute and fluffy but can cause a painful allergic reaction if touched; they can be fatal to smaller animals like dogs and cats.

History

Portugal is a small country with epic history. As one of the world's oldest nations and ruler of what was one of the world's most powerful empires, yet with one of the youngest settled democracies in Europe, Portugal has remarkable historical achievements. Its name is said to derive from the ancient Portus Cale, the name for the city now known as Porto. From ancient and medieval invasions to the 12th-century reconquests and the founding of the nation, through the Age of Discoveries, when Portugal spearheaded global explorations and established itself as a world power, the 17th-century Restoration of Independence, and the more recent Carnation Revolution and implementation of democracy, Portugal has a storied history.

Evidence of these eras can be found throughout the country in relics, architecture, and monuments, which in many cities have been excellently preserved. Portugal's architectural styles are influenced by its wide-ranging history and territorial disputes, and can be loosely divided into five main styles: Romanesque, Gothic, Renaissance, Baroque, and neoclassical. Portugal's hand in shaping the world belies its discreet yet determined positioning today, and it deserves its reputation as a nation with an acute sense of adventure and resilience, having successively and successfully rebuilt and repositioned itself in the wake of natural and economic disasters.

ANCIENT TIMES

Portugal is believed to have been inhabited by humans since Paleolithic times, more than 20,000 years ago. The earliest known people to have invaded Portugal were the Celts of Central Europe, who arrived in waves from the first millennium BC, interbreeding with the local native population to form a number of tribes. Like much of Europe, Portugal was invaded by the Romans, who occupied the territory from the 3rd century BC until their demise in the late 4th and 5th centuries AD.

The Roman occupation of Portugal started from the south and took several decades. Rebellion in the north by local Lusitanians hampered the invasion, but after the Romans bribed three rebels to kill their own leader, Viriathus, the country was finally conquered as a whole, and the Roman Empire began to flourish, laying the foundations of the cities and infrastructure of today's Portugal. The cities of Beja and Braga were key administrative sites during the Roman occupation, and many vivid remnants of the Romans' time in Portugal can still be found there. Two of the best-preserved Roman sites in Portugal are in Conímbriga, near Coimbra, and the Milreu Roman Ruins in Estoi, Algarve.

EARLY HISTORY

In the 5th century AD, the Iberian Peninsula was invaded and conquered by a Germanic tribe known as the Visigoths, vestiges of whose presence can be found in Coimbra, Alenquer, and Lisbon. Despite establishing what went on to become known as the Visigoth Kingdom, the invaders' claim didn't last long, and they were overthrown by the Moors, medieval Muslims from present-day Morocco in North Africa, who invaded Portugal circa 711, claiming and settling across the entire Iberian Peninsula. Small pockets of Christian armies lingered and rebelled against the Moors, over the next few centuries driving them back and reclaiming territory during an era known as the *reconquistas* (reconquests). By the 9th century, the north of Portugal was under Christian rule, and by the 12th century the Moors had been completely driven out. One of the main leaders of the Christian armies, Afonso Henriques, famously declared himself the first king of Portugal in 1139, and a fledgling kingdom was founded.

Portugal's early foundations were shaken

when territorial disputes with the Spaniards broke out, particularly over the south of Portugal. However, Portugal's status as an independent kingdom was reinforced in the Middle Ages when Afonso III (third in succession of founding King Afonsos, in what became known as the Afonsine era) conquered the southern city of Faro in the Algarve in 1249, and an alliance was drawn up with the United Kingdom, the Treaty of Windsor, to protect Portugal from further incursions.

AGE OF DISCOVERIES

With the country firmly under Christian rule and the protection of the Treaty of Windsor, Portugal turned its attentions to exploration, an era that was to become known as the Age of Discoveries. Roughly spanning the 15th and 16th centuries, this golden age saw Portuguese seafarers, spearheaded by Portugal's most famous captain, Prince Henry the Navigator, sail off to explore the world. Henry, the third son of John I (João I), at age 21 commanded a military force that captured the Muslim outpost of Ceuta in North Africa in 1415; this was the initial step in Portugal's Age of Discoveries. First, the Portuguese explored the Atlantic archipelagos and the African coast before rounding the Cape of Good Hope in 1488 under the leadership of Bartolomeu Dias, finally reaching India a decade later in 1498, guided by Vasco da Gama. But what really catapulted Portugal to stratospheric wealth and power was the exploration and claiming of Brazil by Pedro Álvares Cabral in 1500. These discoveries elevated Portugal from a tumultuous territory to a leading global power, along with the imperial peers of England, France, and Spain, in terms of economic, political, and cultural clout.

COLONIALISM

Portuguese explorers continued to establish profitable trading routes around the globe and set up a string of trading colonies, forts, and factories throughout the world as they went; the spice, gold, and slave trades were among the most lucrative. By 1571, a series of naval outposts connected Lisbon to places as far-flung as Nagasaki, along the coasts of Africa, the Middle East, India, and South Asia. This had a huge positive impact on Portuguese economic growth that lasted for three centuries. While Brazil was undoubtedly the jewel in Portugal's colonial crown, major colonies in the African countries of Angola, Mozambique, and Guinea-Bissau also proved profitable. Other important colonies were established in Cape Verde, São Tomé and Príncipe, Goa (India), East Timor, and Macau. For centuries, the Portuguese pioneered global explorations and excelled in trade, and its colonial empire grew to become one of the largest and longest-lived in world history, spanning six centuries until the handover of Macau to China in 1999.

SPANISH ANNEXATION AND INDEPENDENCE

In 1578 Portugal's king, Dom Sebastião I, was killed in the Battle of Alcácer Quibir in northern Morocco. Because the king died without an heir, the throne was claimed by King Phillip II of neighboring Spain, based on a vague family lineage. Phillip II took advantage of Portugal's vulnerability following the king's death and invaded in 1580, forcing a merger that saw Spain protect Brazil from being claimed by the Dutch but also saw Portugal inherit Spain's enemies, among them England. Even though life was relatively tranquil during the reigns of Phillip II and III, with Portugal retaining its own laws and currency, unrest finally reached boiling point during the reign of Phillip IV, who stripped the country's nobility of all powers and effectively attempted to make Portugal a Spanish province. Seizing Spain's fatigue at the end of the Thirty-Year War, Portugal's John of Braganza led a Portuguese resistance, later known as the Portuguese Restoration War, that lasted 28 years. Finally, on February 13, 1668, Spain officially recognized Portugal's independence. Even though Portugal no longer has a monarch, and hasn't since the revolution of October 5, 1910, the House of Braganza is still seen as akin to the country's royal family, and lays claim to the throne.

EARTHQUAKE OF 1755

Portugal was again brought to its knees by the massive 1755 Lisbon earthquake, which razed vast swaths of the country. A succession of three devastating tsunamis and massive fires that raged for days contributed to the apocalyptic chaos that practically wiped out an entire country. In the aftermath, the Marquis of Pombal was nominated by José I to lead the recovery, which, to Pombal's credit, was remarkably swift. Portugal was almost entirely rebuilt in a matter of years, mostly thanks to the wealth coming from Brazil after gold was discovered there. This reconstruction gave way to the distinctly Portuguese Pombaline style of architecture, a mix of late Baroque and neoclassical.

BRITISH ULTIMATUM

In 1890 the United Kingdom issued Portugal an ultimatum that all Portuguese troops should withdraw from the belt of African colonies between Mozambique on the east and Angola on the west. The theories about the reasons for this are that the presence of Portuguese troops hampered British plans to build a railroad between Cairo and Cape Town, or that the British government was pressed into taking action by Cecil Rhodes, whose British South Africa Company was founded in 1888. Rhodes's ambition was to create a zone of British commercial and political influence from Cape Town to Cairo, and the Portuguese settlements were in the way.

Portugal complied with the British demands, which were considered a breach of the Treaty of Windsor as well as a national humiliation by republicans in Portugal, who denounced the government and the king, leading to the collapse of the government. It was considered the most outrageous action by the United Kingdom against its oldest ally and was one of the main causes for the Republican Revolution, which ended the monarchy in Portugal 20 years later. On October 5, 1910, a coup d'état organized by the Portuguese Republican Party, in which at least 37 people died, deposed the constitutional monarchy and proclaimed a republican regime, the Estado Novo (first republic). The iconic red, gold, and green national flag was adopted in 1911.

20TH CENTURY

After siding with the Allies in World War I and suffering postwar turmoil and unrest, on May 7, 1926, Portugal saw another coup d'état that paved the way for the military to seize power and gave birth to the second republic, the Diatdura Nacional (National Dictatorship). This saw the rise of notorious dictator António de Oliveira Salazar, and times of oppression and censorship. Salazar led Portugal through World War II, during which the country remained nominally neutral. Despite supplying troops under the British flag and allowing the Allies to establish air bases in the Azores, Portugal continued to trade successfully with both sides for the duration of World War II. The demise of Salazar came in 1968 when he slipped in a bathtub and suffered a brain hemorrhage; he died in 1970. He handed power to the slightly less radical Marcelo Caetano, who was overthrown in 1974 in what has become known as the Carnation Revolution, the third and last republic.

The Carnation Revolution eradicated dictatorial power without bloodshed or a single shot being fired. This was the start of the democratic republic of Portugal we know today. The revolution also saw the end of the Portuguese colonial empire, with its remaining overseas colonies, including Angola and Mozambique, attaining independence. The Portuguese people who left the colonies to come back to Portugal became known as the *retornados* (returnees). Macau, the nation's last possession, was handed over to China in 1999. But Portugal joining the European Union in 1986 really thrust the country forward, increasing funding for basic infrastructure such as roads, schools, and medical facilities as well as foreign investment, with which Portugal has truly blossomed.

CONTEMPORARY TIMES

Modern-day Portugal is a prospering and socially stable country despite the severe impact of the 2008 global economic crisis. Years of austerity ensued, but Portugal remained true to its resilient roots, and its recovery and payback of its €78 billion bailout have been exemplary. Prior to the 2020 coronavirus pandemic, Portugal had been enjoying a period of financial reestablishment, social and economic recovery, record-breaking tourism, and dropping unemployment, and the country had yet again managed to get back on its feet following a debilitating blow. A number of reforms are in place to underpin future growth.

In recent years, Portugal has also repeatedly topped the list of most peaceful countries in the world, and it has been voted among the best places to live in Europe, to retire in Europe, and to visit in Europe.

Government and Economy

ORGANIZATION

The Republic of Portugal is a sovereign democracy. Its current form of government is unitary and semi-presidential (with a president as well as a prime minister), in which the central government has ultimate power. The prime minister is the head of government, while the president is the head of state. The president is head of the armed forces and is responsible for swearing in new prime ministers, based on election results, and convening or dissolving parliament when required. At the time of writing, Portugal's prime minister is António Costa, of the Socialist Party, and its president is Marcelo Rebelo de Sousa of the Social Democratic Party.

The government of Portugal comprises the president of the republic, the Assembly of the Republic (parliament), and the courts, the country's executive, legislative, and judicial branches, respectively. The government has political, legislative, and administrative functions and comprises a prime minister, ministers, secretaries of state (junior ministers), and their deputies. Portugal's current government is a Socialist Party (PS) minority government, supported by a leftist alliance of the Left Bloc (BE), Portuguese Communist Party (PCP), and the Ecologist (green) Party (PEV). The autonomous regions (Azores and Madeira) have their own regional political and administrative statutes, governments, and presidents.

POLITICAL PARTIES

Since the dawn of democracy following the 1974 Carnation Revolution, Portugal has had two main parties that dominate the political scene: the center-left PS Socialist Party, and the center-right PSD Social Democratic Party. Following those, the other main parties are the conservative Christian-Democratic CDS-PP People's Party, the BE Left Bloc, the PCP Communist Party, the green party Os Verdes, and, more recently, the progressive center-left PAN—Party for People, Animals, and Nature. The country does have a few right-wing and far-right parties, but they have little political expression.

ELECTIONS

Elections take place on the national and local levels. Citizens directly elect a president every five years in the Presidential Election, and a new parliament in the Legislative Election every four years. Portugal's parliament is made up of 230 members elected to four-year terms by proportional district representation. Locally, Portugal has 308 municipal authorities, and every four years local elections choose councils and mayors for four-year terms. Local elections are interspersed with national elections. Portugal also stages European elections for representatives to sit in the European Parliament.

AGRICULTURE

Agriculture plays a large role in the Portuguese economy, with the Alentejo, known as the breadbasket of Portugal and for grazing. Forestry, farming, and fishing support many families in rural and inland areas, reflected in regional gastronomy. The main products of Portugal, beyond cork and wine, are green vegetables, rice, corn, wheat, barley, olives, oilseeds, nuts, cherries, bilberries, table grapes, and mushrooms. Portugal is also a leading producer of tomato paste, olive oil, and sea salt. Despite vast regions of the country still being agriculture-dependent, investment and funding for the sector is low, and environmental issues such as drought, wildfires, and dwindling fish stocks hamper prosperity.

INDUSTRY

Because Portugal is a seafaring nation where trade has historically been a mainstay, it is perhaps unsurprising that it remains an industrious and creative country. The tertiary (services) sector is currently the largest in the country's economy, in which the importance of tourism cannot be overstated. The services sector presently provides jobs for more than two-thirds of the working population and represents over 75 percent of the gross value added (GVA). Industry, construction, energy, and water make up just under a quarter of the GVA and employ one-quarter of the working population, while agriculture, forestry, and fishing are just a tiny slice of the GVA (2.2 percent) and employment (6.9 percent).

Given that in the 1960s fishing and farming were responsible for around a quarter of the country's economy, that sector has suffered a steep and steady downturn over the past half-century.

Although Portugal was a late starter in industrialization—it was one of the last European countries that the Industrial Revolution reached—the economy today is powered by several key drivers, mostly harnessed from the country's natural attributes and ever-developing skills. Chiefly, these are machinery, electrical, and electronics industries; automotive and shipbuilding industries; injection molding; creative clothing, textiles, and footwear; wood pulp, paper, and cork; food processing and fish canning (Portugal's canned fish brands are gastronomic icons); world-class wine and olive oil production; and the all-important tourism.

Industrial production in Portugal soared after World War II, aided by modernization in the 1960s. Portugal's return to democracy in 1974, followed by the nation's joining the European Union in 1986, saw privatized firms liberalized, which allowed the national economy to thrive.

Most of the bigger textile and footwear factories are in the north, while Oeiras, in Lisbon, is home to the country's major multinational companies. Many larger Portuguese companies have also made significant investment in internationalizing, among them retailer Jerónimo Martins, which owns the largest no-frills supermarket chain in Poland and is also investing in Colombia, and national flag-carrier airline TAP Portugal, which is held in high regard for its safety record.

For much of the 1990s the economy grew by more than the EU average, and, despite the crippling economic downturn, it has recently started to regain ground. In 2017, driven by exports and investment, the economy grew at twice the pace of the Eurozone average.

DISTRIBUTION OF WEALTH

Despite gradual industrialization in the late 1800s, prior to the 1974 Carnation Revolution, Portugal was socially divided into two main classes: an affluent elite of mainly landowners and impoverished peasants. The revolution eradicated the dictatorship that had kept the social classes in place, and major changes erupted. The onset of slow modernization in the 20th century saw a new and prosperous middle class begin to emerge, and social indicators began to equalize. Portugal infamously had one of the highest illiteracy rates in Europe, but as education improved, so did development, mainly along the country's coast, which inevitably saw younger people leaving the rural interior for the coast to pursue studies or seek employment. This led to desertification inland, which, while less pronounced today, had an impact on the distribution of investment. With the exception of a handful of major inland cities, the coast is generally a more affluent and desirable place to live, although much of the employment, particularly in the Algarve, is tourism-generated and seasonal.

The economic crisis of 2008 had a debilitating impact on the country's lower-earning families, whose main income came from precarious employment and benefits. Rife unemployment and tough austerity measures saw many families heading for soup kitchens, and young graduates left the country in large numbers to find employment abroad, many in the former Portuguese colonies. That scenario is much improved today, although recent studies have found that Portugal's distribution of wealth is still disparate, one of the most unequal in Europe and with higher-than-average levels of poverty.

TOURISM

Tourism is a buoyant key economic driver in Portugal, particularly in coastal areas and especially in the southern Algarve region, where tourism is the main source of employment. Growth has been gradual since 2011, with new hotels opening every year to welcome a record 21 million tourists in 2017, generating €3.39 billion in revenue. This is up significantly from the 15 million visitors registered in 2014, and the 19 million tourists who stayed in Portugal's hotels in 2016. Tourism currently accounts for approximately 12 percent of the gross domestic product, making tourism the second-biggest element of the national economy.

Foreign visitors to Portugal are predominantly European and of British, German, Spanish, and French nationality, or Brazilian. In recent years, growing numbers of American, Russian, Asian, and Scandinavian tourists have arrived.

While Portugal has always been a popular destination among Northern Europeans, particularly the British, who make up the largest tourist group as well as a major expatriate community, it's safe to say Portugal's allure has never been stronger. Despite the crippling economic downturn and austere bailout, Portugal managed to maintain its quality over quantity image while identifying new niche markets and investing in creative promotions to become increasingly trendy.

Lisbon, the Algarve, and Madeira see the largest numbers of tourists, accounting for almost one-third of visitors to the country, but the Azores and Northern Portugal are enjoying a newfound demand that has seen visitor figures soar. From 2006 to 2016, foreign tourist numbers in Portugal almost doubled. As one of the last Western European countries to develop its tourism, Portugal has more tourists, more revenue, and fuller hotels than ever, and was named the World's Leading Destination at the 24th annual World Travel Awards (WTA) in 2017.

Lisbon and Porto are now revered top European destinations like Barcelona and London, while the Algarve remains one of Europe's leading beach destinations.

People and Culture

DEMOGRAPHY AND DIVERSITY

Portugal has a population of about 10 million. Most densely populated are Lisbon, Porto, Coimbra, Braga, and Funchal (Madeira), and the Algarve and the Silver Coast are popular places to live. As of 2016, the average life expectancy was 81.1 years. However, as life expectancy increases and the birth rate dwindles, Portugal's struggles with an aging population.

Portugal has a literacy rate of 95.7 percent. Education in Portugal is free, as is health care, and is compulsory until the age of 18 or until completing 12th grade.

Portugal's largest minority groups are Brazilians, Eastern Europeans, Asians, and Africans from Portugal's former colonies, such as Cape Verde, Angola, and Guinea-Bissau. Legal immigrants account for about 5 percent of the total population. There are also 40,000-50,000 Roma people in the country. Portugal has strict antiracism and antidiscrimination laws. It is forbidden to collect statistics about race or ethnicity in the country. Racially motivated attacks in Portugal are not unheard of, but they're not daily news either. There has been some concern expressed over a perceived rise in racially motivated hate crimes and hate speech in recent times, and discrimination particularly against Roma and those of African descent.

RELIGION

Portugal is over 80 percent Roman Catholic, although only around one-third of Portuguese are practicing. Traditional religious festivals and customs are widely observed, as are religious ceremonies like baptisms, last rites, and marriages. Religious observance is strongest in the northern regions and less prevalent in the southern regions and cities.

LANGUAGE

The language spoken in Portugal is European Portuguese, distinct from Brazilian Portuguese, which originates from the European version. A West Romance language, Portuguese is the seventh most widely spoken language in the world and the sole official language of Portugal and former Portuguese colonies Brazil, Cape Verde, Mozambique, Angola, and São Tomé and Príncipe, as well as Guinea-Bissau. Portuguese also has co-official language status in East Timor, Equatorial Guinea, and Macau in China.

While Portuguese is spoken throughout the country, some 5,000 people in the villages in the Miranda do Douro speak their own language, Mirandese, recognized as a co-official language.

English is the most widely spoken second language in Portugal, followed by French and Spanish. Most tours will have a guide who speaks very good English, and signage will usually have an English translation, especially at main monuments and attractions. Generally, the less prominent the attraction, the poorer the level of English.

THE ARTS
Literature

Portugal has a rich literary history, with acclaimed and revered writers of international repute. One of the earliest examples of Portuguese literature is medieval Galician-Portuguese poetry, which shaped early Portuguese literature. A superlative example of this style is the great 16th-century master poet Luís de Camões's epic lyrical text *Os Lusíadas (The Lusiads)*. *Os Lusíadas* is an undisputed classic and one of the most important works of Portuguese literature.

The progression of Portuguese literature can be divided into three main classical phases—Renaissance, Baroque, and neoclassical, followed by romanticism and realism.

Other Portuguese literary greats include Eça da Queirós; Fernando Pessoa; Antero de Quental; Alexandre O'Neill, a Portuguese poet of Irish descent; and novelist José Saramago, recipient of the 1998 Nobel Prize in Literature.

Visual Arts

Particularly accomplished in ceramics, architecture, sculpting, and painting, Portuguese artists excel in many genres. Famous for glass and crystal ware as well as ceramics, artisans produce striking and colorful objects, many of which have been elevated from time-honed crafts to true art. The country is perhaps best known for its *azulejos*, hand-painted glazed tiles that historically have been used to create giant plaques depicting everything from battle scenes to drink advertisements. Azulejo murals of myriad sizes and scenes can be found on buildings and monuments throughout the country. Portugal is also famous for terracotta earthenware, a distinctive staple on many of the country's restaurant tables.

Over the centuries, Portugal has produced many fine artists and sculptors, among them Nuno Gonçalves, Joaquim Machado de Castro, Grão Vasco, António Soares dos Reis, and, more recently, Maria Helena Vieira da Silva, Carlos Botelho, and Paula Rego. Portugal is also home to many revered architects, perhaps the most celebrated being Álvaro Siza Vieira, who designed Porto's stunning Serralves Foundation, and Eduardo de Souta Moura, who designed Braga's unique municipal stadium; both have won major international architecture awards.

Music and Dance

Portugal's music and dance originate from its exotic heritage. The country has a huge appetite for traditional festivities, and folk music and dance underpin celebrations nationwide that vary by region. Portuguese folklore is rich and exhilarating, with upbeat music and dizzying dances. Most towns have their own local dance groups, *ranchos*, which perform the traditional dances at local or tourist attractions, such as the themed "Portuguese night" dinners that so many hotels offer.

Portuguese dances include the circle dance, fandango (from the Ribatejo region), two-step waltz, schottische *(chotiça), corridinho* (from the Algarve and Estremadura regions), *vira* (from the Minho region), *bailinho* (Madeira), *vira solto,* and *tau-tau,* among many others. Dances tend to be fast-paced and involve lots of twirling and leg-lifting. Folk dancing is generally accompanied by a traditional band or an accordion player as well as folk singing, with everyone dressed in colorful folky outfits. Typical instruments used in folk bands are the guitar, mandolin, bagpipes, accordion, violin, drums, Portuguese guitar, and a plethora of wind and percussion instruments. Portugal is currently enjoying something of a folk revival, with cool bands making it popular among the younger generations.

A very typically Portuguese form of music is *pimba,* a kitsch genre that mixes traditional instruments like the accordion with up-tempo Latin beats and generally involves lyrics that can be tongue-in-cheek and sometimes rude. It might sound cheesy, but *pimba* has generated some of the country's best-loved artists, including Emanuel, Quim Barreiros, and Ágata, who have become national treasures and pretty wealthy.

Two of Portugal's best-known genres of traditional music are the mournful fado, which has two main styles, deriving from Lisbon and Coimbra, and *cante alentejano,* traditional group folk singing from the Alentejo region. Both fado and the *cante alentejano* are classified by UNESCO as Intangible Cultural Heritage.

It's a little-known fact that many former and current mainstream pop stars are of Portuguese descent—including Nelly Furtado, former Journey lead singer Steve Perry, Aerosmith's Joe Perry (both Perrys' original paternal family names were Pereira), Jamiroquai lead singer Jay Kay, Katy Perry (again, from Pereira), and Shawn Mendes, whose father is from Lagos in the Algarve—which only adds to Portugal's newfound cool.

Essentials

Transportation

GETTING THERE

Traveling to Portugal from anywhere in Europe is quick and easy, with regular direct flights from many European cities as well as from Asia, the Middle East, North and South America, and Africa. Even better, flights can be pretty cheap within Europe, thanks to the growing number of low-cost airlines.

The three main airports on the mainland are **Lisbon,** the biggest and busiest; **Porto** in the north; and **Faro** in the south. **Madeira**

Airport (also known as Funchal) and **Ponta Delgada Airport** are main airports for Madeira and the Azores.

Most flights from outside Europe are to Lisbon, with direct flights from the United States and Canada as well as many other destinations. Porto also has regular direct flights from Newark in the United States, although far fewer than Lisbon. Faro has almost exclusively European flights, the vast majority from the United Kingdom, Germany, and France.

It is easy to travel to Portugal within Europe, with bus and train services connecting Portugal with Spain, France, Belgium, the Netherlands, and the United Kingdom. Driving to Portugal is also possible thanks to a good international road network and the EU (European Union) open-borders policy.

From North America

Some transatlantic cruises include Lisbon, generally just for a short day trip, but the easiest, quickest, cheapest, and most convenient way to travel between the United States and Portugal is without doubt by air. Flights take seven hours eastbound from the Northeast, and nine hours westbound.

Portugal's national carrier, **TAP Air Portugal** (www.flytap.pt), has regular direct flights between mainland Portugal and New York (JFK and Newark), Boston, Miami, and Philadelphia. US airline **United** (www.united.com) also has direct flights to Portugal. TAP has invested heavily in the US market, increasing the number of destinations it serves, and has also created the **Portugal Stopover** (www.portugalstopover.flytap.com) program, where US travelers on TAP to other destinations can spend a few days in Portugal before continuing onward. Portugal's national flag carrier also operates onward connecting flights from Lisbon to Porto, Faro, and the islands.

Regional Azores airline **SATA Azores Airlines** (www.azoresairlines.pt) and **Air Canada** (www.aircanada.com) operate direct flights between Portugal and Canada, including a stop in the Azores archipelago.

From Europe
AIR

The vast majority of European flights to Portugal are from the United Kingdom, France, Germany, the Netherlands, and Belgium, all 2.5-3 hours away. Direct flights also operate from Finland as well as Eastern European countries such as Poland, the Czech Republic, and Hungary. Flights from neighboring Spain are only to Lisbon and Porto; oddly, there are no direct flights between Spain and Faro Airport in southern Portugal.

The ever-expanding availability of European flights include low-cost airlines such as Ryanair (Ireland), easyJet (UK), Vueling (Spain), Eurowings (Germany), and Transavia (France), meaning travel between two European destinations can cost less than €100 round-trip. Prices within Europe are heavily influenced by school holidays at Easter, summer, and Christmas-New Year's, as well as peak tourist seasons in Portugal, especially July-August; pricing can vary widely.

TRAIN

Getting to Portugal from other European countries by train isn't as straightforward as by air and can sometimes be more expensive. The train is slightly quicker than traveling by bus.

From the United Kingdom: Getting to Portugal from the United Kingdom takes around 24 hours and involves catching the **Eurostar** (www.eurostar.com) from London to Paris, then a TGV high-speed train from Paris to Hendaye-Irun at the border of southern France and Spain, and from there the overnight Sud Expresso train to Lisbon.

From Spain: There are two overnight sleeper trains: the **Lusitania Hotel Train** (www.cp.pt), linking Madrid's Chamartin

Coronavirus in Portugal

At the time of writing in February 2021, Portugal was significantly impacted by the coronavirus, but the situation was improving. Periodic lockdowns over the course of 2021 appeared to be causing a noticeable improvement. However, smaller local businesses have been hard hit by the pandemic, as was the country's tourism scene, particularly in the Algarve, where the unemployment rate skyrocketed.

The country's counties were classified into categories of level of risk (by number of cases per 100,000 inhabitants), with containment measures varying accordingly. Risk levels were regularly assessed. Measures for the worst-hit areas included a ban on moving between municipalities, nighttime and weekend curfews, and commercial establishments closing earlier. A blanket ban on travel between municipalities was being applied to all national mainland territory over holiday and bank holiday periods, with varying measures in the archipelagos. Rail and coach travel was reduced during these periods.

Wearing a mask is mandatory in all indoor places in Portugal, and outdoors in situations where social distancing cannot be adhered to. Council-run sports facilities such as indoor pools may be closed. Be aware that in some locations in Portugal, depending on their risk level, establishments such as green grocers and restaurants may be closed at night or take-away only. Most supermarkets and gas stations remain open seven days a week, but, at the time of writing, were prohibited from selling alcohol after 8pm.

Now more than ever, Moon encourages its readers to be courteous and ethical in their travel. We ask travelers to be respectful to residents, and mindful of the evolving situation in their chosen destination when planning their trip.

BEFORE YOU GO

· **Check local websites** (listed below) for restrictions and the overall health status of the destination and your point of origin. If you're traveling to or from an area that is currently a COVID-19 hotspot, you may want to reconsider your trip.

· Get **vaccinated** if your health status allows, and if possible, take a **coronavirus test** with enough time to receive your results before your departure. Some destinations may require proof of vaccination or a negative COVID test result before arrival, along with other tests and

Station to Lisbon in about 10 hours, and the **Sud Expresso** (www.cp.pt), which connects Lisbon to San Sebastian in Spain and Hendaye in southern France in about 11 hours. In Northern Portugal, a high-speed train, the **Celta IC** (www.cp.pt), links Porto to Vigo in 3.5 hours.

From elsewhere: Getting to Portugal by train from Belgium, the Netherlands, or Germany requires passing through an international terminal such as Paris or Madrid.

Train passes: The easiest way to get around Portugal—and the rest of Europe—by train is with a **Eurail Pass** (www.eurail.com). This EU-wide rail travel pass for non-EU citizens covers train travel in first or second class. The Eurail pass comes in three options: the

Global Pass, covering 5 or more of up to 28 European countries; the Select Pass—covering 2, 3, or 4 bordering countries; or a single-country pass. Prices for Portugal range from €82 for a single-country pass to €307 for a basic Global Pass, although prices vary.

An identical pass is available to EU citizens and official residents: the **Interrail Pass** (www.interrail.eu) ranges from €80 for a single-country pass to €208 for a basic Global Pass, although prices vary.

BUS

The main bus lines offering intercity travel within Europe to Portugal are **Eurolines** (Lisbon tel. 218 957 398, Porto tel. 225 189 303, Bragança tel. 273 327 122; www.

potentially a self-quarantine period, once you've arrived. Check local requirements and factor these into your plans.

- If you plan to fly, check with your airline and the destination's health authority, the **Direção-Geral da Saúde** (Directorate-General for Health; www.dgs.pt), for updated travel requirements. Some airlines may be taking more steps than others to help you travel safely, such as limited occupancy; check their websites for more information before buying your ticket, and consider a very early or very late flight, to limit exposure. Flights may be more infrequent, with increased cancellations.

- Check the website of any **museums and other venues** you wish to visit to confirm that they're open, if their hours have been adjusted, and to learn about any specific visitation requirements, such as mandatory reservations or limited occupancy.

- Pack **hand sanitizer,** a **thermometer,** and plenty of **face masks.** Consider packing snacks, bottled water, or anything else you might need to limit the number of stops along your route, and be prepared for possible closures and reduced services over the course of your travels.

- **Assess the risk** of entering crowded spaces, joining tours, and taking public transit.

- **Expect general disruptions.** Events may be postponed or cancelled, and some tours and venues may require reservations, enforce limits on the number of guests, be opem during different hours than the ones listed, or be closed entirely.

RESOURCES

- **Direção-Geral da Saúde** (Directorate-General for Health; www.dgs.pt)

- **Visit Portugal** (www.visitportugal.com/en/content/covid-19-measures-implemented-portugal)

- **TAP Air Portugal** (www.flytap.com/en-us/travel-restrictions)

---

eurolines.com) and **National Express** (www.nationalexpress.com). These generally travel to Lisbon, Porto, and Faro in the Algarve from many European countries. The most popular routes are from the United Kingdom, France, Spain, and the Netherlands. Transfers may be required; from London to Lisbon, for example, a change may be required in Paris. There are at least five buses a week between Paris and Lisbon. Bus prices from Amsterdam to Lisbon start from €110 one-way and take around 36 hours; London to Lisbon is around €115 and 45 hours, and Paris to Lisbon €85 and 29 hours.

The main bus companies operating between Portugal and neighboring Spain are **Avanza** (tel. +34 912 722 832; www.avanzabus.com) and **Alsa** (tel. 902 422 242; www.alsa.com). A one-way trip from Madrid to Lisbon costs around €23, Seville to Lisbon €25, and Corunna to Lisbon €38.

CAR

Europe is connected by a well-maintained motorway network, meaning international travel is straightforward between EU capital cities. Most of Europe exercises an open-borders policy, with no compulsory inspections at borders. Time-wise, for example, driving nonstop from Paris to Lisbon takes around 16 hours; Madrid to Lisbon is 6 hours; and Berlin to Lisbon is 26 hours. Each country has different speed limits, driver alcohol tolerances, and other traffic laws.

Driving from the United Kingdom to Portugal is slightly more complicated, as it requires a ferry between the UK and mainland Europe. There are no direct ferries between the UK and Portugal, so the more common driving routes are from the UK by ferry to France or Spain. Ferries from the UK to France are quicker and cheaper than those to Spain, but also make the journey longer due to added driving time. Ferry trips between the UK and France often take just a few hours, while a ferry to Spain can take over a day. There are many ferry routes between the UK and France, and the website **Direct Ferries** (www.directferries.co.uk) provides a comprehensive map of routes and prices.

The alternative to the ferry between the United Kingdom and mainland Europe is to take the Channel Tunnel, also known as the **Eurotunnel** (www.eurotunnel.com). Taking just 35 minutes to cross under the channel, the tunnel is cheaper and quicker than a ferry but is not for the claustrophobic. It connects Folkestone in the south of England to Calais in northern France via a 50-kilometer (31-mi) rail tunnel. At its lowest point, it is 75 meters (246 ft) below the seabed and 115 meters (377 ft) below sea level. Costs start from £30 per car (including up to nine passengers), but don't fight over the window seats; the views aren't that amazing.

Most of Europe, with exceptions like the United Kingdom and Ireland, drives on the right-hand side of the road. Manual gear shifts are the norm, although automatic transmissions are available on request when hiring a car.

It is without doubt cheaper and quicker to fly to Portugal from anywhere in Europe than to drive, and tolls and the cost of gasoline can vary noticeably from country to country.

From Australia and New Zealand

There are no direct flights between Portugal and Australia or New Zealand. Connecting flights are generally via Dubai in the United Arab Emirates, with a daily direct flight between Lisbon and Dubai on **Emirates** (www.emirates.com), or via Asia. There is also a direct nonstop flight between Australia and London, from where there are many onward flights to Portugal. Most major European air carriers operate code-share flights to major Asian hubs. Singapore, for example, can be reached with just one connection, from Lisbon to Istanbul on Turkish Airlines, or Dubai on Emirates, or via the United Kingdom or Germany with Singapore Airlines.

From South Africa

There are no direct flights from South Africa to Portugal. TAP flies direct to Maputo in Mozambique and Luanda in Angola, also served by Angolan airline TAAG, and connecting flights can be arranged from there, or via a connection in another European hub with major European carriers such as British Airways, Lufthansa, Swissair, Iberia, and Air France.

Package Holidays

From European countries, the United Kingdom particularly, packages for a week or so in the Algarve, Lisbon or Madeira including flights and accommodations can be found at competitive prices at websites such as www.travelsupermarket.com. Packages usually include flights and one to three weeks' lodging, ranging from self-catering to all-inclusive, and in off-peak seasons can start from as little as £120 ($154) pp for self-catering based on double occupancy for seven nights in a three-star hotel; £250 ($322) including two meals; and £350 ($451) all-inclusive. Prices shoot up in high season, but if you're not fussy about where you stay or when you travel, good deals can be found. If you just want a little taste of Portugal, the ports of Portimão in the Algarve, Lisbon, and Leixões in Northern Portugal are included on some European cruise itineraries by companies such as **Fred Olsen** (www.fredolsencruises.com) and **Princess** (www.princess.com).

GETTING AROUND

Once in Portugal, getting around is easy. The travel network is perhaps not as sophisticated as in France, Spain, or Germany, but domestic flights, good motorways (with tolls), and efficient and inexpensive buses and trains link all the main towns and cities, and cars can be hired from every airport and hotel in the country.

Air

Portugal's main destinations—Faro in the Algarve, Lisbon, and Porto—are connected by regular daily domestic flights. **TAP Express** (www.flytap.pt), a subsidiary of the national carrier, operates hourly flights between Lisbon and Porto, while low-cost **Ryanair** (www. ryanair.com) operates regular daily Lisbon-Porto flights, albeit less frequently than TAP. Ryanair also has regular flights between Faro in southern Portugal and Porto at least five times a week, increasing in frequency in summer. TAP has a few flights daily between Faro and Lisbon, with connections to Porto.

TAP, Ryanair, **SATA Azores Airlines** (www.azoresairlines.pt), and **easyJet** (www. easyjet.com) all operate daily flights between Lisbon, Porto, and the archipelagoes of the Azores and Madeira. All of the archipelagoes' islands are connected by regular interisland flights, which also increase in frequency in busier months.

A multistage **national shuttle service** links the south of Portugal to the north. A small plane leaves Portimão airdrome in the Algarve every morning Monday-Saturday and flies to Bragança in the north, stopping en route at Cascais in Lisbon, Viseu in Central Portugal, and Vila Real in Northern Portugal. This trip takes three hours, depending on the duration of the stops, and costs €95-198 round-trip from Portimão to Bragança. Passengers are allowed to carry 10 kilograms (22 pounds) of luggage. The flight is operated by **AeroVip,** which belongs to the Sevenair group, once a day off-season and twice daily during the busier months from the end of March. **Sevenair** (tel. 214 444 545; www.sevenair.com) also operates interisland flights between Madeira and Porto Santo.

Train

Portugal's train service **Comboios de Portugal (CP)** (www.cp.pt/passageiros) is efficient and cheap but complex. It operates on several tiers, from the painfully slow Urbano train service, which stops in every town and village; the modern Intercity service between main cities; and the high-speed Alfa-Pendular, which connects Porto to Lisbon and the Algarve with a few stops between. Taking into account the required time spent at the airport for checking in (passengers are generally advised to arrive two hours before the flight), flying between Faro and Porto can take the same amount of time as the train and often costs the same.

Despite being comprehensive, the national rail network isn't as direct as bus services, and, oddly, some major cities have no train station, while many cities and towns have their train stations on the outskirts, requiring a taxi ride to the center. On the plus side, Portugal's trains tend to be spacious and well-kept on the inside, and offer cheaper second-class tickets and more privacy and comfort in first class, sometimes in private compartments.

Bus

There are many different bus companies in Portugal, including three major intercity long-distance bus companies, Algarve line **Eva Transportes** (www.eva-bus.com), national **Rede Expressos** (www.rede-expressos.pt) and northern **Rodonorte** (www.rodonorte. pt). Local and regional buses link towns, villages, and parishes within municipalities. In Lisbon, the local public transport company is Carris, which operates buses, trams, and funiculars. Bus travel in Portugal is cheap but not always the most comfortable, although long-distance express buses are mostly equipped with air-conditioning, TVs, toilets, and even onboard drinks and snacks. Routes between large cities, such as the Algarve-Lisbon or Lisbon-Porto, depart several times a day, while smaller local services tend to be frequent on weekdays and irregular on weekends and holidays. Pop into a local ticket office to check for updated timetables. The Algarve-Lisbon bus takes 3 hours and costs €18.50 one-way. Lisbon-Porto takes 3.5 hours and costs €19 one-way. Small discounts are given on round-trip tickets.

Car

Driving in Portugal can, in certain places, require nerves of steel and patience. Lisbon and Porto have fast and furious traffic, where delaying at a traffic light will inevitably earn a blast of the horn from behind. There can also be a seeming lack of civility on Portugal's roads, with poor usage of indicators when turning, and overtaking seems to be a national sport. For the most part, navigating Portugal's roads is straightforward, and major road surfaces are of a decent standard.

Portugal has one of the highest accident and road death rates in Europe, but these figures have improved drastically since the 1990s, along with the condition of the country's roads and the policing of them. One road in particular—the N125 road in the Algarve, a major cross-region secondary road that runs parallel to the Algarve's only motorway, the A22 Via do Infante—once was among Europe's deadliest spots. In recent years the N125 road has been significantly overhauled to improve safety and offer a viable alternative to the paid motorway, although congestion, especially in summer, is still a problem. It's widely agreed that while it's much better, the N125 is not yet a good alternative to a motorway.

ROAD SYSTEM

Portugal's road system is decent and major routes are kept in good condition. Some smaller regional roads are in urgent need of repair, particularly in rural areas, and on certain stretches signage could use updating.

Motorways are generally in good condition, although major motorways (autoestradas) have tolls, signaled with a large white V on a green background. Secondary and rural roads can be poorer quality, with potholes and sharp bends. In high-elevation areas, such as the Serra da Estrela, snowfall can close roads for hours or even days.

Roads are categorized as follows:

- **Motorways (autoestrada)** start with an **A** (A1, A22). Most A roads have tolls, paid at booths or electronically. Some motorways, such as the A22, are exclusively electronic and have barriers. Electronic toll payment uses the **Via Verde** (www.viaverde.pt) transponder system. More information on tolls and motorways is available at www.portugaltolls.com. Motorways have service areas with cafés, gas stations, and toilet facilities at regular intervals. Emergency telephones are also found at regular intervals.

- **Main highways (itinerário principal)** start with an **IP** (IP1, IP2). These are major roads that are alternatives to the motorways, although the road conditions are inferior, and generally link main cities.

- **Secondary highways (itinerário complementar)** start with an **IC** (IC1, IC2). These roads complement the IPs by connecting them to big towns and cities.

- **National roads (estrada nacional)** start with an **N** or **EN** (N125, also known as EN125) and are the main roads between towns and cities.

- **Local municipal roads (estrada municipal)** start with an **M** or **EM** and are smaller roads within localities.

Portugal is also connected to the rest of Europe by an **international E-road system,** a numbering system for pan-Europe roads. The main European routes crossing Portugal are the E01, E80, E82, E90, E801, E802, E805, and E806.

GENERAL ROAD RULES

In Portugal traffic runs on the right side of the road. Drivers must be over age 18, and seat belts are compulsory. National speed limits are easy to remember, although many drivers seem to struggle to abide by them: 50 km/h (31 mph) in residential areas, 90 km/h

(56 mph) on rural roads, and 120 km/h (74 mph) on motorways. Cars towing trailers are restricted to 80 km/h (50 mph). The rule on roundabouts (rotaries, or traffic circles) is that the outer lane should only be used if turning off immediately. In practice, this rarely happens. Make allowances for it.

You must park facing the same direction as the traffic flow. It's also illegal to use a mobile phone while driving (although at times you might wonder), and that applies to talking and texting.

Punishment for drunk driving is harsh, ranging from hefty fines to driving bans. The legal limit is 0.5 gram (0.02 ounce) of alcohol per liter (34 ounces) of blood, or 0.2 gram (0.007 ounce) per liter for commercial drivers.

DRIVER'S LICENSES

EU citizens require a valid driver's license with a photo on it, issued by the bearer's home country, to drive in Portugal. Drivers from outside the EU require a license and an International Driving Permit, which must be shown both to rental agencies for hiring a car and to the authorities if asked. When you are driving on Portugal's roads, the vehicle's documents must be in the vehicle at all times, and drivers need a valid ID, such as a passport. It is compulsory to have a reflective danger jacket, a reflective warning triangle, spare bulbs, a spare tire, and approved child seats for children under age 12 or 150 centimeters (5 ft), in the vehicle. Failure to produce them could result in a fine.

CAR RENTAL

The country's airports host many car rental companies, or ask at your hotel. Vehicles can be dropped off at most holiday lodgings. Use price comparison sites like **Auto Europe** (www.autoeurope.pt) or **Portugal Auto Rentals** (www.portugal-auto-rentals.com) to find the best deals. Booking well in advance will mean better prices. Beware of unexpected surprises by double-checking the opening and closing times of the car rental desk at the airport, fuel fees and excess insurance, electronic

toll payments (if you want to use motorways with barriers, such as the Algarve's A22, see www.portugaltolls.com), fees to drop the car in a different location from where you picked it up, and cross-border surcharges if you take the car out of Portugal into Spain.

Even though the minimum legal age to drive is 18, most rental companies require drivers to be age 21 or to have held a license for at least five years. Costs can vary greatly, from as little as €10 per day in low season, rising exponentially in high season. If you're just visiting one or two areas, a small car is useful as most town centers have areas that are a tangle of narrow cobbled streets. To do a lot of touring, a bigger engine is better, which means a more expensive rental.

REFUELING

Diesel (gasóleo) is cheaper than unleaded gasoline (gasolina sem chumbo) in Portugal, and gas stations can be found in abundance (although this is less the case in rural areas). Most large supermarkets and shopping centers have gas stations that offer low-cost fuel, and there is almost always a gas station near an airport. The main gas stations in Portugal belong to BP, Galp, and Repsol. Most petrol stations are open 7am-10pm daily, but stations at service areas on motorways or on main roads should be open 24 hours daily. Unleaded gasoline has a 95 or 98 octane rating, although both can be used in gasoline vehicles; the 98 is more expensive. All petrol stations accept debit and credit cards as well as cash.

PARKING

Parking can be hard to find in town centers given the narrow cobbled streets and tourist demand. Big towns and cities have designated car parks and parking areas, which charge fees, especially in popular places like Faro, Lisbon, and Porto. The closer to the city center, the more expensive the parking will be.

AUTOMOBILE ASSOCIATIONS

A contact number for breakdowns should be provided by the vehicle's insurer. When collecting a rental car, always clarify what to do or who to call in the event of a breakdown or emergency. The **Auto Club Portugal** **(ACP)** (tel. 808 222 222; www.acp.pt) is the Portuguese equivalent of the American Automobile Association.

Visas and Officialdom

To enter Portugal, all travelers are required to have a valid ID. Most European citizens need only a valid ID or a passport and can circulate freely within the EU by land, air, or sea. People from other countries must have a passport and may require a visa. Always check with the relevant authorities before traveling.

PASSPORTS AND TOURIST VISAS

EU nationals traveling within EU or Schengen states do not require a visa for entering Portugal for any length of stay. They do require a valid passport or official ID card (national citizen's card, driver's license, or residency permit, for example).

European citizens traveling between Schengen countries are not required to present an identity document or passport at border crossings. However, it is recommended that travelers have ID documents with them at all times, as they may be requested at any time by the authorities. In Portugal the law requires everyone to carry a personal ID at all times.

The UK is no longer part of the EU, but as COVID had greatly impacted travel, the bureaucratic process for entering and exiting Portugal from the UK was somewhat unclear at the time of writing. As non-European Economic Area (EAA) nationals, different border checks will apply when UK residents travel to other EU or Schengen-area countries. They may have to use separate lanes from EU, EEA, and Swiss citizens when queuing and may also need to show a return or onward ticket. British passport-holders will need to have at least six months left on their passports, which must have been issued within the last 10 years. UK nationals are able to travel to other Schengen-area countries for up to 90 days in any 180-day period without a visa for purposes such as tourism. Furthermore, travel insurance is required to cover healthcare, and roaming charges may apply on cellphone use. Go to www.abta.com/tips-and-advice/brexit-advice-for-travellers, www.gov.uk/visit-europe-1-january-2021, or https://europa.eu/youreurope/citizens/index_en.htm for more information.

People from non-EU countries always require a passport, valid for at least six months, and some may require a visa. Australian, Canadian, and US travelers require a valid passport but do not need a visa for stays of up to 90 days in any six-month period. While it is not obligatory to have an onward or return ticket, it is advisable to have one.

South African nationals need to apply for a Portugal-Schengen visa. This should be done three months before travel. Applicants must have a South African passport valid for six months beyond the date of return with at least three blank pages. They also need a recent passport photo (specify to photographer that it has to meet the Schengen visa requirements), a completed original application form, round-trip tickets from South Africa to Portugal, and proof of prepaid lodging or a letter of invitation if staying with friends or family in Portugal, among other requisites.

CUSTOMS

Customs is mandatory for all travelers arriving in or leaving Portugal carrying goods or money, although certain limits apply to what can be brought in or taken out. Aeroportos de Portugal (ANA) states that all passengers traveling without baggage or transporting cash or monetary assets under the equivalent of €10,000 or carrying personal items not intended for commercial purposes and not prohibited should pass through the "Nothing to Declare" channel. Passengers carrying over €10,000 or whose baggage contains tradable goods in quantities greater than those permitted by law and that are not exempt from value-added tax (VAT) or excise duty must pass through the "Goods to Declare" channel.

Passengers age 17 or older can bring in the following:

From EU member states: 800 cigarettes, 400 cigarillos, 200 cigars, 1 kilogram (2.2 pounds) of smoking tobacco, 10 liters (11 quarts) of alcoholic spirits, 20 liters (21 quarts) of beverages with alcoholic content under 22 percent, 90 liters (95 quarts) of wine, 110 liters (116 quarts) of beer, medications in quantities corresponding to need and accompanied by a prescription.

For travelers from outside the EU: 200 cigarettes, 100 cigarillos, 50 cigars, 250 grams (0.6 pound) of smoking tobacco, 1 liter (1 quart) of alcoholic spirits, 2 liters (2 quarts) of beverages with alcoholic content under 22 percent, 4 liters (4 quarts) of wine, 16 liters (17 quarts) of beer, medications according to need, accompanied by a prescription.

Quantities exceeding these must be declared, and passengers under age 17 don't get an exemption for alcohol or tobacco.

EMBASSIES AND CONSULATES

Australian Embassy: Av. da Liberdade 200, Lisbon; http://portugal.embassy.gov.au; tel. 213 101 500; Mon.-Fri. 10am-4pm

British Embassy: Rua de São Bernardo 33, Lisbon; tel. 213 924 000, emergency tel. 213 924 000; www.gov.uk/world/organisations/british-embassy-lisbon; Mon., Wed., and Fri. 9:30am-2pm

British Vice Consulate: Edifício A Fábrica, Av. Guanaré, Portimão (Algarve); tel. 213 924 000; Mon., Wed., and Fri. 9:30am-2pm

Canadian Embassy: Av. da Liberdade 196, Lisbon; tel. 213 164 600; www.

canadainternational.gc.ca/portugal; Mon.-Fri. 9am-noon

French Embassy: Rua Santos-O-Velho 5, Lisbon; tel. 213 939 292; https://pt.ambafrance.org; Mon.-Fri. 8:30am-noon

Irish Embassy: Av. da Liberdade 200, Lisbon; tel. 213 308 200; www.dfa.ie/irish-embassy/portugal; Mon.-Fri. 9:30am-12:30pm

New Zealand Consulate: Rua da Sociedade Farmacêutica 68, 1st Right, Lisbon; tel. 213 140 780; consulado.nz.pt@gmail.com, www.mfat.govt.nz; office hours by appointment only

South African Embassy: Av. Luís Bívar 10, Lisbon; tel. 213 192 200; lisbon.consular@dirco.gov.za; Mon.-Thurs. 8am-12:30pm and 1:15pm-5pm, Fri. 8am-1pm Fri., the Consular Section (Annex) Mon.-Fri. 8:30am-noon

Spanish Embassy: Praça de Espanha 1, Lisbon; tel. 213 472 381; www.exteriores.gob.es; Mon.-Fri. 9am-2pm

US Embassy: Av. das Forças Armadas 133C, Lisbon; tel. 217 273 300; https://pt.usembassy.gov/embassy-consulate/lisbon; Mon.-Fri. 8am-5pm

US Consulate: Príncipe de Mónaco 6-2F, Ponta Delgada (Azores); tel. 296 308 330; conspontadelgada@state.gov; Mon.-Fri. 8:30am-12:30pm and 1:30pm-5:30pm

POLICE

Portugal has three police forces: the **PSP (Public Safety Police—Polícia de Segurança Pública)** (tel. 218 111 000; www.psp.pt), in cities and larger towns; the road traffic police **GNR (National Republican Guard—Guarda Nacional Republicana)** (tel. 213 217 000; www.gnr.pt), also responsible for policing smaller towns and villages and investigating crimes against animals or nature; and the **PJ (Judiciary Police—Polícia Judiciária)** (tel. 211 967 000; www.pj.pt), the criminal investigation bureau, responsible for investigating serious crimes.

The common European **emergency number** is tel. **112,** which redirects calls to the appropriate services.

Festivals and Events

WINTER
NEW YEAR'S IN MADEIRA
throughout Funchal; Dec. 31
The year's celebrations kick off with fabulous New Year firework displays that take place through the country, but the biggest, most spectacular, and most famous by far is Madeira's.

LOULÉ CARNIVAL
Feb. or early Mar.
New Year's is swiftly followed by colorful Carnival celebrations (usually in February, before Lent). Loulé, in the Algarve, boasts one of the country's best Carnival parades.

SPRING
SEMANA SANTA
Braga; Mar. or Apr.
Starting the Friday before Palm Sunday and ending Easter Sunday, Braga's Holy Week attracts tens of thousands of people to the city to participate in colorful parades and processions.

MADEIRA FLOWER FESTIVAL
Madeira; 4 weeks after Easter

Madeira's weeklong Flower Festival is one of Portugal's most famous celebrations, with flower-decked floats and parades.

SUMMER
FESTA DOS TABULEIROS (FESTIVAL OF THE TRAYS)
Tomar; June or July every 4 years
A spectacle like no other, in which a procession of local girls wearing headdresses made from bread piled staggeringly high parades through the streets.

SANTO ANTÓNIO FESTIVITIES
throughout Lisbon; June
Portugal's biggest traditional religious festival means celebrations are staged throughout the capital for the whole month of June, with jubilant parades and processions into the night.

AUTUMN
MARVÃO CHESTNUT FESTIVAL
Nov.
This celebration of the fall harvest is one of the most authentic in the country, when the smell of roasting nuts fills this hilltop village in the Alentejo.

Recreation

PARKS
Portugal has one excellent national park, the Peneda-Gerês, and a vast variety of outstanding protected parks and reserves. The **Institute for Conservation of Nature and Forests (Instituto da Conservação da Natureza e das Florestas)** (ICNF; www2. icnf.pt) is largely responsible for managing the country's parks and forests. The associated **Natural.PT** website (www.natural.pt) offers plenty of information in English on Portugal's natural parks and protected areas.

HIKING AND BIKING
With glorious lush mountains, undulating plains, and wild coastline, Portugal offers excellent conditions for active travelers. In addition to trails in parks and reserves, there are regional designated hiking and cycling tracks, such as the **Via Algarviana** (www. viaalgarviana.org) in the Algarve and the **Vicentine Route (Rota Vicentina)** (www. rotavicentina.com) in the Alentejo, with networks of well-mapped and signed routes. Many towns also have *eco-vias* or *ciclovias*

(designated cycling tracks) and public bike-sharing schemes.

The website of the national tourism board, **Turismo de Portugal** (www.visitportugal. com), has pages on cycling and walking in Portugal. The website of the tour company **Portugal Bike Tours** (www.portugalbike. com) provides detailed information on cycling routes in Portugal.

Walking Madeira's *Levadas*

Walking the *levadas* (ancient irrigation channels) in Madeira can be challenging. Walkers need to do their research in advance and choose only the *levadas* that are suited to their physical ability. The trails can be narrow, uneven, vertiginous, and slippery. There are sporadic reports of tourists going missing on Madeira after becoming lost or falling down a *levada*. Suitable clothing and footwear are essential, as is taking supplies like water, energy bars, and a lightweight raincoat. It is recommended that less experienced walkers join a group or a guided tour. Leave details of where you intend to walk with your hotel reception, and if you have a mobile phone, take it with you.

BEACHES

Portugal has some of Europe's finest beaches, from the grotto-etched coastline of the Algarve, Portugal's premier beach destination, to the endless, largely undiscovered beaches of the Alentejo, Lisbon's cosmopolitan Estoril coastline, and the rugged beaches of Central and Northern Portugal, popular among surfers. Portugal also boasts one of the highest numbers of Blue Flag-awarded beaches, a European symbol of clean, high-quality beaches.

One of Portugal's less-explored delights is its excellent river beaches (*praias fluviais*), lakes and dams with artificial beaches. Northern and central inland regions are pocked with these little oases of tranquil water and sand, which in warmer months provide a refreshing escape far from the coast. Most have fun water equipment like canoes and pedal boats, sun beds, cafés or restaurants, and toilet facilities. Most are staffed by lifeguards in summer.

SURFING

Portugal is one of Europe's top surfing hot spots. From the Algarve's windswept, rugged west coast to Guincho Beach near Lisbon and Cabedelo Beach in Northern Portugal, the coast has popular surfing hubs that offer consistent conditions for all levels. Portugal's most famous surfing spot is Nazaré, which came onto the global surfing radar in 2011 after US surfer Garrett McNamara set a new world record here for the largest wave ever surfed.

The website of **Turismo de Portugal** (www.visitportugal.com) addresses all kinds of surfing in Portugal (including windsurfing, kite-surfing, and body-boarding), with suggestions on where to go. Surf website **Portuguese Waves** (www.portuguesewaves. com) has detailed information on surf spots and news.

OTHER WATER SPORTS

Bounded by the Atlantic, latticed by rivers, and studded by lakes and dams, Portugal is a boating and water sports playground. Diverse activities for all ages include coastal and champagne sunset cruises and grotto boat trips; parasailing, Jet Skiing, and banana-boating off golden beaches; deep-sea fishing and scuba diving; and stand-up paddleboarding and kayaking along scenic waterways.

The website of **Turismo de Portugal** (www.visitportugal.com) provides information on sailing and mooring. The **Portal do Mar** website (www.portaldomar.pt) offers information on all things nautical.

GOLF

Several dozen first-rate golf courses range in difficulty from amateur to pro. The majority of Portugal's golf courses are in Lisbon and the Algarve, many designed by legendary golfers such as Sir Henry Cotton, Arnold Palmer, and Jack Nicklaus.

WILDLIFE-WATCHING

From whale-watching in the Atlantic to bird-watching on reedy lagoons or observing dolphins in the unique setting of the Sado Estuary, Portugal offers an abundance of special and exhilarating wildlife-watching opportunities.

The website of **Turismo de Portugal** (www.visitportugal.com) offers a wealth of information on nature tourism, including bird-, whale-, and dolphin-watching. The **Portuguese Society for the Study of Birds (Sociedade Portuguesa para o Estudo das Aves)** (SPEA; www.spea.pt) provides information on the birds and bird-watching tourism of Portugal.

ADVENTURE SPORTS

Portugal boasts the only bridge-climb in Europe (in Porto), excellent year-round conditions for skydiving and paragliding, and some canyoneering and climbing in Europe at Peneda-Gerês National Park and Serra da Estrela Natural Park.

WINTER SPORTS

In the coldest months, mainland Portugal's Serra da Estrela mountain range becomes a snowy wonderland and the only place in the country for skiing and snowboarding.

Food and Drink

Portugal's cuisine is fresh, flavorful, comforting, and generous, it is the soul of an unassuming seafaring nation. Largely Mediterranean, the staples are fresh fish, meat, fruit, and vegetables prepared with olive oil and washed down with excellent national wines. Dishes vary from light and fresh along the coast, with grilled fish and seafood, to hearty meaty stews and roasts in rural inland areas and colorful cosmopolitan fusions in larger towns and cities.

Each region touts its own take on national staples such as the *cozido á Portuguesa* (Portuguese stew) and *caldeirada* (fish stew), as well as typical local sweets—all with a story attached to them. Another staple on most menus and one of Portugal's emblematic gastronomic ingredients is salted codfish, or *bacalhau*. The most famous cod dishes are *bacalhau à Brás* (cod mashed with egg, potato, and onion, topped with crunchy matchstick fries), *bacalhau à Gomes de Sá* (flaked cod layered with sliced potato and egg and baked in the oven), *bacalhau espiritual* (like *bacalhau á Bras* but with grated carrot), and *pastéis de bacalhau* (cod fritters), usually a snack with cold beer.

PORTUGUESE CUISINE

Fish

It is perhaps unsurprising that Portugal, an audacious seafaring nation, is renowned for its bounty of seafood. Coastal areas generally serve shellfish as an appetizer. One-pot dishes such as *caldeiradas* and *arroz de tamboril* (monkfish rice) are not to be missed. Salted codfish is a staple throughout Portugal, and grilled sardines are enjoyed voraciously during summer (sardine fishing is limited in winter to allow stocks to replenish); these, along with *dourada* (golden bream), *robalo* (sea bass), and *cavalas* (mackerel), are among the most common fish on menus. Prawns boiled or fried in olive oil and garlic are enjoyed as a snack or appetizer, while more unusual seafood includes razor clams and sea urchins.

Meats

Most restaurants have grilled meat on the menu, most commonly *febras* (pork steaks), *costeletas de porco* (pork chops), *entrecosto* (pork ribs), *entremeada* (pork belly), and the ubiquitous *frango piripiri* (chicken grilled and served with spicy chili sauce). Note that the word *grelhado* (grilled) usually means on charcoal.

Cured and smoked meats, especially the smoky, spicy *chouriço* sausage, *presunto* (cured ham), and *morcela* (black blood sausage), also represent a huge chunk of Portuguese gastronomy. They are often eaten simply as an appetizer, accompanied by fresh rustic bread, olives, and cheese, or added to stews and soups to enhance the flavor.

Soups

Almost all cafés and restaurants have a homemade vegetable soup on the menu. *Caldo verde,* potato and kale soup with hunks of smoky *chouriço* sausage, is a typical soup served at family tables and traditional festivities.

Bread

It is customary in Portugal, especially in restaurants, for a basket of fresh bread to be brought out before a meal, along with olives and butter and fishy pâtés. Don't be misled: These items are not complimentary, and if you eat them, they will be charged on the bill. If you don't want them, ask for them to be taken away. Portugal has amazing bread, almost always freshly made. From rustic hobs to seeded baguettes and pumpkin or carob bread, it's hard not to be sucked in by the amazing carbohydrates on offer, especially to soak up those delicious sauces and juices.

Sweets and Pastries

Portugal is renowned for its range of traditional sweets and pastries. Unique *doces conventuais* (convent sweets), generally based on egg yolk and sugar and made to ancient recipes, are said to originate in the 15th century convents.

Arroz doce (rice pudding with a sprinkling of cinnamon), *bolo de bolacha* (cookie cake), *pudim flan* (custardy pudding with caramel on top), and *tarte de natas* (creamy chilled pie made from condensed milk with a ground cookie topping) are typical desserts, but the ever-present *pastel de nata* (custard tart) is Portugal's iconic sweet.

DRINKS

Perhaps not as eminent as France, Italy, or Spain, modest Portugal nonetheless boasts a gamut of acclaimed wines, including rosés and unique fresh and fizzy green wines. Even ordinary table wine tends to be palatable, and a small jug of house wine in a low-key restaurant costs as little as €3. Besides wine, Portugal produces beer, the most famous being Sagres, Cristal, and Super Bock. A growing number of craft beers are also on the market.

Traditional Portuguese tipples include *ginja* (a sweet cherry liqueur, also called *ginjinha*), *licor beirão* (a medicinal-tasting liqueur said to aid digestion, made from a long-guarded secret blend of herbs), *aguardente* (brain-blowing firewater), and *amarguinha* (a marzipan-tasting, toothachingly-sweet almond liqueur, often chilled). Besides port and madeira liquor-wines, make sure you try the local *poncha* in Madeira, a mix of alcohol distilled from sugarcane, honey, orange or lemon juice, or other fruit juices.

The legal age to drink and buy alcohol in Portugal is 18. Nondrinkers won't be disappointed with canned iced teas and Sumol sparkling fruit juices, the traditional flavors being pineapple and orange. The Algarve, especially the city of Silves, is renowned for incredibly sweet oranges, and fresh orange juice served here with plenty of ice is a real treat.

The Portuguese are big coffee drinkers, and the standard is a small, strong, black expresso. To get milk in it, ask for *café com leite* or *meia-de-leite* (in a cup and saucer), or *galão* (served in a tall glass), differing only in presentation. "Having a coffee" is synonymous with "catching up," and cafés are the social glue of neighborhoods.

DINING OUT

Restaurants in Portugal are incredibly varied, from down-to-earth, no-frills spots to high-end Michelin-starred eateries. Touristy areas have a wider range of well-known chains and international cuisines. Vegetarian and vegan restaurants are on the rise, while traditional Portuguese eateries can be found in spades.

For real local flavor, try to find a *casa de pasto,* literally a "grazing house," basic, cheap, and cheerful little diners found off the beaten track that cater to local laborers with good home-cooked food. These characterful places tout three-course "dish of the day" menus for as little as €7.50, including a bread basket with butter, pâtés, and olives, a fish or meat entrée, a coffee, dessert, and drinks. If your budget allows, head to a high-end eatery where the menu will be a contemporary take on fresh local products and time-honored recipes. If you have a sweet tooth, find a *pastelaria* (there seems to be one on almost every street) to enjoy a coffee and freshly made traditional cake or a toasted sandwich for just a few euros.

PICNIC SUPPLIES AND GROCERIES

A great way to save money, and to enjoy a meal in the fresh, open air, is to buy your own food. Portugal is a veritable buffet of fresh produce. Larger supermarkets have counters for fresh fish, cold meats, cooked meats, and deli, with the likes of olives and slaws, as well as a fresh bread section, baked in-house or supplied by local bakers. There will almost always be a picturesque nearby square with a bench for you to enjoy an alfresco picnic.

Most towns have a farmers market at least once or twice a month, generally on Saturday morning, piled high with locally grown fruit and vegetables as well as treats like dried nuts, dried fruits, sweets, and eggs. Municipal markets, usually open mornings Monday-Saturday, are also great for fish, meats, vegetables, and fruit. Some municipal markets have ready-to-go food counters and sell jams, liqueurs, cured meats, and preserves.

MEALS AND MEALTIMES

Portugal has three main meals: a good breakfast in the continental style, with cereals, bread, cold meats and cheese, and jam, generally eaten before work or school; lunch at 1pm-3pm; and dinner starting from 7:30pm-8pm. Main meals tend to be hearty, and lunch and dinner are often preceded by a bowl of soup. The Portuguese also enjoy *lanche,* a light mid-afternoon snack, as well as a coffee and a pastry midmorning.

Accommodations

Accommodations range from run-of-the-mill hotels and tourist complexes to friendly family-run inns, campsites, budget-friendly hostels, and exclusive luxury retreats. Lisbon and Porto currently exercise a **tourist tax (taxa turística);** Lisbon's has a surcharge of €1 per night per guest up to a maximum of seven nights. This is charged directly at reception on check-in. Porto's tourist tax is €2 per guest over age 13 per night, maximum seven nights.

ACCOMMODATIONS RATINGS

Portugal's rating system is governed by national law and implemented by the national tourism board, **Turismo de Portugal** (www.turismodeportugal.pt). Ratings are based on fulfilled minimum requisites stipulated for each category. Star ratings are generally indicative of the level of comfort and facilities an establishment provides and not necessarily subjective factors such as view or atmosphere. Hotels are classified one to five stars; a one-star property is a basic budget lodging, while a five-star hotel offers a luxurious experience. *Estalagens* (inns) rate four to five stars, *pensões* (guesthouses) one to four stars, and apart-hotels rate two to five stars. Campsites are graded one to four stars.

MAKING RESERVATIONS

Most people make bookings online via price comparison websites or directly with hotels. It's always wise to follow it up with a phone call to ensure everything is confirmed and any special requests are clear. If planning to travel to Portugal in summer, book well ahead, as hotels sell out fast. Prices can also be much higher in peak season than in low season.

TYPES OF ACCOMMODATIONS

Hotel

All of Portugal's main towns and cities offer hotels spanning three to five stars. The more popular the destination, the greater the choice. Lisbon, Porto, and especially the Algarve are awash with smart hotels, most with their own pools. Prices vary greatly by season and the popularity of the resort. Prices are cheaper in winter. Portugal has several major national hotel chains: **Pestana Hotels and Resorts** (www.pestana.com), **Vila Galé** (www.vilagale.com), **Sana Hotels** (www.sanahotels.com), and **Tivoli Hotels & Resorts** (www.tivolihotels.com), part of the Minor Hotel Group, to name a few. A number of international chains also operate within Portugal, from low-cost to high-end.

Minimum requirements for four- and five-star hotels include air-conditioning, TV, and direct phone lines in all rooms; one- to three-star hotels don't necessarily have to have those features. Three- to five-star hotels must also provide room service, laundry service, and air-conditioning in public areas, whereas one- and two-star hotels don't. All categories except one-star hotels must have an on-site bar, a full bath, 24-hour reception, copy and fax service, and safes in the rooms.

Estalagem (Inn)

Portugal's inns *(estalagens)* are hotel-type lodgings in traditional buildings that, due to their architectural characteristics, style of fixtures and furnishings, and services provided, reflect the region and its natural environs. Inns are classified four or five stars. As a whole, inns must comply with criteria similar to corresponding hotels (24-hour reception, room service, restaurant, bar, air-con in public areas, etc.); the main differences are found in the actual rooms, which tend to be smaller. Generally speaking, inns are more modest than hotels and often rustic and family-run.

Pensão Residencial

Smaller towns and villages will usually have a *pensão residencial,* or just *residencial,* private family-run boardinghouses in shared residential buildings. These provide affordable lodgings in central locations. *Pensões* usually have a restaurant. The word *residencial* is added when the unit provides breakfast only. *Residenciais* are simple bed-and-breakfast lodgings.

Apart-Hotel

Apart-hotels are self-contained apartments with the full facilities of hotels. There is no room service.

Pousada

Pousadas are state-owned monuments such as castles, palaces, monasteries, and convents converted into accommodations reflecting the region and era of the monument. **Pousadas de Portugal** (www.pousadas.pt) has iconic monument-hotels in exceptional locations.

Hostel

Portugal is renowned for excellent hostels, regularly earning European awards. That doesn't mean all of the country's hostels are above par. Do some research and read reviews before booking at www.hostelworld.com.

Aldeamento Turístico (Tourist Resort)

Tourist resorts, also known as tourist villages or complexes, are developments comprising different types of independent lodging, such as bungalows, apartments, or villas, in communal spaces. These resorts must also have an on-site four- or five-star hotel, entertainment facilities, and room service.

Camping

Portugal has over 100 campgrounds, classified by stars, from the most luxurious four stars to the minimum basic one star. Privately owned camping sites are classified in the same way, preceded by the letter *P*. Campsites tend to stay open year-round, as Portugal has a growing number of winter motor-home visitors, but prices can double from low to peak season. High-season prices may apply to holidays such as New Year's. Most campsites have on-site toilets and showers as well as facilities such as swimming pools and markets, bungalows, and chalets, which are reflected in the star rating. Some have sanitary facilities for RVs. Not all accept pets. For more on camping in Portugal, see www.campingportugal.org.

Conduct and Customs

The Portuguese are characteristically warm and welcoming and proud to show off their heritage, although they are also modest and conservative. Try striking up a conversation about food or soccer. Conscious that tourism is a main source of income, the Portuguese are generally friendly and helpful toward visitors, although in rural pockets of the country foreigners are still eyed with curiosity. Staunchly traditional and understated, Portugal is a country where recent acquaintances may be greeted like long-lost friends, but raucous behavior, such as drunken rowdiness, is eschewed. Decorum is much appreciated, which is not to say you can't let your hair down and let loose in the appropriate places. As long as you show courtesy and respect to the locals, you can expect the same back.

GENERAL ETIQUETTE

Typically friendly and humble, the Portuguese love to show off their language skills and impress visitors, and few are the people who don't know at least a few key phrases in English. Likewise, the Portuguese very much appreciate efforts by visitors in learning even just a few words of the national language. Modest and somewhat reserved, the Portuguese tend to be quite formal in greetings among those less well acquainted. Men usually shake hands while women give air kisses on each cheek; women hardly ever shake hands in Portugal. Children are greeted in the same way as adults. Family is the foundation of Portuguese households and takes precedence over most other social and professional affairs.

COMMUNICATION STYLES

The Portuguese appreciate polite directness, eye contact, a smile, and a firm handshake. Saying *"Bom dia"* (Good day or Hello), *"Por favor"* (Please), and *"Obrigado/a"* (Thank you) go a long way. Overtly exuberant or loud behavior is not appreciated. The Portuguese tend to socialize on the weekends rather than after work during the week.

BODY LANGUAGE

A big no-no in Portugal is pointing—especially pointing at someone. While conversations can sound heated and loud, the Portuguese are not overly demonstrative with hand gestures or body language. Finger-snapping to get someone's attention is also frowned upon.

TERMS OF ADDRESS

An overtone of formality is required when addressing people, especially strangers. Men should be addressed as *senhor* (abbreviation *Sr.*) and women *senhora (Sra.)* at all times. A young girl would be *menina* (miss), and a boy, *menino*.

TABLE MANNERS

Table manners are relaxed but courteous. Around family tables, it's common to share from a bowl while talking animatedly, although politeness, wishing everyone *"Bom apetite"* (Bon appétit) before a meal and saying "Thank you" afterward, is expected. Domestic dining begins at the say-so of the head of the table or the cook, and feel free to raise a glass to toast *(saúde)* everyone. Dining out depends on the type of establishment; laid-back eateries are a family-style affair, while upmarket venues require upmarket manners and dress. Arriving late to a meal with friends is acceptable; arriving late to a dinner reservation is not. If invited to dine at someone's home, take a small gift, such as a bottle of wine or flowers.

PHOTO ETIQUETTE

Places where photos are banned will be signed. Taking photos inside churches during mass is considered disrespectful. If you want to take a picture of a local, they are generally happy to collaborate, but always ask politely beforehand.

Health and Safety

Overall, travel and health risks in Portugal are relatively low, with food- and water-borne illnesses like traveler's diarrhea, typhoid, and giardia not a concern in Western Europe. Insect-transmitted diseases, such as Lyme disease and tick fever, however, are found in Portugal. A number of precautionary steps can reduce the risk: prevent insect bites with repellents, apply sunscreen, drink plenty of water, avoid overindulging in alcohol, don't approach wild or stray animals, wash your hands regularly, carry hand sanitizer, and avoid sharing bodily fluids.

Basic medications such as ibuprofen and antidiarrheal medication can be bought over-the-counter at any pharmacy in Portugal. For emergency medical assistance, call **112** and ask for an ambulance. If you are taken to a hospital, contact your insurance provider immediately. Portugal also has a 24-hour free health help line (tel. 808 242 424) in Portuguese only. For detailed advice before traveling, consult your country's travel health website: www.fitfortravel.nhs.uk (United Kingdom), wwwnc.cdc.gov/travel (United States), www.travel.gc.ca (Canada), or www.smarttraveller.gov.au (Australia).

VACCINATIONS

At the time of writing, there are no compulsory immunization requirements to enter Portugal, but it remains to be seen what, if any, vaccination requirements may be implemented to prevent the spread of **COVID-19.** The World Health Organization (WHO) recommends all travelers, regardless of destination, are covered for diphtheria, tetanus, measles, mumps, rubella, and polio. See your doctor at least six weeks before departure to ensure your vaccinations are up-to-date.

Rabies

Rabies has been detected in bats in Portugal, but there is a low risk of infection. The US Centers for Disease Control and Prevention (CDC) recommends the rabies vaccine for travelers involved in activities in remote areas that put them at risk for bat bites, such as adventure travel and caving.

Hepatitis A

Recommended for all travelers over age one and not previously vaccinated against hepatitis A. In 2017 a number of European countries, Portugal included, recorded an outbreak of hepatitis A. It is transmitted through contaminated food and water, as well direct contact with infected individuals via the fecal-oral route.

Hepatitis B

The hepatitis B vaccination is suggested for

all nonimmune travelers who may be at risk of acquiring the disease, which is transmitted via infected blood or bodily fluids, such as by sharing needles or unprotected sex.

Yellow Fever

Yellow fever vaccinations are only required for travelers heading to the Azores or Madeira and only if arriving from a yellow-fever-infected country in Africa or the Americas.

HEALTH CONSIDERATIONS
Sunstroke and Dehydration

The sun and heat in Portugal can be fierce, especially June-September and particularly July-August. Apply a strong sunblock and use a hat and sunglasses. Avoid physical exertion when the heat is at its peak (noon-3pm) and keep well hydrated by drinking plenty of water or electrolyte-replenishing fluids. Avoid excessive alcohol during the hottest hours or being out in the sun with a hangover.

Undertow

Some beaches, especially along the western coast, which is fully exposed to the Atlantic, can experience strong undercurrents when the sea is roughest, particularly in winter and spring. During summer, generally May-September, the sea is calmer and beaches are staffed by lifeguards; off-season they are not. Always obey flags.

Tap Water

Tap water is consumable throughout Portugal and is safe to brush teeth, wash fruit, or make ice, although many people drink bottled water, as opposed to tap water, even at home.

Insects

Portugal is home to lots of bugs, including mosquitoes, sand flies, and ticks. There is a low risk in Portugal of catching Lyme disease from ticks, which inhabit long grasses and bushes. There is a higher risk of catching tick fever, ehrlichiosis, and anaplasmosis. To minimize the chance of tick bites, avoid areas of long grass and stray animals.

To avoid mosquito bites, use lightweight, light-colored clothing and avoid places with stagnant water. In the hotter months, particularly in early morning or at dusk, apply a repellent.

An outbreak of *Aedes* mosquito-borne dengue fever was reported on Madeira, concentrated in the city of Funchal, in 2012. More than 2,000 cases had been reported by 2013, including 78 cases in travelers. The outbreak is currently under control. There is no vaccine against dengue. To prevent it, apply insect repellent and keep covered when outdoors.

Stray Animals

Portugal still battles errant and abandoned animals. In some places it's not unusual to see stray dogs and cats, even in packs and colonies. A huge amount of work has been done by private and public entities to sterilize and rehome animals, and things have greatly improved since the 1980s, but more work remains. Travelers are advised to not approach, pet, or feed strays. If you are bitten by a stray animal, wash and disinfect the wound, and seek medical advice promptly.

Sexually Transmitted Diseases

Travelers are at high risk of acquiring sexually transmitted diseases (STDs) if they engage in unprotected sex. According to research, Portugal has one of the poorest control rates of STDs; gonorrhea and syphilis are common.

HEALTH CARE
Medical Services

Portugal's state-funded public health service (SNS, Serviço Nacional de Saúde) provides quality care, particularly in emergency situations and those involving tourists. There are also private hospitals operating throughout Portugal, such as the **Hospital Particular do Algarve** (tel. 707 282 828; www.grupohpa.com) group in the Algarve and the **CUF Hospitals and Health Units** (tel. 210 025

200; www.saudecuf.pt) in Lisbon and the north. For minor illnesses and injuries, head to a pharmacy: Most pharmacists speak good English and can suggest treatment. If the problem persists or worsens, seek a doctor. Portugal has two types of pharmacies: traditional pharmacies (farmácia), identified with a big flashing green cross outside, and parapharmacies (parafarmácia), selling only non-prescription medicines.

Insurance

EU citizens have access to free emergency medical treatment through the European Health Insurance Card (EHIC), which replaces the defunct E111 certificate. Non-EU citizens should consider fully comprehensive health insurance for serious illness, accident, or emergency. Opt for a policy that covers the worst-case event, like medical evacuation or repatriation. Find out in advance if your insurance will make payments to providers directly or reimburse you later for overseas health expenditures. Travelers to the Azores and Madeira are advised to acquire wide-ranging travel insurance that provides for medical evacuation in the event of serious illness or injury.

Prescriptions

If you're traveling from outside the EU, have enough of your prescription medication to cover the trip. Talk to your doctor beforehand and travel with a doctor's note, a copy of any prescriptions, or a printout for the medication. Medications should be carried in labeled original bottles or packaging, although this is not compulsory. Some prescription medicines may require a medical certificate; always check with your doctor. Ask for an extra written prescription with the generic name of the drug. Portuguese pharmacies will accept prescriptions from countries outside the EU, but drugs have to be paid for in full. Even without the state subsidies, drugs are generally cheaper in Portugal than many other EU countries and the United States. Alternatively, visit a Portuguese doctor and obtain a prescription in Portugal.

A prescription issued by a doctor in one EU country is valid in all EU countries. However, a medicine prescribed in one country may not be authorized for sale or available in another, or might be sold under a different name. Opt for paper copies of prescriptions as opposed to electronic copies.

Many types of medication—including heart medication, antibiotics, asthma and diabetes medicines, codeine, injectable medicines, and cortisone creams—can only be acquired in Portugal with a prescription.

It is illegal to ship medication to Portugal. When traveling, always transport medicines in carry-on luggage.

Birth Control

Birth control is widely available throughout Portugal. Female contraceptive pills, patches, and rings can be bought over the counter in pharmacies, as can the morning-after pill, without a prescription. Condoms are also widely available in pharmacies, supermarkets, petrol stations, and some nightlife venues.

SAFETY
Crime

Portugal has a relatively low serious crime rate, but opportunistic crime is recurrent, particularly in busy places popular among tourists, such as Lisbon and the Algarve. Popular beaches are hot spots for car theft, so keep valuables on your person or at least hidden from view. Don't leave anything of value, such as passports or computers, in vehicles. Pickpocketing is also common, particularly on the busy trams in Lisbon and Porto. Use a concealed cross-body pouch to carry cash and your ID, and keep money and documents separate. Take the same precautions you would at home—keep valuables safe and avoid walking alone at night or on backstreets.

Harassment

Harassment is not something visitors to Portugal will usually have to deal with.

Opportunistic petty drug pushers in busy nightspots and overenthusiastic restaurant or bar staff trying to attract clientele are about the extent of the pestering. Saying a polite but firm "No, thanks" and walking away are generally enough to deter unwanted attention.

Drugs

Since 2001, Portugal has a decriminalized drug system. Being caught with a small amount of some recreational drugs, such as marijuana, is no longer a crime but a medical health issue, addressed with rehabilitative action like therapy as opposed to jail.

This health-focused legal shift saw drug-related deaths drop dramatically, but that's not to say it's okay to do drugs in Portugal; drug use is prohibited. The law does not differentiate between citizens and visitors; tourists caught with drugs will be subject to fines or being brought before a dissuasive committee or a doctor. Producing or dealing drugs in Portugal is a serious criminal offense punishable with lengthy jail terms. The use of recreational drugs is common in the nightlife hubs of Lisbon and Albufeira. Beware being approached by people selling drugs.

Practical Details

WHAT TO PACK

Key items to pack include mosquito repellent and sunblock (sunblock is expensive in Portugal) plus a hat for May-October, a windbreaker for all seasons (Portugal can be breezy year-round), and warm sweaters, a jacket, and a light raincoat for winter. Comfortable shoes for walking are advised if your trip is more than a beach holiday, especially if you're traveling to the Azores or Madeira, and don't forget an electrical adapter for chargers. Pack a concealable pouch to carry documents and cash while out and about exploring, and never carry cash and documents together.

LAUNDRY

Most hotels offer a laundry service—usually quite pricy, in which you pay per item—but larger shopping centers generally have self-service machines outside or a launderette (*lavandaria*) inside. Most towns also have self-service launderettes. A self-service wash usually costs €3-5.

LUGGAGE STORAGE

Portugal Luggage (www.portugalluggage. com) offers luggage storage solutions at various points in Lisbon, Porto, Braga, Coimbra, and Cascais. If you ask, most hotels will let

you leave your luggage in their luggage rooms after checkout until you depart for the airport. Most main bus stations, train stations, and airports offer some form of lockers or luggage storage, too. You can also check at local tourism bureaus for suggestions.

MONEY

Currency

Since 1999 Portugal's currency has been the euro; before that it was the escudo. There are 100 cents in 1 euro (€1).

Changing Money

The ability to exchange currency varies greatly by location. In tourist-dense Lisbon, Porto, and the Algarve, foreign currency can be exchanged at almost every hotel, currency exchanges, and even some shops. Airports have exchange bureaus, although their commission rates, along with those in hotels, are more expensive. Keep an eye on exchange rates in the months before you travel to see how they fluctuate, and change some cash beforehand when the rates are favorable. In Portugal, hunt around, do some ground-work, and compare rates to choose the best option. It is almost always more favorable for UK travelers with British pounds to change their cash for euros in the United Kingdom; in Portugal the Scottish pound can sometimes be refused. For up-to-date exchange rates, see www.xe.com.

Banks

Banks in Portugal are generally open 8:30am-4pm Monday-Friday. In larger towns and cities, they will stay open during lunch, but in smaller locales, banks close 1pm-2pm. Portugal's banks close Saturday-Sunday and national holidays. Banks rarely offer foreign exchange services.

ATMs

ATM cash withdrawal machines *(multibanco)* can be found widely in most towns and cities. Smaller villages may have just one or two, normally at bank branches, in supermarkets, on main streets and squares, and at major bus and train stations and airports. Charges apply to foreign transactions. There is an option for instructions in English. Maximum withdrawals are €200 a time, but this can be withdrawn several times a day.

Credit Cards

Credit cards are widely used in bigger towns and cities, but not so much in smaller ones. Visa, Mastercard, and American Express are widely accepted in hotels, shops, and restaurants. Gas stations usually only take debit cards and cash.

Sales Tax

The standard sales tax rate in Portugal is 23 percent. On wine it is 13 percent, and on medications, books, and optical lenses 6 percent. In Madeira the tax is 22 percent, and in the Azores 18 percent. Many stores throughout Portugal have adopted the Europe Tax Free (ETS) system, which allows non-EU shoppers to recover VAT or sales tax as a refund. Stores adhering to this system have a sign at the entrance. For more information, see www.globalblue.com/tax-free-shopping/portugal.

Bargaining

Haggling is increasingly a thing of the past in Portugal, as standardized retail prices are enforced in municipal markets and farmers markets. However, haggling at a flea market is still part of the experience.

Special Discounts

Students, seniors (65 and over), and children generally benefit from discounts on state-run services such as monuments, museums, municipal swimming pools, and public transport.

Tipping

Restaurants tend to be the only places in Portugal where tipping is exercised, and a tip reflects how much patrons have enjoyed the food and service. As a general rule, 10-15 percent of the overall bill is the standard, but in less formal eateries it's okay just to leave any loose change you have, but at least €1. Gratuities are not included on bills. Waitstaff in Portugal appreciate tips, but they are not compulsory.

Budgeting

One of Europe's most affordable countries, Portugal still offers value for money, far cheaper than London, Paris, or Barcelona. As with all the sunshine destinations in Southern Europe and the Mediterranean, hotel rates peak in summer and drop in winter, meaning spring and autumn can offer the best value in terms of lodging and weather. Car hire rates fluctuate with the tourist seasons, and airfares are influenced by EU school holidays. Portugal has a range of inns, vacation rentals, and some of the best hostels in Europe, so how much you spend depends on you.

A British study found Portugal's Algarve was Europe's third-cheapest holiday destination for sun-loving Britons in 2018, mainly driven by a strengthening pound. Including everyday items such as coffee, beer, meals, wine, public transport, and sunblock, it is still much cheaper than other European destinations.

Examples of average costs include:

- small expresso coffee: €0.70
- 1.5-liter bottle of water: €0.50
- sandwich: €2
- local bus ticket: €2
- theme park or water park admission: €15-25
- museums: €2-5
- small glass of wine or beer: €1.50-2
- hotel room: €60-90

COMMUNICATIONS
Phones and Cell Phones

Portugal's country code is +351 (00351). To call a phone number in Portugal from abroad, first dial the country code. Within Portugal, there are regional prefixes (area codes), and all start with 2. Lisbon, for example, is 21, Faro is 289, and Porto is 22. There is no need to dial 0 or 1 before the area code. Mobile phone numbers start with 9. Toll-free numbers start with 8. Portugal's main landline provider is **Portugal Telecom** (www.telecom.pt).

The main mobile providers are **Nós** (www.nos.pt), **Meo** (www.meo.pt), and **Vodafone** (www.vodafone.pt). Mobile coverage is decent throughout the country, particularly in major cities and populous areas along the coast, although it can be patchy in rural or high-elevation areas. Using a prepaid SIM card in Portugal is recommended, particularly for non-EU visitors. They are widely available from major mobile phone providers, found on retail streets and shopping centers. You will need a copy of your passport or ID to buy one.

In 2017 the EU abolished roaming surcharges for travelers, meaning that people traveling within the EU can call, text, and use data on mobile devices at the same rates they pay at home, but this applies only to EU countries. Surcharges may apply if your consumption exceeds your home usage limits.

Internet Access

Portugal has an up-to-date communications network, with good phone lines and high-speed internet. Wi-Fi is widely available, and most hotels will either have free Wi-Fi throughout or in designated Wi-Fi areas. Elsewhere, major cities offer Wi-Fi hotspots, as do some public buildings, restaurants, and cafés. Internet cafés can be found throughout Portugal.

Shipping and Postal Service

Portugal's national postal service is **Correios de Portugal** (tel. 707 262 626; www.ctt.pt), with post offices in all population centers. Postal services range from regular *correio normal* to express *correio azul*. Shipping costs for a 2-kilogram (4.4-pound) package range from €4.50 sent domestically to €15 sent abroad. Postcards and letters up to 20 grams (0.7 ounce) cost €0.86 within Europe, €0.91 to other countries. Express mail letters cost €2.90. Other shipping services operate in Portugal, including **FedEx** (tel. 229 436 030; www.fedex.com) and **DHL** (tel. 707 505 606; www.dhl.pt).

OPENING HOURS

In the past most shops and services in Portugal would close 1pm-3pm for lunch. This is still in practice in some areas, but a growing number of state and private entities such as banks, post offices, and pharmacies now remain open during lunch.

Major national monuments like castles, churches, and palaces are open every day of the week, and those that aren't tend to close on Monday. Almost all close on bank holidays, such as Christmas Day, New Year's Eve, and New Year's Day. Smaller museums and monuments also close for lunch.

Attractions stay open longer in summer, opening an hour or so earlier than in winter and closing an hour or so later. Theme parks, especially water parks, and even some hotels and restaurants close for a month or two in winter.

WEIGHTS AND MEASURES
Customary Units

Portugal was the second country after

France to adopt the metric system, in 1814. Length is in centimeters, meters, and kilometers, and weight is in grams and kilograms. Temperatures are in degrees Celsius.

In addition, shoes and clothing sizes differ from the British and US systems. For example:

- shoe sizes: US men's 7.5, women's 9 = UK men's 7, women's 6.5 = Portugal 40
- women's dresses and suits: US 6, 8, 10 = UK 8, 10, 12 = Portugal 36, 38, 40
- men's suits and overcoats: US and UK 36, 38, 40 = Portugal 46, 48, 50

Time Zone
Mainland Portugal is in the Western European time zone (WET), the same as the United Kingdom and Ireland. Complying with European daylight saving time (DST), clocks advance one hour on the last Sunday in March and lose one hour on the last Sunday in October. The Azores archipelago is always one hour earlier than mainland Portugal. Madeira is in the same time zone as the mainland. In relation to the United States, Portugal is seven or eight hours later than Los Angeles, four or five hours ahead of Miami and New York, five or six hours ahead of Chicago, and ten or eleven hours ahead of Hawaii.

Electricity
Portugal has 230-volt, 50-hertz electricity and type C or F sockets. Type C plugs have two round pins; type F have two round pins with two earthing clips on the side. Travelers from the United Kingdom, the rest of Europe, Australia, and most of Asia and Africa will only require an adapter to make the plugs fit.

Visitors from the United States, Canada, and most South American countries require an adapter and for some devices a voltage converter. These are available in airports, luggage shops, and most electrical shops. Universal adapters are a great investment as they can be used anywhere.

TOURIST INFORMATION
Portugal is a tourism-oriented destination. Each region—Porto and the North, Central Portugal, Lisbon, the Alentejo, the Algarve, Azores and Madeira—has its own tourism board to promote the area, while the national **Turismo de Portugal** (www.turismodeportugal.pt) promotes the country as a whole. Each main town has at least one tourist office, as do popular villages. Most hotels provide good information on what to do and see locally. Portugal's official tourism website, www.visitportugal.com, provides a wealth of information on history, culture, and heritage as well as useful contacts.

Tourist offices can be found in every city, town, and village that has a tourist attraction or monument. Major cities and destinations like Lisbon, Porto, and the Algarve have numerous tourist offices where visitors can drop in with questions and get maps, public transport timetables, and excursion information. Tourist office staffers speak good English.

Maps
Download maps of Portugal and its various regions free from www.visitportugal.com. Most hotel reception desks have maps of the vicinity, or ask at tourist offices.

Traveler Advice

ACCESS FOR TRAVELERS WITH DISABILITIES

Portugal prides itself on being an accessible destination for travelers with disabilities, and massive efforts have been made to become inclusive for all. The main airports have services and facilities for wheelchair users, and infrastructure is gradually being modernized to facilitate mobility. There are a number of wheelchair-friendly accessible beaches along the coast, with equipment and facilities for all to enjoy the beach safely and comfortably. Some monuments, however, are not wheelchair friendly, and people with mobility issues might struggle with cobbled streets and high sidewalks.

In 2018 the national tourism board launched an interactive app, **TUR4all Portugal,** with information about facilities and services for those with special needs visiting Portugal. It can be downloaded for free from www.accessibleportugal.com.

TRAVELING WITH CHILDREN

Youngsters in family-friendly Portugal are fawned over and welcomed practically everywhere. It's not unusual to see children dozing on their parents' laps in a café late on a summer night. Restaurants are very accommodating of younger diners, although kids' menus can be limited to the staple chicken nuggets or fish fingers.

Activities for children range from Lisbon's Oceanarium to Coimbra's Little Portugal and the many water parks in the Algarve; zoos in most major towns; fantastic beaches; and play parks in almost every public garden. Kids also benefit from discounts on public transport, at museums, and at most main attractions.

When the weather is warm, tourist trains and ice cream are found throughout towns and villages, while most resorts and hotels have kids' clubs or at least activities and facilities for children, as well as babysitters.

To enter and leave Portugal, all minors must have their own passport and be with both parents. If children are not traveling with both parents, legal documentation with formalized permission from the other parent is required. Portugal's border and immigration officials will ask for such papers.

Breastfeeding is applauded in Portugal, although it's rarely done in public, and if it is, it's done discreetly.

WOMEN TRAVELERS

Portugal is a great destination for women traveling alone, given that it is one of Europe's safest and most peaceful countries, and people as a whole are respectful and obliging. If you want to share lodging or to meet new people, Portugal has clean and cheap, well-regulated and well-run hostels, a great way to mingle with fellow travelers. Most people speak decent English and are happy to assist. Besides petty crime in major towns and cities, the serious crime rate is low, and lone women travelers should have no problems. As with any place, common sense should prevail, and taking dark backstreets or walking along deserted streets at night should be avoided.

SENIOR TRAVELERS

With a year-round pleasant climate and placid, laid-back lifestyle, Portugal is a magnet for senior travelers and a top destination for Northern European retirees who make it their second home. Compact, peaceful, and well equipped, with medical facilities (providing you have the right insurance coverage), it meets the needs of travelers of all ages. Geographically, Lisbon and Porto are hilly and a challenge on foot; sticking to the flatter downtown and riverside areas and using the plethora of public transport can help travelers avoid issues with aches and pains.

Portugal has discounts for senior travelers (65 and over) with ID on public transport and in museums, and plenty of attractions, like wine-tasting and spa visits, to appeal to the mature tourist.

LGBTQ TRAVELERS

LGBTQ travelers will find Portugal mostly welcoming; it legalized same-sex marriage in 2010, the eighth country in Europe to do so. Portugal is currently a popular destination for same-sex weddings. Most Portuguese have a laid-back attitude toward LGBTQ visitors, although attitudes toward same-sex couples can vary by region. Despite being progressive, Portugal is traditionally a Roman Catholic society, and inhabitants of remote and small towns might raise an eyebrow or scowl at same-sex displays of affection, but rarely will verbal or physical hostility be directed at you.

While the LGBTQ scene is still underground in much of Portugal, Lisbon and Porto, and to a lesser extent the Algarve, have vibrant and inclusive LGBTQ scenes. Lisbon and Porto host colorful pride marches and numerous gay bars and LGBTQ-friendly accommodations, although tourists being denied a room or table based on their sexual orientation or gender identity is not unheard of. The **International Gay & Lesbian Travel Association** (IGLTA; www.iglta.org) provides a wealth of information on LGBTQ travel in Portugal, including organized trips, tours, and travel advice.

TRAVELERS OF COLOR

Portugal is a fairly racially homogenous country. Ninety-five percent of the population is ethnically Portuguese, though this in itself is a complex designation, given Portugal's history of the migration and domination of different ethnic groups, from Celtic and Iberian tribes to the Romans, Moors, and even French. This history is complicated further by the legacy of Portuguese colonialism, in which Portugal played a huge role in the trade of enslaved African people to their colonies in what is now Brazil. Within Portugal's growing immigrant population, the largest group by far is Brazilian. Larger cities, especially Lisbon, are significantly more diverse than the country as a whole.

Portugal is widely regarded as one of Europe's safest, most peaceful, and most tolerant countries, and allegations of color-motivated discrimination and attacks are rare. However, in recent times there have been sporadic reports of incidents involving racial bias, specifically at the doors of popular nightspots in Lisbon. Management of these venues strongly deny that bouncers discriminate against clubgoers' entry based on their race, but allegations to that effect have made the rounds on social media. In 2020, reports of racially motivated street attacks were on the rise, including the high-profile shooting of Black actor Bruno Candé in a Lisbon suburb, after the perpetrator issued a slew of racial insults. If you feel you have been a victim of discrimination, report it to Portuguese law enforcement.

For the most part, travelers and immigrants of all colors are welcomed and accepted in Portugal, which has one of the most integrated immigrant communities in Europe. Groups like **African Lisbon Tour** (africanlisbontour.com) aim to provide resources detailing "the lost, covered, unknown or silenced history of Portugal and the African continent."

Resources

Glossary

adega: wine cellar

arco: arch

autoestrada: motorway (abbreviated A)

avenida: avenue

azulejo: hand-painted ceramic tile, usually blue and white

bacalhau: salted codfish

bairro: neighborhood or district

capela: chapel

castelo: castle

cataplana: seafood stew cooked in a copper pan

cidade: city or town

espetada: skewered meat

estação: station

estalagem: inn

estrada municipal: local municipal road (abbreviated M or EM)

estrada nacional: national road (abbreviated N or EN)

fadista: fado singer

fado: a genre of traditional Portuguese music that is soulful and often mournful

farmácia: pharmacy

feira: fair or open-air market

ferroviária: railway

festa: festival

fortaleza: fortress

forte: fort

foz: river mouth

ginja: cherry liqueur; also known as *ginjinha*

gruta: cave

igreja: church

ilha: island

itinerário complementar: secondary highway (abbreviated IC)

itinerário principal: main highway (abbreviated IP)

jardim: garden

lago: lake

lagoa: lagoon or pond

largo: small square or plaza

levada: irrigation channel

litoral: coastal

livraria: bookshop

loja: shop

lote: lot or unit

Manueline: lavishly ornate Portuguese architectural style, widely employed in the early 16th century; owes its name to the reign of King Manuel I

mercado: market

miradouro: viewpoint

monte: hill or mountain

multibanco: ATM

museu: museum

paço: palace

palácio: palace

parafarmácia: pharmacy with only nonprescription medications

parque: park

pastel: pastry

pensão residencial: boardinghouse or bed-and-breakfast

Pombaline: distinctly Portuguese architectural style of the 18th century that is a mix of late baroque and neoclassical; named after the first Marquis of Pombal, who led the rebuilding of Lisbon after the 1755 earthquake

poncha: alcoholic punch associated with Madeira

ponte: bridge

pousada: monument (such as a castle, palace, monastery, or convent) converted into luxurious accommodations

praça: square or plaza

praia: beach

quinta: wine farm or estate

rabelo: traditional flat-bottomed boat

reconquista: Christian reconquest of Portugal

retornado: Portuguese citizen returned from former colonies

ria: lagoon or estuary

rio: river

rua: street

santuário: sanctuary or shrine

sé: cathedral

serra: mountain range

tasca: simple, small eatery

vila: village or town

vinho: wine

Portuguese Phrasebook

PRONUNCIATION
Vowels

The pronunciation of **nonnasal vowels** is fairly straightforward:

a pronounced "a" as in "apple," "ah" as in "father," or "uh" as in "addition."

e pronounced "eh" as in "pet." At the end of a word, it is often silent or barely pronounced.

i pronounced "ee" as in "tree."

o pronounced "aw" as in "got." At the end of a word or when it stands alone, it is generally pronounced "oo" as in "zoo."

u pronounced "oo" as in "zoo."

The **nasal vowels** are much more complicated. Nasal vowels are signaled by a tilde accent (~) as in *não* (no), or by the presence of the letters **m** or **n** following the vowel, such as *sim* (yes) or *fonte* (fountain). When pronouncing them, it helps to exaggerate the sound, focus on your nose and not your mouth, and pretend there is a hidden "n" (or even "ng") on the end. Note that the **ão** combination is pronounced like "own" as in "town."

Consonants

Portuguese consonant sounds are easy compared with the nasal vowels. There are, however, a few exceptions to be aware of.

c pronounced "seh" as in "say." However, when followed by the vowels **e** or **i**, it is pronounced "s" as in "set." When followed by an "a," "o," or "u," it is pronounced "k" as in "car," and when sporting a cedilla accent (ç), it is pronounced with a longer "ss" sound as in "passing."

ch pronounced "sh" as in "ship."

g pronounced "g" as in "go." However, when followed by the vowels **e** or **i**, it is pronounced "zh" like the "s" in "measure."

h always silent.

j pronounced "zh" like the "s" in "measure."

l usually pronounced as in English. The exception is when it is followed by **h**, when it acquires a "li" sound similar to "billion."

n usually pronounced as in English. The exception is when it is followed by **h**, when it acquires a "ni" sound similar to "minion."

r pronounced with a trill. When doubled (**rr**), it should be pronounced with a longer roll.

s pronounced "s" as in "set" when found at the beginning of a word. Between vowels, it's pronounced like "z" as in "zap." At the end of a word, it's pronounced like "sh" as in "ship."

x pronounced "sh" as in "ship" when found at the beginning of a word. Between vowels, the pronunciation varies between "sh" as in "ship," "s" as in "set," "z" as in "zap," and "ks" as in "taxi."

z pronounced "z" in "zap" when found at the beginning of a word. In the middle or at the end of a word, it is pronounced "zh" like the "s" in "measure."

Stress

Most Portuguese words carry stress on the second-to-last syllable. There are, however, some exceptions. The stress falls on the last syllable with words that end in **r** as well as words ending in nasal vowels. Vowels with accents over them (~, ´, `, ^) generally indicate that the stress falls on the syllable containing the vowel.

PLURAL NOUNS AND ADJECTIVES

In Portuguese, the general rule for making a noun or adjective plural is to simply add an **s**. But there are various exceptions. For instance, words that end in nasal consonants such as **m** or **l** change to **ns** and **is,** respectively. The plural of *estalagem* (inn) is *estalagens,* while the plural of *pastel* (pastry) is *pastéis.* Words that end in nasal vowels also undergo changes: **ão** becomes **ãos, ães,** or **ões,** as in the case of *irmão* (brother), which becomes *irmãos,* and *pão* (bread), which becomes *pães.*

GENDER

Like French and Spanish, all Portuguese words have masculine and feminine forms of nouns and adjectives. In general, nouns ending in **o** or consonants are masculine, while those ending in **a** are feminine. Many words have both masculine and feminine versions determined by their **o** or **a** ending, such as *menino* (boy) and *menina* (girl). Nouns are always preceded by articles—*o* and *a* (definite) and *um* and *uma* (indefinite)—that announce their gender. For example, *o menino* means "the boy" while *a menina* means "the girl." *Um menino* is "a boy" while *uma menina* is "a girl."

BASIC EXPRESSIONS

Hello *Olá*
Good morning *Bom dia*
Good afternoon *Boa tarde*
Good evening/night *Boa noite*
Goodbye *Tchau, Adeus*
How are you? *Como está?*
Fine, and you? *Tudo bem, e você?*
Nice to meet you. *Um prazer.*
Yes *Sim*

No *Não*
I don't know. *Não sei.*
and *e*
or *ou*
Please *Por favor*
Thank you *Obrigado* (if you're male), *Obrigada* (if you're female)
You're welcome. *De nada.*
Excuse me (to pass) *Com licença*
Sorry/Excuse me (to get attention) *Desculpe* (if you're male), *Desculpa* (if you're female)
Can you help me? *Pode me ajudar?*
Where is the bathroom? *Onde é o banheiro?*
What's your name? *Como se chama?*
My name is . . . *Meu nome é . . .*
Where are you from? *De onde é que vem?*
I'm from . . . *Sou de . . .*
Do you speak English? *Fala inglês?*
I don't speak Portuguese. *Não falo português.*
I only speak a little Portuguese. *Só falo um pouquinho português.*
I don't understand. *Não entendo.*
Can you please repeat that? *Pode repetir, por favor?*

TERMS OF ADDRESS

I *eu*
you *você* (formal), *tu* (informal)
he *ele*
she *ela*
we *nós*
you (plural) *vocês*
they *eles* (male or mixed gender), *elas* (female)
Mr./Sir *Senhor*
Mrs./Madam *Senhora*
boy/girl *menino/menina*
child *criança*
brother/sister *irmão/irmã*
father/mother *pai/mãe*
son/daughter *filho/filha*
husband/wife *marido/mulher*
friend *amigo* (male), *amiga* (female)
boyfriend/girlfriend *namorado/namorada*
single *solteiro* (male), *solteira* (female)

divorced *divorciado* (male), *divorciada* (female)

TRANSPORTATION

north *norte*
south *sul*
east *este*
west *oeste*
left/right *esquerda/direita*
Where is . . . ? *Onde é . . . ?*
How far away is . . . ? *Qual é a distância até . . . ?*
far/close *longe/perto*
car *carro*
bus *autocarro, camioneta*
bus terminal *terminal das camionetas*
subway *metro*
subway station *estação do metro*
train *comboio*
train station *estação de comboio*
plane *avião*
airport *aeroporto*
boat *barco*
ship *navio*
ferryboat *ferry, balsa*
port *porto*
first *primeiro*
last *último*
next *próximo*
arrival *chegada*
departure *partida*
How much does a ticket cost? *Quanto custa uma passagem?*
one-way *uma ida*
round-trip *ida e volta*
I'd like a round-trip ticket. *Quero uma passagem ida e volta.*
gas station *bomba de gasolina*
parking lot *estacionamento*
toll *portagem*
at the corner *na esquina*
one-way street *sentido único*
Where can I get a taxi? *Onde posso apanhar um táxi?*
Can you take me to this address? *Pode me levar para este endereço?*
Can you stop here, please? *Pode parar aqui, por favor?*

ACCOMMODATIONS

Are there any rooms available? *Tem quartos disponíveis?*
I want to make a reservation. *Quero fazer uma reserva.*
single room *quarto de solteiro*
double room *quarto duplo*
Is there a view? *Tem vista?*
How much does it cost? *Quanto custa?*
Can you give me a discount? *É possível ter um desconto?*
It's too expensive. *É muito caro.*
Is there something cheaper? *Tem algo mais barato?*
for just one night *para uma noite só*
for three days *para três dias*
Can I see it first? *Posso ver primeiro?*
comfortable *confortável*
change the sheets/towels *trocar os lençóis/as toalhas*
private bathroom *banheiro privado*
shower *chuveiro*
soap *sabão*
toilet paper *papel higiênico*
key *chave*

FOOD

to eat *comer*
to drink *beber*
breakfast *pequeno almoço*
lunch *almoço*
dinner *jantar*
snack *petisco*
dessert *sobremesa*
menu *ementa*
plate *prato*
glass *copo*
fork *garfo*
knife *faca*
spoon *colher*
napkin *guardanapo*
hot *quente*
cold *frio*
sweet *doce*
salty *salgado*
sour *azedo, amargo*
spicy *picante*

I'm a vegetarian. *Sou vegetariano* (if you're male), *Sou vegetariana* (if you're female).

I'm ready to order. *Estou pronto para pedir* (if you're male), *Estou pronta para pedir* (if you're female).

Can you bring the bill please? *Pode trazer a conta, por favor?*

Meat
meat *carne*
beef *carne, bife de vaca, bovino*
chicken *frango, galinha*
pork *porco, leitão*
ham *fiambre*
sausage *salsicha*

Fish and Seafood
fish *peixe*
seafood *frutas do mar, mariscos*
shellfish *marisco*
codfish *bacalhau*
sardines *sardinhas*
tuna *atum*
shrimp *camarão*
crab *caranguejo*
squid *lula*
octopus *polvo*
lobster *lagosta*

Eggs and Dairy
eggs *ovos*
milk *leite*
butter *manteiga*
cheese *queijo*
ice cream *gelado*

Fruit, Vegetables, and Legumes
vegetables *verduras, legumes*
salad *salada*
potato *batata*
beans *feijões*
fruit *fruta*

Seasoning and Condiments
salt *sal*
black pepper *pimenta*
hot pepper *pimenta picante*

garlic *alho*
oil *óleo*
olive oil *azeite*
mustard *mostarda*
mayonnaise *maionese*
vinegar *vinagre*

Baked Goods and Grains
bread *pão*
pastry *pastel*
cookies *biscoitos*
cake *bolo, torta*
rice *arroz*

Cooking
roasted, baked *assado*
boiled *cozido*
steamed *cozido no vapor*
grilled *grelhado*
fried *frito*
well done *bem passado*
medium *médio*
rare *mal passado*

Drinks
beverage *bebida*
water *água*
sparkling water *água com gás*
still water *água sem gás*
soda *refrigerante*
juice *sumo*
milk *leite*
coffee *café*
tea *chá*
with/without sugar *com/sem açúcar*
ice *gelo*
beer *cerveja*
wine *vinho*
Do you have wine? *Tem vinho?*
Red or white? *Tinto ou branco?*
Another, please. *Mais um/a, por favor.*

MONEY AND SHOPPING
money *dinheiro*
ATM *multibanco*
credit card *cartão de crédito*
Do you accept credit cards? *Aceita cartões de crédito?*

Can I exchange money? *Posso trocar dinheiro?*

money exchange *câmbio, troca de dinheiro*

It's too expensive. *É muito caro.*

Is there something cheaper? *Tem algo mais barato?*

more *mais*

less *menos*

a good price *Um preço bom.*

HEALTH AND SAFETY

I'm sick. *Estou doente.*

I have nausea. *Tenho nausea.*

I have a headache. *Tenho uma dor de cabeça.*

I have a stomachache. *Tenho uma dor de estômago.*

Call a doctor! *Chame um doutor!, Chame um médico!*

Call the police! *Chame a polícia!*

Help! *Socorro!*

pain *dor*

fever *febre*

infection *infecção*

cut *corte*

burn *queimadura*

vomit *vómito*

pill *comprimido*

medicine *remédio, medicamento*

antibiotic *antibiótico*

cotton *algodão*

condom *preservativo*

contraceptive pill *pílula*

emergency contraceptive *pílula do dia seguinte*

toothpaste *pasta de dentes*

toothbrush *escova de dentes*

NUMBERS

0 zero

1 *um* (male), *uma* (female)

2 *dois* (male), *duas* (female)

3 *três*

4 *quatro*

5 *cinco*

6 *seis*

7 *sete*

8 *oito*

9 *nove*

10 *dez*

11 *onze*

12 *doze*

13 *treze*

14 *catorze, quatorze*

15 *quinze*

16 *dezesseis*

17 *dezessete*

18 *dezoito*

19 *dezenove*

20 *vinte*

21 *vinte e um*

30 *trinta*

40 *quarenta*

50 *cinquenta*

60 *sessenta*

70 *setenta*

80 *oitenta*

90 *noventa*

100 *cem*

101 *cento e um*

200 *duzentos*

500 *quinhentos*

1,000 *mil*

2,000 *dois mil*

first *primeiro*

second *segundo*

third *terceiro*

once *uma vez*

twice *duas vezes*

half *metade*

TIME

What time is it? *Que horas são?*

It's 3 o'clock in the afternoon. *São três horas da tarde.*

It's 3:15. *São três e quinze.*

It's 3:30. *São três e meia.*

It's 3:45. *São três e quarenta-cinco.*

In half an hour. *Daqui a meia hora.*

In an hour. *Daqui a uma hora.*

In two hours. *Daqui a duas horas.*

noon *meio-dia*

midnight *meia-noite*

early *cedo*

late *tarde*

before *antes*

after *depois*

DAYS AND MONTHS

day *dia*
morning *manhã*
afternoon *tarde*
night *noite*
today *hoje*
yesterday *ontem*
tomorrow *amanhã*
tomorrow morning *amanhã de manhã*
week *semana*
month *mês*
year *ano*
Monday *segunda-feira*
Tuesday *terça-feira*
Wednesday *quarta-feira*
Thursday *quinta-feira*
Friday *sexta-feira*
Saturday *sábado*
Sunday *domingo*
January *janeiro*
February *fevereiro*
March *março*
April *abril*

May *maio*
June *junho*
July *julho*
August *agosto*
September *setembro*
October *outubro*
November *novembro*
December *dezembro*

SEASONS AND WEATHER

season *estação*
spring *primavera*
summer *verão*
autumn *outuno*
winter *inverno*
weather *o tempo*
sun *sol*
rain *chuva*
cloudy *nublado*
windy *vento*
hot *quente*
cold *frio*

Suggested Reading

NONFICTION

Eat Portugal (2017) Lucy Pepper and Célia Pedroso. A go-to read on national cuisine, this is an essential guide to Portuguese gastronomy.

The Portuguese: A Modern History (2011) Barry Hatton. An entertaining and wittily-written book on Portuguese history, peppered with information on the landscape, culture and history, and personal anecdotes.

The First Global Village (2006) Martin Page. This acclaimed book is a fascinating and factual recount of Portugal's links and influences on the rest of the world.

FICTION

Night Train to Lisbon (2018) Pascal Mercier. A well-known thriller-mystery-romance, later made into a movie starring Jeremy Irons, that unfurls in Portugal, showcasing the romantic allure of Lisbon.

Os Lusíadas (1572) Luís de Camões. A poetic and fantastical celebration of the navigation of a sea route to India by Portuguese explorer Vasco da Gama.

The Book of Disquiet (1982) Fernando Pessoa. This work by prolific Portuguese poet and writer Fernando Pessoa is categorized as "existential literature." Described as an unclassifiable and unfinished book of self-reflective fragments, this introspective masterpiece is a lifetime project left unedited by its author.

Internet Resources

TRAVEL AND TOURIST TIPS

www.visitportugal.com
Comprehensive information for tourists on all things related to visiting Portugal.

www.travel-in-portugal.com
A fact-packed guide on what to see and do in Portugal and its major attractions.

www.dgs.pt
Updated information on health matters and services, from Portugal's Directorate General for Health (DGS).

www.portugalwalking.com
A top resource for avid walkers and hikers, offering many different walking tours throughout the country.

www.visitlisboa.com
Lisbon-specific information for visitors, covering where to stay, what to see, and how to get around the vibrant capital.

www.visitalgarve.pt
The official Algarve regional tourism website, providing a wealth of information on accommodations, attractions, events, and activities, to squeeze the most out of a visit to Portugal's sunniest region.

www.visitportoandnorth.travel
Detailed information on the history of the northern region, plus tourist-centred information on what to do and see, where to stay, and, of course, the famous wines. Provides inspiration for a stay in Porto and the North.

www.algarvefun.com
A one-stop shop for tickets for the best sightseeing tours, activities, and excursions in the Algarve.

www.portugalist.com
In-depth information on all things related to visiting and living in Portugal, from local dishes to tax procedures.

www.myguidealgarve.com
A guide to the Algarve written by locals.

TRANSPORTATION

www.cp.pt
Train timetables and fares, plus updated information on rail travel from national train company Comboios de Portugal.

www.rede-expressos.pt
The website by national express coach company Rede Nacional de Expressos and its network in Portugal includes timetables, online purchases, and information on special offers.

NEWS

www.theportugalnews.com
Portugal's largest national English-language weekly newspaper, covering current affairs in Portugal daily.

www.portugalresident.com
Established in 1989, the Portugal Resident is an English news and lifestyle portal, with daily online news and a weekly newspaper.

BLOGS

https://juliedawnfox.com
For an insight on living in the country, award-winning blogger Julie Dawn Fox writes about travelling in Portugal as well as her life as an expat on her website.

Index

List of Maps

Photo Credits

MOON

CHILE

MOON

ECUADOR
& THE GALÁPAGOS ISLANDS

MOON

EGYPT

MOON

GREEK ISLANDS & ATHENS

ICELAND ESCAPES WITH TIMELESS VILLAGES,
SCENIC HIKES, AND LOCAL FLAVORS

MOON

ICELAND

WITH A ROAD TRIP ON THE RING ROAD

MOON

JAPAN

PLAN YOUR TRIP, AVOID THE CROWDS,
AND EXPERIENCE THE REAL JAPAN

MOON

TRIP OF A LIFETIME

MACHU PICCHU

MOON

MOROCCO

PORTUGAL

MOON

PRAGUE, VIENNA & BUDAPEST

MOON

ROME, FLORENCE & VENICE

MOON

CAMINO DE SANTIAGO

SACRED SITES,
HISTORIC VILLAGES,
LOCAL FOOD & WINE

BEEBE BAHRAMI

MOON

Drive & Hike
APPALACHIAN TRAIL

THE BEST TRAIL TOWNS, DAY HIKES,
AND ROAD TRIPS IN BETWEEN

TIMOTHY MALCOLM

MOON

Drive & Hike
PACIFIC CREST TRAIL

THE BEST TRAIL TOWNS, DAY HIKES,
AND ROAD TRIPS IN BETWEEN

CAROLINE HINCHLIFF

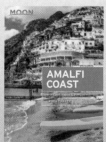

Get inspired for your next adventure

Follow **@moonguides** on Instagram or subscribe to our newsletter at **moon.com**

MAP SYMBOLS

═══════ Expressway	○ City/Town	ⓘ Information Center	♠ Park
Primary Road	◉ State Capital	🅿 Parking Area	⛳ Golf Course
──── Secondary Road	⊛ National Capital	⛪ Church	✦ Unique Feature
═══════ Unpaved Road	✪ Highlight	🍇 Winery/Vineyard	🍂 Waterfall
────── Trail	★ Point of Interest	TH Trailhead	▲ Camping
────── Ferry	● Accommodation	🚆 Train Station	▲ Mountain
━━━━━ Railroad	▼ Restaurant/Bar	✈ Airport	🎿 Ski Area
═══════ Pedestrian Walkway	■ Other Location	✕ Airfield	〰 Glacier
▥▥▥ Stairs			

CONVERSION TABLES

°C = (°F – 32) / 1.8
°F = (°C x 1.8) + 32
1 inch = 2.54 centimeters (cm)
1 foot = 0.304 meters (m)
1 yard = 0.914 meters
1 mile = 1.6093 kilometers (km)
1 km = 0.6214 miles
1 fathom = 1.8288 m
1 chain = 20.1168 m
1 furlong = 201.168 m
1 acre = 0.4047 hectares
1 sq km = 100 hectares
1 sq mile = 2.59 square km
1 ounce = 28.35 grams
1 pound = 0.4536 kilograms
1 short ton = 0.90718 metric ton
1 short ton = 2,000 pounds
1 long ton = 1.016 metric tons
1 long ton = 2,240 pounds
1 metric ton = 1,000 kilograms
1 quart = 0.94635 liters
1 US gallon = 3.7854 liters
1 Imperial gallon = 4.5459 liters
1 nautical mile = 1.852 km

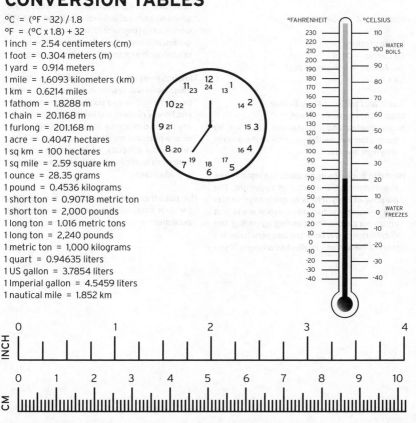

MOON PORTUGAL

Avalon Travel
Hachette Book Group
1700 Fourth Street
Berkeley, CA 94710, USA
www.moon.com

Editor: Megan Anderluh
Managing Editor: Hannah Brezack
Graphics and Production Coordination: Ravina
 Schneider
Cover Design: Faceout Studio, Charles Brock
Interior Design: Domini Dragoone
Moon Logo: Tim McGrath
Map Editor: Kat Bennett
Cartographers: Erin Greb, Kat Bennett, Karin Dahl,
 Alison Ollivierre
Proofreader: Nikki Ioakimedes
Indexer: Grace Fujimoto

ISBN-13: 978-1-64049-519-7

Printing History
1st Edition — 2019
2nd Edition — September 2021
5 4 3 2 1

Text © 2021 by Carrie-Marie Bratley.
Maps © 2021 by Avalon Travel.
Some photos and illustrations are used by
 permission and are the property of the original
 copyright owners.

Front cover photo: Praia de Dona Ana, Lagos. ©
 Michael Howard / Sime / eStock Photo
Back cover photo: Lisbon street scene. © Sepavo /
 dreamstime.com

Printed in Malaysia for Imago